Methodological and Statistical Advances in the Study of Individual Differences

PERSPECTIVES ON INDIVIDUAL DIFFERENCES

CECIL R. REYNOLDS, *Texas A&M University, College Station*
ROBERT T. BROWN, *University of North Carolina, Wilmington*

PERSPECTIVES ON BIAS IN MENTAL TESTING
Edited by Cecil R. Reynolds and Robert T. Brown

PERSONALITY AND INDIVIDUAL DIFFERENCES
A Natural Science Approach
Hans J. Eysenck and Michael W. Eysenck

DETERMINANTS OF SUBSTANCE ABUSE
Biological, Psychological, and Environmental Factors
Edited by Mark Galizio and Stephen A. Maisto

THE NEUROPSYCHOLOGY OF INDIVIDUAL DIFFERENCES
A Developmental Perspective
Edited by Lawrence C. Hartlage and Cathy F. Telzrow

METHODOLOGICAL AND STATISTICAL ADVANCES IN THE STUDY OF INDIVIDUAL DIFFERENCES
Edited by Cecil R. Reynolds and Victor L. Willson

A Continuation Order Plan is available for this series. A continuation order will bring delivery of each new volume immediately upon publication. Volumes are billed only upon actual shipment. For further information please contact the publisher.

Methodological and Statistical Advances in the Study of Individual Differences

Edited by

CECIL R. REYNOLDS

and

VICTOR L. WILLSON

Texas A&M University
College Station, Texas

PLENUM PRESS • NEW YORK AND LONDON

Library of Congress Cataloging in Publication Data

Main entry under title:

Methodological and statistical advances in the study of individual differences.

(Perspectives on individual differences)
Includes bibliographies and index.
1. Difference (Psychology)—Research—Methodology. 2. Difference (Psychology)—
Statistical methods. 3. Individuality—Research—Methodology. 4. Individuality—
Statistical methods. I. Reynolds, Cecil R., 1952–   . II. Willson, Victor L. III. Series.
BF697.M46   1985   155.2   85-17042
ISBN 0-306-41962-9

©1985 Plenum Press, New York
A Division of Plenum Publishing Corporation
233 Spring Street, New York, N.Y. 10013

Printed in the United States of America

Contributors

P. Barrett Institute of Psychiatry, University of London, London, England

John R. Bergan Department of Educational Psychology, University of Arizona, Tucson, Arizona

Hans J. Eysenck Institute of Psychiatry, University of London, London, England

Jason K. Feld Department of Educational Psychology, University of Arizona, Tucson, Arizona

Ronald K. Hambleton Department of Educational Psychology, University of Massachusetts, Amherst, Massachusetts

Merrill Hiscock Department of Psychology and Department of Psychiatry, University of Saskatchewan, Saskatoon, Saskatchewan, Canada

Samuel S. Hung College of Education, University of Illinois, Chicago, Illinois

Arthur R. Jensen School of Education, University of California, Berkeley, California

Randy W. Kamphaus Department of Psychology, Eastern Kentucky University, Richmond, Kentucky

Alan S. Kaufman Department of Educational Psychology, University of Alabama, Tuscaloosa, Alabama

Thomas T. Kratochwill Department of Educational Psychology, University of Wisconson, Madison, Wisconsin

F. Charles Mace School Psychology Program, Lehigh University, Bethlehem, Pennsylvania

Marilyn N. MacKay Department of Psychology and Department of Psychiatry, University of Saskatchewan, Saskatoon, Saskatchewan, Canada

Stacy E. Mott Department of Educational Psychology, University of Arizona, Tucson, Arizona

BEEMAN N. PHILLIPS   Department of Educational Psychology, University of Texas, Austin, Texas

CECIL R. REYNOLDS   Department of Educational Psychology, Texas A & M University, College Station, Texas

ROBERT J. STERNBERG   Department of Psychology, Yale University, New Haven, Connectiticut

CLEMENT A. STONE   Department of Educational Psychology, University of Arizona, Tucson, Arizona

HERBERT J. WALBERG   School of Education, University of Illinois, Chicago, Illinois

VICTOR L. WILLSON   Department of Educational Psychology, Texas A & M University, College Station, Texas

Preface

Differential psychology, or the psychology of individual differences as it is better known, is perhaps the single most important basic psychological science that underlies professional practice in psychology. The recent age of behaviorism all but ignored individual differences, but in this decade the study has emerged from relative dormancy with a new vitality, fueled by new concepts, technologies, statistics, and new viewpoints on old ideas that are moving us forward. This work is intended to be a review of as well as a primer on many of these advances and new approaches to the study of individual differences.

The venerable, interesting, and often controversial Eysenck opens the volume with a review of recent results and new techniques for unlocking the physiological basis of what is commonly understood to be intelligence. Eysenck and his students, in his London laboratory, have been fostering advances in this field for more than four decades. Their latest work could be the most exciting of Eysenck's illustrious, scholarly career. Eysenck's eye-opening, innovative work on the relationship between evoked potentials and performance on traditional psychometric measures, presented with a new slant, is certain to attract much attention in coming years.

Eysenck and Barrett's chapter is followed by a closely related work by Arthur Jensen, who gives us a revitalizing look at the concepts of Sir Francis Galton, the founder of the psychology of individual differences. Through new concepts and statistical procedures, Jensen has linked the general efficiency of the central nervous system to differences in aptitude in a way that updates certain of Galton's early thoughts and that very much complements Eysenck's recent work. From a reading of these two chapters, it appears that we are approaching major new vistas in the psychophysiology of intelligence, ones with many direct clinical applications.

To further complement the first two chapters, clinical neuropsychologists Hiscock and Mackay bring us up to date on how neuropsychologists study individual differences, what they have found, and what the future of neuropsychological research holds for those interested in human differences. The recently published Kaufman Assessment Battery for Children (K-ABC) presents us with a new scale for studying individual differences. Kamphaus, Kaufman, and Reynolds have reviewed this new scale and its most promising applications to the study of how children differ in their intellectual or mental processing skills. The K-ABC, steeped in research and theories taken largely from the neuropsychological theories of Luria and American researchers interested in cerebral specialization of cognitive function, also reflects the various concerns of the preceding three chapters. Aside from describing this new scale, the authors of Chapter 4 provide insight into specific applications of this new technology to a host of present problems in differential psychology. The K-ABC indeed seems to hold promise for new insights into the field.

In Chapter 5, we change gears to take up one of the major cognitive theories of the 1980s, Sternberg's componential theory of intelligence. Cognitive science, as begun by Neisser in the 1960s, has not often been applied to the study of individual differences; individual variations in behavior have most often been seen as nuisances in cognitive research. Sternberg describes the basic results of his own work and how componential analysis of performance on cognitive tasks can contribute to an understanding of individual differences. This area, ripe for the innovative researcher, has gone largely unexplored.

Chapters 6 and 7 present two views of new directions in aptitude × treatment interaction (ATI) research. Phillips, in Chapter 6, briefs us on his views of new concepts and new approaches to the early ideas of ATI. He argues that we have not yet reached the pinnacle of ATI work and that by changing our old views and applying recent, more appropriate methods, new avenues of understanding will become available to us—a conclusion with which we heartily agree; understanding has nowhere near exhausted the study of ATI. Willson follows Phillips's conceptual chapter to present new statistical techniques for more detailed and accurate analyses of interactions in ATI and related research designs. Following Willson's presentation, Hung and Walberg demonstrate the establishment of linear models of individual differences. As many of us have suspected, it does seem that anything ANOVA can do GLM can do better! Perhaps that is a little zealous, but linear models of individual differences data are very powerful and offer potential insights into results that might otherwise be missed.

In the final three chapters, we look at out-of-the-ordinary methods and technologies for studying individual differences that deviate from traditional approaches to the topic. Behaviorism has long been seen, or at least interpreted, as antithetical to the study of individual differences.

In Chapter 9, Kratochwill and his colleagues, Mace and Mott, have taken on the difficult task of relating research methods from behavioral psychology and, more specifically, applied behavior analysis to individual variations in behavior. This intriguing chapter provides clear and concise tutelage in modern behavioral research methodologies and lends itself readily to revealing potential advances in not only how we study individual differences, but also what we find. Hambleton, in Chapter 10, updates current methods of criterion-referenced testing (CRT) a derivation of behavioral *and* instructional psychology, and explains how CRTs can help us understand individual differences in behavior. As one of the pioneers of CRT and one of the most sophisticated researchers in the area, Hambleton is in a unique position to provide the necessary insights. Concepts of CRT are central not only to Kratochwill's behavioral approach to individual differences, but also to Bergan's new approach to the field, which evaluates performance from the vantage point of path-referenced assessment (PRA). Bergan's path-referenced model for assessing individual differences combines behavioral psychology with CRT and causal modeling. Although much remains to be done, Bergan's ideas truly have much to offer the student of individual differences. Path-referenced assessment seeks a hierarchically arranged sequence of skills for learning various tasks, but encounters individual variations in sequences across individuals. The cause of these variations is certainly important to the individual differences researcher.

We hope this work will contribute to the new wave of research in individual differences. We would also like to express our appreciation to those who assisted us in compiling these works. Our Plenum editor, Eliot Werner, was not only helpful, but patient as well, and always came to our aid when needed. To the many chapter reviewers, we appreciated your help, especially that of John Glover. Our graduate assistants, Joan Kappus and Shannon Richardson, were also gracious in running down references and doing other assorted, sundry work. We also much appreciate the work of our many authors and their willingness to revise their work and to do so in a timely fashion. To our department chair, Michael J. Ash, who is always ready to facilitate any worthy scholarly endeavor and who creates an atmosphere of positive regard for all inquiry, we remain indebted in all our work. Editing books always seems a chore, but this book is one that we feel has much to tell us about the future of research in individual differences, and we look forward to additional volumes on the topic.

CECIL R. REYNOLDS
VICTOR L. WILLSON

Contents

Merrill Hiscock and Marilynn MacKay

4 APPLICATIONS OF THE KAUFMAN ASSESSMENT BATTERY FOR CHILDREN TO THE STUDY OF INDIVIDUAL DIFFERENCES

Randy W. Kamphaus, Alan S. Kaufman, and Cecil R. Reynolds

    Ronald K. Hambleton

    John R. Bergan, Clement A. Stone, and Jason K. Feld

1

Psychophysiology and the Measurement of Intelligence

H. J. EYSENCK AND P. BARRETT

THE TWO PARADIGMS OF INTELLIGENCE

Any discussion of the measurement of intelligence is likely to be handicapped by the many different meanings the term has assumed in psychology, to say nothing of popular discourse. It is useful to distinguish the three major meanings of the term, which are shown in Figure 1. Intelligence A is the genotypic, biological underlay of all cognitive activities, responsible for individual differences in the ability to perform cognitive tasks. Intelligence B is the expression of this ability in everyday life, heavily contaminated, of course, by educational, cultural, and socioeconomic factors, as well as by personality and the many accidental features that distinguish one person's life from that of another. Intelligence C is psychometric intelligence, that is, the intelligence that is measured by tests of one kind or another.

Intelligence C can be again subdivided in various ways. For the purpose of this chapter, we recognize three major types of measurement. In the first place, we must distinguish between (1) a general factor of intelligence (called g by Spearman) that underlies all cognitive tasks, but that must be supplemented by (2) a number of group or primary factors involving visuospatial ability, verbal ability, and numerical ability. (Eysenck, 1979). In this chapter, we will be dealing throughout with g, but psychometrically g has itself been subdivided into crystallized ability (g_c) and fluid ability (g_f) by Cattell (1963, 1971). Crystallized ability is clearly more closely related to Intelligence B, fluid ability to Intelligence A. We must also recognize, however, the existence of more direct measures of Intelligence A that have been denoted by g_p in Figure 1, that is, g as measured, physiologically, by instruments. All three types of intelligence are, of

H. J. EYSENCK AND P. BARRETT ● Institute of Psychiatry, University of London, London, England.

1

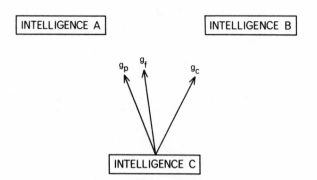

FIGURE 1. Diagrammatic representation of Intelligence A, Intelligence B, and Intelligence C.

course, fairly closely related, but they are not identical, and confusion can hardly be avoided if different discussants use different concepts without being aware of these subtle but important differences.

As regards the measurement of intelligence (i.e., Intelligence C), there have been two rival paradigms ever since the first attempts to investigate a vague and popular concept scientifically. These two paradigms stem from the seminal writings of Sir Francis Galton, on the one hand, and of the French psychologist Alfred Binet, on the other. The division between them is clearly focused on three major points.

Intelligence as a General Factor or Intelligence as an Average. For Galton, *intelligence* constituted a general cognitive ability underlying all mental tasks, differing from one person another, and responsible for individual differences in performances of all kind. For Binet, intelligence was merely the average of a number of disparate and probably unrelated mental abilities, and indeed it might be said that he was illogical in talking about intelligence at all, since he did not really believe in its existence. However, most pioneers in science are less than rigorous in their use of language, and the major question remains: Is psychology justified in positing a general ability underlying all types of cognitive performance, or are there a number of separate abilities that can only be artificially brought together by the use of an averaging procedure?

Psychometrically, this dispute has usually been addressed by means of factor analytic research, with Spearman (1927) advocating the universality of a general factor (*g*) and Thurstone (1938) suggesting the absence of a general factor, and the predominance of a number of primary factors. Eysenck (1939) suggested that a proper analysis of Thurstone's data did suggest the presence of a general factor, as well as of group factors, a point acknowledged in later work by Thurstone and Thurstone (1941). Eysenck

(1979) and Vernon (1979) have discussed the history of this debate and the evidence; they agree that a general factor is indispensable in accounting for all the available evidence, as are a number of group factors similar to the primary factors suggested by Thurstone.

Among present-day psychologists, perhaps the only one to adhere to a strictly Binetian account is Guilford (Guilford, 1967; Guilford & Hoepfner, 1971). Guilford's "structure of intellect model of intelligence" posits 120 independent combinations of five operations (evaluation, convergent production, divergent production, memory, cognition), six products (units, classes, relations, systems, transformations, implications), and four contents (figural, symbolic, semantic, behavioral). Guilford's psychometric approach has been criticized in detail by Eysenck (1979); it is clearly incompatible with the theory of *independent* factors that practically all the reported correlations (even when the range of ability is relatively small) are positive, and significantly so. Furthermore, high correlations have been reported among measures of many of his 120 abilities and a general test of intelligence (g). Finally, factor analytically, Guilford's solution fits less well than a solution in terms of g plus primary factors. For all these and other reasons, Guilford's model is unacceptable psychometrically.

The fact that intercorrelations among all cognitive tests tend to be positive, that is, they produce what Thurstone called a "positive manifold," supports the concept of a general factor, although not conclusively. What is more impressive is that the intercorrelations so observed tend to fall into a pattern in which, as Spearman pointed out, tetrad differences vanish; in other words, the matrix approximates unit rank. In order to obtain unit rank, as Thurstone and Thurstone (1941) pointed out, we have to intercorrelate primary factors and extract g as a second-order factor; Spearman had already warned against including tests in the battery that were too similar and, hence, contained overlapping elements. On this point, then, Galton was clearly right, and Binet was clearly wrong, although Binet was right in suggesting the presence (in addition to g) of special or primary factors.

Some critics still doubt the necessity for introducing g, and statistically it must be admitted that the variance *can* be split up arbitrarily in such a way that g is excluded. This seems a very artificial thing to do, and unlikely to portray reality in a meaningful sort of way, but the fact that it can be done suggests that psychometric considerations alone may be unable to resolve the conflict. It is one important function of this chapter to suggest that an experimental answer to this question is possible and that this answer can be obtained through psychophysiological examinations.

Intelligence as Influenced by Genetic Factors. For Galton, these factors were supreme; for Binet, who as an educationalist was more interested in improving the performance of mentally retarded children, environmental (particularly educational and cultural factors) were far more important, and although he did not dismiss genetic factors, he certainly did not stress them the way Galton did. There is not a necessary contradiction between the two here; Binet's interest was in Intelligence B, Galton's in Intelligence A, and it seems reasonable to suppose that environmental factors are far more important in determining a person's actions in everyday life than they are in determining a person's biological disposition to act intelligently or unintelligently.

Looking at the very large body of evidence relating to the genetics of psychometric IQ, that is, of Intelligence C, the evidence suggests strongly that heredity does play a very important part, but that environmental factors cannot be ruled out. Eysenck (1979) has summarized the extensive literature and reanalyzed available data using a variety of different approaches to estimate the heritability of Intelligence C; his major conclusion is that heritability contributes something like 80% to the phenotypic variance, with environmental variance contributing something like 20%. Of the environmental contribution, two thirds is the between-family kind, one third the within-family kind. Thus, IQ as a measure of Intelligence B is still largely determined by genetic factors; this suggests that Galton was right to a greater extent than was Binet.

It should be noted that other authors (including Vernon, 1979) have estimated lower contributions for heritability. Here again we should note that the term *heritability* has several different meanings, and the fact that two authors report apparently different estimates does not mean that they disagree. Thus, heritability may be interpreted as encompassing the ratio of additive genetic variance over total phenotypic variance; this is the so-called *narrow* heritability. Alternatively, we may add the effects of dominance, of assortative mating, and of epistasis to the genetic term in the equation, thus arriving at the *broad* heritability. Since assortative mating and dominance are known to play a prominent role in the genetic architecture of intelligence, and since epistasis may also play such a role, the broad heritability is significantly larger than the narrow heritability. Last but not least, we may correct our formulas for measurement error (attenuation); this is important, since normally the error would be added to the environmental variance. The results of one and the same investigation may thus be reported as giving a heritability of .6 (narrow heritability), .7 (broad heritability), or .8 (broad heritability corrected for attenuation).

In the usual formulation of heritability, the covariance of genotypes and environments (Cov GE) forms part of the environmental variance, but some geneticists (e.g., Roberts, 1967, p. 217) include Cov GE as part of the total genetic variance rather than as part of the environmental variance, defining the environmental variance component as those environmental effects that are *independent* of the genotype. This would again increase the heritability. It might be thought that a term like *heritability* should only have one meaning and, consequently, lead to one estimate, but this is an unreasonable request. Geneticists know precisely for what purpose any particular definition of heritability can be used and what it means; it is the uninformed readers who may get mixed up and believe that there is a disagreement where none exists. The estimate of 80% heritability is the corrected broad heritability, that is, that portion of the total phenotypic variance not produced by errors of measurement. It does not include Cov GE, although Roberts and other experts might increase the estimate by so including it.

The precise value of heritability, of course, is not very important; heritability is a population parameter, that is, it estimates a quantity that differs from population to population and from time to time. Furthermore, it is characteristic of populations, not of individuals; critics frequently confuse the issue by assuming that heritability applies to individuals. Thus, the often-heard criticism that to try and estimate the relative importance of heredity and environment is as pointless as trying to decide whether length or width is more important in determining the area of a field is clearly incorrect; a field does not constitute a population, and is hence not subject to the analysis of variance that is fundamental to the establishment of heritability.

Intelligence as Measured by Intelligence A or Intelligence B. We now come to the third great difference between Galton and Binet, which derives from the two differences already noted. For Galton, measurement of intelligence should be as direct as possible a measure of Intelligence A, that is, it should be biological and psychophysiological in nature, and he suggested reaction times as the approach most feasible at that time for that purpose. Binet, as noted, was far more concerned with Intelligence B and hence suggested tests that were relevant to ordinary life—demonstrations of cognitive ability, often involving verbal knowledge, experience, and educational factors of one kind or another. Binet's conception, of course, won the day, and intelligence tests ever since have been exclusively devoted to measures that are similar to those contained in his original scale. A possible exception to this rule are measures of what Cattell called "culture-fair intelligence," that is, measures of g of a nonverbal kind, but as critics have pointed out, these, too, are demonstrably influenced by socioeconomic and cultural factors, such as the absence of right angles in the experience of Bushmen and African Blacks living in Kraals. It is recognized that g_f tests are less subject to such cultural factors than g_c tests, but it cannot be maintained that they are completely free of such factors.

The failure of psychologists to follow up Galton's suggestions to use reaction time (RT) measures as indices of intelligence is interesting from the sociological and historical point of view, as indicating a zeitgeist opposed to genetic and biological factors and favorable to environmental and educational factors as determinants of behavior. However, clearly the zeitgeist was wrong, as demonstrated by Jensen (1982a, b). His chapter in this book deals with the possible contribution of RTs to the measurement of intelligence, and nothing will be said here other than to emphasize the major points (1) that g clearly is quite highly correlated with RT in the sense that high IQ subjects are *quicker* than low IQ subjects; (2) that correlations between RT and g are higher, the more complex the stimulus pattern, up to a point; and (3) that *variability* in RT is negatively correlated with g in the sense that high ability subjects show less variability than low ability subjects. These facts have led Jensen (1982b) to a theory emphasizing speed of transmission of neural impulses as a causal factor in intelligence. Eysenck (1982a, b) has suggested an alternative hypothesis better able to account for all the facts, and this will be dealt with later in this chapter. Let us merely note that the quite high correlations between RT and the many different types of IQ tests of the Binet type are incompatible with a theory that does not acknowledge the existence of g. It also goes counter to the many types of cognitive theory of intellectual functioning recently advanced (Sternberg, 1982). This cognitive theory seems to be more relevant to Intelligence B than to Intelligence A and, hence, will form no part of this presentation, other than to be looked at from the point of view of the results of our own studies on the psychophysiological basis of intelligence.

THE ELECTROENCEPHALOGRAM AND THE AVERAGED EVOKED POTENTIAL AS BIOLOGICAL CORRELATES OF IQ

One obvious way of looking at the possible biological substrate of intelligence is by way of brain size (Jerison, 1973). The increase in brain size and brain weight (in relation to body size and weight) with evolutionary development suggests that greater intelligence may be correlated with greater brain size and weight, but although nearly always positive, the range of the correlations has been disappointing, from around .2 to .3, even after various corrections. There are obvious difficulties in the ascertainment of brain size and weight in live humans, but the avenue is not a promising one and has been largely abandoned.

The electroencephalogram is an obvious approach to the problem of psychophysiological recording of events possibly related to IQ, but a careful survey by Lindsley (1961) showed quite early on that there is no clear-cut relation in normal adults, although in early childhood (when slower gamma and delta waves give way to faster and prevalent alpha) and in brain-injured persons (Ostow, 1954) some relationships are found. Among younger children and mental defectives, or deteriorated adults with a mental age of between 6 and 10, the correlations range from .3 to .6 between mental age and more rapid, developed alpha rhythm. Netchine and Netchine (1962) have suggested that correlations with mental age are high if one takes a compound index of alpha frequency with amplitude and certain patterns on the EEG, but the suggestion has not been followed up. Cattell (1971) has suggested that better results might have been obtained had factor analytic studies of EEG measures disclosed the major dimensions inherent in such measurement, but little has been done along these lines, and it is doubtful whether this approach would have had a greater claim to success than the more usual search for meaningful biological interpretations of the various components of the EEG.

However that might be, Ellingson (1966), in his review, stated that there was little he could feel confident about other than the rather obvious fact that EEG signs of gross brain lesions and epilepsy were more common in retarded individuals. Vogel and Broverman (1964, 1966) objected and put forward evidence that in normal children mental age and alpha frequency are correlated, when age and sex are held constant. Callaway (1975) voiced the opinion that it would perhaps be more nearly correct to say that the EEG–intelligence correlations reported thus far are unpromising, rather than to infer that they are invalid, and that the repetitive waves, like aspects of the ongoing EEG, are not the best windows on the mind. This presumably reflects the fact that such repetitive waves in the EEG tell us more about what the mind is *not* doing than about what the mind is doing. Wavelike activities often signal a failure to operate, and if the brain is usually busy on a variety of jobs, the EEG is a jumble of signals appropriate to the jumble of underlying processes and, hence, not likely to reflect such dispositional qualities as g.

Efforts to relate ordinary resting EEGs to intelligence have almost ceased, and instead we have had a spurt of studies using event–related potentials, such as the contingent negative variation (CNV), and more importantly, the averaged evoked potential (AEP). The CNV is the sum of a group of slope potentials, *contingent* in that it develops between a warning signal (S_1) and a second, imperative signal (S_2) that demands some response, usually the pressing of a button. The negative wave that usually follows about 500 milliseconds (ms), upon a novel signal grows and becomes a CNV when S_1 is followed regularly by S_2. The CNV may be regarded as an excitatory state that affects primarily, but not exclusively the anticipated stimulus–response complex. There is little evidence that the CNV is correlated with intelligence; it is more of the nature of a measure of attention or arousal, and will not be dealt with in detail here.

Averaged evoked potentials, their nature and origin, are well described by Shagass (1972), Regan (1972), and more recently, Basar (1980). Figure 2 shows, in very diagrammatic form, the resting EEG (to the left of the arrow), followed by a sensory stimulus (auditory, visual, or somato-sensory); the series of waves, negative and then positive in each case, is the AEP, gradually dying out after approximately 750 to 1,000 ms. Because of the poor signal to noise ratio of the AEP (which is only partly corrected by making the stimulus phase dependent on the resting EEG), a number of time-locked evocations have to be averaged in order to obtain a recognizable and measurable wave. John (1973) has pointed out that averaging may, in fact, obscure event-related potentials. He found that individual evoked potentials, recorded from electrodes implanted in cats, may be quite different even to the same stimuli. As John puts it: "Noise . . . may not be noise but only poorly understood signals." Nevertheless, averaging has been widely used and has become indispensable for the study of AEPs.

The waveform of the AEP differs from person to person and depends on the nature of the stimulus, the location of the electrode, the intensity of the stimulus, and the state of the subject. Descriptively, the AEP is divided into early and late components, with the former easier to characterize from a physiological point of view, while the later components are more interesting to the psychologist.

The earlier components in the scalp AEP are usually called far-field

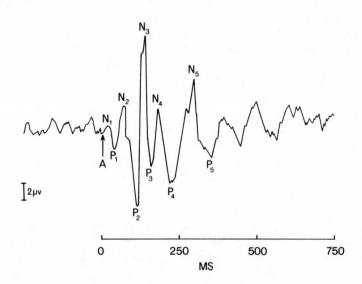

FIGURE 2. Diagram of the evoked potential.

components; they reflect dipoles set up by receptors and peripheral relay stations (Jewett, Romano, & Williston, 1970). Far-field potentials are very small and have very short latencies; they are potentially useful in neurological diagnosis, but have been little used for correlating AEPs with intelligence. Unpublished work by S. Harkin suggests significant correlations of far-field potentials and intelligence in the neighborhood of $r = .40$.

Following the far-field components are the so-called primary cortical-evoked responses. These are near-field components, since small changes in electrode position may have large effects; thus does not occur with far-field components. They are also characterized by larger amplitude and later occurrence (20–100 ms).

Most work has been concerned with the later components of AEP. Even the early AEP is complex, containing far-field and near-field responses, myogenic responses arising from the muscles of the neck and ear, and the ongoing EEG. After 60 to 100 ms, the AEP even more certainly reflects the summation of a variety of events in which some potentials add, others cancel, and the result, as Callaway (1975) says, is a "potpourri."

Electrode placement can be very important, and in our work we have always used monopolar recordings, that is, one active electrode on the scalp and the relatively inactive reference electrode on the mastoid. As we shall see, bipolar recordings have been used by Ertl (1971, 1973) and Ertl and Schafer (1969) and produce results that are often difficult to interpret.

Figure 2 is highly schematic, and the identification of $N_1, P_1,$ N_2, P_2, N_3, P_3, etc., is not as easy as it might appear. Components are not stable entities that can be named, but rather entities that can have changes in amplitude and latency attached to them and be referred to specific physiological underlying variables. Components tend to be labile and may be largely idiosyncratic; nor is it possible to consider positive and negative potentials as being equally significant. Nevertheless, it has become common to refer to such fairly regular waves as the P_{300} (the so-called polaric-latency labeling system).

We will find, in what follows, a great divergency of results, such as the unwary might not expect in what appears to be a clear-cut, definitive line of research, namely, Does the averaged evoked potential correlate with intelligence? The simple question masks a large number of pitfalls, most of them related to the fact that parameter choice determines whether replicable results are obtained. If different investigators use different electrode placements, bipolar versus unipolar recordings, different types and intensities of stimuli, different interstimulus intervals (ISIs), different instructions, different waveform analyses, and other parameters that may be related to attentional and similar psychological factors, and then use correlations with different types of IQ tests—some measures of fluid ability, some measures of crystallized ability, some more likely measures of educational learning—clearly chaos is likely to reign supreme, and we will be lucky if we can disentangle the types of parameter arrangements most likely to yield positive results. Add to that the fact that many investigators have been relatively incompetent and slapdash, and you may imagine that the sum total of the results is highly confusing, particularly to the uninitiated.

To all this confusion we must add one further point relating to the choice of subjects, namely, blacks appear to have different reactions to whites, so much so that correlations are sometimes reversed in direction as we go from one race to the other. Thus, Callaway (1975) reports that in his U. S. Navy studies blacks had lower mean IQs but faster mean latency than whites, although faster mean latency is correlated with IQ! Again, the same author found that white recruits had a higher average variability of AEP than blacks, although black recruits averaged lower on IQ. This is a curious finding because average variability is negatively correlated with IQ! Again, similar contradictory results were obtained with AEP asymmetry. The meaning of these odd reversals is unclear, but it is important to bear them in mind. Thus, for instance, Engel and Henderson (1973) in trying to replicate findings by Ertl (to be discussed presently) were unable to do so, but they were using a group of blacks and whites; possibly the data were contaminated by an extraneous source of latency differences. It must be an absolute rule in studies of this kind that blacks and whites not be analyzed together.[1]

These few paragraphs concerning the AEP are necessary in order that we may understand and evaluate the studies reviewed in the following sections.

The quality of the work done in this field, and the size of the correlations obtained, has constantly improved. We now have a much better understanding of the parameters to be controlled, and it seems likely that in the future much greater replicability will obtain than in the past. Hence, the next section will only present a brief history of the attempts to correlate AEP and intelligence, just sufficient to introduce the newer methods and results.

AEPS AND INTELLIGENCE: EARLY PARADIGMS

The essential novelty of Binet's approach to the measurement of intelligence was that he related intelligence to the concept of mental age,

---

[1] Callaway's findings on black and white differences urgently require replication. Navy personnel (his subjects) presents peculiar difficulties, partly due to the exigencies of the Navy program, and results may not be confirmed when other types of subjects are used.

that is, the development of cognitive capacity from early to late childhood. The AEP can be similarly approached, which suggests that those aspects of the AEP that change from early to late childhood might be measures of mental age, and possibly of IQ. Callaway (1975) has surveyed a large body of evidence, and there seems to be much agreement that with increasing age the *variability* of AEP, and its *latency,* is reduced. In other words, in the older child the frequency of waves increases, and the waves resemble each other more closely than they did at an earlier age. These observations might, therefore, lead to plausible avenues to explore. However, Callaway points out that, in actual fact, age-related measures are not necessarily correlated any more highly with IQ than are non–age-related measures, and hence these relationships should be regarded as suggestive, not conclusive.

The first correlations between AEP measures and IQs were reported by Chalke and Ertl (1965). Short visual AEP latencies were found correlated with high IQ in a group of 48 rather heterogeneous subjects, including 4 mentally retarded subjects. This early work was followed by several other reports (Ertl & Schafer, 1969; Ertl, 1971, 1973; Barry & Ertl, 1965), culminating in Ertl's marketing of a device called the "neural efficiency analyzer." Many frequency-domain measures have been attempted in order to improve correlations, such as Fourier analysis, complex demodulation, and analog spectral analysis, but the time-domain measure has remained the measure of choice. With it, quite large samples have been tested, and correlations with standard IQ tests in the neighborhood of .3 have been obtained fairly consistently.

Several investigators have found no evidence for such a correlation between AEP and IQ (Rhodes, Dustman, & Beck, 1969; Dustman & Beck, 1972; Dustman, Schenkenberg, & Beck, 1974 and, in particular, Davis, 1971); we have also already mentioned the work of Engel and Henderson (1973), in which both black and white children were studied. These negative findings have had a powerful effect on many research workers, but they have to be seen in the context of the particular design of Ertl's experiments, which was quite different from the designs of the people who tried to replicate them; Ertl also used a peculiar bipolar electrode placement and an unusual definition of latency; neither of these was used by other workers. Finally, Ertl's electrode placement was unusual and somewhat esoteric. The most confusing of these, as Callaway (1975) pointed out, has been Ertl's definition of latency. Thus, when the EEG crossed zero voltage in a particular direction, he accumulated these counts in bins according to the time of the stimulation. After trying other methods, he has most recently simply averaged line-crossing periods. Callaway has discussed some of the problems resulting from Ertl's unorthodox procedures. Other difficulties arise from the fact that some of the samples used by Ertl were small and consisted of subjects selected for very high and very low IQs. Also, Ertl paid little attention to the fact that his latency measures are not basic and immutable biological phenomena, but rather are sensitive to age and state of arousal.

Nevertheless, sufficient replications of Ertl's work, with positive results, have been made to assert that correlations between AEP latency and IQ, accounting for some 10% of the variance, are obtained when suitable attention is paid to parameter values. Callaway mentions two unpublished Ph.D. theses by Plum and Shucard; much of the work of the latter was later published in conjunction with Horn (Shucard & Horn, 1972). The Shucard and Horn study is one of the most impressive and detailed in the literature; it used measures of fluid and crystallized intelligence, both of which correlate to about the same magnitude with evoked potential latency measures. Shucard and Horn also found significant correlations between measures representing simple cognitive processes (e.g., motor-perceptual speed) and evoked potential latency. Most importantly, they found that the average size of ability–latency correlations, as well as the number of significant correlations, increased as conditions of evoked potential testing that tended to impose alertness on subjects were relaxed.

Galbraith, Glidden, and Busk (1970), in a study of visual AEPs of retarded and normal young adults, also found long latencies with lower IQ. Callaway (1973) reported similar negative correlations between IQ and AEP latency on large samples of navy recruits. Gucker (1973), using a technique rather more similar to Ertl's than most, also found negative correlations, as did Everhart, Chin, and Auger (1974). Frequency-domain analogs of Ertl's measure have also proved useful, and the results have been positive (Bennett, 1968; Weinberg, 1969).

The evidence on auditory latencies is curiously ambiguous. Callaway (1975) presents evidence for both children and adults for a *positive* relationship between latency and IQ. This is inherently improbable, as there seems to be no reason why auditory and visual AEPs should differ in direction of correlation with intelligence. Our own work (Hendrickson, 1972) does not support Callaway's findings. A summary of the results of Hendrickson's unpublished Ph.D. study are given in Eysenck (1973). Using 93 adults, randomly sampled, Hendrickson administered the AH4 test of intelligence, which gives a verbal, a spatial, and a total score; she also determined latencies and amplitudes of evoked potentials in response to sounds of three different intensities. Table 1 lists the correlations obtained for all intensities combined; a correlation of .27 would be significant at the 1% level. It will be seen that both latency (negatively) and amplitude (positively) are correlated with intelligence; more with verbal than with spatial intelligence; and possibly most of all with the total intelligence score.

TABLE 1. Correlations between Wechsler IQ Test and
Evoked Potential Latency and Amplitude Scores

Latency	Verbal	Spatial	Total
P_1	−.41	−.39	−.44
N_1	−.44	−.38	−.45
P_2	−.48	−.44	−.50
N_2	−.34	−.35	−.38
P_3	−.41	−.29	−.38
N_3	−.29	−.25	−.30
Amplitude			
A3	.31	.10	.22
A4	.45	.25	.37
A5	.31	.19	.27

Note. From *The Measurement of Intelligence* (p. 429) by H. J. Eysenck, 1973, Lancaster, England: MTP. Copyright 1973 by H. J. Eysenck. Reprinted by permission.

The average size of the correlations ranges from .30 to .50 for latency and from .30 to .45 for amplitude, when we are considering verbal ability, and from .10 to .25, when we are considering spatial ability. It should be borne in mind that latency and amplitude are essentially uncorrelated, and we can therefore add variance estimates to predict IQ. Quite roughly, such a combined score of latency and amplitude would have a correlation with IQ of between .50 and .60; if this value were corrected for attenuation, it would give a correlation between .6 and .7.

It was this study that led to the developments to be described in the next section.

An experiment that apparently failed to replicate Hendrickson's (1972) findings, also coming from our laboratory, has been published by Rust (1975). There are, however, certain important differences between the two experiments. Thus, in the Rust study, subjects received 20 stimuli at an intensity of 95 dB, with a regular interstimulus interval of 33 seconds(s). (In his second study, stimuli at 55 dB and at 75 dB were also used, with interstimulus intervals randomized between 4 and 9 s.) Twenty stimuli is much too small a number to obtain meaningful results, and we have found that a minimum of 90 repetitions is needed. Rust sampled the EEG for 500 ms after each stimulus, but in general our work has shown that it is the first 250 ms that are important, with the inclusion of the next 250 ms reducing correlations with IQ. Finally, intensities of 95 dB are too high, producing undesirable startle and similar responses in some subjects, whereas 55 and 75 dB intensities are too low; the best results were obtained with stimuli of 85 dB. Rust's study was useful in arriving at estimates of the most appropriate parameters for the study, and his negative results do not indicate nonreplicability; they merely indicate the importance of choosing parameter values.

In general, it may be useful to lay down a general rule for the evaluation of replication studies in this field, namely, failure to replicate only counts as a failure if and when the study uses the same major parameter values as the original studies. When this is not done, the study is not a replication; it may throw light on the effects of altering parameters, but it cannot, in the nature of things, be used to throw doubt on the adequacy of the original study or its results.

Before leaving the measurement of intelligence by means of evoked potential latencies, it may be relevant to point out that genetic factors have been found to influence latencies to a marked extent, as they do all aspects of the AEP (Lewis, Dustman, & Beck, 1972). This is important in view of the position of the g_p arrow in our Figure 1; if evoked potentials are a more direct measure of the biological dispositions leading to differences in IQ, then one would expect the AEPs to have a high heritability. To find such a high heritability would not be a *sufficient* reason for adopting the hypothesis put forward, but it would seem to be a *necessary* condition; in the absence of high heritabilities, the argument would flounder immediately.

The conclusions of Lewis *et al.* (1972) agree with the earlier work on EEG tracings (Davis & Davis, 1936; Lennox, Gibbs, & Gibbs, 1945; Juel-Nielsen & Harvald, 1958) and work on the cerebral evoked response (Dustman & Beck, 1965; Osborne, 1970). Lennox *et al.* (1945) concluded that the electrical activity of the brain was determined to a large degree by hereditary factors, and Lewis *et al.* (1972) agree, stating that "our results indicated a considerable hereditary component in the wave characteristics of visual, auditory and somatosensory evoked responses" (p. 215).

The results just mentioned have been confirmed by two unpublished studies carried out in our own laboratories (Young, 1969; Rust, 1976). Both differ from the earlier studies in that they used a suitable type of biometrical genetical analysis, in an attempt to go beyond the simple comparison of monozygotic and dizygotic twins and to look at a possible breakdown of the total variance into component parts. Both found strong evidence for genetic factors, and the simple model of D_R: E_I was found to agree with the data. This means essentially that additive genetic variance and within-family environmental variance accounted for the majority of the findings. There were also differences between the investigators, Young finding genetic factors more important in latency than amplitude and Rust finding that the heritability of amplitude was in excess of 80% and stronger than the heritability of latency. Experiments using a larger number of subjects will be needed to reconcile these findings, but the evidence is overwhelming that a strong genetic factor is operating to produce differences in AEP between individuals.

In addition to latency and (to a much lesser extent) amplitude, two other main parameters of the evoked potential have attracted attention in connection with the correlation with IQ. One of these is *variability* in the evoked potential (Callaway, 1979). As evoked potentials are averaged, the AEP, of course, contains no information about the variability of the individual measures on which the AEP is based. It is the variability about the mean with which we are concerned now, and this, as Brazier (1964) pointed out, is related to amplitude: Greater variability reduces amplitude. (This is a consequence of the fact that perfectly time-locked waves yield the largest average, other things being equal; if waves are not time-locked, i.e., if there is variability around the mean at each data point, then any departure from zero voltage in either the positive or the negative direction will be reduced, thus yielding lower amplitude.) Variability, as Callaway (1975) points out, may also account for an increase in latency in an average, so that amplitude, latency, and variability are not independent. Accordingly, he suggested that variability, rather than being something to be gotten rid of, may be a more fundamental factor than the other variables.

Averaged evoked potential variability is high in schizophrenia, and this may be, in part, because evoked potential (EP) variability parallels cognitive variability (Callaway, 1975). Patients with psychotic depression also have been found to have a high EP variability (Borge, 1973). It would seem that variability in EP is connected with psychosis in general, rather than with any specific psychotic disorder.

The fact that EP variability decreases in children aged 6 to 16 suggests a negative correlation between variability and IQ. Callaway (1975) has summarized his own work with children, which in general shows that low EP variability is associated with superior performance. He also notes that linear correlations may not be appropriate because there is a nearly empty quadrant in which poor EP stability and good IQ performance would be located; he suggests that it is as though the opportunity to learn, and other factors, plays an increasingly important role in limiting performance once a neural substrate stabilized sufficiently. In other words, the neural processes producing stable EPs are *necessary* to, but not *sufficient* for superior performance.

In rather larger samples from his research with adult Navy recruits, Callaway used two measures of variability: (1) averaged standard deviation over trials, which correlates positively with amplitude, and (2) averaged normalized standard deviation, which correlates inversely with amplitude. Correlations were in the expected directions, but centered around .20, which, as Callaway points out, is of more theoretical than practical interest. Again, however, as in the case of children, regressions seemed not to be linear; thus, the predictive power of the variability EP measure by using the product–moment correlation coefficient was underestimated.

A final approach that has been used in calculating AEP–IQ correlations has been the use of AEP asymmetry. Asymmetrical AEPs can be obtained by somato-sensory stimulation, which produces a contralateral parietal AEP that has more complex early components than the ipsilateral parietal AEP has. Similarly, one-sided stimulation of other modalities produces asymmetrical AEPs. Cognitive operations can also be used in this context: Propositional (left-hemisphere) cognitive operations tend to suppress the EEG from the left hemisphere and to reduce AEPs to irrelevant stimuli, with appositional (right-hemisphere) tasks suppressing right-hemisphere EEGs and task-irrelevant AEPs.

Greater asymmetry has been found in bright children by Rhodes *et al.* (1969) and Lairy, Remond, Rieger, and Lesevre (1969); two Ph.D. studies are quoted by Callaway (1975) as failing to find significant differences.

The earliest adult study was by Giannitrapanni (1969); his results were positive. Callaway (1975) obtained positive results, but only under nonattending conditions; again he observed the phenomenon of the "empty quadrant." In later studies, however, he failed to find a correlation between asymmetry and IQ. Callaway has suggested that such negative findings could be explained by the fact that verbal people do well on IQ tests and, when left to their own devices, think in propositional verbal symbols; thus individuals show pervasive cognitive modes most clearly when at rest. He further postulated that these cognitive modes are related to differences in performance. Direct evidence is not obtainable to test this hypothesis.

Other aspects of AEP performance have been tested relative to intelligence, for instance, by varying task demands. When tasks demand increasing concentration on a central stimulus, AEPs to peripheral and thus task-irrelevant stimuli diminish. It might be argued that as a simple task is made harder, high IQ subjects concentrate more effectively and demonstrate their superiority by a greater reduction in AEPs in response to peripheral irrelevant stimuli. Dinand and Defayolle (1969) have tested this hypothesis and obtained highly positive results. However, there are alternative explanations, such as the effects of retention on receptor orientation. It seems possible that duller subjects simply look more frequently at the peripheral stimuli when overwhelmed by the difficulty of the central task.

What may we conclude from these early studies? There are suggestions that IQ is correlated with short latency, high amplitude, less EP variability, and AEP asymmetry. Correlations, on the whole, are low, averaging between .2 and .3, and are often difficult to replicate. The indicators mentioned above are not independent functionally or statistically, which makes it difficult to use any form of causal analysis. Conditions of testing are undoubtedly important and suggest that nonattending conditions may be preferable to conditions demanding attention. But, there are so many differences in positioning of the electrodes and the intensity of the stimuli, as well as their modality; arrangement of trials and intertrial intervals; instructions given to subjects; internal states of motivation, etc.; and many other aspects of the situation that it is almost impossible to compare one study with another or to draw any general conclusions. One of the major reasons for the unsatisfactory state of the early work is undoubtedly its almost complete lack of theoretical sophistication and justification; most authors seem to have chosen parameter values almost at random, disregarding theoretical problems. It seems unlikely that this approach would lead to significant results, and more theory-guided approaches, as we shall see in the following sections, have yielded much more impressive results. As Kurt Lewin used to say, there is nothing as practical as a good theory!

AEPs AND INTELLIGENCE: RECENT PARADIGMS

In contrast to the earlier investigations in which attempts were made to relate arbitrary parameters of AEPs to psychometric intelligence test scores, the more recent studies adopt substantial theoretical approaches to the collection and analysis of empirical biophysical data. Not only has this resulted in some exceptional empirical results, it has also provided a framework wherein individual psychological differences may be perceived as the behavioral outcome of physiological system differentiation. Two major models have been proposed to date; they account for a variety of observed electrophysiological and behavioral phenomena in terms of neural ionics and general electrical systems theory. A third, less-well-defined model has been proposed to account for the relationship between levels of stimulus habituation (measured from the AEP) and test intelligence.

THE HENDRICKSON PARADIGM

A. E. Hendrickson (1982) and D. E. and A. E. Hendrickson (1980) have proposed a model of neuron function and cerebral process that challenges both conventional cognitive psychology and neurological science. Two main propositions characterize the model.

Proposition 1. The popular summation hypothesis of neuronal impulse propagation is rejected in favor of a pulse train hypothesis. That is, information within the central nervous system (CNS) is represented as a series of pulses (22 in the human, with 21 interpulse intervals), which forms the pulse train. Four discrete time intervals are proposed between 4 to 18 ms, with a mean of 11 ms. The integrity of the patterning/sequencing of intervals is defined as crucial to the continued propagation of the information, represented by the train, from neuron to neuron. Although not all stimuli are envisaged as being initially encoded as pulse trains, it is suggested that all higher levels of processing are encoded and processed within the brain in pulse train packets.

The summation hypothesis of neural encoding and transmission of information is rejected because of its inability to account for the degree of functional redundancy of the brain. In addition, neuron firing controlled solely by a summated set of inputs would not "store" information as to which inputs arrived at the cell body. Only if an input sequence pattern is stored by the neuron, or if all input and output connections bear some logical predefined relation to each other, will such information be available for subsequent coded transmission. The Hendricksons opted for the plausibility of the former hypothesis—maintenance of information by a nonrandom patterning of pulses within a pulse train packet.

There is some circumstantial neurophysiological evidence (Brink, Bronk, & Larrabee, 1946) with regard to the specified interpulse time intervals, which involves the experimental topical application of sodium citrate to a single nerve fiber dissected from the sciatic nerve of a frog. The post stimulus time stimulus histogram (PSTH) was generated in an unusual way. Instead of the abscissa displaying time from stimulus application in milliseconds, it was defined as the duration of interpulse intervals (milliseconds), the ordinate being the length of each observed interval rather than the usual number of pulses per duration unit after stimulation. From their figure, it is apparent that in this histogram there are three modes at approximately 6, 12, and 18 ms. The Hendricksons also considered modes at approximately 24 ms to be positive.

Unfortunately, this is the only evidence to date of such a patterning of interpulse intervals. Most, if not all, PSTHs are defined in terms of pulse activity rather than interpulse intervals. In addition, as the Hendricksons (1980) have pointed out, the bin size (the minimum measurement unit defining the abscissa) in the few similar studies is generally too large to detect such intervals. Finally, they insist that stimulation/inducement of pulses must be "natural," that is, they must be the result of "spontaneous" firing, not firing initiated by mechanical or chemical means along the nerve axon itself.

Proposition 2. Allied to the temporal events put forward in proposition 1 is a comprehensive range of biochemical and ionic events based on the concept and function of an engram RNA (eRNA) with a molecular weight of approximately 7,000 daltons, containing, between 21 and 9 bases (the actual number depending on the species of the animal), and about 150 Ångstroms in length. The eRNA, as with other more common forms of RNA, consists of an arbitrary sequence of four polynucleotides: guanine, cytosine, adenine, and uracil. This eRNA is posited to reside within the postsynaptic density (PSD), attached to microtubule-associated protein (MAP), just under the postsynaptic membrane (PSM). The temporal events (interpulse intervals) are translated into the chemical concomitants of neurotransmitter release and function, the sequencing of eRNA bases being associated with the postulated release of chemicals and ionic activity induced by the pulse train interpulse interval sequence.

A summary of the biochemical framework—to support neuron pulse train encoding, axon propagation and general CNS transmission—is given below. (The reader is referred to A. E. Hendrickson, 1982, for a complete exposition inclusive of ancillary neurophysiological evidence.) If we assume the attachment of eRNA bases to MAP (via H bonds—a different number and type for each polynucleotide) just under the PSM; the presence of a shield-like structure to prevent exposure of the entire backbone of the eRNA; and the presence of calmodulin (a calcium regulatory protein), calcium, and actin (a muscle protein having the function of kinesis—in this case being inhibited in a contractile state by a high concentration of calcium) in the PSD, the mechanism of pulse propagation may be described. A pulse arrives at the synapse. The synaptic vesicles of the presynaptic side discharge a transmitter molecule, acetylcholine (ACh). The ACh opens channels connecting the PSD to the synaptic cleft, allowing sodium (Na) to enter the postsynaptic side. Because of the positive charge of Na and the negative charge along the eRNA backbone, it is hypothesized that the H bond attachment (between the eRNA and MAP substrate) is weakened. If the Na is sufficiently concentrated, H bonds will be broken. Because of the hypothesized shield structure, however, not all bonds are affected at once. Then, because Na is hypothesized to inhibit the contractile state of the actin is weakened, and the bases of the eRNA move out from under the shield. The control of such movement is a function of the Na concentration, which is itself seen as a function of the number of pulses arriving at the presynaptic membrane; a sodium pump is hypothesized to immediately pump Na out of the PSD into the synaptic cleft at a constant rate—thus, the internal PSD concentration is a function of the amount of ACh discharged by the presynaptic vesicles over time. Assuming that the polynucleotides have a one-to-one correspondence with an interpulse interval (the four intervals put forward in proposition 1 above), a set of incoming pulses might affect the PSD Na level in such a way as to detach sequentially each polynucleotide base as it is "rotated" out from under the shield structure. If the entire eRNA strand is detached from the MAP, an unknown ionic transmitter is hypothesized to enter a microtubule ending that has been exposed because of the eRNA detachment. A new pulse train is now initiated, the synapse having effectively recognized an incoming pulse train. In fact, the Hendricksons go on to posit that this is the physiological basis for recognition memory.

It is proposed that learning and the formation of memory (eRNA templates) take place within the PSD. By hypothesizing the existence of a learning enzyme that will bind free nucleotide diphosphates (the precursors of RNA), and assuming that arrays of such diphosphates exist within the PSD, incoming pulses (equal Na levels) are hypothesized to detach diphosphates selectively in some arbitrary, stimulus-specific order such that they can be "knitted" together by the learning enzyme into the eRNA strand. This "free" eRNA will then form H bonds with a "free" MAP substrate (a MAP not already supporting an eRNA strand).

These two propositions describe the Hendrickson concept of the biological basis of intelligence. Individuals with neuronal circuitry that can best maintain the encoded integrity of stimuli will form accessible memories faster than those individuals whose circuitry is more "noisy." In addition, for individuals of low neural integrity, the maintenance of long sequences of pulse trains will be practically impossible; the total information content can never be stored in a meaningful way; thus no accessible memory can be formed. Hence, there would be observable differences within individuals' knowledge bases. This integrity loss of interpulse intervals within a pulse train was illustrated by A. E. Hendrickson (1982) using a simulation algorithm. Basically, the algorithm generated a series of equispaced (error-free) pulses over a period of 500 ms (500 replications). By adding random jitter (error) to the occurrence of the pulses in a cumulative manner, it was shown that with error values drawn from a normal distribution with mean 0 and standard deviation 2, the plotted output closely resembled a typical AEP form. Drawing upon the evidence of Fox and O'Brien (1965), Vaughan (1969), and Creutzfeldt, Rosine, Ito, & Probst (1969) relating the AEP to individual neuron spike discharges (averaged PSTHs), the Hendricksons concluded that the electrogenesis of the EEG is derived from the summation of individual pulses, if it is assumed that certain pulse trains are being replicated in a proportionately higher number than others. Thus, the AEP represents the pulse train activity recorded from an area of the scalp, following a series of identical stimuli. It was hypothesized that those individuals with noisy channels would produce AEPs of a smoother appearance than the AEPs from individuals with less noisy channels. This follows naturally from the simulation data; the more accurately pulse trains are encoded and replicated, the more such "pulse" information will be contained within the waveform of the AEP. The more error is introduced, the less information will be represented within the AEP, and the waveform will be smoother.

Consequently, the two measures that may be derived on the basis of this reasoning should correlate with psychometric test intelligence scores, given that such test performance is related to neural transmission integrity. The first measure would be the *complexity* of the waveform (assessed by measuring the contour perimeter of the AEP waveform—the "string" measure); the more intelligent the individual, the longer the contour. The second measure would be the *variance* at each point across a number of stimulus waveform epochs; the greater the variance, the less intelligent the individual. These two measures would be expected to correlate reasonably well, since they both derive from the same fundamental property of the pulse train. *We thus have a rational measure that can be objectively quantified and correlated with intelligence.*

The empirical evidence regarding the complexity/variance of the AEP is drawn from two studies. The first, reported by Blinkhorn and Hendrickson (1982), correlated the complexity (string) measure with performance on Raven's Advanced Progressive Matrices (APM) and a variety of verbal ability tests. Specifically, data were collected from 17 male and 16 female subjects. Auditory AEPs were generated, the stimulus consisting of a 1,000-Hz sine wave tone, of 30-ms duration, switched at the zero-crossing point and presented binaurally through headphones at 85-db SPL. The interstimulus interval was quasi-random between 1 and 8 s. The recording derivation was bipolar with montage $Cz-A_1$ (10–20 system) and epoch time was 512 ms with a 0.5-s sample speed (1,024 sample points for each of the 90 epochs). Various correlations between the string measure from variously generated AEPs (90, 64, and 32 epochs) and the APM yielded a mid-range correlation of approximately .45. The verbal test scores did not correlate significantly. However, because the range of the scores on the APM was restricted, Blinkhorn and Hendrickson corrected this value assuming a full range of IQ. The correlation was thus boosted to a maximum of .84. This value is reasonably close to one obtained by the Hendricksons (1980) in an analysis of some published data of Ertl's, for which they obtained a correlation of .77 between WISC IQs and the string score from the EPs; only extreme IQs were reported in the Ertl study.

In the second study (D. E. Hendrickson, 1982) a reasonably random sample of 219 schoolchildren (121 boys, 98 girls) was used. The WAIS (Wechsler, 1955) was used to assess IQ, scores being given for 11 separate subscales, a performance total, a verbal total, and an overall IQ. In addition to the complexity and variance measures defined above, D. E. Hendrickson defined a new *composite* measure. This measure was given simply as the variance score minus the string score. The stimulus presentation, data acquisition, epoch length, EEG derivation, and montage were the same as those reported in the first study.

The main results of the study are shown in Table 2. The correlations among the WAIS IQ and string, variance, and composite AEP measures are .72, −.72, and −.83, respectively. The correlations among the WAIS performance total and the string, variance, and composite measures are .53, −.53, and −.60, respectively. The correlations among the WAIS verbal total and the string, variance, and composite measures are .68, −.69, and −.78, respectively. Thus, contrary to the study of Blinkhorn and Hendrickson, it appears that the string measure (and both other measures) correlates higher with verbal abilities than with performance-related abilities.

We carried out a factor analysis, using the 11 WAIS scales and the composite AEP score. (See Table 5.) Only one general factor was extracted to represent, in a direct form, the g factor common to all the tests. On this factor, the AEP measure had a loading of .77. The highest loading of any of the Wechsler scales was the Similarities test (.82). (Corrections for attenuation due to scale unreliability gave a loading of .88.) The lowest

TABLE 2. Relationship between the EEG Measures and the WAIS Subtests

WAIS test	Variance	String	Variance minus string	Full WAIS IQ (current study)	Full WAIS IQ (published data)
Information	−.64	.55	−.68	.80	.84
Comprehension	−.50	.53	−.59	.74	.72
Arithmetic	−.57	.56	−.65	.79	.70
Similarities	−.69	.54	−.71	.84	.80
Digit span	−.54	.49	−.59	.71	.61
Vocabulary	−.57	.62	−.68	.79	.83
Verb total	−.69	.68	−.78	.95	.96
Digit symbol	−.28	.32	−.35	.45	.68
Picture comprehension	−.47	.52	−.57	.67	.74
Block design	−.50	.45	−.54	.70	.72
Picture arrangement	−.36	.45	−.46	.54	.68
Object assembly	−.32	.45	−.44	.55	.65
Performance total	−.53	.53	−.60	.69	.93
WAIS total	−.72	.72	−.83	1.00	1.00

Note. From *A Model for Intelligence* (p. 205) by H. J. Eysenck, 1982, New York: Springer. Copyright 1982 by H. J. Eysenck. Reprinted by permission.

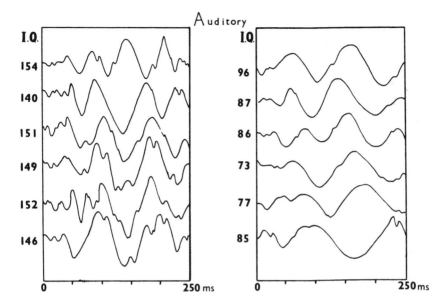

FIGURE 3. Evoked potential waveforms for six high and six low IQ subjects—auditory stimulation.

loading was that for the digit symbol subtest, an uncorrected value of .50 and a corrected value of .52.[2]

The data so far relate to the auditory mode of stimulation; however, D. E. Hendrickson carried out another study (unpublished) on 90 adults, using a visual flash stimulus. Retinal stimulation was indirect insofar as the xenon flash was presented behind the subject, who had closed eyes. A similar set of correlations between the composite measure and the IQ test scores was obtained, although the values were slightly lower. D. E. Hendrickson (personal communication) has indicated that the flash stimulus was not optimal, in that switching transients, eye movements, and differential retinal stimulation would have perhaps led to differential pulse train encoding of each stimulus.

It may be of interest to reproduce typical AEPs, with auditory and visual stimulation, for high and low IQ children. These are given in Figures 3 and 4 and illustrate the fact that high IQ children have more *complex* traces than have low IQ children.

---

[2] A previous analysis (Eysenck, 1982b) used data from a rather different group of Ss, including some high IQ adults as well as the schoolchildren, and hence gave slightly different results.

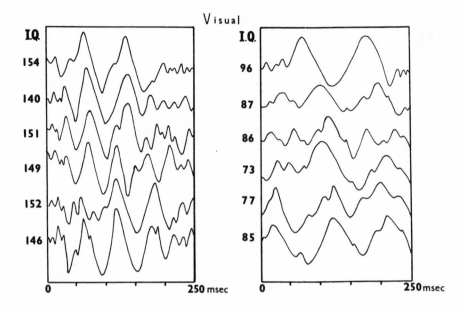

FIGURE 4. Evoked potential waveforms for six high and six low IQ subjects—visual stimulation.

Thus, the two published studies provide clear evidence of a relationship between intelligence test scores and AEP measures, as defined. Both studies provide an explicit methodology for easy replication by other investigators; in addition D. E. Hendrickson (1982) further justifies the use of closely controlled stimuli and random presentations. The evidence is certainly in accord with the model predictions.

Recently, two further studies included the Hendrickson string measure as part of their total methodology. Shagass, Roemer, Straunanis, and Josiassen (1981) attempted to replicate the Hendrickson results on a sample of 20 subjects (14 males and 6 females) ranging in age from 18 to 49. Unfortunately, Shagass *et al.* did not seem to be fully aware of the stimulus conditions required by the Hendrickson measurement paradigm. For example, the auditory stimuli were .1-ms duration clicks presented binaurally at 50-db SPL above a constant white noise level of 75 db. In addition, the subject was asked to look continuously at a constantly illuminated fixation point on a TV screen. Visual checkerboard and somato-sensory stimuli were also presented throughout the experiment. In all, 192 stimuli were presented (between 1.5 and 2.0 s pseudorandom interstimulus time) for each modality, and no two identical stimuli were delivered in succession. Lastly, scores on the measure of IQ adopted by Shagass *et al.* (Raven's Progressive Matrices), were transformed prior to correlation analysis in order to partial out the effects of age. However, given that age relates to fluid intelligence (of which the Raven test is a good measure), this would have the effect of weakening any relationship sought with an alternative measure of IQ.

Needless to say, Shagass *et al.* found no significant relationships among the auditory, visual, and somato-sensory AEPs string measures and IQ. In this experiment, so many conditions were confounded and so little attention was directed toward the separability among the stimulus conditions that it is not surprising that Shagass *et al.* emerged with data of doubtful empirical value. Although they report significant correlations between measures of evoked potential amplitude and IQ ($r = .60$), these were computed from only 14 subjects, 7 high IQ and 7 low IQ. No such data are presented for the 20 subjects used for the Hendrickson string data analysis. No reasons are given for such *a posteriori* selectivity.

Recently, Haier, Robinson, Braden, and Williams (1984) reported a relationship among various AEP waveform amplitude measures, the string measure, and Raven's APM. Twenty-two nursing students took part in the study. Visual AEPs were generated, using light flashes projected onto a translucent screen, with four levels of light intensity. Each light flash had a duration of 500 ms, with a total of 256 flashes presented at a constant rate of one per second, with 64 measurement epochs at each intensity. The order of intensities was pseudorandom, the 256 stimuli being presented in one session. The monopolar derivation EEG was recorded from montage Cz-A_1 (10–20 system), with A_1 as the reference. Sampling speed was 4 ms. Each subject repeated the entire procedure, and eyeblinks occurring during any particular epoch caused the epoch to be rejected. The AEP was computed for each intensity level across the records from both the artifact-rejected epoch set and from the "unfiltered" complete set of epochs. (It is not clear why the authors bothered to reject artifacts in one set and then simply included such errors in the other set.) Haier *et al.* used a different version of the string measure from that originally used by the Hendricksons. Whereas the Hendricksons assessed their measure by taking the mean of the total sum of squared deviations of each point from its adjacent point in time, Haier *et al.* used a value given by the sum of the the the absolute differences between the points. This latter method does not assure monotonicity with the Hendrickson measure.

The results indicated that *intensity of stimulus is important in determining the magnitude of the relationship among both the string and amplitude measures and the APM scores.* The correlations reported for the string measure indicated values around .23 for low-intensity stimulation and up to .45 for high intensities. For the amplitude measures, these values were around .35 and .63, respectively. Notably, the amplitude measures were correlated with the string measure taken over a 508-ms epoch. (The highest correlation was .79.) Although Haier *et al.* digress into arguments concerning the relative importance of stimulus intensity/amplitude measures/their string measure, the essential argument concerning the relationship between the string measure and the APM is missed entirely. All the measurement conditions employed by the Hendricksons were changed completely by Haier *et al.* Therefore, any arguments they may wish to make for or against the Hendrickson model or data are rendered irrelevant by the fact that two different experimental paradigms have been adopted by the investigators. To make a valid statement for or against the Hendrickson data, an investigator must at least *seriously* attempt to replicate their stimuli, sample speed, and measures.

Unlike the Shagass *et al.* (1981) study, this particular investigation did produce empirical results of some note. Although it is unfortunate that the theoretical component of the results is somewhat attenuated by the mismatch of the experimental paradigms, it does nevertheless present more evidence as to the strong relationship between AEP measures and IQ.

In concluding the examination of the Hendrickson paradigm, it must be said that, to date, their EEG results have not yet met the rigorous challenge that is demanded by initial results of such import and clarity. Rather, it appears that a somewhat sporadic, nonchalant approach has been adopted, epitomized by the Shagass *et al.* and Haier *et al.* studies. However, whereas definitive confirmation (or rejection) of the empirical data is urgently required, it nevertheless can be viewed as separate from the biological model proposals. Maintaining an attitude of hard empiricism, the data alone are crucial in their own right, the explanation/models may follow later.

The model *per se* is adventurous, challenging, and powerful. However, there is little or no empirical evidence for most of the fundamental assertions. Proposition 1 is crucial to the main body of the model statements, but the only empirical evidence that pertains to the statements in this proposition is that provided by Brink *et al.* (1946) and Scott (1948), in unpublished records quoted in Brink (1951). Although this evidence is indicative of rhythmic pulse activity with well-defined interpulse intervals, it is not indicative of pulse train activity consisting of discrete 22-pulse "packets." This is a fundamental assertion and must, therefore, be investigated more thoroughly. Obviously, there are difficulties in the arbitrary counting of pulses and interpulse intervals, but the evidence required is simply an instance of a neuron firing trains of pulses with regular (if somewhat jittered) interpulse intervals, corresponding to the four modal intervals hypothesized. Naturally, this would inspire greater confidence in the accuracy of proposition 1 of the model.

Unfortunately, with respect to proposition 2, there is no direct confirmatory empirical evidence. The assertion of the existence of eRNA, its location, associated processes, and function, is simply that. Hence, there is no point in attempting to argue for or against the accuracy of the model. The widespread ancillary physiological and circumstantial evidence is suggestive only, not confirmatory. However, the model represents an ingenious weaving of this evidence into a coherent set of explanations concerning *process*. It is sufficient to state that the model could be expressed as a computer simulation algorithm. Its specifications and assertions are that clear. It is, of course, a matter of conjecture whether this model construction is simply premature or part of an essential scientific methodology of process formulation, statement, and test. We would favor the latter assertion. The depth, scope, and detail of the model allow many assumptions to be tested and verified empirically, and to that end it is successful. It is unfortunate that neither psychologists nor neurophysiologists have yet taken up the challenge implicitly issued to them by the propositions and the corollaries of the model.

THE ROBINSON PARADIGM

Robinson (1982a, b), in direct contrast to the Hendricksons, has generated a model accounting for individual differences in personality and in intelligence. The model deals with physiological events without recourse to hypotheses concerning the behavior of individual neurons. Robinson has taken a more conservative approach, postulating physiological events generally in line with current established evidence. As such, no new physiological mechanisms are proposed for the model. Rather, he has used Pavlovian typology and general systems theory as his framework, generated a very precise model, and then subsequently tested the parameters of the model. We shall briefly discuss the background, logic, and main features of the model.

Pavlov, as a result of his studies on the differential individual behavioral concomitants of conditioning processes in dogs, postulated that specific behavioral types could be explained by the properties and interaction of hypothetical excitatory and inhibitory processes of the CNS. (He further claimed that these concepts also explained human individual differences in personality, performance, and susceptibility to psychopathology.) He proposed that the presence or absence of responses to discrete stimuli depended on whether the excitatory or the inhibitory process dominated and that the intensity of a response, or its suppression, depended upon the degree of dominance. His experimental results led him to conclude, first, that the extent to which a particular stimulus engaged both processes depended, in a lawful manner, on manifest differences in the experienced quality of contiguous stimulation during earlier stimulation. However, his results also demonstrated that the explanation for the variability of learned salivary responses could not be complete without referring to individual differences between subjects. He proposed as an explanation for these differences that apart from the extent to which a stimulus could engage either process, the relative effectiveness of the processes depended on intrinsic differences, which he called differences in "strength." (Mangan, 1982, gives a comprehensive account of this theory.)

He concluded that, in some animals, the excitatory and inhibitory processes were of equal strength and hence "balanced," although either might be stronger or weaker than normal. In other animals, he concluded that these processes were not balanced, and either an excitatory or inhibitory process was predominate. In addition, he inferred that stimuli can produce either diffuse and general patterns of cortical activation (irradiation) or, alternatively, more selective and sharply defined patterns (concentration). This inference has been supported by the electrophysiological recordings of Magoun (1961, p. 818). Concentration was associated with a better performance on discrimination tasks, whereas irradiation was associated with a poorer performance.

Robinson (1982a), after reviewing a large number of physiological studies on the cerebrum, concluded that the identity of neurophysiological subsystems corresponding to Pavlov's hypothetical processes is suggested by findings that define the role of the reticular formation with respect to behavior. In detailing the behavioral effects that Pavlov attributed to the processes of excitation and inhibition, Robinson concluded that the diffuse thalamocortical system (DTS) might also act as a mediator of Pavlovian excitation. Based on Pavlov's speculation—that excitation and inhibition are generated simultaneously (with different effects) in the same cortical cells—the DTS model proposed by Robinson, although identifying the excitatory processes with cortical cells, also identifies the inhibitory process with certain thalamic neurons. Given the reciprocal axonal connections between these neurons, in addition to evidence that both sets of neurons may be activated by the same conditioned stimulus, concordance with Pavlov's speculation is thus maintained.

Although the arguments presented above only suggest the identity of the DTS with Pavlov's typology, Robinson has extended his position by an elaboration on and a test of a transmission system model. Following Magoun's (1963) reference to the observed EEG phenomena accompanying direct DTS stimulation, Robinson proposed testing the DTS in human subjects. The logic behind this proposal is based on the assertion that given an input signal to the DTS and a resultant output scalp-recorded EEG signal, the intrinsic transmission properties of the hypothesized cortical and thalamic neural elements will be manifest in the stimulus–response relationship. More specifically, by drawing upon evidence from Barlow (1956), Brazier (1958), Cohn (1964), and Clynes, Kohn, & Lifshitz (1964) with regard to the rhythmic after-activity in the EEG following visual stimulation, and noting the similar transmission characteristics seen in particularly simple electrical networks, Robinson was able to derive an equation to describe the appropriate evoked EEG phenomena.

The transmission characteristic equation used is that for describing the behavior of the series RLC circuit, a simple oscillatory circuit having a network of inductance, capacitance, and resistive elements in series. The reasoning behind this choice of model is that since the EEG is an oscillatory phenomenon, the kind of relationship linking an input signal, system properties, and an output signal is suggested by other physical systems that oscillate. In general, sinusoidal oscillation tends to occur when a system displaced from equilibrium is subjected to a restoring force that is proportional to the displacement. This is the prototypical case for many oscillatory phenomena, and it is consistent with the reciprocal interaction of excitatory and inhibitory neurons that appears to be an almost universal feature of neural organization. For such a system, the relationship among an excitatory or driving input, system properties (components), and the activity of the system is described by the equation for forced harmonic motion. By virtue of its generality, and on the grounds of parsimony, physicists always use this equation as a model for oscillatory phenomena whenever it can be justified (French, 1971, p. 112).

By activating a system such as the RLC network with a range of input sinusoidal frequencies, the output can be perceived as the frequency response of the system. Plotting the input/output amplitude ratio against frequency yields the frequency response curve of the network. This curve describes the natural frequency (resonant frequency) of the network and its damping ratio (the restoring force). Basar (1982), Basar and Ungan (1976), and Basar, Demir, Gonder, and Ungan (1980) have extended this notion of brain resonance into strong and weak forms, in addition to postulating a probabilistic forced harmonic oscillatory model to explain the interactions of populations of oscillatory systems.

Thus, given the network model and its equation, Robinson developed an ingenious driving stimulus and measurement paradigm to test his assertions; 25 female and 23 male students took part in both the studies reported by Robinson (1982a, b). All subjects took the WAIS, Form A of the Embedded Figures Test (EFT) (Witkin, Oltman, Raskin, & Karp, 1971), and the Eysenck Personality Questionnaire (EPQ) (Eysenck & Eysenck, 1975). To elicit evoked brain responses, each subject was asked to attend to a diffuse field back-projected screen. A continuous sequence of sinusoidally modulated light was flashed onto the screen for 1 min, with up to 15 different frequencies within the range 7 to 13 Hz. (The sequence of frequencies was pseudorandom.) After each 1-min period of modulation, a 2-min rest period was given. During this rest period, the luminance of the screen remained constant. The modulation depth of the stimulus was held constant throughout the entire set of 15 1-min modulation periods: the mean luminance throughout each modulation period also remained constant. For each stimulus frequency between 7 and 13 Hz, an AEP was computed. Using a bipolar EEG derivation with montage $Pz-A_1$, a trigger pulse was delivered to the averaging computer each time the stimulus crossed the mean luminance level in a positive (or increasing) direction. The computer then accepted and stored the portion of the ongoing EEG that corresponded to just less than one cycle of the stimulus frequency. Thus, portions of the EEG corresponding to successive cycles of the sinusoidal stimulus were accepted and summed. (All averaging was, therefore, on line, with no facility to examine individual epochs.) Eye movements/artifacts were detected by examining an output paper trace of the raw EEG and signal source wave.

Fitting the network model equation to each subject's data, Robinson accounted for over 95% of EEG response amplitude variation in all but three subjects. In the worst case, just less than 90% of the variation was accounted for. Using two specific parameters, C and L, analogous to the capacitance and induction of the RLC network, Robinson could account for individual differences among subjects in terms of Pavlov's concepts of strength and balance.

The equation constants C and L were identified with excitation and inhibition, respectively. In combination C and L could be used to define the ST dimension and the B dimension. When subjects with extreme B dimension values were excluded, the variation of ST was correlated up to .95 with E and Stability (Low N) EPQ scores. By standardizing the subject's B and ST values, they could be regarded as Cartesian coordinates in two-dimensional space, and the vector lengths could be calculated in polar coordinates. Given the relationship between the B and ST dimensions and the C and L parameters, Robinson argued that each subject could be assigned a derived score V, using the values on the B and ST dimensions to define a coordinate point in the two-dimensional space of computing the length vector of the point from the origin. Robinson, suggested that when both B and ST took intermediate and similar values, superior intellectual performance would be manifest (the Pavlovian "concentration" concept). Thus, all other combinations of values would tend to be associated with less than optimal performance (the Pavlovian "irradiation" concept). To examine the validity of these statements, Robinson implemented a factor analysis of the WAIS subtests, the EFT score, the P and L EPQ scores, and the V "distance" measure. Table 3 shows the Varimax rotated four-factor solution.

The $-.80$ loading of V on factor 4 was interpreted by Robinson as support for the Pavlovian concepts of concentration and irradiation. Noting the similarity of the loading pattern in factor 4 to Cohen's (1957, 1959) patterns of the WAIS, Robinson designated factor 4 as the attention/concentration factor of the WAIS. Thus, the higher the V score, the lower the attention/concentration factor score; the obvious corollary was that the Pavlovian concept of concentration is measured by this factor. Robinson further speculated that factor 3 is a "mobility" factor (in the Pavlovian sense). However, this factor analysis must be cautiously interpreted. Only 48 subjects were used, and the solution of 4 factors appears to be arbitrary. (There were no tests of factor extraction-quantity or constrained orthogonal rotation.) Also, interpretation of loadings less than at least $|.3|$ is a practice fraught with dangers, especially when the standard error of each correlation

TABLE 3. Matrix of Varimax Rotated Factor Loadings[a]

	I	II	III	IV
Information	.88	.22	.24	.28
Comprehension	.68	.07	−.08	.04
Arithmetic	.51	.30	.18	.28
Similarities	.69	.42	−.10	.08
Digit span	.32	.27	.15	.52
Vocabulary	.72	−.13	.12	.14
Digit symbol	.22	.35	−.04	.48
Picture comprehension	.26	.39	−.05	−.10
Block design	.21	.66	.52	−.02
Picture arrangement	.11	.42	.54	.13
Object assembly	−.06	.64	.02	.16
P	−.10	−.04	.47	.22
L	−.07	−.03	−.63	.00
Field independence	.21	.66	.52	.25
V	−.12	.12	−.24	−.80

Note. From 'Properties of the Diffuse Thalamocortical System, Human Intelligence and Differentiated vs Integrated Models of Learning by D. L. Robinson, 1982, *Personality and Individual Differences*, 3, p. 400. Copyright 1982 by Pergamon Press. Reprinted by permission.

[a] The six highest loadings on each factor have been underlined for clarity.

coefficient is relatively high ($\sim 1/\sqrt{N}$, where N = the number of variables).

However, even a cautious view of the data would suggest that an effect is present, perhaps not in the way Robinson might propose, but there certainly is a correlation with some subset of intelligence test scales, EPQ scores, and the EFT score. Both studies obviously require replication and extension in much the same way as the Hendrickson work. Two completely different models have been specified to account for two sets of experiment results, even though the Pavlovian typology could be explained by the Hendrickson pulse train model. However, given the speculative nature of the model to date and the lack of replicated/validated results from the Robinson studies, this would not be a worthwhile exercise.

THE SCHAFER PARADIGM

In recent years, studies showing the influence of selective attention (Hillyard, Hink, Schwent, & Picton, 1973; Picton & Hillyard, 1974), expectancy (Squires, Wickens, Squires, & Donchin, 1976; Schafer, Amochaev, & Russell, 1981), and information processing workload (Schafer, 1978; Israel, Wickens, Chesney, & Donchin, 1980) on the amplitude of AEPs have all demonstrated a cognitive modulation of EEG activity. This modulation is manifested as the tendency for unexpected or "attended" stimuli to produce AEPs of larger overall amplitude than those generated using stimuli, the nature and timing of which is known by the individual. Schafer has extended the scope of this empirical phenomenon, hypothesizing that individual differences in the modulation of amplitude (cognitive neural adaptability) will relate to individual differences in intelligence. The physiological basis of this relationship is hypothesized to be neural energy as defined by the number of neurons firing in response to a stimulus. A functionally efficient brain will use fewer neurons to process a known stimulus, whereas for a novel, unexpected stimulus, the brain will commit large numbers of neurons.

Given the relationship between individual neuron firing patterns and observed cortical AEPs, the commitment of neural energy will be observed as amplitude differences between AEPs elicited under various stimulus presentation conditions. Schafer defines his operational measures as variations around the concept of an individual's "average amplitude." Thus, individuals with high neural adaptability, characterized by AEPs with much smaller than average amplitude to expected stimuli and much larger than average amplitude to unexpected stimuli, should show a high intelligence test score. Conversely, for individuals with low neural adaptability, the size of such AEP amplitude modulation should be diminished, with a correspondingly low intelligence test score.

Two studies have been implemented by Schafer using a specific stimulus presentation paradigm known as "self-stimulation." Schafer and Marcus (1973) investigated the neural adaptability hypothesis using three groups of subjects ranging in age from 3 to 78 years old. Both visual and auditory AEPs were generated, the visual stimuli being 10-ps light flashes, whereas the auditory stimuli were 1-ms clicks delivered at 60-db SPL through a loudspeaker placed above the subject. Bipolar EEG derivations of $Cz-A_1$ and $Oz-A_2$ (10–20 system) were utilized. Each measurement epoch was 500 ms, with 2-ms sampling speed, and 100 epochs per condition for both stimulus types. Stimuli were presented under four experimental conditions. Condition 1, self-stimulation (SS), in which subjects delivered clicks and flashes to themselves by pressing a hand-held microswitch, with some attempt to deliver the stimuli randomly in time. The stimulus sequence was recorded for subsequent playback in condition 3. Under condition 2, periodic stimulation (PS), clicks and flashes were presented regularly at the rate of one every 2 s. Under condition 3, machine stimulation (MS), the recorded stimulus events generated in condition 1 (SS) were replayed to the same subjects. Condition 4 was a self-stimulation control condition (C), in which the subject pressed the microswitch, but received no stimulus. All conditions were counterbalanced across subjects.

Intelligence was not measured, but rather the groups were selected for intelligence level based upon medical and social/educational criteria. Group 1 (low IQ) was made up of institutionalized Down Syndrome retardates; group 2 (median IQ), technicians; group 3 (high IQ) PhDs. Group composition and age means were not reported.

The results indicated that, overall, auditory stimuli elicited the greatest amplitude changes observable in the AEPs, with the $Cz-A_1$ montage providing the best separation of conditions. Comparison of the integrated waveform amplitude for each AEP from the three conditions of SS, PS, and MS indicated that the MS condition generated AEPs with maximum amplitude; the PS condition was intermediate; and the SS condition, was lowest.

Following these results, Schafer and Marcus developed a self-stimulation score for each individual: the percent difference between the amplitude of SS AEP and MS AEP. Plotting this score against a subset of subjects from the three groups yielded a positive relationship. However, no correlation coefficient was reported.

The importance of the results is, unfortunately, affected by the lack of comprehensive detail in the report. No psychometrically reliable/valid tests of intellectual performance were used to directly measure the intelligence of each individual. No correlations were computed, no indications were given as to the number of subjects within each group, their age, or their sex. In addition, the computations and comparisons that were reported were based upon subjects selected from the original groups. No reasons for these selections were given by the investigators.

The study reported by Schafer (1982) is far superior to that detailed above, both in its methodology and the clarity of its results. In addition, a more direct test of Schafer's concept of cognitive neural adaptability was attempted. Two groups of subjects took part in this investigation. Group 1, the normal sample, consisted of 63 female and 46 male adults recruited from laboratory and hospital staff, with a mean age of 28 years. Group 2, the retarded sample, consisted of 32 male and 20 female subjects, with a mean age of 30 years. All subjects in Group 2 were in a mental institution. The IQ for the 74 subjects in the normal sample of 109 subjects were assessed using the WAIS, yielding a mean full scale IQ of 118, with a range from 98 to 135. The IQ for the retarded sample was assessed using both the Stanford Binet and the Leiter Performance scale, yielding a mean IQ of 37, with a range from 18 to 68.

Fifty auditory click stimuli were presented to each subject, at 60-db SPL, under the same three stimulus conditions as in Schafer and Marcus (1973), reported above (the control condition for postmovement vertex potentials was also included). Bipolar EEG derivation using montage Cz-A was utilized with a 3- to 30-Hz bandpass region. Epochs were 500 ms, digitized at 2 ms intervals. Two sets of AEP scores for each subject were obtained. The total integrated amplitude of each AEP from each condition (SS, PS, and MS) was expressed as a ratio of each subject's average AEP amplitude. Average amplitudes (AV) were then computed from the sum of the integrated amplitude AEP measures under all three experimental conditions divided by the number of conditions: for example, $AV = (SS + PS + MS)/3$. A neural adaptability T score was computed for each subject using the formula $NATS = [(MS - SS)/AV] + 50$.

The results showed that the normal subjects had a significantly smaller than average AEP to self-delivered stimuli (SS condition), which indicated the presence of the temporal expectancy effect. The retarded subjects showed no statistically significant difference. For the PS condition, the results were repeated, although the ratio was slightly larger for the normal group; this indicated less temporal expectancy than was seen under the SS condition. Comparison of the two groups on the MS/AV ratio indicated a significant difference, showing the normal group orienting to the random stimuli with higher amplitude AEPs than the retarded group.

Correlations between the various test scores from the 74 normal subjects with measured IQ are shown in Table 4. A correlation of .66 can be observed between the NATS scores and the WAIS full IQ. Given the somewhat restricted range of the IQ scores, Schafer corrected this value to

TABLE 4. Correlations between Evoked Cortical Potential Amplitude Ratios and Neural Adaptability T Score (NATS), and Psychometric Intelligence

	Age	WAIS full IQ	WAIS verb IQ	WAIS performance IQ	PPVT IQ	NATS	Periodic/av	Self/av	Random/av	P$_{157}$ latency
WAIS full IQ	.28									
WAIS verbal IQ	.48	.90								
WAIS perf IQ	.19	.75	.40							
PPVT IQ	.52	.75	.75	.51						
NATS	.09	.66	.63	.44	.60					
Periodic/average	.07	.40	.38	.25	.30	.63				
Self/average	.06	.44	.42	.31	.52	.60	.13			
Random/average	.10	.65	.61	.43	.59	.97	.53	.63		
P$_{157}$ latency	−.08	.16	.09	.18	.06	.05	.01	.18	.01	
N^a	109	74	74	74	55	109	109	109	109	109
Mean	28.47	117.69	118.86	113.54	121.51	50.62	.903	.775	1.321	115.03
S.D.	6.98	9.20	10.66	9.50	13.99	9.74	.161	.163	.206	20.35

Note. From "Neural Adaptability: A Biological Determinant of Behavioural Intelligence" by E. W. P. Schafer, 1982, *International Journal of Neuroscience, 17,* 187. Copyright 1982 by Gordon & Breach Science Publishers, Inc. Reprinted by permission.

^{a} With $N = 109$, Pearson r coefficient of .25 significant at .01 level; with $n = 74$, r of .30 significant .01 level.

yield a coefficient of .82. Thus, the higher the IQ, the greater the amplitude difference between MS and SS AEP amplitude. This implies greater flexibility in the attentional response to expected stimuli, that is the higher IQ subjects habituate to a greater extent (as indexed by amplitude) to regular, expected stimuli than do the lower IQ subjects.

The results presented above support the differentiation of AEP amplitude under different stimulus conditions, and as a function of measured IQ. However, the operational definition of neural adaptability as variation in amplitude around an arbitrary measure of brain potential mean amplitude is not the most elegant way of demonstrating the concept of neural adaptability. In addition, Schafer appears to ignore the consequences, as reflected in his AEPs, of the very effect he is examining— habituation. The initial EPs in the SS and PS conditions might be expected to have higher amplitudes than the later 40th to 50th EPs. By averaging all the EPs, he is probably missing some valid signal/amplitude effects.

If we recast his paradigm simply as a set of tasks involving a habituation effect, we can then approach the whole data analysis in a completely different way. Neural adaptability may be reflected as speed of habituation provided by a slope coefficient computed from successive epoch group AEP mean amplitude values. If the AEP signal/noise improvement ratio is proportional to $\sqrt{N}$ (N = the number of epochs to be averaged; since Schafer's data is significantly bandwidth compressed, $\sqrt{N}$ is actually a conservative estimate of the "smoothing" function), and it Binnie, Rowan, and Gutter's (1982) assertion that a fairly clear AEP may be computed with about 12 to 15 trials is correct, it would have been useful to group the fifty epochs into at least four successive epoch subgroups. Amplitude slope parameters, computed from the AEPs given by each subgroup, could then have been used for comparative and computational purposes. Thus, the data would be more efficiently examined, in better accord with the underlying hypothesis than the use of "global" averages. Of course, increasing the number of epochs per condition would give better averaging within each epoch subgroup.

Looking at the size of the amplitude change across tasks, and expressing these values as mean difference percentage change values computed from either the regressed subgroup AEP mean integrated amplitude values or the raw data values, we should once again be able to test Schafer's basic hypothesis more directly. Thus, high IQ subjects should habituate faster, with a correspondingly larger amplitude loss than should low IQ subjects. Schafer's analysis cannot validate his hypothesis; however, our form of analysis considers both the speed and level of event adaptation independently of any concept of average brain amplitude. Neural adaptability is, therefore, defined purely in terms of event adaptation as demonstrated by a series of conditions manipulating the periodicity/ regularity of stimulus presentation.

It is interesting to note that Schafer's hypothesis and results can be explained in terms of the Hendricksons' theory. Processing errors would be expected to delay recognition of repetition essential to adaptation; hence, the loss of AEP amplitude with repetition (adaptation) would be less in low IQ than in high IQ subjects. This hypothesis should be tested directly in any repetition of the Schafer experiment.

THEORY AND MEASUREMENT

In science, measurement and theory always go hand in hand. Measurement without theory is meaningless; theory without measurement is impotent. Even in areas in which the methods of measurement are so familiar as to suggest that theory is of no importance, it can be shown historically that such a view is wrong. We are so accustomed to the measurement of heat by means of fluid-in-glass thermometers that we fail to realize how much such measurements depend on theory. Early thermometers of this kind were open at the top, thus making measurement dependent not only on heat, but also on barometric pressure; it was only when theory differentiated between these two effects that heat could be accurately measured. Hence, in a book on measurement, theory is a vital ingredient, and in this section of our chapter, we will try to suggest how theory and measurement are integrated in view of the new data presented.

One aspect of the psychophysiological measurement of intelligence that, at the moment, depends less on theory than on experience is the EEG methodology used. In our experience, even quite small and apparently unimportant details can be critical to the measurement of intelligence. The type of electrode and electrode paste, the intensity and spacing of stimuli, the degree of expectancy of stimuli, and many other variables have turned out to be crucial in the investigation of intelligence by means of EPs, but to date there is little by way of theory to guide the investigator. In view of the importance of the problems raised, however, it seems worthwhile to discuss, at least briefly, some of the general conclusions we have drawn. We will then go on to a theoretical problem relating to the nature of intelligence and the questions posed by the results of the work reported in the literature, and this volume.

We are concerned with the acquisition of approximately 2-Hz and greater frequency signals using percutaneous (scalp) electrode placements, recording over relatively brief periods of time (15 min to 1 hr), with awake and/or attentive subjects. There is evidence to indicate that the use of polarizable gold or nonpolarizable silver/silver chloride cup or disc electrodes is immaterial to the collection of artifact-free EEG data. The use of gold electrodes, however, depends on capacitive input-coupled AC potential amplification, with an input impedance of at least $1\,M\Omega$ (Zablow & Goldensohn, 1969; Cooper, Osselten, & Shaw, 1969; Goff, 1974; Binnie et al., 1982). In addition, the area of the electrode contact surface will determine the efficiency of signal reproduction. Gold conducts only by capacitive coupling to the underlying tissues so the larger the surface contact area, the greater the capacitive coupling.

The specific requirements of multielectrode detailed AEP methodology necessitate data acquisition methods far superior to the more usual laboratory or clinical on-line signal averager. In order to compute within-sample variability coefficients, such as the subset correlation, standard deviations of normalized evoked potentials, and the coefficient of variability (Callaway, 1975), the investigator must have access to individual EP epochs. These records will also be used for selective averaging/artifact-free averaging (Pfurtscheller & Cooper, 1975) and for such post hoc filtering as Wiener, Kalman response adaptive, or generalized bandpass (Barlow, 1979; Basar, 1980). The collection and manipulation of these data is feasible only with the use of a digital computer. Given a signal sampling speed of 1 ms, an epoch length of 1 s, 100 epochs, and four unfiltered input EEG channels, a data acquisition system must sample, digitize (preferably a minimum of 12 bit analogue to digital [A/D] conversion accuracy), and store ~ 400 Kb of information. The cross channel sample sequencing will be determinate upon either a multiplexed or an individual buffer sample and hold A/D process. The storage time will be determined by main memory size of the processor, in addition to the access and write speed of secondary storage. Thus, if contemplating the use of a microcomputer acquisition facility, it is advisable to opt for a 16 bit processor, a 12 bit A/D, a minimum of 128-Kb main memory, and a fixed head, $5\frac{1}{4}$-in., 10-Mb Winchester disc for secondary data storage. Commercial signal acquisition hardware for this equipment is usually some form of multichannel multiplexer combined with a single A/D unit. The total efficiency of the system depends, of course, on the efficiency of the software algorithms designed to drive the equipment.

Given that raw signal data are acquired in this way, speed, efficiency, and long-term storage of all data are possible. Obviously, this system is most suited to AEP work in which short duration epochs are required. For spontaneous EEG and long-term recording, analog tape may perhaps be more efficient. However, signal bandwidth (frequency range) and its relation to the minimum Nyquist frequency will determine the sampling speed and, hence, storage requirements. For example, if the range of frequencies is only between 1 and 40 Hz, then a sample speed of around 10 ms would be acceptable. Assuming 4-hr continuous recording, over four hardware bandpass filtered channels with a 10-ms sampling speed, a total of 5.76 Mb of data will require storage.

Finally, with regard to the specific measures taken from the AEP waveform, such as peak latencies; total integrated and/or peak amplitude; the Hendrickson string, variance, and composite measures; and the Schafer NATS score, it is essential that when possible, most if not all these measures *must* be computed as a matter of course in any study relating AEP parameters to intelligence. If an investigator wishes to introduce a new measure, new stimuli, new responses, or a combination of all three, it is crucial that some reference be made to already established measures. If the study is an attempt at replication and extension, then all conditions and measures for the replication phase of the study *must match those of the original study*. Similarity is no substitute for exactitude when dealing with controversial, novel, and as yet unreplicated results. The further elucidation of the relationship between intelligence and parameters of the AEP requires careful investigative work of particularly high quality. Electrophysiological recording techniques and the electrical activity of the brain are subject to many different influences, most of which cause several nontrivial events to occur. For example, static, rapid, uncontrolled polarization of electrodes, mains voltage fluctuations, earth loops, subject movement, insufficient A/D sampling speed, and component failure all add artifacts to the EEG signals. In addition, stimulus intensity, type, sequencing, EEG montage, derivation, and recording time can all produce nontrivial differences in AEP waveforms. Hence, at present, caution should be viewed as the better part of science.

Given that these various instructions are heeded, what do the recorded measures, in fact, tell us? In what way can we say that the Hendrickson combined measure, for example, is an index of intelligence? The easy way out would be to say that the Wechsler test (or the Raven Matrices) is considered a good measure of intelligence and that any measure that correlates .83 with the Wechsler (or the Matrices) is *eo ipso* a good measure of intelligence. Such an answer, although true as far as it goes, clearly disregards many important differences between such a test as the Wechler and the EP. The Wechsler, following the Binet tradition, is essentially a *cognitive* test and inextricably reflects previously acquired knowledge; problem-solving capacity; learned strategies; factual information; and all sorts of educational, cultural, and socioeconomic factors related to the acquisition of knowledge and the evolvement of strategies. Modern cognitive theories of intelligence, as discussed in great detail in Sternberg's (1982) *Handbook of Human Intelligence*, seem to rely *exclusively* on factors of this kind in explaining individual differences in intelligence; there is no mention in Sternberg's book of work with EPs. Yet none of these factors seem to play any part in the type of measurement used by the Hendricksons, Schafer, or Robinson. This is a paradox that clearly requires some kind of resolution.

The obvious answer that suggests itself is, or course, that underlying individual differences in intelligence, which constitute the core of the concept itself, is the physiological process measured by the EP. Here, as we have seen, various theories differ considerably from each other; let us for the moment simply consider the Hendricksons' theory, namely, the occurrence of errors in transmission as being responsible for differences in intelligence. The argument that follows could just as easily be made about the alternative theories considered, but we feel that at the moment the Hendricksons' theory has the best empirical support and is the most fundamental; it will therefore be used to stand for any kind of psychophysiological theory that postulates processes in the nervous system as underlying differences in intelligence.

The psychophysiological measures used would, based on this assumption, furnish us with a direct measure of the genetic basis of intelligence, unadulterated by socioeconomic, educational, and cultural factors and disregarding acquired knowledge and learned problem-solving strategies, except insofar as the acquisition of such knowledge and such strategies itself depends on intelligence A. We would thus say that the failure of the correlation between the Wechsler and the EP measure to achieve unity results from the fact that the Wechsler, in addition to measuring intelligence, also measures acquired skills of various kinds, such as those dealt with in Sternberg's book. The arrows in Figure 1 indicate the position here taken, with the g_p arrow pointing more directly at intelligence A, while the arrows symbolizing g_f, and, even more, g_c, point more directly at intelligence B.

If this were true, and if we can assume that different IQ tests combine the various cognitive elements in different ways, then we would expect that the psychophysiological measures of intelligence would correlate more highly with different tests of IQ than these do among themselves. This appears to be true. We have seen that correlations above .8 can be obtained between the Hendricksons' measure and the Wechsler or the Matrices; intercorrelations among the Wechsler, the Binet, and the Matrices, for such populations as were used in the Hendricksons' work, are usually below .8. It might of course be possible to construct two tests of IQ very similar with respect to the demands made on nongenetically controlled aspects of intelligence, and here these tests might correlate more highly with each other than either would with the Hendricksons' measure.

This argument can be extended and tested by means of the data from the Hendrickson experiment discussed earlier. If the general factor obtained from the intercorrelations between all the subtests of the Wechsler is our best index of intelligence and if the AEP composite measure represents a good measure of intelligence, then we would expect the *factor loadings on the 11 WAIS subtests and the correlations of the subtests with the AEP composite measure to be proportional.* Table 5 shows the actual data, giving both factor loadings and correlations with the composite AEP measure. In view of the fact that the reliabilities of the different WAIS subtests are not identical, we give both the uncorrected (raw) correlations and the correlations corrected for attenuation. It will be seen that as far as the correlation between factor loadings and composite measure are concerned, the correction makes little difference; the Spearman rho is .95 for the uncorrected values and .93 for the corrected values. Proportionality, therefore, is almost perfect and strongly supports the view that the EP is a true measure of intelligence.

A model of intelligence involving essentially error-free transmission of information through the cortex must be amplified to be made to do the job

TABLE 5. Correlation between WAIS Subsets and Composite AEP Measure and Factor Loadings of WAIS Subtests, Both Uncorrected and Corrected for Attenuation[a]

| WAIS subtests | Correlations with | | | |
| | Composite AEP measure | | Factor loadings | |
	Uncorrected[b]	Corrected[c]	Uncorrected[b]	Corrected[c]
Information	−.68	−.71	.78	.82
Comprehension	−.59	−.66	.73	.82
Arithmetic	−.65	−.73	.78	.88
Similarities	−.71	−.76	.82	.88
Digit span	−.59	−.70	.68	.81
Vocabulary	−.68	−.70	.79	.81
Digit Symbol	−.35	−.36	.50	.52
Picture Completion	−.57	−.63	.68	.75
Block Design	−.54	−.58	.71	.77
Picture Arrangement	−.46	−.57	.58	.71
Object Assembly	−.44	−.55	.58	.72
The AEP Composite Measure	—	—	−.77	—

[a] All rankings were carried out on the full eight decimal precision correlations and loadings.
[b] The Spearman rho between the *Uncorrected* correlations and loadings = .95.
[c] The Spearman rho between the *Corrected* correlations and loadings = .93.

it is intended to do. Thus, if it is to serve as a model for problem-solving in its widest sense (and certainly intelligence is closely related to problem-solving, in any theory), then we must postulate some kind of regular search mechanism, of the kind discussed by Furneaux (1973). Such a search mechanism, involving, of course, accessing short-term and long-term memory, would clearly be much handicapped by frequent errors in transmission and would thus give rise to individual differences in problem-solving ability. We would also have to postulate, as does Furneaux, some kind of comparator, which would compare the solution offered by the search mechanism with the requirements of the problem. The model is, of course, rudimentary, but it does indicate the direction in which we should look, given that differences in correct transmission are basic to differences in intelligence.

It will also be seen that such a model would incorporate all the data that have suggested to previous authors (Jensen, Brand, and others) that the essential feature, in psychophysiology, that is responsible for differences in intelligence is mental speed. Speed itself depends on correct transmission; if information transmission is incorrect, it has to be repeated, thus slowing down the process of problem-solving, and possibly, if too many errors are involved, making problem-solving impossible because of the decay of short-term memory traces. Thus, the theory does not contradict earlier views of the importance of mental speed for intelligence; it merely suggests that speed is possibly a secondary mechanism that depends on the correct transmission of information through the cortex (Eysenck, 1982a).

If some such view were, in fact, correct, and we have here only outlined it in the briefest compass because in this chapter we obviously cannot go into too great detail, then we might claim that we now may be able to measure intelligence in a manner that is more akin to natural science measurement than is the ordinary type of IQ measurement. The EP is not, like the IQ, a *relative* measure, dependent on inter-personal comparisons with no true zero and no equal intervals. It has the same advantages as a yardstick, the thermometer, or the voltmeter and, hence, should greatly simplify the scientific measurement of intelligence.

In addition, the psychophysiological measurement of intelligence has the obvious advantage that it is much less dependent on, and may even be independent of, intruding environmental factors of an educational or a cultural kind. Consider, for instance, the question of differences in intelligence between males and females. Although there are no differences on IQ tests between men and women, on average, it has been suggested that this may be due to the fact that items showing such differences are usually discarded from the construction of IQ tests, making the finding a self-fulfilling prophecy. The Hendricksons have shown that there are no significant differences between males and females on the EP, either, and this would seem to be a much more definitive finding in view of the fact that no exclusion of items could possibly account for the observed identity. Similarly, the greater variance of males on IQ tests has sometimes been suggested to be an artifact, but the fact that on the EP similar significant differences have been observed by the Hendricksons suggests that this is a true biological difference that must be taken into account (Eysenck, 1982a).

It is, of course, possible to suggest that even the EP is influenced by experiences of early childhood, school learning, and other events and is not a "pure" measure of innate ability. Such objections are sometimes based on the work of Rosenzweig (1964), who demonstrated that brain changes in rats depended on conditions of early upbringing, including environmental deprivation. Much other material is summarized in McV. Hunt (1961). It should be noted that the conditions producing such cortical effects are usually extreme and not comparable to the relatively small environmental variations characteristic of upbringing in Western societies. Nevertheless, the point is a valid one, theoretically, and genetic studies will be required to substantiate the heritability of EP measures as compared with IQ measures.

If our theory is along the right lines, can we assume that the EP will supplant ordinary IQ tests in everyday life? The answer to this question is probably "no." Intelligence quotient tests in schools, industry, and the armed forces are used for practical purposes, and for these, a mixture of innate ability and learned knowledge may be more predictive than the EP alone. Hence for many practical purposes, ordinary IQ tests may be a better choice, and they are cheaper and easier to administer as well.

This is, of course, not always true. In many cases the results of IQ tests are misleading, as when the IQs of schizophrenics, deeply anxious patients, or individuals of a very different cultural or socioeconomic and educational background are measured. In such cases, it would seems desirable to have a measure less contaminated than the usual IQ test by cultural, educational, and other environmental factors. Thus, even in the practical plane, the new test may find a secure place.

Its main claim to acceptance, however, lies in the experimental and theoretical plane. Most theoretical questions concerning intelligence are difficult to answer because the 20% variance in IQ tests due to environmental factors usually covers an area larger than the area that is likely to be covered by the social factors to be investigated. Thus, class differences in intelligence are difficult to investigate by means of IQ tests because it is always possible to argue the relative importance of environmental and genetic factors, given the observed differences in IQ. (See Eysenck, 1982a, b, for the use of the AEP in this connection.) Similarly with respect to the decline of IQ with age, different tests give different results, and arguments about the degree or even the presence of the decline in question can arise. In all such cases, recourse may be had to psychophysiological measures as relatively free of such disturbing influences. These new developments hold out exciting prospects for the solution of questions that have plagued students of intelligence almost from the beginning of the scientific study of intelligence in the days of Galton and Binet.

To say this is not to deny, of course, that a great deal of empirical work still remains to be done before the general view here adumbrated can be accepted. Obviously, replication of the work here cited will be essential, and much work also remains to be done on the study of various parameter values, only some of which have been investigated. Indeed, although it may be said that the work here recounted constitutes a revolution in the measurement of intelligence, it must also be said in caution that what we have so far is only the beginnings of such a revolution. As Kuhn has often pointed out, a revolution in science is followed by a long period of problem-solving activity of what he calls "normal science," and what is now needed more than anything is a long period of such "normal science" to solve the many problems that have already arisen, or are likely to arise, in the study of intelligence by means of psychophysiological indices. The model here outlined is only a skeleton; what is required now is the detailed experimental work that alone can transform it into the flesh and blood of a true scientific theory. But whatever future experiments may hold in store for us, it is already obvious that the old Binet-type model of intelligence is no longer tenable, and that something new must take its place.

REFERENCES

Barlow, J. S. *Computerised Clincical Electroencephalography in perspective.* IEEE Transactions on Biomedical Engineering, 1979, BME-26, 7, 377–391.

Barlow, J. S., & Brazier, M. A. B. *The pacing of EEG potentials of alpha frequency by low rates of repetitive flash in man.* Program, American EEG Society, 1956.

Barnet, A. EEG and evoked response correlates of mental retardation. *Clinical Proceedings of the Children's Hospital,* 1971, 27, 250–260.

Barnet, A., & Lodge, A. Click evoked EEG responses in normal and developmentally retarded infants. *Nature,* 1967, 214, 252–255.

Barry, W., & Ertl, J. P. Brain waves and human intelligence. In B. Davis (Ed.), *Modern educational developments: Another look.* New York: Educational Records Bureau, 1965.

Basar, E. *EEG–Brain Dynamics.* New York: Elsevier, 1980.

Basar, E., & Ungan, P. Nonlinearities in biology. E. Basar (Ed.), *Biophysical and physiological systems analysis.* Reading, Mass: Addison-Wesley, 1976.

Basar, E., Demir, N., Gonder, A., & Ungan, P. Combined dynamics of EEG and evoked potentials. 1. Studies of simultaneously recorded EEg-EPograms in the auditory pathway, reticular formation and hippocampus during the waking stage. *Biological Cybernetics,* 1979, 34, 1–19.

Bennett, W. F. Human perception: A network theory approach. *Nature*, 1968, *220*, 1147–1148.

Binnie, C. D., Rowan, A. J., & Gutter, T. H. *A manual of electroencephalographic technology.* New York: Cambridge University Press, 1982.

Blinkhorn, S. F., & Hendrickson, D. E. Averaged evoked responses and psychometric intelligence. *Nature*, 1982, *295*, 596–597.

Borge, G. F. Perceptual modulation and variability in psychiatric patients. *Archives of General Psychiatry*, 1973, *29*, 760–763.

Brazier, M. A. B. Studies of evoked responses by flash in man and cat. In H. H. Jaspers, L. D. Proctor, R. S. Knighton, W. C. Noshay, & R. T. Costello (Eds.), *Reticular formation of the brain.* Boston: Little, Brown, 1958.

Brazier, M. A. B. Evoked response recorded from the depth of the human brain. *Annals of the New York Academy of Science*, 1964, *112*, 33–59.

Brink, F., Jr. Excitation and conduction in the neuron. In S. S. Stevens (Ed.), *Handbook of experimental psychology.* New York: Wiley, 1951.

Brink, F., Bronk, A., & Larrabee, D. W. Chemical excitation of nerve. *Annals of the New York Academy of Science*, 1946, *47*, 457–470.

Callaway, E. Correlations between averaged evoked potentials and measures of intelligence. *Archives of General Psychiatry*, 1973, *29*, 553–558.

Callaway, E. *Brain electrical potentials and individual psychological differences.* London: Grune & Stratton, 1975.

Callaway, E. Individual psychological differences and evoked potential variability. *Progress in Clinical Psychophysiology*, 1976, *6*, 243–257.

Cattell, R. B. Theory of fluid and crystallized intelligence: A critical experiment. *Journal of Educational Psychology*, 1963, *54*, 1–22.

Cattell, R. B. *Abilities: Their structure, growth and action.* Boston: Houghton Mifflin, 1971.

Chalke, F., & Ertl, J. Evoked potentials and intelligence. *Life Sciences*, 1965, *4*, 1319–1322.

Clynes, M., Kohn, M., & Lifshitz, K. Dynamics and spatial behavior of light evoked potentials, their modification under hypnosis, and on-line correlation in relation to rhythmic components. *Annals of the New York Academy of Science*, 1964, *112*, 468–509.

Cohen, J. The factorial structure of the WAIS between early adulthood and old age. *Journal of Consulting Psychology*, 1957, *21*, 283–290.

Cohen, J. The factorial structure of the WISC at ages 7–6, 10–6, and 13–6. *Journal of Consulting Psychology*, 1959, *23*, 285–299.

Cohn, R. Rhythmic after-activity in visual evoked responses. *Annals of the New York Academy of Science*, 1964, *112*, 281–291.

Cooper, R., Osselton, J. W., & Shaw, J. C. *EEG technology.* London: Butterworth, 1969.

Creutzfeldt, O. D., Rosina, A., Ito, M., & Probst, W. Visual evoked response of single cells and of EEG in the primary visual area of the cat. *Journal of Neurophysiology*, 1969, *32*, 127–139.

Davis, F. B. The measurement of mental ability through evoked potential recording. *Educational Record Research Bulletin*, 1971, No. 1.

Davis, H., & Davis, P. Action potentials of the brain in normal persons and in normal states of cerebral activity. *Archives of Neurological Psychiatry*, 1936, *36*, 1214–1224.

Dinand, J. P., & Defayolle, M. Utilisation des potentials evoques moyennes pour l'estimation de la change mentale. *Agressologie*, 1969, *10* (Suppl.), 525–533.

Donchin, E., Kubony, M., Kutas, M., Johnson, R., & Herning, R. Graded changes in evoked response (P300) amplitude as a function of cognitive activity. *Perception and Psychophysics*, 1973, *14*, 319–324.

Dustman, R. E., & Beck, E. C. The visual evoked potential in twins. *Electroencephalography and Clinical Neurophysiology*, 1965, *19*, 570–575.

Dustman, R. E., & Beck, E. C. Relationship of intelligence to visually evoked responses. *Electroencephalographic and Clinical Neurophysiology*, 1972, *33*, 254.
Dustman, R. E., Schenkenberg, T., & Beck, E. C. The development of the evoked response as a diagnostic and evaluative procedure. In R. Karrer (Ed.), *Developmental psychophysiology in mental retardation and learning disability*. Springfield, Ill.: Thomas, 1975.
Ellingson, R. J. Relationship between EEG and test intelligence: A commentary. *Psychological Bulletin*, 1966, *65*, 91–98.
Engel, R., & Henderson, N. B. Visual evoked responses and I.Q. scores at school age. *Developmental and Medical Child Neurology*, 1973, *15*, 136–145.
Ertl, J. Fourier analysis of evoked potentials and human intelligence. *Nature*, 1971, *230*, 525–526.
Ertl, J. I.Q., evoked responses and Fourier analysis. *Nature*, 1973, *241*, 209–210.
Ertl, J., & Schafer, E. Brain response correlates of psychometric intelligence. *Nature*, 1969, *223*, 421–422.
Everhart, J. P., Chin, C. L., & Auger, R. A. Measures of EEG and verbal intelligence: An inverse relationship. *Physiological Psychology*, 1974, *2*, 374–378.
Eysenck, H. J. Primary mental abilities. *British Journal of Educational Psychology*, 1939, *9*, 270–275.
Eysenck, H. J. (Ed.) *The measurement of intelligence*. Lancaster, Penn.: MTP, 1973.
Eysenck, H. J. *The structure and measurement of intelligence*. New York: Springer, 1979.
Eysenck, H. J. *A model for intelligence*. New York: Springer-Verlag, 1982a.
Eysenck, H. J. The psychophysiology of intelligence. In C. D. Spielberger & J. N. Butcher (Eds.), *Advances in personality assessment* (Vol. 1). Hillsdale, N. J.: Lawrence Erlbaum Associates, 1982b.
Eysenck, H. J., & Eysenck, S. B. G. *Manual of the Eysenck personality questionnaire*. London: Hodder and Stoughton, 1975.
Fox, S. S., & O'Brien, J. H. Duplication of evoked potential waveform by curve of probability of firing of a single cell. *Science*, 1965, *147*, 888–890.
French, A. P. *Vibrations and waves*. London: Nelson, 1971.
Furneaux, W. D. Intellectual abilities and problem-solving behaviour. In H. J. Eysenck (Ed.), *The measurement of intelligence*. Lancaster, Penn.: MTP, 1973. pp. 212–237.
Galbraith, G., Gliddon, J., & Busk, J. Visual evoked responses in mentally retarded and non-retarded subjects. *American Journal of Mental Deficiency*, 1970, *75*, 341–348.
Giannitrapani, D. EEG average frequencies and intelligence. *Electroencephalography and Clinical Neurophysiology*, 1969, *27*, 480–486.
Goff, W. R. Human average evoked potentials. In R. F. Thompson & H. M. Patterson (Eds.), *Bioelectric recording techniques*. New York: Academic Press, 1974.
Gucker, D. Correlating visual evoked potentials with psychometric intelligence, variation in technique. *Perceptual and Motor Skills*, 1973, *37*, 189–190.
Guilford, J. P. *The nature of human intelligence*. New York: McGraw-Hill, 1967.
Guilford, J. P., & Hoepfner, R. *The analysis of intelligence*. New York: McGraw-Hill, 1971.
Haier, R. J., Robinson, D. L., Braden, W., & Williams, D. Electrical potentials of the cerebral cortex and psychometric intelligence. *Personality and Individual Differences*, 1984, *5*, 293–301.
Henderson, N., & Engel, R. Neonatal visual evoked potentials as predictors of psycheducational tests at age seven. *Developmental Psychology*, 1974, *10*, 269–276.
Hendrickson, A. E. The biological basis of intelligence: Part 1: Theory. In H. J. Eysenck (Ed.), *A model for intelligence*. New York: Springer-Verlag, 1982.
Hendrickson, D. E. *An examination of individual differences in the cortical evoked response*. Unpublished doctoral thesis, University of London, 1972.

Hendrickson, D. E. The biological basis of intelligence. Part II: Measurement. In H. J. Eysenck (Ed.), *A model for intelligence*. New York: Springer-Verlag, 1982.

Hendrickson, D. E., & Hendrickson, A. E. The biological basis of individual differences in intelligence. *Personality and Individual Differences*, 1980, *1*, 3–33.

Hullyard, S. A., Hink, R. F., Schwent, V. L., & Picton, T. W. Electrical signs of selective attention in the human brain. *Science*, 1973, *182*, 177–180.

Hunt, McV. J. *Intelligence and experience*. New York: Ronald Press, 1961.

Israel, J. B., Wickens, C. D., Chesney, G. L., & Donchin, E. The event related brain potential as an index of display monitoring workload. *Human Factors*, 1980, *22*, 211–224.

Jensen, A. R. The chronometry of intelligence. In R. J. Sternberg (Ed.), *Advances in the psychology of human intelligence*. London: Lawrence Erlbaum Associates, 1982a.

Jensen, A. R. Reaction time and psychometric g. In H. J. Eysenck (Ed.), *A model for intelligence*. New York: Springer-Verlag, 1982b.

Jerison, H. Evolution of the brain and intelligence. New York: Academic Press, 1973.

Jewett, D. L., Romano, M. N., & Williston, J. S. Human auditory evoked potentials: Possible brain stem components detected on the scalp. *Science*, 1970, *107*, 1517–1518.

John, E. R. Brain evoked potentials: Acquisition and analysis. In R. F. Thompson & M. M. Patterson (Eds.), *Bioelectric recording techniques*. New York: Academic Press, 1973.

Juel-Nielsen, N., & Harvald, B. The electroencephalogram in uniovular twins brought up apart. *Acta Genetica*, 1958, *8*, 57–64.

Lairy, G. C., Remond, A., Rieger, H., & Lesevre, N. The alpha average: III. Clinical application in children. *Electroencephalography and Clinical Neurophysiology*, 1969, *26*, 453–467.

Lennox, L. G., Gibbs, E. L., & Gibbs, F. A. The brain-wave pattern, an hereditary trait. *Journal of Heredity*, 1945, *36*, 233–243.

Lewis, E. G., Dustman, R. E., & Beck, E. C. Evoked response similarity in monozygotic, dizygotic, and unrelated individuals: A comparative study. *Electroencephalography and Clinical Neurophysiology*, 1972, *32*, 309–316.

Lewis, G. W. Visual event related potentials of pilots and navigators. In D. Lehman & E. Callaway (Eds.), *Human evoked potentials: Applications and problems*. New York: Plenum Press, 1979, pp. 462ff.

Lindsley, D. B. The reticular motivating system and perceptual integration. In D. E. Sheer (Ed.), *Electrical stimulation of the brain*. Austin: University of Texas Press, 1961.

Magoun, H. W. Electrophysiology of learning. *Annals of the New York Academy of Science*, 1961, *92*, 813–1198.

Magoun, H. W. *The waking brain* (2nd ed). Springfield, Ill.: Thomas, 1963.

Mangan, G. L. *The biology of human conduct: East–West models of temperament and personality*. Oxford: Pergamon Press, 1982.

Netchine, G., & Netchine, S. Organisation psychologique et organisation bioélectrique, cérébrale dans une population d'arrienes mentaux. *Psychologique Française*, 1962, *7*, 241–258.

Osborne, R. T. Heredability estimates for the visual evoked response. *Life Sciences*, 1970, *9*, 481–490.

Ostow, M. Psychodynamic distrubances in patients with temporal lobe disorder. *Journal of Man* (Sinai Hospital), 1954, *20*, 293–308.

Pfurtscheller, G., & Cooper, R. Selective averaging of the intracerebral click evoked responses in man: An improved method of measuring latencies and amplitudes. *Electroencephalography and Clinical Neurophysiology*, 1975, *38*, 187–190.

Picton, T. W., & Hillyard, S. A. Human auditory evoked potentials: Effects of attention. *Electroencephalography and Clinical Neurophysiology*, 1974, *36*, 191–199.

Regan, D. *Evoked potentials in psychology, sensory physiology and clinical medicine*. New York: Wiley-Interscience, 1972.

Rhodes, L., Dustman, R., & Beck, E. The visual evoked response: A comparison of bright and dull children. *Electroencephalography and Clinical Neurophysiology*, 1969, *27*, 364–372.

Roberts, R. C. Some concepts and methods in quantitative genetics. In S. Hirsch (Ed.), *Behavior-genetic analysis*. New York: McGraw-Hill, 1967, pp. 214–257.

Robinson, D. L. Properties of the diffuse thalamocortical system and human personality: A direct test of Pavlovian/Eysenckian theory. *Personality and Individual Differences*, 1982a, *3*, 1–16.

Robinson, D. L. Properties of the diffuse thalamocortical system, human intelligence and differentiated vs integrated modes of learning. *Personality and Individual Differences*, 1982b, *3*, 393–405.

Rosenzweig, M. R. Effects of heredity and environmental on brain chemistry, brain anatomy, and learning ability in the rat. *Kansas Studies in Education*, 1964, *14*, 3–34 (Reprinted in Eysenck, 1973).

Rust, J. *Genetic factors in psychophysiology*. Unpublished doctoral thesis, University of London, 1974.

Rust, J. Cortical evoked potential, personality and intelligence. *Journal of Comparative and Physiological Psychology*, 1975, *89*, 1220–1226.

Schafer, E. W. P. Brain responses while viewing television reflect program interest. *International Journal of Neuroscience*, 1978, *8*, 71–77.

Schafer, E. W. P. Neural adaptability: A biological determinant of behavioural intelligence. *International Journal of Neuroscience*, 1982, *17*, 183–191.

Schafer, E. W. P., & Marcus, M. M. Self stimulation alters human sensory brain responses. *Science*, 1973, *181*, 175–177.

Schafer, E. W. P., Amochaev, A., & Russell, M. J. Knowledge of stimulus timing attenuates human evoked cortical potentials. *Electroencephalography and Clinical Neurophysiology*, 1981, *52*, 9–17.

Shagass, C. *Evoked brain potentials in psychiatry*. New York: Plenum Press, 1972.

Shagass, C., Roemer, R. A., Straunanis, J. J., & Josiassen, R. C. Intelligence as a factor in evoked potential studies in psychopathology. 1. Comparison of low and high I.Q. subjects. *Biology Psychiatry*, 1981, *11*, 1007–1029.

Shucard, D. Evoked potential amplitude change related to intelligence and arousal. *Psychophysiology*, 1973, *10*, 445–452.

Shucard, D., & Callaway, E. Auditory evoked potential amplitude and variability—effects of tasks and intellectual ability. *Journal of Comparative and Physiological Psychology*, 1974, *87*, 284–294.

Shucard, D., & Horn, J. Evoked cortical potentials and measurement of human abilities. *Journal of Comparative and Physiological Psychology*, 1972, *78*, 59–68.

Spearman, C. *The abilities of man*. London: Macmillan, 1927.

Sternberg, R. J. (Ed.) *Handbook of human intelligence*. London: Cambridge University Press, 1982.

Squires, K. C., Wickens, C., Squires, N. K., & Donchin, E. The effect of stimulus sequence on the waveform of the cortical event related potential. *Science*, 1976, *193*, 1142–1146.

Thurstone, L. L. *Primary mental abilities*. Chicago: University of Chicago Press, 1938.

Thurstone, L. L., & Thurstone, T. G. *Factorial Studies of Intelligence*. Chicago: University of Chicago Press, 1941.

Vaughan, H. G. The relationship of brain activity to scalp recording of event related potentials. In E. Donchin & D. B. Lindsley, (Eds.), *Average evoked potentials*. NASA SP-191 Washington, D.C., 1969.

Vernon, P. E. *Intelligence: Heredity and environment*. San Francisco: Freeman, 1979.

Vogel, W., & Broverman, D. M. Relationship between EEG and test intelligence: A critical review. *Psychological Bulletin*, 1964, *62*, 132–144.

Vogel, W., & Broverman, D. M. A reply to "Relationship between EEG and test intelligence: A commentary." *Psychological Bulletin*, 1966, *65*, 99–109.

Weinberg, H. Correlation of frequency spectra of averaged visual evoked potentials with verbal intelligence. *Nature*, 1969, *224*, 813–814.

Witkin, H. A., Oltman, P. K., Raskin, E., & Karp, S. *A manual for the Embedded Figures Test*. Palo Alto: Consulting Psychologists Press, 1971.

Young, J. P. R. An investigation of the role of genetic factors in certain spontaneous and induced changes in the human electroencephalogram. Unpublished doctoral thesis, University of London, 1969.

Zablow, L., & Goldensohn, E. S. A comparison between scalp and needle electrodes for the EEG. *Electroencephalography and Clinical Neurophysiology*, 1969, *26*, 530–533.

2

Methodological and Statistical Techniques for the Chronometric Study of Mental Abilities

ARTHUR R. JENSEN

The study of individual differences in reaction time (RT) had its origin not in psychology, but in astronomy. The Prussian astronomer F. W. Bessel, in 1823, coined the term *personal equation* for the consistent differences among telescopic observers in recording the exact moment that the transit of a star crosses a hairline in the visual field of the telescope. The need to make corrections for the personal equation led to the invention, in 1828, of the chronograph, an instrument for the precise measurement of RT, which was later to become useful to psychologists.

But it was not until the 1860s that RT was taken up by psychologists. In that same decade, psychology was launched as an empirical science. Its founding fathers were Sir Francis Galton (1822–1911), in England, and Wilhelm Wundt (1832–1920), in Germany.

The measurement of RTs figured prominently in the laboratories of both Galton and Wundt, but their purposes were quite different and led them in separate directions. Galton's interest was mainly in the nature and measurement of individual differences. He has been claimed as the father of differential psychology, which also subsumes mental measurement, or psychometrics. Wundt is recognized as the founder of experimental psychology; he aimed to discover the general principles of mind and behavior, much as physicists had established the fundamental laws of matter and energy.

This division between the methods and aims of differential and experimental psychology has existed from psychology's very beginnings as

---

ARTHUR R. JENSEN ● School of Education, University of California, Berkeley, California 94720.

an empirical science. Distinct lines of descent, from Galton and Wundt to the present, are discerned through the history of psychology, not just as the normal division of investigative labor, which necessarily exists in every science, but also as a difference in philosophical attitude and theoretical orientation with regard to psychology's development, both as pure science and as technology. Psychology's historical duality is often referred to today, in terms of Cronbach's (1957) well-known characterization, as "the two disciplines of scientific psychology." Cronbach deplored the theoretical and methodological separateness of the two disciplines and suggested that a proper marriage would prove fruitful, and indeed was necessary, for the advancement of psychology as a science.

This bit of history is recounted as relevant to RT research because it is exactly in this specialized domain that, finally, we are seeing the rapid development of what may well be the most promising example of the kind of marriage that Cronbach had envisaged between the two disciplines of scientific psychology.

In Galton's laboratory, RT was simply used as one among several measures of individual differences in "human faculties." In addition to RT, Galton also measured other elemental sensory–motor functions and physical traits that he judged to be significant in human evolution and believed to be more strongly influenced by heredity than by environment. He hoped that some weighted combination of such measurements would afford an objective index of an individual's largely innate general mental capacity. The practical application of this effort, as Galton (1908) stated in his autobiography, "would be to estimate the combined effect of these separately measured faculties. . . and ultimately to ascertain the degree with which the measurement of sample faculties in youth justifies a prophecy of future success in life, using the word 'success' in its most liberal meaning" (p. 267). So it was that Galton's work foreshadowed what was later to become one of the most controversial aspects of applied psychometrics—the prediction of an individual's future educational or occupational performance from current measurements of ability or aptitude.

Although Galton himself invented a novel device for measuring RT accurately (to one one-hundredth of a second), there is no evidence that he had any interest in RT as a phenomenon to be studied experimentally in its own right. He viewed RT only as one of many different means of mental measurement. Unfortunately for the history of psychometrics, Galton's overly simple method of RT measurement could only reveal a scarcely impressive relationship to other criteria of intellectual capacity, although it is noteworthy that several of Galton's laboratory tests, including RTs to auditory and visual stimuli, showed statistically significant mean differences between several occupational levels, from professional to unskilled worker. The use of only *simple* RT, and with too few trials for adequate reliability, doomed it to failure. (The average test–retest reliability of Galton's RT measurements was only about .17.) The same mistakes, repeated by Galton's immediate disciples (most notably James McKeen Cattell), led to the premature abandonment of RT as a technique for the study of individual differences in mental ability; the technique was not to be revived for at least half a century.

In Wundt's laboratory, however, with its strong experimental emphasis, its search for general principles, and its lack of interest in individual differences (except as "error" variance), RT measurement served a very different purpose in psychological research. At that time, it proved to have a scientifically more influential purpose, so much so, in fact, that Boring, in this *History of Experimental Psychology* (1950), refers to the late nineteenth century as "the period of mental chronometry." Reaction time was used then as the principal technique for the objective analysis, or decomposition, of mental activity, identifying, and measuring in real time, such processes as perception, apperception, cognition, association, discrimination, choice, and judgment.

The essential idea for this application of RT in psychological research is credited to F. C. Donders, a Dutch physiologist, whose innovative method, first published in 1862, was taken up and developed further in Wundt's laboratory in Leipzig in the 1880s. Donders' essential methodological contribution was the *subtraction method,* which is the notion that the different speeds of reaction to experimentally varied tasks represent additive components of time for the execution of the various mental processes occasioned by the task conditions and that the differences between the reaction times to the systematically varied tasks could be used to isolate and determine the duration of each of the component processess of a complex mental act (Donders, 1868/1969). The assumption is made that the time for all such processes intervening between stimulus and reaction summate in a strictly additive fashion and therefore can be precisely decomposed by subtracting the RT to simpler tasks from the RT to more complex tasks. Although this assumption has since been seriously criticized, the basic idea was an especially important one for psychology at that time, for it demonstrated that mental events take place in real time that could be precisely measured and quantitatively analyzed, as are physical events in the natural sciences. And thus, with the advent of RT measurement, psychology took a large step on its path, from speculative philosophy to empirical science.

Then, shortly after the turn of the century, interest in RT markedly waned as experimental psychologists became increasingly engrossed in the laboratory study of conditioning and learning as pioneered by Pavlov and Thorndike. Except for an occasional study using RT (which now takes on retrospective significance), there was slight interest in RT research among academic psychologists for almost 50 years. In the 1970s, RT was rediscovered by researchers in experimental cognitive psychology. This field has adopted RT techniques, now more broadly termed *mental chronometry*, as its most important methodology. Although a number of psychologists were instrumental in this recent revival of mental chronometry, it probably owes most to the initial work of Michael I. Posner and Saul Sternberg, who are both still active in this field.

CATEGORIES OF REACTION TIME RESEARCH

Today, RT research can be conveniently divided into three categories, although the three are not always distinct in the research literature. Each is important for our purpose.

Reaction Time per se *as a Dependent Variable.* Reaction time can be studied experimentally as a dependent variable in its own right. This research aims to comprehend all the stimulus and response conditions, and the effects of practice, on all the measurable parameters of RT performance, including the overt error rate. The main focus is on the measurement properties of RT itself. Research in this area goes beyond empirical description of functional relationships. It is now concerned with the construction and testing of theories or models of the RT process that can include all the observed variation in RT as a function of experimentally manipulable variables (Smith, 1968). A recent example of this kind of model, and the evidence brought to bear on it, is found in the recent work of Grice, Nullmeyer, and Spikes (1982). There is no generally accepted theory or model of choice for RT yet. But this type of experimental investigation of RT, along with testable hypotheses to explain the results, is valuable and necessary for the other two categories of uses of RT. The essential nature of RT cannot be ignored when RT is used as a measurement technique for the primary study of other, more complex, cognitive phenomena. Many lines of research on RT *per se,* in addition to such other lines of investigation as time perception (e.g., Pöppel, 1978), the latency of conscious awareness (Libet, 1965), and evoked brain potentials (e.g., A. E. Hendrickson, 1982; D. E. Hendrickson, 1982) must all converge on the "black box" of hypothetical cognitive or neurological processes that mediate stimulus and response in mental tasks, if this black box is ever to be scientifically fathomed. Only then we can hope to understand the basic mechanisms responsible for individual differences in performance on mental tasks. The attempt to formulate testable models of the brain, for which RT affords a promising methodology, among others, is essentially a search for simplicity. The achievement of simplicity in science is greatly aided by sensitive and precise measurements. A scientist cannot wallow in unquantified complexity if he is to escape hopelessly vague or untestably complex causal theories. Good scientists succeed in *achieving* simplicity. Newton expressed this idea in his famous dictum "Nature is simple." In truth, however, neither simplicity nor complexity is inherent in nature. Simplicity or complexity are constructions of the scientist's effort to understand nature, an effort that is often abetted by more powerful techniques of observation and measurement. Such is the role of RT in the study of higher mental processes.

Reaction Time as an Analytic Technique in Experimental Cognitive Psychology. Research in cognitive psychology using RT techniques has been called *mental chronometry* by Posner (1978), who defines mental chronometry as "the study of the time course of information processing in the human nervous system" (p. 7). The growth of interest in RT in recent years has paralleled the growth of experimental cognitive psychology, for which the precise measurement of time has become the most frequent dependent variable used for the analysis, or decomposition, of the processes involved in *cognitive* tasks.

The emphasis here is on *cognition,* because RT measurement has too long been popularly thought of as the assessment of sensory–motor ability. It is taken for granted even by many psychologists, for example, that highly skilled athletes should outperform, say, university students in all RT tasks. Yet Mohammed Ali, perhaps the greatest boxer of all time, in his prime was found to show a very average RT (Keele, 1973). The fact is that only a small part of a person's total RT is attributable to peripheral sensory–motor functioning. The total RT sequence between stimulus onset and the initiation of response includes sense organ lag, peripheral nerve transmission time, muscle latency, and brain time. Most of the total time consists of brain activity, which is what cognitive psychologists are especially interested in evaluating. Moreover, experimental techniques permit the separation of the times required for the sensory–motor activity from brain time in a particular RT task. For example, it has been determined that only 15 to 30 milliseconds (ms) is required from sense organ to brain, whereas the fastest human RT to a single stimulus is about 150 ms. The stimulus–response (S–R) time for a spinal or subcortical reflex is more than twice the simple RT (SRT), showing that the cerebral cortex is the main source of delay in RT.

Another important fact that emphasizes the relative importance of cerebral activity in RT, as contrasted with sensory–motor mechanisms, is the finding that there is quite a large general factor in individual differences (ID) in various RT tests, which cuts across all different stimulus and response modalities—visual, auditory, tactile, left and right hands and feet, and biting. Hence, there seems little doubt that RT is more central than a peripheral phenomenon. Even if this were not the case, it would be possible, experimentally, to determine the amount of time attributable to peripheral processes and that attributable to central processes.

An extremely simple example of how processes can be determined is the decomposition of the time required to name visually presented words. It has been observed that words that are longer, in number of syllables, take more time to name, when time is measured from the onset of visual presentation to the initiation of the spoken word, recorded by a voice-activated key. The question is, Do longer words take longer to name because they take longer to be visually encoded, that is, recognized, or because the vocal response takes longer? The experimental paradigm for answering this question is simple. In the first condition, the person sees single words projected one at a time on a screen and reads each word aloud as fast as possible. The average S–R interval, or RT, is recorded for words of different numbers of syllables. This interval comprises the amount of time it takes the person to *encode* the stimulus and to *prepare* the appropriate vocal response, an act that involves the complex coordination of breath, vocal cords, tongue, and lips. In the second condition, the person sees single words projected on a screen, but is instructed to delay the vocal response until a light flashes on, there being a brief interval between the presentation of the word and the light. The average interval between the flash of light and the initiation of the vocal response is also recorded as a function of word length. This interval represents the time taken for the first condition *minus* the time required for the *encoding* of the stimulus word. What the experiment reveals may seem surprising: the time variation in naming words, as a function of their number of syllables, is attributable to differences in encoding time and not to differences in response preparation time (Eriksen, Pollack, & Montague, 1970). This simple experiment illustrates a general assumption in mental chronometry, which is that information processing takes place in real time in a sequence of stages and that the total measured time from the initiation of a mental task can be analyzed in terms of the time required for each stage. It can also be determined whether the stages are temporally discrete, or overlap or interact for any given task.

Another possible separation of cognitive processes by mental chronometry is the important distinction between *structural* and *functional* components of information processing, which are analogous to the "hardware" and "software" components of a computer, respectively. The structural components, for example, would be less easily influenced by practice or special training than would the functional components. The functional components involve the control of processing within the structure and would involve different responses to instruction for various strategies applied to a cognitive task. Individual differences in the structural and functional aspects of information processing would seem to correspond rather closely to Cattell's distinction between fluid and crystallized ability (Cattell, 1971). Piaget's theory of cognitive development similarly distinguishes among structure, function, and content of mental operations (Flavell, 1963, Ch. 2).

Although at present there is no general theory of information processing, practically all workers in this field view the structural, or hardware, components as consisting of such elemental processes as sensory encoding, or the mental representation of a stimulus; short-term and long-term memory storage; memory scanning and retrieval systems; and response execution. But the extent to which each of these processes can be characterized as structural or functional is still open to question and investigation, as is even the clearness of the distinction between structure and function as it applies to the brain. Analogizing from computer components to a neurological system can suggest hypothetical cognitive models, but the limitations of such a method for understanding biological systems are recognized.

The list of substantive topics in psychology to which analysis by chronometric methods has already been applied is extensive—sensory coding; selective attention; apprehension; perceptual integration; pattern recognition; stimulus comparison, matching, and transformation; retrieval of information from short-term and long-term memory; psychological refractoriness; parallel and serial information processing; the mental representation of semantic and logical relations; inference in verbal, pictorial, and figural analogies; spatial reasoning; and the selection and execution of responses, to name only the most commonly researched processes. Chronometry has also been used to study such complex phenomena as *reading skills* (e.g., Carpenter & Just, 1975; Ehri & Wilce, 1983; Posner, Lewis, & Conrad, 1972; Spring, 1971), *dyslexia* (Spring & Capps, 1974), *mental retardation* (Baumeister & Kellas, 1968), and even *personality* (Brebner, 1980).

Reaction Time in the Analysis of Individual Differences in Mental Abilities. The elementary information processes discovered in the kind of studies described in the preceding section display a wide range of individual differences (IDs). In studies of elemental cognitive processes, even in groups with a highly restricted range of ability, such as university students, IDs constitute a much large source of variance in RT measurements than do the experimentally manipulated task conditions. For example, 85% of the total variance is ascribable to IDs and only 15% to the experimental conditions in Posner's (1978, Ch. 2) letter-matching task, in which subjects, under one condition, must respond *same* or *different* to pairs of letters in terms of their physical characteristics (upper *versus* lower case type) or, under another condition, must respond *same* or *different* to their letter names. The latter condition has longer RTs, because in addition to sensory encoding of the stimuli, semantic encoding is required, which involves access to overlearned letter names in long-term memory. The IDs in such processes can be the main object of investigation in their own right.

If the rank order of IDs in RT measurements were found to be no more consistent than if the order were determined with a table of a random numbers, between one experimental paradigm and another, then the measurements, however reliable they may be in any one paradigm, would be so task-specific as to be too trivial for scientific study. Hence the study of IDs in elementary cognitive tasks must rely heavily on methods of correlation analysis to identify sources of IDs that are not too task-specific. The investigator seeks evidence for the generality of IDs in the chrono-metric measurements obtained in a particular experimental paradigm. Unfortunately, this quest is made difficult by the fact that a very substantial part of the IDs variance in fine-grained laboratory measurements is task-specific. That is to say, IDs do not remain in the exact rank order from one task to another, even when, formally, the tasks would seem to elicit the same processes. In the terminology of the analysis of variance, IDs *interact* with the specific or unique features of each task. In terms of correlation, IDs are imperfectly correlated among various tasks, even after the correlations are corrected for attenuation as a result of errors of measure-ment. In terms of factor analysis, the single tasks have rather large *specifics*, that is sources of reliable IDs variance that are not shared with other tasks. Hence, analyses of variance, correlations, and factor analysis are the obvious methods for determining sources of IDs in elementary cognitive tasks that have enough generality across tasks to be of theoretical or practical interest.

Two main strategies have been adopted in this pursuit. The first, but least developed, looks for correlations among RT measurements of theoreti-cally similar cognitive processes (e.g., sensory encoding, choice, response selection) as they are hypothesized to occur in different experimental paradigms. Reliable and even fairly substantial correlations that demon-strate IDs in the hypothesized elementary processes involved in different tasks have been found. Evidence for the distinct processes depends on the finding of higher correlations among chronometric variables hypothesized to arise from the same process than among variables hypothesized to arise from different processes (e.g., Keating & Bobbitt, 1978). However, the observed correlations, even after correction for attenuation, are usually smaller than those we are accustomed to find among various tests in traditional psychometrics. The most probable reason for this is that the individual experimental paradigms used for chronometric analysis yield scores (time measurements) that are factorially more like scores on single items in psychometric tests than total scores on tests with many different items. In psychometric tests composed of varied items, more of the total IDs variance consists of item covariance than of item specificity. The total variance in test scores comprises the sum of the item variances plus twice the sum of the item covariances, and the item covariances increase at a greater rate, by a factor of $n^2 - n$, than do the item variances, as the number of items, n, increases. It should be recalled that the single items in psychometric tests have large specifics, the average correlation among single items being usually in the .2 to .3 range. The larger the number of various items, the more is the specificity "averaged out," so to speak, accentuating whichever factors the items measure in common. To be sure, the use of many repeated trials in chronometric tasks can ensure high internal consistency reliability, but it does not diminish task specificity. Given the great homogeneity of the repeated measures in RT tasks, what is really most surprising is the finding that such homogeneous measures are as highly correlated as they are with certain other measures of ability. Generally, correlations among highly homogeneous RT parameters obtained in a single paradigm and scores on psychometric tests of ability fall between .2 and .5.

Indeed, the second method for "validating" the generality of chronometric scores is to show their correlations with psychometric tests, especially those that measure well-established factors of ability, such as general intelligence, or g, and verbal, quantitative, and spatial visualization abilities. The fact that these psychometric abilities, which have emerged in countless factor analyses over the past 75 years, can be very reliably measured by standardized tests, and are known to have substantial predictive validity for educational and occupational criteria, lends further interest and importance to those RT paradigms, or combinations thereof, that show the highest correlations with psychometric scores.

Analysis of the correlations between chronometric and psychometric scores is probably the "richest vein," in terms of potential, for advancing our theory of human mental ability. For some time there has been a growing consensus among differential psychologists that the traditional methodology of studying mental ability in terms of classical psychometrics, factor analysis, and external validation, over the last 75 years or so, has accumulated an impressive amount of solid empirical facts on the range, correlational structure, and practical consequences of IDs in ability, but has not contributed to the further development of theoretical explanations of the main abilities identified by factor analysis of psychometric tests. In the traditional framework, explanations of IDs have not advanced beyond statements that, to put it in the simplest form, individuals A and B differ in performance on task X, because X is highly saturated (or loaded) with ability factor Y, and A and B differ in ability factor Y. But ability Y is a hypothetical or mathematical construct that is not invariant to the method of factor analysis used to identify it. There is unfortunately nothing in the raw psychometric data that can compel the factor theorist to explain A's and B's difference in performance on task X in terms of their differing in factor Y. Factor rotation could displace the IDs variance on factor Y and divide it between two other factors P and Q, so that then the difference between A and B would be attributed to their differing in factors P and Q. And factors P and Q would be different from factor Y, according to the usual method for psychologically describing factors in terms of the characteristics of those content-homogeneous tests that show the highest loadings on the factor. This, in essence, is the theoretical blind alley that differential psychologists find themselves in if they confine their methodology to traditional psychometric tests and factor analysis. The measurements and methods of psychometry reveal only the end products of mental activity, and, by themselves, cannot expose the processes intervening between problem presentation and a subject's response. It is in these intervening processes, at some level of analysis, that the explanation for IDs is to be sought. Mental chronometry and electroencephalography afford the chief tools for such process analysis at the interface of brain and behavior. The tools themselves do not interfere with the normal functioning of the intact brain.

Scores on traditional tests represent a complex amalgam of causes that are not amenable to analysis in terms of elemental processes by any classical psychometric methods. Factor analysis reveals common sources of variance among various tests, but does not reveal the nature of these sources. Within this framework, we cannot answer such questions as why there are quite large correlations between tests that differ as much say, as, vocabulary, block designs, and number series, except to state that all these seemingly dissimilar tests measure a common factor, often termed *g* (for *general* ability). But that is hardly more than a tautology, not an explanation, as the emergence of the *g* factor merely reflects our original observation that scores on all the tests are positively correlated with one another. (In addition, factor analysis shows precisely the degree to which each test shares the common variances in all the tests entered into the factor analysis.) In fact, the analysis of correlations among variables, such as factor analysis, should probably be called *synthesis* rather than *analysis*, since syntheses represent a higher level of abstraction or generalization from the observed phenomena, not a decomposition of it into less complex causal elements. An important aim of chronometric analysis, in contrast to factor analysis, is to achieve a decomposition of complex abilities and to measure the IDs in the common elemental processes that effect the correlations among complex tests.

Elemental processes are hypothetical and inferential constructs, as are factors; processes are truly *analytical* constructs, whereas factors are really principles of synthesis, or classification. Factors only signify the presence of common causal elements that remain to be identified and measured. Iron, copper, and gold, although different, have certain properties in common: They are malleable, they melt at specific temperatures, and they conduct heat and electricity. By analogy with factor analysis, we would explain these commonalities by going to a higher level of abstraction and noting that iron, copper, and gold are all metals. A process analysis, by analogy, would explain their similarities (and differences) in conductivity, in terms of the number and arrangement of their orbital electrons. When a person faces a task, such as a test item, certain things must happen, in some sequence in time, for the person to arrive at the appropriate response. The analysis of these activities in terms of the time they take is the aim of mental chronometry. The term *activity* here can refer to any level of analysis, from observed, overt behavior to inferred, hypothetical brain processes.

DIFFERENCES BETWEEN PSYCHOMETRIC AND CHRONOMETRIC DATA

Psychometric and chronometric data differ in three main ways.

Scale Properties. Scores on psychometric tests based on number of correct answers (or some transformation of the raw scores) measure ability on an arbitrary, relativistic, or norm-referenced (i.e., standardized) scale. There is no true zero point, and the interval property of the scales depends on the acceptance of certain theoretically based assumptions, however plausible, about the form of the distribution of the ability in the population. A scale for which equal intervals are claimed, based on an assumption of the true form of the population distribution of the trait, obviously cannot be used to test hypotheses about the form of the distribution. Also, without the assurance of an interval scale, one cannot meaningfully plot the form of mental growth curves. Without an absolute or ratio scale (i.e., an interval scale with a true zero point), one cannot meaningfully compare *proportions* of mental growth from one period of time to another.

Norm-referenced or standardized score scales also have the disadvantage of a questionable comparability of norm groups, across different tests and for the same test (or equivalent forms) normed at different times. Consequently, for example, Wechsler and Stanford-Binet IQs may differ because of non-comparable norm-reference groups. It is virtually impossible to determine why scores on such tests are higher (or lower) from one generation or decade to the next. Is it because of true changes in the level of ability in the population or because some of the test items are merely easier due to familiarization of the item contents or because of sampling differences in obtaining norm-reference groups at different points in time? A "random" or "representative" sample of a national population, although a theoretically definable concept, is a mythical concept, practically speaking.

Chronometric data on IDs, in marked contrast to psychometric test scores, surmounts most of these difficulties and disadvantages because they consist of absolute measurements of real time, expressed in seconds or milliseconds, which are standard units in the universally adopted *Système Internationale* for all physical and scientific measurements.

Precision and Sensitivity. The smallest unit of measurement on psychometric tests is the scale on which single items are graded. This is usually a 2-point scale ("right" or "wrong," 1 or 0), or, as in some of the subtests of the Wechsler scales, a graded scale of several points, depending on the quality or speed of the individual's performance. In either case, performance at the item level is scored in terms of a relatively coarse scale.

The unit of measurement for RT is usually the millisecond. The obvious advantage of such a refined measurement is its extreme sensitivity. Extremely small differences in ability or performances, undetectable by tests scored right or wrong at the item level, can be detected. For example, a paper-and-pencil test of simple addition of pairs of single numbers (e.g., $5 + 2 = 7$, which is answered *true* or *false*) will hardly discriminate between sixth-graders and college students. Yet such an age discrimination is very marked when true–false response latencies are measured. Other interesting phenomena, which reveal the nature of the cognitive processes involved in this simple task, are also evident from an analysis of the mean latencies for each item. For example, the mean latency is directly related to the size of the smaller of the two addends. That is, response latency increases as the smaller addend increases in size, which suggests that subjects begin with the larger addend and count up the number of the smaller addend. This strategy is also suggested by the observation of corresponding finger movement in younger children. The interesting point, however, is that the same rank order of differences in mean response latencies for different problems is observed in children *and* adults, although in adults the latencies are shorter and the relative differences between problems are less pronounced. But the chronometric data reveal that adults use the same counting strategy for simple addition as do children. Without a precise chronometric apparatus and repeated measurements, it would be virtually impossible to obtain such data. Error rates scarcely differ across various number combinations for simple addition, and the subjects have no subjective feeling that such easy problems differ at all in difficulty. The small differences in response latencies are not detectable by direct observation. But with a suitable reaction timer, even more subtle cognitive effects are revealed. For example, why should the response (*false*) to $4 + 3 = 12$

have a significantly longer latency than to either $5 + 2 = 12$ or $5 + 3 = 12$? It is evidently because of the extra time required to discriminate between $4 + 3 = 12$ (*false*) and $4 \times 3 = 12$ (*true*), whereas no such discrimination is called for in $5 + 2 = 12$ or $5 + 3 = 12$.

Range of Ability. Because psychometric test items are scored *right* or *wrong* (quantized as 1 or 0), they must be at a suitable level of difficulty for any given group if they are to detect IDs reliably. As item difficulty departs in either direction from a p value (p = proportion of a group passing the item) of .50, item variances and covariances decrease and the detection of IDs becomes less reliable. Hence, the same set of test items cannot be used for subjects with a wide ability range. For example, there is no common set of test items on which it is possible to compare, say, five-year-olds or retarded adults and college students and also reliably measure IDs *within* each group. The usual solution is to use different sets of items of the same type (e.g., vocabularly, figure analogies, matrices), but of widely differing levels of difficulty, and then show, by means of factor analysis of the tests in the overlapping ability groups, that the factor composition of the various tests is the same for all levels of ability. This procedure is often difficult to follow, practically, and is problematic, theoretically. A sameness of factor composition across widely varying ability levels does not solve the problem of comparability of scale units across the full range of ability.

Chronometric techniques have a great advantage in all these respects. Because of the great sensitivity of RT measurements, as described in the preceding section, the tasks used can be so simple that they can be performed correctly by persons who differ even as extremely in ability as severely retarded adults (with IQs below 40) and the brightest university students. The IDs are measured not in terms of "right" or "wrong," but rather in terms of response latency, or RT. Of course, some RT tasks are somewhat more limited in this respect because of their greater complexity or the knowledge or skills required. Even so, chronometric tasks are generally applicable over a much wider range of ability than is any one-and-the-same psychometric test.

BASIS OF CORRELATION BETWEEN CHRONOMETRIC AND PSYCHOMETRIC INDICES OF INDIVIDUAL DIFFERENCES

If IDs in chronometrically and psychometrically obtained indices correlate significantly, it can be hypothesized that they both tap the same sources of variance involving the speed or the efficiency of mental processes. The importance of a time element in mental efficiency can be understood in terms of certain well-established concepts and principles of cognitive psychology. The conscious brain acts as a single-channel, or *limited capacity,* information processing system. Limited capacity also restricts the number of operations that can be performed simultaneously on the information that enters the system from external stimuli or from retrieval of information stored in short-term or long-term memory (STM or LTM). Hence, speediness of mental operations is advantageous because more operations per unit of time can be excuted without overloading the system. Also, because there is a *rapid decay* of stimulus traces and information, speediness is an advantage for any operations that must be performed on the information while it is still available. Finally, to compensate for limited capacity and rapid decay of incoming information, a person resorts to *rehearsal and storage* of the information into LTM, which has a practically unlimited capacity. But the storage process itself takes time and ties up channel capacity, so there is a trade-off between storing and processing incoming information. The more complex the information and the operations required on it, the more time is required and the greater the advantage of speediness in the elemental processes involved. Loss of information because of overload interference and the decay of traces that were inadequately encoded or rehearsed for storage or retrieval from LTM result in a failure to grasp all the essential relationships among the elements of a complex problem needed for its solution. Speediness of processing, therefore, should be increasingly related to success in dealing with cognitive tasks to the extent that their information load strains the individual's limited channel capacity. The most discriminating test items, scored in terms of right or wrong, thus would be those that bring the information processing system to the threshold of breakdown. In a series of items of graded complexity, such breakdown would occur at different points for different persons. If IDs in the speed of the elemental components of information processing can be measured in RT tasks that are so simple as to rule out breakdown failure, it should be possible to predict IDs from the point of breakdown for more complex tasks, such as the most discriminating items in psychometric tests.

Seemingly small but reliable IDs in the speed of performing certain elementary cognitive tasks, amounting to less than 100 ms, may show up on certain psychometric tests as very large differences, such as one person's vocabularly being only one-half as large as another person's. Small absolute differences in rate of information processing, involving encoding and storage, can result in large IDs in the amount of information and skills acquired over long periods of time. A good analogy would be that of two cars on the highway travelling side by side at only slightly different average rates, say, 50 and 51 mph, respectively. Within a few hours, they will be miles apart. Thus, full siblings reared together, with the same exposure to language and the same educational opportunities, may, by the time they enter high school, show large differences in vocabulary, general information, and the intellectual skills important for success in school and in the world of work. Such IDs are found to be correlated with IDs in RT to elementary tasks for which the task requirements are easily within the capability of perhaps 98% or 99% of the school-age and adult population, with the exception of those persons who have such severe sensory or motor handicaps as to rule out the possibility of their performing most RT tasks.

The Speed–Complexity Paradox

This is the name of the observation that speed of reaction correlates most highly with scores on complex psychometric tests only when the RT task is fairly easy, but still more complex than SRT (i.e., single stimulus–single response) and when RTs fall within the range of about 200 to 1,000 ms for normal adults. The paradox is that, whereas the RT in such undemanding tasks is correlated with IQ, as measured by complex psychometric tests, the response latencies to the IQ test items themselves are not correlated with IQ. However, if IQ test items of a difficulty level appropriate for, say, second-graders were administered to university students as stimuli in a RT paradigm, their response latencies would probably be correlated with the students' IQs as obtained on an IQ test suitable for university students. The reasons for this seeming paradox are not yet fully understood, but it appears that for very complex tasks (such as highly discriminating test items), different individuals resort to different strategies, or distribute the various elemental component processes disproportionately. For example, in solving verbal and pictorial analogies, higher IQ persons tend to allot more time to stimulus encoding and less time to response selection, whereas lower IQ persons do the reverse (R. Sternberg, 1977; R. Sternberg & Rifkin, 1979). Also, when the task is highly complex, personality factors affecting persistence, impulsiveness, and involuntary rest pauses become noncognitive sources of IDs in the response latencies.

MOST RELEVANT REFERENCES IN THE
REACTION TIME LITERATURE

Before reviewing the methodology of RT studies in more detail, it would seem worthwhile to provide an annotated list of the books or chapters this writer considers to be the most essential reading for anyone who expects to do empirical research in this field. All these references themselves have extensive bibliographies. They are listed here in alphabetical order, by author.

Carroll (*Individual Difference Relations in Psychometric and Experimental*

Cognitive Tasks, 1980) is a detailed, critical, integrative review of recent research in experimental cognitive psychology, most of it based on chronometric methods. An excellent, comprehensive, and critical overview of the state of the art.

Eysenck (*A Model for Intelligence*, 1982) reviews in detail the research on mental speed, RT, inspection time, evoked potentials, and componential analysis as these concepts and methods have figured in studies of general intelligence.

Pachella (*The Interpretation of Reaction Time in Information-Processing Research*, 1974) discusses the major methodological problems in RT research; emphasized are the characteristics of RT in terms of the experimental conditions that affect it as a dependent variable. It contains probably the best available introduction to the subtraction method of Donders and the *additive factors* method of S. Sternberg, and detailed criticisms of these methods. It also thoroughly considers the *speed–accuracy* (error rate) problem in RT research.

Posner (*Chronometric Exploration of Mind*, 1978) is already a classic. Probably no other single reference shows the many ways that chronometric techniques can be used in psychological research. However, relatively very little of the book deals with IDs or with psychometric abilitities *per se*.

Welford (*Reaction Times*, 1980) is the most advanced and comprehensive work on RT *per se*, dealing largely with theoretical formulations of RT phenomena. It is also a mine of information on empirical research on RT.

Woodworth (1938) and Woodworth and Schlosberg (1954) (*Reaction Time*) are chapters in the classic textbook of experimental psychology. For their relatively short length, they are the most thoroughly informative and lucid introductions to RT research, and certainly the best places to begin one's reading in this field. These chapters, of course, antedate the modern revival of chronometry in experimental cognitive psychology, but the material they cover is basic and essential. Although there is considerable overlap in contents between the original (1938) and revised (1954) editions, both are well worth reading. In some respects, the earlier version is better for our purpose in that it gives more consideration to IDs in RT and to the correlation of RT with psychometric intelligence.

TYPES AND TERMINOLOGY OF REACTION TIME

DEFINITIONS OF REACTION TIME

Reaction time has been defined in a number of ways. Warren's (1934) *Dictionary of Psychology* defines RT as "the interval of time between the onset of a stimulus and the beginning of the observer's overt intentional response . . . . The term *reaction time* is historically established; *intentional response time* is a more accurate term" (pp. 223–224). The qualification of *intentional* is now ambiguous, since we know that many RTs are faster than the speed of conscious awareness of a peripheral stimulus, which is about 500 ms (Libet, 1965). Another definition of RT is that it is the minimum amount of time needed for the observer to produce a *correct* response. This definition expresses the important fact that *false* responses can occur in an RT experiment and that the RT for false responses cannot be treated in the same manner as that for correct responses. But the qualification *minimal* amount of time makes the definition theoretical rather than operational because we cannot reliably measure the *minimal* RT of a given subject without some operational specification of what we mean by *minimal* RT (e.g., the mean of the shortest 5% of the subject's RTs in *n* number of trials). Actually all that is important for a definition of RT is that it be made explicitly operational in terms of the details of the experimental paradigm that is being used to measure RT.

CLASSICAL REACTION TIME PARADIGMS

The classic paradigms and their terminology originated with the work of Donders and Wundt. These can be described most easily by means of the five schemata shown in Figure 1.

1. *Simple reaction time (SRT)*, which Donders called the *A*-reaction, describes a single response (*R*) to a single stimulus, the *reaction stimulus* (*RS*). The single-stimulus–single-response condition for SRT distinguishes it from all the other paradigms (2–5) in Figure 1, which are examples of

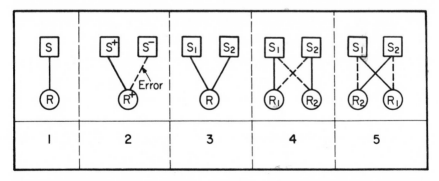

FIGURE 1. Schemata for classical RT paradigms. S, stimulus; R, response; solid lines, correct response; dashed lines, error response. (See the text for the name and an explanation of each schema.)

what Wundt originally called *compound* (or *complex*) reactions. These compound RT paradigms generally result in a longer RT than does the SRT paradigm. This is especially true of paradigms 4 and 5, which are examples of what is called *choice reaction time (CRT)*. In SRT, the subject is instructed to respond (e.g., by either releasing or pressing a Morse key) as quickly as possible on the occurrence of the RS (e.g., a sound, or a light going on). Typically, a *preparatory stimulus (PS)* precedes the RS, usually by a random interval of from one to several seconds. The PS, which is often in a different sensory modality from the RS (e.g., PS, auditory signal; RS, visual signal), focuses the subject's attention on the RS and determines his readiness to respond. The duration of the *warning interval (WI)* is usually randomized from trial to trial to prevent the subject's learning to anticipate the occurrence of the RS precisely. Figure 2 shows the typical RT procedure. In this example, the beginning of the subject's response (R) terminates the RS. In another procedure, the RS has a set duration independent of the subject's response.

2. *Discriminative reaction time (DRT)*, or Donders' *C-reaction*, requires that the subject discriminate between a *positive* and a *negative stimulus* (S^+ and S^-), but allows only one response. The subject should respond only to the S^+, and inhibit response on the occurrence of S^-. The task of discriminating between S^+ and S^- can be made easy or difficult, depending on the experimenter's purpose. It should be understood that S^+ and S^- (and all other alternative Ss in Figure 1) may appear in the same place or in different places. The DRT affords the possibility of false responses or errors (i.e., responding to S^-). To minimize the error rate, subjects may be

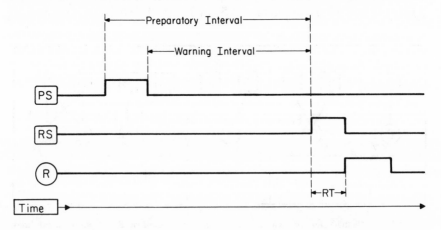

FIGURE 2. Paradigm for simple reaction time (SRT), and for all the other RT paradigms shown in Figure 1. PS, preparatory stimulus; RS, reaction stimulus; R response.

instructed to respond only as fast as they can without making errors. Even then, some errors will be made, and they are recorded as an essential part of the RT data.

3. *Nondiscriminative reaction time* (*NDRT*) (or *conjunctive reaction time*) was introduced by Wundt, who called it the *D-reaction*, in keeping with Donders' terminology of A, B, and C reactions. The NDRT differs from the DRT only in that the subject makes the only possible response to whichever stimulus occurs. It is a rarely used paradigm because the results are often only slightly different from those for the SRT. (Separate spatial locations of S_1 and S_2 tend to increase the RT.) Merely the *uncertainty* of the occurrence of S_1 or S_2 on each trial causes the RT in this paradigm to be slighly longer than in the SRT paradigm. As in SRT, there is virtually no chance for errors.

4. *Discriminative-choice reaction time,* or *CRT,* also known as Donders' *B-reaction* or *disjunctive reaction time* requires that different responses be made to different stimuli. Hence it involves *discrimination* between stimuli and *choice* of the appropriate response from among a number of alternatives. Paradigm 4 represents CRT with a high degree of S–R *compatibility,* that is, there is a close spatial correspondence (or some other form of close correspondence) between the S and R alternatives.

5. *Discriminative-choice reaction time* is here shown with a *low* degree of S–R compatibility. Both RT and error rate generally increase, the lower the S–R compatibility.

ANALYSIS OF ELEMENTARY COGNITIVE PROCESSES

The basic RT paradigms shown in Figure 1 can be used to illustrate simply how elementary cognitive processes can be distinguished and measured in terms of the time taken by each component process.

Two main methods have dominated the field: Donders' (1868/1969) *subtraction method* and S. Sternberg's (1969) *additive factor method.* (Because there are two noted psychologists in this field with the name *Sternberg,* Saul Sternberg of Bell Laboratories and Robert J. Sternberg—no relation—of Yale University, it is less confusing to affix their first initials whenever we refer to him.)

The Subtraction Method

In this method, it is assumed that information processing proceeds in a sequence of discrete mental events, each taking a certain amount of time. If the processing requirements of two tasks differ only in the presence or absence of one of these mental events, or processing stages, the difference between the total time taken for each task is the time required for the one mental event in which the task requirements differ. Conversely, if the time taken by each of two tasks differs, it is presumed that the tasks differ either in the duration or the number of different processes required, or both.

To illustrate this in terms of Donders' classic paradigms, consider the processing requirements for SRT, DRT, and CRT (paradigms 1, 2, and 4 in Figure 1).

The SRT involves (1) sense organ lag; (2) afferent neural conduction time, from sense organ to brain; (3) apprehension of the S; (4) efferent neural conduction time from brain to muscle; and (5) muscle lag.

The DRT involves everything involved in SRT, *plus* (6) time for *discrimination* between S^+ and S^-.

The CRT involves everything involved in DRT, plus (7) time to *choose* between R_1 and R_2.

Hence, subtracting SRT from DRT (i.e., DRT − SRT) yields the *discrimination* time. And CRT − DRT yields the time taken to choose the correct response.

Interestingly, the first measurement of the speed of afferent nerve conduction in humans, by Helmholtz, in 1850, was based on the subtraction method, using only SRT. He applied the RS to the person's toe and to the thigh, and noted the difference in the RT. With this information, the speed of the sensory nerve impulse was calculated to be between 50 and 100 meters per second—less than one-third the speed of sound.

Donders' subtraction method has met with a number of criticisms. One is that its application presupposes that the investigator already has a rather clear concept of the discrete processes or stages involved in each of the tasks compared by the subtraction method. Thus, it begs the questions it is intended to answer. Another class of criticisms centers on the fact that the method does not allow the components of a task to interact: It is assumed that additional processing requirements can be inserted into a given task, or deleted, without in any way affecting the other processes involved in the task. The subtraction method, by itself, affords no means of objectively testing the validity of its assumption of "pure insertion" or complete additivity of the time required by each of the information processing elements involved in the task. Consider three tasks, A, B, C, which have reaction times $t_A < t_B < t_C$, respectively. We hypothesize that $t_B > t_A$ because task B involves all the processes involved in task A, *plus* process x, which is not involved in task A; and $t_C > t_B$ because task C involves process y (in addition to all the processes involved in task B). By subtraction, then, $t_B - t_A = t_x$ and $t_{C'} - t_B = t_y$. Now, if the processing stages x and y are purely additive, as we have assumed in order to obtain their time values, then $t_C - t_A$ should be exactly equal to $t_x - t_y$. But it is obvious that this is a mere tautology, since, if $t_x = t_B - t_A$, and $t_y = t_C - t_B$, then $t_x + t_y$ *must* be equal to $t_C - t_A$ (i.e., $t_B - t_A + t_C - t_B = t_C - t_A$). It is therefore not an independent proof of the additivity of x and y. What is required is some way to determine whether stages x and y act in an additive or an interactive manner.

THE ADDITIVE FACTOR METHOD

Introduced by S. Sternberg (1969) as an improvement over Donders' more limited subtraction method, the additive factor method also begins with the assumption that information processing proceeds in a sequence of stages, each involving different processes. Although it is assumed that the times for each of the processing stages are additive, the question of which inserted or deleted task requirements, or *factors* (in the analysis of variance sense), act additively or interactively is left open to empirical investigation. The finding of pure additivity of the factors, as shown by the absence of significance interactions in an analysis of variance, identifies the factors with different and separate processing stages, whereas the finding of an interaction between factors is interpreted as signifying that of the two (or more) factors, each affects some one-and-the same stage of processing. By means of a converging series of ingeniously planned factorial experiments, it is possible to infer a processing model for a given type of cognitive task in which the experimentally manipulable factors in the task and their interactions are assignable to different processing stages. S. Sternberg has applied the method to a number of RT tasks, including what is referred to later in this chapter as the S. Sternberg short-term memory scanning paradigm. More detailed expositions of the additive factor method are to be found in S. Sternberg (1969), Pachella (1974), and Welford (1980, see index).

As a simple example of how the additive factor method works, consider the RT paradigms 4 and 5 in Figure 1. The factors here are presumed to be (1) stimulus discrimination (S_1 vs. S_2) and (2) response choice (R_1 vs. R_2). Each of these factors can be experimentally varied. For simplicity, say we have two *levels* of factor 1—high *versus* low stimulus similarity (discriminability)—and two levels of factor 2—high *versus* low S–R compatibility (e.g., paradigm 4 *vs.* paradigm 5 in Figure 1). The RT tasks with every possible combination of the 2 factors × 2 levels—four tasks in all—would be administered to four independent randomized samples of a pool of subjects. The analysis of variance of all the RT data (i.e., the *mean*

RTs of each subject as the unit of analysis) would have four terms:

	Source of variance	df
Main effects	Between factors	1
	Between levels	1
Interaction	Factors × Levels	1
Residual	Subjects within groups	N − 4

If the main effect of factors is significant and substantial and the interaction term is nonsignificant (Figure 3A), we would conclude that the two factors (stimulus discrimination and response choice) occur in two separate stages of information processing. A significantly large Factors × Levels interaction (Figure 3B), however, would mean that some stages of processing involve *both* factors, perahaps to the exclusion of separate stages involving one factor each. It should be noted that for the interaction term to be cogently interpreted, the data used for the analysis must consist of the RT measurements *per se* (or the *arithmetic means* of these measurements), which are expressed in units of real time, rather than any scale transformation of the measurements. Also, *median* RTs are ruled out for this type of analysis, as medians are not necessarily additive, whereas arithmetic means are always additive.

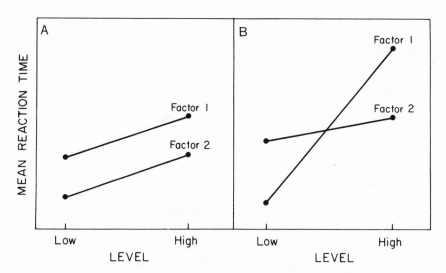

FIGURE 3. Graphical representation of the analysis of variance of the factorial experiment described in the text in which (A) there is a main effect for both factors and levels, but no interaction between them, and (B) a main effect for both factors and levels and an interaction between factors and levels.

Inferential ambiguities are now recognized in both the subtraction method and the additive factor method, and most present-day investigators hold that each method has valid uses under the special conditions for which it is appropriate and that both methods can be used in a complementary fashion. Carroll (1980) expresses a consensus that "the method of 'converging operations' (i.e., the accumulation of evidence from a variety of related studies) can be expected eventually to produce scientifically valid results and interpretations" (p. 63).

ELABORATIONS OF CLASSICAL REACTION TIME PARADIGMS

The classical RT paradigms just described are the prototypes for almost countless modifications and elaborations designed to study a variety of cognitive phenomena. There are many variations in the number and character of the stimulus and response alternatives. In addition to presenting some stimulus situation (S) and having some mode of overt response (R) to it, the only common feature of all paradigms is the precise measurement, usually in milliseconds, of the amount of time that elapses between S and R.

The main experimental variations most commonly encountered in the literature are the following.

Experimenter-Paced versus Subject-Paced Presentation of the Stimulus. Reaction time experiments always use repeated trials in order to minimize measurement error. Each trial can be conceived of as a cycle comprising the sequence of events as depicted in Figure 2. The cycle may be initiated by either the experimenter or the subject. We have found that self-pacing of trials by the subject is especially desirable when the task requirements are fairly complex and repeated trials may incur fatigue.

Presence or Absence of a Preparatory Stimulus (PS). Experimenters now rarely omit the PS (see Figure 2) because its use not only focuses attention on and shortens the RT, but it also decreases its trial-to-trial variability, thereby yielding a more reliable measure when the RTs are averaged over n trials.

Single Location versus Separate Locations of Multiple Stimuli. In discriminative RT or choice RT, the two (or more) stimuli may be randomly presented (sequentially), either in the same location (e.g., different-colored lights appearing in a single aperture) or in spatially separate locations. When the different stimuli to be discriminated appear at the same visual fixation point on every trial, variance due to eye movements, or visual scanning, is minimized, as compared with random presentation of the stimuli in separate locations.

Sequential versus Simultaneous Presentation of Stimuli. When multiple stimuli are presented, such as a string of numbers, letters, words, or symbols, they may be displayed either sequentially or simultaneously. An example of a paradigm that has used both sequential and simultaneous displays in different studies is S. Sternberg's short-term memory scan paradigm. A set of digits (varying in number from one to seven) is displayed, either simultaneously or sequentially (at a rate of, say, two digits per second), and is followed immediately by a single "probe" digit, which serves as the RS. The subject responds *yes* or *no* (usually by pressing buttons labeled *yes* and *no*), depending on whether the probe digit was or was not a member of the previously displayed set of digits. The RT is the interval between the onset of the probe digit and the subject's response.

Variations of Response Mode. The RT for verbal responses can be measured by a voice-activated key. Except when the experimenter is studying the speed of word associations or features of vocalization *per se*, the use of a voice key has certain disadvantages, for example, time variations in the initiation of pronouncing different words.

When only a small number of alternative responses is presented, finger-activated response keys are usually preferable. In the classical CRT experiment, the subject poises the index fingers of the left and right hand lightly on two Morse keys, ready to make the appropriate response. The response to the RS may consist of *releasing* one of the keys (when both keys are initially depressed) or of *pressing* one of the keys.

When more than two response alternatives are required, any number of keys, up to ten, can be used, each one activated by a different finger. At the beginning of each cycle, the subject's fingers are poised lightly on the keys (for a press response by one finger) or they depress all the keys (for a release response). Multiple response keys used this way have the distinct disadvantage of unwanted variance because the muscular capabilities of the right and left hands, and of the different fingers of each hand, differ. As every pianist knows, the ring finger of each hand is comparatively weak and inept.

To overcome this problem, we have introduced a procedure that uses a *home button* (Jensen & Munro, 1979). It has been effectively adapted to several different RT paradigms. The procedure divides the subject's response into two separately measurable acts, RT and *movement time (MT)*. The simplest example of this procedure can be described for the CRT paradigm, as shown in Figure 4. At the beginning of a cycle, instead of the subject's having the index fingers of each hand readied for responding to the R_1 or R_2 buttons, the index finger of the preferred hand depresses H. Immediately on the appearance of the reaction stimulus ($RS = S_1$ or S_2), the subject removes the index finger from H and presses R_1 or R_2. The RT, also called *decision time (DT)* in this procedure, is the interval between the onset of the RS and the release of H. The interval between releasing H and

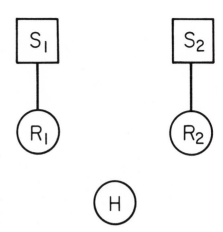

FIGURE 4. Choice reaction paradigm, using a home (H) button. The cycle begins by the subject depressing H with the index finger. As soon as S_1 or S_2 appears, the subject presses the appropriate response button (R_1 or R_2) as quickly as possible.

pressing R_1 or R_2 is the MT. The spatial distance between H and R is usually not more than a few inches. The same procedure can, of course, be used for simple RT and for CRT involving many more than just two S–R alternatives. (In subject-paced trials, each cycle is initiated by the subject's pressing down H.) The main advantage of the H procedure is that it permits RT to be measured by exactly the same form of response (i.e., simply raising the index finger of the preferred hand) regardless of the number of S–R alternatives. It is a remarkable fact that RT rather than MT increases as a function of the number of S–R alternatives, at least within a range of one to eight alternatives. The response alternative buttons should be so arranged that they are located at equal distances from H.

An apparatus, shown in Figure 5, for measuring both SRT and varying degrees of multiple-choice RT (all with maximal S–R compatibility), based on the H procedure, has been used extensively in our Berkeley laboratory (Jensen & Munro, 1979). The subject's console of the apparatus for measuring the subject's RT and MT consists of a panel, 13×17 in., painted flat black, and tilted at a 30° angle. At the lower center of the panel is a red pushbutton, $\frac{1}{2}$ in. in diameter, H. Arranged in a semi-circle above the H are eight red pushbuttons, all equidistant (6 in.) from H. One half an inch above each button (except H) is a $\frac{1}{2}$ in. faceted green light. Different flat black panels can be fastened over the whole array, to expose arrays having any number of light–button combinations. (We usually use one, two, four, and eight alternatives, which correspond to zero, one, two, and three bits of information, when information is measured as $\log_2$ of the number of S–R alternatives.)

The subject is instructed to place the index finger (of the preferred

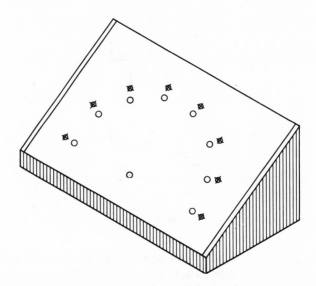

FIGURE 5. Subject's console of the RT–MT apparatus. Pushbuttons are indicated by circles, faceted green lights by crossed circles. The home button is in the lower center, 6 in. from each response button.

hand) on H. Then an auditory preparatory signal is sounded (a high-pitched tone of 1 s duration), followed, after a continuous random warning interval of from 1 to 4 s, by one of the green lights going "on," which the subject must turn off as quickly as possible by touching the sensitive microswitch button directly under it. The RT is the time the subject takes to remove his finger from the H after the green light goes on. The MT is the interval between removing the finger from H and touching the button that turns the green light off. The RT and MT on each trial are separately registered in milliseconds by two electronic timers.

   Carroll (1980) has devised a useful method for representing, in a highly detailed fashion, both the task requirements and the hypothesized cognitive processes involved. Carroll calls this type of diagram the *dual time representation (DTR) of elementary cognitive tasks (ECTs)*. It is most useful for highlighting the precise (and often crucial) procedural differences between various chronometric paradigms as actually performed in the laboratory. It is illustrated in Figure 6 with respect to the RT–MT procedure just described. The DTR of another variant of the choice RT paradigm, used in a study by Keating and Bobbitt (1978), is shown in Figure 7 to illustrate how the DTR flow diagram depicts all the fine-grained procedure differences between tasks that can yield differences in results.

Carroll (1980) describes the DTR representation as follows:

> Objective (observable) stimulus and response events are shown along the central time axis that runs from upper left to lower right. The remaining space in the chart is available for other purposes. The upper triangle (above the diagonal axis) is used for representing presumed mental or "cognitive" processes, their duration and effects over time, and their interrelationships and interactions with stimulus and response events and with each other. The lower triangle can be used for such purposes as annotating stimulus variations, depicting repetitions of events (as by the "repeat signs" of musical notation), and showing measurement procedures (e.g., time measurements). The distances on a DTR chart are regarded only topologically, i.e., they show only temporal order relationships among events, but do not necessarily represent, to scale, the exact occurrence times or the durations of events.
>
> Various further conventions can be established in designing DTR charts. In representing objective events, those that are obligatory (i.e., that are always present and are characteristic of the task) are shown in solid-line boxes. Optional events are shown in broken-line boxes. Broken lines bordering the lower right of a box can be used to indicate that an event (e.g., the shining of a light) persists for an indefinitive period, or until some other event supersedes it . . . .
>
> "Cognitive" (nonobservable, but presumed) events may be shown in "cartouches" [boxes with rounded corners] placed in the upper triangle of the chart in such a way as to show assumed precursors and consequences of such events and their temporal relationships. . . . Lines, generally with direction of effect shown by arrows, show presumed causal connections and interactions of cognitive events with objective events and with each other. (pp. 13–14)

Double Stimulation. It is often of interest to measure the change in RT that occurs when the subject has to process two sources of information simultaneously rather than just one. Invariably, RTs to double stimulation are slower than RTs to a single stimulus. A simple example of the double-stimulation discrimination paradigm would be the simultaneous presentation of a tone (high or low) and a light (blue or yellow), with two response keys, and instructions to press (or release) the left key (with the left index finger) only when the high tone is sounded and to press (or release) the right key (with the right index finger) only when the blue light goes on. Such double tasks strain the subject's limited channel capacity and generally increase RT, as well as the error rate, considerably.

Double-stimulation tasks can also use successive stimuli, as in the study of processing-storage trade-off. For example, say the subject must respond "true" or "false" (by pressing keys labeled T and F) to simple addition problems (e.g., 3 + 4 = 7) that are either correct or incorrect. Two such problems, labeled A and B, respectively, are presented one after the other in quick succession, immediately followed by the reaction stimulus (letter A or B) that post-cues the problem to which the subject must respond T or F. More complex variations of this paradigm have been

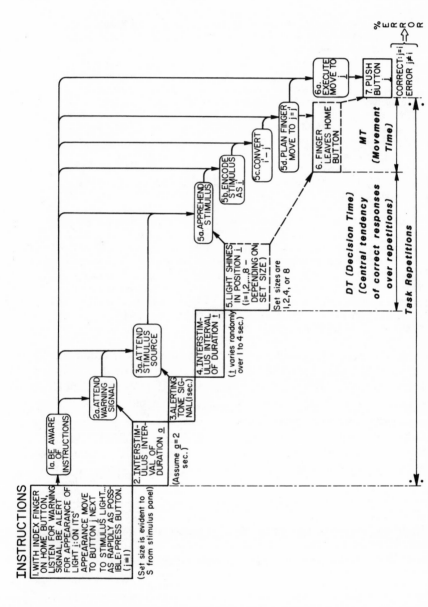

FIGURE 6. Carroll's dual time representation (DTR) of Jensen's RT–MT procedure. From *Individual Difference Relations in Psychometric and Experimental Cognitive Tasks* (p. 18) by J. G. Carroll, 1980, Chapel Hill, N.C.: L. L. Thurstone Psychometric Laboratory, University of North Carolina. © 1980 by J. G. Carroll. Adapted by permission.

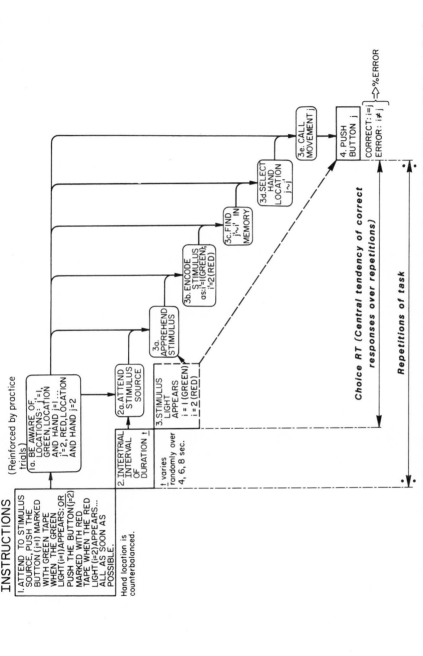

FIGURE 7. Dual time representation (DTR) of Keating's and Bobbitt's choice RT procedure. From *Individual Difference Relations in Psychometric and Experimental Cognitive Tasks* (p. 15) by J. G. Carroll, 1980, Chapel Hill, N.C.: L. L. Thurstone Psychometric Laboratory, University of North Carolina. © 1980 by J. G. Carroll. Adapted by permission.

used. (Double-stimulation paradigms, theoretical models, and sample experiments have been thoroughly reviewed by Kantowitz, 1974.) There is evidence that RTs measured by double-stimulation procedures are somewhat more highly correlated with IDs in general mental ability than are RTs to either stimulus presented singly, probably because of the greater information load and the strain on channel capacity occasioned by the double stimulation.

PROCEDURAL VARIABLES THAT AFFECT REACTION TIME

The results of RT studies are extraordinarily sensitive to a large number of factors in which procedures and subjects may differ. Investigators should be fully aware of all these factors in designing their experiments and in comparing the results of different studies. Variations in results of studies cannot be evaluated in the absence of explicit reports of the procedural and subject variables that are known to affect RT. A knowledge of these variables and of their interrelationships is also of importance theoretically, in that they afford an essential part of the network of empirical clues to the psychological and physiological nature of mental speed and its manifestations in performance on psychometric tests, as well as their practically significant correlates.

PREPARATORY FACTORS

The subject's state of expectancy and attention just before the RS is called *preparatory set*. It is largely a function of the experimenter's instructions to the subject (e.g., emphasizing speed *or* accuracy), and especially, of the PS and warning interval (*WI*). The RT will be shorter and less variable from trial to trial if a PS precedes the RS than if there were no PS. The duration and intensity of the PS should be sufficient so as to leave no doubt of its occurrence. We have found a constant PS duration of 1 s to be about optimal. The subjective intensity of the PS should not exceed that of the RS, especially if they are in the same sensory modality. The optimal WI is 1 to 2 s, but WIs in the range of 1 to 4 s are approximately equivalent in their effect on RT. Warning intervals shorter than 1 s or longer than 4 s result in a slower RT. A WI of constant length results in a gradual shortening of RT as the subject develops an expectancy of the precise occurrence of the RS. This expectancy effect can be overcome by using *random* WIs within the range 1 to 4 s. A PS of a different sensory modality than the RS (e.g., PS, auditory; RS, visual) is a decided advantage, especially when the subjects are young children or the mentally retarded. Distinct sensory modalities for the PS and the RS offer much less chance for confusion and help to minimize the role of learning in the subject's RT performance.

Little attention is paid in the RT literature to the *intertrial interval* (*ITI*), also called *afterperiod*, that is, the interval between the subject's last response to the RS and the reappearance of the PS. The ITI should always be distinctively longer than the WI. The risk of mental fatigue in complex RT tasks is reduced by the subject pacing the trials. Each cycle is initiated by the subject's pressing H, whereupon the preprogrammed cycle runs off automatically. There should be a constant interval between the subject's depressing H and the occurrence of the PS. (We have used a constant H–PS interval of 1 s with good results.)

STIMULUS FACTORS

The RT varies according to the *sensory modality* of the RS because of differences in peripheral mechanisms. For example, visual lag is greater (by 30 to 40 ms) than auditory lag, probably because the former is initiated by a chemical process and the latter by a mechanical process. Also, central (foveal) vision results in a faster RT than peripheral vision. Tactile stimuli and a mild electric shock result in about the same RT as auditory stimuli.

Stimulus *intensity*, *area* (as of a light source), and *duration* are all positively related to a faster RT, but there is not a monotonic relationship at the extremes of these variables.

A greater *complexity* of the stimulus or a greater *number of alternatives* in the location or form of the RS or less *discriminability* of the alternate RS all result in a slower RT. Hick (1952) has noted that in CRT, the RT increases linearly as a function of the number of *bits* of information. A *bit* is defined in information theory as $\log_2 n$, where n is the number of choice alternatives. A *bit* can be thought of as the amount of information that will reduce uncertainty by one-half. Figure 8 shows this relationship, now known as *Hick's Law*.

RESPONSE FACTORS

The RT is facilitated by moderate increases in *muscle tension*, which, under normal conditions, is an index of cortical arousal. It has been found that the forearm muscles to the hand that executes the response become tense during the WI (see Woodworth & Schlosberg, 1954, pp. 30–32). The subject's *concentration* on the response to be made also speeds the RT.

When the subject's fingers are poised closely above the keys, ready to respond, *finger tremor* will affect RT in a variable fashion from trial to trial. Responses are synchronized with the tremor, so that RT is faster if the RS occurs when the tremor is in the downward phase of its movement. Control of the subject's *motivation* for fast response by means of a reward or

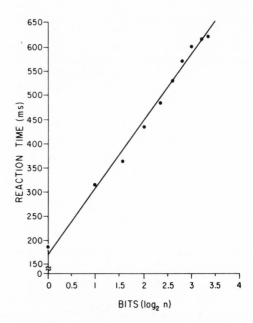

FIGURE 8. Mean choice RTs to stimulus arrays conveying various amounts of information scaled in bits; n is the number of choice alternatives. Data from Merkel (1885) as reported in *Experimental Psychology* (p. 33) by R. S. Woodworth and H. Scholsberg, 1954, New York: Holt, Rinehart and Winston. Copyright 1954 by Holt, Rinehart and Winston. Adapted by permission.

punishment or an immediate knowledge of the results will speed up RT beyond the subject's normal "best" effort without such incentives.

Practice Effects speed the RT (and lower the error rate in CRT) and are generally found over the course of many repeated trials, but they are often so small as to be practically negligible, especially for SRT. Practice effects become more prominent as the task requirements are made more complex. But practice effects differ greatly in magnitude and in number of trials to asymptotic performance, depending upon the task requirements and the characteristics, such as age and ability, of the subjects.

EXTRINSIC ORGANISMIC FACTORS

Anoxia, as at high altitudes, slows RT, and CRT is more sensitive than SRT. Stimulant drugs, such as caffeine, tobacco, and amphetamine, speed the RT. Depressant drugs generally slow the RT, but alcohol has a diphasic effect, at first speeding and later slowing the RT. In general, drugs that alter synaptic thresholds and hence synaptic connectivity also alter RTs in the predictable direction.

INTRINSIC ORGANISMIC FACTORS

Age greatly affects the RT, which decreases in a negatively accelerated fashion from early childhood to maturity, plateaus between about 25 and 55 years of age, and gradually increases again in old age. The RT increases rapidly the few months before death, just as performance on IQ tests has also been found to deteriorate markedly in the few months before death.

Sex differences in RT generally are found to favor males slightly, but in studies in our laboratory, using H that permits separation of the subject's response into RT (or decision time) and movement time (MT), we have found a significant sex difference (males faster) only for MT. *Physical exercise* and general *fitness* speed the RT.

The RT varies throughout the day as a function of changes in body *temperature*, with higher temperatures making for faster reactions. The SRT varies about 9 or 10 ms per degree Fahrenheit change in body temperature in the normal range of diurnal variation. Woodworth and Schlosberg (1954) note that "the amount of [RT] change [with temperature] corresponds pretty well to what would be expected from the temperature coefficient of chemical processes, and suggests that the cerebral process in reaction depends closely upon chemical activity" (p. 38). It is theoretically noteworthy that CRT shows much greater shifts with change in temperature than does SRT.

Food intake also slows the RT, over and above the drop in temperature that follows eating. There is a post-lunch slowing of RT, which, of course, contributes to the variability among subjects who are tested at different hours throughout the day and may slightly attenuate the correlation between RT and other variables that are less sensitive to physiological state or are measured at some other time of the day.

Strangely, *body build* affects RT, with more slender persons having the faster RT. The index of body build found to show the highest correlation (about .3) with SRT is the ratio of $(\text{height})/(\text{weight})^{\frac{1}{3}}$.

In general, factors that slow RT also tend to increase its trial-to-trial variability.

CHRONOMETRIC APPARATUS AND TECHNIQUES

APPARATUS

A great diversity of mechanical, electrical, and electronic equipment has been used to measure RT. The common aim is the precise and reliable measurement of very brief time intervals, and this has been largely achieved since the earliest studies of RT. What has changed in this field is not so much the precision of the measuring instruments, but rather their dependability of operation and the silence, compactness, general efficiency, convenience, and ease of reading or recording measurements. The older chronoscopes, for example, required frequent adjustment and calibration, which is virtually obviated by modern electronic equipment using crystal timing devices that oscillate at constant frequencies ranging above 10^3 cycles per second (cps).

The RT should be measured in units of 10^{-3} s, or in milliseconds, with an error of less than .1%. This is routine with modern electronic timers.

Aside from the precision of the timers, there is virtually no standardization of the chronometric equipment used by experimenters. The reason for this lack of standardization of the stimulus and response modes is the great diversity of purposes served by chronometry in modern cognitive psychology. Every investigator adapts the experimental arrangements idiosyncratically to the requirements of a particular kind of study. The commercially produced RT apparatuses, which can be purchased from the suppliers of psychological laboratory equipment, usually have a sufficiently accurate timer, are relatively inexpensive, and, for any particular manufacturer, the S–R features are highly standardized. But these apparatuses are so simple and so inflexible as to be hardly adaptable to the great variety of experimental task arrangements required for mental chronometry experiments. The commercially available RT apparatuses are scarcely useful for anything but simple demonstrations and exercises in the undergraduate psychology laboratory. Hence, most professionals today use equipment that is custom-built to their specifications.

The great disadvantage of each experimenter using his or her own custom-built RT equipment is the lack of standardization from one laboratory to another. Consequently, attempts to replicate experiments in different laboratories, using highly comparable groups of subjects, often result in replication of the same *relationships* among RTs obtained under various experimental conditions, but not the same *absolute values* of RT. This always poses the question of whether the absolute differences in RT found in different studies result from the use of nonstandardized apparatus or from a difference between subject pools. This is an especially undesirable state of affairs when chronometric techniques are used to study individual or group differences, for one of the potential advantages of chronometry, as compared with traditional psychometry, is that measurements can be made on an absolute or ratio scale. Nonstandardized RT equipment lessens this advantage when findings from different laboratories are compared. The significance of this observation has been impressed upon the present writer as a result of his contacts with other investigators who have duplicated the particular RT–MT equipment (shown in Figure 5) that was originally devised by the writer for his own chronometric studies of the relationships between SRT and CRT and the *g* factor of intelligence tests (Jensen, 1982a,b). At last count, this apparatus, or the subject's response console, has been nominally duplicated in nine different laboratories in the United States. Despite the attempt to make the consoles as much like the original as possible, from the dimensions and descriptions provided, they all differ slightly, not in the physical measurements between the various S and R and H components or in the precision of the reaction timers, but rather in such subtle (but crucial) features as the lag in the microswitch response buttons and the pressure required. When we have tested the same subjects on different instruments, we find significant variations in the average RT because of these seemingly slight differences in equipment. Although the same *relative* differences and correlations with other variables replicate dependably, comparisons of absolute RT values between experiments performed even with only subtly differing apparatus is scarcely justified. (In order to compare RTs between groups that have had to be obtained in different localities validly, we have lent and transported our original apparatus to laboratories as far separated as Canada, northern and southern California, and Arizona.) It is clear that if S–R consoles are to be properly standardized, every component must be standardized. Ideally, prototype apparatuses that are intended to replicate experimental results with exactly the same absolute values of RT (except for sampling error) should all be constructed by the same manufacturer, using identical components, materials, and so forth.

The most expensive parts of any RT apparatus are the timers, but they are now also highly perfected and standardized, even when obtained from different manufacturers. They are the least of the problem, which resides in the lack of standardization of the stimulus display and the response console.

We have found the modern microcomputers, such as the Apple II and Apple III, to be a boon to mental chronometry. These computers are equipped with highly precise timing mechanisms and display screens and are programmable, so that the entire sequence of stimulus and response events can be run automatically. The whole program for an experiment lasting an hour or so can be stored on a magnetic tape cassette, and with a suitable (commercially available) attachment, can be read into the computer in just a few minutes. Also, with available attachments, all the subject's RTs can be recorded on magnetic tape and/or printed out on paper tape for a later detailed analysis. The computer can also be programmed to calculate summary statistics (e.g., mean, median, standard deviation) or frequency distributions of the subject's RTs over trials for each experimental condition—all available within a few seconds of the end of the testing.

The only component of the commercial microcomputers that we have found inadvisable for the laboratory measurement of RT is the computer's keyboard as the subject's response console. The computer's keyboard should be reserved only for programming the computer and for giving it "instructions" by the experimenter. In the first place, if it is used as a response console, parts of the keyboard have to be masked, exposing only those few keys germane to the requirements of the experiment, and these exposed keys usually have to be relabeled. Also, the small size and close spacing of the keys tends to inhibit fast response. But the main disadvantage is that the relatively delicate, expensive keyboard mechanisms of computers are not ideally suited to take the constant "beating" a response console is subjected to when many persons are run through hundreds of trials in RT experiments. Therefore, we have devised special response consoles that can be connected by a cable to the computer. In addition to the RT–MT console shown in Figure 5, we have a general-purpose response console that permits the measurement of RT and MT in all chrometric paradigms that call for any form of binary response (e.g., yes–no, true–false, same–different, odd–even, red–green, + −). It consists of a panel with a home button and two response buttons; each button is equidistant from the others, with the apex of the "triangle" toward the subject. The microswitch buttons, which make instant contact with a very light touch, are about the size of a half-dollar; their centers are about 6.4 cm apart. Appropriate magnetized labels that can be easily changed are placed just above each response button. Inside the console is a small sound generator that delivers a computer-programmed "beep" as the PS. The elementary cognitive task, including the RS, is presented visually on an alphanumeric display screen attached to the response console. (Videoscreens are ideal for stimulus display.) The computer itself, which controls the experiment, need not be in view of the subject. In any case, its operation is silent and thus unobtrusive. The subject's console is shown in Figure 9. As a general rule, the home button and response buttons should be fairly large, to minimize the purely motor-skill aspects of the task, and should make contact with very little pressure, to minimize the effect of differences in finger strength and fatigability. Work, in the physical sense of Force × Distance, should be reduced to the absolute minimum in the response requirements of a chronometric apparatus. This becomes especially important when young children or elderly persons are tested.

Also, it is essential that the subject's console of any RT–MT apparatus be designed so that the RT timer will not register the subject's response if the subject's finger releases H before the RS appears. In other words, it should be impossible to activate the electrical connection between H and the reaction timer until the instant the RS appears. This arrangement helps to

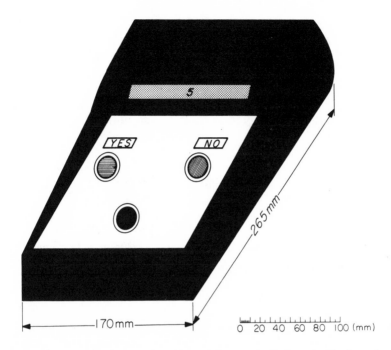

FIGURE 9. A binary response console, with an alphanumeric display unit. The lower button is the home, the upper two buttons are for binary choice responses (here labeled Yes and No) for indicating the presence (or absence) of the probe digit (shown in the display) in the "positive set," in S. Sternberg's short-term memory-scan paradigm.

prevent anticipatory flukes being included with authentic RT measurements.

PROCEDURES

The most general procedural principle for RT studies has been succinctly stated by Nettelbeck (1980): "First, all subjects . . . must understand what is required, and no subject should be influenced or disadvantaged by factors in the experimental situation not accounted for—for example, insufficient practice, fatigue or undetected sensory or physical disabilities" (p. 384).

Subjects should be seated during testing to avoid fatigue. An adjustable chair or stool is advisable, especially for children of varying age, to ensure approximately the same physical relationship betwen the subject and the S–R console for all subjects.

In our experience, a session involving any one type of RT should not last longer than about one-half an hour when testing normal young adults. We usually make the testing sessions even shorter, often using the remainder of the hour the subject is in the laboratory to administer paper and pencil tests or individually administer such IQ tests as the Wechsler. The attentional requirements of RT tests make them more demanding and fatiguing than the usual psychometric tests, and unless the experimenter is explicitly studying persistence of attention and resistance to fatigue, the testing sessions should be kept short. Subjects can more easily take two rather different RT tasks, each lasting 15 min, than they can take either task alone if it lasts 30 min. Children and older adults and the mentally retarded must be given even greater consideration in this respect.

The RT varies throughout the day for a given person, and there are IDs in this variation. The best time of day for testing, therefore, is problematic when the main object of study is IDs in RT. Generally, the individual diurnal variations in RT simply constitute error variance in the measurement of IDs in RT. The only way it can be reduced is by testing the same subject on two or more days at different times each day and using the average RT over days (see the later section, *Reliability and Stability*)· The least desirable time for measuring RT is any time within 1 hr or so after the subject has eaten lunch. Alcohol, drugs, medication, or illness of any kind may also affect the measurement of IDs in RT. It should be kept in mind that RT is considerably more sensitive to the subject's momentary physiological state than are psychometric tests.

Instructions to the subject are a crucially important part of the procedure for measuring RT. Variations in instructions can significantly affect the results, even when the testing procedure is the same in every other way. It is most important that the subject fully understand the task requirements and the features of his performance (e.g., speed and accuracy) that are being measured. The subject's ability to grasp and retain the instruction throughout the testing should not be a significant source of variance in the measurements. They are merely prerequisites for taking the test, and the experimenter must obtain evidence that all subjects are virtually equal in ability to comply with the task requirements, even if different subjects need different amounts of time for instruction and practice trials. Young children and retarded persons often need a demonstration of the required performance by the experimenter, so as to learn the procedure by imitation. Practice trials should be given until the subject performs confidently and consistently all the task variations that will be used in the experiment proper. For this purpose, we have made up brief practice sets that incorporate all the conditions of the experiment the subject will encounter. Subjects who cannot perform easily and consistently on the practice set after a number of attempts (the number depending upon the time available and the supply of subjects) are dismissed as being unable to meet the minimal prerequisite skills to serve as subjects, whatever the reason. The task demands of most chronometric experiments are so simple as to be easily mastered almost immediately by normal young adults. For a new procedure, a pilot study with several subjects who are typical of those to be tested in the study proper should be performed to discover any problems that may arise in instructing subjects and to determine the effect of practice on the subjects' performance of the task. If there is a marked practice effect (i.e., improvement in performance) over the first n trials before an approximately asymptotic level of performance is attained, it is advisable to require n practice trials before beginning the experiment proper. (A typical learning curve can be plotted, with mean RT shown as a function of number of practice trials.) The reason for this requirement is that in chronometric studies we are usually more interested in the speed of reaction to various stimulus conditions than in the rate of learning the particular skills that are prerequisite for the subject's performance. Hence, a significant practice effect over trials usually indicates a source of variance that is extraneous to the experimenter's interest. The importance of measuring only RT performances that are close to asymptote, however, can be determined only by the particular purpose of the study.

Another important consideration is the relative emphases on speed and accuracy in the instructions. The speed–accuracy operating characteristic of a task depends on its complexity. The simpler the task, the less will be the effect on RT or on error rate of instructions that differentially emphasize speed and accuracy of responses. A speed–accuracy operating characteristic curve is shown in Figure 10. In this graph, the theoretical definition of RT is the minimal time required for correct response. It is seen that both PT and performance accuracy increase as accuracy is emphasized at the expense of speed. *Normal instructions* would be something like "We want to measure how fast you can respond without making errors." With these instructions, even highly practiced subjects will make 2% to 3% errors in fairly simple RT tasks, and the error rate will be considerably higher in complex tasks. Error rates are lowered if the subject immediately receives informative feedback as to whether each response was "correct" or "an error." It should be made clear to subjects that in addition to the measurement of RTs, the number of correct and error responses is recorded. Task difficulty and instructions should be adjusted in such a way as to maintain a low error rate and one that is fairly uniform across the various experimental conditions of the chronometric paradigm (e.g., the different numbers of light-button alternatives in the RT–MT paradigm). When error rates differ markedly across different experimental conditions, the interpretation of the cor-

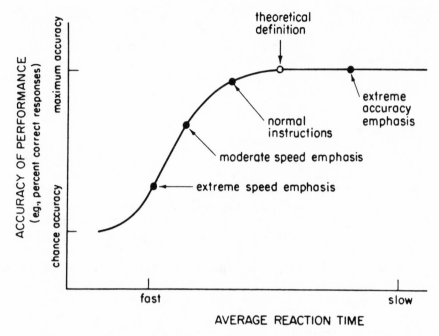

FIGURE 10. An idealized speed-accuracy operating characteristic. From "The Interpretation of Reaction Time in Information-Processing Research" by R. G. Pachella in *Human Information Processing: Tutorials in Performance and Cognition* (p. 59), B. H. Kantowitz, Ed., 1974, Hillsdale, N.J.: Lawrence Erlbaum Associates. Copyright 1974 by Lawrence Erlbaum Associates. Adapted by permission.

responding observed differences in RT becomes problematic. (See *Speed-Accuracy Trade-Off* in the following section.)

Finally, investigators should be aware that IDs and experimental effects can hardly be studied in-one-and-the-same procedure. Experimental psychologists are accustomed to thinking in terms of experimentally varying task conditions across subjects so as to randomize out certain unwanted sources of variance. This is rarely feasible in a single study of IDs and, moreover, it is usually undesirable. Beyond slight variations in instructions and preliminary practice to ensure that all subjects understand the task, the conditions must be *uniform* for all subjects. For example, the entire sequence of the particular S–R conditions over trials must be invariant for all subjects. Even if the sequence is *random,* it should be the *same* random order for everyone. Response repetition on successive trials (as contrasted with making different responses on successive trials) is known to affect RT, which is faster for a repeated response than for a varied response (Kirby,

1980). Hence, in measuring IDs in RT, it is essential that the conditions for sequential effects be the same for all subjects.

INDIVIDUAL DIFFERENCE VARIABLES DERIVED FROM CHRONOMETRIC PARADIGMS

SPEED–ACCURACY TRADE-OFF

One of the prominent methodological problems in RT research concerns the relationship between speed and accuracy of response. (A thorough discussion of this problem is provided by Pachella, 1974.) In all but the simple RT paradigm, there is the possibility of errors, either in the failure to respond to the appropriate signal or in the selection of the wrong response in a choice situation. For a given task, the subject cannot maximize *speed* of response and *accuracy* of response simultaneously. Hence we speak of a *speed–accuracy trade-off*. The direction and degree of the speed–accuracy trade-off are influenced by the degree of complexity or difficulty of the task, the emphasis given to the importance of speed or accuracy in the experimenter's instructions to the subject, and individual differences among subjects. An objective index of the degree of speed–accuracy trade-off for a single subject is the point-biserial correlation between RT and response accuracy (scored 1 and 0 for correct and error responses, respectively) over trials. A *negative* correlation indicates a speed–accuracy trade-off. This index may be entered into a multiple correlation, along with other RT parameters, in studying the relationship among IDs in RT and psychometric test scores.

The speed–accuracy trade-off has always been of special concern to experimental psychologists who study RT because they are interested mainly in comparing average RTs obtained under different experimental conditions of task complexity, etc., which affect both speed and accuracy of response, and the relationship between speed and accuracy is almost always inverse when the same instructions for responding are used for all conditions. The problem lies in the interpretation of differences in RT among various experimental conditions when there are also differences in error rates. How much accuracy has been sacrificed for speed?

The speed–accuracy problem is generally less problematic to the differential psychologist than to the experimentalist. If IDs in speed and accuracy were *negatively* correlated, the differential psychologist would face the same trade-off problem as the experimental psychologist. But in fact, IDs in speed and accuracy are *positively* correlated. We have not found an exception to this generaliztion in our own work on IDs in RT or in any studies reported in the literature. In other words, the speed–accuracy trade-off is only a *within*-subjects phenomenon, that is, speed and accuracy are *negatively* correlated *within* subjects between different task conditions. However, speed and accuracy are *positively* correlated *between* subjects within task conditions. These relationships may be easier to grasp in terms of Figure 11. On the *simple task*, persons A, B, and C are shown to have the same short RT and low error rate. On the *complex task*, the latent ability differences between persons A, B, and C are manifested as variation in their RTs and error rates. Their performances, as reflected jointly by RT and errors, will tend to fall somewhere on each of the arcs that describe the speed–accuracy trade-off; they are different for each person. If the same low error rate of the simple task is to be maintained for the complex task, the RT is greatly increased for all persons (vertical line, zero speed–accuracy trade-off). If the RT in the simple task is to be maintained in the complex task, the error rate is greatly increased for all persons (horizontal line, 100% speed–accuracy trade-off). So the arc for each person describes an *inverse* relationship (or *negative* correlation) between RT and error rate. But *between* persons, RT and error rate show a *direct* relationship (or *positive* correlation). The line marked x in Figure 11 indicates a fairly high

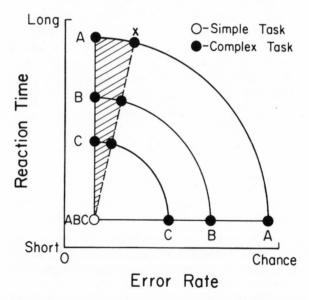

FIGURE 11. The relationship between RT and error rate for simple and complex tasks. The arcs describe the speed–accuracy trade-off for persons A, B, and C, who are shown here as performing equally well on the simple task. The shaded area represents the most desirable region of speed–accuracy trade-off for RT studies.

speed–accuracy trade-off for a typical RT study, if the error rate (on the abscissa) is assumed to range between *zero* and *chance*. Thus, the shaded area represents the most desirable region for performance when studying IDs in RT, in that it spreads out IDs in RT more than IDs in error rate.

As both RT and number (or percentage) of errors are ratio scales, Pearson's coefficient of variation ($V = \sigma/\mu$) (i.e., the ratio of standard deviation/mean) can be used to compare intersubject variability in RT and error rates. The more desirable condition for which procedures and instructions should aim is a larger V for RT than for errors. If the reverse is found, the investigator should question the procedures and instructions. A relatively high variability in errors often indicates that some subjects have not fully understood the task requirements or are too lacking in motivation or concentration to yield useful data. Subjects whose error rates are *outliers* by the some reasonable criterion (e.g., more than 3σ above the group mean) are probably better eliminated from subsequent data analyses.

It is especially important to take into account the speed–accuracy trade-off in studies in which subjects vary widely in age, because the speed–accuracy relationship interacts with age. Error rate decreases monotonically as a function of age, from early childhood to later maturity, whereas speed of response increases from childhood to early maturity and thereafter gradually decreases. Interestingly, in this respect, mentally retarded young adults resemble very old normal persons more than they resemble young children, that is, they have quite slow RTs, but relatively low error rates.

Several methods can be used to deal with errors in the treatment of RT data. Each method has advantages and disadvantages; none is ideal.

1. The central tendency (mean or median) of the subject's RT over trials can be based only on RTs for correct responses. The RTs for error responses are not used. This method is defensible only when error rates are very low (less than 4% or 5%) for every subject. With higher error rates, there is the risk that the subjects who have greatly sacrificed accuracy for speed are favorably overrated in terms of RT. A variation of this is to treat RTs for correct and error responses separately. If the correlation between RTs for correct and error responses is as high as the internal consistency reliability of either set, then there is no point in treating them separately.

2. The subject's RT is "adjusted" in terms of his or her error rate. This is accomplished by a regression equation in which RT is the dependent variable and error rate is the independent variable. The subject's "adjusted" RT score, then, is the difference between his or her *obtained* RT and *predicted* RT (using error rate as the predictor variable). Because the regression between RT and errors may be nonlinear, it is advisable to use a multiple regression equation, entering errors[1], errors[2], errors[3] (or higher

powers if necessary) as the predictor variables. The multiple prediction is justifiable only if the multiple correlation (R) between RT and the several predictor variables is significantly higher (after correction for bias or shrinkage) than the simple Pearson correlation (r) betwen RT and errors.

3. If the investigator is interested in the correlation between IDs in RT and some psychometric variable, error rate may be partialed out of the correlation. The error rate can act as a *suppressor variable* in such a correlation, that is, a variable, z, which, when partialed out of the correlation r_{xy}, results in a larger partial correlation, $r_{xy \cdot z}$.

CENTRAL TENDENCY OF RESPONSE TIME AND MOVEMENT TIME

Chronometric testing always involves repeated trials. In the study of IDs, we are interested in the central tendency of the subject's performance over n trials under a given set of task conditions. The number of trials (n) will depend upon the amount of testing time that is available and feasible in terms of the task demands and the degree of reliability deemed desirable for the purposes of the study.

Because there is an absolute lower limit to RT (and MT)—the so-called *physiological limit*—and RT theoretically has no upper limit, it is inevitable that the distribution of a subject's single RTs obtained in n trials will be *positively skewed*. In such a case, the *median*, rather than the *arithmetic mean*, is the preferred measure of central tendency, because the median is much less influenced by extreme values or outliers. The median has long been the usual measure of central tendency for the RT over trials of individual subjects. It should be remembered, however, that, unlike arithmetic means, medians are not additive, that is, the median value of the medians of each of two or more equal-sized groups is not equal to the median for the combined groups. For analyses in which this may be an important consideration, as in S. Sternberg's additive factor method, the arithmetic mean RT should be used instead of the median. Arithmetic mean is explicitly specified, because the *harmonic* mean (i.e., the reciprocal of the arithmetic mean of the n reciprocals of x) minimizes the effect of large outliers, and in a skewed distribution it has a value closer to the median than does the mean. But harmonic means are not additive. When additivity of RTs is an important consideration for subsequent analysis, only the arithmetic mean will do.

When the arithmetic mean is used, however, it is often advisable to apply certain uniform criteria for "cleaning up" each subject's RT data, to rid them of outliers—a practice known to statisticians as *Winsorizing* the distribution. It can greatly improve the reliability of the subject's mean RT over trials. (Winsorizing will have much less effect on the median.) Various methods can be used to Winsorize RT and MT data.

1. Eliminate all RTs of *less* than some specified value, as these are merely anticipatory flukes and not really measures of the subject's RT. True SRTs in alert young adults are rarely as short as 150 ms and certainly never shorter than 100 ms. One may safely use 100 ms as the cut-off for eliminating RTs at the lower end of the distribution. Winsorizing, or "trimming," the upper end is more problematic.

2. Eliminate all RTs (or MTs) of *greater* than some specified value. For normal subjects, we have used 999 ms as the cut-off in the one to eight light/button RT–MT paradigm; RTs or MTs that exceed 999 ms are not averaged, and the eliminated trial is repeated at the end of the scheduled trials to avoid a repetition effect.

3. Eliminate all RTs (or MTs) that exceed the subject's own *median* by some specified number of standard deviations, such as $3SD$, with the SD based on the subject's own RTs over the n trials given to all subjects.

INTERCEPT AND SLOPE OF REACTION TIME

When the chronometric experiment consists of two or more S–R tasks of varying complexity, we usually want to characterize the subject's performance with respect to (1) an overall level or base level and (2) the amount of increase in RT as s function of task complexity. When there is an approximately linear relationship between RT and task conditions, the *intercept* and *slope* of the regression of RT on conditions efficiently describe the subject's performance. Figure 12 shows the mean RT and MT as a function of bits of information conveyed by the task conditions (one, two, four, or eight light-button alternatives, n) in the RT–MT paradigm (see Figure 5). The intercept and slope of the regression of RT on bits can be calculated for each subject. (Since we have never found a significant slope for MT, we now do not bother to compute its regression on bits, but obtain only the median MT for each subject.) Intercept and slope may also be calculated for the S. Sternberg memory-scan paradigm, in which RT is a linear function of the actual number of digits in the "positive set." (After being shown the "positive set," i.e., a series of from one to seven digits, the subject is shown a single "probe" digit and must respond *yes* or *no* according to whether or not it was a member of the "positive set." The RT is the interval between the probe and the subject's response.)

To determine how closely individuals conform to a linear relationship between RT and task conditions (e.g., bits in the RT–MT paradigm or set size in the S. Sternberg paradigm), one can compute the correlation (Pearson r) between RT and the task conditions. We have generally found the rs to be in the high .90s for the medians of individual subjects in the RT–MT paradigm, which clearly indicates that Hick's Law (i.e., the linear increase in RT as a function of bits) holds for individuals and is not merely

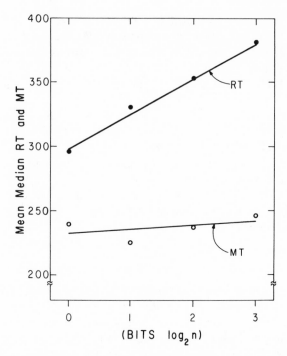

FIGURE 12. Mean median RT and MT on the RT–MT apparatus (see Figure 5) for 280 university students. Each subject's median RT (or MT) is based on 15 trials at each level of bits.

an artifact of averaging RTs over many subjects. Thus, an individual's RT in the RT–MT, or Hick, paradigm can be expressed in terms of the regression equation $RT = a + bH$, where a is the intercept, b is the slope, and H is the number of bits of information that must be processed for a correct response.

The a and b regression parameters call for distinct psychological interpretations. The *intercept* (a) is probably the most complexly determined feature of RT. It reflects not only the purely sensory and motor lags and peripheral nerve conduction, but also the apprehension and encoding of the stimulus and the preparation and initiation of the response, as well as all nonexperimental factors that may affect the subject's RT, such as the subject's general physiological state at the time. The *slope* (b), on the other hand, reflects such purely central processes as discrimination, comparison, choice, retrieval of information from short-term or long-term memory, and response selection. In terms of Hick's Law, the slope of RT on bits is the *speed* of information processing expressed as *milliseconds per bit*. The *reciprocal* of the slope is the *rate* of information processing, which is conventionally multipled by 1,000 to express rate as *bits per second*.

The fact that MT is much shorter than RT, and that MT does not vary significantly or systematically with the amount of information to be processed, would seem to suggest that MT reflects only sheer speed of response after all the other functions involved in the intercept and slope have already occurred. Considerable doubt is cast on this simple interpretation of MT, however, by the fact that median MT, like the RT parameters, is correlated with IQ, which certainly involves central processesses. But RT and MT are not highly correlated with each other. *Within* subjects, the average correlation between RT and MT is *zero*, indicating that there is no trade-off between RT and MT (which would result in a negative correlation). *Between* subjects, we generally find a low correlation between RT and MT, mostly tin the range +.2 to +.4 for relatively homogeneous samples of young adults. It has also been noticed that RT (for 0 bit) is relatively greater than MT in groups with higher intelligence, as shown in Figure 13. The reason for this relationship between RT/MT and IQ remains speculative (Jensen, 1980a, p. 114; 1980b, pp. 286–289).

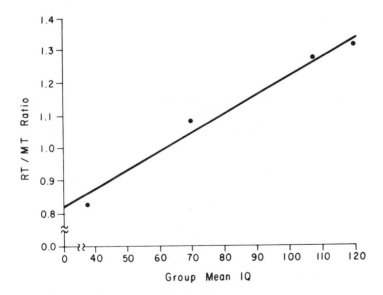

FIGURE 13. Ratio of mean of simple RT to mean MT as a function of the average intelligence levels of adult criterion groups: severely retarded ($N = 60$), borderline retarded ($N = 46$), vocational students ($N = 200$), and university students ($N = 50$).

INTRAINDIVIDUAL VARIABILITY IN RESPONSE TIME AND MOVEMENT TIME

This has been a neglected variable in chronometric research, probably because it is less obviously a measure of "goodness" of performance than is speed of reaction *per se*; also, variability does not lend itself so neatly to such simple analytic techniques as Donders' subtraction method. Yet it now warrants our attention, mainly for three reasons: (1) There are reliable IDs in trial-to-trial intraindividual variability in RTs; (2) these IDs have been found to be at least as highly correlated with psychometric g as any other parameter of RT paradigms; and (3) intraindividual variability in RT seems to be a more fundamental phenomenon than RT itself, in the sense that it is theoretically easier to explain IDs in mean (or median) RT in terms of IDs in intertrial variability than the reverse. There is always a high *positive* correlation between IDs in the central tendency of RT and IDs in the intertrial variability of RT. If persons differ relatively little in the *shortest* RTs of which they are capable, but differ greatly and reliably in the *variability* of their RTs from trial to trial, they would also necessarily differ in the central tendency of their RTs and IDs in variability, and the central tendency of RTs would always be positively correlated. (Intraindividual variability is always more highly correlated with IDs in the *mean* RT than in the *median* RT over trials.) This is what we find. Hence, the causes of IDs in average RT may have to be sought in the causes of IDs in variability. It is also noteworthy that intraindividual variability in RT decreases markedly from childhood to maturity and increases again in old age.

Intraindividual variability in RT (or MT) is best measured as the standard deviation of the person's RTs over trials. It is symbolized σ_i (or when a distinction is required between RT and MT, $RT\sigma_i$ and $MT\sigma_i$). When RT is measured at a number of different levels of S–R complexity, and an overall measure of σ_i is obtained, it should be obtained *within* levels, so as not to mix up variability between mean RTs for different levels of task complexity with intertrial variability. The average of σ_i (symbolized $\bar{\sigma}_i$) over levels (or other conditions) should be obtained as follows: $\bar{\sigma}_i = \sqrt{\sum \sigma_i^2/n}$, where n is the number of conditions. (Note: Variances $[\sigma^2]$ are additive, whereas standard deviations are not.)

The σ_i also increases as a function of task complexity, and for certain purposes it is useful to compute the intercept and slope of the regression of σ_i on the levels of complexity. In the Hick RT–MT paradigm, σ_i increases systematically as a function of bits of information in the stimulus array, as shown in Figure 14. Interestingly, σ_i increases in a perfectly linear fashion as a function of the actual *number* of light-button alternatives (i.e., the antilog$_2$ of bits).

The σ_i should be calculated *after* the RT data have been Winsorized by the methods previously described. This will appreciably improve the

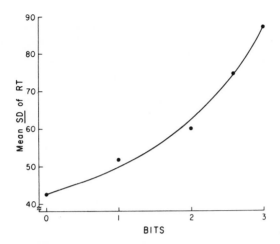

FIGURE 14. Mean intraindividual variabilty (measured by the σ_i of RTs in milliseconds on 30 trials) as a function of bits on the RT–MT apparatus, for 160 schoolchildren in grades four to six.

reliability of σ_i, which tends to have a lower reliability than the mean or the median RT.

Group differences in σ_i can be viewed more analytically by plotting RTs on each trial in their rank order of magnitude (from shortest to longest) for each subject averaging all RTs at each rank order over subjects. The RT data should first be Winsorized to minimize outlier flukes, such as by

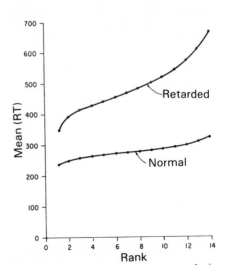

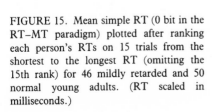

FIGURE 15. Mean simple RT (0 bit in the RT–MT paradigm) plotted after ranking each person's RTs on 15 trials from the shortest to the longest RT (omitting the 15th rank) for 46 mildly retarded and 50 normal young adults. (RT scaled in milliseconds.)

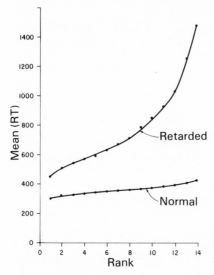

FIGURE 16. Mean choice RT (three bits in the RT–MT paradigm) plotted in the same fashion as in Figure 15.

omitting the one (or more) longest RT(s) for each subject. Figure 15 shows such a plot for normal and borderline retarded (IQs 60 to 80) young adults who were given 15 trials of SRT (one light button on the RT–MT apparatus). (The longest RT in 15 trials was eliminated for each subject.) This type of plot here reveals two theoretically important facts: (1) Retarded and normal persons differ (on average by about 100 ms) in SRT, even in their *shortest* RTs produced in 15 trials, and (2) the RTs are much more variable for retarded than for normal persons (as indicated by the marked divergence of the two curves). The group differences on SRT shown in Figure 15 are greatly exaggerated for CRT (with three bits of information), as shown in Figure 16.

The *relative variability* of RT is indicated by Pearson's coefficient of variability, $V = \sigma_i/\mu_i$. In this case, μ_i is the individual's mean RT over trials; V, like σ_i, is found to be positively correlated with mean (or median) RT and negatively correlated with intelligence level. Thus, slower (and less intelligent) subjects how greater intraindividual variability in RT in terms of both *absolute* variability and variability *relative* to their own average RT.

STATISTICAL TREATMENT OF CHRONOMETRIC DATA

RELIABILITY AND STABILITY

It is convenient in chronometric research to distinguish clearly between *reliability* and *stability* of the RT or MT measurements or the parameters derived from them, such as intercept, slope, and intraindividual variability. *Reliability* refers to the "internal consistency" of the measurements across trials within a single test session. *Stability* refers to the consistency of measurements (derived from all trials) across test sessions. The stability coefficient will usually be more informative if the sessions are at least one day apart. The main reason the distinction between the coefficients of *reliability* and *stability* is important is that they differ greatly for RT (much less so for MT). The reliability of RT, when based on 15 trials or more, is usually very high—as high as the reliability of good psychometric tests, that is, above .90. The day-to-day stability of RT, however, is generally much lower than the reliability. Stability coefficients for RT mostly range from about .50 to .70, when test sessions are one or two days apart, because of the sensitivity of RT to slight changes in a subject's physiological state.

Correlations between RT (and its derivatives) and psychometric variables cannot be properly evaluated without knowing the reliability and stability of the measurements. Stability is probably the more important, because it is this nonrandom, physiological state source of variability that is most likely responsible for attenuating the correlation between RT and other variables. But the reliability coefficient is needed to evaluate the stability coefficient. Since the stability cannot be higher than the reliability, we want to be sure that a low stability coefficient is not the result of low reliability, since it is usually easier to improve the reliability (by increasing the number of trials in a session) than to improve the stability of the measurements (by increasing the number of test sessions).

For a chronometric technique that is to be used in a series of studies to measure IDs, it is advisable to determine the reliability and stability of all the derivative measurements in at least one sample that is typical of the study population.

Reliability of IDs in RT (or MT) is best measured by *coefficient alpha* (α) (Cronbach, 1951). It can be derived from a two-way ANOVA of the subjects × trials matrix. The three sources of variance are *between trials*, *between subjects* (*BS*), and *within subjects* (*WS*). Coefficient α, then, is derived from the mean squares (*ms*), thus:

$$\alpha = (BSms - WSms)/BSms$$

Coefficient α is the reliability of the *mean* of n trials.

Because the *median* is more popular than the mean in RT work, how can we determine the reliability of the median? There is no very satisfactory way. However, we can reason as follows. Coefficient α is the average of all possible split-half reliability coefficients (boosted by the Spearman-Brown formula). Therefore, we can determine the split-half reliability of the median by splitting the number of trials into two equal sets in various ways (e.g., odd–even trials, odd–even pairs of trials, odd–even triplets or purely random sets), determining the median within each half, and correlating the two medians over subjects. We have done this analysis for 50 subjects given 30 trials on each of the four levels of bits $(0, 1, 2, 3)$ on the RT–MT paradigm; we found that the S-B–boosted, split-half reliabilities for the median are as high as or higher than the same split-half determination for the mean. Therefore, it would seem reasonable to assume that coefficient α does not overestimate the reliability of the median and is probably the best estimate we can obtain, short of the wholly unfeasible prospect of calculating every possible split-half reliability coefficient. Coefficient α is undoubtedly more dependable than any *single* split-half determination.

Stability of the mean or median RT (over trials) is obtained from the Pearson correlation of these statistics between test sessions (boosted by the Spearman-Brown formula) to obtain the reliability of the composite score for two sessions. (The *composite* mean or median is the mean of the means or medians across sessions.) If there are more than two sessions, the reliability (coefficient α) can be computed from a two-way ANOVA, with the sources of variance being between sessions, between subjects, and within subjects (WS). The reliability of the composite of n sessions then is

$$\alpha = [BSms - WSms]/[BSms + (n - 1)WSms]$$

where n is the number of sessions.

All the essential reliability and stability coefficients information can be obtained from a three-way ANOVA of RT data obtained by administering the task (or a parallel form of it) for $t + 1$ *trials* on each of $d + 1$ *days* to $s + 1$ *subjects*. The full ANOVA design is shown in Table 1. The reliability coefficient α for the composite scores, derived from the mean squares (MS) in Table 1, is $\alpha = (MS_S - MS_{ST})/MS_S$. The *stability* coefficient for the composite scores is $\alpha = (MS_S - MS_{SD})/MS_S$.

TABLE 1. Analysis of Variance of RT Data for Calculating Coefficient Alpha for Reliability and Stability

Source	SS	df	MS
Between days (D)	SS_D	d	MS_D
Between trials (T)	SS_T	t	MS_T
D × T	SS_{DT}	dt	MS_{DT}
Between subjects (S)	SS_S	s	MS_S
S × D	SS_{SD}	sd	MS_{SD}
S × T	SS_{ST}	st	MS_{ST}
Within subjects (W)	SS_W	sdt	MS_W

The reliability of complexly determined parameters, such as the intercept and slope of the regression of RT on bits and intraindividual variability (σ_i), can only be estimated by the odd–even split-half method. These parameters are calculated separately on the odd and even trials for each subject. The Pearson r between the odd and even sets (boosted by the Spearman-Brown formula, i.e., boosted $r' = 2r/(1 + r)$) estimates the reliability of the particular parameter based on all the trials. Reliability and stability coefficients are generally much lower for these complex parameters than for the mean or the median RT.

We have discovered that when there is no significant practice effect, the RT over *trials* conforms perfectly to the basic assumption underlying the use of the Spearman-Brown formula, namely, that increasing the number of measurements by a factor of n boosts the reliability (r) such that the boosted reliability (r') is equal to $r' = nr/[1 + (n - 1)]$, *provided* that the measurements in the additional trials by which the total number of trials is increased are *equivalent* (but not necessarily identical) to the original set of measurements. Two crucial tests of the equivalence of RTs over all trials are tests of the *homogeneity* of all the *covariances* between trials and of all the *correlations* between trials. In other words, we test the null hypothesis (H_0) that all the covariances between trials are equal, and we test the same hypothesis for correlations. Statistical tests, based on chi square, for the homogeneity of covariances and correlations have been provided by Wilks (1946) and Lawley (1963), respectively. When these tests were applied to RT data from the RT–MT paradigm, they completely failed to reject the null hypothesis. (The obtained chi square was less than 1/70th as large as the chi square required to reject the null hypothesis at the .05 level of confidence.) It was concluded that neither the covariance matrix nor the correlation matrix was significantly heterogeneous, but rather appeared as if the RTs on each trial were a random sample from the total distribution of all RTs the given subject could produce during that particular testing session. There is naturally some limit to this generalization because testing cannot be prolonged to the point of fatigue without damaging the equivalence of trials. Such equivalence, or homogeneity, of RTs was not found when these statistical tests were applied to the matrix of covariances or of correlations of RT obtained in 10 sessions, each on *different* days, two days apart. The matrix of correlations between days closely resembles a *simplex*, i.e., a matrix in which the correlations systematically decrease as the number of days between test sessions increases. This simplex pattern of the correlation matrix indicates that for individuals there is some systematic change, or nonequivalence, of the RT across days, even though there is no overall significant or appreciable day-to-day variation in mean RT, mean σ_i, mean intercept, or mean slope for the group as a whole.

Factors that generally tend to decrease reliability and stability for any given number of trials are low-ability subjects (for whatever reason—age, IQ, etc.), greater task complexity, insufficient practice, variable experimental conditions across subjects, and non-Winsorized RT data.

RELATIONSHIP OF CHRONOMETRIC VARIABLES TO PSYCHOMETRIC VARIABLES

Much of our theoretical interst in chronometric variables stems from their relationship to psychometric variables, particularly general intelligence, or g. Verbal, numerical, spatial, and other group factors found in psychometric tests, as well as tests of scholastic achievement, are also of interest.

There are two main ways to demonstrate a relationship between a chronometric variable x and a psychometric variable y: (1) test the significance of the difference between the means on x of two or more criterion groups selected from discrete regions of the distribution of y (e.g., IQs 80–90, 100–110, 120–130) and (2) compute the correlation between x and y obtained from a sample with continuously distributed scores on y.

The first method is most economical in exploratory studies, when we are seeking those chronometric paradigms and variables that are most strongly related to psychometric variables. When significant differences are found on various chronometric variables between psychometrically distinct criterion groups, the magnitudes of the differences can be compared in terms of standard scores or mean sigma ($\bar{\sigma}$) units, where $\bar{\sigma}$ is the average within-group σ for all groups; that is, each of the group mean differences based on raw measurements is divided by $\bar{\sigma}$, so that all differences are expressed in terms of the same standard units. Given the standard deviation (σ) of raw measurements within each of n groups, the mean sigma is

$$\bar{\sigma} = \sqrt{\frac{N_1\sigma_1^2 + N_2\sigma_2^2 + ... N_n\sigma_n^2}{N_1 + N_2 + ... N_n}}$$

where N is the number of subjects in a group. The mean difference between groups expressed in $\bar{\sigma}$ units may be corrected for attenuation (unreliability of the measurements) by dividing it by the square root of the reliability, that is, $\sqrt{r_{xx}}$.

The correlation coefficient is the most satisfactory method for expressing degree of relationship, but its interpretation and generalizability rest heavily upon a number of conditions.

1. The form of the distribution of the psychometric measurements (y) will determine the generalizability of r_{xy} to some population. If y is not

randomly sampled from a designated population, or if its frequency distribution departs significantly from the population distribution of which it is supposedly a sample, the correlation coefficient r_{xy} may be used to determine whether there is a significant relationship between x and y, but beyond the fact that r_{xy} is significantly greater than zero, its magnitude is meaningless with respect to any population; it is not generalizable. Such a correlation can be useful in exploratory research to discover those particular chronometric variables with the possibly closest relationship to the psychometric variable of interest. For such exploratory work, it is economical to test a small sample with a wide range on the psychometric variable and an approximately rectangular distribution, that is, the frequencies of each score are more or less evenly distributed over the entire range of scores. It would be as if we had a total of 60 subjects, with one subject at every IQ point over the range from, say, IQ 70 to IQ 130. The correlation of such IQ data with any other cognitive variable would, of course, be much higher than it would be in a large random sample of the population in which the distribution of IQs between 70 and 130 would closely approximate a Gaussian distribution.

2. Random or representative samples of particular natural populations (e.g., sixth-traders in a middle-class neighborhood, institutionalized retarded with IQs between 50 and 70, college students) can yield correlations that can be generalized to their respective populations, but these correlations *understimate* the true correlation in the *general* population. The reason, of course, is that almost any natural group from which we obtain our study sample has a more restricted variance than that of the general population. This is especially true for measures of intelligence, scholastic aptitude and attainments, and most other cognitive variables. If we know the standard deviation of the psychometric variable in a broader sample of the general population, such as the normative group for most standardized tests, we can use this *SD* along with the *SD* and the obtained correlation r_{xy} of our more restricted sample to obtain an estimate of what the correlation would be in the unrestricted population; the formula is given by McNemar (1949, p. 126):

$$R = \frac{r(\Sigma/\sigma)}{\sqrt{1 - r^2 + r^2(\Sigma/\sigma)^2}}$$

where R is the correlation in unrestricted sample, r is the correlation in restricted sample, Σ is the *SD* for unrestricted sample, and σ is the *SD* for restricted sample.

3. When estimates of the reliability and stability of the chronometric variables are available, the correlation can be corrected for attenuation to estimate the theoretical error-free correlation between x and y. The stability

coefficient will usually afford the more realistic correction. Simultaneous corrections for attenuation and restriction of variance are not advisable. Each correction in effect adds an increment to r_{xy}. If each of these added increments were completely independent, there would be no problem. But they are indeterminately nonindependent; the reliability coefficients used to correct for attenuation are themselves decreased by the restriction of variance. Hence, simultaneous correction for attenuation and restriction causes some indeterminate degree of overestimation of the true correlation in the unrestricted population.

4. The true degree of relationship between x and y will be underestimated by r_{xy} if the regressions are not linear. Scatter diagrams should be plotted and examined, and if there is any suspicion of nonlinearity, it should be confirmed by a suitable statistical test, such as a statistical comparison of the magnitudes of r_{xx}^2 and the squared correlation ratio, or eta^2, which is explicated in most statistics textbooks.

5. Outliers in the distributions of variable x or variable y will inflate the correlation. The distributions are best rid of outliers, or Winsorized, by some reasonable criterion before correlations are calculated. Another solution to the same problem, which has been suggested but which has little merit, is a *reciprocal transformation* of the x or y scores (or both). A reciprocal transformation of the scores (on both variables) will indeed minimize the effect of correlated outliers at the high end of the scale, but it also has disadvantages, and there is little else to recommend it. It should be noted that the correlation r_{xy} between variables x and y is not simply $-r_{xy}$, that is, the same correlation reversed in sign, by correlating $1/x$ and y, or x and $1/y$. The numerical value of r will differ, as well as its sign, and if x and y are linearly related, there will not be a linear relationship between one variable and the reciprocal of the other. For the same set of data, with linearity of the regressions of x and y and without any discontinuities or outliers on either variable, the correlation between x and y and the correlation between the reciprocals of x and y can be markedly different. Only the rank order correlation (Spearman's rho) remains invariant in magnitude under a reciprocal transformation (or any other monotonic transformation). But the rank order correlation also has the advantage of being little affected by discontinuities and outliers in the bivariate distribution and may be a useful safeguard when the Pearson r is a suspect for such reasons.

Multiple correlation, R, is called for when we want to determine the degree of linear relationship between an optimally weighted composite of chronometric variables (the independent variables) and a particular psychometric variable (the dependent variable). The independent variables need not be *experimentally* independent, that is, two or more of them may be derived from the same set of data, such as the intercept, slope, and σ_i of RT and the mean and σ_i of MT in the Hick paradigm. The aim is simply to find the optimal set of predictors of the dependent variable. The stepwise order in which the variables come out in the multiple regression equation has virtually no theoretical significance and can be largely a matter of chance. The investigator may elect to force the order of the variables in the stepwise regression to determine if a particular variable adds a significant increment to R^2 over the the variance already accounted for by certain other variables.

If there are a number of psychometric variables, they may play the role of independent variables to predict a chronometric variable. A set of n psychometric variables often yields a greater R with a chronometric variable than is found for the converse relationship, probably because the typical psychometric variables involve more different cognitive processes than the typical chronometric variables. Complex variables are better predictors of simple variables than simple variables of complex variables. In all cases, however, the multiple R should always be corrected for bias (or "shrinkage") by the formula given in most statistics textbooks.

A *canonical correlation* expresses the degree of linear relationship between a number of independent variables and a number of dependent variables considered simultaneously. This is useful for testing a hypothesis concerning overall relationships between two sets of variables and for exploratory studies that seek those variables in each of the two domains that contribute most to the canonical correlation and, therefore, seem most promising for further experimental and correlation analysis. Unfortunately, there is no convenient correction for bias (or shrinkage) of a canonical correlation, and with a considerable number of variables and a relatively small sample of subjects, the canonical correlation will be spuriously inflated. (Dempster, 1966, has proposed a "jackknifing" method for the removal of bias from estimates of the canonical correlation.)

Age variance must be attended to in a chronometric study if the subject sample is at all heterogeneous in age. Both RT and MT are strongly affected by age in the range from early childhood to early maturity. For a sample from this age range having an age spread of more than about six months, it is advisable to control for age (in months) in all the subsequent statistical treatment of the chronometric data. The same consideration applies to age-heterogeneous samples over about the age of 30 years, beyond which age increasingly contributes to the variance in RT. With respect to the correlations between chronometric and psychometric variables, the partial correlation coefficient, with *age in months* partialed out, is called for. The regression of chronometric and psychometric variables on age is generally linear within relatively short age ranges. But if the subjects' ages range over more than about three years, one should test the correlation for nonlinearity. Usually, when there is nonlinearity, partialing out age, age^2, and age^3 will rid the correlation of all the unwanted age variance.

In a multiple correlation, R, one can enter age (or also age^2, age^3, etc.) ahead of any other variable in the stepwise regression, so that all the variance associated with age in the dependent variable is accounted for, permitting evaluation of the contributions of the remaining independent variables free of age effects.

Psychometric variables are often measured by such age-standardized tests as IQ tests, the IQs on which, at least in the standardization sample, are made to be uncorrelated with age. One now and then comes across the (mistaken) notion that if either variable x or y entering into the correlation r_{xy} is not correlated with age (a), it is unnecessary to partial out age, presumably (but mistakenly) because r_{xy} would remain unchanged by partialing out age when it has zero correlation with x (or y). Actually, in this situation, age acts as a *suppressor variable*, and partialing out age will increase the correlation, that is $r_{xy \cdot a} > r_{xy}$. If $r_{xa} = 0$ and $r_{ya} > 0$, then the partial correlation is

$$r_{xy \cdot a} = r_{xy} / \sqrt{1 - r_{ya}^2},$$

which is necessarily larger than r_{xy}.

One should not assume that scores on an age-standardized test are uncorrelated with age in any particular study sample. In sampling from regular classrooms, for example, one typically finds a low negative correlation between IQ and chronological age; that is, the younger children within any grade level tend to be brighter.

Factor Analysis of Chronometric and Psychometric Data

When a large number of variables is to be analyzed in terms of interrelationships, some type of factor analysis affords the most informative technique. The particular type of factor analysis to be used will depend, in part, upon the investigator's analytical purpose and theoretical stance. The writer has expressed his own views on these matters with reference to chronometric research in some detail elsewhere (Jensen, 1982b, pp. 263–268).

The factors that emerge from a collection of tests have greater generality than do the particular test scores, and factors are therefore of more general psychological interest. Factor analysis, in a sense, separates the psychologically more important sources of variance from the chaff of test specificity, which usually attenuates the correlations between psychometric test variables and the cognitive process variables reflected in chronometric paradigms.

From a theoretical standpoint, common factor analysis (or principal factor or principal axes analysis) is preferable to principal components analysis, but the arguments on this issue are beyond the scope of this chapter. Factor analysis generally yields more clear-cut and more replicable results than principal components analysis, since each principal component contains some part of each test's *uniqueness* (i.e., that part of the test variance that is not shared by any other test in the battery), whereas factors reflect only common factor variance (i.e., only that variance that all tests or some subsets of tests share). Principal components, however, have the advantage that the *factor scores* (they should actually be called *component scores*) derived from them are completely determinate and exact, whereas factor scores derived from common factor analysis are mathematically indeterminate and are really *estimated factor scores*, which are imperfectly correlated with the indeterminable "true" or exact factor scores. The seriousness of this limitation of factor scores for most purposes, however, has often been exaggerated. If it is important that factor scores for different factors be perfectly uncorrelated, it is preferable that they be derived exactly from principal components and not estimated from factors. When principal components are *orthogonal* (i.e., uncorrelated), the factor scores derived from them will also be perfectly uncorrelated. The estimated factor scores derived from different perfectly orthogonal principal factors, however, may be (and usually are) correlated with one another. But in general, principal factors and principal components are, in fact, highly correlated, and rarely, if ever, would these two types of analysis result in substantially different conclusions.

As for types of factor rotation, this writer takes a definite position, which is based on the overwhelming evidence for a large general factor in the domain of cognitive abilities. R. Sternberg and Gardner (1982) have stated it well: "We interpret the preponderance of the evidence as overwhelmingly supporting the existence of some kind of general factor in human intelligence. Indeed, we are unable to find convincing evidence at all that mitigates against this view" (p. 231). The most obvious evidence for a general factor is the fact that all tests of cognitive ability, however diverse, show positive intercorrelations in any large, unrestricted samples of the general population—a fact of nature termed *positive manifold* by Thurstone (1947). This means that cognitive ability tests of all sorts have a common source of variance, which Spearman discovered in 1904 and labeled g for *general factor*. Therefore, any form of factor rotation that submerges the g factor, that is, distributes its variance among a number of rotated factors so as to obscure its identity completely, is simply an inappropriate factor model for research on mental abilities. This is precisely what is accomplished by what, at least until recent years, has been the most popular analytical method of orthogonal factor rotation, Kaiser's (1958) *varimax*, a criterion for rotation intended to approximate Thurstone's concept of orthogonal *simple structure*, which of mathematical necessity absolutely precludes the emergence of a *g* factor, even from a correlation matrix that perfectly exemplifies positive manifold. Hence, orthogonal rotation of factors, by varimax or any other method, should be avoided in this field.

What is recommended? If the investigator is only interested in the general factor of a matrix, there are essentially two choices: (1) The first *unrotated* principal factor is a good representation of the general factor of the correlation matrix, particularly when the tests are diverse and no one type of test is overrepresented. (The first unrotated principal component [FPC] will scarcely differ from the first principal factor [FPF]. Congruence coefficients between the FPC and FPF and the correlation between FPC and FPF factor scores are generally above .95.) (2) Hierarchical factor analysis of the correlations among obliquely rotated primary, or first-order, factors will yield a single *g* factor for cognitive tests. This second-order *g* factor accounts for somewhat less of the total variance than is accounted for by the first principal factor, but it is usually very highly correlated with the FPF—an empirical generalization, not a mathematical necessity.

If the investigator is interested in other factors besides the *g* factor in his collection of variables, he should resort to a method of factor rotation that completely rids the remaining factors of any trace of *g* variance. The ideal method for achieving this is by means of a hierarchical factor analysis, using the Schmid–Leiman (Schmid & Leiman, 1957) orthogonalization transformation (cf. Wherry, 1959). This method, in effect, partials *g* (or any other higher order factor) out of the first-order factors, leaving them all perfectly orthogonal to one another and to *g* or all other higher order factors.

Factor analysis is used in chronometric research on IDs in three ways.

1. Factor analysis is used to identify the best *marker* or *reference* tests for different factors in a battery of psychometric tests properly selected to measure certain hypothesized cognitive ability factors of interest to the investigator. It is more economical to use the factor reference tests than to use the whole battery of tests that was required to identify the factors, for subsequent correlation with chronometric variables.

2. Factor analysis can be used to obtain factor scores to be correlated with chronometric variables. Factor scores are usually of more general interest, psychologically, than scores on any single test. The *specificity* of any given test may affect its correlation with a chronometric variable more than the factor the test supposedly measures and there would be no way of knowing this without the use of factor analysis. The use of properly derived *factor scores* obviates this problem.

3. Chronometric and psychometric variables can be factor analyzed

together to see which variables of both types have the largest loadings on the same factors. This is a reasonable procedure if there are a great many psychometric variables and just a few chronometric variables, because the factor structure will be predominantly determined by the psychometric variables. If about equal numbers of variables of both classes are factor analyzed together, however, there is the possibility that a clear-cut and interpretable factor structure will not be achieved, because of what is termed *method variance,* which is variance peculiar to each of the two classes of measurements. For this reason, most factor analysts recommend performing a factor analysis separately within each domain of variables—the psychometric and the chronometric. Factor scores obtained within each domain are then correlated *across* domains to reveal more clearly interpretable common sources of variance between the psychometric and the chronometric domains.

It is advisable in this type of study to minimize as much as possible the effect of a *speed factor* in the psychometric tests. Their correlation with chronometric variables should not be attributable merely to the speed of taking psychometric tests. Therefore, the psychometric tests used in chronometric studies should be administered with no time limit, or at least with a very liberal time limit. The tests should be viewed as *power tests,* and subjects should be urged to take all the time they need to attempt every item. There should be absolutely no sense of time pressure on the subjects. Research has already established, however, that the correlations between psychometric tests of g and chronometric variables are not attributable to a speed factor in the psychometric tests. Timed tests are no more highly correlated with chronometric variables than are untimed tests. The recommended precautions for unspeeded tests are still important, however, to rule out the overly simple interpretation of the observed relationship between psychometric and chronometric variables as being the result of a common test-taking speed factor.

It is a general rule in factor analysis that all the variables entering into the analysis should be *experimentally independent,* which means variables based on measurements obtained from separate acts or observations, not from mathematical manipulations of other variables that are entered into the same analysis. If we give subjects two different tests, x and y, the scores are experimentally independent, but the "difference score," $x - y$, and the ratio score, x/y, are not independent. In the RT–MT paradigm, RT and MT are experimentally independent measurements, whereas the *intercept* and *slope* of the regression of TR on bits are not independent variables, because they are mathematically derived from the same set of measurements. The same thing is true for mean (or median) RT and σ_i of RT. The argument against including variables that are not experimentally independent into the same factor analysis is that the correlation between such variables may simply represent an artifact of their mathematical derivation, rather than a true psychological or causal relationship. (Of course, the correlation between *any* two variables may or may not represent a causal relationship.) In short, the interpretation of factors with significant loadings on two or more experimentally dependent measures is always suspect and problematic. Yet a factor analysis or components analysis that includes experimentally dependent measures may be performed, keeping this problem in mind, for the explicitly limited purpose of seeing which variables cluster together (i.e., load on uncorrelated factors), in order to select the one variable from each cluster that best represents the cluster, as indicated by the magnitude of its factor loading. If one needs to use such experimentally dependent measures as intercept and slope in a factor analysis and wishes to give an acceptably rigorous interpretation of the results, or base a theoretically important argument on them, then the RT data should be obtained in two separate test sessions, S_1 and S_2, so that the intercept and slope parameters can be obtained in experimentally independent sets of RT data. The factor analysis can be repeated, as well, the first analysis including the correlation between the S_1 intercept and the S_2 slope and the second analysis including the correlation between the S_2 intercept and the S_1 slope.

Such chronometric variables as RT, MT, intercept, slope, and σ_i are *positively* correlated among themselves, but are all *negatively* correlated with scores on various psychometric tests of ability, which are always *positively* correlated with one another. This condition can confuse anyone examining the results of a factor analysis that comprises both chronometric and psychometric variables, even though, of course, the mixture of positive and negative correlations could have no effect on the factor structure or the magnitudes of the factor loadings. It is advisable to avoid this unnecessary difficulty in "reading" the factor matrix by reflecting the signs of some variables in the original correlation matrix so that superior performance on any variable will always show a *positive* correlation with superior performance on any other variable, thereby allowing the appearance of positive manifold when it, in fact, exists.

Factor analysis has not yet been widely or rigorously used in chronometric studies of IDs, perhaps because other methods of data analysis are more economical and, with a limited number of variables, other methods are more defensible in the initial exploratory stages of this work. Practically all the chronometric studies that have used factor analysis or have produced data that would justify factor analysis (30 data sets in all) have been quite thoroughly reviewed, and in many cases factor analyzed by a uniform method, by Carroll (1980). Carroll (pp. 81–82) has noted the five most common deficiencies of the factor analyses applied so far to the study of IDs in elementary cognitive tasks, which include chronometric variables:

1. There was little deliberate attempt to design sets of variables that would reasonably be expected to produce clear simple structures and/or test hypotheses about factors.
2. The variables included in the factor analysis exhibited too much overlap and experimental dependence on each other.
3. The analysis used only principal component techniques (analysis of total variance), whereas a principal factor procedure (analysis of only common factor variance) would have been preferable.
4. The data were either under- or over-factorized, in that there was slavish dependence on the Guttman-Kaiser rule that the number of factors analyzed be taken as equal to the number of eigenvalues in a principal component solution that are equal to or greater than unity.
5. The factors were rotated, if at all, only orthogonally, usually by Kaiser's (1958) varimax procedure, whereas the structure of the data may have suggested that the results could be clarified by the use of oblique rotations.

CHRONOMETRIC VARIABLE CORRELATED WITH PSYCHOMETRIC INTELLIGENCE

It is a seemingly remarkable and almost counterintuitive fact that chronometric variables derived from elementary cognitive tasks that include virtually no intellectual *content* that would be a source of IDs nevertheless show significant, even substantial, correlations with scores on complex psychometric tests of general intelligence and of scholastic achievement, the item contents of which comprise a great variety of acquired knowledge and skills (Carlson & Jensen, 1982; Jensen, 1979, 1980, 1981, 1982a,b; Jensen & Munro, 1979; Jensen, Schafer, & Crinella, 1981; Vernon, 1981, 1983; Vernon & Jensen, 1984). Therefore, psychometric tests of intelligence and achievement actually tap much more fundamental sources of IDs than the superficial aspects of the information content that can be gleaned from casual inspection of the test items. Thus, IDs in mental test performance must also reflect IDs in fundamental cognitive and even neural processes that lie below the level of information content and scholastic skills *per se*. Galton's original intuition would seem to be vindicated. But much research remains to be done. The prospect of measuring IDs in human intelligence in terms of IDs in such basic and content-irrelevant processes is still a major challenge for researchers in differential psychology and mental chronometry. Research aimed toward this goal is still exploratory. The techniques are too undeveloped and too lacking in sufficiently substantiated theoretical underpinnings and construct validity for chronometric techniques to be recommended as replacements for standard psychometric tests of intelligence. Yet, judging from the buregoning research in mental chronometry in the study of IDs, the time does not seem far off—less than a decade, perhaps—when we will see the practical application of sophisticated chronometric techniques to individual assessment, at least as a valuable adjunct to the standard psychometric instruments used in clinical work, in the diagnosis and remediation of school-learning disabilities, and in educational and personnel selection.

REFERENCES

Baumeister, A. A., & Kellas G. Reaction time and mental retardation. In N. R. Ellis (Ed.), *International review of research in mental retardation*. Vol. 3. New York: Academic Press, 1968.

Boring, E. G. *A history of experimental psychology* (2nd ed.). New York: Appleton-Century-Crofts, 1950.

Brebner, J. M. T. Reaction time in personality theory. In A. T. Welford (Ed.), *Reaction times*. New York: Academic Press, 1980.

Carlson, J. S., & Jensen, C. M. Reaction time, movement time, and intelligence: A replication and extension. *Intelligence*, 1982, *6*, 265–274.

Carpenter, P., & Just, M. Sentence comprehension: A psycholinguistic processing model of verification. *Psychological Review*, 1975, *82*, 45–73.

Carroll, J. G. *Individual difference relations in psychometric and experimental cognitive tasks*. Chapel Hill, N.C.: L. L. Thurstone Psychometric Laboratory, University of North Carolina, 1980.

Cattell, R. B. *Abilities: Their structure, growth, and action*. Boston: Houghton Mifflin, 1971.

Cronbach, L. J. Coefficient alpha and the internal structure of tests. *Psychometrika*, 1951, *16*, 297–334.

Cronbach, L. J. The two disciplines of scientific psychology. *American Psychologist*, 1957, *12*, 671–684.

Dempster, A. P. Estimation in multivariate analysis. *Proceedings of the Symposium on Multivariate Analysis*. New York: Academic Press, 1966.

Donders, F. C. Over de snelheid van psychische processen. *Onderzoekingen gedan in het Physiologisch Laboratorium der Utrechtsche Hoogschool*, 1868, 2nd series, *2*, 92–120. (On the speed of mental processes. Trans. by W. G. Koster, *Acta Psychologica*, 1969, *30*, 412–431.)

Ehri, L. C., & Wilce, L. S. Development of word identification speed in skilled and less skilled beginning readers. *Journal of Educational Psychology*, 1983, *75*, 3–18.

Eriksen, C. W., Pollack, M. D., & Montague, W. Implicit speed: Mechanism in perceptual encoding? *Journal of Experimental Psychology*, 1970, *84*, 502–507.

Eysenck, H. J. (Ed.) *A model for intelligence*. New York: Springer-Verlag, 1982.

Flavell, J. *The developmental psychology of Jean Piaget*. New York: Van Nostrand, 1963.

Galton, F. *Memories of my life*. London: Methuen, 1908.

Grice, G. R., Nullmeyer, R., & Spikes, V. A. Human reaction time: Toward a general theory. *Journal of Experimental Psychology: General*, 1982, *111*, 135–153.

Hendrickson, A. E. The biological basis of intelligence. Part I: Theory. In H. J. Eysenck (Ed.), *A model for intelligence*. New York: Springer-Verlag, 1982.

Hendrickson, D. E. The biological basis of intelligence. Part II: Measurement. In H. J. Eysenck (Ed.), *A model for intelligence*. New York: Springer-Verlag, 1982.

Hick, W. On the rate of gain of information. *Quarterly Journal of Experimental Psychology*, 1952, *4*, 11–26.

Jensen, A. R. *g*: Outmoded theory or unconquered frontier? *Creative Science and Technology*, 1979, *2*, 16–29.

Jensen, A. R. Chronometric analysis of mental ability. *Journal of Social and Biological Structures*, 1980, *3*, 103–122.

Jensen, A. R. Reaction time and intelligence. In M. P. Friedman, J. P. Das, & N. O'Connor (Eds.), *Intelligence and learning*. New York: Plenum Press, 1981.

Jensen, A. R. Reaction time and psychometric *g*. In H. J. Eysenck (Ed.), *A model for intelligence*. New York: Springer-Verlag, 1982a.

Jensen, A. R. The chronometry of intelligence. In R. J. Sternberg (Ed.), *Advances in the psychology of human intelligence*. Vol. 1. Hillsdale, N.J.: Lawrence Erlbaum Associates, 1982b.

Jensen, A. R., & Munro, E. Reaction time, movement time, and intelligence. *Intelligence*, 1979, *3*, 121–126.

Jensen, A. R., Schafer, E. W. P., & Crinella, F. M. Reaction time, evoked brain potentials, and psychometric *g* in the severely retarded. *Intelligence*, 1981, *5*, 179–197.

Kaiser, H. F. The varimax criterion for analytic rotation in factor analysis. *Psychometrika*, 1958, *23*, 187–200.

Kantowitz, B. H. Double stimulation. In B. H. Kantowitz (Ed.), *Human information processing: Tutorials in performance and cognition*. Hillsdale, N.J.: Lawrence Erlbaum Associates, 1974.

Keating, D. P., & Bobbitt, B. Individual and developmental differences in cognitive processing components of mental ability. *Child Development*, 1978, *49*, 155–169.

Keele, S. W. *Attention and human performance*. Pacific Palisades, Cal.: Goodyear, 1973.

Kirby, N. Sequential effects in choice reaction time. In A. T. Welford (Ed.), *Reaction times*. New York: Academic Press, 1980.

Lawley, D. N. On testing a set of correlation coefficients for equality. *Annals of Mathematical Statistics*, 1963, *34*, 149–151.

Libnet, B. Cortical activation in conscious and unconscious experience. *Perspectives in Biology and Medicine*, 1965, *9*, 77–86.

McNemar, Q. *Psychological statistics*. New York: Wiley, 1949.

Merkel, J. Die zeitlichen Verhältnisse der Willensthatigkeit. *Philosophische Studien*, 1885, *2*, 73–127.

Nettelbeck, T. Factors affecting reaction time: Mental retardation, brain damage, and other psychopathologies. In A. T. Welford (Ed.), *Reaction times*. New York: Academic Press, 1980.

Pachella, R. G. The interpretation of reaction time in information-processing research. In B. H. Kantowitz (Ed.), *Human information processing: Tutorials in performance and cognition*. Hillsdale, N.J.: Lawrence Erlbaum Associates, 1974.

Pöppel, E. Time perception. In R. Held, H. W. Leibowitz, & H.-L. Teuber (Eds.), *Handbook of sensory physiology: Vol. VIII. Perception*. Berlin: Springer-Verlag, 1978.

Posner, M. I. *Chronometric explorations of mind*. Hillsdale, N.J.: Lawrence Erlbaum Associates, 1978.

Posner, M. I., Lewis, J. L., & Conrad, C. Component processes in reading: A performance analysis. In J. F. Kavanagh & I. G. Mattingly (Eds.), *Language by ear and by eye: The relationships between speech and reading*. Cambridge, Mass.: MIT Press, 1972.

Schmid, J., & Leiman, J. The development of hierarchical factor solutions. *Psychometrika,* 1957, *22,* 53–61.

Smith, E. E. Choice reaction time: An analysis of the major theoretical positions. *Psychological Bulletin,* 1968, *69,* 77–110.

Spring, C. Perceptual speed in poor readers. *Journal of Educational Psychology,* 1971, *62,* 492–500.

Spring, C., & Capps, C. Encoding speed, rehearsal, and probed recall of dyslexic boys. *Journal of Educational Psychology,* 1974, *66,* 780–786.

Sternberg, R. J. *Intelligence, information processing, and anological reasoning: The componential analysis of human abilities.* Hillsdale, N.J.: Lawrence Erlbaum Associates, 1977.

Sternberg, R. J. (Ed.) *Advances in the psychology of human intelligence* (Vol. 1). Hillsdale, N.J.: Lawrence Erlbaum Associates, 1982.

Sternberg, R. J., & Gardner, M. K. A componential interpretation of the general factor in human intelligence. In H. J. Eysenck (Ed.), *A model for intelligence.* New York: Springer-Verlag, 1982.

Sternberg, R. J., & Rifkin, B. The development of anological reasoning processes. *Journal of Experimental Child Psychology,* 1979, *27,* 195–232.

Sternberg, S. The discovery of processing stages: Extensions of Donders' method. (Attention and performance II.) *Acta Psychologica,* 1969, *30,* 276–315.

Thurstone, L. L. *Multiple-factor analysis: A development and expansion of the vectors of mind.* Chicago: University of Chicago Press, 1947.

Vernon, P. A. Reaction time and intelligence in the mentally retarded. *Intelligence,* 1981, *5,* 345–355.

Vernon, P. A. Speed of information processing and general intelligence. *Intelligence,* 1983, *7,* 53–70.

Vernon, P. A., & Jensen, A. R. Individual and group differences in intelligence and speed of information processing. *Journal of Educational Psychology,* 1984, *5,* 411–423.

Warren, H. C. (Ed.) *Dictionary of psychology.* Boston: Houghton Mifflin, 1934.

Welford, A. T. (Ed.) *Reaction times.* New York: Academic Press, 1980.

Wherry, R. J. Hierarchical factor solution without rotations. *Psychometrika,* 1959, *24,* 45–51.

Wilks, S. S. Sample criteria for testing equality of means, equality of variances and equality of covariances in a normal multivariate distribution. *Annals of Mathematical Statistics,* 1946, *17,* 275–281.

Woodworth, R. S. *Experimental psychology.* New York: Holt, 1938.

Woodworth, R. S., & Schlosberg, H. *Experimental psychology.* New York: Holt, Rinehart & Winston, 1954.

3

Neuropsychological Approaches to the Study of Individual Differences

MERRILL HISCOCK AND MARILYNN MACKAY

The main objective of human neuropsychology is to map mental functions onto the brain. The desired result is a set of general facts and organizing principles that relate specific behaviors to neural activity at specific brain locations. Insofar as individual variation may qualify those facts and obfuscate the underlying principles, such variation often is viewed as unwanted noise that lowers the correlation between brain and behavior. Cerebral speech regions would be easier to define if topographic landmarks did not vary so much from brain to brain (Rubens, 1977); dichotic listening would be a more useful measure of language lateralization if there were not so many normal people who fail to show the expected performance asymmetries (Satz, 1977); poor performance on a neuropsychological test would be easier to interpret if test performance were not affected by the patient's educational level (Lezak, 1983). In many respects, the work of neuropsychologists would be less problematic if the human brain and its behavioral repertoire were as invariant as the brain and behavior of the laboratory rat.

Alternatively, one may view diversity among humans not as a hindrance to understanding brain–behavior relationships, but rather as an opportunity to be exploited. If some people are, for example, more verbally fluent or more aggressive than others, perhaps these characteristics can be related to specific aspects of brain structure or function. It is often claimed

MERRILL HISCOCK AND MARILYNN MACKAY ● Department of Psychology and Department of Psychiatry, University of Saskatchewan, Saskatoon, Saskatchewan, Canada. Preparation of this chapter was supported by a grant to Merrill Hiscock from the Medical Research Council of Canada.

that the left and right cerebral hemispheres provide different—perhaps even opposite—sets of skills and behavioral tendencies. One may carry this claim one step further and assert that a person who relies more on one hemisphere than on the other will exhibit hemisphere-specific abilities, strategies, and behavioral traits (e.g., Ornstein, 1972).

Irrespective of whether individual differences are regarded as a nuisance or as a source of insight, there is a neurological and behavioral diversity among humans, and that diversity must be dealt with in any attempt to demonstrate an orderly relationship between brain structure and brain function, on the one hand, and behavioral characteristics, on the other hand. Nature makes no guarantee of isomorphism between individual differences in behavior and individual differences in neurological structure or function. Often, however, the pathology of a certain brain region produces a characteristic pattern of behavioral alteration. That kind of anatomical–behavioral correlation is well documented in the neuropsychological literature, and we may be tempted to extrapolate such findings to people with no known neurological disorder. We may note that someone's behavior resembles the characteristic behavior of a particular group of neurologically imparied patients. Are we justified in attributing that behavior to some neurological anomaly, even though the person is without detectable brain pathology? If damage to the frontal lobes of the cerebrum often leads to impulsive behavior, can we infer that the impulsivity of a criminal offender or a hyperactive child is the result of some occult "dysfunction" in the frontal region? At what point does neuropsychological inference become a fanciful "new phrenology" (Parsons, 1977)?

The question of invididual differences is a pivotal one. If findings from lesion studies can be extrapolated to differences among people without neurological abnormality, then neuropsychological methods and concepts would indeed be relevant to the study of such individual differences. If not, there would be no point in using neuropsychological techniques in the study of individual differences. The central question of this chapter, then, is not how one uses neuropsychological methods to study individual differences, but rather whether anything of importance is learned.

If neurological sources of behavioral variability are regarded as predictor variables in a multiple regression equation, then these predictors may be grouped into three categories. The first category consists of factors—mostly pathological—that are known to affect behavior in a fairly uniform way across individuals. These factors are analogous to surgical and pharmacological manipulations in physiological psychology. For example, the size of a lesion influences the severity of the behavioral impairment, and damage to the left cerebral hemisphere is likely to impair certain linguistic functions. Generalizations of this kind constitute the basic principles that neuropsychologists traditionally have sought to establish. The second category of predictor variables consists of grouping variables such as sex, handedness, and age. These variables may be used to predict behavior directly, as when a particular skill is expected to diminish with increasing age, or they may interact with factors within the first category, as when it is hypothesized that left-hemisphere lesions in the male lead to different behavioral outcomes than such lesions in the female (e.g., McGlone, 1980). Finally, there are true individual differences, such as nonpathological differences among people in the relative size of different cortical gyri or in the rate of blood flow through the left and right cerebral hemispheres. These individual differences also may affect behavior, either directly or as the result of an interaction with factors in the first and second categories.

This chapter is divided into three parts. The first part concerns certain group differences, *viz.*, neurological and behavioral differences between left- and right-handers, between males and females, and among people in different age groups. We examine the rationale underlying the neuropsychological study of these groups. Are there neurological differences between groups? Are there behavioral differences? Do neurological differences account for behavioral differences? The second part of the chapter emphasizes individual differences. We discuss differences in the relative size of different brains and brain regions, differences in brain physiology, and differences in "hemisphericity." Topics in this part have been chosen to illustrate some potentially useful means of studying individual differences and to reveal some of the limitations and pitfalls inherent in the neuropsychological investigation of individual differences. The third part of the chapter summarizes the major principles presented and the conclusions drawn from the topics discussed in the first two parts.

DIFFERENCES BETWEEN GROUPS

HANDEDNESS DIFFERENCES

Among the countless ways of dividing human beings into groups, none is more salient to the neuropsychologist than classification of people as left- or right-handers. The dichotomy admittedly is a false one. Not only are there various degrees of handedness (e.g., Annett, 1972; Oldfield, 1971; Woo & Pearson, 1927), but there also are several orthogonal components of manual skill (Fleishman, 1972), any of which might be used as a criterion to define handedness. In other words, there is a continuum of handedness for each of the various manual skill factors, and it is not known which factors most reflect individual differences in neurological organization.

Handedness can be defined either as hand preference or as a difference between the hands in some skill. The distribution of hand preference, as measured by questionnaire, takes the form of a J-shaped curve, with a large concentration of scores at the right-hand pole, a much smaller concentration of scores near the left-hand pole, and a relative paucity of scores at intermediate points (Oldfield, 1971). In contrast, hand differences in skill (e.g., in speed or strength) tend to have unimodal, bell-shaped distributions, with the mean displaced from zero in the direction indicating right-hand superiority (Annett, 1972; Woo & Pearson, 1927). These latter distributions, in particular, demonstrate that handedness is not a discrete, but rather a continuous variable (Annett, 1976), and that the classification of people as left- or right-handers depends on criteria chosen by the investigator.

Measuring skill differences between the left and right hands is no easy undertaking. First, even though the reliability of scores for either hand may be satisfactory, the difference between those scores often is unreliable (Provins & Cunliffe, 1972). It seems that the reliability of difference scores is limited by characteristically high correlations between left- and right-hand performance (Hiscock & Kinsbourne, 1980). Because difference scores are not very reliable, and perhaps because different tasks tap different orthogonal components of handedness, correlations among measures of manual asymmetry tend to be low and, in some instances, not significantly different from zero (Shankweiler & Studdert-Kennedy, 1975). Moreover, asymmetric performance on some tasks (e.g., cursive writing) probably reflects differential practice to a greater degree than it reflects a constitutional limitation of the nonpreferred hand. Even novel tasks may be susceptible to transfer of training or of interference from highly practiced tasks. The magnitude of performance asymmetries within the testing situation often is influenced by such factors as task complexity, fatigue, practice, and the order in which the hands are tested (Briggs & Brogden, 1953; Hicks & Kinsbourne, 1978; Provins, 1967; Steingrueber, 1975).

If the problems of skill measurement are avoided by defining handedness in terms of hand preference, then an equally challenging set of new problems is encountered. What are the most representative manual activities, and how is each to be weighted? Is a person's preference for holding a tennis racquet in the right hand as meaningful as that person's preference for left-hand writing? Some of the activities listed on handedness inventories (e.g., holding a glass for drinking) seem to be performed by many people equally often with either hand (Raczkowski, Kalat, & Nebes, 1974). One may question whether a person is less right-handed because he or she sometimes uses the left hand to perform a nondemanding, highly practiced act. With the exception of Annett's (1970) classification by association analysis, handedness scores have been derived from question-naires with the implicit assumption that all items contribute equally. The neurological relevance of different questionnaire items is not known, but there are other reasons to believe that some items are more useful than others. Whereas many questionnaire items have very high retest reliability, responses to other items are less stable over time (Raczkowski et al., 1974). Items also vary in validity, that is, in the degree to which responses predict actual hand usage during behavioral testing (Raczkowski et al., 1974). Factor analyses of handedness inventories (Bryden, 1977; White & Ashton, 1976) reveal a handedness factor and at least one other factor, which seems to depend on the way questions are worded. For some items, factor loadings of the extraneous factor are higher than those of the handedness factor. Among the least satisfactory of inventory items, judging from the factor analyses, are those relating to bimanual acts, such as sweeping with a broom, threading a needle, and opening a box. Annett (1970) found, in two different samples, that people claiming to shovel, sweep, or thread needles, in the supposedly left handed manner were more right handed than pure right-handers in a test of manual skill. Another factor of importance is the degree to which hand preference for a particular activity is shaped by cultural pressure. A study by Teng, Lee, Yang, and Chang (1976) suggests that handedness for some activities, but not others, is susceptible to cultural influence.

For all the reasons outlined above, classifying people with respect to handedness is an imprecise and somewhat arbitrary undertaking. Strong left- and right-handers can be distinguished from each other without great difficulty, but uncertainty increases as one attempts to differentiate among people whose handedness is less extreme. For most purposes in neuro-psychological research, handedness has been treated simply as a dichoto-mous variable, with ambidextrous people often considered to be sinistrals (e.g., Rasmussen & Milner, 1975). People frequently have been classified according to self-report or the hand they use to write with. In some cases, investigators have attempted to subdivide left-handers by taking into account the presence or absence of sinistrality among members of the persons' immediate family (cf. Lake & Bryden, 1976) or the posture in which the hand is held while writing (Levy & Reid, 1976, 1978). Even though it has been claimed that both familial sinistrality and writing posture vary with the cerebral organization of left-handers, neither variable has been consistently useful in discriminating left-handers with left-hemisphere linguistic functions from those with language represented in the right hemisphere (cf. Bradshaw, Nettleton, & Spehr, 1982; Bryden, 1983a; Hicks & Kinsbourne, 1978; Levy, 1982; Moscovitch & Smith, 1979; Weber & Bradshaw, 1981). Thus, as we explain further in the following paragraph, the current definitions of left-handedness leave us with a group that is heterogeneous not only with respect to the strength and consistency of left-hand preference (and, presumably, degree of left-hand superiority in skill), but also with respect to the neurological organization of higher mental processes.

The importance of handedness to the neuropsychologist stems from knowledge that language often is represented differently in the brains of left- and right-handers. Little is known about differences in the organization of higher mental functions other than language, and even differences in language representation can be variously interpreted (Satz, 1980). However, there is much convergent evidence—from patients with unilateral brain damage (e.g., Gloning, Gloning, Haub, & Quatember, 1969; Hécaen & Ajuriaguerra, 1964; Hécaen & Sauget, 1971; Zangwill, 1960); from depressed patients who have had unilateral electroconvulsive therapy (Warrington & Pratt, 1973); and from neurosurgical patients who have had a barbiturate injected into the carotid artery supplying such hemisphere (e.g., Rasmussen & Milner, 1975)—that language representation in left-handers is more variable and more often bilateral than in right-handers. At one extreme, Rasmussen and Milner (1975) suggest that 70% of sinistrals have left-hemispheric speech representation, as do almost all dextrals. According to their data, from intracarotid injection of sodium amytal, 15% of left-handers have speech control lateralized to the right hemisphere and 15% have bilateral speech representation. Satz (1979) exemplifies the opposite extreme in estimating, from the incidence of aphasia after left- and right-sided injury, that 70% of left-handers have bilaterally represented speech. Despite these huge differences in the estimated occurrence of bilateral and right-hemispheric speech in left-handers, there is general agreement that left-handers are much more likely than right-handers to deviate from the norm of exclusively left-sided language representation.

If it were possible to know which left-handers have bilateral or right-hemispheric speech representation, then it would be a simple matter to determine whether certain behavioral anomalies are associated with these less common forms of language representation. It is possible to determine the side of expressive speech representation quite conclusively, but only with invasive procedures that cannot ethically be used in normal, healthy people. Nevertheless, one may capitalize on the knowledge that a group of left-handers is more likely than a comparable group of right-handers to include a number of people with language representation that deviates from the norm. The rationale is as follows (Kinsbourne & Hiscock, 1977). If anomalous representation of speech (and associated linguistic functions) is associated with impaired cognitive functioning, then a sample of normal left-handers should show poorer average performance and greater variability on an appropriate cognitive test when compared to a sample of normal right-handers.

Even if the null hypothesis of equal intelligence in left- and right-handers cannot be proven, the preponderance of evidence supports that conclusion. Despite a few studies finding a relative lack of nonverbal ability among left-handers (Levy, 1969; Miller, 1971; Nebes, 1971), most studies have failed to detect any notable differences between left- and right-handers (Briggs, Nebes, & Kinsbourne, 1976; Fagin-Dubin, 1974; Hardyck, Petrinovich, & Goldman, 1976; Keller, Croake, & Riesenman, 1973; Newcombe & Ratcliff, 1973; Orme, 1970; Roberts & Engle, 1974; Wilson & Dolan, 1931). Moreover, many of the negative outcomes derive from studies in which the samples were much larger and more representative of the general population than those in which a difference between groups was found. For example, Roberts and Engle (1974) reported a failure to differentiate 762 left-handed children from 6,350 right-handed children on the basis of scores from the Block Design and Vocabulary subtests of the Wechsler Intelligence Scale for Children (WISC). Hardyck *et al.* (1976) failed to find any significant differences between 741 left-handed and 6,947 right-handed children who were given an extensive battery of cognitive ability and academic achievement tests. The 7,688 children in this study constituted the entire grade one through six population of a medium-sized community.

The importance of within-group variability seems to have been overlooked by most investigators, but Newcombe and Ratcliff (1973) did note the variability as well as the mean performance levels of their 26 pure left-handers, 658 pure right-handers, and 139 adults with mixed hand-edness. The investigators found no significant differences in either Verbal IQ or Performance IQ, as computed from a shortened version of the Wechsler Adult Intelligence Scale (WAIS), but the scores of the pure left-handers were notable for their *small* variance. A subsequent analysis showed that the variance for the 26 pure left-handers was significantly less than that for 26 matched right-handers.

The data then do not support either prediction, *viz.*, that left-handers, on the average have less cognitive ability than right-handers or that their performance varies more from one person to another. Even the previous claim that left-handers are selectively handicapped in performing nonverbal tasks is not confirmed by large-scale studies. Consequently, we may infer that anomalous patterns of language representation—at least those kinds found among sinistrals—do not lead to decreased cognitive ability. It appears that mental faculties need not be organized within the brain in one standard way in order to be expressed normally.

Admittedly, the studies of left-handers leave some important questions unanswered. First, although we know that left- and right-handers differ in the likelihood of having deviant speech representation, we know much less about the representation of other functions in the brains of dextrals and, especially, sinistrals (Levy, 1982). Even the lateralization of receptive speech functions, in contrast to expressive functions, is poorly understood (Searleman, 1977, 1983; Sperry, 1982; Whitaker & Ojemann, 1977; Zaidel, 1978). The expectation that left- and right-handers will differ in nonverbal abilities rests either upon the assumption that those abilities also tend to be represented anomalously among left-handers or that the coexistence of speech and nonlinguistic functions within the same cortical territory (of sinistrals) will disrupt the holistic processes necessary for effective performance of the nonverbal skills (Levy, 1969). In either case, the rationale for comparing left- and right-handers is weaker if nonverbal skills, rather than language functions, are being considered. A second problem concerns the assessment of cognitive skills. The putative deficits associated with anomalous cerebral organization may not be detected by such broad-band tests as IQ tests (cf. Dennis & Whitaker, 1977). Failure to find a difference in Performance IQ between left- and right-handers in the large-scale studies does not refute Nebes's (1971) claim that sinistrals are deficient in one specific nonverbal skill (although Kutas, McCarthy, & Donchin, 1975, failed to replicate Nebes's finding). Finally, we must account for the various reports that the incidence of left-handedness is elevated in clinical samples of mentally retarded and learning-disabled people (e.g., Bakwin, 1950; Burt, 1950; Critchley, 1970; Doll, 1933; Gordon, 1920; Hicks & Barton, 1975; Porac, Coren, & Duncan, 1980; Vernon, 1971; Wilson & Dolan, 1931; Zangwill, 1960) and in other pathological groups (see Harris, 1980). It has been suggested that all left-handedness is attributable to brain damage consequent to birth stress (Bakan, 1971; Bakan, Dibb, & Reed, 1973). If so, any behavioral deficits found among left-handers could be ascribed more plausibly to brain pathology than to anomalous neurological organization *per se*. Most studies, however, fail to show an association between birth stress and sinistrality (Annett & Ockwell, 1980; Coren, Searleman, & Porac, 1982; Dusek & Hicks, 1980; Hicks, Elliot, Garbesi, & Martin, 1979; Hicks, Dusek, Larsen, Williams, & Pelligrini, 1980; Hicks, Evans, & Pelligrini, 1978; Hubbard, 1971; McManus, 1980; Schwartz, 1977; Spiegler & Yeni-Komshian, 1982), and it seems more probable that only a minority of sinistrals ("pathological left-handers") are left-handed because of brain damage (Bullard-Bates & Satz, 1983; Gordon, 1920; Satz, 1972, 1974; Silva & Satz, 1979). One would expect an overrepresentation of these pathological left-handers in clinical samples, and this would account for the reports of frequent sinistrality among the mentally retarded and the learning disabled. The inclusion of pathological left-handers in a sample of sinistrals would tend to decrease the average performance of left-handers for reasons unrelated to the manner in which language is represented in the brains of normal left-handers.

If methods become available for differentiating, among normal left-handers, different forms of cerebral speech representation, a more direct assessment of the consequences of anomalous neurological organization may be made. As noted previously, attempts to divide left-handers according to familial handedness or the position in which the hand is held while writing have failed thus far to reduce the ambiguity surrounding the organization of higher mental functions in the brains of left-handers. We are left only with evidence that left-handers are heterogeneous in cerebral speech representation and with no compelling evidence for any deleterious effects of that heterogeneity (provided that the left-handers are sampled from the general population and not from clinical populations).

SEX DIFFERENCES

The logic implicit in studies of sex differences often is the reverse of that underlying studies of left- and right-handedness. As described above, one may begin the study of handedness with the knowledge that left- and right-handers are likely to differ in the cerebral organization of certain higher mental functions and proceed to look for behavioral correlates of those neurological differences. Where sex differences are concerned, it has been traditional to start with behavioral differences, whether real or mythical, and then proceed to seek a neural or other biological basis for those differences (cf. Buffery & Gray, 1972; McGee, 1979, Shields, 1975). In addition, however, there are many instances in which a sex difference appears unexpectedly in clinical or experimental neuropsychological data, and is regarded, *post hoc,* as evidence of sexual dimorphism in brain organization.

The neuropsychology of sex differences revolves about three questions: (1) Are there sex differences in the performance of higher mental functions? (2) Are there sex differences in brain anatomy, physiology, or neurochemistry? (3) Can the performance differences be related to the brain differences? Each of these questions is complex and controversial, and none can be answered definitively, as of yet.

Of the three questions, the first perhaps is the easiest to address. Although most performance differences between males and females tend to be small in magnitude and to vary from sample to sample, a few average differences are found consistently (Maccoby & Jacklin, 1974). Those of greatest interest to neuropsychologists thus far are an average female superiority in certain verbal skills and an average male superiority in spatial ability. Females tend to outperform males on measures of verbal fluency, speed of articulation, and grammatical skill (Maccoby & Jacklin, 1974). Males tend to outperform females on a variety of visuospatial tasks that include Embedded Figures and Rod-and-Frame tests, mental rotation, geometry problems, chess playing, maze solving, map reading, left–right discrimination, aiming and tracking, and certain spatial Piagetian tasks (Harris, 1978; Jensen & Reynolds, 1983; Maccoby & Jacklin, 1974; McGee, 1979). Less controversy surrounds the existence of these sex differences than surrounds their magnitude and importance. For example, Plomin and Foch (1981), upon computing a point-biserial correlation from data tabulated by Maccoby and Jacklin (1974), determined that the statistically significant sex difference in children's verbal ability accounted for only 1% of the total variance. The magnitude of the sex difference did not increase appreciably when only subjects of age 12 or above were considered. Plomin and Foch suggested that any attempt to attribute so miniscule an effect to such a factor as differential lateralization seems "doomed from the outset." They pointed out that, even if lateralization differences between males and females account for half of the sex difference, the differences in lateralization would account for only .5% of the total variance of verbal ability. From a similar but more comprehensive meta-analysis of data cited by Maccoby and Jacklin, Hyde (1981) confirmed Plomin and Foch's (1981) conclusion that sex differences in verbal ability account for only 1% of the total variance and, in addition, found that sex differences in two categories of visuospatial ability accounted for less than 5% of the variance within each of those categories. However, Sanders, Soares, and D'Aquila (1982) showed that the magnitude of sex differences may be substantially larger on certain tasks. Sex accounted for 9% of the variance on the Primary Mental Abilities spatial test (Yen, 1975) and for 13 to 17% of the variance on tests of mental rotation (Bouchard & McGee, 1977; Sanders et al., 1982; Yen, 1975). These analyses of the magnitude of sex differences are important, for they suggest that—irrespective of whether there are differences between the brains of females and males—there is only a trivial sex difference in performance to be explained in the case of verbal tasks as well as some nonverbal tasks, but a much larger mean difference in the case of certain visuospatial tasks.

The question of sex differences in cognitive abilities may elicit different answers if one examines distributions, not central tendencies. A trivial mean difference between females and males does not preclude large sex differences at either tail of the frequency distribution. Even though boys may be nearly equal to girls in average verbal proficiency, the ratio of boys to girls among children with a specific reading disability is at least 3:1 (e.g., Yule & Rutter, 1976); and despite a modest mean difference between boys and girls in quantitative ability (Maccoby & Jacklin, 1974), boys outnumber girls by a ratio of 13 : 1 at the extreme top end of the distribution of scores from the mathematical part of the Scholastic Aptitude Test (Benbow & Stanley, 1983). There are no obvious explanations for these large sex ratios, but the findings at least show that mean differences alone provide only a partial picture of sex differences in cognitive ability. Important sex differences may be found at the ends of the distribution, even in the absence of large mean differences.

Since much of the evidence concerning sex differences in cerebral organization comes from the examination of Verbal and Performance IQ following unilateral brain damage, a few points about sex differences in IQ within the general population should be made. In developing his series of IQ tests, Wechsler made every effort to eliminate a bias in favor of either sex (Matarazzo, 1972). Items and tests that favored either males or females were expunged or else counterbalanced by other items and tests that showed the opposite tendency. Consequently, the average difference between females and males in Full Scale IQ, Verbal IQ, and Performance IQ is so small as to be of no practical significance. For this reason, a failure to find sex differences in Verbal or Performance IQ does not show that there is no average difference between the sexes in verbal or nonverbal ability. One corollary of this contrived equivalence between the scores of females and males is that neither Verbal IQ nor Performance IQ reflects the kind of abilities in which one sex shows superiority. If brain damage on one side or the other tends to affect the Verbal IQ of women more than that of men, for instance, one cannot conclude that the damage is specifically affecting those skills that are more highly developed in women. There are some fairly large, consistent sex differences in performance on component subtests, however. Most notable is the tendency of females to outperform males on symbol substitution tasks, that is, the Digit Symbol subtest of the Wechsler tests for adults and the Coding subtest of the children's scale (Jensen & Reynolds, 1983; Wechsler, 1958). Digit Symbol and Coding subtests are classified as Performance tests. The largest difference favoring adult males is found on the Arithmetic subtest, which is included among the Verbal tests (Wechsler, 1958).

At the anatomical, biochemical, and physiological levels of analysis, the main question is not whether there are any differences between male and female brains, but rather whether there are any differences that might be related to differences in higher mental functioning. It is well known that the skull of the adult female is smaller than that of the male and that the cranial capacity of the female is about 10% less (Williams & Warwick, 1980). However, because sex differences in brain size and weight correspond to differences in overall body size and weight, early attention to that facet of sex differences has led nowhere (Shields, 1975). There is one report that the brains of adult females are more likely than the brains of males to show reversed asymmetry of the planum temporale, which usually is larger on the left side than on the right (Wada, Clarke, & Hamm, 1975). Since the planum temporale is known to play a major role in speech perception, one might speculate that a sex difference in the size of this region would be associated with a difference in linguistic skill. However, other investigations of cerebral surface area have failed to substantiate this reported difference in the planum temporale or to find other differences in neuroanatomical asymmetry between the sexes (Witelson, 1980). Studies of nonhuman animals suggest that hormonal influences may lead to differential prenatal or perinatal organization of the hypothalamus in females and males (Harris & Levine, 1965) and to differential neurochemical activity within the hypothalamus and other limbic-mesencephalic structures known to play major roles in reproductive behavior (Fischette, Biegon, & McEwen, 1983; Goy, 1970; Levine, 1966). Even though some of these findings have been extrapolated to sex differences in human characteristics, such as aggression, depression, and emotionality, the actual effect of sex differences in neural anatomy and chemistry upon nonreproductive behavior in humans remains uncertain. Even in nonhuman animals, such effects are often specific to certain species, certain experimental situations, and certain behaviors (Hoyenga & Hoyenga, 1979).

Prenatal exposure to either androgens or progestins is associated with above-average intellectual level in both males and females (e.g., Baker & Ehrhardt, 1974; Dalton, 1976; Money & Ehrhardt, 1972), but it has not been established that prenatal androgens or masculinizing progestins alter brain structure (or even that they increase IQ, since the affected individuals do not differ significantly in IQ from their unaffected siblings [Baker & Ehrhardt, 1974; Money & Lewis, 1966; Reinisch, 1977]). Sex chromosome abnormalities, as in Turner's syndrome (karyotype 45, X) and Klinefelter's syndrome (karyotype 47, XXY), have been related to certain intellectual characteristics (see Hoyenga & Hoyenga, 1979), and one might reasonably assume that the relationships are mediated by anatomical or chemical changes within the brain. There is, in fact, electrophysiological and neuropsychological evidence of brain abnormality in patients with anomalous numbers of sex chromosomes (e.g., Money, 1973; Netley & Rovet, 1985; Nielsen & Tsuboi, 1974; Waber, 1979), although there is inadequate evidence to allow us to specify exactly how the brain is altered by even the most dramatic abnormalities in sexual differentiation. Moreover, there is no satisfactory answer to the question of how cognitive skills are related to sex hormone levels within normal females and normal males (Broverman, Klaiber, Kobayashi, & Vogel, 1968; Peterson, 1976). The available findings suggest that some balance of estrogen and androgen is optimal for spatial ability, irrespective of the individual's sex. Thus, spatial ability would be greatest among males who are relatively low in androgen and among females who are relatively high in androgen (McGee, 1979).

The brain characteristic of males and females most frequently studied in recent years is hemispheric specialization. Consequently, we shall summarize the arguments in favor of a sex difference in the neurological organization of certain higher mental functions.

It is claimed that unilateral cerebral lesions produce different patterns of behavioral deficits in males, as compared to females (Inglis & Lawson, 1981, 1982; Inglis, Ruckman, Lawson, MacLean, & Monga, 1982; Kimura, 1983; Lansdell & Urbach, 1965; McGlone, 1977, 1978, 1980). For example, Lansdell and Urbach (1965) and McGlone (1978) found that men with left-hemisphere lesions showed greater impairment on tests of Verbal IQ than of Performance IQ, whereas men with right-hemisphere lesions showed greater impairment on tests of Performance IQ. In neither study did women show selective verbal or nonverbal impairment irrespective of the side of the lesion. These differential patterns have been construed as evidence that "typical" lateralization of higher mental functions—verbal skills represented in the left hemisphere and nonverbal skills in the right—is more prominent in adult males than in adult females. There are, however, negative findings as well (Bornstein, 1984; Kertesz & Sheppard, 1981; Snow & Sheese, 1985).

In reviewing the neuropsychological evidence for sex differences in hemispheric specialization, McGlone (1980) distinguished between the effects of unilateral lesions on verbal functions and the effects of such lesions on nonverbal functions. She noted three kinds of evidence regarding verbal functions: (1) Speech disorders following brain injury are more common or more severe among males than among females (e.g., Edwards, Ellams, & Thompson, 1976); (2) verbal deficits other than aphasia are related to left-hemisphere lesions in men, but not in women (Lansdell, 1961, 1968a, 1973); and (3) negative findings, that is, there were no differences related to sex in the effect of left- and right-hemisphere damage on verbal skills (Lansdell, 1968b,c). McGlone (1980) speculated that the likelihood of finding differential effects for males and females following left- and right-hemisphere lesions depends on the degree to which the task entails speech production. She suggested that sex differences are more likely as the demand for expressive speech increases. Nevertheless, as McGlone (1980) acknowledged, sodium amytal studies (e.g., Rasmussen & Milner, 1975) suggest that very few right-handers—whether female or male—have bilateral or right-hemispheric representation of expressive speech. In addition, Kertesz and Sheppard (1981) found no sex differences in the results of a comprehensive aphasia test battery administered to 192 patients with left-hemisphere strokes.

With respect to nonverbal impairment, McGlone (1980) conceded that there is no consistent interaction between sex and side of brain injury if the task entails only form or pattern recognition (Benton, Hannay, & Varney, 1975; Edwards et al., 1976; Lansdell, 1962, 1968b; McGlone & Kertesz, 1973). There is some evidence of a sex difference when constructional praxis is required (Lansdell, 1968a: McGlone, 1977), although there are also negative findings (Levine & Mack, 1979; McGlone & Kertesz, 1973) and qualified positive results (McGlone, 1977). When sex differences are observed (e.g., McGlone, 1977), there is an association between impaired nonverbal skills and right-sided lesions in males, but approximately equal impairment of verbal and nonverbal skills in females, irrespective of side of lesion. Thus, the evidence concerning nonverbal impairment, although weak, again seems to suggest that males are more strongly lateralized than females.

The literature summarized above has a number of shortcomings. Sample size often is limited; lesion site and extent often are poorly defined; no differentiation usually is made among lesions of different etiology; and patients seldom are matched for such factors as age, education, hand preference, lesion location, lesion size, time since onset of pathology, and medication. As McGlone (1980) pointed out, results may be distorted significantly by including cases in which lesion effects are bilateral and cases in which speech representation is known to be atypical. A study that excluded cases with evidence of bilateral damage or anomalous speech representation yielded no sex differences (Kertesz & Sheppard, 1981). Nevertheless, the argument for sex differences is bolstered by a recent study (Inglis et al., 1982) in which a large number of patients with either left- or right-sided stroke was grouped according to the chronicity of the damage and matched for age, education, family history of sinistrality, and severity of brain damage. The results of this study were similar to those reported previously by McGlone (1978) insofar as the average discrepancy between Verbal IQ and Performance IQ, in men, but not in women, depended on the side of the damage. Men with left damage had relatively impaired Verbal IQs; men with right damage had relatively impaired Performance IQs; and women showed no significant difference between Verbal IQ and Performance IQ irrespective of the side of the stroke. In contrast to McGlone's (1978) findings, however, women with left-sided damage had lower Verbal IQs than women with right-sided damage, and women with left-sided damage were nearly as impaired in Performance IQ as were males with right-sided damage. In other words, left-sided strokes in women tended to affect both Verbal IQ and Performance IQ to a greater degree than did right-sided strokes, although the difference was statistically significant only for Verbal IQ.

Meta-analyses of clinical data gleaned from several studies further support the claim that males are more likely than females to show differential verbal and nonverbal impairments, depending on the side of the lesion. Inglis and Lawson (1981) computed the mean Verbal versus Performance IQ discrepancy (Verbal IQ minus Performance IQ for patients with right-hemisphere lesions; Performance IQ minus Verbal IQ for patients with left-hemisphere lesions) for samples of patients with unilateral damage and found a significant rank order correlation of +.51 between the average magnitude of the discrepancy and the proportion of males in each sample. Regression analyses performed on an overlapping collection of clinical data (Inglis & Lawson, 1982) yielded similar results, that is, the magnitude of the average Verbal IQ minus Performance IQ discrepancy (in the "typical" direction) increased as a function of the percentage of male patients in the sample.

Although the data compiled by Inglis and his colleagues show at least a superficial resemblance to those of McGlone, the interpretations are quite different. Whereas McGlone (1980) suggested that both verbal and non-verbal functions are represented less asymmetrically in the brains of females than in the brains of males, Inglis and Lawson (1982) found that unilateral lesions have similar effects on the Verbal IQ of both men and women. They speculate that sex differences in the effect of left- and right-hemisphere lesions upon Performance IQ can be attributed to strategy differences, that is, to women's tendency to process Performance IQ test items relatively more verbally. Thus, left-sided lesions in women tend to impair both Verbal IQ and Performance IQ, whereas right-sided lesions have relatively little effect on either Verbal or Performance IQ (Inglis & Lawson, 1981, 1982; Inglis et al., 1982).

It also has been claimed that males and females differ in the way in which higher mental functions are represented within each hemisphere. Kimura (1983) reported that, among 49 males with damage confined either to the anterior or posterior left hemisphere, the incidence of aphasia was about 40%, irrespective of lesion location. Among 32 females, however, the incidence of aphasia was 62% following anterior damage and only 11% following posterior damage. Kimura suggested that the left anterior region of the cerebral cortex is of special importance in females for the control of speech and praxic functions, but that the left posterior cortex is at least equally important in subserving those functions within the male brain. Some evidence was presented for an analogous sex difference in patients with right-hemispheric damage, that is, females with anterior damage performed significantly worse on the WAIS Block Design test than did females with posterior damage, but the performance of males with anterior lesions did not differ significantly from the performance of males with posterior lesions. In the same report, Kimura substantiated McGlone's

(1977, 1980) report that right-hemisphere damage affects the Verbal IQ of women more than that of men. This finding is consistent with McGlone's claim that the right hemisphere subserves language to a greater degree in women than in men.

The case for sex differences in cerebral organization does not rest entirely upon clinical studies, for there is evidence that normal males and females differ in laterality (see Bryden, 1979, 1982, 1983b; Fairweather, 1976; Harshman & Remington, 1974; Lake & Bryden, 1976; McGlone, 1980). Males sometimes show greater right-ear superiorities in dichotic listening for verbal material, and they also are likely to show greater asymmetries in the visual perception of both verbal and nonverbal stimuli. If the sex difference is not reflected in the magnitude of the asymmetry, it may appear as a difference in the frequency of asymmetric performance (Bryden, 1983b). However, females seem to be more asymmetric than males in both hand preference (Annett, 1972; Barnsley & Rabinovitch, 1970; Searleman, Tweedy, & Springer, 1979) and manual skill (Annett, 1972, 1978). Moreover, sex differences in perceptual asymmetry vary across samples and tasks. McGlone's (1980) conclusion that males are more asymmetric than females in dichotic listening is based on 4 positive findings out of 14 studies and, as Annett (1980) pointed out, one of those positive findings was not statistically significant and another was the result of combining 3 studies, each of which yielded a nonsignificant sex difference. Table 1, which summarizes dichotic listening data accumulated by the present authors in five consecutive experiments, illustrates the elusive nature of sex differences. Even when laterality scores were pooled across experiments, there was no significant difference between females and males. By applying a test of statistical power (Cohen, 1977) to the data from all 477 subjects, we determined that there is a probability of .95 that a significant sex difference would have been detected if it had accounted for only 3% of the total variance in ear asymmetry. Consequently, although we cannot accept the null hypothesis, we can state that any difference between females and males in the magnitude of the dichotic right-ear advantage is sufficiently weak as to appear only sporadically or in extremely large samples. Laterality differences between females and males are absent more often than present, although apart from studies of handedness, there are only a few instances in which adult females show the greater asymmetry (Buffery, 1976; Healey, Goodglass, & Waldstein, 1983).

Is it possible, given the available data, to draw any simple conclusions regarding sex differences in the functional organization of the brain? Probably not. However, it is possible to divide the question into two components: the acceptability of the evidence in favor of sex differences and the proper interpretation of whatever evidence is judged to be acceptable.

TABLE 1. Mean Left- and Right-Ear Scores of Right-Handed Men and Women in Five Consecutive Dichotic Listening Experiments

Experiment number	Stimuli	(N)	Correct responses (%)		Significance test of sex × ear interaction
			Left ear	Right ear	
1	Digit names				
	Females (47)		74.4	76.3	$F < 1$
	Males (46)		79.9	82.7	
2	Consonant–vowel nonsense syllables				
	Females (35)		44.7	53.0	$F = 2.59$
	Males (35)		43.7	59.0	$p = .11$
3	Digit names				
	Females (47)		75.3	78.0	$F = 2.81$
	Males (46)		73.3	81.8	$p = .10$
4	Consonant–vowel nonsense syllables				
	Females (48)		47.0	52.3	$F = 1.85$
	Males (47)		47.3	56.7	$p = .18$
5	Digit names				
	Females (64)		63.1	67.2	$F < 1$
	Males (62)		63.2	67.0	

Note. "The sex difference in dichotic listening: Multiple negative findings" by M. Hiscock and M. Mackay, *Neuropsychologia*, 1985, in press. Copyright 1985 by Pergamon Press Limited. Adapted by permission.

As we have seen, the evidence is deficient in many respects, and there is some justification for dismissing positive findings as artifacts of biased sampling, selective reporting, and flawed methodology. Perhaps the valid findings are those showing no differences between women and men. If some of the evidence for sex differences is to be accepted, exactly which findings do we accept? Do we believe McGlone's findings that left- and right-hemisphere lesions have comparable effects on verbal functioning in women or do we believe the findings of Inglis and his colleagues that left-hemisphere lesions in women have a more adverse impact than right-hemisphere lesions on both verbal and nonverbal functioning? Since relatively little evidence supports Buffery and Gray's (1972) argument that females are more strongly lateralized, the field of contending claims is narrowed to the two remaining alternatives: Males are more lateralized than females, and there is no difference between males and females. If males are more lateralized, are they more lateralized for verbal functions, for visuospatial functions, or for both?

If one grants that lesion effects are different in males and females, one may attribute such effects, as well as any laterality differences between normal females and males, to sex differences in strategy rather than neurological organization. As noted, Inglis and Lawson (1982) have proposed that their clinical findings can be explained in terms of women's tendency to accomplish Performance IQ subtests verbally. Verbal IQ items, being inherently verbal, are processed by the left hemisphere of both men and women; Performance IQ items, being amenable to verbal as well as nonverbal processing, tend to be processed by the right hemisphere in men and by the left hemisphere in women. Consequently, left-hemisphere damage diminishes Verbal IQ in both women and men, but Performance IQ is affected by left-hemisphere damage in women and by right-hemisphere damage in men. McGlone's (1977, 1978, 1980) data do not fit this explanation, nor do findings of a sex difference in asymmetry on verbal dichotic listening tasks. Nevertheless, strategy explanations for sex differences in neuropsychological functioning are attractive for at least two reasons. First, such explanations can account for findings—for example, contradictory results from two putatively nonverbal tasks—that might otherwise be uninterpretable. There is considerable evidence, for instance, that strategy affects performance on laterality tasks (Bryden, 1978; Kinsbourne, 1970). Strategy explanations also are attractive because they do not entail bold inferential leaps from behavioral data to the "hard-wiring" of the brain. Of course, it is possible—although not necessary—that the cognitive strategies themselves are neurologically determined.

Having reviewed the evidence for sex differences in cognitive skill and in the organization of the brain, we now address briefly the third fundamental question of the neuropsychology of sex differences, viz., Can performance differences be related to underlying brain differences? In discussing handedness, we concluded that different patterns of brain organization need not imply differences in behavior. This principle may very well apply to sex differences. Even if it is proven that there are neurological differences between females and males, such differences may be irrelevant to differences between the sexes in cognitive ability or other behaviors. Traditionally, however, brain differences have been looked for to "explain" behavioral differences (Shields, 1975), and this reductionistic objective is not absent from contemporary neuropsychology.

If sex differences in brain organization are responsible for certain sex differences in cognitive ability, then we have a criterion for evaluating different proposed models of sex differences in brain organization: The neurological sex difference should explain the cognitive sex difference. For example, if sex differences in cerebral lateralization are assumed to underlie the tendency for females to outperform males on certain verbal tasks and for males to outperform females on certain visuospatial tasks, then some of the models outlined above seem more adequate than others. McGlone's (1980) interpretation of the neuropsychological evidence, with its emphasis on sex differences in the organization of verbal skills, seems superfluous if the sex difference in verbal abilities is indeed too minute to account for much of the variance in those verbal abilities (Plomin & Foch, 1981). An emphasis on sex differences in the organization of visuospatial skills would be more promising. However, the apparent mismatch between a sex difference in the lateralization of *verbal* function, on the one hand, and a sex difference in *visuospatial* performance, on the other hand, is easily rectified. One has only to hypothesize that bilateral representation of language disrupts the holistic, nonverbal processors of the right hemisphere (Levy, 1969). Thus, even if visuospatial functions are represented exclusively within the right hemisphere of men and women, those functions in women might be affected adversely by interference from linguistic activity within the same hemisphere. This example illustrates a major problem in contemporary neuropsychology, that is, the Procrustean nature of its explanations. Models of hemispheric specialization, in particular, can be modified to account for almost any behavioral finding (Hiscock & Kinsbourne, 1982).

The search for a link between neurological and behavioral sex differences has led to some new hypotheses and research strategies. Harris (1980) has suggested that studying each sex in isolation may yield some useful information. Harris cited the example of a study by Zoccolotti and Oltman (1978), in which males who performed well on the Rod-and-Frame and Embedded-Figures tests also tended to show the expected asymmetries on verbal and nonverbal tests of visual laterality. As Harris (1980) pointed out, the absence of an association between cerebral lateralization and skill level, within either sex, would cause one to doubt the validity of differential lateralization as an explanation for sex differences in cognitive performance. Waber (1977) suggested that sex differences in verbal and spatial ability might be attributed to differential rates of maturation. She hypothesized that early maturation favors the development of verbal ability and that later maturation favors the development of spatial ability. Although Waber (1977) failed to find the expected relationship between verbal ability and early maturation, she did find that late-maturing individuals, irrespective of sex, tended to have more spatial ability than early-maturing individuals. Other tests of this hypothesis have yielded mixed results (Carey & Diamond, 1980; Herbst, 1980; Herbst & Peterson, 1979; Peterson, 1976; Strauss & Kinsbourne, 1981; Waber, Bauermeister, Cohen, Ferber, & Wolff, 1981). Irrespective of whether Waber's hypothesis is correct, it illustrates one way in which an apparent sex difference may be attributable to a factor other than sex *per se*. Still another perspective is provided by

Harshman, Hampson, and Berenbaum (1983), who claim that sex interacts with handedness and reasoning ability to affect performance on cognitive tests. These investigators found that, among subjects with relatively high reasoning ability, the spatial performance of left-handed males was lower than that of right-handed males, but the spatial performance of left-handed females was higher than that of right-handed females. The opposite pattern of handedness differences within each sex was found for subjects who fell below the median in reasoning ability. On the basis of these results, Harshman et al. (1983) concluded that both sex and handedness differences in cognitive performance stem from factors that are partly neurological. This work shows that sex differences may be manifested not only as main effects, but also as interactions between sex and one or more other variables.

AGE DIFFERENCES

Age is another important factor in neuropsychological research. Of course, age is not intrinsically a categorical variable, but it often is convenient to classify people arbitrarily by age. Especially in children and in elderly adults, one finds age-related changes in cognitive ability that presumably are related to processes or changes within the brain. Thus, to a degree not possible when dealing with either handedness or sex differences, the investigator who addresses questions of age differences may know that groups differ in both neurological and behavioral characteristics. The objective of such research then is to establish that one particular aspect of the age-related neurological difference is responsible for a particular age-related difference in behavior.

There are various aspects of brain maturation, including axonal growth, dendritic branching, myelination of axons, and increase in arterial blood supply (Dobbing & Sands, 1973; Epstein, 1978). Presumably, each of these developmental changes is related to increasing mental capacity during childhood. More attention, however, has been devoted to the question of cerebral dominance and to how increasing hemispheric specialization might affect the development of cognitive processes. Lenneberg (1967) has persuasively argued for the traditional view that the two cerebral hemispheres of the infant's brain are equally good substrates for language development, but that language representation normally shifts from a bilateral to an exclusively left-hemispheric base during the critical period between the beginning of language acquisition and puberty. This principle of progressive lateralization was generally accepted in the 1960s and 1970s, and was invoked to explain not only age differences in cognitive ability, but also individual differences among children of a given age (e.g., Bakker, 1973; Sparrow & Satz, 1970). Recent evidence, however, suggests that the cerebral hemispheres became specialized very early in life and that the degree to which the left hemisphere is dominant for language processing does not change during childhood (e.g., Kinsbourne & Hiscock, 1977; Segalowitz & Gruber, 1977; Woods & Teuber, 1978). Instead of confirming an association between cognitive ability and developmental changes in cerebral lateralization, recent advances in neuropsychology have made such an association seem increasingly less plausible (Hiscock & Kinsbourne, 1982; Kinsbourne & Hiscock, 1983).

The neuropsychological study of people at the opposite end of the life-span can be characterized in a similar way. First, although the question of cognitive decline in "normal" aging is complicated and somewhat controversial (cf. Horn & Donaldson, 1976; Schaie, 1974), it is well documented that some mental functions are diminished in samples of elderly people (Bak & Greene, 1980; Botwinick, 1981; Corkin, Davis, Growdon, Usdin, & Wurtman, 1982; Lezak, 1983). Moreover, there is an increased likelihood of various degenerative changes in the brains of old people. Such changes include neuronal depletion; vascular insufficiency; changes associated with Alzheimer's disease, multi-infarct dementia or Parkinson's disease; and changes in cholinergic and other neurotransmitter systems (Albert, 1981; Bartus, Dean, Beer, & Lippa, 1982; Bondareff, 1980; Coyle, Price, & DeLong, 1983; Wang, 1973). Thus, as in children, there is evidence of age-related changes in the brain as well as behavior, and there have been some attempts to relate the degree of brain degeneration to the degree of behavioral decline. For instance, Blessed, Tomlinson, and Roth (1968) reported a correlation of .77 between the behavioral competence of hospitalized elderly people, as rated by their relatives, and a postmortem estimate of the degree of neuronal loss.

As in the literature on children, one of the most popular hypotheses regarding age-related neurological change in adults concerns hemispheric specialization. At least three different assertions have been made. One is that the cerebral hemispheres become increasingly specialized throughout life and that, as a consequence, the right hemisphere in older people has less ability to compensate for linguistic deficits following damage to the left hemisphere (Brown & Jaffe, 1975). It has also been claimed that communication between the cerebral hemispheres increases with aging (Kocel, 1980) and that the right hemisphere deteriorates more rapidly than the left with age (Klisz, 1978; Stern & Baldinger, 1983). As pointed out by Kinsbourne and Hiscock (1983), none of these claims is convincing. If the right hemisphere of elderly people has only a limited ability to compensate for damage to the left, that limitation may be ascribed to deterioration of the right hemisphere without the additional assumption of increased hemispheric specialization. Kocel's (1980) claim of increased interhemispheric communication in the aged brain rests on indirect evidence from a single study, and the concept of accelerated right hemisphere deterioration seems to arise from a confound between two dimensions of mental functioning: fluid versus crystallized intelligence and verbal versus nonverbal processing. Nonverbal tests tend to tap fluid (age-sensitive) intelligence (Cattell, 1963; Horn & Cattell, 1967) to a greater degree than do verbal tests. Consequently, there may appear to be a disproportionate decline in nonverbal ability with age (e.g., Wechsler, 1981, Table 7). When verbal and nonverbal performance in the aged is compared, with other factors held constant, there is no difference between verbal and nonverbal scores (Elias & Kinsbourne, 1974). Moreover, neither auditory nor visual laterality appears to change significantly as a consequence of aging (Borad & Goodglass, 1980; Byrd and Moscovitch, in press). On neuropathological examination of the aged brain, the two hemispheres show a comparable degree of abnormality (Bondareff, 1977; Roth, 1980).

Another popular hypothesis is that cognitive deficits in the aged resemble those observed in younger, brain-damaged people. Many of the investigators who have addressed this issue defined both cognitive ability and brain damage nonspecifically. Thus, elderly people are compared with diverse "organic" patients on a variety of neuropsychological tests (e.g., Goldstein & Shelly, 1975; Hallenbeck, 1964; Overall & Gorham, 1972; Reed & Reitan, 1963). Not surprisingly, the results differ somewhat from study to study, presumably as a function of differences in samples, tests, and research designs. In general, however, these investigators conclude that, although there may be certain similarities between the effects of brain damage and those of so-called normal aging, the pattern of cognitive decline in the aged is distinct from the pattern of deficits seen in the younger, brain-damaged individual.

More specific comparisons of elderly and brain-damaged people may prove to be of greater value. Of particular interest in contemporary neuropsychology is the resemblance between the learning and memory ability of old people and that of amnesic patients with Korsakoff's disease. First, there is evidence that both groups have sustained degenerative changes in the frontal and medial temporal regions of the brain (Bondareff, 1980). Second, there is substantial evidence that the two groups show similar patterns of performance in various tests of learning and memory, which include free recall and recognition tasks, short- and long-term memory tests, and tests of paired-associate learning (see Winocur & Moscovitch, 1983). Winocur and Moscovitch (1983), however, found that only their institutionalized old subjects resembled the brain-damaged amnesic patients on tests of paired-associate learning and inter-list interference. In qualitative as well as quantitative aspects of paired-associate learning under various conditions, elderly people who lived in their own homes showed a performance that was more similar to that of normal young adults than to that of institutionalized old people. These findings illustrate the great heterogeneity of performance among the elderly and the risks inherent in generalizing from institutionalized samples to the general population of old people.

Although the parallels between learning and memory impairments of the aged (at least some subgroups of the aged) and those of amnesic patients are suggestive, the data do not prove that the same causal factors are responsible for the impaired performance of both groups. The analogy is strengthened, however, by evidence that frontal and medial temporal brain structures are particularly vulnerable to damage in both populations (Bondareff, 1980). Nevertheless, many deteriorative processes affect the aging brain, and the neural basis of memory deterioration in the aged may vary considerably from one person to the next. Further information about the importance of specific structures and neurotransmitters in memory decline will be obtained by correlating performance deficits with brain pathology for each individual. Parallels between the performance of elderly people and that of people with well-defined neuropathology can point the way to the brain structures most likely to underlie the deficits of the aged. In addition, the detailed examination of cognitive functioning in the elderly, such as that performed by Winocur and Moscovitch (1983), provides insight at the behavioral level of analysis into the nature of cognitive decline in aging, and such insight may be of considerable theoretical and practical value.

DIFFERENCES AMONG INDIVIDUALS

Although classifying people into groups may be convenient and potentially informative, there is almost always more variability within than between groups. Knowing that a person belongs to one or another group seldom leads to accurate predictions about that person's brain or behavior. A second limitation is inherent in neuropsychological studies of group differences, viz., the inability of such studies to establish a causal link between neurological and behavioral variables. Even if we know that two groups differ with respect to brain variable X and behavioral variable Y, we cannot be sure that X is responsible for Y. The group differences can only alert us to the likelihood that Y is related to X. A logical next step would be to measure X directly in each individual and correlate that measurement with Y, after partialling out the effects of group membership. Finding a correlation would still not establish causality, but it would confirm that X and Y are associated and that the association is not an artifact of some other difference between the two groups. In some cases, it might be possible to take still another step, that is, to manipulate X and measure the effect on Y. In short, information on neuropsychological differences between groups may be viewed as preliminary information, which can be used to direct investigators to underlying individual differences. These true individual differences should prove, ultimately, to be more instructive than group differences. However, as we shall see, few advances have been made thus far.

STRUCTURAL DIFFERENCES

The most obvious prediction that can be made about brain–behavior correspondence is that larger brains are more effective than smaller brains. Considerable attention has been paid to phylogenic differences in brain size (Blinkov & Glesner, 1968; Jerison, 1973; Sarnat & Netsky, 1974), and it is clear that the human brain is substantially larger than other primate brains, even when the figures are adjusted for differences in body size. Much of the increase in brain size from nonhuman primates to humans can be attributed to the neocortex, especially the so-called association (nonsensory, non-motor) cortex (Kolb & Whishaw, 1980).

Cross-species comparisons constituted only a starting point for studies of brain size. Throughout much of the nineteenth century, such respected scientists as Samuel Morton and Paul Broca reported race and sex differences in cranial size that corresponded to assumed race and sex differences in intellectual capacity (Gould, 1981; Shields, 1975). Nevertheless, individual differences among male Caucasians were not overlooked. One particularly interesting source of information about the relation of brain size to brain functions is a fairly large series of postmortem analyses performed on the brains of eminent men. The results are summarized by Gould (1981), who notes that "the dissection of dead colleagues became something of a cottage industry among nineteenth-century craniometricians" (p. 92). Table 2 shows some of the more notable findings. Although some men of eminence did have brains larger than average, the brains of equally eminent men proved to be ordinary in size or even much smaller. The doctrine of correlation between brain size and intelligence was further embarrassed by reports of large brains in criminals, women, and people of low social class (Gould, 1981). The question of brain size and its relation to intellectual ability has been set aside without a definitive answer. In fact, the question would appear to be unanswerable unless one knows precisely how to correct brain volume and weight for the influence of such confounding variables as body size and musculature, age, cause of death, and general health before death. New methods of

TABLE 2. Brain Weights for Eminent Men and Others

Name/other identification	Occupation/ other categorization	Recorded brain weight (g)
Ivan Turgenev (1818–1883)	Russian novelist	Over 2,000
Brain measured by J. Marshall, 1892–93	Mechanic	1,986
Georges Cuvier (1769–1832)	French naturalist	1,830
Le Pelley (reported by T. Bischoff, 1880)	Assassin	1,809
Brain measured by T. Bischoff, 1880	Murderess	1,565
Karl Friedrich Gauss (1777–1855)	German mathematician and physicist	1,492
Paul Broca (1824–1880)	French anthropologist and physician	1,424
Average for European males		Approx. 1,400
Hermann von Helmholtz (1821–1894)	German physiologist and physicist	1,277
Franz Josef Gall (1758–1828)	German physician, founder of phrenology	1,198
Anatole France (1844–1924)	French novelist and literary critic	1,017

Note. From *The Mismeasure of Man* (pp. 92–95) by S. J. Gould, 1981, New York: Norton. Copyright 1981 by Stephen Jay Gould. Adapted by permission. Brain weights for von Helmholtz and the anonymous mechanic were obtained from *Brain and Personality*, by W. H. Thomson, 1907.

computer-assisted medical imaging make it possible to estimate the size of brains *in vivo*, thus eliminating some but not all the ambiguities inherent in postmortem assessments. However, neuropsychological interest in brain structure has shifted from the question of overall differences in brain size to somewhat more refined questions about differences within different brain regions.

Even in the nineteenth century, investigators such as Broca pursued their craniometric interests beyond the issue of total brain size and computed the size of the frontal, parietal, and occipital regions, as well as such other individual characteristics as the cranial index (ratio of maximal width to maximal length of the skull) and the position of the foramen magnum relative to the frontal and occipital poles of the cerebrum (Gould, 1981; Shields, 1975). No readily interpretable findings resulted from this work, although considerable variability among individuals was found. In the modern era, attention has focused, instead, on asymmetries in the size of certain cortical regions, which, in the left hemisphere, are associated with linguistic functions (see Galaburda, 1984; Le May, 1984; Rubens, 1977; and Witelson, 1977, 1980, for reviews).

Of particular interest is the report of Geschwind and Levitsky (1968), subsequently confirmed by several other investigators (Teszner, Tzavaras, Gruner, & Hécaen, 1972; Wada et al., 1975; Witelson & Pallie, 1973), that the planum temporale is significantly larger on the left side than on the right. Since the planum temporale on the left constitutes a large portion of Wernicke's area, the cortical region associated with language perception, some investigators regard the asymmetry of this region to be a significant anatomical factor underlying the specialization of the left hemisphere for linguistic processing (e.g., Geschwind, 1974). A number of problems are encountered, however, in attempting to relate this neuroanatomical asymmetry to functional asymmetries. First, only 65% of the specimens in Geschwind and Levitsky's (1968) sample showed left-greater-than-right asymmetry. The proportion is higher in other studies (e.g., Wada et al., 1975), but Witelson (1977) calculated that about 70% of brains in the various series show the expected asymmetry. Even allowing for a representative number of brains from left-handers in these series, the incidence of the expected asymmetry is considerably lower than would be predicted on the basis of currently accepted estimates of the incidence of left-hemisphere dominance of language. A finding by Yeni-Komshian and Benson (1976) also seems problematic insofar as it suggests similar asymmetries in chimpanzee brains. Other findings regarding great apes and other primates are mixed (cf. Rubens, 1977), and, in any event, one could defend the putative structural–functional link by citing evidence that the great apes have some degree of linguistic ability (e.g., Premack, 1971; Gardner & Gardner, 1975). A third source of interpretive difficulty is the finding that two other language areas of the left hemisphere—the angular gyrus and the frontal operculum—appear to be smaller than the homologous regions of the right hemisphere (Rubens, 1977; Wada et al., 1975). Wada et al. (1975) suggested that the left frontal operculum may be more convoluted and thus have more surface area than the right operculum, despite the fact that their own measure of surface area revealed an asymmetry favoring the right operculum. This ambiguity exemplifies a fourth problem inherent in this research, that is, the questionable meaningfulness of cortical surface area calculations. A greater measurable area in one region may be more than offset by deeper fissures or a thicker cortical mantle in another region. The smaller area may have the greater number of neurons. Finally, the expected asymmetries seem to occur most reliably and most markedly in the posterior regions of the cortex, which are associated with receptive language functions, and it is for these functions that lateralization appears to be relatively incomplete and ambiguous (cf. Zaidel, 1976).

Neuroradiological techniques, such as arteriography, pneumoencephalography, and computed tomography (CT scanning), permit the measurement of structural features of the brain *in vivo*. Although none of these techniques is ideal for measuring the surface area of different cortical regions, they do enable the investigator to correlate structural and functional characteristics of the same brain. The results of these radiological studies can be summarized as follows. First, asymmetries within the temporo-parietal and occipital regions are consistent with those reported on the basis of postmortem examination (Hochberg & LeMay, 1975; LeMay, 1984; LeMay & Culebras, 1972; Pieniadz & Naeser, 1984; Ratcliff, Dila, Taylor, & Milner, 1980). In addition, it appears that the frontal cortex is usually wider on the right side than on the left, and that the reverse is true of the occipital cortex (LeMay, 1977). If, however, the length of the posterior horns of the lateral ventricles is taken as an index of occipital tissue volume, then the left side appears to be smaller than the right (McRae, Branch, & Milner, 1968). With the exception of the lateral ventricle measure, for which the results differed from one sample to another (McRae *et al.*, 1968), each of these asymmetries was reported to be less common or less pronounced in left-handers than in right-handers (Hochberg & LeMay, 1975; LeMay, 1977, 1984; LeMay & Culebras, 1972). These anatomical asymmetries also seem to vary with speech lateralization (LeMay & Culebras, 1972; McRae *et al.*, 1968; Ratcliff *et al.*, 1980), although data for patients with verified atypical speech representation are quite sparse. In at least some of these patients, the association between anomalous structural asymmetry and anomalous speech lateralization may be an artifact of long-standing brain pathology. In any event, there does not appear to be a direct correspondence between speech lateralization and morphological asymmetry, but only a tendency for the usual anatomical asymmetry to be reduced or absent in people with atypical speech representation. Pieniadz, Naeser, Koff, and Levine (1983) found that, even though left hemisphere strokes produced aphasia irrespective of the relative size of the two hemispheres, recovery was better for those patients having atypical asymmetry, i.e., greater occipital length on the right side.

The implications of these neuroanatomical data are debatable. One may find it encouraging that, despite the methodological inadequacies, there is reasonably consistent evidence of asymmetry in certain cortical regions. Better methods probably will bring more definitive findings. For example, detailed examination of architectonic zones promises to be much more satisfactory than crude measurement of surface distances or areas (Galaburda, LeMay, Kemper, & Geschwind, 1978). However, more accurate measures of anatomical features do not necessarily mean that a consistent association between structure and function will be found. As measurement of brain structure becomes more refined, investigators may discover only that the brain differences most relevant to behavioral differences lie at a molecular level of analysis, that is, the neurochemical level. Moreover, the findings currently available pose some conceptual difficulties for the investigator who would link behavioral differences among people to differences in brain morphology. The great neuroanatomical variability found among behaviorally normal people makes it seem unlikely that an isomorphic association between behavior and brain structure will ever be found. If 30% of the general population lacks the usual asymmetry of the planum temporale (without demonstrable consequences), is it plausible that small variations in degree of asymmetry will have important behavioral consequences? The possibility that some speech areas in the left hemisphere are smaller than homologous areas in the right hemisphere (Rubens, 1977) raises some questions about the expectation that left-hemispheric areas should be larger. What assumptions underlie this expectation, and are they justified? Are linguistic processes "higher" or more complex than other cognitive processes? Is the adaptive value of language greater than that of nonverbal skills? Is the size of a neural region associated with the complexity or with the adaptive significance of the function it subserves?

A curious instance of individual differences in neuroanatomy involves the massa intermedia, a band of tissue connecting the left and right halves of the thalamus. In general agreement with previous reports, Lansdell and Davie (1972) found that the massa intermedia was absent (i.e., not visible on X-ray films obtained during pneumoencephalography) in a substantial minority of right-handed neurological patients. The massa intermedia was not found in 40% of their 47 males and 33% of their 27 females. Lansdell and Davie reported that male patients without the massa intermedia scored significantly higher on nonverbal tests from the Wechsler-Bellevue Intelligence Scale than did men with the massa intermedia, although no such difference was found for the female patients. Verbal scores were not related to the presence or absence of the massa intermedia in either women or men. When the massa intermedia was present, its size correlated positively with nonverbal performance ($r = .43$), although the correlation may have been an artifact of the tendency for both massa intermedia size and nonverbal ability to decrease with age. The authors suggested that absence of the massa intermedia might be associated with greater hemispheric specialization, reduced competition between the hemispheres, and decreased vulnerability to neurological impairment. These speculations, and the findings themselves, must be regarded with some skepticism until confirmatory data are available. As pointed out by Lansdell and Davie, investigation of the consequences of massa intermedia absence in the healthy brain will be especially valuable. Even a cautious interpretation of Lansdell and Davie's findings, however, allows us to conclude that the absence of a particular brain structure is not necessarily associated with cognitive impairment.

PHYSIOLOGICAL DIFFERENCES

Any relationship between brain structure and the behavior of an organism presumably is mediated by a complex set of physiological variables, for example, cerebral blood flow, metabolism, chemical processes at the synapses, and axonal action potential patterns. In view of the large number of potentially relevant physiological factors, it is improbable that any single factor would account for individual differences in any major aspect of behavior. Yet, there should be closer correspondence between neurophysiology and behavior than between gross neuroanatomy and behavior. Two categories of physiological variables will be discussed briefly: perfusion of blood in the left and right hemispheres and electrical activity of the brain.

As noted by Carmon and his associates (Carmon & Gombos, 1970; Carmon, Harishanu, Lowinger, & Lavy, 1972), humans differ from most other mammals in having an asymmetrical cerebrovascular system. In most mammals, the left and right carotid arteries branch symmetrically from the brachiocephalic artery, which supplies the right subclavian artery as well. In the majority of humans, the right carotid artery branches from the right subclavian artery but the left carotid artery arises from the arch of the aorta. Variants of this configuration in humans are not uncommon, and most of these deviant configurations are not associated with any known defect of cerebrovascular functioning (see Krayenbuhl & Yasargil, 1968; Lie, 1968). Of 14 alternative configurations described by Lie (1968), only one is considered to be clinically significant. Nonetheless, differences in blood supply to the respective cerebral hemispheres might be associated with individual differences that fall within the normal range of human variability.

Carmon and Gombos (1970) speculated that differences in blood pressure between the left and right carotid arteries would vary with the subjects' handedness. Using ophthalmic artery pressure at each eye to measure pressure in the respective carotid arteries indirectly, the investigators found a weak but statistically significant correlation between degree of right-handedness and the degree to which systolic pressure on the right side exceeded that on the left. They inferred that most right-handers have higher systolic pressure in the right carotid artery than in the left and that left-handers are more likely to have either higher pressure in the left carotid or equal pressure in both carotids. In a subsequent study Carmon *et al.* (1972) injected a radioactive isotope of iodine to measure, more directly, blood flow through the two hemispheres of normal left- and right-handers. The blood flow in each hemisphere was consistent with the previously reported differences in blood pressure, that is, there appeared to be a greater volume of blood in the hemisphere ipsilateral to the preferred hand.

A separate analysis showed a significant association between asymmetry of blood flow and ear differences on a dichotic digits task. Subjects with a right-ear superiority in dichotic listening (i.e., subjects having the ear asymmetry associated with left-hemisphere language dominance) tended to have more flow through the right side than the left, and subjects with left-ear superiority tended to show the opposite asymmetry of blood flow. It has also been reported that the relative size of the three primary superficial veins of each hemisphere varies with the individual's speech lateralization (De Chiro, 1962), although the significance of that relationship is obscure.

The most provocative implication of the studies by Carmon et al. is that the so-called nondominant hemisphere of most right-handers receives a greater volume of blood than does the dominant left hemisphere. This runs counter to the common assumption that the hemisphere specialized for language should be anatomically and physiologically superior to its non-verbal counterpart. A second important implication of the research concerns individual differences. Regardless of whether subjects were grouped according to hand preference or ear superiority in dichotic listening, 12% showed no difference in blood flow in the left and right hemispheres, and another 26% to 27% showed an asymmetry opposite to that of the majority. The variability for left-handers might be attributed to the heterogeneity of speech representation in a relatively small sample ($N = 25$). There should, however, be few if any deviations from left-hemisphere speech representation in the sample of 60 young and healthy right-handers (the dichotic listening variability notwithstanding). Thus, we are left with only a loose association between hand preference and inferred asymmetry of blood flow, and little reason to believe that speech lateralization is linked causally to blood flow.

Regional cerebral blood flow (rCBF) studies are an even more powerful and refined means of relating higher mental functions to the hemodynamics of the brain (e.g., Ingvar & Risberg, 1967; Obrist, Thompson, Wang, & Wilkinson, 1975; Risberg & Ingvar, 1973; Wood, 1980). The technique, which is similar in principle to that used by Carmon et al. (1972) to estimate global blood volume in the left and right hemispheres, usually entails the introduction of radioactive xenon-133 into the subject's blood and measurement of the radioactivity of different brain regions. Changes in blood flow in the gray and white matter of each region are obtained by computer. Different tasks, such as speaking, reading, reasoning, and moving the hands, enhance cerebral blood flow differentially in various brain regions (e.g., Ingvar & Schwartz, 1974; Larsen, Skinhøj, & Lassen, 1978; Risberg & Ingvar, 1973; Risberg, Halsey, Wills, & Wilson, 1975; Wood, 1980). Verbal task performance tends to increase blood flow in the left hemisphere more than in the right, and spatial task performance tends to increase blood flow in the right hemisphere (Gur, Gur, Obrist,

Hungerbuhler, Younkin, Rosen, Skolnick, & Reivich, 1982; Gur & Reivich, 1980; Risberg et al., 1975), although negative results have been reported (Risberg, 1980).

In a few instances, investigators have reported handedness and sex differences in rCBF patterns, but no simple conclusions can be drawn. Prohovnik, Hakansson, and Risberg (1980) reported several significant correlations between the degree of asymmetry in rCBF and strength of hand preference in normal right-handed males. Since larger blood flow differences favoring the right hemisphere were associated with greater right-handedness, these findings support those of Carmon and Gombos (1970) and Carmon et al. (1972). Other findings are less straightforward. Gur et al. (1982) reported a significant four-way interaction among handedness, sex, task, and hemispheres in their study of blood flow associated with the accomplishment of verbal and spatial tasks. Task-related asymmetries were statistically significant only for right-handed females and left-handed males, who showed greater right- than left-hemisphere rCBF increase during spatial activity (relative to a resting baseline), and either the reverse asymmetry or an equal left- and right-hemisphere increase during verbal activity. Gur et al. (1982) found higher overall blood flow among females than males, while resting and while performing both tasks, but other workers have failed to show significant differences between females and males in overall rCBF or in rCBF pattern (Hannay, Leli, Falgout, Katholi, & Halsey, 1983). Quite possibly, rCBF is differentially related to task performance, depending on the individual's sex. In two different studies (Hannay et al., 1983; Leli, Hannay, Falgout, Wilson, Wills, Katholi, & Halsey, 1982), the rCBF in males during a left–right discrimination task was negatively correlated with performance on the task, but the association was not found in females. In contrast, Gur and Reivich (1980) reported a significant positive correlation ($r = .35$), for a sample of males, between the degree of lateralized rCBF change during spatial task performance and the level of performance on the task. The degree of lateralized blood flow increase during verbal activity was not correlated with performance on the verbal task.

If cerebral blood flow is taken as an index of cortical activation during cognitive processing (Gur & Reivich, 1980), then one could explain either a positive or a negative association between increases in amount of flow and task performance. A positive correlation would reflect activation of the entire cortex or of the hemisphere or cortical region appropriate for the performance of the task. A negative correlation would reflect less activation (i.e., effort) among those people more skilled in performing the task. No significant correlation might reflect heterogeneity in the cerebral organization of that particular skill (Hannay et al., 1983) or, conversely, a 'hard-wired' activation pattern in which all individuals, irrespective of skill, have identical activation patterns (Gur & Reivich, 1980). The correct interpretation of any association between cerebral blood flow and behavior is academic until consistent relationships are found. The data are sparse, and the findings may not be comparable because of differences across studies in such important factors as the subjects' age, the tasks used, the measure or measures of rCBF used, and the manner in which the data are reduced and analyzed.

Although much more voluminous, the literature on electrophysiological asymmetries is similar in many respects to that on cerebral blood flow. There are many reports of task-related asymmetries in spontaneous electroencephalographic (EEG) activity (e.g., Butler & Glass, 1974; Doyle, Ornstein, & Galin, 1974; Galin & Ornstein 1972; Harmon & Ray, 1977; McKee, Humphrey, & McAdam, 1973; Morgan, McDonald, & Macdonald, 1971) and of either stimulus- or task-related asymmetries in averaged evoked scalp potentials (e.g., Cohn, 1971; Hillyard & Woods, 1979; Matsumiya, Tegliasco, Lombroso, & Goodglass, 1972; Neville, 1974; Schucard, Schucard, & Thomas, 1977; Wood, Goff, & Day, 1971). Typically, when such asymmetries are found, verbal tasks are associated with less EEG amplitude or power over the left hemisphere (presumably because the EEG is increasingly desynchronized with increasing activation) than over the right, or with higher amplitude evoked potentials (EPs) over the left hemisphere than over the right. Nonverbal stimuli and tasks frequently yield either the opposite asymmetry, or else there is little difference between hemispheres. However, the predicted EP asymmetries often are absent (e.g., Friedman, Simson, Ritter, & Rapin, 1975; Galambos, Benson, Smith, Shulman-Galambos, & Osier, 1975; Mayes & Beaumont, 1977; Shelburne, 1972, 1973), and EEG asymmetries thought to be associated with cognitive factors may be attributable, in many instances, to stimulus, response, and eye-movement artifacts (Gevins, Zeitlin, Doyle, Yingling, Schaffer, Callaway, & Yeager, 1979). In general, studies of EEG and EP asymmetry are characterized by diverse and often unsatisfactory methods and experimental designs and by findings that are either weak or unreliable (Donchin, Kutas, & McCarthy, 1977; Gevins *et al.*, 1979; Hillyard & Woods, 1979).

The difficulty of establishing reliable stimulus- and task-dependent asymmetries in EEG and EP studies is hardly ideal for studies of individual differences. Findings from studies of between-group differences are equally diverse. The EEG differences between left- and right-handers are inconsistent across studies (see Butler & Glass, 1974; Donchin *et al.*, 1977; Galin, Ornstein, Herron, & Johnstone, 1982), as are differences between males and females (cf. Davidson, Schwartz, Pugash, & Bromfield, 1976; Galin *et al.*, 1982; Ray, Morell, Frediani, & Tucker, 1976; Rebert & Mahoney,

1978; Tucker, 1976; Wogan, Kaplan, Moore, Epro, & Harner, 1979). The influence of the subjects' handedness and sex on EP asymmetries apparently has not been investigated extensively, but the available evidence fails to establish any clear and consistent differences between left- and right-handers (Culver, Tanley, & Eason, 1970; Davis & Wada, 1978; Eason, Groves, White, & Oden, 1967; Gott & Boyarsky, 1972) or between males and females (Davis & Wada, 1978; Molfese & Molfese, 1979; Shucard, Shucard, Cummins, & Campos, 1981). Contrasting views regarding sex differences in the asymmetry of auditory EPs in infants have been expressed by Molfese and Radtke (1982) and by Shucard, Shucard, Campos, and Salamy (1982), respectively.

In spite of—or perhaps because of—the incoherent nature of the electrophysiological laterality literature with respect to stimulus, task, and group factors, some investigators have focused on individual differences. This line of research is related to the older tradition of correlating electrophysiological characteristics and intellectual ability (e.g., Ertl & Schafer, 1969; Rhodes, Dustman, & Beck, 1969), but currently, specific abilities and strategies rather than general intelligence are emphasized. Some results have been negative. Dumas and Morgan (1975) obtained the expected task-related asymmetries of EEG alpha, but failed to find any significant differences between nine male artists and eight male engineers. Two attempts to demonstrate differences in EEG laterality between groups differing in hypnotic susceptibility also failed (Morgan, Macdonald, & Hilgard, 1974; Morgan et al., 1971), although highly susceptible subjects in one of the studies showed higher alpha amplitude over both hemispheres than did less susceptible subjects. Furst (1976), however, reported a rank order correlation of .55 between alpha asymmetry and the latency of solving visuospatial problems in a sample of 16 right-handed university students. Since a relatively high right-to-left ratio of alpha amplitude during the task was associated with long latency (or incorrect responses, in some instances), the author concluded that subjects with more right-hemisphere activation perform better on tasks for which the right hemisphere is thought to be specialized. Furst suggested that Dumas and Morgan (1975) might have failed to find a difference in EEG laterality between engineers and artists because people within an occupational group may approach a task with diverse strategies. Although Furst's (1976) finding is encouraging, it should be accepted with caution, since it consists of a single correlation, based on 16 subjects and significant only at the .05 level of probability. Moreover, interpretation of this finding is complicated by the fact that the correlation between latency to respond and alpha asymmetry in a resting baseline condition was statistically significant and nearly as strong as that between latency to respond and asymmetry during problem-solving. As Furst concedes, the magnitude of this second correlation indicates that the relationship between EEG asymmetry and task performance reflects some tonic characteristic of the subjects' EEG, not a task-specific activation pattern.

Other studies have addressed such variables as arousal (Shucard & Horn, 1973), expectancy (Ledlow, Swanson, & Kinsbourne, 1978), strategy (Wogan, Moore, Epro, & Harner, 1981), task difficulty (Dumas & Morgan, 1975), and meaningfulness of stimuli (Matsumiya et al., 1972) as factors that may alter EEG and EP asymmetries, as well as other aspects of electrophysiological activity. Wogan et al. (1981), using simultaneous EEG and video recording of subjects as they performed block design problems, showed that changes in alpha activity in the right hemisphere were influenced significantly by the strategy being used at a particular time. Right-hemisphere alpha activity was greater when subjects were actively placing blocks into a pattern or manipulating blocks prior to adding them to the pattern than when subjects seemed to be using a combination of strategies or were "just sitting" without manipulating any blocks. Wogan et al. interpret this finding as evidence that the right hemisphere is more actively involved in the problem-solving process in the latter two instances than in the first two. Although explanations other than strategy—for example, differential motor activity—seem plausible, the Wogan et al. study implies that a putatively right-hemisphere task may not be equally right hemispheric for all people or even for a particular person at different times.

Given the complexity of electrophysiological methods and the large number of variables that can alter the asymmetry of scalp potentials, one might be inclined to dismiss individual differences as artifacts. If an individual's pattern of asymmetry is not due to some idiosyncratic shift of attention or use of strategy, perhaps it can be ascribed, instead, to an asymmetrical motor activity or to small irregularities in the placement of the electrodes (Donchin et al., 1977). Perhaps the asymmetry would disappear if the task were made slightly easier or more difficult, or more or less interesting. Although these possibilities cannot be excluded altogether, it appears that individual differences in EEG alpha asymmetry—differences within subjects with respect to different tasks, as well as among subjects with respect to the same task—are quite stable (Amochaev & Salamy, 1979; Ehrlichman & Wiener, 1979). Ehrlichman and Wiener (1979) computed an average coefficient of .75 for the consistency of left-to-right alpha ratios within subjects across four verbal and four spatial tasks. The reliability of ratios from the first to the second testing session was .88 for the 11 subjects in that sample. This consistency within and between subjects shows that individual variation in EEG asymmetry is not simply experimental error. However, consistency might be attributed to certain constant artifacts, such as individual variation in scalp thickness on the left and right sides (Donchin *et al.*, 1977) or individual differences in oculomotor or manual activity (Anderson, 1977; Gevins *et al.*, 1979).

Interpreting individual differences in EEG or EP laterality is especially difficult because of the ambiguities and controversies surrounding task-related asymmetries (e.g., Davidson & Ehrlichman, 1980; Donchin *et al.*, 1977; Gevins *et al.*, 1979). If the meaning, and even the existence, of task-dependent electrophysiological asymmetries is a matter of dispute, then the meaning of individual differences is even more obscure. Yet, if individual differences can be related to performance (Furst, 1976) and if those relationships prove reliable, the study of individual differences will be of value even though the underlying mechanisms remain obscure.

DIFFERENCES IN LEFT- AND RIGHT-HEMISPHERE UTILIZATION

Suppose there are no important differences among normal people in brain anatomy or physiology, even though there are distinct differences between the functions of the left and right hemispheres of all people. Behavioral diversity among people then could be attributed to differences in the utilization of each hemisphere. Humans could be divided into those who rely heavily on the left hemisphere and those who rely heavily on the right. The thinking and behavior of each group presumably would reflect the nature of the preferred hemisphere. From the currently popular characterizations of the "style" of each hemisphere (Bakan, 1969; Bogen, 1969; Ornstein, 1972), one would expect the left-hemisphere type of person to be verbal, analytical, rational, propositional, and so forth, and the right-hemisphere type to be nonverbal, holistic, emotional, appositional, and so forth. This notion of a habitually preferred or more frequently utilized hemisphere is referred to as hemisphericity.

Hemisphericity could be defined operationally in terms of any laterality characteristic of a person, for example, asymmetry of EEG alpha, ear asymmetry in dichotic listening, or handedness. Alternatively, one could classify people according to some cognitive or personality variable, for example, difference between Verbal IQ and Performance IQ, and then attempt to relate that classification to laterality or to some more direct measure of brain function. Hemisphericity need not be viewed as a typology, for people could be assigned to intermediate positions on a continuum from extremely right hemispheric to extremely left hemispheric.

We shall illustrate hemisphericity research by focusing on the paradigm that probably best exemplifies this approach, *viz.*, the investigation of lateral eye movements (LEMs). This research can be traced to the work of Day (1964, 1967a,b, 1968), who found that people tend to avert their eyes to one side or the other after being asked a question that requires reflection. Day speculated that the eye movement marks a shift in attention from a "passive listening mode" to an "active expressive mode" and that left- and right-movers differ in certain physiological, perceptual, and cognitive characteristics. Bakan (1969) subsequently claimed that individual differences in eye-moving tendency are related to a functional asymmetry of the brain. He reported that left-movers, in comparison to right-movers, scored higher on a measure of hypnotic susceptibility, had a greater verbal-minus-mathematics discrepancy on the Scholastic Aptitude Test, reported clearer visual imagery, and tended more often to major in the humanities or the social sciences. These findings were attributed by Bakan (1969) to a difference between left- and right-movers in the ease with which the left and right hemispheres are "triggered": a tendency to move the eyes in either direction was ascribed to a general prepotency of the contralateral cerebral hemisphere. Thus, the LEM became an indicator of hemisphericity.

Although several investigators have undertaken to establish correlates of left or right eye-moving tendency, no consistent findings have emerged. Hypnotic susceptibility is perhaps the variable most often linked to LEM characteristics. Whereas some investigators have confirmed Bakan's (1969) finding that left-moving is associated with hypnotic susceptibility (Bakan & Svorad, 1969; DeWitt & Averill, 1976; Gur & Gur, 1974; Morgan et al., 1971), others have failed to confirm the finding (Gur & Reyher, 1973; Smith, 1980; Spanos, Pawlak, Mah, & D'Eon, 1980; Spanos, Rivers, & Gottlieb, 1978). Even some of the confirmatory findings offer only qualified support. Gur and Gur (1974) found an association between hypnotic susceptibility and left-moving of the eyes only for right-handed males. Morgan et al. (1971) had to include data from pilot subjects in order to obtain a statistically significant difference between the hypnotic susceptibility scores of left- and right-movers. Moreover, Morgan et al. found that neither LEM tendency nor hypnotic susceptibility was associated with the asymmetry of EEG alpha. Among the negative findings, that of Spanos et al. (1980) is especially notable insofar as the investigators used a large sample of subjects ($N = 82$), three different indices of hypnotic susceptibility, and questions (for elicting eye movements) that were taken from three different studies in which the expected association between eye-moving tendency and hypnotic susceptibility had been obtained. Despite these precautions, none of the 24 correlation coefficients between LEM measures and hypnotic susceptibility scores was significantly different from zero.

Correlations between LEM direction and visual imagery are similarly inconsistent and unconvincing. Although Bakan (1969) reported that left-movers gave their images higher ratings for clarity than did right-movers, the difference failed to reach the .05 level of probability. A similar finding by Harnad (1972) was also weak: the point-biserial correlation between eye-movement classification and self-reported reliance upon visual imagery for problem solving was .34 in a small sample of mathematicians and graduate students in mathematics. However, the general notion that left-moving is associated with nonverbal thinking was reinforced by Tucker and Suib's (1978) report of a point-biserial correlation of .65, in the expected direction, between LEM tendency and the difference between scores on selected Verbal and Performance subtests from the WAIS. Richardson (1978) found that male "visualizers" move their eyes leftward more often than do male "verbalizers," but this effect was not found for females. In contrast, Ray, Georgiou, and Ravizza (1979) reported a significant relationship between LEM direction and spatial performance for females, but not males. Several other studies of eye-moving tendency and spatial ability or self-reported imagery have yielded negative results (Barnat, 1972; Bruce, Herman, & Stern, 1982; Ehrlichman, 1972; Galin & Ornstein, 1974; Hiscock, 1977b; Spanos et al., 1978, 1980; Stam & Spanos, 1979; Wolf-Dorlester, 1976) and at least one significant correlation in the direction opposite to that expected (Otteson, 1980).

Some other putative correlates of eye-movement directionality are outlined in Table 3, which by no means constitutes an exhaustive accounting of the extant claims. Although investigators almost invariably attribute these characteristics to the preeminence of one or the other hemisphere, most of these abilities and behavioral characteristics have no obvious relationship to the known specialized functions of either hemisphere. Even if it were true, beyond a reasonable doubt, that left- and right-movers differ with respect to creativity (Harnad, 1972) or values (Weiten & Etaugh, 1973), there is very little independent evidence to support the inference that one cerebral hemisphere or the other is primarily responsible for creative thinking or the acquisition of particular values (see Corballis, 1980). The more immediate problem with these studies, however, is not the weakness of their conceptual underpinnings, but rather the questionable robustness and reliability of the findings themselves.

Three assumptions are implicit in these studies of eye-moving tendencies and in other approaches to the study of hemisphericity: (1) The chosen index of hemisphericity (e.g., direction of lateral eye movements) indicates selective activation of one hemisphere or the other; (2) the putative correlate of the hemisphericity index (e.g., hypnotic susceptibility) depends on the specialized processing of one hemisphere or is manifested differentially, depending on the hemisphere being used; and (3) people show consistent tendencies to rely on one hemisphere for thinking and behaving, that is, to be consistently left- or right-brained. The first assumption pertains to the

TABLE 3. Some Characteristics of Left-Movers as Claimed by Various Investigators

Study	Sample	Questions to elicit eye movements	Left-mover characteristics (compared with right-movers)
Bakan & Shotland (1969)	53 university students (24 females, 29 males)	4 or more mental arithmetic problems	Slower reading
Harnad (1972) Exp. 1	10 mathematics professors, 21 graduate students in mathematics	An unreported number of questions concerning the person's work	More likely to participate in artistic activities; more creative (professors only)
Harnad (1972) Exp. 2	20 college-educated people	Not reported	Higher score on Remote Associates Test; less likely to make neutral responses when evaluating prose
Etaugh (1972)	89 university students	5 miscellaneous questions	Less affected by feelings; more assertive; more suspicious; shrewder
Sherrod (1972)	300 under-graduates	5 miscellaneous questions	Greater attitude change after hearing persuasive message
Libby & Yaklevich (1973)	70 university undergraduates (35 females, 35 males)	54 questions (6 "neutral" questions and 48 questions that were varied on four dimensions)	Higher abasement score from the Edwards Personality Preference Schedule
Weiten & Etaugh (1973)	40 university undergraduates (consistent eye-movers)	20 questions (content not reported)	Poorer performance on a concept identification task
Gur, Gur & Marshalek (1975)	74 university undergraduates (33 females, 41 males)	10 verbal and 10 spatial questions	Greater preference for sitting on the right side of a classroom

Table 3 (continued)

Study	Sample	Questions to elicit eye movements	Left-mover characteristics (compared with right-movers)
Schroeder (1976)	33 children, 4–6 years old	Age-appropriate questions (number of questions not reported)	Used more adjectives and fewer nouns to describe objects
Graves & Natale (1979)	40 right-handed female undergraduates	10 verbal and 10 spatial questions	More accurate in communicating disgust and fear, but not happiness, via facial expression
Otteson (1980)	136 university undergraduates (72 females, 64 males)	10 verbal and 10 spatial questions	Less dogmatic and less "external" (females only)
Katz & Salt (1981)	25 right-handed college students (9 females, 16 males)	Miscellaneous questions (number of questions not reported)	More likely to major in "soft" subjects, e.g., English, history, theatre, education
Stern & Baldinger (1983)	64 right-handed adults (32 females, 32 males); half, 18–32 years old & half, 60–72 years old	Not reported	Poorer performance on vocabulary, block design, and scrambled word tests (older group only)

validity and reliability of the particular hemisphericity index being considered and, consequently, may be correct or not, depending on that index. Even if LEM direction proves to be an invalid or unreliable index of hemisphericity, EP asymmetry or some other measure could prove to be satisfactory. The second and third assumptions pertain to the concept of hemisphericity itself. As suggested previously, some attributes are more readily related than others to the specialized functioning of one hemisphere. Comparing verbally adept people with spatially adept people would be more defensible on theoretical grounds than comparing people with different, arbitrarily selected personality characteristics, for instance. The assumption that people tend to be consistently left- or right-brained is suspect. We have cited two reports of individual differences in EEG asymmetry that remain relatively stable over time (Amochaev & Salamy, 1979; Ehrlichman & Wiener, 1979), but these reports show that task-related differences within subjects are stable as well. If the activation balance between hemispheres varies with the task, then there must be limits to the influence of hemisphericity. The concept of hemisphericity cannot be demonstrated directly insofar as cognitive processes are occult, but the concept would be supported by convergent evidence from different putative indices of hemisphericity— EEG asymmetry, cerebral blood flow asymmetry, lateral eye movements, etc.—that some people activate the left hemisphere more consistently than the right and that other people show a consistent asymmetry in the opposite direction.

Lateral eye-moving tendency, as an index of hemisphericity, can be evaluated with respect to the first assumption—its validity and reliability. Does a reflective lateral eye movement indicate activation of the contralateral hemisphere during cognitive processing? The affirmative argument is supported by several studies that report an association between verbal questions and rightward LEMs and between nonverbal questions and relatively more leftward movements (Galin & Ornstein, 1974, Experiment 2; Gur, Gur, & Harris, 1975; Hiscock & Bergstrom, 1981, Experiment 1; Katz & Salt, 1981; Kinsbourne, 1972; Kocel, Galin, Ornstein, & Merrin, 1972; O'Gorman & Siddle, 1981; Schwartz, Davidson, & Maer, 1975; Weiten & Etaugh, 1974). However, negative findings have been at least as numerous (Ahern & Schwartz, 1979; Berg & Harris, 1980; Ehrlichman, Weiner, & Baker, 1974, Experiments 1, 2, & 3; Galin & Ornstein, 1974, Experiment 1; Greschner, 1978; Hiscock & Bergstrom, 1981, Experiments 2 & 3; Reynolds & Kaufman, 1980; Richardson, 1978; Rodin & Singer, 1976; Säring & von Cramon, 1980; Takeda & Yoshimura, 1979; Tucker, Roth, Arneson, & Buckingham, 1977, as cited by Ehrlichman & Weinberger, 1978; Wolf-Dorlester, 1976). In two of the studies that failed to show the predicted association between task and LEM direction, an association opposite to that predicted was found (Richardson, 1978; Wolf-Dorlester, 1976). It appears that the task may influence gaze in the manner predicted, but, then, the effect is often overwhelmed by certain uncontrolled biasing factors that have not been identified (Ehrlichman & Weinberger, 1978; Hiscock, 1985).

The situation, then, is similar to that encountered in electrophysiological work. In both instances, one's ability to make inferences about individual differences in the relative activation of the left and right hemispheres is undermined by the difficulty of showing reliable and unequivocal task-related asymmetries. Perhaps the most convincing validation for LEM direction as an index of asymmetrical brain activation is the association between LEM tendency and cerebral blood flow asymmetry

(Gur & Reivich, 1980) and between LEM tendency and asymmetry of the cortical EP (Shevrin, Smokler, & Kooi, 1980). Gur and Reivich (1980) reported that left-movers had relatively more blood flow in the right hemisphere than in the left, and right-movers relatively more in the left hemisphere. Shevrin *et al.* (1980) found that left-movers showed greater amplitude of occipital event-related potentials over the right hemisphere than over the left, and right-movers the reverse asymmetry. However, these findings are based on small samples and should be regarded as inconclusive until repeated. As noted previously, Morgan *et al.* (1971) found no difference in the asymmetry of occipital EEG in left- and right-movers.

Relatively little attention has been paid to the reliability of individual differences in eye-movement direction, possibly because Day (e.g., 1967a) implied that people could be dichotomized unequivocally into left- and right-movers. It now is clear that the direction of a person's LEMs varies from one trial to another and that the average proportion of LEMs to the preferred side within a testing session may be only slightly above 70% (cf. Bakan, 1969; Bakan & Svorad, 1969; Duke, 1968; Ehrlichman & Weinberger, 1978; Hiscock, 1977a; Weiten & Etaugh, 1973). Even when a nonstringent criterion, such as 70% consistency, is used to select consistent left- and right-movers, the majority of people may be classified as "bidirectional" or mixed (Hiscock, 1975). Nevertheless, individual differences in LEM tendency do seem to be adequately reliable across trials and between raters (Libby, 1970; Shevrin *et al.*, 1980; Templer, Goldstein, & Penick, 1972). The stability of individual differences from one testing session to another is less impressive. Estimates of test–retest reliability range from .65 to .80 (Bakan & Strayer, 1973; Crouch, 1976; Ehrlichman & Weinberger, 1978; Etaugh & Rose, 1973), but only a minority of subjects is likely to be classified identically on different occasions (Templer *et al.*, 1972; Weiten & Etaugh, 1973). Weiten and Etaugh (1973), beginning with 90 subjects, ended with only eight left-movers and ten right-movers after excluding those who failed to make at least 75% of their LEMs in the same direction on each of three occasions. If LEM tendency is an accurate index of hemisphericity, these data suggest that only a small proportion of the population can be characterized as having strong and consistent hemisphericity.

Studies of the LEM phenomenon lead to two conclusions regarding individual differences: (1) Some people (although perhaps a minority) show a fairly consistent tendency to look leftward or rightward while thinking, and (2) there is preliminary evidence that this asymmetry of gaze is associated with activation of the hemisphere contralateral to the direction of gaze (Gur & Reivich, 1980; Shevrin *et al.*, 1980). These modest beginnings, however, leave us far short of establishing that gaze tendency indicates hemisphericity or that there is such a phenomenon as hemisphericity. The relationship between gaze asymmetry and asymmetrical cortical activation requires confirmation. We need to know that left- and right-movers differ consistently along some dimension of behavioral preference or skill, and ideally we will be able to obtain independent evidence of an association between that behavioral dimension and the specialized functions of the cerebral hemispheres. Until such evidence is obtained, claims for hemisphericity differences between left- and right-movers must be regarded as speculations that are supported by only a subset of the methodologically problematic and empirically inconsistent studies that deal with eye-movement tendencies (Ehrlichman & Weinberger, 1978; Hiscock, 1985).

The very concept of hemisphericity is of questionable scientific value (Beaumont, Young, & McManus, 1984; Corballis, 1980). The meaning of hemisphericity is vague. Are left-hemisphere people unable to use right-hemisphere strategies, or do they differ from right-hemisphere people only in preference? Perhaps a difference in preference derives from a difference in ability. Are there degrees of hemisphericity? Are there people who show no hemisphericity or whose hemisphericity changes from situation to situation? How does the concept of hemisphericity relate to the various contemporary models of hemispheric specialization (Allen, 1983)? In view of the popularity of the concept of hemisphericity in the general culture and in certain disciplines (education, in particular, e.g., Grady, 1976; Hunter, 1976; Rennels, 1976; Samples, 1975), it is essential that neuropsychologists point out the vacuity of the concept and the lack of empirical justification for the diverse claims. People do show various intellectual strengths and weaknesses, as well as various strategies and styles, but these human differences are not known to be derived from a characteristic reliance on one cerebral hemisphere in preference to the other.

CONCLUDING COMMENTS

New methods in electrophysiology, clinical medicine, and experimental psychology have given the neuropsychologist access to information about the brain and behavior of humans that was inaccessible only a decade or two ago. The new methods have generated a new wave of widespread interest in the classical problem of brain–behavior correspondence. Although neuropsychologists have emphasized general principles over individual variation as they have used these methods, there are several indications of individual differences, many of which have been described here. If the new opportunities for neuropsychological investigation have failed thus far to yield many reliable facts—whether these facts relate to general principles or to individual differences—the shortcomings of the research may be attributed less to the inadequacy of the methods than to our inability to comprehend the data obtained. The factors that limit the progress of neuropsychological research seem to be conceptual, not technological (see Kinsbourne, 1978; Kinsbourne & Hiscock, 1983).

One conceptual problem concerns the localization of functions. Many neuropsychological studies are based on the assumption that the location of a processor within the cortex determines the efficiency of processing. Although this assumption is not unreasonable, it may be incorrect. As we pointed out in connection with left-handedness, even a marked anomaly in the localization of a major function, that is, speech control, seems to have no measurable effect on the efficiency of that function or on the overall efficiency of the brain, provided the brain is healthy and the anomalous organization is not the result of some earlier pathology. The same may be said of differences in degree of specialization: There is no compelling evidence that relatively diffuse representation of functions, with overlap among regions, is less efficient than more discrete, sharply demarcated localization. If higher mental functions were, in fact, organized differently in males and in females, that difference would not necessarily lead to a sex difference in overall intellectual ability or in any specialized cognitive ability. Until it is established that one topographic pattern of localization, or one degree of regional specialization, is superior to any normal variant, there is no justification for claiming that (putative) differences in brain organization are associated with (putative) differences in performance. Obviously, the consequences of a focal brain lesion will vary with differences in brain organization (e.g., Semmes, 1968), but this is not necessarily relevant to normal functioning.

A similar problem concerns the size of brain regions. We have seen that, in an earlier era, great importance was ascribed to the size of one's brain. Now great importance is attributed to the size of different regions of the brain. This is a good example of today's technology being tethered to yesterday's concepts. Again, the assumption is not unreasonable. It is not unreasonable to assume that there is some correlation between the size of a brain region and the excellence of its function, but reasonable assumptions are not always correct. In fact, many findings suggest that this assumption is incorrect. A substantial minority of normal brains does not show the common pattern of planum temporale asymmetry, and there are no known consequences of this deviation from the norm. In the case of the massa intermedia, it has even been claimed that the absence of this brain structure is associated with higher intellectual ability. The apparent correlation between asymmetry of cortical surface area and language dominance is undermined by the discovery of language areas that are smaller than the homologous areas of the nondominant hemisphere. It is not known why one brain, or one part of a brain, is more efficient than another brain, or the part of the latter brain. However, it seems unlikely that the critical property is the amount of tissue present.

Doubts on the functional significance of structural, static characteristics of the normal brain lead to an emphasis on physiological and behavioral techniques as means of identifying the more "dynamic" neurological correlates of individual differences in higher mental functioning. Such techniques as electrophysiological recording, regional cerebral blood flow measurement, and laterality tasks should prove particularly useful. We must concede, however, that the evidence accumulated thus far from physiological and behavioral studies has not contributed greatly to our understanding of the brain basis of individual differences. Again, conceptual limitations have slowed progress. For example, the traditional connectionistic or "switchboard" models of brain functioning often seem inadequate to account for laterality phenomena (see Studdert-Kennedy, 1975), and laterality work perhaps is handicapped by the lack of a general, unifying theoretical framework (Allen, 1983). The neuropsychology of individual differences is made particularly difficult by the absence, in many instances, of stable task-related effects. Without consistent stimulus and task effects, it is difficult to educe general mechanisms and principles; and, without some understanding of the underlying mechanisms and principles, it is difficult to interpret individual differences. We are left with an empirical, inductive science of individual differences in which the findings of each study depend not only on characteristics of the sample, but also on numerous methodological parameters, the effects of which are largely unknown. Progress under such adverse circumstances is bound to be slow, and investigators may often by misled by chance findings. Thus, it is imperative that findings be replicated before they are accepted as valid and that researchers and readers alike develop an appropriate "respect for the null hypothesis" (Soper, Satz, Light, & Orsini, 1983).

Let us return to our regression model, in which we attempt to predict some aspect of people's behavior on the basis of (1) neurological factors that, when present, have similar effect on all brains; (2) neurological factors that differ between groups of people; and (3) neurological factors that differ among people within each group. The first set of predictors is the best understood, although our knowledge is restricted largely to the deleterious effects of various pathological influences on behavior. The grouping variables add relatively little to predictive ability at our present level of understanding, but the reason for the lack of predictive power varies according to the grouping variable. Handedness groups appear to differ somewhat in brain organization, but there are no certain consequences for higher mental functioning. Males and females seem to differ, on the average, in a few aspects of cognitive functioning, but the presence of corresponding brain differences is a matter of dispute. With regard to different age groups, there is evidence of behavioral differences and several covarying neurological differences. Here the challenge is to isolate the specific neurological factors that are responsible for specific behavioral changes. Not much can be said about the predictive power of true individual differences among brains, except that these differences presumably account for most of the behavioral variability among humans. The critical brain factors are yet to be identified.

REFERENCES

Ahern, G. L., & Schwartz, G. E. Differential lateralization for positive versus negative emotion. *Neuropsychologia*, 1979, *17*, 693–698.

Albert, M. S. Geriatric neuropsychology. *Journal of Consulting and Clinical Psychology*, 1981, *49*, 835–850.

Allen, M. Models of hemispheric specialization. *Psychological Bulletin*, 1983, *93*, 73–104.

Amochaev, A., & Salamy, A. Stability of EEG laterality effects. *Psychophysiology*, 1979, *16*, 242–246.

Anderson, S. W. Language-related asymmetries of eye-movement and evoked potentials. In S. Harnad, R. W. Doty, L. Goldstein, J. Jaynes, & G. Krauthamer (Eds.), *Lateralization in the nervous system*. New York: Academic Press, 1977.

Annett, M. A classification of hand preference by association analysis. *British Journal of Psychology*, 1970, *61*, 303–321.

Annett, M. The distribution of manual asymmetry. *British Journal of Psychology*, 1972, *63*, 343–358.

Annett, M. A coordination of hand preference and skill replicated. *British Journal of Psychology*, 1976, *67*, 587–592.

Annett, M. Genetic and nongenetic influences on handedness. *Behavior Genetics*, 1978, *8*, 227–249.

Annett, M. Sex differences in laterality—meaningfulness versus reliability. *The Behavioral and Brain Sciences*, 1980, *3*, 227–228.

Annett, M., & Ockwell, A. Birth order, birth stress and handedness. *Cortex*, 1980, *16*, 181–188.

Bak, J. S., & Greene, R. L. Changes in neuropsychological functioning in an aging population. *Journal of Consulting and Clinical Psychology*, 1980, *48*, 395–399.

Bakan, P. Hypnotizability, laterality of eye-movements and functional brain asymmetry. *Perceptual and Motor Skills*, 1969, *28*, 927–932.

Bakan, P. Handedness and birth order. *Nature*, 1971, *229*, 195.

Bakan, P., & Shotland, R. L. Lateral eye movement, reading speed, and visual attention. *Psychonomic Science*, 1969, *15*, 93–94.

Bakan, P., & Strayer, F. F. On reliability of conjugate lateral eye movements. *Perceptual and Motor Skills*, 1973, *36*, 429–430.

Bakan, P., & Svorad, D. Resting EEG alpha and asymmetry of reflective lateral eye movements. *Nature*, 1969, *223*, 975–976.

Bakan, P., Dibb, G., & Reed, P. Handedness and birth stress. *Neuropsychologia*, 1973, *11*, 363–366.

Baker, S. W., & Ehrhardt, A. A. Prenatal androgen, intelligence, and cognitive sex differences. In R. C. Friedman, R. M. Richart, & R. L. Vande Wiele (Eds.), *Sex differences in behavior*. New York: Wiley, 1974.

Bakker, D. J. Hemispheric specialization and states in the learning-to-read process. *Bulletin of the Orton Society*, 1973, *23*, 15–27.

Bakwin, H. Psychiatric aspects of pediatrics: Lateral dominance, right- and left-handedness. *Journal of Pediatrics*, 1950, *36*, 385–391.

Barnat, M. R. Some personality correlates of the conjugate lateral eye-movement phenomenon. *Dissertation Abstracts International*, 1972, *33*, 2337–2338.

Barnsley, R., & Rabinowich, A. Handedness proficiency versus stated preference. *Perceptual and Motor Skills*, 1970, *30*, 343–362.

Bartus, R. T., Dean, R. L., III, Beer, B., & Lippa, A. S. The cholinergic hypothesis of geriatric memory dysfunction. *Science*, 1982, *217*, 408–417.

Beaumont, J. G., Young, A. W., & McManus, I. C. Hemisphericity: A critical review. *Cognitive Neuropsychology*, 1984, *1*, 191–212.

Benbow, C. P., & Stanley, J. C. Sex differences in mathematical reasoning ability: More facts. *Science*, 1983, *222*, 1029–1031.

Benton, A. L., Hannay, H. J., & Varney, N. R. Visual perception of line direction in patients with unilateral brain disease. *Neurology*, 1975, *25*, 907–910.

Berg, M. R., & Harris, L. J. The effect of experimenter location and subject anxiety on cerebral activation as measured by lateral eye movements. *Neuropsychologia*, 1980, *18*, 89–93.

Blessed, G., Tomlinson, B. E., & Roth, M. The association between quantitative measures of dementia and of senile changes in the cerebral grey matter of elderly subjects. *British Journal of Psychiatry*, 1968, *114*, 797–811.

Blinkov, S., & Glezer, I. *The human brain in figures and tables*. New York: Basic Books, 1968.

Bogen, J. E. The other side of the brain II: An appositional mind. *Bulletin of the Los Angeles Neurological Societies*, 1969, *37*, 49–61.

Bondareff, W. The neural basis of aging. In J. E. Birren & K. W. Schaie (Eds.), *Handbook of the psychology of aging*. New York: Van Nostrand Reinhold, 1977.

Bondareff, W. Neurobiology of aging. In J. E. Birren & R. D. Sloane (Eds.), *Handbook of mental health and aging*. Englewood Cliffs, N.J.: Prentice-Hall, 1980.

Borad, J. C., & Goodglass, H. Lateralization of linguistic and melodic processing with age. *Neuropsychologia*, 1980, *18*, 79–83.

Bornstein, R. A. Unilateral lesions and the Wechsler Adult Intelligence Scale—Revised: No sex differences, *Journal of Consulting and Clinical Psychology*, 1984, *52*, 604–608.

Botwinick, J. Neuropsychology of aging. In S. B. Filskov & T. J. Boll (Eds.), *Handbook of clinical neuropsychology*. New York: Wiley, 1981.

Bouchard, T. J., Jr., & McGee, M. G. Sex differences in human spatial ability: Not an X-linked recessive gene effect. *Social Biology*, 1977, *24*, 332–335.

Bradshaw, J. L., Nettleton, N., & Spehr, K. Sinistral inverters do not possess an anomalous visuomotor organization. *Neuropsychologia*, 1982, *20*, 605–609.

Briggs, G. E., & Brogden, W. J. Bilateral aspects of the trigonometric relationship of precision and angle of linear pursuit-movements. *American Journal of Psychology*, 1953, *66*, 472–478.

Briggs, G. G., Nebes, R. D., & Kinsbourne, M. Intellectual differences in relation to personal and family handedness. *Quarterly Journal of Experimental Psychology*, 1976, *28*, 591–602.

Broverman, D. M., Klaiber, E. L., Kobayashi, Y., & Vogel, W. Roles of activation and inhibition in sex differences in cognitive abilities. *Psychological Review*, 1968, *75*, 23–50.

Brown, J. W., & Jaffe, J. Hypothesis on cerebral dominance. *Neuropsychologia*, 1975, *13*, 107–110.

Bruce, P. R., Herman, J. F., & Stern, J. Lateral eye movements and the recall of spatial information in a familiar, large-scale environment. *Neuropsychologia*, 1982, *20*, 505–508.

Bryden, M. P. Measuring handedness with questionnaires. *Neuropsychologia*, 1977, *15*, 617–624.

Bryden, M. P. Strategy effects in the assessment of hemispheric asymmetry. In G. Underwood (Ed.), *Strategies of information processing*. London: Academic Press, 1978.

Bryden, M. P. Evidence for sex-related differences in cerebral organization. In M. Wittig and A. C. Peterson (Eds.), *Sex-related differences in cognitive functioning: Developmental issues*. New York: Academic Press, 1979.

Bryden, M. P. *Laterality: Functional asymmetry in the intact brain*. New York: Academic Press, 1982.

Bryden, M. P. *Laterality: Studies of functional asymmetry in the intact brain*. Paper presented at the meeting of the Canadian Psychological Association, Winnipeg, Manitoba, 1983.(a)

Bryden, M. P. *Sex-related differences in perceptual asymmetry*. Paper presented at the meeting of the American Psychological Association, Anaheim, California, 1983.(b)

Buffery, A. W. H. Sex differences in the neuropsychological development of verbal and spatial skills. In R. M. Knights & D. J. Bakker (Eds.), *The neuropsychology of learning disorders*. Baltimore, Md.: University Park Press, 1976.

Buffery, A. W. H., & Gray, J. A. Sex differences in the development of spatial and linguistic skills. In C. Ounsted & D. C. Taylor (Eds.), *Gender differences: Their ontogeny and significance*. London: Churchill, 1972.

Bullard-Bates, P. C., & Satz, P. A case of pathological left-handedness. *Clinical Neuropsychology*, 1983, *5*, 128–129.

Burt, C. *The backward child*. London: University of London Press, 1950.

Butler, S. R., & Glass, A. Asymmetries in the electroencephalogram associated with cerebral dominance. *Electroencephalography and Clinical Neurophysiology*, 1974, *36*, 481–491.

Byrd, M., & Moscovitch, M. Lateralization of peripherally and centrally masked words in young and elderly people. *Journal of Gerontology*, 1984, *39*, 699–703.

Carey, S., & Diamond, R. Maturational determination of the developmental course of face encoding. In D. Caplan (Ed.), *Biological studies of mental processes*. Cambridge: MIT Press, 1980.

Carmon, A., & Gombos, G. M. A physiological vascular correlate of hand preference: Possible implications with respect to hemispheric cerebral dominance. *Neuropsychologia*, 1970, *8*, 119–128.

Carmon, A., Harishanu, Y., Lowinger, E., & Lavy, S. Asymmetries in hemispheric blood volume and cerebral dominance. *Behavioral Biology*, 1972, *7*, 853–859.

Cattell, R. B. Theory of fluid and crystallized intelligence: A critical experiment. *Journal of Educational Psychology*, 1963, *54*, 1–22.

Cohen, J. *Statistical power analysis for the behavioral sciences*. New York: Academic Press, 1977.

Cohn, R. Differential cerebral processing of noise and verbal stimuli. *Science*, 1971, *172*, 599–601.

Corballis, M. C. Laterality and myth. *American Psychologist*, 1980, *35*, 284–295.

Coren, S., Searleman, A., & Porac, C. The effects of specific birth stressors on four indices of lateral preference. *Canadian Journal of Psychology*, 1982, *36*, 478–487.

Corkin, S., Davis, K., Growdon, J., Usdin, E., & Wurtman, R. (Eds.) *Aging, Vol. 19, Alzheimer's disease: A report of progress in research*. New York: Raven Press, 1982.

Coyle, J. T., Price, D. L., & DeLong, M. R. Alzheimer's disease: A disorder of cortical cholinergic innervation. *Science*, 1983, *219*, 1184–1190.

Critchley, M. *The dyslexic child* (2nd ed.). London: Heinemann, 1970.

Crouch, W. Dominant direction of conjugate lateral eye movements and responsiveness to facial and verbal cues. *Perceptual and Motor Skills*, 1976, *42*, 167–174.

Culver, C. M., Tanley, J. C., & Eason, R. G. Evoked cortical potentials: Relation to hand dominance and eye dominance. *Perceptual and Motor Skills*, 1970, *30*, 407–414.

Dalton, K. Prenatal progesterone and educational attainments. *British Journal of Psychiatry*, 1976, *129*, 438–442.

Davidson, R. J., & Ehrlichman, H. Lateralized cognitive processes and the electroencephalogram. *Science*, 1980, *207*, 1005–1006.

Davidson, R. J., Schwartz, G. E., Pugash, E., & Bromfield, E. Sex differences in patterns of EEG asymmetry. *Biological Psychology*, 1976, *4*, 119–138.

Davis, A. E., & Wada, J. A. Speech dominance and handedness in the normal human. *Brain and Language*, 1978, *5*, 42–55.

Day, M. E. An eye-movement phenomenon relating to attention, thought, and anxiety. *Perceptual and Motor Skills*, 1964, *19*, 443–446.

Day, M. E. An eye-movement indicator of individual differences in the physiological organization of attentional processes. *Journal of Psychology*, 1967a, *42*, 51–62.

Day, M. E. An eye-movement indicator of type and level of anxiety; Some clinical observations. *Journal of Clinical Psychology*, 1967b, *23*, 438–441.

Day, M. E. Attention, anxiety and psychotherapy. *Psychotherapy: Theory, Research and Practice*, 1968, *5*, 146–149.

Dennis, M., & Whitaker, H. A. Hemisphere equipotentiality and language acquisition. In S. J. Segalowitz & F. A. Gruber (Eds.), *Language development and neurological theory*. New York: Academic Press, 1977.

DeWitt, G. W., & Averill, J. R. Lateral eye movements, hypnotic susceptibility and field-dependence. *Perceptual and Motor Skills*, 1976, *43*, 1179–1184.

Di Chiro, G. Angiographic patterns of cerebral convexity veins and superficial dural sinuses. *American Journal of Roentgenology, Radium Therapy and Nuclear Medicine*, 1962, *87*, 308–321.

Dobbing, J., & Sands, J. Quantitative growth and development of human brain. *Archives of Diseases in Childhood*, 1973, *48*, 757–767.

Doll, E. A. Psychological significance of cerebral birth lesions. *American Journal of Psychology*, 1933, *45*, 444–452.

Donchin, E., Kutas, M., & McCarthy, G. Electrocortical indices of hemispheric utilization. In S. Harnad, R. W. Doty, L. Goldstein, J. Jaynes, & G. Krauthamer (Eds.), *Lateralization in the nervous system*. New York: Academic Press, 1977.

Doyle, J. C., Ornstein, R., & Galin, D. Lateral specialization of cognitive mode: II. EEG frequency analysis. *Psychophysiology*, 1974, *11*, 567–578.

Duke, J. D. Lateral eye movement behavior. *Journal of General Psychology*, 1968, *78*, 189–195.

Dumas, R., & Morgan, A. EEG asymmetry as a function of occupation, task, and task difficulty. *Neuropsychologia*, 1975, *13*, 219–228.

Dusek, C. D., & Hicks, R. A. Multiple birth-risk factors and handedness in elementary school children. *Cortex*, 1980, *16*, 471–478.

Eason, R. G., Groves, P., White, C. T., & Oden, D. Evoked cortical potentials: Relation to visual field and handedness. *Science*, 1967, *156*, 1643–1646.

Edwards, S., Ellams, J., & Thompson, J. Language and intelligence in dysphasia: Are they related? *British Journal of Disorders of Communication*, 1976, *11*, 83–94.

Ehrlichman, H. *Hemispheric functioning and individual differences in cognitive abilities*. Doctoral dissertation, New School for Social Research, New York, 1971. (*Dissertation Abstracts International*, 1972, *33*, 2319B.)

Ehrlichman, H., & Weinberger, A. Lateral eye movements and hemispheric asymmetry: A critical review. *Psychological Bulletin*, 1978, *85*, 1080–1101.

Ehrlichman, H., & Wiener, M. S. Consistency of task-related EEG asymmetries. *Psychophysiology*, 1979, *16*, 247–252.

Ehrlichman, H., Weiner, S. L., & Baker, A. H. Effects of verbal and spatial questions on initial gaze shifts. *Neuropsychologia*, 1974, *12*, 265–277.

Elias, M. F., & Kinsbourne, M. Age and sex differences in the processing of verbal and non-verbal stimuli. *Journal of Gerontology*, 1974, *29*, 162–171.

Epstein, H. T. Growth spurts during brain development: Implications for educational policy and practice. In J. S. Chall & A. F. Mirsky (Eds.), *Education and the brain* (Yearbook of the National Society for Study of Education). Chicago: University of Chicago Press, 1978.

Ertl, J., & Schafer, E. W. P. Brain response correlates of psychometric intelligence. *Nature*, 1969, *223*, 421–422.

Etaugh, C. F. Personality correlates of lateral eye movement and handedness. *Perceptual and Motor Skills*, 1972, *34*, 751–754.

Etaugh, C., & Rose, M. Lateral eye movement: Elusive personality correlates and moderate stability estimates. *Perceptual and Motor Skills*, 1973, *37*, 211–217.

Fagin-Dubin, L. Lateral dominance and development of cerebral specialization. *Cortex*, 1974, *10*, 69–74.

Fairweather, H. Sex differences in cognition. *Cognition*, 1976, *4*, 231–280.

Fischette, C. T., Biegon, A., & McEwen, B. S. Sex differences in serotonin 1 receptor binding in rat brain. *Science*, 1983, *222*, 333–335.

Fleishman, E. A. On the relation between abilities, learning, and human performance. *American Psychologist*, 1972, *27*, 1017–1032.

Friedman, D., Simson, R., Ritter, W., & Rapin, I. Cortical evoked potentials elicited by real speech words and human sounds. *Electroencephalography and Clinical Neurophysiology*, 1975, *38*, 13–19.

Furst, C. J. EEG alpha asymmetry and visuospatial performance. *Nature*, 1976, *260*, 254–255.

Galaburda, A. M. Anatomical asymmetries. In N. Geschwind & A. M. Galaburda (Eds.), *Cerebral dominance*. Cambridge, Mass.: Harvard University Press, 1984.

Galaburda, A. M., LeMay, M., Kemper, T. L., & Geschwind, N. Right–left asymmetries in the brain. *Science*, 1978, *199*, 852–856.

Galambos, R., Benson, P., Smith, T. S., Shulman-Galambos, C., & Osier, H. On hemispheric differences in evoked potentials to speech stimuli. *Electroencephalography and Clinical Neurophysiology*, 1975, *39*, 279–283.

Galin, D., & Ornstein, R. Lateral specialization of cognitive mode: An EEG study. *Psychophysiology*, 1972, *9*, 412–418.

Galin, D., & Ornstein, R. Individual differences in cognitive style. I. Reflective eye movements. *Neuropsychologia*, 1974, *12*, 367–376.

Galin, D., Ornstein, R., Herron, J., & Johnstone, J. Sex and handedness differences in EEG measures of hemispheric specialization. *Brain and Language*, 1982, *16*, 19–55.

Gardner, B. T., & Gardner, R. A. Evidence for sentence constituents in the early utterances of child and chimpanzee. *Journal of Experimental Psychology: General*, 1975, *104*, 244–267.

Geschwind, N. The anatomical basis of hemispheric differentiation. In S. J. Dimond & J. G. Beaumont (Eds.), *Hemisphere function in the human brain*. London: Paul Elek, 1974.

Geschwind, N., & Levitsky, W. Human brain: Left–right asymmetries in temporal speech region. *Science*, 1968, *161*, 186–187.

Gevins, A. S., Zeitlin, G. M., Doyle, J. C., Yingling, C. D., Schaffer, R. E., Callaway, E., & Yeager, C. Electroencephalogram correlates of higher cortical functions. *Science*, 1979, *203*, 665–667.

Gloning, I., Gloning, K., Haub, G., & Quatember, R. Comparison of verbal behavior in right handed and non-right handed patients with anatomically verified lesions of one hemisphere. *Cortex*, 1969, *5*, 41–52.

Goldstein, G., & Shelly, C. H. Similarities and differences between psychological deficit in aging and brain damage. *Journal of Gerontology*, 1975, *30*, 448–455.

Gordon, H. Left-handedness and mirror writing, especially among defective children. *Brain*, 1920, *43*, 313–368.

Gott, P. S., & Boyarsky, L. L. The relation of cerebral dominance and handedness to visual evoked potentials. *Journal of Neurobiology*, 1972, *3*, 65–77.

Gould, S. J. *The mismeasure of man*. New York: Norton, 1981.

Goy, R. W. Early hormonal influences on the development of sexual and sex-related behavior. In F. O. Schmitt (Ed.), *The neurosciences: Second study program.* New York: Rockefeller University Press, 1970.

Grady, M. P. Students need media for a balanced brain. *Audiovisual Instruction*, 1976, *21*, 46–48.

Graves, C. A., & Natale, M. The relationship of hemispheric preference, as measured by conjugate lateral eye movements, to accuracy of emotional facial expression. *Motivation and Emotion*, 1979, *3*, 219–234.

Greschner, J. J. *A test of the cerebral asymmetry model of lateral eye-movements.* Unpublished Master's thesis, University of Saskatchewan, Saskatoon, 1978.

Gur, R. C., & Gur, R. E. Handedness, sex, and eyedness as moderating variables in the relation between hypnotic susceptibility and functional brain asymmetry. *Journal of Abnormal Psychology*, 1974, *83*, 635–643.

Gur, R. C., & Reivich, M. Cognitive task effects on hemispheric blood flow in humans: Evidence for individual differences in hemispheric activation. *Brain and Language*, 1980, *9*, 78–92.

Gur, R. E., & Reyher, J. Relationship between style of hypnotic induction and direction of lateral eye movements. *Journal of Abnormal Psychology*, 1973, *82*, 499–505.

Gur, R. E., Gur, R. C., & Harris, L. J. Cerebral activation, as measured by subjects' lateral eye movements, is influenced by experimenter location. *Neuropsychologia*, 1975, *13*, 35–44.

Gur, R. E., Gur, R. C., & Marshalek, B. Classroom seating and functional brain asymmetry. *Journal of Educational Psychology*, 1975, *67*, 151–153.

Gur, R. C., Gur, R. E., Obrist, W. D., Hungerbuhler, J. P., Younkin, D., Rosen, A. D., Skolnick, B. E., & Reivich, M. Sex and handedness differences in cerebral blood flow during rest and cognitive activity. *Science*, 1982, *217*, 659–661.

Hallenbeck, C. E. Evidence for a multiple process view of mental deterioration. *Journal of Gerontology*, 1964, *19*, 357–363.

Hannay, H. J., Leli, D. A., Falgout, J. C., Katholi, C. R., & Halsey, J. H., Jr. *Sex differences in activation of rCBF by a test of right–left discrimination.* Paper presented at the meeting of the International Neuropsychological Society, Mexico City, 1983.

Hardyck, C., Petrinovich, L. F., & Goldman, R. D. Left-handedness and cognitive deficit. *Cortex*, 1976, *12*, 266–279.

Harmon, D. W., & Ray, W. J. Hemispheric activity during affective verbal stimuli: An EEG study. *Neuropsychologia*, 1977, *15*, 457–460.

Harnad, S. R. Creativity, lateral saccades and the nondominant hemisphere. *Perceptual and Motor Skills*, 1972, *34*, 653–654.

Harris, L. J. Sex differences in spatial ability: Possible environmental, genetic, and neurological factors. In M. Kinsbourne (Ed.), *Asymmetrical function of the brain.* Cambridge: Cambridge University Press, 1978.

Harris, L. J. Left-handedness: Early theories, facts, and fancies. In J. Herron (Ed.), *Neuropsychology of left-handedness*. New York: Academic Press, 1980.

Harris, G. W., & Levine, S. Sexual differentiation of the brain and its experimental control. *Journal of Physiology*, 1965, *181*, 379–400.

Harshman, R., & Remington, R. *Sex, language and the brain, part I: A review of the literature on adult sex differences in lateralization*. Paper presented at UCLA conference on human brain function, Los Angeles, 1974.

Harshman, R. A., Hampson, E., & Berenbaum, S. A. Individual differences in cognitive abilities and brain organization, part I: Sex and handedness differences in ability. *Canadian Journal of Psychology*, 1983, *37*, 144–192.

Healey, J. M., Goodglass, H., & Waldstein, S. *Sex differences in the lateralization of receptive and expressive language functions*. Presented at the meeting of the International Neuropsychological Society, Mexico City, 1983.

Hécaen, H., & Ajuriaguerra, J. *Left-handedness: Manual superiority and cerebral dominance*. New York: Grune & Stratton, 1964.

Hécaen, H., & Sauget, J. Cerebral dominance in left-handed subjects. *Cortex*, 1971, *7*, 19–48.

Herbst, L. *Timing of maturation, brain lateralisation and cognitive performance*. Paper presented at the meeting of the American Psychological Association, Montreal, 1980.

Herbst, L., & Peterson, A. C. *Timing of maturation, brain lateralisation and cognitive performance in adolescent females*. Paper presented at the 5th Annual Conference on Research on Women and Education, Cleveland, Ohio, 1979.

Hicks, R. E., & Barton, A. K. A note on left-handedness and severity of mental retardation. *Journal of Genetic Psychology*, 1975, *127*, 323–324.

Hicks, R. E., & Kinsbourne, M. Handedness differences: Human handedness. In M. Kinsbourne (Ed.), *Asymmetrical function of the brain*. Cambridge: Cambridge University Press, 1978.

Hicks, R. A., Evans, E. A., & Pellegrini, R. J. Correlation between handedness and birth order: Compilation of five studies. *Perceptual and Motor Skills*, 1978, *46*, 53–54.

Hicks, R. A., Elliot, D., Garbesi, L., & Martin, S. Multiple birth risk factors and the distribution of handedness. *Cortex*, 1979, *15*, 135–137.

Hicks, R. A., Dusek, C., Larsen, F., Williams, S., & Pellegrini, R. J. Birth complications and the distribution of handedness. *Cortex*, 1980, *16*, 483–486.

Hillyard, S. A., & Woods, D. L. Electrophysiological analysis of human brain function. In M. S. Gazzaniga (Ed.), *Handbook of behavioral neurobiology*, (Vol. 2.) New York: Plenum Press, 1979.

Hiscock, M. *Some situational antecedents and dispositional correlates of lateral eye-movement direction*. (Doctoral dissertion, University of Texas at Austin, 1975.) *Dissertation Abstracts International*, 1975, *36*, 942B.

Hiscock, M. Effects of examiner's location and subject's anxiety on gaze laterality. *Neuropsychologia*, 1977a, *15*, 409–416.

Hiscock, M. Eye-movement asymmetry and hemispheric function: An examination of individual differences. *Journal of Psychology*, 1977b, *97*, 49–52.

Hiscock, M. Lateral eye movements and dual-task performance. In H. J. Hannay (Ed.), *Experimental techniques in human neuropsychology*. New York: Oxford University Press, 1985.

Hiscock, M., & Bergstrom, K. J. Ocular motility as an indicator of verbal and visuospatial processing. *Memory and Cognition*, 1981, *9*, 332–338.

Hiscock, M., & Kinsbourne, M. Asymmetry of verbal–manual time sharing in children: A follow-up study. *Neuropsychologia*, 1980, *18*, 151–162.

Hiscock, M., & Kinsbourne, M. Laterality and dyslexia: A critical view. *Annals of Dyslexia*, 1982, *32*, 177–228.

Hiscock, M., & Mackay, M. The sex difference in dichotic listening: Multiple negative findings. *Neuropsychologia*, 1985.

Hochberg, F. H., & LeMay, M. Arteriographic correlates of handedness. *Neurology*, 1975, *25*, 218–222.

Horn, J. L., & Cattell, R. B. Age differences in fluid and crystallized intelligence. *Acta Psychologica*, 1967, *26*, 701–719.

Horn, J. L., & Donaldson, G. On the myth of intellectual decline in adulthood. *American Psychologist*, 1976, *31*, 701–719.

Hoyenga, K. B., & Hoyenga, K. T. *The question of sex differences*. Boston: Little, Brown, 1979.

Hubbard, J. I. Handedness not a function of birth order. *Nature*, 1971, *232*, 276–277.

Hunter, M. Right-brained kids in left-brained schools. *Today's Education*, November–December, 1976, 45–49.

Hyde, J. S. How large are cognitive gender differences? *American Psychologist*, 1981, *36*, 892–901.

Inglis, J., & Lawson, J. S. Sex differences in the effects of unilateral brain damage on intelligence. *Science*, 1981, *212*, 693–695.

Inglis, J., & Lawson, J. S. A meta-analysis of sex differences in the effects of unilateral brain damage on intelligence test results. *Canadian Journal of Psychology*, 1982, *36*, 670–683.

Inglis, J., Ruckman, M., Lawson, J. S., MacLean, A. W., & Monga, T. N. Sex differences in the cognitive effects of unilateral brain damage. *Cortex*, 1982, *18*, 256–276.

Ingvar, D. H., & Risberg, J. Increase of regional cerebral blood flow during mental effort in normals and in patients with focal brain disorders. *Experimental Brain Research*, 1967, *3*, 195–211.

Ingvar, D. H., & Schwartz, M. S. Blood flow patterns induced in the dominant hemisphere by speech and reading. *Brain*, 1974, *97*, 273–288.

Jensen, A. R., & Reynolds, C. R. Sex differences on the WISC-R. *Personality and Individual Differences*, 1983, *4*, 223–226.

Jerison, H. J. *Evolution of the brain and intelligence*. New York: Academic Press, 1973.

Katz, J., & Salt, P. Differences in task and use of language: A study of lateral eye movement. *Perceptual and Motor Skills*, 1981, *52*, 995–1002.

Keller, J. F., Croake, J. W., & Riesenman, C. Relationships among handedness, intelligence, sex, and reading achievement of school age children. *Perceptual and Motor Skills*, 1973, *37*, 159–162.

Kertesz, A., & Sheppard, A. The epidemiology of aphasic and cognitive impairment in stroke: Age, sex, aphasia type and laterality differences. *Brain*, 1981, *104*, 117–128.

Kimura, D. Sex differences in cerebral organization for speech and praxic functions. *Canadian Journal of Psychology*, 1983, *37*, 19–35.

Kinsbourne, M. The cerebral basis of lateral asymmetries in attention. *Acta Psychologica*, 1970, *33*, 193–201.

Kinsbourne, M. Eye and head turning indicates cerebral lateralization. *Science*, 1972, *176*, 539–541.

Kinsbourne, M. Biological determinants of functional bisymmetry and asymmetry. In M. Kinsbourne (Ed.), *Asymmetrical function of the brain*. Cambridge: Cambridge University Press, 1978.

Kinsbourne, M., & Hiscock, M. Does cerebral dominance develop? In S. J. Segalowitz & F. A. Gruber (Eds.), *Language development and neurological theory*. New York: Academic Press, 1977.

Kinsbourne, M., & Hiscock, M. The normal and deviant development of functional laterization of the brain. In P. H. Mussen (Ed.), *Handbook of child psychology*, (4th ed.) *Vol. II: Infancy and developmental psychobiology*. New York: Wiley, 1983.

Klisz, D. Neuropsychological evaluation in older persons. In M. Storandt, I. C. Siegler, & M. F. Elias (Eds.), *The clinical psychology of aging*. New York: Plenum Press, 1978.

Kocel, K. M. Age-related changes in cognitive abilities and hemispheric specialization. In J. Herron (Ed.), *Neuropsychology of left-handedness*. New York: Academic Press, 1980.

Kocel, K., Galin, D., Ornstein, R., & Merrin, E. L. Lateral eye movement and cognitive mode. *Psychonomic Science*, 1972, *27*, 223–224.

Kolb, B., & Whishaw, I. Q. *Fundamentals of human neuropsychology*. San Francisco: W. H. Freeman, 1980.

Krayenbuhl, H. A., & Yasargil, M. G. *Cerebral angiography*. London: Butterworths, 1968.

Kutas, M., McCarthy, G., & Donchin, E. Differences between sinistrals' and dextrals' ability to infer a whole from its parts: A failure to replicate. *Neuropsychologia*, 1975, *13*, 455–464.

Lake, D. A., & Bryden, M. P. Handedness and sex differences in hemispheric asymmetry. *Brain and Language*, 1976, *3*, 266–282.

Lansdell, H. The effect of neurosurgery on a test of proverbs. *American Psychologist*, 1961, *16*, 448.

Lansdell, H. A sex difference in effect of temporal lobe neurosurgery on design preference. *Nature*, 1962, *194*, 852–854.

Lansdell, H. The use of factor scores from the Wechsler-Bellevue Scale of Intelligence in assessing patients with temporal lobe removals. *Cortex*, 1968a, *4*, 257–268.

Lansdell, H. Effect of extent of temporal lobe ablations on two lateralized deficits. *Physiology and Behaviour*, 1968b, *3*, 271–273.

Lansdell, H. Evidence for asymmetrical hemispheric contribution to an intellectual function. *Proceedings of the American Psychological Association*, 1968c, 337–338.

Lansdell, H. Effect of neurosurgery on the ability to identify popular word associations. *Journal of Abnormal Psychology*, 1973, *81*, 255–258.

Lansdell, H., & Davie, J. C. Massa intermedia: Possible relation to intelligence. *Neuropsychologia*, 1972, *10*, 207–210.

Lansdell, H., & Urbach, N. Sex differences in personality measures related to size and side of temporal lobe ablations. *Proceedings of the American Psychological Association*, 1965, 113–114.

Larsen, B., Skinhøj, E., & Lassen, N. A. Variations in regional cortical blood flow in the right and left hemispheres during automatic speech. *Brain*, 1978, *101*, 193–210.

Ledlow, A., Swanson, J. M., & Kinsbourne, M. Reaction times and evoked potentials as indicators of hemispheric differences for laterally presented name and physical matches. *Journal of Experimental Psychology: Human Perception and Performance*, 1978, *4*, 440–454.

Leli, D. A., Hannay, H. J., Falgout, J. C., Wilson, E., Wills, E. L., Katholi, C. R., & Halsey, J. H., Jr. Focal changes in cerebral blood flow produced by a test of right-left discrimination. *Brain and Cognition*, 1982, *1*, 206–223.

LeMay, M. Asymmetries of the skull and handedness. *Journal of the Neurological Sciences*, 1977, *32*, 243–253.

LeMay, M. Radiological, developmental, and fossil asymmetries. In N. Geschwind & A. M. Galaburda (Eds.), *Cerebral dominance*. Cambridge, Mass.: Harvard University Press, 1984.

LeMay, M., & Culebras, A. Human brain morphologic differences in the hemispheres demonstrable by carotid arteriography. *New England Journal of Medicine*, 1972, *287*, 168–170.

Lenneberg, E. H. *Biological foundations of language*. New York: Wiley, 1967.

Levine, R., & Mack, J. L., *The basis of visual constructional ability in patients with lateralized brain lesions.* Paper presented at the meeting of the International Neuropsychological Society, New York, 1979.

Levine, S. Sex differences in the brain. *Scientific American*, 1966, *214*, 84–90.

Levy, J. Possible basis for the evolution of lateral specialization of the human brain. *Nature*, 1969, *224*, 614–615.

Levy, J. Handwriting posture and cerebral organization: How are they related? *Psychological Bulletin*, 1982, *91*, 589–608.

Levy, J., & Reid, M. Variations in writing posture and cerebral organization. *Science*, 1976, *194*, 337–339.

Levy, J., & Reid, M. Variations in cerebral organization as a function of handedness, hand posture in writing, and sex. *Journal of Experimental Psychology: General*, 1978, *107*, 119–144.

Lezak, M. D. *Neuropsychological assessment* (2nd ed.). New York: Oxford University Press, 1983.

Libby, W. L. Eye contact and direction of looking as stable individual differences. *Journal of Experimental Research in Personality*, 1970, *4*, 303–312.

Libby, W. L., & Yaklevich, D. Personality determinants of eye contact and direction of gaze aversion. *Journal of Personality and Social Psychology*, 1973, *27*, 197–206.

Lie, T. A. *Congenital anomalies of the carotid arteries.* Amsterdam, The Netherlands: Excerpta Medica Foundation, 1968.

Maccoby, E., & Jacklin, C. N. *The psychology of sex differences.* Stanford, Calif.: Stanford University Press, 1974.

Matarazzo, J. D. *Wechsler's measurement and appraisal of adult intelligence* (5th ed.). New York: Oxford University Press, 1972.

Matsumiya, Y., Tagliasco, V. L., Lombroso, C. T., & Goodglass, H. Auditory evoked response: Meaningfulness of stimuli and interhemispheric asymmetry. *Science*, 1972, *175*, 790–792.

Mayes, A., & Beaumont, G. Does visual evoked potential asymmetry index cognitive activity? *Neuropsychologia*, 1977, *15*, 249–256.

McGee, M. G. Human spatial abilities: Psychometric studies and environmental, genetic, hormonal, and neurological influences. *Psychological Bulletin*, 1979, *86*, 889–918.

McGlone, J. Sex differences in the cerebral organization of verbal functions in patients with unilateral brain lesions. *Brain*, 1977, *100*, 775–793.

McGlone, J. Sex differences in functional brain asymmetry. *Cortex*, 1978, *14*, 122–128.

McGlone, J. Sex differences in human brain asymmetry: A critical survey. *Behavioral and Brain Sciences*, 1980, *3*, 215–264.

McGlone, J., & Kertesz, A. Sex differences in cerebral processing of visuospatial tasks. *Cortex*, 1973, *9*, 313–320.

McKee, G., Humphrey, B., & McAdam, D. W. Scaled lateralization of alpha activity during linguistic and musical tasks. *Psychophysiology*, 1973, *10*, 441–443.

McManus, I. C. Handedness and birth stress. *Neuropsychologia*, 1980, *18*, 347–355.

McRae, D. L., Branch, C. L., & Milner, B. The occipital horns and cerebral dominance. *Neurology*, 1968, *18*, 95–98.

Miller, E. A. Handedness and the pattern of human ability. *British Journal of Psychology*, 1971, *62*, 111–112.

Molfese, D. L., & Molfese, V. J. Hemisphere and stimulus differences as reflected in the cortical responses of newborn infants to speech stimuli. *Developmental Psychology*, 1979, *15*, 505–511.

Molfese, D. L., & Radtke, R. C. Statistical and methodological issues in "Auditory evoked potentials and sex-related differences in brain development." *Brain and Language*, 1982, *16*, 338–341.

Money, J. Turner syndrome and parietal lobe functions. *Cortex*, 1973, *9*, 313–320.

Money, J., & Ehrhardt, A. A. *Man and woman, boy and girl*. Baltimore, Md.: Johns Hopkins University Press, 1972.

Money, J., & Lewis, V. IQ, genetics and accelerated growth: Adrenogenital syndrome. *Bulletin of the Johns Hopkins Hospital*, 1966, *118*, 365–373.

Morgan, A. H., McDonald, P. J., & Macdonald, H. Differences in bilateral alpha activity as a function of experimental task with a note on lateral eye movements and hypnotizability. *Neuropsychologia*, 1971, *9*, 459–469.

Morgan, A. H., Macdonald, H., & Hilgard, E. R. EEG alpha: Lateral asymmetry related to task and hypnotizability. *Psychophysiology*, 1974, *11*, 275–282.

Moscovitch, M., & Smith, L. L. Differences in neural organization between individuals with inverted and noninverted handwriting postures. *Science*, 1979, *205*, 710–713.

Nebes, R. D. Handedness and the perception of part–whole relationships. *Cortex*, 1971, *7*, 350–356.

Netley, C., & Rovet, J. Atypical hemispheric lateralization in Turner syndrome subjects. *Cortex*, 1982, *18*, 377–384.

Neville, H. Electrographic correlates of lateral asymmetry in the processing of verbal and nonverbal auditory stimuli. *Journal of Psycholinguistic Research*, 1974, *3*, 151–163.

Newcombe, F., & Ratcliff, G. Handedness, speech lateralization and ability. *Neuropsychologia*, 1973, *11*, 399–407.

Nielsen, J., & Tsuboi, T. Electroencephalographic examinations in the XYY syndrome and Klinefelter's syndrome. *British Journal of Psychiatry*, 1974, *125*, 236–237.

Obrist, W. D., Thompson, H. D., Wang, H. S., & Wilkinson, W. E. Regional cerebral blood flow estimated by [133] xenon inhalation. *Stroke*, 1975, *6*, 245–256.

O'Gorman, J. G., & Siddle, A. T. Effects of question type and experimenter position on bilateral differences in electrodermal activity and conjugate lateral eye movements. *Acta Psychologica*, 1981, *49*, 43–51.

Oldfield, R. C. The assessment and analysis of handedness: The Edinburgh Inventory. *Neuropsychologia*, 1971, *9*, 97–113.

Orme, J. E. Left-handedness, ability and emotional instability. *British Journal of Social and Clinical Psychology*, 1970, *9*, 87–88.

Ornstein, R. E. *The psychology of consciousness*. San Francisco: W. H. Freeman, 1972.

Otteson, J. P. Stylistic and personality correlates of lateral eye movements: A factor analytic study. *Perceptual and Motor Skills*, 1980, *50*, 995–1010.

Overall, J. E., & Gorham, D. R. Organicity versus old age in objective and projective test performance. *Journal of Consulting and Clinical Psychology*, 1972, *39*, 98–105.

Parsons, O. A. Human neuropsychology: The new phrenology. *Journal of Operational Psychiatry*, 1977, *8*, 47–56.

Peterson, A. C. Physical adrogyny and cognitive functioning in adolescence. *Developmental Psychology*, 1976, *12*, 524–533.

Pieniadz, J. M., & Naeser, M. A. Computed tomographic scan cerebral asymmetries and morphologic brain asymmetries: Correlation in the same cases post mortem. *Archives of Neurology*, 1984, *41*, 403–409.

Pieniadz, J. M., Naeser, M. A., Koff, E., & Levine, H. L. CT scan cerebral hemispheric asymmetry measurements in stroke cases with global aphasia: Atypical asymmetries associated with improved recovery. *Cortex*, 1983, *19*, 371–391.

Plomin, R., & Foch, T. T. Sex differences and individual differences. *Child Development*, 1981, *52*, 383–385.

Porac, C., Coren, S., & Duncan, P. Lateral preference in retardates: Relationship between hand, eye, foot and ear preference. *Journal of Clinical Neuropsychology*, 1980, *2*, 173–187.

Premack, D. Language in chimpanzee? *Science*, 1971, *172*, 808–822.

Prohovnik, I., Hakansson, K., & Risberg, J. Observations on the functional significance of regional cerebral blood flow in "resting" normal subjects. *Neuropsychologia*, 1980, *18*, 203–217.

Provins, K. A. Motor skills, handedness, and behaviour. *Australian Journal of Psychology*, 1967, *19*, 137–150.

Provins, K. A., & Cunliffe, P. Motor performance tests of handedness and motivation. *Perceptual and Motor Skills*, 1972, *35*, 143–150.

Raczkowski, D., Kalat, J. W., & Nebes, R. Reliability and validity of some handedness questionnaire items. *Neuropsychologia*, 1974, *12*, 43–47.

Rasmussen, T., & Milner, B. Clinical and surgical studies of the cerebral speech areas in man. in K. J. Zülch, O. Creutzfeldt, & G. C. Galbraith (Eds.), *Cerebral localization*. Berlin, Heidelberg, New York: Springer-Verlag, 1975.

Ratcliff, G., Dila, C., Taylor, L. B., & Milner, B. Arteriographic correlates of cerebral dominance for speech. *Brain and Language*, 1980, *11*, 87–98.

Ray, W., Morell, M., Frediani, A., & Tucker, D. Sex differences and lateral specialization of hemispheric functioning. *Neuropsychologia*, 1976, *14*, 391–394.

Ray, W. J., Georgiou, S., & Ravizza, R. Spatial abilities, sex differences, and lateral eye movements. *Developmental Psychology*, 1979, *15*, 455–457.

Rebert, C., & Mahoney, R. Functional cerebral asymmetry and performance III. Reaction time as a function of task, hand, sex, and EEG asymmetry. *Psychophysiology*, 1978, *15*, 9–16.

Reed, H. B. C., & Reitan, R. M. A comparison of the effects of the normal aging process with the effects of organic brain-damage on adapative abilities. *Journal of Gerontology*, 1963, *18*, 177–179.

Reinisch, J. M. Prenatal exposure of human foetuses to synthetic progestin and oestrogen affects personality. *Nature*, 1977, *266*, 561–562.

Rennels, M. R. Cerebral symmetry: An urgent concern for education. *Phi Delta Kappan*, 1976, *57*, 471–472.

Reynolds, C. R., & Kaufman, A. S. Lateral eye movement behavior in children. *Perceptual and Motor Skills*, 1980, *50*, 1023–1037.

Rhodes, L. E., Dustman, R. E., & Beck, E. C. The visual evoked response: A comparison of bright and dull children. *Electroencephalography and Clinical Neurophysiology*, 1969, *27*, 364–372.

Richardson, A. Subject, task, and tester variables associated with initial eye movement responses. *Journal of Mental Imagery*, 1978, *2*, 85–100.

Risberg, J. Regional cerebral blood flow measurements by ^{133}Xe-inhalation: Methodology and applications in neuropsychology and psychiatry. *Brain and Language*, 1980, *9*, 9–34.

Risberg, J., & Ingvar, D. M. Patterns of activation in the gray matter of the dominant hemisphere. *Brain*, 1973, *96*, 737–756.

Risberg, J., Halsey, J. H., Wills, E. L., & Wilson, E. M. Hemispheric specialization in normal man studied by bilateral measurements of the regional cerebral blood flow: A study with the Xe-inhalation technique. *Brain*, 1975, *98*, 511–524.

Roberts J., & Engle, A. *Family background, early development, and intelligence of children 6–11 years*. In National Center for Health Statistics, Data from the National Health Survey, Series II, No. 142, DHEW No. (HRA) 75–1642. Washington, D.C.: U. S. Government Printing Office, 1974.

Rodin, J., & Singer, J. L. Eye-shift, thought, and obesity. *Journal of Personality*, 1976, *44*, 594–610.

Roth, M. Senile dementia and its borderlands. In J. O. Cole & J. E. Parett (Eds.), *Psychopathology and the aged*. New York: Raven Press, 1980.

Rubens, A. B. Anatomical asymmetries of human cerebral cortex. In S. Harnad, R. W. Doty, L. Goldstein, J. Jaynes, & G. Krauthamer (Eds.), *Lateralization in the nervous system*. New York: Academic Press, 1977.

Samples, R. Are you teaching only one side of the brain? *Learning*, 1975, *3*, 25–28.

Sanders, B., Soares, M. P., & D'Aquila, J. M. The sex difference on one test of spatial visualization: A nontrivial difference. *Child Development*, 1982, *53*, 1106–1110.

Säring, W., & von Cramon, D. Is there an interaction between cognitive activity and lateral eye movements? *Neuropsychologia*, 1980, *18*, 591–596.

Sarnat, H., & Netsky, M. G. *Evolution of the nervous system*. New York: Oxford University Press, 1974.

Satz, P. Pathological left-handedness: An explanatory model. *Cortex*, 1972, *8*, 121–135.

Satz, P. Left-handedness and early brain insult: An explanation. *Neuropsychologia*, 1974, *11*, 115–117.

Satz, P. Laterality tests: An inferential problem. *Cortex*, 1977, *13*, 208–212.

Satz, P. A test of some models of hemispheric speech organization in the left- and right-handed. *Science*, 1979, *203*, 1131–1133.

Satz, P. Incidence of aphasia in left-handers: A test of some hypothetical models of cerebral speech organization. In J. Herron (Ed.), *Neuropsychology of left-handedness*. New York: Academic Press, 1980.

Schaie, K. W. Translations in gerontology—from lab to life: Intellectual functioning. *American Psychologist*, 1974, *29*, 802–807.

Schroeder, N. Lateral eye-shift related to preschoolers' use of descriptive language. *Perceptual and Motor Skills*, 1976, *42*, 865–866.

Schwartz, G. E., Davidson, R. J., & Maer, F. Right hemisphere lateralization for emotion in the human brain: Interactions with cognition. *Science*, 1975, *190*, 286–288.

Schwartz, M. Left-handedness and high risk pregnancy. *Neuropsychologia*, 1977, *15*, 341–344.

Searleman, A. A review of right hemisphere linguistic capabilities. *Psychological Bulletin*, 1977, *84*, 503–528.

Searleman, A. Language capabilities of the right hemisphere. In A. W. Young (Ed.), *Functions of the right cerebral hemisphere*. London: Academic Press, 1983.

Searleman, A., Tweedy, J., & Springer, S. Interrelationships among subject variables believed to predict cerebral organization. *Brain and Language*, 1979, *7*, 267–276.

Segalowitz, S. J., & Gruber, F. A. (Eds.) *Language development and neurological theory*. New York: Academic Press, 1977.

Semmes, J. Hemispheric specialization: A possible clue to mechanism. *Neuropsychologia*, 1968, *6*, 11–26.

Shankweiler, D., & Studdert-Kennedy, M. A continuum of lateralization for speech perception? *Brain and Language*, 1975, *2*, 212–225.

Shelburne, S. A., Jr. Visual evoked responses to word and nonsense syllable stimuli. *Electroencephalography and Clinical Neurophysiology*, 1972, *32*, 17–25.

Shelburne, S. A., Jr. Visual evoked responses to language stimuli in normal children. *Electroencephalography and Clinical Neurophysiology*, 1973, *34*, 135–143.

Sherrod, D. R. Lateral eye movements and reaction to persuasion. *Perceptual and Motor Skills*, 1972, *35*, 355–358.

Shevrin, H., Smokler, I., & Kooi, K. A. An empirical link between lateral eye movements and lateralized event-related brain potentials. *Biological Psychiatry*, 1980, *15*, 691–697.

Shields, S. A. Functionalism, Darwinism, and the psychology of women. *American Psychologist*, 1975, *30*, 739–754.

Shucard, D. W., & Horn, J. L. Evoked potential amplitude change related to intelligence and arousal. *Psychophysiology*, 1973, *10*, 445–452.

Shucard, D. W., Shucard, J. L., Campos, J. J., & Salamy, J. G. Some issues pertaining to auditory evoked potentials and sex-related differences in brain development. *Brain and Language*, 1982, *16*, 342–347.

Shucard, D. W., Shucard, J. L., & Thomas, D. G. Auditory evoked potentials as probes of hemispheric differences in cognitive processing. *Science*, 1977, 1295–1298.

Shucard, J. L., Shucard, D. W., Cummins, K. R., & Campos, J. J. Auditory evoked potentials and sex-related differences in brain development. *Brain and Language*, 1981, *13*, 91–102.

Silva, D., & Satz, P. Pathological left-handedness: Evaluation of a model. *Brain and Language*, 1979, *7*, 8–16.

Smith, D. E. Hypnotic susceptibility and eye movement during rest. *American Journal of Clinical Hypnosis*, 1980, *22*, 147–155.

Snow, W. G., & Sheese, S. *Lateralized brain damage, intelligence, and memory: A failure to find sex differences*. Manuscript in preparation, Sunnybrook Medical Centre, Toronto, 1985.

Soper, H. V., Satz, P., Light, R., & Orsini, D. Dangers of improper respect for the null hypothesis in neuropsychology. *Bulletin of the Psychonomic Society*, 1983, *22*, 355.

Spanos, N. P., Rivers, S. M., & Gottlieb, J. Hypnotic responsivity, meditation, and laterality of eye movements. *Journal of Abnormal Psychology*, 1978, *87*, 566–569.

Spanos, N. P., Pawlak, A. E., Mah, C. D., & D'Eon, J. L. Lateral eye-movements, hypnotic susceptibility and imaginal ability in right-handers. *Perceptual and Motor Skills*, 1980, *50*, 287–294.

Sparrow, S. S., & Satz, P. Dyslexia, laterality and neuropsychological development. In D. J. Bakker & P. Satz (Eds.), *Specific reading disability: Advances in theory and method*. Rotterdam, The Netherlands: Rotterdam University Press, 1970.

Sperry, R. Some effects of disconnecting the cerebral hemispheres. *Science*, 1982, *217*, 1223–1226.

Spiegler, B., & Yeni-Komshian, G. H. *Birth trauma and left-handedness: Test of a theory*. Paper presented at the meeting of the International Neuropsychological Society, Pittsburgh, 1982.

Stam, H., & Spanos, N. Lateral eye-movements and indices of nonanalytic attending in right-handed females. *Perceptual and Motor Skills*, 1979, *48*, 123–127.

Steingrueber, H. J. Handedness as a function of test complexity. *Perceptual and Motor Skills*, 1975, *40*, 263–266.

Stern, J. A., & Baldinger, A. C. Hemispheric differences in preferred modes of information processing and the aging process. *International Journal of Neuroscience*, 1983, *18*, 97–106.

Strauss, E., & Kinsbourne, M. Does age of menarche affect the ultimate level of verbal and spatial skills? *Cortex*, 1981, *17*, 323–326.

Studdert-Kennedy, M. Dichotic studies II: Two questions. *Brain and Language*, 1975, *2*, 123–130.

Takeda, M., & Yoshimura, H. Lateral eye movement while eyes are closed. *Perceptual and Motor Skills*, 1979, *48*, 1227–1231.

Templer, D. I., Goldstein, R., & Penick, S. B. Stability and inter-rater reliability of lateral eye movement. *Perceptual and Motor Skills*, 1972, *34*, 469–470.

Teng, E., Lee, P., Yang, K., & Chang, P. Handedness in a Chinese population: Biological, social and pathological factors. *Science*, 1976, *192*, 1148–1150.

Teszner, D., Tzavaras, A., Gruner, J., & Hécaen, H. L'asymétrie droite–gauche du planum temporale: A propos de l'étude anatomique de 100 cerveaux. *Revue Neurologique*, 1972, *126*, 444–449.

Thomson, W. H. *Brain and personality*. New York: Dodd, Mead, 1907.

Tucker, D. Sex differences in hemispheric specialization for synthetic visuospatial functions. *Neuropsychologia*, 1976, *14*, 447–454.

Tucker, D. M., Roth, R. S., Arneson, B. A., & Buckingham, V. Hemisphere activation during stress. *Neuropsychologia*, 1977, *15*, 697–700.

Tucker, G., & Suib, M. Conjugate lateral eye movement (CLEM) direction and its relationship to performance on verbal and visuospatial tasks. *Neuropsychologia*, 1978, *16*, 251–254.

Vernon, M. *Reading and its difficulties*. London: Cambridge University Press, 1971.

Waber, D. P. Sex differences in mental abilities, hemispheric lateralization and rate of physical growth at adolescence. *Developmental Psychology*, 1977, *13*, 29–38.

Waber, D. P. Neuropsychological aspects of Turner syndrome. *Developmental Medicine and Child Neurology*, 1979, *21*, 58–70.

Waber, D. P., Bauermeister, M., Cohen, C., Ferber, R., & Wolff, P. H. Behavioral correlates of physical and neuromotor maturity in adolescents from different environments. *Developmental Psychobiology*, 1981, *14*, 513–522.

Wada, J. A., Clarke, R., & Hamm, A. Cerebral hemispheric asymmetry in humans. *Archives of Neurology*, 1975, *32*, 239–246.

Wang, H. S. Cerebral correlates of intellectual function in senescence. In L. F. Jarvik, C. Eisdorfer, and J. E. Blum (Eds.), *Intellectual functioning in adults*. New York: Springer, 1973.

Warrington, E. K., & Pratt, R. T. C. Language laterality in left-handers assessed by unilateral E.C.T. *Neuropsychologia*, 1973, *11*, 423–428.

Weber, A. M., & Bradshaw, J. L. Levy and Reid's neurological model in relation to writing hand/posture: An evaluation. *Psychological Bulletin*, 1981, *90*, 74–88.

Wechsler, D. *The measurement and appraisal of adult intelligence* (4th ed.). Baltimore, Md. Williams & Wilkins, 1958.

Wechsler, D. *WAIS-R Manual*, New York: Harcourt Brace Jovanovich, 1981.

Weiten, W., & Etaugh, C. F. Lateral eye movement as related to verbal and perceptual-motor skills and values. *Perceptual and Motor Skills*, 1973, *36*, 423–428.

Weiten, W., & Etaugh, C. Lateral eye-movement as a function of cognitive mode, question sequence, and sex of subject. *Perceptual and Motor Skills*, 1974, *38*, 439–444.

Whitaker, H. A., & Ojemann, G. Lateralization of higher cortical functions: A critique. In S. J. Dimond & D. A. Blizard (Eds.), *Evolution and lateralization of the brain. Annals of the New York Academy of Sciences*, 1977, *299*, 459–473.

White, K., & Ashton, R. Handedness assessment inventory. *Neuropsychologia*, 1976, *14*, 261–264.

Williams P. L., & Warwick, R. (Eds.) *Gray's Anatomy* (36th ed.). London: Churchill Livingstone, 1980.

Wilson, M. O., & Dolan, L. B. Handedness and ability. *American Journal of Psychology*, 1931, *43*, 261–276.

Winocur, G., & Moscovitch, M. Paired-associate learning in institutionalized and noninstitutionalized old people: An analysis of interference and context effects. *Journal of Gerontology*, 1983, *38*, 455–464.

Witelson, S. F. Anatomical asymmetry in the temporal lobes: Its documentation, phylogenesis, and relationship to functional asymmetry. *Annals of the New York Academy of Sciences*, 1977, *299*, 328–356.

Witelson, S. F. Neuroanatomical asymmetry in left-handers: A review and implications for functional asymmetry. In J. Herron (Ed.). *Neuropsychology of left-handedness*. New York: Academic Press, 1980.

Witelson, S. F., & Pallie, W. Left hemisphere specialization for language in the newborn: Neuroanatomical evidence of asymmetry. *Brain*, 1973, *96*, 641–646.

Wogan, M., Kaplan, C. D., Moore, S. F., Epro, R., & Harner, R. N. Sex difference and task effects in lateralization of EEG-alpha. *International Journal of Neuroscience*, 1979, *8*, 219–223.

Wogan, M., Moore, S. F., Epro, R., & Harner, R. N. EEG measures of alternative strategies used by subjects to solve block designs. *International Journal of Neuroscience*, 1981, *12*, 25–28.

Wolf-Dorlester, B. Creativity, adaptative regression, reflective eye movements, and the Holtzman movement responses. *Dissertation Abstracts International*, 1976, *36*, 6458B–6459B.

Woo, T. L., & Pearson, K. Dextrality and sinistrality of hand and eye. *Biometrika*, 1927, *19*, 165–199.

Wood, C. C., Goff, W. R., & Day, R. S. Auditory evoked potentials during speech perception *Science*, 1971, *173*, 1248–1251.

Wood, F. (Ed.) Noninvasive blood flow studies. *Brain and Language*, 1980, *9*, 1–148.

Woods, B. T., & Teuber, H. L. Changing patterns of childhood aphasia. *Annals of Neurology*, 1978, *3*, 273–280.

Yen, W. M. Sex-linked major-gene influences on selected types of spatial performance. *Behavior Genetics*, 1975, *5*, 281–298.

Yeni-Komshian, G. H., & Benson, D. A. Anatomical study of cerebral asymmetry in the temporal lobe of humans, chimpanzees and Rhesus monkeys. *Science*, 1976, *192*, 387–389.

Yule, W., & Rutter, M. Epidemiology and social implications of specific reading retardation. In R. M. Knights & D. J. Bakker (Eds.), *The neuropsychology of learning disorders: Theoretical approaches*. Baltimore, Md.: University Park Press, 1976.

Zaidel, E. Auditory vocabulary of the right hemisphere following brain bisection or hemidecortication. *Cortex*, 1976, *12*, 191–211.

Zaidel, E. Auditory language comprehension in the right hemisphere following cerebral commissurotomy and hemispherectomy: A comparison with child language and aphasia. In A. Caramazza & E. B. Zurif (Eds.), *Language acquisition and language breakdown: Parallels and divergencies*. Baltimore, Md. Johns Hopkins University Press, 1978.

Zangwill, O. L. *Cerebral dominance and its relation to psychological function*. London: Oliver & Boyd, 1960.

Zoccolotti, P., & Oltman, P. K. Field dependence and lateralization and configurational processing. *Cortex*, 1978, *14*, 155–163.

4

Application of the Kaufman Assessment Battery for Children to the Study of Individual Differences

RANDY W. KAMPHAUS, ALAN S. KAUFMAN, AND CECIL R. REYNOLDS

The Kaufman Assessment Battery for Children (K-ABC) is a new test of intelligence and achievement for children ages $2\frac{1}{2}$ through $12\frac{1}{2}$ (Kaufman & Kaufman, 1983a,b). Released in the spring of 1983, the K-ABC has received a good deal of attention from professionals (Reynolds, 1984) and the public (Starr, 1983, West, 1982) alike.

The K-ABC is a multi-subtest intelligence and achievement battery with intelligence scales based on the sequential/simultaneous processing model, a processing dichotomy gleaned from a remarkable convergence of research and theory in neuropsychology and cognitive psychology. Sequential/Simultaneous mental processing styles have been identified by Luria (1966) and his followers (Das, Kirby, & Jarman, 1975, 1979), cerebral specialization researchers (Bogen, 1969; Sperry, 1968), and cognitive psychologists (Neisser, 1967).

The intelligence scales consist of 10 subtests combined to form scales of Sequential processing, Simultaneous processing, and the Mental Processing Composite, a summary score reflecting the Sequential and Simultaneous scales. On the separate achievement scale, subtests are combined to form a

RANDY W. KAMPHAUS ● Department of Psychology, Eastern Kentucky University, Richmond, Kentucky, 40475. ALAN S. KAUFMAN ● Department of Educational Psychology, University of Alabama, Tuscaloosa, Alabama 35486. CECIL R. REYNOLDS ● Department of Educational Psychology, Texas A & M University, College Station, Texas 77843.

global Achievement score. The K-ABC also includes a special short form of the Mental Processing Composite known as the Nonverbal Scale (comprised of tasks that can be given in pantomime and that are responded to motorically) to assess the intelligence of children with speech or language handicaps, of hearing-impaired children, and of children who do not speak English.

Simultaneous processing refers to the ability of the child to mentally integrate input simultaneously in order to solve a problem correctly. Simultaneous processing often involves spatial, analogic, or organizational abilities (Kaufman & Kaufman, 1983b). The Triangles subtest on the K-ABC (an analog of Wechsler's Block Design task) is a prototypical measure of simultaneous processing. In order to solve these items correctly, one must mentally integrate the components of the design to "see" the whole. Similarly, the Spatial Memory subtest (a novel task) requires that the child memorize the spatial locations of stimuli and then identify the correct locations of the stimuli on a blank grid. Whether the tasks are spatial or analogic, the unifying characteristic of simultaneous processing is the mental synthesis of the stimuli to solve the problem.

Sequential processing, however, emphasizes the arrangement of stimuli in sequential or serial order for successful problem-solving. Each stimulus is linearly or temporally related to the previous one (Kaufman & Kaufman, 1983b), creating a form of serial independence. An example from the K-ABC is the Word Order subtest, a task that requires the child to point to a series of silhouettes of common objects (e.g., tree, shoe, hand) in the same sequence as the objects were named by the examiner—sometimes following a color-interference activity. In this task and in other Sequential processing subtests, the child has to place the stimuli in their proper order; it is not enough merely to reproduce the input without regard to the serial order. Other Sequential processing tasks include Hand Movements, which involves visual input and a motor response, and Number Recall, which involves auditory input and a verbal response. Therefore, the mode of presentation or response is not what determines the scale placement of a task, but rather the *mental processing demands* of the task are important.

An equally important component of the K-ABC is the Achievement Scale. This Scale measures abilities that serve to complement the intelligence scales. The Achievement Scale contains measures of what have traditionally been identified as verbal intelligence (verbal concept formation and vocabulary), general information, and acquired school skills (arithmetic, letter and word reading, and word and sentence comprehension). Performance on the Achievement Scale is thought to be a valid estimate of a child's success in the application of mental processing skills to the acquisition of knowledge from the environment (Kaufman, Kaufman, &

Kamphaus, 1985). A more detailed overview of the K-ABC scales is provided in the next section.

Some researchers have argued that existing intelligence tests are not very useful for the study of individual differences (Buss & Poley, 1976; Tyler, 1974). This criticism seems valid in many cases because of the lack of a theoretical basis for many existing tests of intelligence, including the Wechsler and Binet scales. Both the Wechsler and Binet test manuals devote a couple of sentences, at most, to defining intelligence. Horn (1968) charges that intelligence tests are based on "relatively crude *omnibus* designs and rest on *a priori* subtests, factored, if at all, after the construction." Nonetheless, the tests Horn was referring to are still the most widely used tests today. The importance of a scientific theory for studying individual differences is that it typically yields hypotheses that can be empirically tested. This has been another pervasive problem in the study of personality, since theories tend to be unscientific, that is, not amenable to adequate or accepted investigative methods (Eysenck & Eysenck, in press). Just having a theory is of little use; it must yield testable hypotheses. A theory predicts behavior and guides practitioners, as well as researchers, in assessing the correlates and causes of individual variations in behavior.

The K-ABC, as indicated earlier, stresses the necessity of assessing intelligence from a sound theoretical basis consistent with Kaufman's (1979) philosophy of intelligent testing. For practical purposes, a theoretical base leads to the generation of hypotheses about the best method of providing psychoeducational intervention to a given child. For research purposes, the K-ABC mental processing theory leads to hypotheses for the study of individual differences. It is this latter topic that is the focus of this chapter, although the former certainly lends itself to much research and, indeed, there exists a great need for just such work.

After presenting a brief overview of the K-ABC, the theory and research relevant to the Sequential/Simultaneous processing model is presented in detail. In subsequent sections, the Sequential/Simultaneous model is discussed in terms of its utility in studying ethnic group differences, sex differences, developmental differences, the relationship of the processing scales to other tests, and group differences for selected samples of exceptional children. Finally, potential future trends for K-ABC research are discussed.

OVERVIEW OF THE K-ABC

All the K-ABC Global scales (Sequential processing, Simultaneous processing, Mental Processing Composite, Achievement, and Nonverbal) yield standard scores with a mean of 100 and a standard deviation of 15 to provide a commonly understood metric and to permit comparisons of mental processing with achievement for children suspected of learning disabilities. Furthermore, the use of this metric allows an easy comparison of the K-ABC Global scales to other major tests of intelligence, as well as to popular, individually administered tests of academic achievement.

The K-ABC is comprised of 16 subtests, not all of which are administered to any one age group (see also Kaufman & Kaufman, 1983a, Figure 1.2). Children age $2\frac{1}{2}$ are given 7 subtests, age 3 receives 9 subtests, ages 4 and 5 receive 11 subtests (but not precisely the same set of tasks due to developmental changes), age 6 receives 12 subtests, and the peak of 13 subtests is given to children age 7 through $12\frac{1}{2}$. The Mental Processing subtests yield standard scores with a mean of 10 and a standard deviation of 3, modeled after the familiar Wechsler scaled score. Achievement subtests, on the other hand, yield standard scores with a mean of 100 and a standard deviation of 15, which permits direct comparisons of the mental processing global scales with individual achievement areas.

A brief description of the 16 K-ABC subtests, along with their age range, is given below. An asterisk identifies the subtests that are part of the K-ABC Nonverbal Scale, a scale that is offered only for children aged 4 through $12\frac{1}{2}$ years.

Mental Processing subtests
  Sequential processing scale
    ⋆ *Hand Movements* (ages $2\frac{1}{2}$–$12\frac{1}{2}$ years)
      Imitating a series of hand movements in the same sequence as the examiner performed them
    Number Recall (ages $2\frac{1}{2}$–$12\frac{1}{2}$ years)
      Repeating a series of digits in the same sequence as the examiner said them
    Word Order (ages 4–$12\frac{1}{2}$ years)
      Touching a series of pictures in the same sequence as they were named by the examiner, with more difficult items employing a color-interference task
  Simultaneous processing scale
    Magic Window (ages $2\frac{1}{2}$–4 years)
      Identifying a picture that the examiner exposes by moving it past a narrow slit or "window," so that only part of the picture is visible at any one time
    ⋆ *Face Recognition* (ages $2\frac{1}{2}$–4 years)
      Selecting from a group photograph the one or two faces that were shown briefly in a preceding photograph

Gestalt Closure (ages $2\frac{1}{2}$–$12\frac{1}{2}$ years)
Naming the object or scene shown in a partially completed "inkblot" drawing
* *Triangles* (ages 4–$12\frac{1}{2}$ years)
Assembling several identical triangles into an abstract pattern that matches a model
* *Matrix Analogies* (ages 5–$12\frac{1}{2}$ years)
Selecting the picture or abstract design that best completes a visual analogy
* *Spatial Memory* (ages 5–$12\frac{1}{2}$ years)
Recalling the placement of pictures on a page that was shown briefly
* *Photo Series* (ages 6–$12\frac{1}{2}$ years)
Placing photographs of an event in chronological order
Achievement subtests
Expressive Vocabulary (ages $2\frac{1}{2}$–4 years)
Naming the object shown in a photograph
Faces & Places (ages $2\frac{1}{2}$–$12\frac{1}{2}$ years)
Naming the well-known person, fictional character, or place in a photograph or an illustration
Arithmetic (ages 3–$12\frac{1}{2}$ years)
Answering a question that assesses an arithmetic ability
Riddles (ages 3–$12\frac{1}{2}$ years)
Naming the object or concept described by a list of characteristics
Reading/Decoding (ages 5–$12\frac{1}{2}$ years)
Naming letters and reading words
Reading/Understanding (ages 7–$12\frac{1}{2}$ years)
Acting out commands given in written sentences

As noted earlier, the Nonverbal Scale is intended for use with hearing-impaired, speech- or language- disordered, other communications-handicapped, and limited-English-proficient children, for whom administration of the regular K-ABC (and virtually all other well-normed, standardized measures of intelligence) would be inappropriate. The Nonverbal Scale yields a global estimate of intelligence; a method for profile interpretation of subtest scaled scores is offered in the *K-ABC Interpretive Manual* (Kaufman & Kaufman, 1983b). Most well-normed intelligence tests that are applicable to communications-handicapped children are very narrow and give a quite limited view of these children's intelligence (e.g., the Columbia Mental Maturity Scale). Although the K-ABC Nonverbal Scale is limited in this regard, of those tests of mental ability that can be used with this population with adequate technical/psychometric characteristics, the K-ABC Nonverbal Scale provides the broadest sampling of abilities. This breadth should enhance studies of these children and their development. The lack of adequately normed scales with any breadth has hindered not only the clinical assessment of children with communications disorders, but also research in the area (Reynolds & Clark, 1983).

The K-ABC was standardized on a sample of 2,000 children, using primarily 1980 U.S. Census figures. The sample was stratified by age, sex, geographic region, race/ethnic group, parental educational attainment (used as a measure of socioeconomic status), community size, and educational placement (regular class placement versus placement in a program for exceptional children). Educational placement is an infrequently utilized stratification variable. Typically, exceptional children are excluded from the standardization samples for individually administered tests. An attempt was made to include representative learning-disabled, mentally retarded, gifted and talented, and other special populations in the standardization sample according to data provided by the National Center for Education Statistics and the U.S. Office of Civil Rights. When all exceptional populations are combined, the total percentage of exceptional children included in the K-ABC standardization sample was 6.9% compared to 8.9% for the U.S. school-age population. An overview of the K-ABC standardization sample and its match to the U.S. Census data for the variables of geographic region, race/ethnic group, parental education, and community size are shown in Table 1.

Split-half reliability coefficients for the K-ABC Global scales ranged from .86 to .93 (mean = .90) for preschool children, and from .89 to .97 (mean = .93) for children age 5 to $12\frac{1}{2}$ years. Mean internal consistency reliability coefficients for the Global scales and the subtests are shown in Table 2. A test–retest reliability study was conducted with 246 children retested after a two- to four-week interval (mean interval = 17 days). This study resulted in good estimates of stability that improved with increasing age. For the Mental Processing Composite, coefficients of .83, .88 and .93 were obtained for age groups $2\frac{1}{2}$ through 4, 5 through 8, and 9 through $12\frac{1}{2}$, respectively. Excellent test–retest coefficients in the .95 to .97 range were obtained for the Achievement Scale at each age group. Further details of the test–retest study can be found in the *K-ABC Interpretive Manual* (Kaufman & Kaufman, 1983b, pp. 81–84).

The test–retest reliability coefficients for the Global scales and, to a lesser extent, the internal consistency (split-half) coefficients show a clear developmental trend, with those for the preschool ages being lower than those for the school age children. This trend is consistent with the known variability that characterizes preschool children's intelligence test performance.

TABLE 1. Representation of the K-ABC Standardization Sample[a] by Geographic Region, Race or Ethnic Group, Parental Education, and Community Size

Region	K-ABC sample N	%	U.S. population (%)	Race or Ethnic group	K-ABC sample N	%	U.S. population (%)
East	401	20.0	20.3	White	1,450	72.5	73.1
North central	565	28.2	26.5	Total minorities	550	27.5	26.8
South	628	31.4	34.0	Black	311	15.6	14.5
West	406	20.3	19.2	Hispanic	157	7.8	9.1
				Native American, Asian, or Pacific Islander	82	4.1	3.2

Parental education	K-ABC sample N	%	U.S. population (%)	Community size	K-ABC sample N	%	U.S. population (%)
Less than high school	384	19.2	21.1	Central city	579	28.9	27.9
High school	813	40.6	41.1	Suburb or small town	876	43.8	43.8
Some college	413	20.6	19.8	Rural area	545	27.2	28.3
College degree	390	19.5	18.0				

[a] Sample, ages $2\frac{1}{2}$ through $12\frac{1}{2}$.

As is shown in Table 2, the reliability coefficients of the K-ABC subtests typically meet or exceed those for comparable intelligence tests (Kaufman & Kaufman, 1983b). Mean internal consistency reliability coefficients for the K-ABC subtests ranged from .72 to .89 for preschool children and from .71 to .92 for school-age children. The test–retest coefficients for the subtests (Kaufman & Kaufman, 1983b) show the same predictable developmental trend identified for the Global Scales.

Also reported (Kaufman & Kaufman, 1983b) are the results of 43 validity studies. These studies assessed various aspects of the construct, concurrent, and predictive validity of the K-ABC. They were carried out using a variety of samples, among them, children classified as gifted, mentally retarded, hearing impaired, learning disabled, and behaviorally disordered.

TABLE 2. Average Reliability Coefficients for the K-ABC Scales and Subtests

Scale or subtest	Preschool children[a] (N = 500)	School-age children[a] (N = 1,500)
Global scales[b]		
Sequential processing	.90	.89
Simultaneous processing	.86	.93
Mental processing composite	.91	.94
Achievement	.93	.97
Nonverbal	.87	.93
Mental processing subtests[c]		
1. Magic Window	.72	
2. Face Recognition	.77	
3. Hand Movements	.78	.76
4. Gestalt Closure	.72	.71
5. Number Recall	.88	.81
6. Triangles	.89	.84
7. Word Order	.84	.82
8. Matrix Analogies		.85
9. Spatial Memory		.80
10. Photo Series		.82
Achievement subtests[c]		
11. Expressive Vocabulary	.85	
12. Faces & Places	.77	.84
13. Arithmetic	.87	.87
14. Riddles	.83	.86
15. Reading/Decoding		.92
16. Reading/Understanding		.91

[a] The values shown for preschool children (ages $2\frac{1}{2}$–4) are the mean coefficients for three age groups ($2\frac{1}{2}$, 3, 4), and the values shown for school-age children are the mean coefficients for eight age groups.
[b] Composite score reliability coefficients were computed based on Guilford's (1954, p. 393) formula.
[c] All coefficients for the subtests were derived using the split-half method and corrected by the Spearman-Brown formula.

Of particular interest is the relationship of the K-ABC to the WISC-R. Numerous studies involving the K-ABC and WISC-R have been reported (Kaufman & Kaufman, 1983b). In a study of 182 children enrolled in regular classrooms, the Mental Processing Composite correlated .70 with a WISC-R Full Scale IQ. Hence, the K-ABC Mental Processing Scales and the WISC-R have a 49% overlap in variance. The findings indicate that the K-ABC is substantially related to the widely used WISC-R, and yet, these data also indicate that the K-ABC is hardly a duplicate of the WISC-R, since it makes its own unique contribution to the field of intelligence measurement. Also of interest in this sample is the standard score difference between the MPC and FSIQ. The K-ABC, based on 1980 U.S. Census data, was shown to be about three points tougher (mean MPC = 113.6) than the WISC-R (mean FSIQ = 116.7), based on a sample of 182 children from regular classes (Kaufman & Kaufman, 1983b).

Administration and scoring procedures for the K-ABC are available in the *K-ABC Administration and Scoring Manual* (Kaufman & Kaufman, 1983a). One important aspect of K-ABC administration deserves special mention, and that is the notion of teaching items. The first three items (the sample and the first two items designated for a child's age group) of each mental processing subtest are designated as teaching items. The examiner is required to "teach the task" on these items if the child fails on the first attempt at solving the item. "Teaching the task" means that the examiner is allowed to use alternate wording, gestures, physical guidance, or even a language other than English to communicate the task demands to the child. This built-in flexibility is particularly helpful to preschoolers, minority group children, or exceptional children who sometimes perform poorly on a task in a conventional IQ test, not because of a lack of ability, but because of the inability to understand the instructions. This feature may account, in part, for the smaller minority group/white differences obtained for the K-ABC. Kaufman (1983) discusses the concept of teaching items in greater detail, and he notes, as is evident from Table 2, that this built-in flexibility has not adversely affected the reliability of the K-ABC.

The extensive use of sample practice items and teaching items on the K-ABC helps to ensure that the various subtests actually measure what they are intended to measure. Many intelligence tests contain such basic language concepts as next, same, alike, opposite, backwards, and after, words that less than one-half of the preschoolers and a significant number of primary-grade children do not understand (Kaufman, 1978). Thus, a child may perform poorly on a test because of a very specific language deficit when the test is really intended to measure psychomotor speed, memory, verbal reasoning, spatial ability, or some other intellectual ability. Violations of standardized procedure to explain the directions to children make the obtained scores essentially unusable, since the amount of error introduced through such procedures is unknown and not constant across children. Since the K-ABC was standardized using the sample and teaching items to ensure the child's understanding of the task, influences on performance are built-in for the normative data, and the error introduced is included in the standard errors of measurement reported in the K-ABC *Manual*. When using the K-ABC in research on individual differences, fewer confounding variables are introduced by the test itself.

Finally, Chapter 7 of the *K-ABC Interpretive Manual* (Kaufman &

Kaufman, 1983b) provides a framework for educational intervention. In this chapter, various approaches to remediating academic problems in children are reviewed (e.g., modality training and processing training) and their advantages and disadvantages discussed. From this review of other approaches to remediation, the K-ABC authors propose that interventions based on K-ABC results should focus on the design of instructional programs that teach the relevant academic skill using curriculum materials that capitalize on a child's mental processing strength and that deemphasize the child's weakness. Some pilot studies using this model, which produced positive results, are also described.

SEQUENTIAL AND SIMULTANEOUS PROCESSING

The utility of the K-ABC for the study of individual differences rests in part on the robustness of the Sequential/Simultaneous processing model. Das *et al.* (1975, 1979) have conducted numerous factor-analytical investigations that have successfully identified the Sequential and Simulations constructs. Others (Kaufman, Kaufman, Kamphaus, & Naglieri, 1982; McCallum & Merritt, 1983; Naglieri, Kaufman, Kaufman, & Kamphaus, 1981; Willson, Reynolds, Chatman, & Kaufman, in press) have successfully cross-validated and extended the findings of Das *et al.* (1975, 1979). Vernon, Ryba, and Lang (1978) conducted a study with an older sample than was used in other studies (college age) and did not find evidence to support the existence of successive and simultaneous processes. However, the interpretation of the results of the latter study have been challenged by Das *et al.*; in addition, Vernon *et al.*'s study is the exception to the overwhelming research support offered in behalf of the dichotomous processing model. Hence, overall, there is considerable evidence for the existence of sequential and simultaneous modes of processing information. Kaufman and Kamphaus (1984) added to this bulk of literature with their factor analysis of the K-ABC standardization sample ($N = 2,000$) in a large-scale study of Sequential and Simultaneous processing.

Kaufman and Kamphaus conducted factor analyses of the K-ABC separately for 11 age groups from $2\frac{1}{2}$ to $12\frac{1}{2}$. The first aim of the study was to determine the existence of Sequential and Simulations factors across the K-ABC age range. In addition, all K-ABC subtests were factor analyzed together to determine if the Sequential and Simultaneous factors maintain their integrity when the Achievement subtests are added to the matrix of Mental Processing subtests.

In the factor analysis of the Mental Processing subtests, two distinct factors emerged for each of the 11 age groups. These factors corresponded

closely to the successive and simultaneous factors identified by Das *et al.*
(1975, 1979), thus cross-validating their work and also clearly identifying
the K-ABC factors as the Sequential and Simultaneous processing dimensions. Mean factor loadings for the analyses of the Mental Processing
subtests are given in Table 3. The component subtests of the K-ABC
Sequential processing scale had the highest mean loadings on the factor
labeled Sequential (.43–.75), whereas the Simultaneous processing scale
subtests loaded highest on the Simultaneous factor (.40–.69). Only Hand
Movements, from the Sequential scale, had a substantial mean loading on
the Simultaneous factor.

The Sequential and Simultaneous dimensions also emerged intact in
the analyses that included the Achievement subtests. A clear three-factor
solution was evident for ages 4 to $12\frac{1}{2}$, indicating the existence of three
factors corresponding to the K-ABC Sequential processing, Simultaneous
processing, and Achievement scales for all but the young preschool
children. At ages $2\frac{1}{2}$ and 3, an Achievement factor was not evident; only
factors corresponding to Sequential and Simultaneous processing were
identified, with the Achievement subtests producing high loadings primarily
on the Simultaneous dimension.

Mean factor loadings for the factor analysis of all K-ABC subtests are
given in Table 4. Inspection of this table reveals that the six Achievement
Scale subtests had average loadings of .49 to .77 on the Achievement factor,

TABLE 3. Mean Sequential/Simultaneous Factor Loadings[a]

	Preschool children[b]		School age children[b]	
Scale	Sequential	Simultaneous	Sequential	Simultaneous
Sequential processing				
3. Hand Movements	*.60*	.19	*.37*	*.43*
5. Number Recall	*.64*	.28	*.77*	.15
7. Word Order	*.69*	.32	*.75*	.26
Simultaneous processing				
1. Magic Window	.21	*.63*		
2. Face Recognition	.28	*.40*		
4. Gestalt Closure	.23	*.59*	.08	*.53*
6. Triangles	*.36*	*.47*	.20	*.72*
8. Matrix Analogies			.30	*.57*
9. Spatial Memory			.24	*.60*
10. Photo Series			.26	*.69*

[a] Factor loadings were obtained by principal factor-analysis with varimax rotation. Factor loadings of .35 and above are italicized.
[b] Preschool children, aged $2\frac{1}{2}$ through 4; school-age children, aged 5 through $12\frac{1}{2}$.

TABLE 4. Mean Sequential, Simultaneous, and Achievement Factor Loadings for Children Ages $2\frac{1}{2}$ through $12\frac{1}{2}$

	Factor loadings[a]		
Scale	Sequential	Simultaneous	Achievement
Sequential processing			
3. Hand Movements	.46	.43	.18
5. Number Recall	.66	.16	.24
7. Word Order	.68	.22	.29
Simultaneous processing			
1. Magic Window	.24	.53	.23
2. Face Recognition	.24	.44	.33
4. Gestalt Closure	.10	.49	.28
6. Triangles	.21	.63	.27
8. Matrix Analogies	.30	.50	.26
9. Spatial Memory	.26	.58	.15
10. Photo Series	.25	.64	.26
Achievement			
11. Expressive Vocabulary	.25	.61	.77
12. Faces & Places	.21	.37	.67
13. Arithmetic	.46	.48	.49
14. Riddles	.34	.42	.62
15. Reading/Decoding	.39	.26	.68
16. Reading/Understanding	.37	.28	.76

[a] Factor loadings of .35 and above are italicized.

with five of the six subtests having mean loadings above .60. Only the Arithmetic task loaded about equally well on all three factors. In addition, each of the other five Achievement subtests had a sizable loading on either the Sequential factor (Reading/Decoding, Reading/Understanding) or the Simultaneous factor (Expressive Vocabulary, Faces & Places, Riddles), thus supporting the contention of the K-ABC authors (Kaufman & Kaufman, 1983b) that Sequential and Simultaneous processing skills are important for various types of school- and environment-related achievement.

A study by Kamphaus and Naglieri (personal communication) further supports the notion that *both* Sequential and Simultaneous processing are important for various types of achievement. Instead of a correlational approach, they performed several 2×2 analyses of variance (with five Achievement subtests serving as dependent variables, excluding Expressive Vocabulary), using data from the K-ABC standardization sample. One grouping variable was a significant processing difference (a standard score difference of 12 points or more, $p < .05$), indicating a preference for one of the processing dimensions (Sequential > Simultaneous or Simultaneous > Sequential). The other grouping variable was the overall level of processing ability (both Sequential and Simultaneous standard scores at or above the 63rd percentile or both scores at or below the 37th percentile).

Kamphaus and Naglieri (personal communication) found that for all the dependent variables, those children who scored higher on *both* processing scales obtained significantly ($p < .05$) higher Achievement subtest standard scores than those who scored at or below the 37th percentile on the two processing scales. This is not surprising, but it does demonstrate that *both* mental processing abilities are important for school achievement.

On the other variable (Sequential > Simultaneous or Simultaneous > Sequential), only two significant findings were obtained: Those children with a Simultaneous > Sequential pattern obtained significantly ($p < .05$) higher scores on Faces & Places ($M = 98.6$) and Riddles ($M = 98.8$) than did those children with the Sequential > Simultaneous profile (Faces & Places, $M = 95.2$; Riddles, $M = 95.3$). Apparently, Simultaneous processing ability is relatively more important for performance on these tasks. These findings are consistent with those of Kaufman and Kamphaus (1984) that showed Faces & Places and Riddles to be correlated more highly with Simultaneous than Sequential factor scores for several age groups. It is interesting that for such academic tasks as arithmetic and reading, *both* Sequential and Simultaneous processing appear to be important. Further data on the relationship of Sequential and Simultaneous processing to achievement have been summarized by Kaufman (1983).

All the data of Kaufman and Kamphaus (1984), taken together, provide clear-cut support for the composition of the K-ABC Mental Processing and Achievement scales. The data cross-validate and extend the findings of Das *et al.* (1975, 1979).

The data presented in Tables 3 and 4 reveal that Number Recall and Word Order are clearly the best measures of Sequential processing across the age range. Number Recall is essentially an analog to Wechsler's digits forward task, which has a rich clinical history as a measure of sequencing ability. Word Order is inspired by a task from Luria's neuropsychological clinical assessment techniques.

The third measure of Sequential processing, Hand Movements, shows the most distinct developmental trend of any of the Mental Processing subtests. For ages $2\frac{1}{2}$ through 4, the Hand Movements subtest had a mean loading of .60 on the Sequential factor versus .19 on the Simultaneous factor. At age 5 and above, however, Hand Movements loads substantially on *both* the Sequential and Simultaneous factors (mean loadings of .37 and .43, respectively). There are a variety of possible explanations for this phenomenon, including the possibility that the longer series of stimuli administered to school-age children require a simultaneous approach, whereas the shorter series administered to preschoolers are processed efficiently by a sequential approach. The Hand Movements subtest, however, is appropriately placed on the Sequential scale, since at 9 of the 11 age groups, it is the first, second, or third best measure of Sequential processing.

The Simultaneous factor is marked by strong loadings by Magic Window and Gestalt Closure for preschool children and by Triangles and Photo Series for school-age children. The strong loadings by Triangles and Gestalt Closure are predictable, since these tasks resemble the Wechsler Picture Completion and Block Design subtests, which have been shown to be good measures of Simultaneous processing (Naglieri, Kamphaus, & Kaufman, 1983). The loadings by Magic Window and Photo Series, however, are less predictable because, at first glance, they both appear to have sequential components. On Magic Window, the stimuli are presented bit by bit in a seemingly sequential fashion. Photo Series items require the child to solve the problems by placing the stimulus pictures in the examiner's hand in the proper sequence. The strong loadings by these subtests on the Simultaneous factor support the contention of Das et al. (1979) and Kaufman and Kaufman (1983b) that it is not the content of the stimuli or the nature of the stimulus or response format that determines a task's factor loadings, but rather the nature of the mental process used by the child to solve the problems that determines the factor loadings. Presumably, the preschool children who do well on Magic Window are able to integrate the parts and revisualize the intact object, a decidedly Simultaneous process; similarly, the school-age children who are successful on Photo Series can organize a large array of photographs they are not permitted to rearrange manually.

ETHNIC GROUP DIFFERENCES IN SEQUENTIAL AND SIMULTANEOUS PROCESSING

As part of the K-ABC prepublication research program, 807 blacks and 1,569 whites were tested. Data from this sample are shown in Table 5. For the total samples, black children achieved mean Sequential processing, Simultaneous processing, and Mental Processing Composite standard scores of 98.2, 93.8, and 95.0, respectively; on these same scales, white children achieved standard scores of 101.2, 102.3, and 102.0, respectively (Kaufman & Kaufman, 1983b). This seven-point discrepancy on the Mental Processing Composite halves the balck/white mean standard score difference found on such traditional intelligence tests as the WISC-R (Kaufman & Doppelt, 1976).

TABLE 5. Means and Standard Deviations of K-ABC Global Scales for Four Ethnic Groups[a]

| | Global scale standard scores | | | | | | | | | | | |
| | Sequential processing | | | Simultaneous processing | | | Mental processing composite | | | Achievement | | |
Ethnic group	(N)	(Mean)	(SD)	(N)	(Mean)	(SD)	(N)	(Mean)	(SD)	(N)	(Mean)	(SD)
Blacks												
As 2½ to 4–11	161	103.1	16.3	161	97.9	16.2	161	100.2	16.9	159	96.7	15.8
As 5–0 to 12½	646	97.0	14.9	644	92.8	14.5	644	93.7	14.2	643	92.9	13.6
Hispanics												
As 2½ to 4–11	32	103.2	14.6	32	104.3	17.6	32	104.4	16.2	32	99.2	16.3
As 5–0 to 12½	128	97.5	14.0	128	98.3	14.1	128	97.5	13.7	128	92.2	12.9
Navajos												
As 5–5 to 12–4	33	87.7	11.3	33	99.8	10.2	33	94.2	10.3	33	81.7	11.2
Sioux												
As 8–2 to 12–0	40	99.6	12.4	40	101.3	10.7	40	100.6	10.7	40	93.3	12.8

[a] From The K-ABC Interpretive Manual (p. 151) by A. S. Kaufman and N. L. Kaufman, 1983, Circle Pines, Minn.: America Guidance Service. Copyright 1983 by A. S. Kaufman and N. L. Kaufman. Adapted by permission.

Further inspection of the data in Table 5 reveals a characteristic pattern for the black children; that is, for this large sample they scored over *four* standard score points higher on the Sequential processing scale than on the Simultaneous processing scale. For the white children, there was a trivial one-point discrepancy in favor of Simultaneous processing. One could argue that black children really do not show a strength in Sequential processing, that it is an illusory difference that is explained better by Jensen's Level I/Level II processing model (Jensen, 1973). The data, however, do not support this contention.

Level I skills are characterized as being rote memory, so the Level I/Level II model is certainly tempting. However, there are two memory tasks on the Simultaneous processing scale, Face Recognition and Spatial Memory, and, when g is removed as an influence on black/white score differences, white children outscore black children on these two "rote memory" tasks. On Word Order and Number Recall, memory tasks on the Sequential scale, black children outperform white children. On Hand Movements, the third Sequential scale subtest, which is also highly memory dependent, black/white differences follow a trend dictated by the tests factor loadings. At the youngest ages, where Hand Movements has its highest Sequential scale loadings, black children tend to outperform white children. At the older ages (7 to $12\frac{1}{2}$ years), where Hand Movements has large Simultaneous scale loadings, white children score significantly higher than black children (Reynolds et al., 1984). Such data are difficult to explain outside the context of the K-ABC processing model.

Data for the Hispanic children who were tested as part of the K-ABC standardization program are also shown in Table 5. For all ages combined, this group only scored three points below the white sample on the Mental Processing Composite. This result is in contrast to an 11–point difference found between white children and Hispanic children on the Full Scale IQ of the WISC-R (Mercer, 1979). As was the case for the black children, the Hispanic sample scored considerably better at the preschool (MPC mean = 104.4) than at the school-age level (MPC mean = 97.5).

In contrast to the black sample, the Hispanic sample did not show a strong preference for a particular processing style. At both the preschool and school-age ranges, the Hispanic sample scored about one point higher on the Simultaneous than on the Sequential scale. The Hispanic group, however, did show larger differences between the MPC and Achievement Scale score than did the black sample. Overall, the Hispanic children scored about five points lower on the Achievement Scale. Although the Hispanic children tested were fluent enough in English to take the K-ABC, it is conceivable that their lower scores on the Achievement Scale are primarily the result of linguistic and cultural differences. Inspection of subtest data provided in the K-ABC Interpretive Manual (Kaufman & Kaufman, 1983b) reveals that Faces & Places and Riddles were two of the most difficult subtests for Hispanic children. This finding is logical given the nature of these two tasks: Faces & Places is a measure of general information that heavily depends on exposure to the "dominant school culture," and Riddles requires the ability to comprehend and combine English language concepts. The other difficult subtest for the Hispanic group was Reading/ Understanding, the K-ABC measure of word and sentence comprehension. The strengths for the school-age Hispanic children were Arithmetic and Reading/Decoding, both skills that depend heavily on school instruction.

The Navajo sample showed the greatest discrepancy between the Mental Processing Composite (mean = 94.2) and the Achievement (mean = 81.7) scales. This is not a surprising finding, given the separation of the Navajo sample from English-speaking society. The Navajo sample lived on an isolated reservation, attended reservation schools, and spoke primarily Navajo. Less than half this sample lived in homes with electricity or running water. In fact, for this sample a mean MPC in the mid 90s seems quite remarkable.

The Navajo sample did show a strong preference for Simultaneous processing, obtaining a mean (99.8) near that for white children. Further research is needed, but this difference may be partially the result of linguistic factors. The group's lowest scores were on the Number Recall, Word Order, and Riddle subtests, all of which require manipulation of English language stimuli. However, linguistic differences do not entirely explain the Sequential/Simultaneous discrepancy, since Gestalt Closure, a measure of Simultaneous processing that requires an English language response, was the third best Mental Processing subtest for this group. Possibly the low scores on Number Recall, Word Order, and Riddles reflect the Navajo children's difficulties with verbal *comprehension,* since these tasks are the only ones on the K-ABC in which spoken words are the only stimuli. It is of interest to note that the scoring rules for the K-ABC give credit for correct responses given in a foreign language such as Navajo. Hence, Navajo children with a verbal *expression* problem in English can respond in Navajo and receive credit, but those with receptive difficulties cannot easily compensate.

The Sioux children, on the other hand, did not show a preference for a particular processing style. They did, however, show a discrepancy in favor of Mental Processing ability (MPC mean = 100.6) over Achievement (mean = 93.3) consistent with the pattern observed for the Hispanic and Navajo samples. It is interesting that the most difficult Achievement subtest for this sample, Faces & Places, is the most "culture loaded," that is, it measures knowledge, much of which is specific to American society. This is an interesting finding for the Sioux group because the sample was taken from an urban area rather than from an isolated setting, as was the case for the Navajo sample.

Overall, the data obtained on the K-ABC for a variety of minority groups are consistent with the findings of Das et al. (1975, 1979), which demonstrated that different cultures may show preferences for particular processing styles (e.g., white Canadian versus native Canadian and high-caste children from India). There are important implications for researchers and clinicians alike should future research continue to replicate the findings of different preferences for Sequential or Simultaneous processing styles for various cultural groups. For the researcher, cultural differences will have to be considered before conclusions regarding relative levels of Sequential and Simultaneous processing for individual children can be drawn. Clinicians will have to consider the possibility that a child's performance in Sequential and Simultaneous processing may merely reflect that child's cultural heritage. The implications of these findings may be even more far reaching, affecting such enterprises as curriculum design.

SEX DIFFERENCES IN SEQUENTIAL AND SIMULTANEOUS PROCESSING

Kaufman and Kaufman (1983b) report that sex differences on the K-ABC favor girls at the preschool ages. Preschool-age girls performed better than preschool-age boys on all K-ABC Global scales and on all subtests but one (Gestalt Closure), a finding that is consistent with previous research indicating that girls' mental development is more rapid than boys' (Ames, Gillespie, Haines, & Ilg, 1979). The differences were largest on the Face Recognition, Number Recall, Word Order, Faces & Places, and Arithmetic subtests.

At the school-age level, the differences between boys and girls virtually disappeared (Kaufman & Kaufman, 1983b). Standard scores on the Mental Processing Composite and the Achievement Scale differed by less than one-half a standard-score point. The largest difference was obtained on the Sequential processing scale where girls (mean = 100.6) scored about two points higher than boys (mean = 98.7). This difference is not large enough, however, to have practical import for clinicians; in addition, it was partially offset by the school-age boys' one-point advantage on Simultaneous processing (101.3 vs. 100.2). There was an interesting split for school-age children on the Achievement Scale: Girls tended to perform better on the two reading subtests, but boys outscored girls on Faces & Places and Riddles, and had a slight advantage on Arithmetic. These data would seem to indicate that girls performed a little better than boys on tasks assessing basic school skills, whereas boys performed better on tasks more closely related to out-of-school learning.

Kamphaus and Kaufman (personal communication) have investigated the construct validity of the K-ABC via factor analysis of separate groups of males and females. For this study, principal components and principal factor analyses were conducted separately for males and females at different age levels, using the K-ABC standardization sample. Essentially, the procedure was the same as that used in the Kaufman and Kamphaus (1984) investigation.

Results of the principal factor analysis of the Mental Processing subtests are summarized in Table 6 for both girls and boys. First, the results of these analyses support the construct validity of the K-ABC Mental Processing scales for males and females. Two factors, closely approximating the dimensions shown in Table 3, emerged for the preschool and school-age ranges. Secondly, overall, the Sequential processing dimensions for girls and boys are strikingly similar and so are the Simultaneous processing factors for each sex. This congruence at both the preschool and school-age level indicates that the grouping of Mental Processing subtests into separate scales on the K-ABC is equally applicable to both groups. There are, however, a few noteworthy differences among the factor solutions for the two groups.

At the school-age range, Hand Movements appears to be a less integrated task (a task requiring both mental processes) for females. The mean loadings for this task on the Sequential and Simultaneous factors for boys are identical (.38 and .38), but girls show greater dependence on Simultaneous abilities (mean = .49) than Sequential skills (mean = .36) to solve these items. However, even for girls, Hand Movements emerged as the third best measure of the Sequential factor; in addition, despite the higher Simultaneous than Sequential loading for Hand Movements in the analysis for girls, this subtest only had the fifth best loading on the Simultaneous factor.

An unusual finding is that Triangles loaded only .27 on the Simultaneous factor for boys at age 4. This subtest's loading of .39 on the Sequential factor is similar to the loading of .37 for girls. It is unwise to overemphasize factor loading of a subtest for a particular age group, but it is interesting that girls (mean scaled score = 10.4) did perform better than boys (mean scaled score = 9.9) on this task at age 4, whereas for ages 5 through $12\frac{1}{2}$, when the loadings are very similar for both sexes, boys (mean scaled score = 10.7) scored higher than girls (mean scaled score = 10.0) (Kaufman & Kaufman, 1983b). these findings suggest that boys either do not possess the Simultaneous skills or do not apply them as well as girls do to

TABLE 6. Mean Sequential and Simultaneous Factor Loadings[a] for Preschool[b] and School-Age Children for Girls (N = 1,000) and Boys (N = 1,000)

	Preschool				School age[c]			
	Sequential		Simultaneous		Sequential		Simultaneous	
Scale	(Girls)	(Boys)	(Girls)	(Boys)	(Girls)	(Boys)	(Girls)	(Boys)
Sequential Processing subtests								
3. Hand Movements	.66	.54	.19	.20	.36	.38	.49	.38
5. Number Recall	.61	.69	.33	.20	.76	.78	.16	.12
7. Word Order	.62	.68	.35	.33	.69	.78	.25	.25
Simultaneous Processing subtests								
1. Magic Window	.16	.17	.61	.69				
2. Face Recognition	.22	.28	.38	.46				
4. Gestalt Closure	.20	.32	.57	.54	.16	.05	.49	.54
6. Triangles	.37	.39	.66	.27	.24	.22	.71	.69
8. Matrix Analogies					.35	.30	.53	.54
9. Spatial Memory					.30	.22	.58	.58
10. Photo Series					.28	.23	.65	.73

[a] Loadings of .35 and above are italicized.
[b] Preschool children; ages $2\frac{1}{2}$ through 4.
[c] School-age children, ages 5 through $12\frac{1}{2}$.

the Triangles task, at this first age group for which Triangles is administered. This limitation may well be due to the fact that boys mature more slowly than girls, a developmental difference that was quite evident in the girls' superiority on the K-ABC at ages $2\frac{1}{2}$ to 4, as noted previously.

Kaufman and Kamphaus (1984) found that Matrix Analogies was consistently an excellent measure of Simultaneous processing in their factor analyses of data for boys and girls combined, but noted an increase in this subtest's Sequential loadings at the older age levels. They suggested that Matrix Analogies' increased Sequential loadings at ages 11 and 12 were consistent with the onset of Piaget's (1950) stage of formal operations, in which thought is characterized by more analytical and logical problem-solving strategies. Again, although it is difficult to generalize too much from factor loadings at a couple of age groups, Kamphaus and Kaufman (1985) did find extremely high loadings by Matrix Analogies on the Sequential factor for boys at age 11 (.70) and girls at age 12 (.60). Do these data suggest that boys reach formal operations sooner than girls? That is probably not the case, since the factor loadings for boys at age 12 show the more frequent factor pattern for Matrix Analogies (loadings of .22 on Sequential and .71 on Simultaneous). The data do suggest, however, that Matrix Analogies does have a more distinct Sequential component for children at the upper end of the K-ABC age range for both boys and girls.

DEVELOPMENTAL DIFFERENCES IN SEQUENTIAL AND SIMULTANEOUS PROCESSING

Unfortunately, the area of developmental changes in Sequential and Simultaneous processing is essentially virgin territory within the research domain. There are many more questions than answers. The most obvious questions have to do with the growth curves for Sequential and Simultaneous processing abilities. Do they have distinctly different growth curves as have been found for other dichotomous models of intelligence, such as Jensen's (1973) Level 1/Level II model?

Mean raw scores for the K-ABC subtests by age, which are given in the *K-ABC Interpretive Manual* (Kaufman & Kaufman, 1983b, Table 4.13), raise some questions regarding developmental differences. Why is it that Hand Movements, an excellent measure of Sequential processing at the preschool level, is so difficult for children at ages $2\frac{1}{2}$ and 3? Hand Movements and Number Recall have items with the same number of stimuli (two to three stimuli per item) at these ages, and yet Hand Movements is more difficult. By comparison, Simultaneous processing subtests yield higher raw scores than Sequential processing subtests at age

3. Is it possible that Simultaneous processing abilities develop more rapidly than Sequential abilities at these early ages? Given that the Simultaneous subtests at this age use concrete meaningful stimuli, this trend may be explained by Bruner's (1964) concept of moving from iconic to symbolic modes of representation. For older children, it is interesting to note considerable raw score increases between ages 10 and 12½ for four of the Simultaneous processing subtests (Photo Series is the only exception), whereas negligible increases are noted on the three Sequential processing subtests. Perhaps Sequential processing develops rather slowly in pre-schoolers and yet peaks rapidly in middle childhood. Only well-controlled studies using more credible data than raw score distributions will answer these questions.

Although little is known about developmental changes on the two mental processes, more is known about changes in the processing demands of specific tasks. As discussed earlier, Hand Movements is a decidedly Sequential subtest for preschool children, both boys and girls, but depends about equally on each mental process for children age 5 to 12½ years; similarly, developmental trends were noted earlier for Triangles and Matrix Analogies. In fact, however, a factor-analytical investigation of an earlier, expanded version of the K-ABC revealed numerous developmental trends (Kaufman et al., 1982). Since the results of that study were used to select subtests for the final version of the K-ABC and to determine the age placement of each selected subtest, not surprisingly the analyses of the K-ABC standardization data revealed relatively few developmental trends.

In the earlier study by Kaufman et al. (1982), Face Recognition was found to be a Simultaneous task only for preschool children, but became decidedly more Sequential for children age 5½ and above. In fact, Face Recognition was one of the best measures of Sequential processing for the oldest group studied (ages 10 to 12½) by Kaufman et al. Magic Window, a clear-cut Simultaneous task for preschoolers, also showed increasing Sequential loadings with age. These findings were interpreted from a theoretical perspective, since the data were consistent with Gibson's (1969) and Braine's (1972) notions of perceptual development in children. Similarly, Piaget's theory of cognitive developmental changes from preoperational thought to formal operations was considered a suitable framework for explaining the fluctuations in Sequential and Simultaneous factor loadings across the age range for Concept Formation, a test of logical classification skills adapted from one of Bruner's experimental tasks (Kaufman et al., 1982).

Research on the development of Sequential and Simultaneous proces-ses is crucial for advising psychologists and educators on the design of effective remedial programs. If, for example, Sequential processing tends to develop slowly in the early years, then perhaps it is unwise to design an instructional program that capitalizes on a child's Simultaneous processing strength and de-emphasizes Sequential abilities. Perhaps the child is merely developmentally delayed; ignoring the Sequential aspects of a curricular area might actually inhibit the development of Sequential processing skills and, hence, ensure the permanence of the Sequential handicap. Furthermore, we need to understand better the nature of the developmental changes in individual K-ABC subtests, and other tasks as well, to be able to interpret K-ABC profiles better for individual children. For example, Kaufman *et al.* (1982) found that the subtests that were forerunners of Matrix Analogies (one with all concrete, meaningful stimuli, the other with only abstract stimuli) were clearly *Sequential* for children aged 3 to $4\frac{1}{2}$. This finding suggests that mentally retarded children age 5 and above may conceivably use a developmentally more primitive method to solve the Matrix Analogies items (i.e., Sequential), despite this task's placement on the Simultaneous processing scale. Knowledge of this possibility can help us in understanding a child's profile.

RESEARCH ON EXCEPTIONAL SAMPLES

Kaufman and Kaufman (1983b) summarize the results of numerous prepublication validity studies using the K-ABC, including samples of learning-disabled, educable mentally retarded (EMR), trainable mentally retarded (TMR), behaviorally disordered, physically impaired, high risk preschool, hearing-impaired, and gifted children. The search for a consistent pattern of Sequential/Simultaneous discrepancies for these exceptional populations has produced few clear-cut results.

For the samples of children diagnosed as learning disabled, the largest mean discrepancy (about five to six points in favor of Simultaneous processing) was obtained for the most homogeneously defined sample, dyslexics (Kaufman & Kaufman, 1983b). The dyslexic sample achieved a mean Sequential processing standard score of 86.09 and Simultaneous processing standard score of 91.53. Furthermore, a discriminant function analysis found that the Mental Processing subtests were able to differentiate normal and dyslexic readers with 85% accuracy.

Characteristic patterns of Sequential/Simultaneous processing were not evident for the identified learning-disabled and learning disabilities referrals samples cited in Kaufman and Kaufman (1983b). This is not a surprising finding, however, given the heterogeneous nature of samples identified as learning disabled. Shepard, Smith, and Vojir (1983) present considerable evidence that the lack of uniformity in placement decisions for learning-disabled children impedes research on the nature of learning disabilities. In summary, for a well-defined group of dyslexic children, a characteristic

Simultaneous greater than Sequential pattern is evident. This not only has a potentially important diagnostic value, but is also useful for designing remediation programs. It was also found that the mean Achievement Scale standard score for this group was 87.00, a value consistent in magnitude with the dyslexic sample's Sequential processing weakness. Hence, for dyslexic children, these data suggest that capitalizing on their Simultaneous processing integrity may hold the key to effective educational intervention.

Kaufman and Kaufman (1983b) summarize the results of three studies of EMR children (total $N = 73$). No clear-cut Sequential/Simultaneous discrepancy was evident for these groups. The EMR children had particular difficulty with the Number Recall, Word Order, and Photo Series subtests. Perhaps Photo Series behaved like a Sequential processing subtest for these children. As Kaufman and Kaufman (1983b) note, it is possible to use a variety of strategies to solve particular tasks. Researchers should attempt to record the test-taking behaviors of mentally retarded children systematically as they solve Mental Processing tasks to determine if they use a Sequential strategy to solve the Photo Series task. Research on the WISC and WISC-R suggests that retarded children may well employ Sequential strategies under circumstances in which normal children use Simultaneous approaches. That is to say, Picture Arrangement, which bears a definite relationship to Photo Series, consistently loads on Wechsler's Perceptual Organization factor (akin to Simultaneous processing) in factor-analytical investigations of normal children, but it loads just as consistently on the Freedom from Distractibility dimension (akin to Sequential processing) in factor analyses of mentally retarded children (Kaufman, 1979). These findings are further supported in the reanalysis of WISC-R data on normal and retarded children from the vantage point of the sequential-simultaneous model (Naglieri et al., 1983).

The remainder of the data for the exceptional samples is presented and discussed in the *K-ABC Interpretive Manual* (Kaufman & Kaufman, 1983b). Because of the recent release of the K-ABC, there are little data on exceptional samples available in professional journals to replicate these findings (Kaufman & Kaufman, 1983b). Because of this lack of replication and cross-validation it is too early to draw conclusions regarding the use of the K-ABC with gifted, TMR, behavior-disordered, or other groups.

RELATIONSHIP OF THE K-ABC MENTAL PROCESSING
SCALES TO OTHER TESTS

Sternberg (1977, 1979) has used componential analysis to try to determine the processing demands of tests of cognitive ability. Similarly, the relationship of the K-ABC Mental Processing scales to existing tests of intelligence provides a methodology for understanding the processing demands of existing tests of intelligence. Table 7 summarizes the correlations of several major tests of intelligence with the K-ABC Sequential and Simultaneous processing scales for normal children. This table also includes correlations with the Mental Processing Composite to show how the global measure of intelligence on the K-ABC relates to IQs and global scores on other tests of intelligence or cognitive ability. The Table 7 data were gleaned from several tables in the *K-ABC Interpretive Manual* (Kaufman & Kaufman, 1983b).

The pattern of correlations for the large WISC-R sample is quite clear. Performance on the Verbal Scale is related to both Sequential and Simultaneous processing, whereas the Performance IQ is more closely related to Simultaneous processing. The high degree of relationship between Performance IQ and Simultaneous processing is sensible, given the obvious similarities between subtests, such as Block Design and Triangles, and given the overall nonverbal nature of the K-ABC Simultaneous processing scale. WPPSI Performance IQ also correlated higher with Simultaneous than Sequential processing for a group of 40 black preschoolers, with WPPSI Verbal IQ showing the opposite pattern of correlations. However, the differences in correlations are not significant in view of the small sample size, and additional studies with the WPPSI and K-ABC for a variety of samples are needed.

Although Wechsler provides *two* separate IQs (Verbal and Performance), the WISC-R has been shown to possess *three* factors for a wide variety of samples (Kaufman, 1979). Naglieri *et al.* (1983) investigated the match of the WISC-R to the Sequential/Simultaneous processing model by factor analyzing the data for the WISC-R standardization sample after eliminating subtests that seem to be heavily influenced by such factors as school learning and sociocultural environment (Information, Vocabulary, Arithmetic, and Comprehension). The results of this study revealed two factors closely resembling the Sequential and Simultaneous dimensions. In effect, the results suggested that the WISC-R Freedom from Distractibility factor (Kaufman, 1975) might well be labeled a Sequential processing factor, as noted earlier.

The Stanford Binet IQ appears to correlate equally with Sequential and Simultaneous processing abilities. Three of four samples presented in Table 7 showed correlations in the 50s and 60s between the K-ABC processing dichotomy and the Binet IQ. The tendency of the Binet IQ to correlate equally well with Sequential and Simultaneous processing is a pattern consistent with correlations of the two processing styles with tests of academic achievement. The K-ABC Sequential and Simultaneous process-

TABLE 7. Correlations of Sequential and Simultaneous Processing with Various Tests of Intelligence for Normal Samples

Criterion	r with Sequential processing	r with Simultaneous processing	r with Mental Processing Composite
WISC-R (N = 182)			
Verbal IQ	.49	.51	.59
Performance IQ	.30	.68	.61
Full Scale IQ	.47	.68	.70
WPPSI (N = 40)			
Verbal IQ	.37	.28	.37
Performance IQ	.41	.50	.55
Full Scale IQ	.46	.47	.55
Stanford-Binet IQ			
School Age (N = 121)	.53	.50	.61
Kindergarten (N = 38)	.63	.65	.72
Preschool (N = 39)	.58	.58	.65
Preschool (N = 28)	.39	.15	.36
McCarthy Scales of Children's Abilities (N = 32)			
Verbal	.42	.46	.51
Perceptual Performance	.47	.45	.54
Quantitative	.55	.18	.40
General Cognitive Index	.56	.49	.60
Memory	.55	.38	.54
Motor (N = 40)	.42	.40	.47
Verbal	.56	.47	.58
Perceptual Performance	.61	.50	.62
Quantitative	.76	.38	.64
General Cognitive Index	.70	.51	.68
Memory	.59	.34	.52
Motor (N = 51)	.44	.32	.42
Verbal	.38	.30	.38
Perceptual Performance	.21	.42	.37
Quantitative	.57	.61	.68
General Cognitive Index	.46	.50	.55
Memory	.58	.47	.59
Motor	.20	.52	.43
Woodcock-Johnson Psycho-educational Battery (n = 25)			
Broad Cognitive Ability Scale Deviation IQ	.17	.43	.41
Cognitive Abilities Test (N = 42)			
Verbal	.56	.53	.62
Quantitative	.43	.66	.64
Nonverbal	.44	.70	.68

Note. Data from *The K-ABC Interpretive Manual* (pp. 113, 117, 133) by A. S. Kaufman and L. N. Kaufman, 1983, Circle Pines, Minn.: American Guidance Services. Copyright 1983 by A. S. Kaufman and N. L. Kaufman. Adapted by permission.

ing scales, for example, correlate equally well with the K-ABC reading subtests (Kaufman & Kaufman, 1983b) and a variety of external criteria of academic Achievement (Kaufman, 1983). In terms of correlations with processing dimensions, then, the Binet IQ "behaves" like a complex school learning (achievement) task.

The pattern of correlations of the K-ABC Mental Processing dichotomy with the McCarthy scales shows approximately equal correlations of the Sequential and Simultaneous processing scales with the Verbal, Perceptual-Performance, and Motor scales, and with the GCI. Two scales, Quantitative and Memory, tended to correlate relatively more highly with Sequential than with Simultaneous processing. This result is consistent with the finding that the K-ABC Arithmetic subtest is more highly related to Sequential processing at ages 3 and 4 (Kaufman & Kamphaus, 1984). It is interesting that the mean ages of the samples for the McCarthy studies, in which the Quantitative scale correlated more highly with Sequential than Simultaneous processing, were 4–10 and 4–0. The only study in which the Quantitative scale did not show a higher correlation with the Sequential scale used an older sample (mean age = 7–8).

There is very little that can be concluded from the small Woodcock–Johnson study ($N = 25$). If regarded as pilot data, the results suggest that, for preschoolers, the deviation IQ for the Broad Cognitive Ability scale is more closely related to the Simultaneous processing scale of the K-ABC than it is to the Sequential scale. Data from the correlational study with the Cognitive Abilities Test repeat some of the above-mentioned findings: Verbal IQ correlated about equally with Sequential and Simultaneous standard scores, but Nonverbal IQ correlated much more highly with Simultaneous processing. Quantitative IQ also showed a much higher correlation with Simultaneous than Sequential processing with this school-aged sample of 42 children (mean age = 10–11). The pattern of correlations between quantitative ability on the McCarthy Scales, for three separate samples, and on the Cognitive Abilities Test reveals stronger Sequential relationships for preschool children and stronger Simultaneous relationships for school-age children. This pattern is mirrored in the changing factor loadings for Arithmetic in the factor analyses reported by Kaufman and Kamphaus (1984) across the 3- to $12\frac{1}{2}$-year age range and also in the age-related changes in correlations between the K-ABC Arithmetic subtest and the Sequential and Simultaneous factor scores reported by these authors.

As shown in Table 7, the K-ABC Mental Processing Composite correlated about equally well verbal and nonverbal intelligence scores in samples assessed on the WISC-R, McCarthy Scales, or Cognitive Abilities Test. Only on the WPPSI was any difference observed, as MPC correlated .55 with Performance IQ versus .37 with Verbal IQ.

For samples of at least 30 cases reported in Table 7, the MPC correlated .70 with WISC-R Full Scale IQ (as discussed earlier in this chapter), .55 with WPPSI Full Scale IQ, .61 to .72 with Stanford-Binet IQ, and .55 to .68 with McCarthy General Cognitive Index; no global score is yielded by the Cognitive Abilities Test, although the Mental Processing Composite correlated .62 to .68 with each separate section of that battery. Thus, the K-ABC global intelligence score overlaps the Global scores yielded by other batteries to the extent of 30 to 50%, a moderate degree of overlap.

CONCLUSIONS

Early research with the K-ABC would indicate that this intelligence test holds great promise for the study of individual differences because of the care taken to establish the construct validity of the K-ABC intelligence scales, Sequential and Simultaneous processing. The validity of the Sequential and Simultaneous processing scales of the K-ABC has been supported in numerous investigations, some of which have used very large samples (Kaufman & Kamphaus, 1984).

Data cited in earlier sections have shown the utility of the K-ABC for studying ethnic group differences, sex differences, developmental differences, processing differences between groups of exceptional children, and the processing components of other tests of intelligence. Many other potential areas of research were not discussed. The Sequential/Simultaneous processing model may be applied to understanding the processing components of musical talent, creativity, and even personality variables, to name but a few of the areas not studied to date. There is also a need to replicate much of the research cited here, using larger samples and different age ranges.

To date, the Sequential/Simultaneous processing model has shed new light on ethnic/cultural group differences in intelligence. Das et al. (1979) have shown that children of different cultures have different preferences for processing styles. The results discussed by Reynolds et al. (1984) and Kaufman and Kaufman (1983b) support these findings of processing differences between cultural groups. These findings serve to highlight the fact that differences, which are not necessarily deficiencies, are at the root of some of the mean score differences observed in the past. The realization of these differences provides an impetus to the movement to expand curricula to better serve the educational needs of all schoolchildren.

Also, research similar in intent to the componential analysis techniques of Sternberg (1979) should be performed to clarify further the essence of the

Sequential/Simultaneous processing dichotomy. This effort will then clarify existing K-ABC research and could serve to guide the efforts of future researchers to produce more clearly interpretable findings, although Simultaneous processing is not particularly amenable to componential analysis.

Finally, the K-ABC is built on the notion that intelligence tests should produce tangible benefits, in this case, the design of remedial programs to improve children's school learning (Kaufman & Kaufman, 1983b). Because of this focus, a considerable effort should be made to assess the utility of the Sequential/Simultaneous processing model for designing educational treatment plans. Critical areas of research include determining individual differences in Sequential and Simultaneous processing and differences in response to treatment based on the processing dichotomy. The elegance with which the K-ABC can be used to design educational interventions will ultimately be one important variable in determining the popularity of the K-ABC as a clinical and research tool.

REFERENCES

Ames, L. B., Gillespie, C., Haines, J., & Ilg, F. L. *The Gesell Institute's child from one to six: Evaluating the behavior of the preschool child.* Lumberville, Penn.: Modern Learning Press, 1979.

Bogen, J. E. The other side of the brain: Parts I, II and III. *Bulletin of the Los Angeles Neurological Society,* 1969, *34,* 73–105, 135–162, 191–203.

Braine, L. G. A developmental analysis of the effect of stimulus orientation on recognition. *American Journal of Psychology,* 1972, *85,* 157–187.

Bruner, J. S. The course of cognitive growth. *American Psychologist,* 1964, *19,* 1–15.

Buss, A. R., & Poley, W. *Individual differences: Traits and factors.* New York: Gardner Press, 1976.

Das, J. P., Kirby, J. R., & Jarman, R. F. Simultaneous and successive syntheses: An alternative model for cognitive abilities. *Psychological Bulletin,* 1975, *82,* 87–103.

Das, J. P., Kirby, J. R., & Jarman, R. F. *Simultaneous and successive cognitive processes.* New York: Academic Press, 1979.

Eysenck, H. J., & Eysenck, M. *Personality and individual differences: A natural science approach.* New York: Plenum Press, 1985.

Gibson, E. J. *Principles of perceptual learning and development.* New York: Appleton-Century-Crofts, 1969.

Guilford, J. P. *Psychometric Methods* (2nd ed.). New York: McGraw-Hill, 1954.

Horn, J. L. Organization of abilities and the development of intelligence. *Psychological Review,* 1968, *75,* 242–259.

Jensen, A. R. Level I and level II abilities in three ethnic groups. *American Educational Research Journal,* 1973, *10,* 263–276.

Kaufman, A. S. Factor analysis of the WISC-R at eleven age levels between $6\frac{1}{2}$ and $16\frac{1}{2}$ years. *Journal of Consulting and Clinical Psychology,* 1975, *43,* 135–147.

Kaufman, A. S. The importance of basic concepts in the individual assessment of preschool children. *Journal of School Psychology*, 1978, *16*, 207–211.

Kaufman, A. S. *Intelligent testing with the WISC-R*. New York: Wiley-Interscience, 1979.

Kaufman, A. S. Some questions and answers about the Kaufman Assessment Battery for Children (K-ABC). *Journal of Psychoeducational Assessment*, 1983, *1*, 205–218.

Kaufman, A. S., & Doppelt, J. E. Analysis of WISC-R standardization data in terms of the stratification variables. *Child Development*, 1976, *47*, 165–171.

Kaufman, A. S., & Kamphaus, R. W. Factor analysis of the Kaufman Assessment Battery for Children (K-ABC) for ages $2\frac{1}{2}$ through $12\frac{1}{2}$ years. *Journal of Educational Psychology*, 1984, *76*, 623–637.

Kaufman, A. S., & Kaufman, N. L. *Kaufman Assessment Battery for Children (K-ABC) administration and scoring manual*. Circle Pines, Minn: American Guidance Service, 1983a.

Kaufman, A. S., & Kaufman, N. L. *K-ABC interpretive manual*. Circle Pines, Minn. American Guidance Service, 1983b.

Kaufman, A. S., Kaufman, N. L., Kamphaus, R. W., & Naglieri, J. A. Sequential and simultaneous factors at ages $3–12\frac{1}{2}$: Developmental changes in neuropsychological dimensions. *Clinical Neuropsychology*, 1982, *4*, 74–81.

Kaufman, A. S., Kaufman, N. L., & Kamphaus, R. W. The Kaufman Assessment Battery for Children (K-ABC). In C. S. Newmark (Ed.), *Major psychological assessment instruments*. Newton, Mass: Allyn & Bacon, 1985.

Luria, A. R. *Human brain and psychological processes*. New York: Harper & Row, 1966.

McCallum, R. S., & Merrit, F. M. Simultaneous–successive processing among college students. *Journal of Psychoeducational Assessment*, 1983, *1*, 85–93.

Mercer, J. R. *System of Multicultural Pluralistic Assessment (SOMPA): Technical manual*. New York: The Psychological Corporation, 1979.

Naglieri, J. A., Kaufman, A. S., Kaufman, N. L., & Kamphaus, R. W. Cross-validation of Das' simultaneous and successive processes with novel tasks. *Alberta Journal of Educational Research*, 1981, *27*, 264–271.

Naglieri, J. A., Kamphaus, R. W., & Kaufman, A. S. The Luria–Das successive–simultaneous model applied to WISC-R data. *Journal of Psychoeducational Assessment*, 1983, *1*, 25–34.

Neisser, U. *Cognitive psychology*. New York: Appleton-Century-Crofts, 1967.

Piaget, J. *The psychology of intelligence*. New York: Harcourt, Brace, 1950.

Reynolds, C. R. (Ed.) The K-ABC: A critical appraisal (Special issue). *Journal of Special Education*, *18*, 1984.

Reynolds, C. R., & Clark, J. H. (Eds.) *Assessment and programming for children with low incidence handicaps*. New York: Plenum Press, 1983.

Reynolds, C. R., Willson, V. L., & Jensen, A. R. *Black-white differences in sequential and simultaneous processing independent of* g. Paper presented at the meeting of the American Educational Research Association, New Orleans, La., April 1984.

Shepard, L. A., Smith, M. L., & Vojir, C. P. Characteristics of pupils identified as learning disabled. *American Educational Research Journal*, 1983, *20*, 309–331.

Sperry, R. W. Hemisphere deconnection and unity in conscious awareness. *American Psychologist*, 1968, *23*, 723–733.

Starr, D. Split-brain I.Q. test. *Omni*, 1983, *5*, 35.

Sternberg, R. J. *Intelligence, information processing, and analogic reasoning; The componential analysis of human abilities*. Hillsdale, N.J.: Lawrence Erlbaum Associates, 1977.

Sternberg, R. J. Stalking the IQ quark. *Psychology Today*, 1979, *13*, 42–54.

Tyler, L. E. *Individual differences: Abilities and motivational directions*. New York: Appleton-Century-Crofts, 1974.

Vernon, P. E., Ryba, K. A., & Lang, R. J. Simultaneous and successive processing: An attempt at replication. *Canadian Journal of Behavioral Science*, 1978, *10*, 1–15.

West, S. A smarter test for intelligence? *Science*, 1982, *3*, 14.

Willson, V. L., Reynolds, C. R., Chatman, S., & Kaufman, A. S. Confirmatory analysis of sequential and simultaneous processing factors for children ages $2\frac{1}{2}$ to $12\frac{1}{2}$ years. *Journal of School Psychology*, in press.

5

Applying Componential Theory to the Study of Individual Differences in Cognitive Skills

ROBERT J. STERNBERG

Many psychological phenomena are so very complex that no single approach can do justice to their complexity. *Intelligence* would seem to be a prime example of such a phenomenon. No matter how one defines intelligence, its complexity seems to overwhelm the conceptual resources any one approach can bring to bear on understanding it. Even limited aspects of intelligence seem almost staggering in their complexity. Consider, for example, that aspect of intelligence measured by conventional IQ tests. If almost a century of research on IQ test performance has shown anything, it is that no simple conceptual scheme or methodological approach has led, or perhaps can lead to an understanding of all the complexities that underlie test performance. The conceptual scheme and methodology one chooses will, of course, depend in large part upon the kinds of questions one wishes to ask.

Two classes of questions that have been particularly salient in the literature on intelligence concern the origins of subject variation in test performance and the origins of item or stimulus variation in such a performance. The first question deals with what makes some individuals score higher than others on intelligence tests; the second question deals with what makes some intelligence test items easier than others. Traditionally, these questions were asked by different investigators and through different research paradigms.

The question of individual differences has traditionally been addressed

ROBERT J. STERNBERG ● Department of Psychology, Yale University, New Haven, Connecticut 06520.
Preparation of this chapter was supported by Contract N0001483K0013 from the Office of Naval Research and Army Research Institute to Robert J. Sternberg.

through the use of psychometric methodologies. These methodologies have had in common their reliance upon correlational techniques and, especially, factor analysis, which is used to discover the latent psychological sources of observed variation on psychometric tests, including tests of intelligence. Factor analysis starts with a matrix of intercorrelations among all possible pairs of tests in a battery and ends with a matrix of correlations among these tests and a set of factors that is postulated to underlie the observed individual differences on the tests. This final matrix thus tells the investigator the extent to which each test measures each factor identified in the analysis. The factors are generally considered to represent latent "mental abilities."

Although the problems associated with the use of traditional factor analysis are of some consequence (e.g., Sternberg, 1977b), many investigators believe that factor analysis is a useful method for exploratory theorizing and data analysis (e.g., Humphreys, 1962; Sternberg, 1977b, 1980c; Thurstone, 1947). Moreover, its usefulness for providing a sort of broad topographical map for the structure of human intelligence seems almost unquestionable (Burt, 1940; Carroll, 1981; Vernon, 1971). If traditional factor analysis has been unilluminating in any respect, at least to date, it would seem to be in the inability to reveal the mental processes underlying human intelligence (Eysenck, 1967; Sternberg, 1977b). Not all investigators would agree with this (Carroll, 1981; Guilford, 1967). But I am not aware of any instance in which traditional (i.e., exploratory) factor analysis has isolated the processes underlying intelligent performance, whether on tests or on anything else.

An alternative approach to understanding human intelligence has been to address precisely those questions that the psychometric approach seems least adept at addressing, in particular, those questions regarding the processes people use in task performance. This approach, the cognitive or information-processing approach, uses a variety of methods of task analysis to identify these latent processes. One method, the "thinking-aloud" method, has subjects describe how they are performing a task at the time they are performing it. These protocols are then used to formulate or test a theory of mental processing. A second method, computer simulation, is sometimes used in conjunction with the thinking-aloud method. In this method, a computer program that is alleged to mimic the processes human subjects use in performing the task or tasks under study is written. Outputs from program execution are sometimes compared to data from human subjects to evaluate the validity of the computer model. Indeed, just getting the program to run is often considered a major accomplishment, in that it demonstrates the sufficiency (if not the validity) of the model for the performance of the given task. A third method, mathematical modeling, simulates task performance with a set of equations that, with the correct substitutions for quantified variables, predict human performance on the cognitive tasks in question. All these methods, then, have in common an attempt to isolate the processes and strategies underlying cognitive task performance.

Information-processing methodologies, like psychometric methodologies, are not above question or reproach (e.g., Sternberg, 1977b). Few people, however, seem to have questioned their usefulness for process analysis. If there is any respect in which they have fallen short, it would seem to be in their utilization for the analysis of individual differences and of the latent structures underlying task performance. Traditionally, information-processing researchers have simply not been terribly interested in individual-differences analysis. This lack of interest was expressed in papers that analyzed task variation while subject variation was treated as unwelcome "noise" in the data.

Cronbach (1957), recognizing the complementarity of the substantive questions that psychometric and experimental (cognitive) methods address, proposed that attempts be made to unify the "two disciplines of scientific psychology." After some years of inactivity, aggressive attempts have recently been made to do just that. Componential analysis, the subject of this chapter, is one such attempt that seeks to bring together the best of the psychometric and cognitive approaches to understanding human intelligence.

The goal of this chapter is to present the techniques of componential analysis, a methodology for studying cognitive skills that draws upon psychometric and cognitive methodologies. I will present a series of steps for executing a componential analysis, and illustrate the techniques of componential analysis with examples from my research.

In order to achieve some uniformity and continuity in the chapter, I will draw especially from my componential theory of analogical reasoning (Sternberg, 1977b), which seeks to understand reasoning by analogy in terms of six mental processes. Consider the analogy, LAWYER: CLIENT:: DOCTOR: (a) PATIENT, (b). MEDICINE. According to the theory, a person must *encode* the terms of the problem, perceiving each item and retrieving relevant attributes from long-term memory; *infer* the relation between LAWYER and CLIENT, recognizing that a lawyer renders professional services to a client; *map* the higher order relation from the first to the second half of the analogy, in this case, recognizing that both halves of the analogy (those headed by LAWYER and by DOCTOR) deal with professional services rendered; *apply* the relation inferred in the first half of the analogy to the second half of the analogy so as to recognize that a DOCTOR renders professional services to a PATIENT, not to a

MEDICINE; optionally, *justify* PATIENT as close enough to an ideal response to be correct; and *respond* with the chosen answer.

OVERVIEW OF COMPONENTIAL ANALYSIS

SELECTING OR GENERATING A THEORY OF RELEVANT COGNITION

The first thing one has to do is to decide what it is one wishes to analyze. Such a decision requires a theory of that aspect of cognition one wishes to analyze componentially. Any number of criteria might be used to evaluate either preexisting theories or one's own new theory. I have proposed five criteria that I believe are particularly useful for this purpose.

1. *Completeness.* A complete theory is one that accounts for all processes involved in the area of cognition of interest.

2. *Specificity.* A specific theory describes in detail the workings of each aspect of cognition. A theory can be complete, but not specific, if it accounts for all processes, representations, structures, and so on, but does not describe the workings of the processes in detail. A theory can be specific, but not complete, if it describes in detail a proper subset of processes, structures, and representations involved in the relevant area of cognition.

3. *Generality.* A theory is general if it is applicable across a wide range of problems within the relevant domain of cognition.

4. *Parsimony.* A theory is parsimonious if it can account for performance in the relevant domain of cognition with a relatively small number of parameters and working assumptions. Parsimony is difficult to evaluate, in part, because many theories that appear parsimonious on their surface have hidden assumptions, whereas other theories that appear less parsimonious can be taken more easily at face value. As might be expected, there tends to be a trade-off between parsimony, on the one hand, and completeness and specificity, on the other. A difficult problem facing theorists is to strike a reasonable balance.

5. *Plausibility.* A theory is plausible if it is able to account for experimental (or other) data that provide a test of the theory. Plausibility also involves intuitive judgments about the reasonableness of the theory. If one theory seems less reasonable on its face than another theory, skeptics may require more compelling evidence to convince them of the plausibility of the former theory than to convince them of the plausibility of the latter theory.

Consider, as an example of the application of these criteria, the componential theory of analogical reasoning.

The theory does quite well by the completeness criterion: The analogical reasoning process is described from beginning to end. This specification is in terms of rather detailed flow chart models for the six processes described earlier. (Explicit flow charts for various models under the theory are presented in Sternberg, 1977b.) All necessary processes are explicitly stated in the flow chart, and their interrelations shown. Of course, the componential theory does not address all aspects of reasoning by analogy: For example, it does not specify the decision rule by which people choose one response over the other(s). This specification requires supplementation of the componential theory with a theory of response choice (which is, in fact, presented in Sternberg & Gardner, 1983).

The theory is quite *specific* in describing the details of the three attribute-comparison processes (inference, mapping, and application). It is less specific in describing the encoding process.

The theory is quite *general*: It has been shown to apply to items presented in both true–false and forced-choice formats; to apply to items with schematic-picture, verbal, and geometric content; and to apply to subjects of ages ranging from about 7 years to adulthood.

The theory achieves a reasonable degree of *parsimony* by specifying all operations, but assigning separate information-processing components only to psychologically significant operations. The theory thus manages to be complete while retaining parsimony. The major aspects of analogical reasoning are accounted for in the five mandatory components and the one optional one. But the minor aspects are represented in flow charts and, in most cases, are absorbed into the response component, which is estimated as a regression constant (including within it all operations that are constant across analogies of varying difficulties and kinds).

Finally, the *plausibility* of the theory has been tested rather extensively through a series of experimental investigations (Sternberg, 1977a,b; Sternberg & Gardner, 1983; Sternberg & Nigro, 1980; Sternberg & Rifkin, 1979). Methods for testing plausibility of the theory will be described later. But to date, the empirical evidence has been very supportive in suggesting that the theory provides a good account of a variety of data with various experimental paradigms and subjects.

SELECTING ONE OR MORE TASKS FOR ANALYSIS

Tasks can be selected for componential analysis on the basis of their satisfaction of four criteria originally proposed by Sternberg and Tulving (1977) in a different context (see also Sternberg, 1982): quantifiability, reliability, construct validity, and empirical validity.

1. *Quantifiability*. The first criterion, quantifiability, assures the pos-

sibility of the "assignment of numerals to objects or events according to rules" (Stevens, 1951, p. 1). Quantification is rarely a problem in research on intellectual abilities. Occasionally, psychologists are content to use individuals' introspective reports or protocols as their final dependent variable. Such protocols, used in and of themselves, fail the test of quantification. If, however, aspects of the protocols are quantified (e.g., Newell & Simon, 1972) and thus rendered subject to further analysis, these quantifications can be acceptable dependent variables as long as they meet the other criteria.

2. *Reliability.* The second criterion, reliability, measures true-score variation relative to total-score variation. In other words, it measures the extent to which a given set of data is systematic. Reliability must be computed in two different ways, across item types and across subjects. Because the two indices are independent, a high value of one provides no guarantee or even indication of a high value of the other. Each of these types of reliability can be measured in two ways, at a given time or over time.

3. *Construct validity.* The third criterion, construct validity, assures that the task has been chosen on the basis of some psychological theory. The theory thus dictates the choice of tasks, rather than the other way around. A task that is construct-valid is useful for gaining psychological insights through the lens provided by some theory of cognition.

4. *Empirical validity.* The fourth criterion, empirical validity, assures that the task serves the purpose it is supposed to serve. Thus, whereas construct validity guarantees that the selection of a task is motivated by theory, empirical validity tests the extent to which the theory is empirically supportable. Empirical validation is usually performed by correlating task performance with an external criterion.

These four criteria are related to each other in a number of ways. First, they fall into two natural and orthogonal groupings of two criteria each. The first and second criteria are ones of measurement theory; the third and fourth are ones of substantive psychological theory. The first and third criteria are discrete and dichotomous, being either satisfied or not; the second and fourth criteria are continuous, being satisfied in greater or lesser degree. Second, the criteria fall into a natural ordering. The first two criteria, those of measurement theory, are prerequisite for the second two criteria, those of psychological theory: The tasks must satisfy certain measurement properties before their psychological properties can be assessed. Moreover, the criteria are ordered within these groupings as well as between them. The first criterion within each grouping is prerequisite for the second. Reliability presupposes quantification, in that reliability measures the extent to which the measurement obtained by the quantification is consistent. Empirical validity presupposes construct validity, in that empirical validity measures the extent to which the measurements dictated by the theory correspond to that theory.

Consider, as an example of the application of these criteria, performance on the analogical problem type to which my componential theory of analogical reasoning has been applied. Performance on analogies satisfies the four criteria described above. First, performance can be quantified in terms of response latency, error rate, or distribution of responses given among the possible responses that might be given. Second, performance on analogical reasoning tasks can be measured reliably. I have shown reliabilities across items of .97 and .89 for schematic-picture and geometric analogies, respectively (Sternberg, 1977a), and standard psychometric tests, including sections measuring analogical reasoning, typically report reliabilities across subjects in the .80s and .90s. The construct validity of performance on tests of analogical reasoning is unimpeachable: Analogies have served as a major source of theorizing in psychometric, Piagetian, and information-processing investigations of cognition and intelligence. Third, the empirical validity of performance on analogy items has been demonstrated in my own research and that of others: Analogies (along with figural matrix problems) have served as a primary basis for measuring g (general intelligence) because performance on these items has been found to correlate about as highly with a variety of criteria as any other single item type that has been tried (see Sternberg, 1977b, for documentation of these claims).

DECOMPOSING TASK PERFORMANCE

Most tasks, indeed, all the tasks my collaborators and I have investigated, can be decomposed into subtasks, where a subtask is defined in terms of its involvement of a subset of the information-processing components that are involved in the full task. There are a number of reasons for attempting to isolate information-processing components from subtasks rather than from composite tasks. First, it is often possible to isolate information-processing components from subtasks that cannot be isolated from composite tasks. The smaller the number of information-processing components involved in any single subtask, the greater the likelihood that the individual components will be susceptible to isolation. Second, the use of subtasks requires that the investigator specify in which subtask or subtasks each information-processing component is executed and thus requires a tighter, more nearly complete specification of the relationship between task structure and the components that act on that structure. Third, the use of subtasks increases the number of data points to be accounted for and thus helps to guard against the spurious good fit between model and data that can result when the number of parameters to be estimated becomes large relative to the number of data points to be predicted. Fourth, the use of subtasks results in component-free estimates of performance for a series of nested processing intervals. These estimates can be valuable when one wants to test alternative predictions about global stages of information processing. The decomposition of composite tasks into subtasks, then, represents a useful intermediate step in the analysis of the nature of mental abilities. There are a number of different ways of decomposing composite tasks into subtasks. Some of these will be considered below.

The Precueing Method of Task Decomposition

In the method of precueing, the first step in a componential analysis is to form interval scores from the decomposition of the global task into a series of nested subtasks, as was done by Johnson (1960) in his pioneering method of serial analysis. The method yields *interval scores* for each of the nested subtasks. Each interval score is a score on one of the series of subtasks and measures performance on a subset of the information-processing components required by the total task. Each subtask in the series of subtasks requires successively less information processing and, hence, should involve reduced processing time and difficulty. Consider two examples of the use of precueing.

Analogies. An example of the use of precueing can be found in the decomposition of performance in analogical reasoning (Sternberg, 1977a,b). Consider the analogy "FOUR SCORE AND SEVEN YEARS AGO": LINCOLN:: "I'M NOT A CROOK": (a) NIXON, (b) CAPONE. In order to decompose the task, one can eliminate from the subject's information processing successive terms of the analogy. Since the analogy has five terms, up to five subtasks can be formed, although there seems to be no good reason for splitting up the two answer options. Consider, then, four subtasks. In each case, we divided presentation trials into two parts. In the first part, the experimenter presents the subject with some amount of precueing to facilitate solution of the analogy. In the second part, that of primary interest, the experimenter presents the full analogy. Solution of the analogy, however, is assumed to require merely a subset of the full set of components (that is, to be a subtask of the full task), because the experimenter assumes that the individual used the precueing presented in the first part of the trial to reduce his or her processing load in the second part of the trial. Indeed, subjects are encouraged to use the precueing information in order to help their processing in the second part of the trial.

In the description of task decomposition that follows, it will be assumed that the analogies are presented either tachistoscopically or via a computer terminal.

In the first subtask (which is identical to the full task), the subject is presented with a blank field (null precueing) in the first part of the trial. The subject indicates when he or she is ready to proceed, and then the full analogy appears. The subject solves the analogy, and then presses a button indicating response (a) or (b). In the second subtask, the subject still needs to perform most of the task in the second part of the trial. The first part of the trial consists merely of precueing with the first term of the analogy. The subject presses a button to indicate that this term has been processed, and then the whole analogy appears on the screen. The subject solves it, and then indicates his or her response. Note that although the full analogy was presented in the second part of the trial, only the last four terms had to be processed, since the first term had been preprocessed during precueing. The third subtask involves a smaller subset of the task to be performed in the second part of the trial. The first part of the trial consists of presentation of the first two terms of the analogy; the second part consists of full presentation. The fourth subtask involves a very small subset of the full task in the second part of the trial. The first part of the trial consists of presentation of the first three terms of the analogy; the second part consists of a full presentation, but requires processing of only the last two terms.

The task decomposition described above serves to separate components of information processing that would be confounded if only the full task were presented. Suppose only the full task were presented to subjects. Then, according to certain information-processing models of analogical reasoning (described in detail in Sternberg, 1977b) under the general theory, (1) encoding and response would be confounded, since response is constant across all analogy types (five analogy terms always need to be encoded); and (2) inference and application would be confounded, since the relation between the third term and the correct option is always the same as that between the first two terms. But precueing permits disentanglement of components by the selective dropping out of components required for processing. By varying the amount of encoding required for various subtasks, the method of precueing permits separation of encoding from the response constant. By eliminating the inference components from the third and fourth subtasks (while retaining the application component), the method makes it possible to distinguish inference from application. Recall that in these two subtasks the first two terms of the analogy were presented during precueing, so that inference could be completed before the full analogy was presented.

The precueing method obviously assumes additivity across subtasks.

Two methods of testing additivity have been proposed (Sternberg, 1977b).

The first requires testing of interval scores for simplicial structure. This test enables one to determine whether the assumption is justified that subtask (interval) scores requiring less processing are contained in subtask scores requiring more processing. If the scores are indeed additive, they should form a simplex. One tests for simplicial structure by examining the intercorrelation matrix between the complete set of subtask scores, with the scores arranged in order of increasing amounts of information processing required for item solution. If the scores form a simplex, then the intercorrelation matrix for the subtask scores should show a certain property: Correlations near the principal diagonal of a matrix should be high, and they should taper off monotonically as entries move farther away from the principal diagonal. In other words, each successive diagonal of the intercorrelation matrix should show decreasing entries as one moves away from the main diagonal. Because of the overlapping nature of the subtask scores, a second prediction can be made. If each subtask score is predicted from every other subtask score, then only predictor subtask scores immediately adjacent to the predicted score will contribute significant variance to the prediction. The reason for this is that since nonadjacent subtask scores either contain or are contained in adjacent scores, any variance contained in the nonadjacent scores that is not also contained in the adjacent ones should not correlate with the predicted variable. Thus, in predicting one subtask score from all the others, only the adjacent scores (those with one more and one less precue) should have significant regression weights.

The second method involves comparison of parameter estimates for the uncued condition alone with those for all the conditions combined. Ideally, this comparison would be done between subjects (just in case the very use of precueing affects performance even on items receiving only null precueing); in practice, the comparison may end up being within-subject. The parameter estimates should be the same, whether or not precueing was used. The data from three experiments on analogical reasoning showed reasonable conformity to the assumption of additivity. More importantly, even when the assumption of additivity was violated to some degree, the method of precueing proved to be robust, yielding sensible and informative data nevertheless. The method was quite successful in its application to analogy problems. The best model under the theory of analogical reasoning accounted for 92%, 86%, and 80% of the variance in the latency data for experiments using People Piece (schematic-picture), verbal, and geometric analogies.

Linear Syllogisms. The method of precueing has also been applied in two experiments on linear syllogisms, or three-term series problems

(Sternberg, 1980b). In the first experiment, subjects were presented with problems such as "John is taller than Pete. Pete is taller than Bill. Who is tallest? John, Pete, Bill." The order of names was counterbalanced. Trials again were in two parts. In the first part, subjects were shown either a blank field or the two premises of the problem. (A third condition, involving presentation of only the first premise, might have been used, but was not.) In the second part, subjects were shown the whole problem. In each trial, subjects indicated when they were ready to be shown the whole item, and then indicated as their response one of the three terms of the problem. A possible limitation of this manner of presentation is that it seems to force serial-ordered processing, whereas when left to their own devices, subjects might process the problems differently, for example, by reading the question first. A second experiment was therefore done.

In the second experiment, the same type of problem was used, except that the question was presented first: "Who is tallest? John is taller than Pete. Pete is taller than Bill. John Pete Bill." Again, the order of names was counterbalanced. There were three precueing conditions. In the first, a blank field was presented during the first part of the trial. In the second, only the question was presented during the first part of the trial. In the third, the question and the premises were presented during the first part of the trial, so that in the second part of the trial the subjects needed to discover only the ordering of the answer options. The full problem was always presented in the second part of the trial.

The methodology was again quite successful. The best model, my own mixed model (Sternberg, 1980b), accounted for 98% of the variance in the latency data from the first experiment and 97% of the variance in the latency data from the second experiment. In these experiments (unlike the analogy experiments), model fits were substantially lower in the conditions comprising the full problems only: 81% and 74%. Worth noting, however, is that the reliabilities of these subsets of the latency data were only .86 and .82, meaning that even here most of the reliable variance was accounted for. The higher fits of the models to data with precueing resulted from a disentanglement of encoding from response. When only full problems are presented, it is impossible to separate premise encoding time from response time, as both are constant over problem types: There are always two premises and one response. Separation of the encoding component substantially increased the variance in the latency data, and hence the values of R^2.

Other Problem Types. The method of precueing has also been applied in the presentation of classification and series completion problems (Sternberg & Gardner, 1983). In the classification problems, subjects were presented with two groups of two items each and a target item. The subjects had to indicate in which group the target belonged. For example, one group might be (a) ROBIN, SPARROW, and the other, (b) HADDOCK, FLOUNDER. If the target were BLUEJAY, the correct answer would be (a). Precueing was accomplished by presenting either a blank field in the first part of the trial or just the two groups of items without the answer. Further precueing might have been accomplished by presenting just one group of items in the first part of the trial, although this was not done in this particular experiment.

In the series completion problems, subjects were presented with a linear ordering that they had to complete, for example, INFANT, CHILD, ADOLESCENT, (a) ADULT, (b) TEENAGER. Precueing was accomplished by presenting either a blank field or just the first three terms of the item in the first part of the trial. Again, more fine-grained precueing might have been done, but was not.

Precueing in these experiments, as in the analogies and linear syllogisms experiment, was quite successful. Models provided good fits to the latency data for schematic-picture, verbal, and geometric items. Details can be found in Sternberg and Gardner (1983).

Evaluation of Method. The method of precueing has both positive and negative aspects. On the positive side: (1) It permits disentanglement of components that otherwise would be confounded; (2) by so doing, it permits comparison of models that otherwise would be indistinguishable; (3) it increases the number of data points to be modeled, thereby helping to guard against the spurious good fit that can result when relatively large numbers of parameters are estimated for relatively small numbers of observations; (4) it requires that the investigator specify in what interval(s) of processing each mental operation takes place, thereby forcing the investigator to explicate his or her model in considerable detail; and (5) it provides scores for performance in a series of nested processing intervals, rather than merely for the total task. On the negative side: (1) The method requires at least a semblance of additivity across subtasks; (2) it requires the use of tachistoscopic or computer equipment to present each trial; (3) it requires individual testing; and (4) it is not suitable for young children because of its complexity. In the uses to which the method has been put so far, the advantages of precueing have more than offset its limitations.

Method of Partial Tasks

In the method of partial tasks, complete items are presented involving either a full set of hypothesized components or just some subset of these components. The method differs from the method of precueing in that trials are not split into two parts. Decomposition is effected with unitary trials. The partial and full tasks, however, are assumed to be additively related, as in the method of precueing. Consider two examples of the use of this method.

Linear Syllogisms. The method of partial tasks has been used in four experiments on linear syllogisms (Sternberg, 1980a,b). The full task consisted of the standard linear syllogism (three-term series problem) as described earlier. The partial task consists of two-term series problems, for example, "John is taller than Pete. Who is tallest?" (The ungrammatical superlative was used in the question to preserve uniformity with the three-term series problems.) The mixed model of linear syllogistic reasoning specified components processes involved in both the two- and three-term series problems, specifying the processes involved in the former as a subset of the processes involved in the latter. The values of R^2 were .97, .97, and .97 with all items considered, and .84, .88, and .84 with only three-term series problems considered. Note that these values are quite similar to those obtained under the method of precueing. Values of parameters were also remarkably similar, with two exceptions (predicted by the mixed model).

Categorical Syllogisms. The method of partial tasks has also been applied in the investigation of categorical syllogisms (Sternberg & Turner, 1981). The full task was a standard categorical syllogism with premises like "All B are C. Some A are B." The subject was presented with a conclusion, such as "All A are C," and had to indicate whether this conclusion was definitely true, possibly true, or never true of the premises. The partial task involved presentation of only a single premise, such as "Some A are B." The subject again had to decide whether a conclusion, such as "All A are B," was definitely, possibly, or never true of the (in this case, single) premise.

Whereas the primary dependent variable of interest in the previously decribed experiments was solution latency, the primary dependent variable in this experiment was response choice. The preferred model of syllogistic reasoning, the transitive-chain model, accounted for 96% of the variance in the response-choice data from the full task and 96% of the variance in the response-choice data from the partial task. Fits were not computed for the combined data, since in this particular experiment we happened to be interested in the full task as an "encoding plus combination task" and in the partial task as an "encoding only" task. These data indicate not only that the method of partial tasks can be applied successfully to categorical syllogisms, but also that it can be applied to response-choice as well as to latency data.

Evaluation of Method. This method seems to share all the advantages of the method of precueing, but only one of its disadvantages, namely, the assumption of additivity, in this case between the partial and the full task.

The method of partial tasks therefore seems to be the preferred method when one has the option of using either of the two methods. Two additional points need to be considered. First, additivity may be obtained across precueing conditions but not from partial to full tasks, or vice versa. Thus, some amount of pilot testing may be needed to determine which method is more likely to yield additivity across conditions. Second, some tasks are decomposable by either method, but others may be decomposable only by one or the other method. I have found the method of precueing applicable to more tasks than the method of partial tasks, although the differential applicability may be a function of the particular tasks I have investigated. In any case, the decision of which method to use can be made only after a careful consideration of task demands and decomposability. In some cases, the investigator may choose to use both methods [as in Sternberg (1980b)].

Method of Stem-Splitting

The method of stem-splitting involves items requiring the same number of information-processing components, but different numbers of executions of the various components. It combines features of the method of precueing with those of the method of partial tasks.

Analogies. So far, the method has been applied only to verbal analogies. Using the method of stem-splitting, we presented verbal analogies in three different formats (Sternberg & Nigro, 1980):

1. RED: BLOOD:: WHITE: (a) COLOR, (b) SNOW
2. RED: BLOOD:: (a) WHITE: SNOW, (b) BROWN: COLOR
3. RED: (a) BLOOD:: WHITE: SNOW, (b) BRICK:: BROWN: COLOR

The number of answer options was allowed to vary from two to four for individual items. Consider how the different item types involve different numbers of executions of the same components. The first item requires encoding of five terms, inference of one relation, mapping of one relation, application of two relations, and one response. The second item requires encoding of six terms, inference of one relation, mapping to two relations, application of two relations, and one response. The third item requires encoding of seven terms, inference of two relations, mapping of two relations, application of two relations, and one response. (In each case, exhaustive processing of the item is assumed.) Varying the number of answer options also creates further variance in the numbers of operations required.

This method has been used with subjects as young as third-graders and as old as college students. The data from the experiment were quite encouraging, both for the tested theory and the method. Multiple correlations (R) between predicted and observed data points were .85, .88, .89, and .92 for the preferred models in grades 3, 6, 9, and college, respectively.

Evaluation of Method. This method has barely been tried, and so I am not in a position to evaluate it fully. On the positive side: (1) It could be (although it has not yet been) used for group testing in conjunction with booklets of the kind described in the next section; (2) it requires no special equipment to administer items; (3) it is feasible to use with young children; and (4) it seems to create a certain added interest to the problems for the subjects. On the negative side: (1) The success of the method has not yet been adequately tested; (2) the generality of the method to problems other than analogies has not yet been shown; and (3) the method seems more likely than the preceding ones to generate special strategies that are inapplicable to standard (complete) tasks.

Method of Systematically Varied Booklets

In previous methods, the unit of presentation was the single item. In this method, the unit of presentation is the booklet. In previous methods, subjects were given as much time as they needed to complete each individual item. In this method, subjects are given a fixed amount of time to complete as many items as they can within a given booklet. The number of items in the booklet should exceed the number of items that subjects can reasonably be expected to complete in the given time period. The key to the method is that all items in the booklet should be homogeneous with respect to the theory or theories being tested. Although the same items are not repeated, each item serves as a replication with respect to the sources of difficulty specified by the theory, and although items within a given booklet are homogeneous, items are heterogeneous across booklets. In this method, specifications of the items within a booklet are varied in the same way that specifications of single items are varied in the preceding methods.

Analogies. The method of systematically varied booklets has been employed only with two types of schematic-picture analogies (Sternberg & Rifkin, 1979). In the two experiments done so far, the method has been used successfully with subjects as young as second-grades and as old as college students. Subjects at each grade level were given 64 seconds in which to solve the 16 analogies contained in each booklet. Independent variables were numbers of schematic features changed between the first and second analogy terms, first and third analogy terms, and the first and second analogy answer options. Items within a given booklet were identical in each of these respects. Three dependent variables were derived from the raw data. The first was latency for correctly answered items, obtained by dividing 64 by the number of items correctly completed. This measure takes into account both quality and quantity of performance. The second dependent variable was latency for all answered items, obtained by dividing 64 by the number of items completed, whether they were completed correctly or incorrectly. This measure takes into account only quantity of performance. The third dependent variable was error rate, obtained by dividing the number of items answered incorrectly by the number of items answered at all. This measure takes into account only quality of performance.

In a first experiment, model fits (R^2) for the best model were .91, .95, .90, and .94 for latencies of correct responses at grades 2, 4, 6, and college, respectively; they were .87, .94, .93, and .94 for latencies of all responses at each grade level; and they were .26, .86, .52, and .65 for error rates at each level. The fits for errors, although lower than those for the latencies, were almost at the same levels as the reliabilities of each of the sets of data, indicating that only slightly better fits could possibly have been obtained. Model fits in a second experiment were slightly lower than in the first experiment, but so were the reliabilities of the data.

Evaluation of Method. The method of systematically varied booklets has three distinct advantages and two distinct disadvantages. Its advantages are that (1) it is practical even with very young children; (2) it requires no special equipment for test administration; and (3) it is adaptable for group testing. Its disadvantages are that (1) it is not possible to obtain a pure measure of time spent only on items answered correctly (or incorrectly), because times are recorded only for booklets, not for individual items, and (2) the method is not particularly well suited to disentangling components. In some of the models tested, for example, encoding and response and inference and application were confounded.

Method of Complete Tasks (Standard Method of Presentation)

The method of complete tasks is simply the standard method of presenting only the composite item. It is suited to items in which no confoundings of components occur. Consider two examples of the use of the method.

Categorical Syllogisms. The method of complete tasks was used in the presentation of categorical syllogisms (Guyote & Sternberg, 1981). In a first experiment, subjects were presented with syllogistic premises, such as "All B are C. All A are B," plus four conclusions (called A, E, I, and O in the literature on syllogistic reasoning), "All A are C. No A are C. Some A are C. Some A are not C," plus the further conclusion "None of the above." Subjects had to choose the preferred conclusion from among the five. In a second experiment, concrete rather than abstract terms were used. Premises were either factual (No cottages are skyscrapers), counterfactual (No milk cartons are containers), or anomalous (No headphones are planets). In a third experiment, the quantifiers "most" and "few" were used instead of "some." In a fourth experiment, premises were presented in the form "All A are B. X is an A," and subjects were asked simply to judge whether a conclusion such as "X is a B" was valid or invalid. Our transitive-chain model outperformed the other models of response choice to which it was compared, yielding values of R^2 of .97 for abstract content, .91 for concrete factual content, .92 for concrete counterfactual content, .89 for concrete anomalous content, .94 when "most" and "few" were substituted for "some," and .97 for the simpler syllogisms requiring only a valid–invalid judgment. Latency models were also fit to some of the data, with excellent results.

Conditional Syllogisms. The method of complete tasks was also used in testing the transitive-chain model on conditional syllogisms of the form "If A then B. A. Therefore, B." The individual's task was to evaluate the conclusion as either valid or invalid. The model accounted for 95% of the variance in the response-choice data.

Evaluation of Method. The main advantages of this method are that it is the simplest of the methods described and that it does not require any assumptions about additivity across conditions of decomposition. The main disadvantage of the method is that in many, if not most tasks, information-processing components will be confounded. These confoundings can lead to serious consequences, as discussed in Sternberg (1977b). The method is the method of choice only when it is possible to disentagle all component processes of interest.

QUANTIFICATION OF COMPONENTIAL MODEL

Once scores have been obtained for the various subtasks (if any) involved in task performance across conditions, it is necessary to quantify the information-processing model (i.e., the model expressed as a flow chart or in other information-processing terms). The exact method of quantification will depend upon the task being studied and the method used to decompose the task. I will therefore first state some general principles of quantification and then give a single example of a quantification—analogies. Other examples of quantifications can be found in my writings (e.g., Guyote & Sternberg, 1981, for categorical and conditional syllogisms; Schustack & Sternberg, 1981, for causal inferences; Sternberg, 1980b, for linear syllogisms; Tourangeau & Sternberg, 1981, for metaphors).

Generally, quantification is done so as to use multiple regression as a means of predicting a dependent variable from a series of independent variables. The dependent variable will usually be reaction time, error rate, or probability of a given response or response set. Independent variables will usually be the number of times each of a given set of information-processing components is performed. Thus, one predicts latency, error rate, or response probability from number of times each of the operations in the model are performed.

Latency parameters (raw regression weights) represent the durations of the various components. Response time is usually hypothesized to equal the sum of the amount of time spent on each component operation. Hence, a simple linear model can predict response time as the sum across the different component operations of the number of times each component operation is performed (as an independent variable) multiplied by the duration of that component operation (as an estimated parameter).

Proportion of response errors is hypothesized to equal the (appropriately scaled) sum of the difficulties encountered in executing each component operation. A simple linear model predicts proportion of errors to be the sum across the different component operations of the number of times each component operation is performed (as an independent variable) multiplied by the difficulty of that component operation (as an estimated parameter). This additive combination rule is based upon the assumption that each subject has a limit on processing capacity (or space) (cf. Osherson, 1974). Each execution of an operation uses up capacity. Until the limit is exceeded, performance is flawless except for constant sources of error (such as motor confusion, carelessness, momentary distractions). Once the limit is exceeded, however, performance is at a chance level. For a discussion of other kinds of error models, see Mulholland, Pellegrino, and Glaser (1980).

In the response-time models (with solution latency as the dependent variable), all the component operations must contribute significantly to solution latency, since by definition each execution of an operation consumes some amount of time. In the response-error models (error rate as the dependent variable), however, all component operations need not contribute significantly to the proportion of errors. The reason for this is that some operations may be so easy that no matter how many times they are executed, they contribute only trivially to prediction of errors.

An Example of a Quantification: Analogies. In the analogy experiments of Sternberg (1977a,b), mathematical modeling was done by linear multiple regression. Parameters of the model were estimated as unstandardized regression coefficients.

Consider the basic equations for predicting analogy solution times in the Sternberg (1977a,b) experiments described earlier. In these experiments, subjects received precueing with 0, 1, 2, or 3 cues and were then asked to solve the full item as rapidly as possible. The equations shown here are for the simplest model, the so-called Model I, in which all operations are assumed to be executed exhaustively. Other models introduce further degrees of complication, and other publications should be consulted for details of their quantification (Sternberg, 1977a,b; Sternberg & Gardner, 1983).

$$RT_0 = 4a + fx + gy + fz + c$$
$$RT_1 = 3a + fx + gy + fz + c$$
$$RT_2 = 2a + \quad + gy + fz + c$$
$$RT_3 = \quad a + \quad + \quad + fz + c$$

In these equations, RT_i refers to reaction time for a given number of precues, i. Among the parameters, a refers to exhaustive encoding time; x, exhaustive inference time; y, exhaustive mapping time; z, exhaustive application time; and c, constant response time. Among the independent variables, the number of encodings to be done in each condition are given numerically (4, 3, 2, 1); f refers to the number of attributes to be inferred or applied (in the exhaustive model, they are confounded); g, the number of attributes to be mapped.

All parameters of each model enter into analogy processing in the 0-cue condition. The subjects must encode all four terms of the analogy, and perform the inference, mapping, application, and response processes as well. The 1-cue condition differs only slightly. The first term was presented during precueing and is assumed to have been encoded at that time. Hence, the 1-cue condition requires the encoding of just three analogy terms, rather than all four. In the 2-cue condition, the A and B terms of the analogy were precued, and it is assumed that inference occurred during precueing. Hence, the inference parameter (x) drops out, and there is again one less term to encode. In the 3-cue condition, the A and C terms were precued, and hence it is assumed that mapping as well as inference occurred during precueing. The mapping parameter (y) therefore drops out, and there is again one less term to encode. In general, the successive cueing conditions are characterized by the successive dropout of model parameters.

Parameter dropouts also resulted from null transformations in which no changes occurred from A to B and/or from A to C. These dropouts occurred in degenerate analogies (0 A to B and 0 A to C attribute changes) and in semidegenerate analogies (0 A to B or 0 A to C attribute changes, but not both 0). Indeed, these degenerate and semidegenerate analogies were originally included to provide a zero baseline for parameter estimation. For example, in the 0-cue condition, the inference and application parameters drop out when no changes occur from A to B, and the mapping parameter drops out when no changes occur from A to C. The same type of selective dropout occurs in all four cueing conditions.

The models make separate attribute-comparison time or error "charges" only for non-null value transformations. This type of "difference parameter" was used throughout these and other experiments and has been used by many others, as well (e.g., Clark & Chase, 1972). Value identities are not separately charged. Subjects are assumed to be preset to recognize null transformations ("sames"), and the parameter is assumed to represent amount of time or difficulty in alteration of the initial state.

The optional justification parameter was estimated as a function of the product of the distance from the keyed answer option to the ideal option times the number of previous attribute-comparison operations to be checked, both as determined by ratings provided by subjects otherwise uninvolved in the experiments. The idea is that the further the keyed option is from the ideal one, the more likely is checking to be necessary. If the keyed and ideal options are identical, then the value of the justification parameter will be 0, and it will be irrelevant to analogy solution. If, however, not even the best presented option corresponds to the ideal option, then justification is required. This parameter was used only in the forced-choice geometric analogies.

This description does not contain all the details included in the models, nor is it intended to be used to reproduce the data in the experiments. Instead, it is intended to illustrate the kinds of procedures used in the quantification of a particular task.

MODEL TESTING: INTERNAL VALIDATION

Once the model is formulated, it is necessary to test it, either by multiple regression or by other means. Any number of tests may be used. I have found the following tests useful in internally validating a componential model. I will illustrate the tests with examples from a study I did with Bathsheva Rifkin on the development of analogical reasoning processes (Sternberg & Rifkin, 1979), sketching in the example only on the adult data:

R² for Model

This descriptive statistic gives the overall squared correlation between predicted and observed data, and, thus, represents the proportion of variance in the data the model is able to account for. It is a measure of relative goodness of fit. In our analogies experiment, the best model showed an R^2 of .94 in the prediction of solution latencies.

Root Mean Square Deviation for Model

The root-mean-square deviation (RMSD) statistic gives the overall RMSD of observed from predicted data. It is a measure of absolute badness of fit. Because it is an "absolute" measure, its value will be affected by the variance of the observed and predicted data. In the Sternberg–Rifkin experiment, we calculated standard errors of estimate rather than RMSDs. (The two statistics are closely related for linear models.) The standard error of estimate for the latency data was .32 second.

$F_{Regression}$ for Model

This statistic is the basis for deciding whether to reject the null hypothesis of no fit of the model to the data. Higher values are associated with better fits of the model to the data. Because the inferential statistic takes into account the number of parameters in the model, I have found the statistic useful in deciding among alternative models with differing numbers of parameters. The regression F for the preferred model in the Sternberg–Rifkin data was 159.94, which was highly significant in rejecting the null hypothesis of no fit of the model to the data.

$F_{Residual}$ for Model

This statistic is the basis for deciding whether to reject the null hypothesis of no discrepancy between the proposed model and the data. Lower values are associated with better fits of the model to the data. It is important to compute this statistic or an analog, in that a model may account for a large proportion of variance in the data and yet be rejected relative to the "true" model. Unfortunately, the residual F was not calculated in the Sternberg–Rifkin data, although it seems highly likely, given the systematicity of residuals described below, that it would have been statistically significant in rejecting the proposed model relative to the "true" one.

Relative Values of Statistics 1–4 for Alternative Models

It is highly desirable to compare the fit of a given model to alternative models. The fact that a given model fits a set of data very well may merely reflect the ease with which that data set can be fit. In some cases, even relatively implausible models may result in good fits. Testing plausible alternative models guards against fits that are good, but nevertheless trivial. In the Sternberg–Rifkin experiment, we tested three alternative models of information processing (for schematic-picture analogies with separable attributes). The models differed in terms of their specifications regarding which components of information processing (inference and application) are exhaustively executed and which are executed with self-termination. The model that best fit the data, in terms of the combined criteria, was the one that was maximally self-terminating (i.e., both inference and application self-terminating).

$F_{\text{Regression}}$ *for Individual Parameter Estimates*

Significance of the overall regression F does not imply that each parameter contributes significantly to the model. Thus, individual parameters should be tested for significance in order to assure their nontrivial contribution to the model. In the preferred model of analogical reasoning for the Sternberg–Rifkin data, all parameters contributed significantly to the model.

ΔR^2 *for Individual Parameter Estimates*

The ΔR^2 statistic indicates the contribution of each parameter when that parameter is added to all others in the model. When independent variables in the model are intercorrelated, this descriptive statistic gives information different from that obtained in the step above. A parameter may be statistically significant and yet contribute only a very small proportion of variance when added to all the others. These values were not computed in the Sternberg–Rifkin study.

Interpretability of Parameter Estimates

Parameters may pass the two tests described above and, yet, have nonsensical values. The values may be nonsensical because they are negative (for real-time operations!) or because their values, although positive, are wildly implausible. In the Sternberg–Rifkin study, interpretability of parameter estimates was a key basis for distinguishing among models. One model yielded statistically significant *negative* parameter estimates for real-time operations and was disqualified on this basis alone.

Examination of Residuals of Observed from Predicted Data Points

Residuals of observed from predicted data points should be assessed in order to determine the specific places in which the model does and does not predict the data adequately. The residuals will usually be useful later in reformulating the model. In the Sternberg–Rifkin data, examination of residuals revealed a systematic discrepancy between predicted and observed data. Subjects tended to be even more self-terminating than the maximally self-terminating model would allow. This discrepancy suggests that for items with very bad answer options, subjects may be able to short-circuit the full amount of normal processing and to disconfirm a false option on the basis of some kind of preliminary scan (see Sternberg, 1977b).

Substantive Plausibility of the Model

This criterion is a substantive rather than a statistical one. The model may "fit" statistically, and yet make little or no psychological sense. The model should therefore be considered for its substantive plausibility. In the Sternberg–Rifkin data, the model not only made sense psychologically, but also corresponded well to the model people indicated they used when they were asked how they solved the problems.

Heuristic Value of the Model

This criterion is again substantive rather than statistical. One should ask whether the model is at the right level of analysis for the questions being asked, whether it will be useful for the purposes to which it will later be put, and whether it is likely to generalize to other tasks and task domains. I believe that the model of analogical reasoning proposed by Sternberg and Rifkin has had at least some heuristic value, in that my colleagues and I have been able to elaborate upon it in subsequent research (e.g., Sternberg & Gardner, 1983; Sternberg & Ketron, 1982).

Consideration of Model for Individual–Subject as Well as Group-Average Data

The analyses described above can be applied to both group-average and individual data. It is important to test the proposed model on individual-subject as well as group-average data. There are at least two reasons for this. First, averaging of data can occasionally generate artifacts whereby the fit of the model to the group data does not accurately reflect its fit to individual subjects. Second, there may be individual differences in strategies used by subjects that can be discerned only through individual-subject model fitting. One wishes to know what individual subjects do, as well as what subjects do "on the average." I have found in at least several cases that what individual subjects do does not correspond in every case to the strategy indicated by the best group-average model (e.g., Sternberg & Ketron, 1982; Sternberg & Weil, 1980). In the Sternberg–Rifkin experiment, the preferred model fit individual data well: The mean R^2 for individual subjects was .78, a respectable fit when one considers that model fitting was done on the basis of just one observation per data point.

MODEL TESTING: EXTERNAL VALIDATION

External validation requires testing the parameters of the proposed model against external criteria. Such validation actually serves at least two distinct purposes.

First, it provides an additional source of verification for the model. Often, one will make differential predictions regarding correlations of individual parameter estimates with external criteria. The external validation can serve to test these predictions and, thus, the validity of the model. Consider, for example, my research on linear syllogisms. Some of the components in the mixed model were predicted to operate upon a linguistic representation for information, and others to operate upon a spatial representation for information (Sternberg, 1980b). It was important to show that the parameters theorized to operate upon a linguistic representation showed higher correlations with verbal than with spatial ability tests; similarly, it was important to show that the parameters theorized to operate upon a spatial representation showed higher correlations with spatial than with verbal ability tests. These predicted patterns were generally confirmed.

Second, it provides a test of generality for the proposed model. If interesting external criteria cannot be found that show significant and substantial correlations with the individual parameter estimates for the proposed model, then it is unclear that the model, or perhaps the task, is of much interest. For example, for parameters of analogical reasoning to be of theoretical interest, they should be shown to correlate with scores on a variety of inductive reasoning tests, but not with scores on perceptual-speed tests. This differential pattern of correlations was, in fact, shown (Sternberg, 1977b).

The above examples may serve to point out that two kinds of external validation must be performed. The first, convergent validation, assures that parameters do, in fact, correlate with external measures with which they are supposed to correlate; the second, discriminant validation, assures that parameters do not, in fact, correlate with external measures with which they are not supposed to correlate, but with which they might be plausibly correlated according to alternative theories. Some investigators have performed convergent, but not discriminant validation (e.g., Shaver, Pierson, & Lang, 1974), with what seem to be auspicious results. The problem, though, is that obtained correlations may result from the general factor in intellectual performance, rather than the particular operations specified as of interest in the theory. Thus, convergent validation without discriminant validation is usually of little use.

Although I have emphasized correlations of parameters with external measures, it is an unfortunate fact of life that oftentimes parameter estimates for individual subjects will not be as reliable as one would like. In these cases, and even in cases where the estimates are fairly reliable, it is desirable to correlate total task scores as well as subtask scores with the external measures. Although such correlations may reflect various mixtures of operations in the tasks and subtasks, they are likely to be more stable than the correlations obtained for the parameter estimates, simply because of the higher reliability of the composite scores and because of the fact that obtaining correlations for these scores does not depend on the correctness of one's theory, as it does for component scores.

The value of external validation for theory testing can be seen, in different ways, in my work on analogical reasoning as well as in my work on linear syllogistic reasoning.

In the former work, initial correlations between parameter estimates and standardized tests of inductive reasoning abilities yielded a curious pattern. Although the attribute-comparison components—inference, mapping, and application—showed relationships with the mental test scores, the highest relationship emerged from the response constant component! Thus, the internal validation procedures showed that the proposed quantified model was doing an excellent job in accounting for the latency data; the external validation procedures, however, showed that some very important ingredient in analogical reasoning, at least in terms of its relationship to intelligence, was being relegated to the least interesting component. It was this finding that led to the development, in my theorizing, of the notion of metacomponents, or executive control processes that, although "constant" over standard experimental manipulations of the analogies, nevertheless are key elements in intellectual performance. Thus, the external validation served the purpose of showing an aspect of the theory that was in need of review. Internal validation—the kind used exclusively by many cognitive psychologists—was insufficient to show this need.

In the latter work, my theory of linear syllogistic reasoning made explicit predictions regarding which components of information processing should correlate with verbal ability tests and which should correlate with spatial ability tests. Although internal validation can address the question of whether a given component contributes to real-time latency or to the commission of errors, it cannot really address the question of whether a given component operates upon one kind of representation or another. Latencies and error rates are simply nondefinitive in indicating forms of representation used. But correlating individual-subject component scores with verbal and spatial ability tests revealed essentially the pattern of convergent and discriminant validation predicted by the theory. With one exception, components theorized to operate upon a linguistic representation correlated with verbal, but not spatial tests; components theorized to operate upon a spatial representation correlated with spatial, but not verbal tests. Thus, additional validation of the theory was possible beyond that which could be obtained merely from internal validation procedures.

REFORMATION OF THE COMPONENTIAL MODEL

In practice, most first-pass (and even subsequent) models, whether componential or otherwise, are not correctly formulated. It will often be necessary to reformulate one's model on the basis of a given data set and then to cross-validate the revised model on subsequent sets of data. It is worth underscoring that cross-validation is essential. With enough fiddling, almost any data set can be fit by some model. What is hard is showing that the model fits data sets other than the set that was used in its formulation. The steps described above provide a wealth of data to use in revising one's model. The investigator should use the data to best advantage in reformulating the model. Once the reformulation is complete, the model is ready to be tested again on new data.

In the analogies work, for example, my original fits of model to data were only mediocre, with values of R^2 in the .50s. Clearly, something was either wrong with or missing from the model. An investigation of residuals revealed that the model was incomplete: Certain kinds of analogies—in particular, those with either identical A and B terms or identical A and C terms (or both), and also those with extremely inadequate incorrect response options—could be processed more quickly than was predicted by the theory. It appeared that subjects were using dual processing, whereby they would process a given analogy both holistically and analytically, at the same time. If the holistic processing yielded an answer, then analytical processing was terminated, and a response was emitted. Thus, the holistic processing essentially bypassed the detailed attribute-by-attribute comparison needed for the analytical processing. This dual-processing theory (Sternberg, 1977b), when it replaced the uni-processing theory, raised the value of R^2 by close to .3 and replicated in subsequent experiments beyond the first. In this and other instances (as noted above), the componential procedures proved useful for reformulation of the theory so as to better account for subject performance.

GENERALIZATION OF COMPONENTIAL MODEL

Once a given task has been adequately unaerstood in componential terms, it is important to show that the proposed model is not task-specific. If the model is, in fact, task-specific, then it is unlikely to be of much psychological interest. My own strategy has been to extend componential models from a single task, task format, and task content first to multiple task formats and contents, and later to other tasks. For example, the componential model of analogical reasoning was originally tested on true–false People Piece analogies, then extended to true–false verbal analogies, then extended to forced-choice geometric analogies, and finally generalized to other tasks, including classifications and series completions, both of which were theorized to involve the same inductive components as are required for analogical reasoning (and for each other). This process of generalization is needed in order to establish the priority of the information-processing theory, rather than of the task analysis, *per se*. Inevitably, one can start with only the analysis of one or a small number of tasks. But eventually, one must extend one's analysis to multiple tasks, with the choice of tasks being guided by the theory that generated the first task that was studied.

In my analogies work, for example, a criticism that was sometimes made after publication of the initial work (Sternberg, 1977a,b) was that the theory was one of analogical reasoning, but not clearly one of anything else. Although I claimed in my 1977 book that the theory could be extended to other kinds of induction items, it was not until this extension was made (Sternberg & Gardner, 1983) that I could claim that the theory truly showed some generality as an account of how individuals solve the kinds of induction problems most frequently used to measure general intelligence (namely, analogies, series completions, and classifications).

INDIVIDUAL AND GROUP DIFFERENCES IN STRATEGY

An important use of componential analysis is in the analysis of strategies differences in performance between groups and between individuals. For example, a large literature has evolved around the question of the strategy subjects use in solving linear syllogism problems. It turns out, however, that there are substantial individual differences in the strategies subjects use for solving these problems (Sternberg & Weil, 1980). Most subjects use a mixture of linguistic and spatial processes; but some use primarily a linguistic strategy, others primarily a spatial strategy, and still others primarily an algorithmic short-cut strategy. Attempting to find one model that best fits the group data can be a meaningless task because of the individual differences in strategy subjects spontaneously adopt. Similarly, in analogical reasoning, most but not all subjects spontaneously adopt a primarily self-terminating strategy (Sternberg & Ketron, 1982). It is important to consider the strategy of the individual as well as his or her component values: Poorer analogical reasoning may be due to a nonoptimal strategy rather than an inefficient execution of components.

The above kind of logic serves as the basis for understanding certain puzzling results in the abilities literature. One result is the seeming difficulty of obtaining aptitude–treatment interactions in educational and psychological research. A possible reason for this difficulty is the assumption of most investigators that instructed subjects adopt the strategy in which they are instructed. Using this assumption, experimenters sort subjects into groups on the basis of the instructional manipulation they receive. But the two studies cited above (Sternberg & Ketron, 1982, and Sternberg & Weil, 1980) indicate that subjects often do not use the strategy they are instructed to use. If they believe that they have an efficient strategy that is different from the instructed one, they may well decide to use that strategy. In such cases, componential analysis of individual-subject strategies is essential for re-sorting subjects into groups representing their true strategies. Indeed, in the Sternberg and Weil study, no pattern of aptitude–treatment interaction was obtained for the instructed groups. It was only after subjects were re-sorted into their true strategy groups—on the basis of componential modeling of individual subject data—that a strong aptitude–treatment interaction was obtained.

Another kind of finding that bears scrupulous examination is that of group differences obtained between members of different cultures or even subcultures. Differences in global scores may, of course, reflect less efficient componential execution of a given strategy. But they may also indicate differences in strategies that result in different patterns as well as levels of scores. Even if the strategies of the various groups are the same, at the very least, it may be possible to localize those components in which the groups show differences and those components in which they do not.

A potential future use of componential analysis is in studies of the heritability of intelligence. Past work has emphasized heritability of overall scores on intelligence and specific ability tests. Occasionally, the work has looked at factors of intelligence as well. But it is possible that a more interesting level of analysis would be the component process. For example, in a reasoning test, it is possible to decompose overall performance into components of encoding, comparison (e.g., inference, mapping, application), and response. Patterns of heritability on each of these kinds of components would probably be somewhat more interesting than patterns of heritability for the different kinds of components considered together.

CONCLUSIONS

I have described in this chapter a set of procedures—collectively referred to as componential analysis—that can be used in the formulation and testing of theories of cognitive processing. A componential analysis generally involves decomposition of a task into subtasks and then the internal and external validation of one or more componential models of task performance.

Several advantages accrue to the decomposition of a global task into subtasks. Scores from subtasks (1) allow separation of components that otherwise would have been confounded, (2) enable comparison of models that otherwise would have been indistinguishable, (3) increase degrees of freedom for the residual in prediction, (4) require precise specification of the temporal ordering and location of components, (5) prevent distortion of results from external validation, and (6) provide component-free estimates of performance for nested processing intervals.

Further advantages accrue from the use of component scores representing subjects' performance on each of the information-processing components used in task performance. Component scores (1) are estimated by inferentially powerful componential models, (2) interpret performance in terms of mental processes, (3) pinpoint individual sources of particular strength and weakness for diagnosis and training, and (4) can derive estimates of measurement error from data for individual subjects.

Finally, the use of reference ability scores that are correlated with subtask and component scores (1) allows identification of correlates of individual differences in performance for each component, (2) prevents overvaluation of task-specific components, and (3) potentially provides for both convergent and discriminant validation of a componential model.

In sum, then, componential procedures have been shown to be applicable to a large number of cognitive domains and have shown themselves to be valuable in understanding human cognitive performance. But I by no means claim that componential analysis is suitable for all kinds of analyses of cognitive skills. The methodology is not appropriate when parallel processing is used to any great extent, and it is also not appropriate where problems are of such great complexity that quantitative modeling simply becomes impractical, and other kinds of modeling, such as computer modeling, become more appropriate. Moreover, there exist some tasks that, although not apparently highly complex, resist the kinds of methods described here. For example, we have found that classical insight problems of the kinds used by Gestalt psychologists are resistant to straightforward componential task decomposition. Perhaps if we had a better grasp of what insight is and how it occurs, we would be in a better position to study such problems componentially, but for the time being, we have found other methods of study superior for understanding performance on these very ill-structured kinds of problems. Thus, although componential analysis is useful for the analysis of many kinds of cognitive skills, it is clearly not useful for the analysis of all kinds of cognitive skills, and the investigator will have to decide whether the methodology can be tailored so as to be suitable for a given use. In the past, many methodologies have been extended beyond the task domains in which they tend to be most successful (e.g., factor analysis, multidimensional scaling, hierarchical clustering), and I have no desire to see this overextension happen with componential analysis. I believe the methodology has shown itself to be useful in a wide variety of domains and expect that the methodology will continue to be extended (but, I hope, not overextended) to new domains.

One final caveat is in order regarding the application of componential analysis. Methodologies are often originally used in the service of theory formulation and testing, but later on they can acquire a life of their own. It becomes too easy to generate research using a methodology that is not particularly well motivated theoretically. The methodology then acquires a bad name. This happened to factor analysis, and I believe it has happened more recently to multidimensional scaling. It is important to emphasize in closing, therefore, that componential analysis, like other methodologies, is not better than the uses to which is is applied. Methods cannot be judged independently of their uses. If it is well used, I believe it will continue to provide investigators with substantial rewards. If it is ill used, it will not. No method can salvage poor ideas. Hence, one would hope that the methodology will be used in ways that will reap maximal rewards for psychological theory and practice. In any case, the methodology should be subservient to, not a substitute for, good ideas.

REFERENCES

Burt, C. *The factors of the mind*. London: University of London Press, 1940.

Carroll, J. B. Ability and task difficulty in cognitive psychology. *Educational Researcher*, 1981, *10*, 11–21.

Clark, H. H., & Chase, W. On the process of comparing sentences against pictures. *Cognitive Psychology*, 1972, *3*, 472–517.

Cronbach, L. J. The two disciplines of scientific psychology. *American Psychologist*, 1957, *12*, 671–684.

Eysenck, H. J. Intelligence assessment: A theoretical and experimental approach. *British Journal of Educational Psychology*, 1967, *37*, 81–98.

Guilford, J. P. *The nature of human intelligence*. New York: McGraw-Hill, 1967.

Guyote, M. J., & Sternberg, R. J. A transitive-chain theory of syllogistic reasoning. *Cognitive Psychology*, 1981, *13*, 461–525.

Humphreys, L. G. The organization of human abilities. *American Psychologist*, 1962, *17*, 475–483.

Johnson, D. M. Serial analysis of thinking. In *Annals of the New York Academy of Science* (Vol. 91). New York: New York Academy of Sciences, 1960.

Mulholland T., Pellegrino, J., & Glaser, R. Components of geometric analogy solution. *Cognitive Psychology*, 1980, *12*, 252–284.

Newell, A., & Simon, H. A. *Human problem solving*. Englewood Cliffs, N.J.: Prentice-Hall, 1972.

Osherson, D. N. *Logical abilities in children. Logical inference: Underlying operations* (Vol. 2). Potomac, Md.: Laurence Erlbaum Associates, 1974.

Schustack, M. W., & Sternberg, R. J. Evaluation of evidence in causal inference. *Journal of Experimental Psychology: General*, 1981, *110*, 101–120.

Shaver, P., Pierson, L., & Lang, S. Converging evidence for the functional significance of imagery in problem solving. *Cognition*, 1974, *3*, 359–375.

Sternberg, R. J. Component processes in analogical reasoning. *Psychological Review*, 1977a, *84*, 353–378.

Sternberg, R. J. *Intelligence, information processing, and analogical reasoning: The componential analysis of human abilities*. Hillsdale, N.J.: Lawrence Erlbaum Associates, 1977b.

Sternberg, R. J. The development of linear syllogistic reasoning. *Journal of Experimental Child Psychology*, 1980a, *29*, 340–356.

Sternberg, R. J. A proposed resolution of curious conflicts in the literature on linear syllogisms. In R. Nickerson (Ed.), *Attention and performance VIII*. Hillsdale, N.J.: Lawrence Erlbaum Associates, 1980b.

Sternberg, R. J. Sketch of a componential theory of human intelligence. *Behavioral and Brain Sciences*, 1980c, *3*, 573–584.

Sternberg, R. J. Reasoning, problem solving, and intelligence. In R. J. Sternberg (Ed.), *Handbook of human intelligence*. New York: Cambridge University Press, 1982.

Sternberg, R. J., & Gardner, M. K. Unities in inductive reasoning. *Journal of Experimental Psychology: General*, 1983, *112*, 80–116.

Sternberg, R. J., & Ketron, J. L. Selection and implementation of strategies in reasoning by analogy. *Journal of Educational Psychology*, 1982, *74*, 399–413.

Sternberg, R. J., & Nigro, G. Developmental patterns in the solution of verbal analogies. *Child Development*, 1980, *51*, 27–38.

Sternberg, R. J., & Rifkin, B. The development of analogical reasoning processes. *Journal of Experimental Child Psychology*, 1979, *27*, 195–232.

Sternberg, R. J., & Tulving, E. The measurement of subjective organization in free recall. *Psychological Bulletin*, 1977, *84*, 353–378.

Sternberg, R. J., & Turner, M. E. Components of syllogistic reasoning. *Acta Psychologica*, 1981, *47*, 245–265.

Sternberg, R. J., & Weil, E. M. An aptitude–strategy interaction in linear syllogistic reasoning. *Journal of Educational Psychology*, 1980, *72*, 226–234.

Stevens, S. S. Mathematics, measurement and psychophysics. In S. S. Stevens (Ed.), *Handbook of experimental psychology*. New York: Wiley, 1951.

Thurstone, L. L. *Multiple factor analysis*. Chicago: University of Chicago Press, 1947.

Tourangeau, R., & Sternberg, R. J. Aptness in metaphor. *Cognitive Psychology*, 1981, *13*, 27–55.

Vernon, P. E. *The structure of human abilities*. London: Methuen, 1971.

6

New Directions in Aptitude–
Treatment Interaction Research

Concepts and Methods

BEEMAN N. PHILLIPS

This chapter contains two messages. One message is methodological and conceptual. Aptitude–treatment interaction (ATI) research strategies must be powerful enough to forge generalizations about instruction. In the future, more treatments should involve learning through instruction rather than learning through practice, be longer in duration, and be more realistic, educationally. The other message is substantive. Aptitude–treatment interactions exist and can be practically important. In addition to being directly useful in instruction, ATI effects can suggest mechanisms in learning from instruction that can be the basis of a framework for learning-from-instruction theory.

The sections that follow address several topics. The first section covers a few key ideas about the status of ATI research and draws attention to the complexity of the ATI concept. The second section reviews the relationship between psychology and education and emphasizes that education has been on the periphery of ATI research. The third section concentrates on the need for new directions, examines conceptual and methodological problems, and reviews suggestions for improvement in ATI research. The fourth section reflects on how ATI effects can be taken into account in educational practice.

RESEARCH STATUS

The basis for an aptitude-matching strategy in instruction is the demonstration of aptitude–treatment interaction. That is, research is needed

BEEMAN N. PHILLIPS ● Department of Educational Psychology, University of Texas, Austin, Texas 78712.

to show that particular individuals with a particular aptitude profile do better under one instructional treatment than another. Extensive reviews of the research literature and the problems encountered have been reported by Berliner and Cahen (1973), Cronbach and Snow (1977), and Snow (1976). They report that most research has been limited to differentiating samples in terms of test scores and then applying grossly defined instructional interventions to these subsamples. The result is that only the most general conclusions can be drawn about how to match aptitude to instructional strategies.

ANXIETY–INSTRUCTIONAL INTERVENTION INTERACTION: AN EXEMPLAR OF TRADITIONAL STUDIES OF APTITUDE–TREATMENT INTERACTION

Research on anxiety and instruction exemplifies the status, problems, and future directions of ATI research. The amount of research linking anxiety to the ability of students to benefit from instruction is substantial (Cronbach & Snow, 1977; Tobias, 1976, 1977a, 1980). In general, high anxiety interferes with learning in a wide variety of settings, and it seems likely that instructional adaptations or anxiety-reduction programs can significantly modify such negative outcomes.

As a case in point, highly anxious subjects tend to do less well on intellectual tasks. Utilizing treatments that include aids, for example, memory aids in problem-solving tasks, tends to minimize the debilitating effects of anxiety. The Gross and Matenbrook (1980) study is an example of such a treatment. They found that high state-anxious subjects are impaired in problem-solving when memory aids are not present. Their performance was, in fact, significantly improved with aids, so that performance was comparable to that of middle and low state-anxious subjects. They further interpreted their findings as emphasizing the use of memory support systems rather than training in the use of rules and efficient problem-solving strategies. Such rules and strategies apparently are available to such subjects and can be used with the help of memory support systems.

A further example of the interactive role of memory support systems in instructional intervention is provided by Corno (1980). The rationale for her study is that one aim of ATI research is to find ways to help children to adapt to different instructional interventions. This can be done by adapting instruction to the learner. In this study, however, the complex character of the classroom environment was taken into account, and data analyses were carried out at both the class and the individual level.

The focus in the instructional intervention utilized was on teacher structuring and participation demands, an adoption of a teaching strategies treatment earlier used by Peterson (1977). This learning skills program (LSP) included such structuring strategies as reviewing, stating goals, summarizing, and making important points and participation activities such as encouraging students in asking questions, volunteering, answering when called upon, and talking about lesson material in class (Corno, 1980, p. 279).

The pattern of results was complex, with students and classes receiving the LSP treatment outperforming the controls. But only class-level interactions were significant, with classes of at least average ability and high anxiety groups profiting from the treatment. In contrast, low ability, low anxiety classes did better *without* the LSP experience. The role of the LSP as an instructional intervention in this study illustrates the further important point that an intervention itself may place demands on subjects that some of them cannot meet. In this particular case, the LSP has a strongly verbal emphasis so that students who did not have the necessary verbal fluency were hampered in utilizing the treatment offered.

Program implementation efforts in this study also illustrate the problems of naturalistically oriented ATI research. Student attrition was a problem, reflecting, in part, variations in teacher support of the program. The degree of teacher support, which went so far in some cases as to include teachers discussing the LSP excercises in class and substituting them for homeroom, covaried with the percentage of students completing all the LSP exercises. Thus, teacher support became an additional variable that entered indirectly into some of the intervention effects, although such interaction effects were separable from those described earlier.

To put the problem of ATI research in perspective, studies of the interaction of anxiety and instructional methods have been plagued by conceptual ambiguities and methodological problems so that the interaction findings were not consistent (Cronbach & Snow, 1977; Tobias, 1977a). One source of such interaction is presumed to be the differential influence of instructional methods on learning processes required by those instructional methods utilized, or how anxiety specifically influences those processes.

To clarify what might be happening, Tobias (1977b, 1979) has developed a research model using information-processing theory to explain how aspects of anxiety might relate to aspects of instruction. He reviews the research from the perspective of hypotheses that can be generated from the model and reports that the results were generally consistent with the predictions.

In addition to adapting instructional methods to individuals, so that the interference of anxiety is minimized, an alternative approach is to reduce anxiety itself. The outcomes of anxiety-reduction programs have been very favorable in terms of reductions of self-reported anxiety (Allen, Elias, & Zlotlow, 1980; Denny, 1980). However, such programs have had considerably less impact on performance, that is, reductions in self-reported anxiety are not usually accompanied by improvement in tests and other forms of scholastic performance. This lack of improvement may be due to a number of factors, of course, including deficiencies in conceptualizations that postulate anxiety as a cause of inferior performance, when the relationship probably is bidirectional in a causal sense. It is also possible that there are problems in the treatment programs, such as inadequate implementation of the program as intended or failure to teach for transfer to performance in real-life situations. In addition, there is the possibility that treatment approaches are not maximally compatible with the background and other relevant characteristics of individuals with high anxiety. In essence, there probably is no one anxiety-reduction program that is maximally effective for all types of anxious individuals.

REASONS FOR THE LACK OF APTITUDE–TREATMENT INTERACTIONS

According to Cronbach and Snow (1977), few reliable and replicable ATIs have been demonstrated. One reason may be that the phenomena simply do not exist in large numbers. From a general psychological perspective, however, this does not seem likely.

Another possibility is that research has been methodologically inadequate. Cronbach and Snow (1977) examine this proposition at great length and make a convincing case that, in much ATI research, the methodologies used were deficient in a number of respects, and often the presence of interaction could not be fully determined.

A third consideration is that inadequate psychological theories have been utilized to conceptualize ATI. Along with this, experimental manipulations developed as interventions have been theoretically weak, and conceptualizations have frequently been developed in ways not likely to tap intrinsic possibilities for interaction.

APTITUDE–TREATMENT INTERACTION VERSUS TREATMENT–APTITUDE INTERACTION

Research in the area of ATI may be suffering from a misplaced emphasis on aptitudes. Turning to the area of personality research, Mischel and others have argued that personality traits seem to have little consistency over time and place. Although others have challenged this position, even if personality traits are consistent and persistent, they appear to control little of the variation in behavior when compared to situational variables. The conclusion some would draw from this is that since so much of the total variance in behavior is unexplained, it is more promising to study situational factors.

When one moves to interaction effects, the question posed is whether one should use personality variables as moderator variables that increase the "best fit" of situation to behavior relationships. Of course, if one accepts Mischel's view of personality traits, this secondary role for personality variables seems justified and necessary.

We have an analogous situation in ATI conceptualization and research, except that it is more ambiguous. Although aptitudes are construed as moderators of instruction to outcome relationships, they are at the same time assigned a primary, rather than a secondary, role in ATI studies. They have received more attention, theoretical concern, and so forth, than instructional variables. Although there seems to be an emphasis on aptitudes, it is not known if aptitude variables control a major, or minor, percentage of the interaction variance when compared to instructional variables. However, the central focus of the ATI concept is adaptation of instruction to individuals, and this implies that instructional variables control a major percentage of the interaction variance. If this is true, the field would be better served by more theoretical and methodological emphasis on instructional variables than has occurred in the past.

THE NEED FOR FURTHER RAPPROCHEMENT BETWEEN PSYCHOLOGY AND EDUCATION

In a recent article, Glaser (1982) traces the history of relations between psychology and education. From the close affinity of the early 1900s that was achieved through the efforts of such men as E. L. Thorndike and J. Dewey, psychology and education moved into a period of estrangement between World War I and World War II. This was followed by a rejuvenation of the partnership in the 1950s and 1960s under the aegis of a developing instructional psychology.

A major distinction crucial to this development is one made by Bruner (1964) between descriptive theories of learning and prescriptive theories of learning. In the process, the boundaries between basic and applied research have been blurred, and a study of the educational process has led to an interactive network involving behavioral scientists and educational researchers. Cognitive psychology oriented toward understanding the complexity of reading processes, mathematical skills, and intelligence and aptitudes measured through tests has been a dominant force in these developments, and new concepts and measures of these aspects of human performance will be valuable in planning instructional interventions and guiding learning.

LACK OF A SCIENTIFIC BASIS FOR UNDERSTANDING COMPLEX SCHOOL-RELATED SKILLS

However, educators, psychologists, and other behavioral scientists still do not have a clear idea of what abilities are necessary for skilled performance in reading, writing, and mathematics or how those abilities and school-related skills can best be taught. Nonetheless, some progress is being made. For example, provocative ideas are emerging in the study of oral communication (Dickson, 1981), writing (Gregg & Steinberg, 1980), reading (Lesgold & Perfetti, 1981; Spiro, Bruce, & Brewer, 1980), and mathematics (Resnick & Ford, 1981) that may lead to a systematic and scientific basis for understanding these skills. But among the general points to be learned from such scientific reports, one is that reading and mathematics, and so forth, are more complex processes than we realize, and we really still know little about how such skills develop. Further, there is little published to serve as a basis for designing instructional strategies or to be useful in teaching.

As an example of this latter point, the book edited by Loch'head and Clement (1979) is specifically intended for teachers as well as researchers. It contains both a research and a teaching section, with the latter emphasizing prescription and instruction. One of the premises of teaching is that one can specify what ought to be taught. In this case, however, there is great disagreement among the contributors on what problem-solving strategies ought to be taught. One source of disagreement was in whether the skills should be "general" or "specific" to particular subject matter areas. Regarding instruction, overviews of a number of instructional programs are provided, but there is little evidence of their effectiveness.

NEED FOR PRESCRIPTIVE THEORIES OF LEARNING

The rapprochement between psychology and education has led to a parallel interest in and a growing body of research on teaching behaviors and class-room practices (Brophy, 1979). Initially, studies designed to evaluate curriculum and other innovations in the classroom often did not provide detailed information on the differences between more and less effective classroom processes or relate the results obtained to systematically developed models of classroom instruction. More recent efforts, however, have begun to uncover important dimensions of classroom instruction and have the potential for the development of prescriptive theories of learning as envisioned earlier by Bruner (1964).

Recently, Resnick (1981) outlined five components of a prescriptive theory of learning or the conditions necessary to guide the process of teaching as well as to describe the process of learning. Paraphrasing Resnick (p. 692), these components are

1. a description of the state of knowledge to be achieved;
2. a description of the initial state in which the learner begins;
3. a specification of actions which can be taken to transform the initial state;
4. an assessment of specific instructional effects;
5. an evaluation of generalized learning outcomes.

The emphasis of research up to now has been on components 1 and 2, with few studies of direct instructional interventions as required in 3. But the necessary concepts and tools are at hand, at least in theory, to describe in greater detail the processes involved in learning under various instructional conditions and to assess specific and general outcomes. With these components, it also is possible to obtain knowledge that would guide more systematic investigation of ATIs.

New prescriptive theories, however, cannot continue to regard the individual as an independent learner and ignore the school learning situation. Prescriptive theories need to be developed in terms of both the individual and the situation, and interactions at the class as well as the individual level must be recognized.

More Focus on a Broader Spectrum of Educational Outcomes

Aptitude–treatment interaction research also has traditionally focused on achievement outcomes, although other educational outcomes are also important, in their own right, and may mediate, more traditional, achievement-oriented educational outcomes. Examples of such variables include satisfaction with school (Epstein & McPartland, 1976), school motivation (Maehr, 1976), and teacher grades and student absenteeism (Moos & Moos, 1978).

These latter variables, that is, teacher grades and student absenteeism, are examples of some of the difficulties we have in determining educational outcome measures. In the Moos and Moos (1978) study of classroom social climate, teachers gave higher average grades in classes students perceived as high in involvement, affiliation, and teacher support. In contrast, lower teacher grades and higher student absenteeism were associated with classrooms perceived as higher in teacher control, rules clarity, and competition.

Such findings raise considerations relevant to choice of educational outcome. Research suggests that classrooms that are intellectually challenging encourage academic achievement. Although children learn more in classrooms that emphasize competition and difficulty, this apparently is at a greater personal cost to some children who experience increased anxiety, tension, and failure. In essence, cognitive outcomes are different from, and sometimes contradictory to, affective outcomes. Therefore, multiple or different educational outcome criteria can be expected to have a different and sometimes opposite impact on aptitude–treatment relations.

An example of such differences is found in ATI research in which achievement and satisfaction are both considered. Clark (1982) recently reviewed ATI studies that included both outcomes. He points out that although students are generally more satisfied with instructional methods from which they learn more, there are many exceptions. Correlations between enjoyment and achievement range from −.80 to .75, and such variations occur most often where there is some student choice of instruction method. Clark further examined a selected number of ATI studies and classified the instructional methods used according to their information-processing demand. In general, he found that high ability students learned more from methods having a high information-processing load and low ability students learned better from a low information-processing load. In contrast, high ability students typically prefer, and report that they enjoy, low load instructional methods more. Conversely, low ability students prefer and like higher load instructional methods from which they learn less. Clark offers an explanation for this discrepancy, but acknowledges that more research is needed. Other factors also may contribute to negative and positive relationships between enjoyment and achievement, and the apparent incompatibility of some educational outcomes indicates the importance of outcome considerations and the role of student perceptions in ATI studies.

Toward a Taxonomy of Student Performance in School Subjects

The progression of cognitive complexity in school academic tasks should be described more systematically to be useful in ATI research and in the application of ATI generalizations to schooling. Biggs and Collis (1982) present the rationale for a taxonomy that categorizes student learning into levels of "learning quality," and the reliability of category assignments is promising. The five levels of their structure of observed learning outcome (SOLO) are prestructural, unistructural, multi-structural, relational, and extended abstract. Each of these levels can be characterized in terms of capacity, type of relating operation, and consistency and closure. They also attempt to relate SOLO categories to developmental stages, using Piaget stages of cognitive development as guidelines.

The value of systems like SOLO in ATI research is that they help to deal with the problem of sequencing increasingly complex ideas in designing instructional interventions for different subjects. Such systems also might be useful in developing instruments to assess achievement in ways that relate more closely to the objectives of teaching.

TEACHER BEHAVIOR AND ITS EFFECTS

A review of research on teacher behavior and its effects bring out important features that have implications for future ATI research. First, as Brophy (1979) has pointed out, most of the variables studied have been "educational" rather than "psychological." Second, most such research has been empirical rather than systematically theoretical. Third, most such research has not included systematic measurement of classroom processes, although a substantial amount of data has been collected.

In addition, research on teacher behavior and its effects has concentrated on basic cognitive skills instruction in the early elementary grades in schools serving primarily low socioeconomic status populations (Brophy, 1979). This limits generalization and reduces the opportunity for at least some types of interactions to appear, and as research accumulates, the importance of such individual differences and context factors is increasingly recognized. This is particularly noteworthy, since contrasting classroom process–educational outcome results have been obtained when student ability and socioeconomic status, grade level, subject matter, cognitive versus affective outcomes, and other factors have been studied (Brophy, 1978; Good & Beckerman, 1978; Good, Ebmeier, & Beckerman, 1978; Solomon & Kendall, 1976). But beyond these individual differences and context-specific relations, there is the question of the degree of generalizability of teaching principles. On this issue, Gage (1979) takes a somewhat different view from Brophy, arguing in favor of greater generality for the major dimensions of teaching.

APTITUDE–TREATMENT INTERACTION RESEARCH IN THE 1980s

What is needed now is further integration of cognitive and other subdisciplines of psychology and school learning, classroom instruction, and teacher behavior and its effects. It is this interface that best exemplifies future prospects for successful ATI research. First, there is the need to emphasize that real classrooms and real teachers are not static phenomena, and that students, classes, instructional designs, and teachers develop and change over time and impact on dependent educational outcome variables as a system of components.

Second, the realization that individual differences impact educational outcomes through systems brings researchers to the reality of multicollinearity among many of these independent variables. It is apparent that much of our new knowledge of ATI will depend on the researchers' ability to disentangle the effects of jointly impacting independent variables that operate as a system. The need to accommodate to this reality is increasingly recognized in analyses of data. This forces researchers to use multivariate analyses with regard to both independent and dependent variables.

Third, ATI research on individual differences, learning processes, and the acquisition of performance will need to be based on longer time spans. Too much past research has been governed by experimental convenience and has not been long enough to take into account the extended periods of time, that is, the hours and even years of learning and experience, that students require to attain the higher levels of knowledge and skill.

Fourth, less attention needs to be given to common or standard independent and dependent variables upon which much of ATI research has focused in the past. The time is ripe for a new infusion of constructs and theory, and a different set of such variables is likely to emerge in the 1980s. Clearly, the process has begun with the utilization of cognitive psychology. But ATI will benefit from the creative use of concepts from other subdisciplines of psychology as well. In addition to the more careful selection of such variables, their construct validity needs to be fully explored, and they need to be more carefully measured.

Fifth, one way to study instructional interventions, teacher behaviors, and classroom processes and their effects on educational outcomes is to view them as social constructions as opposed to objective realities. That is to say, these realities are essentially phenomenological, and exist to some degree in the learner's perceptions. Thus, to understand fully the effects these factors have on educational outcomes one must shift the typical paradigm in ATI research to an analysis of these perceptions. This also emphasizes information-processing models as they apply to the phenomena ATI researchers study.

CONCEPTUALIZING APTITUDE–TREATMENT INTERACTION: SOME ADDITIONAL PERSPECTIVES

Typically, ATI research does not capture the complexity needed to understand relationships between characteristics of learners and the classroom/instructional environments within which school learning occurs. A full understanding of these interactive effects on educational outcomes depends on the simultaneous examination of multilevels of student, class, teaching, and outcome variables. But the need for educationally realistic

ATI research that recognizes social–psychological factors operating at the class or group level is especially important.

Classroom/Teacher Effects

Recognition of such effects has serious implications for the traditional ATI model. For example, Cronbach and Snow (1977) point out that the effects of the class require a radical change in approach to ATI research. Individual differences often do not operate independently of the effects of the class and teacher. In looking for interactions, therefore, it is necessary to separate between-class from within-class effects. A recent example of this interdependency is a study of Greene (1980). Motivational and cognitive aptitudes were investigated in nine classes, using educational treatments that involved choice of learning procedures for some students and no choice for others. Stepwise multiple regression analyses were utilized, and although significant results related to individual differences in aptitude were obtained, between-class analyses suggested even larger class differences, Other research (e.g., Cronbach & Webb, 1975; Gustafsson, 1978) on specific class effects confirms the importance of this phenomenon in ATI research.

This salience of class effects emphasizes the importance of Brophy's (1979) observations on the normative character of actual classrooms. He points out that classrooms typically have a number of prominent features, including those outlined in Figure 1. Moreover, in addition to describing these classroom contexts and activities, teacher behavior and its effects should be studied. This raises further questions concerning the relation of teacher behavior to specific classroom contexts and activities.

Of particular importance and relevance to the study of ATI in the classroom is the study of small groups and whether small group, as well as individual, characteristics enter into ATI effects on achievement and other educational outcomes. Intraclass grouping for instructional purposes is common in reading, and it is used for other subjects as well. That small group characteristics do make a difference in outcomes is indicated by recent studies. Webb (1980, 1982) found that small group ability led to differentiated outcomes, with middle-ability students profiting more from being in uniform-ability than in mixed-ability small groups. Peterson, Janick, and Swing (1981) obtained similar results, although they also varied the size of the groups.

A major feature distinguishing these studies, in addition to the emphasis on small group composition, was the systematic analysis of interaction. It not only is important to have detailed information on student–teacher and student–student interaction, but the *sequential* nature

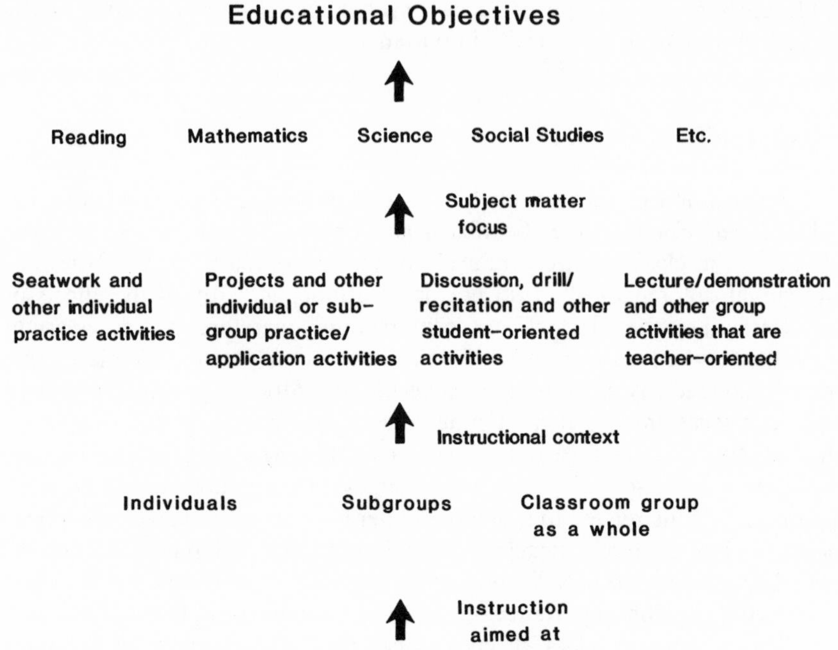

Educational Objectives

↑

Reading   Mathematics   Science   Social Studies   Etc.

↑ Subject matter
focus

Seatwork and	Projects and other	Discussion, drill/	Lecture/demonstration
other individual	individual or sub-	recitation and other	and other group
practice activities	group practice/	student–oriented	activities that are
	application activities	activities	teacher–oriented

↑ Instructional context

Individuals   Subgroups   Classroom group
as a whole

↑ Instruction
aimed at

FIGURE 1. Scheme for examining educational experiences in the classroom.

of such interaction also needs to be recorded, analyzed, and related to outcomes.

It also is important to recognize that classroom settings involve not only a range of individual student characteristics interacting with an array of instructional resources, but also that students in the *same* classroom group are allocated different combinations of resources and attention. An example of such a variable, on which there are marked differences within classroom groups, is academic learning time (Berliner & Cahen, 1973). Since the theory of the research cited is that such engaged time is crucial to student achievement, it is important to understand what student, teacher, classroom process, instruction, and group factors combine to produce individual differences in engaged time. In the same report, large differences between *classes* in engaged time were also noted. Thus, *each* student in a classroom, and *each* classroom group, can be seen as receiving a potentially distinct "treatment." The identification of the characteristics of these individual and group differences in "instructional treatments," and the sources of these differences, is a major challenge to ATI researchers.

Although some progress has been made in research on teacher

behaviors and its effects, dimensional analysis that focuses on curriculum content, specific contexts, and instructional methods needs more attention. Taking classroom situations as they are found, ATI researchers should determine just what transpires in different classes, including the adaptations teachers make in the course of teaching. The variables to be taken into account are numerous, and the instructional adaptations that ocur may often be unique to a particular situation or student.

To facilitate such an analysis, Dunkin and Biddle (1974), in their review of research on teaching, identified four broad categories of variables including (1) *presage,* that is, background, attitudes, abilities, and other characteristics that teachers and students bring into the classroom situation; (2) *content,* that is, grade level, subject matter, and other situationally specific considerations; (3) *process,* that is, teacher and student observable behavior and interactions; and (4) *product,* that is, educational outcomes. They and other reviewers emphasize the importance of context-specific variables, especially in relation to process phenomena. Brophy (1979) also stresses specific contexts in research on classroom processes and describes measurement, design, and curricular issues in such research. In essence, conventional hypothesis-testing and statistics-based research strategies will prove sterile until ATI researchers find out what happens in the course of educational experiences and derive taxonomic descriptions of learning environments, use of pupil time, and methods of instruction that can be used in instructional research.

The Need for "Interactive" Conceptions of Classroom Variables

However, separating between-class and within-class components of ATI effects presents problems. One reason for this is that ATI effects may not result solely from differential responses of individuals, or classes as units, to treatment. In some circumstances, the meaning of a particular student's score may differ functionally in different classes. This methodological issue was demonstrated in a study by Gustafsson (1978). It showed that when tests used to measure dependent variables are administered in classes, and these tests are highly sensitive to the way instructions are given, the mental alertness of the students and other events during administration may influence all the students in essentially the same way. The effect of this would be to produce a large intraclass correlation for errors of measurement, and since these correlated errors may be of different kinds in different treatments, a "significant" ATI may appear. Thus, it is important to keep track of or systematically measure such class-mediated effects, in addition to considering individual aptitude variables.

Investigations of the characteristics of classes ordinarily look upon such variables as objective properties of the class. But the source of such information often is *individual* student reports and ratings, which are then aggregated as macro-level (group) variables. An alternative is to consider these perceptions individually and as phenomenal descriptions of the student's experience in the classroom. This recognizes that these perceptions of the classroom may directly reflect the students' own personalities or they may be products of a personality × treatment interaction. Cronbach and Snow (1977) cite several studies that suggest that variations in students' perceptions of teachers account for at least as much variance as actual differences between teachers. In fact, student perception of a treatment may be as important as the treatment *per se*. This leads logically to the need for studies of the phenomenology, as well as the objective reality, of instructional treatments. As a case in point, in ATI research that matches student and instruction it must be recognized that student perceptions mediate the interaction of teacher style and instructional method, even when the teacher and the instructional method are "constant." One form such research can take, for example, is to give students the kind of teachers they say they want.

Burstein (1980) takes this general point further, arguing that the *same* variable can measure different constructs at different levels of aggregation. This is the case when the mean ability of classroom groups is related to individual educational outcomes, after the effects of individual ability are controlled. In this instance, aggregated ability may reflect the opportunity rather than the ability to learn. According to Burstein, group mean ability affects instructional practices. That is, teachers adjust instruction to the average level of ability of their classes. For high ability classes, they teach at a faster pace and offer more content and thus increase opportunities for learning.

Process measures used in investigations of process–process and process–outcome relationships are subject to similar interpretative problems (Borich, Malitz, & Kugle, 1978). Such variables frequently have different functions and meanings, depending on specific content, and to be fully understood they must not be seen in isolation, but rather as reflections of a larger, dynamic, ongoing system.

A "CORRELATES" VERSUS A "COMPONENTS" APPROACH TO THE STUDY OF APTITUDES

It is useful in ATI research to distinguish between a "correlates" approach and a "components" approach to the study of aptitudes. Pelligrino and Glaser (1979) make such a distinction for the study of intelligence. The correlates approach uses an aptitude test as a criterion measure and looks for more elementary processes that are highly correlated with the criterion. The purpose of research is to identify basic processes that differentiate between high and low scores on a particular test. The search for such "primitive" processes is guided by drawing upon the mainstream of basic psychological research.

An example of this effort is the work of Hunt (1978). He suggests that verbal performance requires specific verbal knowledge as well as the use of certain mechanistic processes by which information is manipulated. According to Hunt, people with less efficient mechanistic processes have to work harder at learning tasks that involve verbal information. Over time, this handicap produces relatively large differences in verbal skill and knowledge. That is, Hunt theorizes that differences in mechanistic processes accumulate over time to produce large differences in verbal skill and knowledge.

If this is true, it suggests that the apparent promise of ATI lies in research that focuses on the identification of such mechanistic processes at an early age, and then if they are amenable to training, to provide such aptitude training early in schooling. If the possibilities of teaching such aptitudes or learning skills are less than anticipated, then research adapting instruction to these mechanistic processes should be pursued in the hope of finding that individuals with a particular mechanistic processing profile make more progress under particular instructional interventions.

The components approach is well represented by the work of Sternberg and Weil (1980) on intelligence. Their analysis begins with components hypothesized to be involved in the performance of a task related to intelligence. Several models, differing in components called upon and the way they are sequenced, are then specified. With these models, reaction time and patterns of errors under varying conditions of presentation of the task can then be predicted. Such research can identify "best fit" models that have the potential of suggesting what instructional treatments best utilize such models. Efforts can also be made to train individuals to use the processing models that most facilitate certain task performances or which are most effective, given a particular instructional treatment.

PROBLEMS OF MEASURING INDIVIDUAL DIFFERENCES

Procedures for converting psychological observations into numerical form is a source of problems as well as promise in ATI research and applications. More specifically, what is at issue is the general problem of measuring individual differences, using approaches based on what is commonly referred to as "test theory." Lumsden (1976) has been one of the critics of classical test theory, pointing out that one of its major weaknesses is the sample-based nature of its estimation procedures. For example, precision of measurement estimates are a function of the particular set of items and sample of individuals on which the data have been collected.

One problem this creates for ATI research is found in reliability estimation. What is crucial to ATI studies is the precision of *individual* measurement. In this context, reliability estimation in classical test theory, which justifies the use of a particular instrument, is only one step in obtaining estimates of the precision of individual measurement. That is, in ATI research and applications, concern needs to shift to the standard error of measurement. Or to put the matter another way, the problem is one of individual differences rather than an experimental focus, with classical test theory being preoccupied with experimentation.

Latent trait test theory has been developed and applied to problems for which classical test theory has proved inadequate, with item response theory perhaps having the most relevance to applications involving the ATI paradigm. Hambleton and Cook (1977), for example, provide a number of illustrations of the uses of item response theory. One advantage of this approach is its potential to measure individuals on the same ability scale, regardless of the difficulty of the subset of items on which they are measured. This implies the capability to equate measurements from different tests and across group and different aptitude levels. Ultimately, though, the model's potential value to ATI work lies in its strong assumptions about the behavior of individuals and its ability to describe their behavior. Lumsden (1977), for example, shows how person reliability and group reliability are related, and that group reliability is a function of person reliabilities. This also permits the identification of individuals who show a lack of fit. The further development of person indices of this type can serve to improve planning for ATI intervention.

THE PSYCHOLOGICAL STATUS OF INDIVIDUAL DIFFERENCES

Regardless of how individual differences are measured, their psychological status still poses questions. Carroll and Maxwell (1979) survey these issues, especially those raised by Sternberg (1977). Excerpting their main points, Are factor analytically identified dimensions actual psychological processes? Or, do they reflect the mental and psychophysical "architecture" of the individual? If they represent processes, are they fundamental, critical to task performance, and generalizable over different types of tasks? Or do they reflect particular types of performance for individuals who might readily select other strategies given the appropriate cues? Further, what is the significance of individual differences manifested at a particular point in time and in a particular group? Are they reliable and consistent over time? If so, what is the course of their development, and to what extent are they subject to change through maturation, learning, short-term physiological effects, and other influences?

They go on to point out that the posing of such questions may imply particular theories and views about behavior and performance. In any event, there is as yet only very limited information available for answering these questions. Possibly, a major virtue of attention to ATI theory, research, and application is that it will prompt increased efforts to provide theory and data for answering such questions, not only about cognitive abilities, but also about other individual difference dimensions in the affective, motivational, psychomotor, personality, sensory, and perceptual, areas. Differential psychology therefore holds the promise for better ATI theory and research, with the further payoff of better ways to adapt individuals to instruction and instruction design to individuals.

The Effect of Subjects' Propensities

A problem in research involving treatments or interventions that are hypothesized to interact with aptitudes is that subjects in particular treatment groups do not follow instructions. That is, subjects with particular aptitude characteristics who are placed in particular treatment groups designed to maximize the fit between aptitude and treatment, and thus maximize the effects of such intervention, do not follow the strategies of their treatment. In other words, the treatment is designed to induce subjects to use certain strategies or to behave in certain ways, and when a substantial number do not, the chance of obtaining a significant interaction effect is diminished. What is needed, therefore, are methods for increasing homogeneity within treatment groups so as to enhance the number of subjects with a best fit. In other words, the failure to obtain a good match results in a mixture of treatments within as well as among groups.

Nonlinear Relationships Among Aptitude and Instruction Variables

A potential limitation on past ATI research that must be recognized is the possibility of nonlinear relationships among variables that manifest interaction. Such a possibility might be represented by an inverted U-shaped curve. As a case in point, Koester and Farley (1982) predict such a relationship between arousal and stimulation-seeking, that is, stimulation-seeking decreases as arousal level increases. In essence, individual differences in physiological arousal levels lead to different needs for external stimulation to maintain an optimal level. Low arousal subjects will seek stimulation so as to raise arousal level, whereas high arousal subjects will attempt to reduce stimulation so as to lower their general arousal.

As an application of this theory, hyperactive children seem to have very low arousal levels, and such children also tend to exhibit more maladaptive classroom behaviors, including impulsivity, restlessness, distractibility, and attentional problems (Whalen & Henker, 1980). If correct, the often recommended placement of hyperactive children in stimulus-reduced classrooms is inappropriate.

Such evidence for nonlinearity complicates the promise of causal modeling in ATI research. Causal modeling that utilizes linear structural equation models is particularly relevant to quasi-experimental ATI research in naturalistic settings and for extended educational experiments and longitudinal studies of ATI. Since the basic building block of these causal models is the linear regression equation, nonlinearity and associated nonnormality present serious problems, although nonlinear programming for such models is being developed (Bentler, 1980).

INSTABILITY OF APTITUDE-LEARNING RELATIONS OVER TIME

The prototypic paradigm for ATI research assumes stability of aptitude–learning relations over time. This can be viewed in a purely methodological sense when analyses for interaction are derived from the full duration of the treatment. But there is a body of evidence indicating that aptitudes required at different stages of learning shift as task demands and learning processes change (Fleishman, 1972; Hultsch, Nesselroade, & Plemons, 1976). In general, it might be argued that aptitudes required at one stage of learning are not necessarily the most important aptitudes at another stage.

Following the logic of this situation, one would collect learning data at different points during treatment, using sequential statistical analyses (Burns, 1980). As Burns further notes, this might not be a bad idea for all instructional research, whether or not one is interested in interactions. Changes that occur *during* learning are as important as changes that show up at the end of learning, and the process of change should be a focus of instructional intervention research.

At a more fundamental level, changes in aptitude–learning relations over the course of learning should be expected by the nature of learning itself. All learning theory at least implicitly assumes that learning extends in time and that learners change during the course of learning. This point is explicated by Glaser (1976) in his description and conceptualization of differences between early learning, as characterized by the novice, and the later stages of learning the expert engages in. From his description, it is clear that early forms of learning differ from later forms, and it is reasonable that shifts in aptitude–learning relations may accompany movement from novice to expert performance.

Burns (1980) suggests that the form of such shifts might relate to different aptitudes associated with the *method* of instruction compared to the *content* of instruction. Drawing upon Snow's (1980) analyses of aptitude processes, he argues that a general set of skills, which represent general learning to learn skills that transcend specific knowledge, are an important source of instructional methods differences. Such sources of influence would be relatively stable during the course of an instructional intervention.

In contrast, there are specific cognitive and other processes that later enter into the course of learning in different ways and at different points in time during instructional intervention. In such cases, aptitude–learning relations would be unstable over time, that is, during the course of instructional treatment, as the requirements of the content of instruction change.

THE APTITUDE–TREATMENT INTERACTION CONCEPT AND TESTS OF SIGNIFICANCE

In their summary chapter, Cronbach and Snow (1977) ask the question, Do ATIs exist? They go on to answer the question in the affirmative, presenting a generally optimistic outlook, although noting the many challenges to finding dependable ATIs. Hunt (1975), in his analysis of person-environment interaction, also presents a positive view, but realizes the demanding challenge of the interaction concept and believes that it has not been fully tried. Others have expressed their support more indirectly. For example, Walberg, Pascarella, Haertel, Junker, and Boulanger (1982) describe a psychological theory of educational productivity derived from classical economic theory of productivity that they believe is applicable to ATIs. The Cobb-Douglas economic production function they apply to educational productivity is itself inherently interactional in the sense that increasing any production factor while holding the others constant leads to diminishing returns. In addition, production factors can substitute or trade off for one another; but when this occurs there is a diminishing rate of return. A further extension of the economic production function is that when any factor reaches zero there is zero educational productivity or learning, although educational productivity factors may not have valid zero points, as in economic productivity.

In contrast to this broad and generally optimistic perspective, the ATI concept has, at times in the past, been viewed in terms of statistically significant disordinal interaction in a restrictive way. Hunt (1975) discusses the statistical definition utilized by Bracht (1970), which is later discussed at length by Cronbach and Snow (1977) who believe that Bracht was unnecessarily pessimistic about the existence of ATIs. Bracht (1970) and Bracht and Glass (1968) used a severe test for disordinality, applying a *t*-test, or a comparable statistic, to differences in the distribution on *each* side of the crossover point. To be considered disordinal, both *t*-tests would have to be significant, with one of the two differences having the opposite sign. Such a test is strongly biased against disordinality, and Cronbach and Snow (1977) recommend against it, preferring the use of confidence intervals for analyzing regression effects instead of tests of the null hypothesis. In support of Cronbach and Snow's position, and to facilitate the computation of confidence intervals, Serlin and Levin (1980) recently presented a "user"-oriented discussion of such procedures that should help make the use of confidence intervals more popular.

But more importantly, Cronbach and Snow (1977) present a "philosophy" of significance testing that they consider necessary because ATI researchers have, in the past, placed too much reliance on conventional levels of significance in studies of interaction. As they put it, (in a modification of Plato), "all the findings of statistical studies are shadows on the wall of the cave" (1977, p. 52). The ATI researcher should use significance tests to discipline himself and to help the scholarly community focus its attention, since "in developing a body of knowledge it is necessary to restrict attention to some fraction of the propositions suggested by the shadows" (1977, p. 52). They go on to note that "interactions that do not reach significance should be described along with those that do" because "*consistent* nonsignificant results are at least as valuable to a science as are incoherent significant results" (1977, p. 53). The prospects of productive work on interactions is considerably enhanced by the position Cronbach and Snow take, and the belief in being able to individualize instruction along ATI lines has more hope of eventual realization.

EXTENDING THE INTERACTIONAL VIEWPOINT

As Cronbach and Snow (1977) have pointed out, most ATI research over-simplifies the educational situation, assuming that treatments are applied to independent individuals. But instead, educational instruction is conducted in classes, in schools, and in communities, and students are influenced by each other, their classes and teachers, and their school's culture. When we attempt to take these effects into account the situation becomes much more complicated, and the conception of ATI needs to be expanded. The nature of aptitude changes, as does the nature of treatments; and the search for new aptitude constructs takes on a greater urgency.

Rather than thinking only about individual differences, one must think in terms of class, school, and community differences. Distinctions between classes and schools also need to be conceptualized. The dimensions required to characterize them adequately need to be identified, and a taxonomy of such treatment variations developed. ⸴

An example of such an effort is provided by Burstein (1980) who has developed a multilevel approach to the analysis of educational performance. The methods he proposes acknowledge that students in school structures are affected by both the individual and group features of those structures and that appropriate models of these effects can be specified. Glasman and Biniaminov (1981) have also reviewed the literature on input–output analyses of schools and offer a structural causal model that identifies school, in addition to individual, variables and the direction of their effects. Teacher–student and student–student interaction variables, however, are not included in the model developed. Model specification, measurement, and analysis problems that arise when both individual-level and group-level effects are taken into account, are given extended attention by Burstein (1980), although he points out that the properties and range of utility of these methods have not been fully elucidated.

Another effort to extend conceptualization and analysis along these lines is that by Walberg et al. (1982). They apply the Cobb–Douglas model of educational productivity to a series of input measures correlated with science achievement, using two-stage least-squares regression analyses, in which a distinction is made between endogeneous and exogenous variables. Endogenous variables, such as quality of instruction and class environment, may cause each other and be caused by other variables, but they do not cause such exogenous variables as race, socioeconomic status, and sex.

Related to this, analyses using grossly defined school resources input variables, such as teacher degree and years of experience and size of school library have not shown consistently significant relationships to educational output (Hanushek, 1979). One likely reason for the lack of a consistent relationship between school resources and student achievement is that the school resource variables usually included are not really "inputs" into the learning process, but rather are a poor proxy for aptitudes and instructional variables. Another limitation of production–function approaches is that the organization of classrooms and schools, and the behavior and learning of students in such settings is not usually taken into account.

It also is evident from these examples, as well as from reviews of the ATI literature, that the interactional viewpoint upon which the ATI concept rests needs to be extended in still another direction (Phillips, 1982). We can no longer exclusively support ATI research that assumes one-way causality, regards individuals as independent, thinks of interaction only at the individual level, and ignores two-way causation, group effects, and interaction at the group level. Not only is two-way causation a likely possibility in real school environments, but ATI research that is adept at analyzing two-way causality is essential if the theoretical and practical significance of ATI is to be ascertained. In addition to determining when a reciprocal causal process is operating, it also is necessary to determine which causal effect is more important. This question cannot be fully answered unless ATI research resorts to a greater use of representative designs (Snow, 1974). Such research designs will have greater ecological validity, permitting the variables in the causal model to reflect their natural variances. Correlational techniques, especially structural equation models such as those referred to earlier (Bentler, 1980), must be more often utilized in situations in which reciprocal causation is likely. This means that the style of ATI research that has dominated in the past will have to change.

TOWARD THE INTEGRATION OF APTITUDE–TREATMENT INTERACTION AND EDUCATIONAL PRACTICE

Adaptation of instruction to the learner is a hallmark of modern education, although adaptation has never been very systematic. The definitive information that is necessary to match learners with instructional environments is lacking. Thus, ATI research seeks to provide such information by establishing principles that relate characteristics of individuals to instructional interventions. But individuals and instructional treatments vary in numerous ways, creating many combinations of variables and the possibility of almost countless interactions. For this reason, the search for generlizations that could be the basis of instruction policies is a formidable task.

Is Optimal Matching Feasible?

We begin by offering a definition of optimality: namely, placement decisions that maximize some explicit and measurable outcome that, in turn, is conditional on certain assumptions. The importance of this definition is that it stresses the conditional nature of optimality. For example, because of the complexity of outcomes of learning from instruction, one can build optimal matching models that make simplifying assumptions or build heuristic models that maintain greater realism. One can use a single outcome criterion, although actual placement decisions are based on multiple educational goals. When such goals conflict, as when they are negatively correlated, there can be no optimal matching decision. That is, the most one can do is to trade off goals or compromise between goals that reflect different values. This leads to the rejection of strictly "objective" optimality and replaces it with the criterion of consistency with one's goals and educational values.

The Utility of Aptitude–Treatment Interactions in Placement Decisions

The cost relative to benefits of different instructional interventions also has seldom been considered in ATI research. One of the main reasons for failure to apply cost–benefit analysis may be the difficulties that are perceived in developing utility theory that is appropriate to educational outcomes. To make such analyses requires careful estimates of the dollar costs of various aspects of instructional intervention. Although it should be possible to develop these kinds of estimates, it is difficult, and for some elements of instruction it may be almost impossible to conceive of a way to make such estimates.

Another possible reason for the disinterest in cost–benefit analyses is that it may be assumed that utility equations relating sources to outcomes are not appropriate when the data do not fit a linear model. Results for such relationships also may be assumed to be situation-specific, making the application of cost–benefit results to different educational settings inappropriate. Although cost–benefit is important in instructional research generally, it takes on added importance when adaptation of instruction to the individual is the major consideration, and utility formulations should become a central concept in ATI research.

Cronbach and Snow (1977) briefly analyze the utility of placement decisions, basing their analysis on the earlier mathematical rationale developed by Cronbach and Gleser (1965). One point that they make is that although small differences may deserve scientific attention, when they are the basis of operating decisions, the question of what size of difference has a practical benefit must also be considered. When the costs of placement decisions have been evaluated, the utility of a proposed treatment can then, in principle, be determined.

"Ordinal" and "disordinal" interactions are distinguished in Figure 2. In Panels 1 and 2 the lines cross, indicating disordinal interaction. In the other two, they do not, at least within the range of the sample. When one regression line remains above the other, the interaction is ordinal. Bracht (1970), among others, has tended to dismiss the value of ordinal interactions. Cronbach and Snow, on the other hand, stress the potential significance of ordinal interaction when the cost of treatment is to be taken into account For example, if Treatment A in Panel 3 costs a lost more than

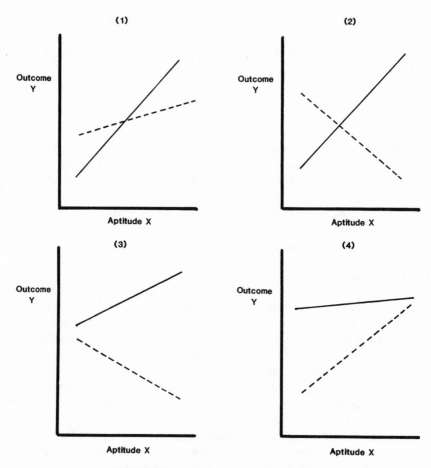

FIGURE 2. Aptitude–treatment interaction.

Treatment B, the ordinality of the interaction may change, becoming disordinal when cost is considered. If the cost-corrected interaction is still ordinal, treatment A might still be justified for those persons high in Aptitude X, for whom the payoff in outcome is greatest. Another reason ordinal interactions should be taken more seriously than in the past is that aptitudes higher or lower than the range of those hypothetically sampled in Panels 3 and 4 might exist. In each panel, if such extrapolation occurred, the regression lines might cross, creating disordinal interactions. If Aptitude X were general ability, and a population of college students had been sampled, disordinal interaction might reasonably be expected if all college-aged youth had been sampled instead.

It is not only important to recognize that the educational decision-maker cannot determine only on the basis of outcome whether a certain treatment should be applied, it is also important that know its cost per unit of educational outcome and how this compares to the per unit cost of other treatments. Beyond this, consideration should be given to the *values* of the decision-maker in the school, institution, or community, since other values and benefits, as in the case of handicapped children, may take precedence over relative costs in terms of educational outcomes. In this case, costs typically average at least twice those for normal children, in spite of the lack

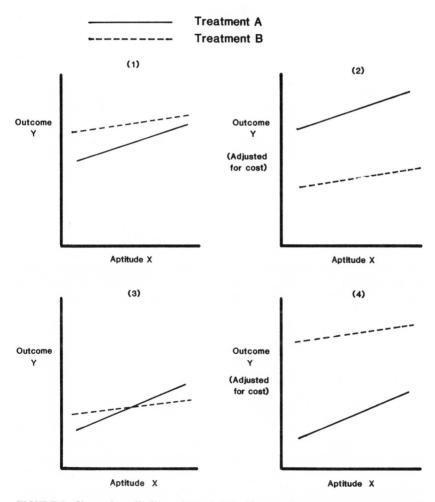

FIGURE 3. Change in ordinality and practical significance when cost–benefit is considered.

of evidence that these extra expenditures improve the educational outcomes for handicapped children.

Moreover, when the differences in costs between two treatments is large, relative to outcomes, the potential value of ATI information is enhanced. Two illustrations of this practically important situation are shown in Figure 3.

Panels 1 and 3 show an ordinal and disordinal interaction, respectively; neither is statistically significant. In Panels 2 and 4, outcomes obtained with each treatment are adjusted for the cost of the treatment relative to outcome. The interaction results are still assumed to be statistically nonsignificant, that is, making the adjustment for costs does not change the slope of the regression lines. But in Panel 2, Treatment A would be preferred to Treatment B on the basis of cost-benefit, which produced a significant "main effects" difference. In Panel 3, the insignificant interaction attaches no advantage to either Treatment A or B. In Panel 4, however, the situation has changed. Now one can make a good case for assigning all students to Treatment B. The slopes of the regression lines have not changed, of course, although the shift in the regression line for Treatment A, after adjustment for cost, has produced a significant ordinal interaction.

STRATEGIES FOR ADAPTING TO INDIVIDUAL DIFFERENCES

In an earlier article, Salomon (1972) conceptualizes several models for the generation of aptitude–treatment hypotheses. Later, Cronbach and Snow (1977) discuss three forms of matching aptitudes and educational treatments: capitalization on strengths, compensation, and remediation. These and one additional strategy are shown in Table 1. In capitalization, one modifies instructional strategies to take advantage of strengths. In compensation, instruction is designed to compensate for the learner's weaknesses. For example, an emphasis on organization in instructional design can compensate for the learner's inability to organize materials effectively. In such matching, inaptitudes are bypassed through compensatory interventions. In remediation, however, weaknesses are remedied. Such remediation may be specific, such as when there are knowledge gaps, or general, as in the case of deficient learning abilities. To these forms of matching, another, educational goal differentiation, should be added; this is reflected in the traditional policy of taking ability into account in assigning curricular tasks and stating objectives for students. At a more general, pervasive level, schools typically operate in terms of an age-graded curriculum that is an application of matching aptitude and curriculum content and objectives on the basis of age or general developmental level.

However, all these tactics assume that ATI effects operate on the

TABLE 1. Strategies for Matching

Matching strategy	Elements in instructional intervention		
	Aptitude	Instructional intervention	Educational outcome (criterion performance)
Normative	Fixed	Fixed	Fixed
Capitalize on strengths	Fixed	Modify to capitalize on aptitude strengths	Fixed
Compensation	Fixed	Modify to compensate for or bypass aptitude deficiencies	Fixed
Remediation	Modify instructional intervention to train deficient aptitudes, and if successful, assign to normative instructional intervention		Fixed
Differentiated expectations	Fixed	Fixed	Individualized

individual student, and social–psychological effects operating at the group or class level are ignored. For example, if there is disordinal interaction between general ability and particular instructional interventions, one might match students to these educational treatments by establishing an appropriate cutting score. But this regards individuals as independent and ignores the distinction between within-class and between-class interactions. If there is between-class interaction, we might alternately assign *classes* rather than individuals to treatments, although classes are formed according to some policy or practice, and such between-class interaction would apply only to classes formed in the same way. This implies an extended matching concept and illustrates that adaptations differ with respect to scope, as well as tactics.

The most far-reaching adaptions are those at the school district level, such as alternative schools for students who have failed to succeed in regular schools. At a second level are differentiations within schools, on the basis of different teaching styles, such as student–teacher matching models based on Conceptual Systems Theory (Miller, 1981). In his approach, students are matched with teachers on the basis of their, and the teachers', level of cognitive complexity. Other levels of adaptation are those for subject matter, subgrouping within classes (as when students are organized into slow, intermediate, and fast reading groups), and adaptations at the level of the individual student.

We can also consider that aptitudes and instructional treatments can be differentiated at both coarse and fine levels. Adaptations in terms of specialized abilities, that is, microadaptations, may account for many interactions. Such fine distinctions are possible, and potentially important, in instructional intervention as well as, for example, in computer-assisted instruction, individually prescribed instruction methods, and "mastery" procedures.

Ultimately, ATIs concern processes within individuals, yet inferences about ATI effects are based on data averaged over students and treatments, although not to the same degree as in main effects research. This averaging may, in turn, conceal or distort the nature of intraindividual processes and miss important idiosyncratic ATI effects. That is one reason for the importance of single-student or response-guided instructional intervention. For example, determining whether a certain instructional treatment will help a particular student is worthwhile, regardless of the intervention's effectiveness for other students. Response-sensitive or response-guided intervention is an alternative, therefore, to traditional ATI approaches. Response-guided instruction is a common form of intervention in teaching, and one strength of this approach is that it allows a competent ATI researcher to increase the utility of an instructional study by modifying it during its course. The weakness of response-sensitive instructional intervention research is that it does not permit statistical tests of treatment effects. However, Kazdin (1982, pp. 324–333), in two examples, shows that if the introduction of treatments is properly handled, valid statistical inferences can be drawn from single-student research designs.

It is evident that the ATI generalizations that could be the basis of educational placement policies would be complicated for other reasons. After reviewing the research included in their book, Cronbach and Snow reaffirmed their earlier conclusion that at least fourth-order interactions of the nature of ability × age × subject matter × treatment × outcome are necessary if placement policies are to derived from ATI research. But even with the establishment of such relationships, application is further complicated by the multidimensional nature of aptitudes and educational interventions.

Considerable progress also has been made in developing a variety of theories of instruction, and a number of these theories have been briefly described by Gagné and Dick (1983). Individual difference variables have a role in all of them, although the potential significance of such variables to learning outcomes seems to vary. In addition, models of instruction that formulate procedures through which efficient instruction programs can be designed are available, and have been reviewed by Andrews and Goodson (1980). But such models are less than theories of instruction because they do not explicitly account for causal relations between learning processes and instructional activities. Taken together, these developments are important to the future of the ATI concept because they provide a different perspective for ATI research, one in which instructional theory and design is the major influence on identification of student characteristics. In large part, these may be learnable student capabilities that mediate the action of instructional variables on learning. They, thus, have the potential of attaining prominence as sources of interactive effects that, in turn, would be amenable to modification through training and ultimately the variation in learning outcomes among students.

There is the challenge, therefore, for ATI research that is potentially more useful to educational practice. For example, Cronbach and Snow (1977) indicate their serious reservations throughout their book about the dominant style of ATI research, and they have much to say about research strategy and procedure. In addition to arguing that the research methods commonly used are inefficient and often produce misleading results, they make a series of recommendations to improve matters. But beyond this, the point has to be made that, although ATI research can establish guidelines to match students and educational environments, it cannot provide clear-cut prescriptions for educational policy or be used directly in making particular placement decisions.

The point here is not to de-emphasize scientific rigor, or the importance of ATI generalizations appropriate to schooling, but rather to acknowledge that educational policy and decisions by professional educators involve more than the *direct* application of scientific knowledge. The classroom teacher, as a professional, attempts to serve the instructional needs of students as effectively as possible, regardless of the adequacy of the knowledge base underlying such practice. In fact, it is between the areas of complete scientific certainty and complete scientific uncertainty that *professional* practice is most manifested.

CONCLUDING COMMENT

Despite the likely persistence of pessimism about the prevalence and strength of ATI effects and the criticism of the ATI approach on philosophical grounds, the search for principles by which adaptation of instruction can be more systematic and productive will continue. Cronbach and Snow (1977), in their book that has already become a classic, laid the foundation with the hope that others would build on it. They agreed then that there is much to be built, and provided no lack of suggestions. But for such research efforts to be more effective than they have been in the past, the logic of research into interactions needs to become clearer, and special methodological and statistical requirements need more attention. Most educationally significant questions about adaptation of instruction, however, cannot be answered by ATI research alone, since with even well-established interactions, the field of application would be too narrow to be directly useful in school policies and practices.

REFERENCES

Allen, G. J., Elias, M. J., & Zlotlow, S. F. Behavioral interventions for alleviating test anxiety: A methodological overview of current therapeutic practices. In I. G. Sarason (Ed.) *Test anxiety: Theory, research, and applications.* Hillsdale, N.J.: Lawrence Erlbaum Associates, 1980.

Andrews, D. H., & Goodson, L. A. A comparative analysis of models of instructional design. *Journal of Instructional Development,* 1980, *3,* 2–16.

Bentler, P. M. Multivariate analysis with latent variables: Causal modeling, *Annual Review of Psychology,* 1980, *31,* 419–456.

Berliner, D. C., & Cahen, L. L. Trait-treatment interaction and learning. *Review of Research in Education,* 1973, *1,* 58–94.

Biggs, J. B., & Collis, K. F. *Evaluating the quality of learning: The SOLO taxonomy (structure of the observed learning outcome).* New York: Academic Press, 1982.

Borich, G. D., Malitz, D., & Kugle, C. L. Convergent and discriminant validity of five classroom observation systems: Testing a model. *Journal of Educational Psychology,* 1978, *70,* 119–128.

Bracht, G. H. Experimental factors related to aptitude–treatment interventions. *Review of Educational Research,* 1970, *40,* 627–646.

Bracht, G. H., & Glass, G. V. The external validity of experiments. *American Educational Research Journal,* 1968, *5,* 437–474.

Brophy, J. Interactions between learner characteristics and optimal instruction. In D. Bar-Tal & L. Saxe (Eds.), *Social psychology of education: Theory and research.* Washington, D.C.: Hemisphere, 1978.

Brophy, J. Teacher behavior and its effects. *Journal of Educational Psychology,* 1979, *71,* 733–750.

Bruner, J. S. Some theorems on instruction illustrated with reference to mathematics. In E. R. Hilgard (Ed.), *Theories of learning and instruction. The 63rd yearbook of the NSSE, Part I.* Chicago: University of Chicago Press, 1964.

Burns, R. B. Relation of aptitudes to learning at different points in time during instruction. *Journal of Educational Psychology,* 1980, *72,* 785–795.

Burstein, L. The analysis of multilevel data in educational research and evaluation. *Review of Educational Research,* 1980, *50,* 158–233.

Carroll, J. B., & Maxwell, S. E. Individual differences in cognitive abilities. *Annual Review of Psychology,* 1979, *30,* 603–640.

Clark, R. E. Antagonism between achievement and enjoyment in ATI studies. *Educational Psychologist,* 1982, *17,* 92–101.

Corno, L. Individual and class level effects of parent-assisted instruction in classroom memory support strategies. *Journal of Educational Psychology,* 1980, *72,* 278–292.

Cronbach, L. J., & Gleser, G. C. *Psychological tests and personnel decisions* (2nd ed.). Urbana: University of Illinois Press, 1965.

Cronbach, L. J., & Snow, R. E. *Aptitudes and instructional methods.* New York: Irvington, 1977.

Cronbach, L. J., & Webb, N. Between-class and within-class effects in a reported aptitude × treatment interaction: Reanalysis of a study by G. L. Anderson. *Journal of Educational Psychology,* 1975, *67,* 717–724.

Denny, D. R. Self-control approaches to the treatment of test anxiety. In I. G. Sarason (Ed.), *Test anxiety: Theory, research, and applications.* Hillsdale, N.J.: Lawrence Erlbaum Associates, 1980.

Dickson, W. P. (Ed.) *Children's oral communication skills.* New York: Academic Press, 1981.

Dunken, N. J., & Biddle, B. J. *The study of teaching.* New York: Holt, Rinehart and Winston, 1974.

Epstein, J., & McPartland, J. The concept and measurement of the quality of school life. *American Educational Research Journal,* 1976, *13,* 15–30.

Fleishman, E. On the relation between ability, learning, and human experience. *American Psychologist,* 1972, *27,* 1017–1032.

Gage, N. The generality of dimensions of teaching. In P. Peterson & H. Walburg (Eds.), *Research on teaching: Concepts, findings, and implications.* Berkeley, Cal.: McCutchan, 1979.

Gagné, R. M., & Dick, W. Instructional psychology. *Annual Review of Psychology,* 1983, *34,* 261–295.

Glaser, R. Components of a psychology of instruction: Toward a science of design. *Review of Educational Research,* 1976, *46,* 1–24.

Glaser, R. Instructional psychology: Past, present, and future. *American Psychologist,* 1982, *37,* 292–305.

Glasman, N. S., & Biniaminov, I. Input–output analyses of schools. *Review of Educational Research,* 1981, *51,* 509–539.

Good, G., Ebmeier, H., & Beckerman, T. Teaching mathematics in high and low SES classrooms. *Journal of Teacher Education,* 1978, *29,* 85–90.

Good, T., & Beckerman, T. An examination of teachers' effects on high, middle, and low aptitude students. *American Educational Research Journal,* 1978, *15,* 477–482.

Greene, J. C. Individual and teacher/class effects in aptitude treatment studies. *American Educational Research Journal,* 1980, *17,* 291–302.

Gregg, L. W., & Steinberg, E. R. *Cognitive processes in writing.* Hillsdale, N.J.: Lawrence Erlbaum Associates, 1980.

Gross, T. F., & Mastenbrook, M. Examination of the effects of state anxiety on problem-solving efficiency under high and low memory conditions. *Journal of Educational Psychology,* 1980, *72,* 605–609.

Gustafsson, J. A note on class effects in aptitude × treatment interactions. *Journal of Educational Psychology,* 1978, *70,* 142–146.

Hambleton, R. K., & Cook, L. L. Latent trait models and their use in the analysis of educational test data. *Journal of Educational Measurement.* 1977, *14,* 75–96.

Hanushek, E. Conceptual and empirical issues in the estimation of educational production functions. *Journal of Human Resources,* 1979, *14,* 351–388.

Hultsch, D., Nesselroade, J., & Plemons, J. Learning–ability relations in adulthood. *Human Development,* 1976, *19,* 234–247.

Hunt, D. C. Person–environment interaction: A challenge found wanting before it was tried. *Review of Educational Research,* 1975, *45,* 209–230.

Hunt, E. Mechanics of verbal ability. *Psychological Review,* 1978, *85,* 109–130.

Kazdin, A. *Single-case research designs: Methods for clinical and applied settings.* New York: Oxford University Press, 1982.

Koester, L. S., & Farley, F. H. Psychophysiological characteristics and school performance of children in open and traditional classrooms. *Journal of Educational Psychology*, 1982, *74*, 254–263.

Lesgold, A. M., & Perfetti, C. A. (Eds.) *Interactive processes in reading*. Hillsdale, N.J.: Lawrence Erlbaum Associates, 1981.

Lochead, J., & Clement, J. (Eds.) *Cognitive process instruction*. Philadelphia: Franklin Institute Press, 1979.

Lumsden, J. Test theory. *Annual Review of Psychology*, 1976, *27*, 251–280.

Lumsden, J. Person reliability. *Applied Psychological Measurement*, 1977, *1*, 477–482.

Maehr, M. Continuing motivation; An analysis of a seldom considered educational outcome. *Review of Educational Research*, 1976, *46*, 443–462.

Miller, A. Conceptual matching models and interactional research in education. *Review of Educational Research*, 1981, *51*, 33–84.

Moos, R. H., & Moos, B. S. Classroom social climate and student absences and grades. *Journal of Educational Psychology*, 1978, *70*, 263–269.

Pellegrino, J. W., & Glaser, J. Cognitive correlates and components in the analysis of individual differences. *Intelligence*, 1979, *3*, 187–214.

Peterson, P. L. Interactive effects of student anxiety, achievement orientation, and teacher behavior on student achievement and attitudes. *Journal of Educational Psychology*, 1977, *69*, 779–792.

Peterson, P. L., Janick, T. C., & Swing, S. R. Individual characteristics and children's learning in large-group and small group-approaches: Study II. *American Educational Research Journal*, 1981, *18*, 453–474.

Phillips, B. N. Reading and evaluating research in school psychology. In C. R. Reynolds & T. B. Gutkin (Eds.), *The handbook of school psychology*. New York: Wiley, 1982.

Resnick, L. B. Instructional psychology. *Annual Review of Psychology*, 1981, *32*, 659–704.

Resnick, L. B., & Ford, W. W. *The psychology of mathematics for instruction*. Hillsdale, N.J: Lawrence Erlbaum Associates, 1981.

Salomon, G. Heuristic models for the generation of aptitude–treatment hypotheses. *Review of Educational Research*, 1972, *42*, 327–343.

Serlin, R. C., & Levin, J. R. Identifying regions of significance in aptitude-by-treatment interaction research. *American Educational Research Journal*, 1980, *3*, 389–399.

Snow, R. E. Representative and quasi-representative designs for research on teaching. *Review of Educational Research*, 1974, *44*, 265–291.

Snow, R. E. Research on aptitudes for learning: A progress report. *Review of Research in Education*, 1976, *4*, 50–105.

Snow, R. Aptitude processes. In R. Snow, P. Federico, & W. Montagne (Eds.), *Aptitude, learning, and instruction: Cognitive process analyses of learning and problem solving, Vol. 1*. Hillsdale, N.J.: Lawrence Erlbaum Associates, 1980.

Solomon, D., & Kendall, A. Individual characteristics and children's performance in "open" and "traditional" classroom settings. *Journal of Educational Psychology*, 1976, *68*, 613–625.

Spiro, R. J., Bruce, B. C., & Brewer, W. F. (Eds.) *Theoretical issues in reading comprehension: Perspectives from cognitive psychology, linguistics, artificial intelligence, and education*. Hillsdale, N.J.: Lawrence Erlbaum Associates, 1980.

Sternberg, R. J. *Intelligence, information processing, and analogical reasoning: The componential analysis of human abilities*. Hillsdale, N.J.: Lawrence Erlbaum Associates, 1977.

Sternberg, R. J., & Weil, E. M. An aptitude × strategy interaction in linear syllogistic reasoning. *Journal of Educational Psychology*, 1980, *72*, 226–239.

Tobias, S. Achievement treatment interactions. *Review of Educational Research*, 1976, *46*, 61–74.

Tobias, S. Anxiety and instructional methods: An introduction. In J. E. Sieber, H. F. O'Neil, Jr., & S. Tobias (Eds.), *Anxiety, learning, and instruction*. Hillsdale, N.J.: Lawrence Erlbaum Associates, 1977a.

Tobias, S. A model for research on the effect of anxiety on instruction. In J. E. Sieber, H. F. O'Neil, Jr., & S. Tobias (Eds.), *Anxiety, learning, and instruction*. Hillsdale, N.J.: Lawrence Erlbaum Associates, 1977b.

Tobias, S. Anxiety research in educational psychology. *Journal of Educational Psychology*, 1979, *71*, 573–582.

Tobias, S. Anxiety and instruction. In I. G. Sarason (Ed.), *Test anxiety: Theory, research and application*. Hillsdale, N.J.: Lawerence Erlbaum Associates, 1980.

Walberg, H. J., Pascarella, E., Haertel, G. D., Junker, L. K., & Boulanger, F. D. Probing a model of educational productivity in high school science with national assessment samples. *Journal of Educational Psychology*, 1982, *74*, 295–307.

Webb, N. M. A process–outcome analysis of learning in group and individual settings. *Educational Psychologist*, 1980, *15*, 69–83.

Webb, N. M. Peer interaction and learning in cooperative small groups. *Journal of Educational Psychology*, 1982, *74*, 642–655.

Whalen, C. K., & Henker, B. (Eds.) *Hyperactive children: The social ecology of identification and treatment*. New York: Academic Press, 1980.

7

Analysis of Interactions in Research

VICTOR L. WILLSON

The scientific side of psychology has been concerned with describing and understanding human and animal behavior for over a century and a half. The engineering or technological side of psychology, concerned with the treatment of individuals' illnesses, is beginning its second century. The distinction between science and engineering is important for the study of psychological treatments and the extent of their generality and complementarity. Cronbach (1957) has termed the issue the *aptitude–treatment interaction* (ATI). These interactions occur at the interface between the psychology of individual differences, the most basic of the psychological sciences, and the therapy and treatment of individuals.

The similarity between engineering and psychological therapy is real. Engineers are problem-solvers who begin with scientific laws. Real-world constraints, the departure from the ideal conditions of the scientific laws, separate the engineers from the scientists. To a great degree, this is the difference between therapists and experimental psychologists. Their meeting ground is the ATI.

Therapists today are infrequently rigid, orthodox practitioners of one school, with perhaps the exception of psychoanalytic schools of thought, which continue to find little use for other doctrines or techniques. The trend toward using what appears to work in a given situation, eclecticism, is more esteemed today than in earlier decades (Smith, 1982). Rather than forcing all problems into a single frame of reference for developing a therapeutic plan, today's therapist may invoke a Pavlovian paradigm to treat a 9-year-old bedwetter, an operant paradigm to remove attentional deficits in the classroom, and a Rogerian view to improve the self-concept of a depressed child. Thus, therapists must read a wide range of research

VICTOR L. WILLSON ● Department of Educational, Psychology, Texas A & M University, College Station, Texas 77843.

dealing with various treatments. They must attempt to match situations to the most efficacious method of treatment available to them; this is, in its most common form, an ATI problem.

Experimental psychologists approach the ATI problem more from the perspective of internal and external validity rather than from that of a problem-solver. Their training in experimental design has led them to the analysis of variance and factorial and functional design (Edgington, 1974; Willson, 1980). Their methodological training promotes the search for treatment effects and ATIs. Since the 1940s, ANOVA has been a major methodological tool of experimental and educational psychology. It seems that the ATI holds great interest for both therapists and experimental psychologists. Thus, an examination of the current state of knowledge of the statistical properties of ATIs is important for both groups. This chapter deals with current knowledge and some issues for investigation in the field of aptitude–treatment interactions.

MODELS

Treatments are manipulable activities and actions that are typically categorical or nominal scale variables, although they occasionally are ordinal or even interval (as with drug dosages, duration of treatment, or degree of concentration of treatment). *Aptitudes* are characteristics of individuals that are relatively stable and/or slowly changing with respect to treatment durations. They may be categorical (type of talent), ordinal (severity of neurosis or psychosis), or interval (intelligence score, locus of control score). Dependent variables may be either nominal (behavior present or absent), ordinal (worsening, no change, or lessening of phobic response), or interval (achievement score). Thus, a three-by-three-by-three matrix of scale conditions represents the possible models for an ATI study in its simplest form. This chapter will examine only interval scale dependent variables, as the other conditions have methodological issues of sufficient importance to warrant full treatment by themselves, and an attempt to examine all in detail would result in a monograph-length work.

Linear Models

The general form of the ATI model with single treatment, single aptitude, and interval dependent variable y is, for subject j nested in group i

$$y_{j(i)} = B_{0i} + B_{j(i)}X_{j(i)} + e_{j(i)} \qquad (1)$$

The treatment is assumed to be constant for all members of group i, but the aptitude value may vary with the individual, and the regression amount contributed by aptitude X may depend on the individual person. For n persons in each of I treatments, this would result in nI separate regression coefficients to estimate plus I treatment parameters or $(n + 1) * I$ parameters, too many for unique estimation with only nI values of y available. Multiple replications of y will not help, since X is not expected to change. As ATIs are usually conceived, all persons with the same aptitude X' are expected to respond the same way to treatment. If this is not true, the aptitude still may be adequate to the task of aiding in treatment selection. That is, treatment efficacy is a probabilistic concept. Smith and Glass (1977) concluded that the average psychotherapy effect was .68 across all kinds of therapy, but the effect could vary for neurotics on average from .52 with systematic desensitization to .85 for behavior modification. Even with average differences of such a magnitude, an individual can be expected to vary considerably in response to a particular treatment. The client might be expected to gain on average .85 standard deviations (SD), yet gain only .3. The difference is attributed to error, but error is often our representation of yet other interactions of the client with treatment conditions, such as therapist characteristics or treatment duration.

The ATIs are most commonly conceived in terms of different smooth curves of the dependent variable across the aptitude range. The simplest are nonparallel straight lines that intersect (disordinal) in the range of X or that do not intersect (ordinal). Curved lines may take many forms, and polynomial functions have been investigated; only quadratic functions have been investigated in any detail. Examples are given in Figure 1.

Figure 1a represents an ordinal interaction. Treatment A is uniformly better than B across all levels of aptitude X. Although such cases are of interest, theoretically, for the practitioner these may be little concern, since A will be the therapy of choice. In Figure 1b, there are three distinct situations: use of treatment A for low values of aptitude X, use of either treatment around values of X where the lines intersect, and use of treatment B for high values of X. Where one condition stops and another begins is of considerable interest. In Figure 1c, the conclusion may be as in 1a: Choose treatment A. There may be a substantial range of X for which differences between A and B are negligible, however. Perhaps therapist Jones prefers B as a technique. With which clients might he use B instead of A if the curvilinear relationship holds?

The questions posed in the cases discussed above have not been addressed in most ATI literature to date, although the general solution to the problem has been known for many years. Details are given below.

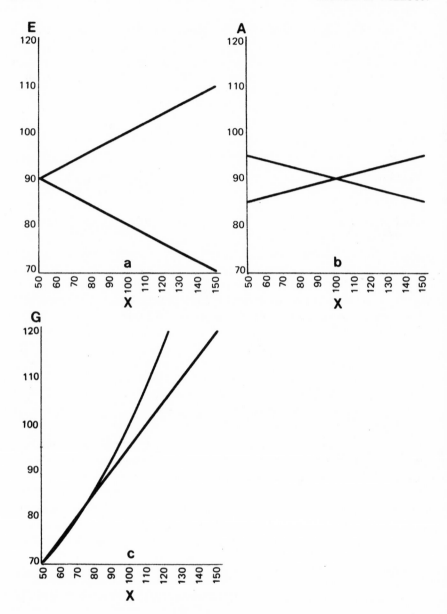

FIGURE 1. Linear regressions for aptitude–treatment interactions: (a) ordinal interaction, (b) dirordinal interaction, and (c) quadratic interaction.

TESTS OF SIGNIFICANCE

NONSIMULTANEOUS REGION OF SIGNIFICANCE

For the two curves associated with the regressions of the dependent variable on the aptitude within treatments, a new function corresponding to the difference between them can be defined as follows,

$$D = f_1(X) - f_2(X) \tag{2}$$

where $f_1(X)$ is the function for the population regression in treatment group 1 and $f_2(X)$ represents this function for group 2. The function $D(X)$ for Figure 1a is given in Figure 2.

The functions f_1 and f_2 may be formulated in the simple linear regression case as follows (after Rogosa, 1981):

$$f_i(X) = B_1 + B_2 T_i + B_3 X + B_4 T_i X \tag{3}$$

and T_i represents a treatment design variable where $T_1 = 1$ and $T_2 = 0$. Thus, the general model of Eq. (1) becomes

$$Y_{j(i)} = B_1 + B_2 T_i + B_3 X_{j(i)} + B_4 T_i X_{j(i)} + e_{j(i)} \tag{4}$$

for $j = 1, \ldots, N$, $i = 1, 2$.

Also, B_2, the difference in means, and B_4, the difference in aptitude slopes, of the two groups become

$$B_2 = B_{02} - B_{01}$$
$$B_4 = B_{j(2)} - B_{j(i)} \tag{5}$$

under an assumption that $B_{j(2)} = $ constant and $B_{j(1)} = $ constant for all j (linear regression).

An equivalent way to conceive of D is as the partial contribution of X to Y holding treatment constant:

$$D = \frac{\partial}{\partial T} Y$$

which results in (from Darlington & Rom, 1972)

$$D = B_2 + B_4 X \tag{6}$$

The model Eq.(4) carries all the usual regression assumptions (Darlington, 1968). The usual least-squares estimates can be made.

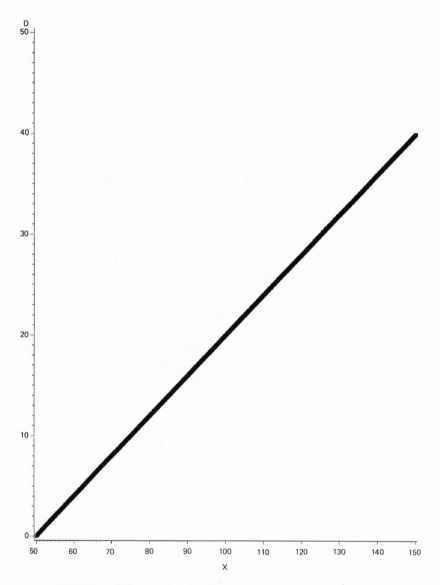

FIGURE 2. Difference Function $D(X)$ for two regressions in Figure 1a.

Of major interest is the estimate of D, $\hat{D}$:

$$\hat{D}(X) = \hat{B}_2 + \hat{B}_4 X \tag{7}$$

Johnson and Neyman (1936) showed $\hat{D}(X)$ is the best linear unbiased estimator (BLUE) of $D(X)$, and $\hat{D}(X)$ is normally distributed with mean $B_2 + B_4 X$, and variance $\sigma^2_{D(X)}$. An unbiased estimate of $\sigma^2_{D(X)}$ is

$$S^2_{D(X)} = S_{22} + S_{24}X + S_{44}X^2 \tag{8}$$

(Rogosa, 1981). The values S_{22}, S_{24}, and S_{44} are elements of $(X^T X)^{-1}$

Thus, for a given value of aptitude, say X', we can test where $D(X')$ is significantly different from zero. This tells us where an individual in treatment 1 with aptitude value X' will differ in score on Y from an individual in treatment 2 with aptitude score X'. We infer the same individual would also differ by $D(X')$ if placed in one treatment or the other. The statistical test is

$$F = \frac{[D(X')]^2}{S^2_{D(X')}} \tag{9}$$

and it is compared with a central F-distribution with 1 and $N - 4$ degrees of freedom at alpha significance level.

The procedure, since it depends on a point-value for X, is termed a nonsimultaneous test. The alpha level applies to similar experiments on random samples at the same value for X'. Thus $(1 - \alpha) \times 100$ is the number of experiments for which the F in Eq. (9) will be nonsignificant when $D(X') = 0$.

When two or more values for X are tested, the experimentwise error rate must be adjusted, just as with multiple comparisons or multiple t-tests. The upper bound for experimentwise error rate will be K_α for K separate values of X. Of course, both $D(X)$ and $S^2_{D(X)}$ must be recalculated for each value of X examined.

EXAMPLE OF A NONSIMULTANEOUS REGION-OF-SIGNIFICANCE CALCULATION

Let us assume the situation in Figure 1b has been found for two reading programs A and B for reading aptitude X. We have determined that the two regressions are (Eq. 3), using fictitious results,

$$f_A = 20 + 5T_A + 3X + .3T_A X$$
$$f_B = 10 + 0T_B + 5X + 1T_B X$$

then

$$B_2 = 5 - 0 = 5,$$
$$B_4 = .3 - 1 = -.7,$$

and

$$D = 5 - .7X$$

If X ranges from 0 to 10 and we are interested in a high value of X, say 8, then

$$D(8) = 5 - .7X$$
$$= 5 - 5.6$$
$$= -.6$$

This indicates that the difference is negative, favoring treatment B, at the aptitude value of 8. To test whether this difference is significantly different from a zero difference, we must use a computer to estimate the covariances of Eq. 8. An option of the statistical analysis system (SAS) procedure PROC REG, can do this. We obtain the values

$$S_{22} = 2 \quad S_{24} = .5 \quad S_{44} = .001$$

so that

$$S_{D(8)}^2 = 2.1 + .5(8) + .001(64)$$
$$= 2.564$$

Then, from Eq. 9, with 104 subjects,

$$F_{1,100} = -.36/2.564$$
$$= -.140$$

a nonsignificant difference at $\alpha = .05$. Thus, although treatment B is slightly better in our study, if the study were replicated we would not expect consistent results favoring A or B for clients with aptitude 8.

Nonparallelism of Slopes

Although $D(X)$ gives a method of examining treatment effects at various values of X, it does not tell us anything about the difference between treatments across all values for X and whether this difference is constant. A constant difference is taken as a definition of noninteraction. That is,

$$D(X) = 0 \tag{10}$$

for all X. From Eq. (5), an omnibus test for this is based on the null hypothesis $B_4 = 0$. From Rogosa (1981),

$$F = \hat{B}_4/S_{44} \tag{11}$$

distributed under the null hypothesis as a central F with 1 and $N - 4$ degrees of freedom. It is quite possible that nonsimultaneous tests for selected values of X will be significant when the overall F for B_4 is not. A Bonferoni type adjustment in Eq. (9) would correct this, as with ANOVA. For many comparisons, however, the power for the tests for D would likely become quite low. In the previous example we can use the information provided, using Eq. 11:

$$F_{1,000} = -.7/.001$$
$$= 700$$

a highly significant value, indicating nonparallel slopes.

Certain values of X are particularly interesting. One is the value $\bar{X}$, the weighted mean for X based on the two groups.

$$D(\bar{X}) = \frac{1}{N} \sum_i \sum_j (B_2 + B_4 X_{j(i)}) \tag{12}$$

This quantity is estimated by

$$\hat{D}(\bar{X}) = \frac{1}{N} \sum_i \sum_j (\hat{B}_2 + \hat{B}_4 X_{j(i)}) \tag{13}$$

The quantity in Eq. (13) is the distance between regression lines for the person with average aptitude $\bar{X}$. It is also the average distance between regression lines.

Another value of X of interest is that value where $D(X)$ has minimum variance, termed the center of accuracy, or $C_a = -\sigma_{24}/\sigma_{44}$. It is estimated by solving the equation that follows:

$$\hat{B}_2 + \hat{B}_4 C_a = \bar{Y}_{\cdot(1)} - \bar{Y}_{\cdot(2)} - B_p(\bar{X}_{\cdot(1)} - \bar{X}_{\cdot(2)}) \tag{14}$$

where B_p is the pooled common regression slope

$$\hat{B}_p = \frac{B_1 \sum_j (X_{j(1)} - \bar{X}_{\cdot(1)})^2 + B_2 \sum_j (X_{\cdot j(2)} - \bar{X}_{\cdot(2)})^2}{\sum_j (X_{j(1)} - \bar{X}_{\cdot(1)})^2 + \sum_j (X_{j(2)} - \bar{X}_{\cdot(2)})^2} \tag{15}$$

Since C_a will always be in the middle of the values of X, $D(C_a)$ is another point to use as an estimate of treatment effect for an average individual.

By definition, $\sigma^{-2}_{D(C_a)}$ is less than or equal to $\sigma^{-2}_{D(X)}$. The latter is estimated by

$$S^2_{D(\bar{X})} = MS_e \left[\frac{1}{n_1} + \frac{1}{n_2} + \frac{(\bar{X}_{\cdot(1)} + \bar{X}_{\cdot(2)})^2}{N^2} \right.$$
$$\left. \times \left(\frac{n_1^2}{\sum_j (X_{j(1)} - \bar{X}_{\cdot(1)})^2} + \frac{n_2^2}{\sum (X_{j(2)} - \bar{X}_{\cdot(2)})^2} \right) \right] \tag{16}$$

The two varainces will be identical, as will $\bar{X} = C_a$ when $\bar{X}_{\cdot(1)} = \bar{X}_{\cdot(2)}$ or $n_1 \sum_j (X_{j(1)} - \bar{X}_{\cdot(1)})^2 = n_2 \sum_j (X_{j(2)} - \bar{X}_{\cdot(2)})$. The first condition is not likely to be fulfilled in nonrandomized studies. The latter may be reasonable for nearly equal samples with similar variances.

For the two values of X, $D(\bar{X})$ seems more useful, since it gives a measure of the average distance between regression lines. An F test is performed as follows for null hypothesis $D(\bar{X}) = 0$.

$$F = [D(\bar{X})]^2 / S^2 D(\bar{X}) \tag{17}$$

with 1 and $N - 4$ degrees of freedom.

Confidence intervals around any value $\hat{D}(X)$ are constructed by the use of

$$\hat{D}(X) \pm (\alpha F_{1,N-4} S^2_{D(X)})^{\frac{1}{2}} \tag{18}$$

to estimate $D(X)$.

SIMULTANEOUS REGIONS OF SIGNIFICANCE

Instead of focusing on one value of X at a time, we may wish to know, at significance level alpha, which regions of X correspond to which values of $D(X)$ that are nonzero. All points in the significance region of X will have no values of $D(X) = 0$ in $1 - \alpha$ of the intervals so constructed. Potthoff (1964) constructed the confidence band corresponding to this probability statement. The interval is constructed as follows:

$$D(X) \pm \sqrt{2F_{2,N-4}S^2_{D(X)}} \tag{19}$$

Since this is a function around $D(X)$, and $S^2_{D(X)}$ generally increases as X deviates, R_X, the region for X will be determined by an hyperbolic function in $D(X)$ at the points where the function crosses the X axis. Thus, regions R_s of X, where $D(X)$ is nonzero, can include three cases, for a, b finite values:

a. $a \leq R_s \leq b$
b. $R_s \leq a$ and $b \leq R_s$
c. $R_s \leq a$ or $R_s \leq b$

Figure 3 shows examples of the three cases. Which case holds depends upon the slope of $D(X)$ and $S^2_{D(X)}$. Rogosa (1980) has worked out the conditions for these cases in terms of $\hat{B}_4/S_{44}$.

When $\hat{B}_4^2/S_{44} < 2_\alpha F_{2,N-4}$, case a holds. When $\hat{B}_4^2/S_{44} > 2_\alpha F_{2,N-4}$, case b holds, and when $\hat{B}_4^2/S_{44} = 2_\alpha F_{2,N-4}$, case c holds. The latter case is termed degenerate. There is a special case of c in which neither points a nor b are finite and there is no region.

To calculate the points a and b, one must solve the quadratic equation implied by the following:

$$[D(X)]^2 - 2_\alpha F_{2,N-4}S^2_{D(X)} = 0 \tag{20}$$

$D(X)$ and S^2 are written in their parametric forms using Eqs. (7) and (8) to yield

$$[\hat{B}_2 + \hat{B}_4X]^2 - 2_\alpha F_{2,N-4}[S_{22} + 2S_{24}X + S_{44}X^2] = 0$$

which is put in quadratic form $AX^2 + BX + C = 0$, solved as

$$X_{R_s} = \frac{-B \pm \sqrt{B^2 - 4AC}}{2A} \tag{21}$$

where

$$A = \hat{B}_4^2 - 2\alpha F_{2,N-4}S_{44}$$
$$B = \hat{B}_2\hat{B}_4 - 2_\alpha F_{2,N-4}S_{24}$$
$$C = \hat{B}_2^2 - 2_\alpha F_{2,N-4}S_{22}$$

When Eq. (21) has two real solutions, one must calculate $\hat{B}_4^2/S_{44}$ to

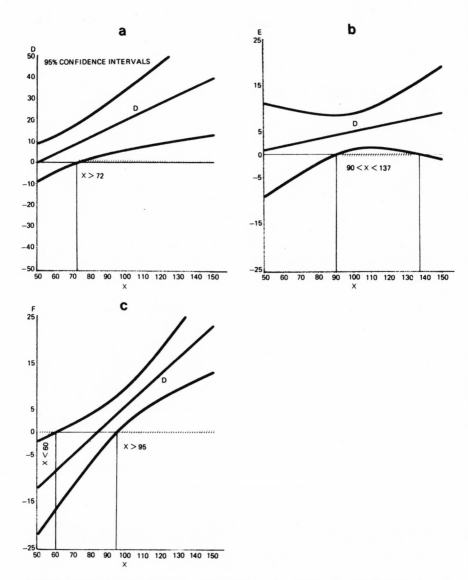

FIGURE 3. Simultaneous Regions of Significance for $D(X)$: (a) right-hand region of significance, (b) central region of significance, and (c) left and right regions of significance.

determine whether case a or b holds. Case c will hold when there is only one real solution $(B^2 - 4AC = 0)$. The case with no points in R_s is equivalent to the solutions of both being imaginary $(B^2 < 4AC)$.

The region R_s is interpreted as the region in which the treatment effect is nonzero. In the application to individual differences, any person whose aptitude score X lies in region R_s will benefit more from the superior treatment than the inferior treatment.

EXAMPLE OF SIMULTANEOUS REGIONS OF SIGNIFICANCE

Using the same data as that given in the previous example, we wish to determine the region of significance for aptitude values between 0 and 10. We solve Eq. 21 to obtain

$$A = (-.7)^2 - 2(3.09)(.001) = .484$$
$$B = (5)(.-7) - 2(3.09)(.5) = -6.509$$
$$C = (5)^2 - 2(3.09)(2) = 12.64$$

Then

$$x_{R_s} = \frac{-(-6.509) \pm \sqrt{(-6.509)^2 - 4(.484)(12.64)}}{2(.484)}$$
$$= \frac{6.509 \pm 4.23}{.968}$$

Thus, the treatments differ for persons with aptitudes at or below 2.35 on X or above 11.09. Since the latter is above the range of interest, we can expect not to find differences between the treatments for high aptitude individuals.

TWO APTITUDES

For two aptitudes X_1 and X_2, analytic results are available. The linear model of Eq. (5) is expanded to include the second aptitude regression and an ATI for the second aptitude. The difference function $D(X_1, X_2)$ is expanded in Eq. (7) to include a third term for the second aptitude. Nonsimultaneous and simultaneous regions are based on a ratio of $D^2(X_1, X_2)d$ to the variance of D. Significance for nonsimultaneous regions (single values of X_1, X_2) for the ratio is given by comparison with an F with $1, N - 6$ degrees of freedom; the simultaneous regions are tested against $3F$ with $3, N - 6$ degrees of freedom. Details are given in Rogosa (1981). The simultaneous region of significance with two predictors is in general bounded by a conic section, just as the hyperbolas for a single predictor bound the region R_s. Since the ATI now is concerned with nonparallel regression planes, the R_s surface may be a hyperbola, an ellipse, or a parabola, depending on the observed ratio of F to initial values $F_2 = 3F_{3,N-6}$ and $F_s = 2F_{2,N-6}$:

    a. Hyperbola if $F > F_2$
    b. Ellipse if $F_s < F < F_2$
    c. Parabola if $F = F_2$

DESIGN CONSIDERATIONS

In ANOVA, factors are considered either fixed or random according to the relation of the levels present to the population they represent. A fixed factor has present in the experiment all levels in the population for which a generalization is to be made. Sex (male or female) is a typical fixed factor. Subject (typically nested in treatments) is usually considered a random factor, since results are generalized to subjects *like those of the experiment.*

Rogosa (1977) has discussed the history of conditional inference, a related situation, in which units are drawn randomly from a population and their aptitude scores are observed or known after sampling. Generalization is restricted to those aptitude scores that actually appear as with fixed levels.

This state of affairs is basically unsatisfactory unless the set of aptitude scores exhausts the population of practical interest. In some designs it may, for the particular experiment, produce sample distributions of the aptitude with intermittent gaps or holes, yet generalization across the range of the aptitude may generally be desired and warranted.

A distinction between conditional and unconditional inference, noted in Rogosa (1977) is that the distribution of the aptitude variable is not needed in conditional inference methods and estimation, but must typically be included in the unconditional, random factor cases. The difference in the two is illustrated in the conditional and unconditional distributions of the sample intercept in a simple regression of Y and X. The unconditional distribution depends on σ_X^2, whereas the conditional distribution does not. The result can be extended to include the treatment effects of a fixed factor by extension to multivariate theory. The distributions of the B-weights are, however, identical in both conditional and unconditional cases (Rogosa, 1977; Bertlett, 1933).

ERROR RATES FOR JOHNSON-NEYMAN TECHNIQUE

Under unconditional sampling of X, the Type I error rate seems to be unaffected (Mendo, 1975). The Type II error rate is expected to be larger, however, since the variance of the regression coefficient estimates is made larger in expectation (Sampson, 1974).

Another consideration, not directly related to the ATI, concerns the test for overall treatment effect. If X is treated as a random factor in a mixed model, the expected mean square for a fixed crossing variable A is

$$\varepsilon(MS_A) = \sigma_e^2 + \eta\sigma_{AX}^2 + nK\sigma_A^2 \qquad (22)$$

which includes a term for the population interaction of X with levels of A. Linear constraints on the levels of X decide the degrees of freedom K associated with factor X (here 1 df). The power of the test of A from this perspective is greatly reduced since MS_{AX} is the appropriate error term. The AX interaction disappears in the conditional or fixed case.

ERRORS OF MEASUREMENT

In psychological research, it is a basic assumption that error exists in the scores of mental measurements. Such concern was far less evident in the agricultural models of ANOVA developed by Fisher. The independent variables (treatments, blocks, etc.) were assumed to be known without error, just as it is assumed that the treatment variables in an ATI study have no error in their coding. The dependent variable was thought to be fallible, but measurement error was bumped into the general error term and no further attention was paid it. In ATI research, errors of measurement of both the dependent variable Y and the aptitude X are expected. True score theory is invoked to account for measurement errors; for variables Y and X in Eq. (1), a useful model for true scores is

$$T_{Yj(i)} = \tau_{0i} + \tau_i T_{Xj(i)} + \eta_{j(i)} \qquad (23)$$

with a common slope for all subjects in group i. The observed scores are related as in Eq. (1) with common slope β_i for all subjects in group i. Reliabilities for Y and X are defined as ratios of true score variance to observed score variance. It can be shown that the observed regression weights are related to the true score regression weights as follows (dropping subscripts for i):

$$\beta_{0i} = \tau_0 + (1 - \rho_{xx})\tau\mu_x \quad \text{and} \quad \beta = \rho_{xx}\tau \qquad (24)$$

The true score models for Y and X are

$$Y_{j(i)} = T_{yj(i)} + \Delta_{j(i)} \qquad (25)$$

$$X_{j(i)} = T_{xj(i)} + E_{j(i)} \qquad (26)$$

The variance error of estimate can be given as follows for each group i:

$$\sigma_e^2 = \sigma_{y.x}^2 = [\sigma_\eta^2 + \sigma_{e_{T_x T_y}}^2 \sigma_y^2 + \sigma_\Delta^2][1 - \rho_{yy}\rho_{xx}\rho_{T_x T_y}^2] \qquad (29)$$

and the true score variance error of estimate is

$$\sigma_\eta^2 = \sigma_{T_y.T_x}^2 = \sigma_y^2(1 - \rho_{T_x T_y}^2) \qquad (28)$$

which is clearly smaller than the observed score error variance. From true score theory, by disattenuation,

$$\rho_{T_x T_y} = \frac{\rho_{xy}}{\sqrt{\rho_{xx}}\,\sqrt{\rho_{yy}}} \qquad (29)$$

The implication of this for the Johnson–Neyman (J–N) technique is to increase $\sigma_{D(X)}^2$ for all X, thus reducing the region of significance R_s, proven by Rogosa (1977), who showed the relationship between the observed score point of significance X_s and the true score point T_{Xs}:

$$X_s = \rho_{XX}T_X + (1 - \rho_{XX})\mu_T \qquad (30)$$

for homogeneous reliabilities within-group for X.

ALTERNATIVE APPROACHES

Jöreskog (1970, 1973) and his coauthors have developed the analysis of covariance structures into an impressive array of techniques that allow for imperfectly measured indicator variables, latent variables, and complex error structures. This leads to another approach to analysis of ATIs with error in the aptitudes, treatments, and dependent variables using the LISREL (linear structural relations) methods that rely on maximum likelihood techniques. Although readers are referred to Jöreskogs' writings for detail, the ATI model with error will be examined here.

The linear model of Eqs. (23), (25), and (26) can be reformulated into Jöreskog's model with a slight notation change

$$\begin{aligned} BT_y &= \Gamma T_x + \eta \\ Y &= T_y + \Delta \\ X &= T_x + E \end{aligned} \qquad (31)$$

Then, from Jöreskog (1973),

$$\Sigma = \left[\begin{array}{c|c} B^{-1}\Gamma\Phi\Gamma'B'^{-1} + B^{-1}\Psi B'^{-1} + \theta_\Delta^2 & B^{-1}\Gamma\Phi \\ \hline \Phi\Gamma'B'^{-1} & \Phi + \theta_E^2 \end{array}\right] \quad (32)$$

Where Φ is the covariance matrix of T_x; Ψ, the covariance matrix of T_y; θ_E, and θ_Δ, the error covariance matrixes; and Σ, the covariance matrix of $(Y', X')'$.

Although Darlington and Rom (1972) dismissed such models from consideration in path analysis, Alwin and Tessler (1974) and Bagozzi (1977) take a more positive view of the use of LISREL in experimental settings. Sörbom (1978) has presented ANCOVA in much this fashion.

Solution of such models is straightforward, using LISREL. The resultant regression weights for the structural exogenous variables are then used in the J–N technique. For reasonably large samples, normal distribution theory is invoked and the results of the first part of this chapter apply.

GENERALIZABLY THEORY AND APTITUDE–TREATMENT INTERACTION

Cronbach and his associates have written extensively about ATIs and their analysis. Much of the work presented here is an outgrowth of their attention to the topic. The work of Cronbach, Gleser, Nanda, and Rajaratnam (1972) on generalizability theory also has interesting applications to ATI research by virtue of the attention paid to variance components in designs.

Of major interest is the generalizability of the ATI component of a design. Recall that, in general, the generalizability coefficient is given in the form

$$g = \frac{\sigma_{ATI'}^2}{\sigma_{ATI'}^2 + \sigma_{E'}^2} \quad (33)$$

where $\sigma_{ATI'}^2$ is a linear combination of components related to the ATI terms, including main effects lower order interactions, and fixed facets, and $\sigma_{E'}^2$ is a linear combination of terms that interact with ATI terms plus true error variance σ_e^2. Rentz (1980) has discussed the formation of g coefficients from variance components.

Generalizability coefficients for ATI components in complex designs provide information concerning the dependability of the ATI under the conditions observed (Cronbach et al., 1972) and form the basis for modification of a test in a subsequent D (decision)-study, presumably to improve the dependability when it is low. Cronbach and Snow (1977)

reported variance components on a 2 (sex) × 2 (IQ) × 3 (treatment) design
on teaching the Archimides principle in physics from a study by Babikian
(1971). One interesting side issue is the estimation of the full IQ variance
component instead of an artificial dichotomy, as was performed by
Cronbach and Snow, who suggest a normal curve correction analogous to
that used for the biserial correlation. In this chapter, we recommend a
direct estimation of the covariate variance, using maximum likelihood or
some other technique suitable to the design (if σ_x^2 is known from other
research, such as a national norm sample, it should be used). In some cases,
the ATI variance can be estimated from the mean square term, if no other
components are included. [Cronbach and Snow's (1977) reported results for
total test (p. 316, Table 10.3).] The g coefficient for $T \times$ IQ, with sex a
fixed facet and assuming IQ is random, is

$$\rho_{AT}^{2(S)} = \frac{\sigma_{AT}^2 + \sigma_A^2 + \sigma_T^2 + (\sigma_{ATS}^2/2)}{[\sigma_{AT}^2 + \sigma_A^2 + \sigma_T^2 + (\sigma_{ATS}^2/2) + (\sigma_{AS}^2/2) + (\sigma_{TS}^2/2) + \sigma_\varepsilon^2]}$$

$$= \frac{.00 + .24 + .22 + (.09/2)}{.00 + .24 + .22 + (.09/2) + (.00/2) + (.03/2) + 1.00}$$

$$= \frac{.505}{1.52} = .33$$

This result suggests a quite modest generalizability for this ATI and
also indicates the large contribution of the ATI-by-sex interaction.

When this coefficient can be improved through a more refined
treatment, a D-study be undertaken. It is not insignificant that such small g
coefficients have been consistently reported (as variance components or as
relatively small F statistics) in the ATI education literature over the last
decade. Although psychologists have pursued the ATI for over 20 years,
perhaps the greatest effort has occurred in education in attempting to find
efficacious educational treatments for students of varying ability and
different sex. A perusal of such studies, including those of Cronbach and his
associates, does not inspire confidence in the ATI search.

USES OF THE JOHNSON–NEYMAN TECHNIQUE

Willson (1982) reviewed the literature in several journals that publish
ATI studies. Of 23 studies, three used the J–N technique. Only three (one
in the group above) examined or tested the effects of unreliability. Only one
specifically examined mixed model effects. The rest all assumed fixed factor
models. These studies represent the mainstream of current ATI research

and suggest a great capacity for misinterpretation of ATI results due to Type I errors. As Willson noted, the potential for misinterpretation of ATI effects over a large number of studies is great if models are inadequately specified. If factors are indeed random (such as subjects, teachers, classrooms, or schools), and they are treated as fixed, the result is to increase power for detecting interactions such as ATIs. It should not be surprising that ATIs will not replicate as significant effects in other studies, because the fixed effect ATI does not allow generalizability to settings that vary from those found in the first study. If such a procedure is taken as the standard technique, an entire body of literature could be built upon ungeneralizable, one-time ATI results.

TOPICS NOT COVERED

One aspect of ATI methodology not covered here is the analysis of nonlinear ATIs, especially quadratic regression. Rogosa (1977, 1980) and Corno, Mitman, and Hedges (1981) have discussed these in some detail. Rogosa (1977) reported particularly unsalutary effects of measurement error for quadratic regressions on Type I error rate, typically increasing it while decreasing power.

Another area not treated here is that of multiple covariates. The problems of multicollinearity are well known, and measurement errors compound the problems of Type I error rates, generally increasing them.

NEW AREAS FOR INVESTIGATION

The movement to merge statistical inferential theory with psychometrics seems to continue. Cronbach *et al.* (1972), Sörbom (1978), Novick (1980), and others have all indicated points of merger. Perhaps it is safe to predict that major areas of psychometric research will be brought to bear on the ATI problems, especially in the measurement of aptitudes. Multidimensional scaling and latent trait theory generate scales and scores. How they can be usefully incorporated into ATI models is not yet clear, but the possibilities are intriguing.

Longitudinal research has far to go before any degree of maturity is reached, but LISREL models can handle some data sets and time-series models can handle others. The dynamic quality of the ATI makes it a difficult but interesting problem for longitudinal research on individuals and on groups. Little has been done.

SUMMARY

This mathematical treatment of ATIs will be tough going for many readers, but they are encouraged to keep at the chapter. The major emphasis of the chapter has been on the Johnson–Neyman technique, which performs a task similar to that of the confidence interval for comparison of means. Significance *per se* is almost never useful by itself. One must always return to the data, in *a priori* or *a posteriori* fashion, to interpret significance. The J–N technique permits a realistic evaluation of the useful ranges for an aptitude treatment interaction. The applications of J–N depend upon the design of the ATI. Nonsimultaneous tests may be especially useful for cases in which a threshold or minimum score is involved. At the cut-off score X, is treatment A better than treatment B? For most applications, however, simultaneous estimation will be preferred. Over which values of aptitude will A be superior to B and over which values will they not differ? Applications abound in special education, bilingual education, and education for the gifted. Comparable problems exist for psychotherapy modes with personality (aptitude) variables interacting. We have not even begun to find bounds for such ATIs. It is hoped that this chapter, to a large degree based on David Rogosa's great effort over the last decade, will encourage further investigation of aptitude–treatment interactions.

REFERENCES

Alwin, D. F., & Tessler, R. C. Causal models, unobserved variables, and experimental data. *American Journal of Sociology*, 1974, *80*, 58–86.

Babikian, Y. An empirical exposition to determine the relative effectiveness of discovery, laboratory, and expository methods of teaching science concepts. *Journal*, 1971, *8*, 201–210.

Bagozzi, R. P. Structural equation models in experimental research. *Journal of Marketing Research*, 1977, *14*, 209–226.

Bartlett, M. S. On the theory of statistical regression. *Proceedings of the Royal Society of Edinburgh*, 1933, *53*, 260–283.

Corno, L., Mitman, A., & Hedges, L. The influence of direct instruction on student self-appraisals: A hierarchical analysis of treatment and aptitude–treatment interaction effects. *American Education Research Journal*, 1981, *18*, 39–61.

Cronbach, L. J. The two disciplines of scientific psychology. *American Psychologist*, 1957, *12*, 671–684.

Cronbach, L. J., & Snow, R. E. *Aptitudes and instructional methods: A handbook for research on interactions*. New York: Irvington/Naiburg, 1977.

Cronbach, L. J., Gleser, G. C., Nanda, H., & Rajaratnam, N. *The dependability of behavioral measurements: Theory of generalizability for scores and profiles*. New York: Wiley, 1972.

Darlington, R. B. Multiple regression in psychological research and practice. *Psychological Bulletin*, 1968, *69*, 161–182.

Darlington, R. B., & Rom, J. F. Assessing the importance of independent variables in nonlinear causal laws. *American Educational Research Journal*, 1972, *9*, 449–462.

Edgington, A. S. A new tabulation of statistical procedures used in APA journals. *American Psychologist*, 1974, *29*, 25–26.

Johnson, P. O., & Neyman, J. Tests of certain linear hypotheses and their applications to some educational problems. *Statistical Research Memoirs*, 1936, pp. *1*, 57–93.

Jöreskog, K. G. A general method for analysis of covariance structures. *Biometrika*, 1970, *57*, 239–251.

Jöreskog, K. G. A general method for estimating a linear structural equation system. In A. S. Goldberger & O. D. Duncan, (Eds.), *Structural equation model in the social sciences*. New York: Seminar Press, 1973.

Mendro, R. L. *A Monte Carlo study of the robustness of the Johnson–Neyman technique.* Paper presented at the annual meeting of the American Educational Research Association, Washington, D.C., March 31, 1975.

Novick, M. R. Statistics as psychometrics. *Psychometrika*, 1980, *45*, 411–424.

Potthoff, R. F. On the Johnson–Neyman technique and some extensions thereof. *Psychometrika*, 1964, *29*, 241–256.

Rentz, R. R. Rules of thumb for estimating reliability coefficients using generalizability theory. *Educational and Psychological Measurement*, 1980, *40*, 575–592.

Rogosa, D. *Some results for the Johnson–Neyman technique.* Unpublished doctoral dissertation, Stanford University, 1977. (University Microfilms, 78–2225).

Rogosa, D. Comparing nonparallel regression lines. *Psychological Bulletin*, 1980, *88*, 307–321.

Rogosa, D. On the relationship between the Johnson–Neyman region of significance and statistical tests of parallel within group regressions. *Educational and Psychological Measurement*, 1981, *41*, 73–84.

Sampson, A. R. A tale of two regressions. *Journal of the American Statistical Association*, 1974, *69*, 682–698.

Smith, D. Trends in counseling and psychotherapy. *American Psychologist*, 1982, *37*, 802–809.

Smith, M. L., & Glass, G. V. Meta-analysis of psychotherapy outcome studies. *American Psychologist*, 1977, *32*, 752–760.

Sörbom, D. An alternative to the methodology for analysis of covariance. *Psychometrika*, 1978, *43*, 381–396.

Willson, V. L. Research techniques in AERJ articles: 1969–1978. *Educational Researcher*, 1980, *9*, 5–10.

Willson, V. L. *Misuses of regression approaches to ANOVA and ANCOVA in educational research.* Paper presented at the Southwest Educational Research Association, Austin, Texas, February, 1982.

8

General Linear Models of Individual Differences

SAMUEL S. HUNG AND HERBERT J. WALBERG

In faith or in hope, all humans may be created equal. By nature or by nuture, all individuals are different, different in certain, if not all, characteristic attributes. Individuals may be said to be different physically, mentally, or socially, based on certain specific attributes that are observable or measurable.

By observing a group of individuals on a given specific attribute, say X or sex, the observed values on X (in this case, dichotomous categories) may be "male" or "female" that are different in kind only. When two individuals, say i and j, are compared based on their values obtained from observation on X (in which females and males may be coded quantitatively as 0 and 1 in this case), these two individuals are said to be different in kind if and only if $X_i \neq X_j$. Otherwise, these two individuals are not different, as long as X is the only attribute in concern.

By measuring a group of individuals on another specific attribute, say Y or body weight, in this case a continuous variable, the observed values on the scale, may range from fifty to several hundred pounds. When two individuals, say i and j, are compared based on their values obtained from measurement on Y, these two individuals are said to be different in amount if and only if $Y_i \neq Y_j$, that implies $Y_i > Y_j$ or $Y_i < Y_j$. The amount in their differences on Y may be readily computed or expressed as either $(Y_i - Y_j)$, $(Y_j - Y_i)$, or $|Y_i - Y_j|$.

Values obtained from imperfect measurement or, say, Y, are subjected to measurement errors, say $e = Y_{obs} - Y_t$, where Y_{obs} is Y (observed) and Y_t is Y (true). If an individual i is measured repeatedly with the same instrument for many times, say N, the measurement errors e_i are said to

SAMUEL S. HUNG AND HERBERT J. WALBERG ● College of Education, University of Illinois at Chicago, Chicago, Illinois 60680.

distributed according to some Gaussian error function with the expected value of e_i equal to zero, namely

$$E(e) = E(Y_{obs} - Y_t) = E(Y_{obs}) - Y_t = 0$$

It implies that

$$Y_t = E(Y_{obs}) = \sum Y_{obs}/N$$

In other words, in repeated measurements on a certain attribute of an individual, the random errors of measurement are expected to balance out such that the average of the observed values may very well serve as an estimate of the true value of the attribute.

If the instrument has a known measurement error of Y_e, a single observed value of Y may be said to represent the true value of Y within measurement error of Y_e, particularly when Y_e is very small relative to the true value, namely; $Y_{obs} = Y_t + Y_e$. In the study of differences between two individuals, say i and j, on attribute Y, we can hardly say with certainty that Y_i and Y_j are different unless their difference $|Y_i - Y_j|$ equals or exceeds twice of measurement errors Y_e. Otherwise, the two individuals, although with $Y_i \neq Y_j$, must be said to be indifferent within measurement errors Y_e.

In study of individual differences on attribute that cannot be directly observed or measured, the basis of comparison of individuals is some inferred difference indirectly observed or measured. Parallel to the black box in physical sciences, the measurement of a construct in social or behavioral sciences may be subject to unknown random or systematic errors. It is hoped, however, that the random part may be balanced out through repetitions of measurement; the systematic part may or may not be adjusted by calibration if the nature of the systematic errors is not yet known.

Not knowing what happens inside the black box or what the construct really is, the attribute, say, Z, may be indirectly or partially represented by some other variable, say, Y, that is either observable or measurable. Suppose that Z is indirectly measurable by an instrument on Y; then individual differences on Z may then be inferred from differences on Y, subject to errors Y_e of the measuring instrument. The difference $|Y_i - Y_j|$ may be interpreted as the difference $|Z_i - Z_j|$ between two individuals i and j.

In a study of a group of individuals, measurements are replicated with the same instrument on each of the N individuals. Assuming that all these individuals are, in fact, indifferent on a certain attribute, say, X, except for the random errors of measurement e, we have

$$X_1 = X_t + e_1$$
$$X_2 = X_t + e_2$$
$$\cdots \quad \cdots \quad \cdots$$
$$X_i = X_t + e_i$$
$$\cdots \quad \cdots \quad \cdots$$
$$X_N = X_t + e_N$$

where X_t is the true value on X. By summing up both sides, the random errors are balanced out, namely; $\sum X = NX_t$ over N measurements. We have $\sum X/N = X_t$, the mean of the N measurements on X. This mean value may very well be used as an estimate for the true value on X (X_t), common for all the individuals in the same group.

In case the individuals differ on an attribute, say, Y, other than the measurement errors e alone, we have

$$Y_1 = Y_{1t} + e_1$$
$$Y_2 = Y_{2t} + e_2$$
$$\cdots \quad \cdots \quad \cdots$$
$$Y_i = Y_{it} + e_i$$
$$\cdots \quad \cdots \quad \cdots$$
$$Y_N = Y_{Nt} + e_N$$

where Y_{it} is the true value of Y for individual i. By summing up both sides, while the random errors are balanced out, we have $\sum Y = \sum Y_t$ or $\sum Y/N = \sum Y_t/N$ over N replicated measurements. In other words, the mean of the N observed values of Y may now be used as an estimate of the average true value over the whole group, say M_y. Under such a circumstance, the difference $|Y_i - M_y|$ represents the difference between the individual i and the group as a whole.

Suppose we have k mutually exclusive groups of individuals, we may be interested in comparing these k groups in terms of their group means on a certain attribute, say, Y, regardless of whether the individuals are different among themselves. The question of interest is whether $M_{1y} = M_{2y} = \ldots = M_{ky}$, within errors of the measuring instrument. If $M_{1y} \neq M_{2y} \neq \ldots \neq M_{ky}$, how different are these groups of individuals? Regardless of whether the individuals are different, based on the attribute Y alone, the group memberships are defined, and the individuals are assigned or classified into groups based on some attribute or attributes other than Y, say, X. Thus, X could be a categorical variable, distinguishable in kinds. Based on sex, for example, we could have groups of males and females. Then X could be a categorized variable, distinguishable in levels. Based on income, we could have a group of low-income, a group of middle-income, or a group of high-income people, although income as a variable could have values ranging over a broad continuum (but it should be said that categorizing continuous variables eliminates within-category numerical information and should ordinarily be avoided).

TIME AS A VARIABLE

When we compare, on a given attribute, say, an individual with individuals, an individual with groups, or a group with groups of individuals, we have assumed either that X is a time-independent variable or that X is measured at the same instant of time. When time is disregarded as a variable of concern, the observed or measured values on the attribute are said to be a set of cross-sectional data. Regardless of when the individuals are actually observed or measured, the ordering of a set of cross-sectional data is considered arbitrary.

When the attribute X is observed or measured sequentially at certain periods or intervals along the continuum of time, we have obtained a set of longitudinal or time-series data. The ordering of a set of sequential data is unique. The data are said to be stationary or time independent if the sequentially measured values fluctuate randomly about a certain constant value. If the data exhibit some definite trend or some regular periodic pattern, the attribute is said to be time dependent. In other words, if there exists a one-to-one correspondence between time and the measured values on X, X may be expressed by some function of time, namely $X = f(t)$.

As a result of indivudual growth and development, certain attributes may change continuously over time. We may speak of individual difference between X_t at time t and $X_{t'}$ at any other time t', at least in principle. By plotting the observed value of a time-dependent variable X versus time t, we may attempt to discover the trend or to uncover a pattern if one exists. Once we succeed in fitting the best smoothed curve graphically or analytically with a certain function of time, we may study the differences of an individual, measured or projected at different point or points of time. It will permit us to study not just the changes over time, but also the rate or velocity or acceleration of change.

By nature or by nuture, the human does continue to grow and to develop, for better or for worse, over the whole life span. The question is not whether the individual difference over time should be studied, but how the individual differences over time can be studied. In most longitudinal studies, the same individuals are repeatedly measured on certain attributes over an extended period or interval of time. When repeated measurements of the same individuals are not feasible or are impractical, the attributes under study may be measured at different time cross sectionally with relevant replicates of individuals.

TOOLS FOR THE STUDY OF INDIVIDUAL DIFFERENCES

Given a set of data on a group or groups of individuals, various tools are available to study the differences among the individuals. These mathematical and statistical techniques have been available for half a century (and the least-squares criterion goes back more than 200 years to F. Gauss). Since the late 1950s, along with advances in high-speed computing, statistical packages have made computation more convenient and efficient. Following the Biomedical Computers Programs, the Statistical Package for the Social Sciences became available at any large computer facility. Joining their ranks, the Statistical Analysis System, available for IBM computers, has greatly enhanced graphic capabilities, which is particularly rewarding for exploratory studies. Its graphic output illustrates the statistical concepts presented in this and subsequent sections.

Table 1 presents a bird's-eye view of the tools readily applicable to the study of individual differences. Before using more complicated techniques or confirmatory analysis of data, it is good general practice to explore the data, both analytically and graphically, using a broad variety of descriptive measures. With better understanding of the nature or characteristics of the data for each variable, one can critically decide whether certain data points of extreme values should be excluded or included with or without adjustment. With a greater comprehension of the relationship between the variables, one may parsimoniously construct models that are easier to interpret or to validate.

This chapter covers a limited area of general linear models in multiple regression and analysis of variance. After brief accounts of how these techniques may be applied to studies of individual differences, two working examples, one on longitudinal data and one on cross-sectional data, are presented to illustrate how the graphs may guide selection or improvement of models.

ANOVA VERSUS REGRESSION ANALYSIS

The analysis of variance is, of course, variance oriented. This technique was originally developed to compare the mean effects on groups

TABLE 1. Tools for the Study of Individual Differences

Objective	Univariate single variable	Bivariate function of one variable	Multivariate function of many variables
Descriptive	Summary statistics for Central tendency Dispersion Symmetry Peakedness	Covariance and correlation for linear relationship	Dispersion and correlation matrices
or			
Explanatory	Frequency distribution (density function) Transformations	Curve-fitting for Linear relationship Nonlinear relationship Joint frequency distribution (contigency or association) Linearization of curves	Linear combination of variables for optimization of canonical, multiple, and partial correlations Component and factor analysis for simple structures
Inferential	Comparison of individual with group	General linear models Simple regression Polynomial regression	General linear models Multiple regression
or			
Applied	Analysis of variance for group comparisons	Analysis of covariance for Group comparisons	Discriminant analysis for Classification of individuals Dispersion analysis of variance and covariance for group comparisons

that have received different treatments. Given k groups of individuals, the treatment effect on an individual, say, i in group g, may be measured and recorded as X_{gi}. For group g of N_g individuals, the mean effect M_g may be obtained by taking the average over the group of individuals. By comparing the effect on each individual X_{gi} with the mean effect M_g, the difference or deviate from the mean $(X_{gi} - M_g)$ measures the dispersion along the distribution of data. The average of the square of the deviates from group mean M_g, say $\sum (X_{gi} - M_g)^2/(N_g - 1)$ is defined as the variance within group g. This is repeated for each group. Summing over all k groups, $\sum\sum (X_{gi} - M_g)^2/\sum (N_g - 1) = \sum\sum (X_{gi} - M_g)^2/(N - k)$, the within-group variance, which measures the dispersion within the k groups.

Parallel to the within-group variance, the weighted average of the square of the deviates of the group means M_g from the grand mean M, say, $\sum N_g(M_g - M)^2/(k - 1)$, is defined as the between- or among-group variance, which measures the dispersion among the k groups. To determine if the k groups are significantly different, based on the set of data on X, the ratio between the among-group variance and the within-group variance gives us a test-statistic T for testing the null hypothesis:

$$H_0 : M_1 = M_2 = \ldots = M_g = \ldots = M_k = M$$

At one extreme, when all M_g are equal to the grand mean M, the computed test-statistic $T = 0$. It implies that H_0 (no difference among groups) is true. At the other extreme, when all M_g greatly differ with one another, the among-group variance is much greater than the within-group variance. Then T is much much greater than zero, and H_0 should be rejected outright. Otherwise, under the assumption of normality and equal variances, the test-statistic T is said to distribute as an F statistic with $(k - 1)$ and $(N - k)$ degrees of freedom. By referring to the appropriate entry on an F-table, a probability statement can be readily made on the significance level that the null hypothesis (no difference) should or should not be rejected.

Analysis of variance as a tool for group comparisons has been generalized for cases dealing with many variables. Being multivariate, it is thus referred to as MANOVA, or dispersion analysis of variance and covariance. Applied to data collected from the field or the laboratory, with rigid control of treatment variables, such techniques for group comparisons might have been instrumental in the agricultural research, which led to our success in the so-called Green Revolution of this century.

Curve-fitting or the fitting of the equation to data may be a technique as old as any of the activities that we are engaged in in applying mathematics to empirical sciences, predominantly in the physical sciences.

By plotting stress versus strain, we observe the linear relationship of Hooke's Law. In studies of the behavior of gases, Boyle (1627–1691) found that, at constant temperature, the volume of a given mass of gas was inversely proportional to its pressure. Charles (1746–1823) found that at constant pressure, the volume of gas expands uniformly with a rise in temperature. By combining Boyle's and Charles' laws, we have the general gas law $PV = RT$ for ideal gases (see Figure 1). Another century passed before Johannes Diderik van der Waals (1837–1923) proposed the equation of $(P + a/V^2)(V - b) = RT$ for real gases, applicable throughout a far greater range than is Boyle's Law. Progress was steady, but slow indeed.

Studies of individual differences might be said to begin with Francis Galton (1822–1911) in his works on heredity or eugenics. In Galton and Pearson's "legendary" study of the relationship between the heights of fathers and sons, Karl Pearson (1857–1936) first worked out a measure for the linear relationship. Based on the positive correlation between the heights, tall fathers are likely to have tall sons, and short fathers are likely to have short sons. However, based on the best straight line fitted to the data with least-square errors, a very tall father tends to have sons shorter than he himself is, and a very short father tends to have sons taller than himself. This tendency of regressing toward the means might have given the linearly fitted line its new name. Since then, we speak of a regression line, the regression equation for the line, and regression analysis for fitting the equation to a given set of data on a dependent variable as related to a given independent variable.

When we deal with a single dependent variable as related to the linear combination of several independent variables, we compute the maximized multiple correlation and work out its associated multiple linear regression equation. When we deal with two sets of several independent and dependent variables, we compute the maximized canonical correlation by obtaining the two vectors of coefficients on the two linear combinations of variables. In this sense, canonical correlation analysis is an extension of regression analysis, or regression analysis is a special case of canonical correlation analysis. All these analyses are correlation oriented. The higher the linear correlation, the stronger the linear relationship between the variables or sets of variables.

Although ANOVA is used to compare group means based on the ratio between among-group and within-group variances, regression analysis is used to determine the functional relationship between dependent and independent variables. They are complementary techniques. Given a set of multigroup, multivariate data, the findings from a regression analysis is supplementary to that from an analysis of variance, and sometimes the reverse is true.

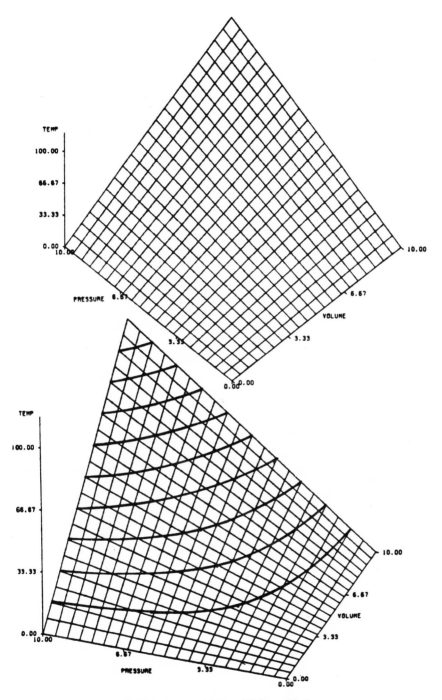

FIGURE 1. Model of $PV = KT$ for an ideal gas.

With the availability of a great variety of packages of statistical programs, numerical computation is no longer a burden. Our problem is not in how to fit the best equation to a given model, but rather in how to build or to choose a model that is a better representation of the functional relationship among the variables. A better model is one that is easier to interpret and to revalidate or one that is applicable to a broader range of data, with smaller squared errors between the estimated and the actual values on the dependent variable. If the maximized multiple correlation is not high enough to have practical value, we may continue to include more relevant variables. Meanwhile, we must consider the trade-off between the full model and a reduced model as long as it is within the bounds of measurement errors. It is generally agreed in science that a simpler model is a better model and a simpler theory is a better theory, granted both explain the same phenomena under study as well as a more complex model or theory.

FITTING WITH GENERAL LINEAR MODELS

Geometrically, two points are necessary to define a straight line, say, $Y = A + BV$, uniquely, with intercept A and slope B. This is said to be a linear model, linear in the variables V and Y and linear in the parameters A and B. Algebraically, $Y = A + BV$ may be said to be a general linear model in the parameters A and B, if we allow the variables V and Y to be functions of some other variables, although not necessarily first-degree functions. In other words, $Y = A + BV$ may represent a straight line or one of the many non-linear curves that can be perfectly fitted into any two given points in space, as shown in Figure 2.

It could be a convex-upward curve with an ever-increasing slope, such as in curves a.1, a.2, or a.3 for $V = e^x$, 2^x, or 1.5^x or in curves b.1, b.2, or b.3 for $V = X^3$, X^2 or $X^{\frac{3}{2}}$. It could be a concave-downward curve with an ever-decreasing slope, such as in curves a.4, a.5, or a.6 for $V = \log_{1.5} X$, $\log_2 X$, or $\log_e X$ or in curves b.4, b.5, or b.6 for $V = X^{\frac{2}{3}}$, $X^{\frac{1}{2}}$, or $X^{\frac{1}{3}}$. The bottom curves are enlargements of the b-curves for $0 \le X \le 1$ to show their degrees in curvature. It is readily seen that over a narrow range, or interval, the segment of curve can almost be represented by a straight line, particularly when either the dependent or the independent variable is fairly large. This explains why we would like to fit a straight line to the data, at least as the first approximation before attempting other curves.

Similarly, $Y = A + BV + CW$ may be said to be a general linear model in parameters A, B, and C. As shown in Figure 3, $Z_1 = 1X + 2Y$ is

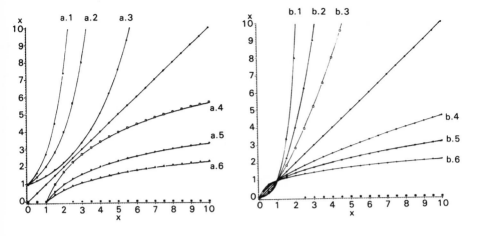

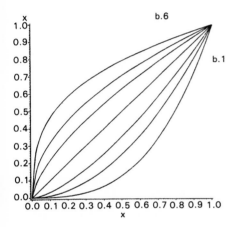

FIGURE 2. General linear models of $Y = A + BV$, where $V = f(X)$, which may or may not be linear in X.

a plane. As shown in Figure 4, $Z_2 = 1X + 2Y + .2X^2 - .1Y^2$ is a surface that X is convexing upward and Y is concaving downward or, with similar curvatures. As shown in Figure 5, $Z_3 = 1X + 2Y + .2X^2 - .1Y^2 + .5XY$ is a twisted surface with varying curvatures caused by the interaction or the cross-product term of X and Y.

A close examination of Figure 6 shows a surface obtained by a three-dimensional plot of Z versus X and Y; we may observe the following

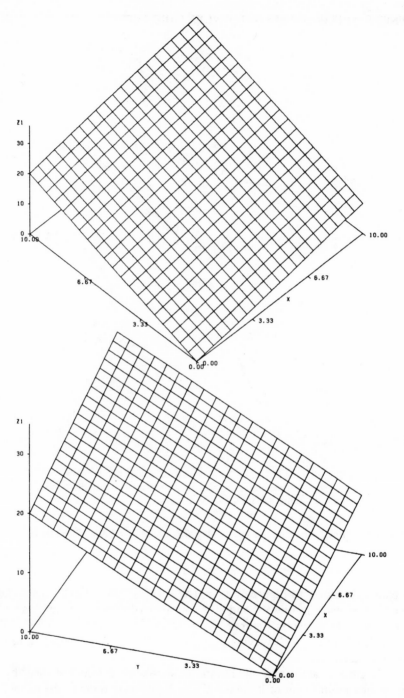

FIGURE 3. Plot of $Z_1 = 1X + 2Y$.

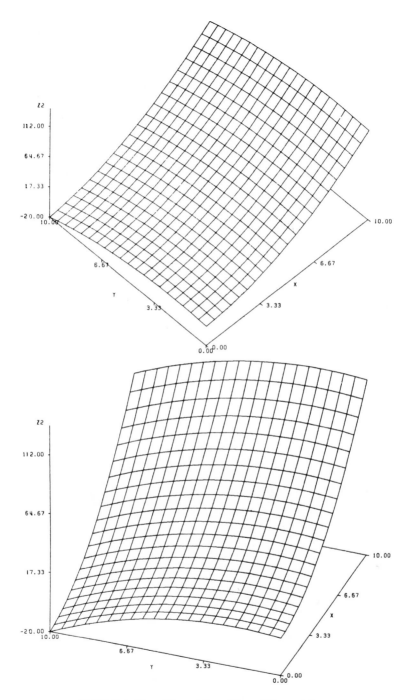

FIGURE 4. Plot of $Z_2 = 1X + 2Y + .2X^2 - .1Y^2$.

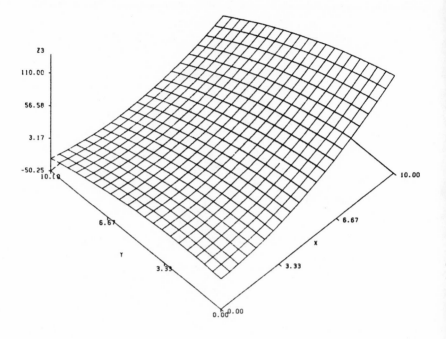

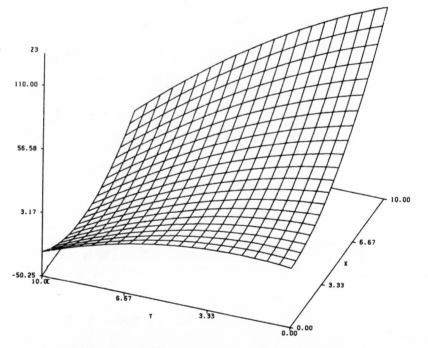

FIGURE 5. Plot of $Z_3 = 1X + 2Y + .2X^2 - .1Y^2 + .5XY$.

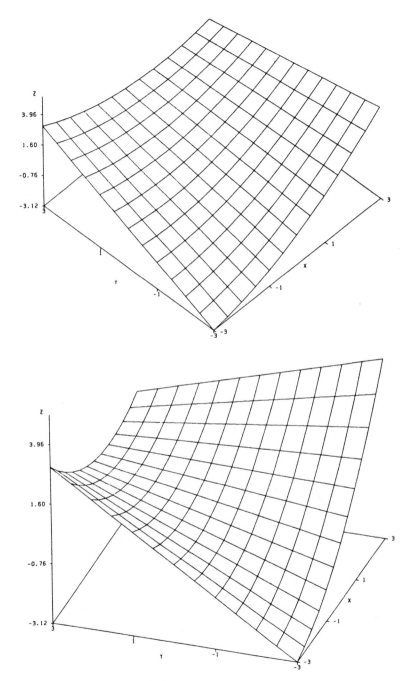

FIGURE 6. Plot of $Z = .43X + .28Y - .25XY + .14X^2$.

functional relationships:

(a) For any given Y, Z is convexing upward as X increases from -3 to $+3$. It implies that Z varies similarly with $a_1X + a_2X^2$.

(b) For any given X, Z is increasing linearly with Y from -3 to $+3$. It implies that Z varies with a_3Y.

(c) The surface appears somewhat twisted with changing curvatures. It implies that Z might vary with a_4XY.

We are tempted to represent the convex-up surface with a general linear model, such as

$$Z = a_0 + a_1V_1 + a_2V_2 + a_3V_3 + a_4V_4$$

where $V_1 = X$, $V_2 = X^2$, $V_3 = Y$, and $V_4 = XY$. In fact, the surface is a three-dimensional plot of data generated from the regression equation: $Z = .43X + .28Y - .25XY + .14X^2$ relating physics achievement test gains Z with student ability X and class difficulty Y (see Walberg, 1971; Anderson, 1970). Similarly, in Figure 7, we might represent the concave-down surface with some general linear models, such as

$$P = a_1C - a_2C^2 + a_3L - a_4L^2 \quad \text{or} \quad \ln P = a_0 + a_1 \ln C + a_2 \ln L$$

this is, $P = kC^{a_1}L^{a_2}$, as originally generated from the Cobb-Douglas equation of $P = 1.01C^{.75}L^{.25}$ (see Walberg, 1981).

In general, a linear model of Y, as a function of a set of p independent variables Xs, can always be represented as

$$Y = a_0 + a_1X_1 + a_2X_2 + \ldots + a_pX_p$$

that is linear in the $(p + 1)$ parameters yet to be determined. The Xs may be some algebraic or transcendental functions.

Given a set of data on the dependent variable Y and the p independent variables Xs, we may perform a regression analysis by using the least-square method of minimizing the sum of the squares of residuals, $(Y_{obs} - Y_{est})$. By solving the system of linear equations, we obtain a set of coefficient as for the linear combination of Xs such that the linear correlation between the observed and the estimated values of Y is maximized. Given a set of values on the independent variables Xs, we readily compute an estimated value for the dependent variable Y based on the general linear model thus obtained. In this sense, regression analysis provides us with a tool to fit analytically the best linear or linearized model to data. It gives us the functional relationship between the dependent

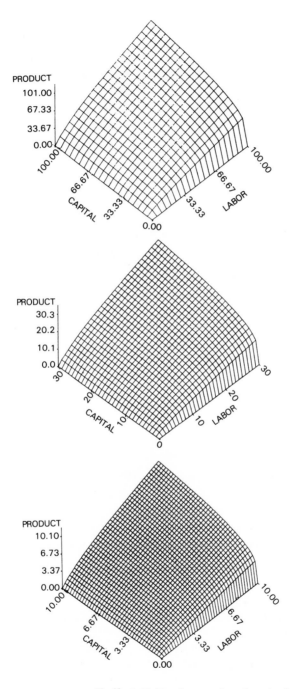

FIGURE 7. Plot of $P = 1.01\ C^{.75}L^{.25}$. Cobb-Douglas equation of productivity as a function of labor and capital.

variable and a unique linear combination of the independent variables and permits us to extend, from a set of known values on the independent variables, to the corresponding unknown dependent variable.

The plot of a set of observed and estimated values on the dependent variable gives us a visual impression of how well the model fits the data. By plotting the residuals against the dependent variable or any particular independent variable, one may gain insight as to whether the model can be improved.

To extend the scope of usefulness of general linear models, it is feasible to include some specially constructed "dummy" variables. Associated with group comparisons in experimental or nonexperimental studies, a dummy variable may be added to represent various effects due to such factors as time, space, or some other categorical or categorized variables that define the groups being compared. The appropriate use of dummy variables allows us to test the relationship between the dependent effect and the different treatment as uniquely defined by the dichotomized values on the dummy variables. In other words, for either a designed experiment or a non-experimental study, we may construct one general linear model to meet our objective in performing an ANOVA or a regression analysis (see Bock, 1975; Graybill, 1961; Johnston, 1972).

INDIVIDUAL DIFFERENCES CLASSIFIED

When we speak of individual differences, we often mean different things under different circumstances. Thus, so we can to be sure of what we are interested in under different circumstances, let us clarify the three basic classes of differences:

Class A: differences among individuals
Class B: differences among groups of individuals
Class C: differences between individuals and groups

For Class A, we need nothing other than simple arithmetic operations. For Class B, we need tools for multigroup comparison, namely univariate or multi-variate ANOVA.

In this chapter, we will focus mainly on Class C, namely, the difference between an individual and the group or groups. The comparison of an individual with a group of individuals is straightforward once we have found some model or representation for the whole group of individuals.

Given a set of data on a group or sample of individuals, we first compute certain descriptive summary statistics. Knowing the mean or means, we can compare the individual with the group in terms of the group mean or means. Knowing the frequency distribution or density function, we can then speak of individual differences in terms of a probability statement. On obtaining the linear model that best describes the whole set of data for the group of individuals, we can then speak of individual differences in terms of comparing the observed value with the value expected or estimated, based on the model for the group or groups.

In a study of individual difference, we can, in fact, compare an individual with a group based on data collected on (1) a single time-independent variable, say, X; (2) a single time-dependent variable, say, $X = f(t)$; or (3) a single dependent variable that is a function of one or more variables, say, $Y = f(V_1, V_2, \ldots, V_p)$.

INDIVIDUAL DIFFERENCES BASED ON A
SINGLE VARIABLE

Given a set of data on a single variable, the computation of certain summary statistics, such as skewness and kurtosis, can show us any marked departures from normality. If the variable under study is approximately distributed as a normal distribution, the difference between an individual and the group can be interpreted within the context of the standard normal distribution.

In case of doubt, a graphic representation of the frequency distribution provides a fast check for outliers or extreme values that might be the cause of a departure from normality. The exclusion or replacement of such data with less extreme values may bring the distribution back to an acceptable approximation of normality. Markedly skewed data may require a transformation to approach a distribution of known density function. For positively skewed data, taking the reciprocal, logarithm, or the square root may have the effect of pulling the long tail on the right toward the center of the distribution. For negatively skewed data, square or cubic transformations may be worth a trial.

Although it is easy to determine the distribution of categorical or discrete data, it is often arbitrary to categorize interval data. Analytically, it is easier to detect departures by plotting the cumulative densities with that of a normal distribution, as illustrated in Figures 8 and 9 (Bock, 1975, pp. 157–160).

As alternatives, either a stem-and-leaf display or a box-and-whisker plot (Tukey, 1977) provides a fast check for normality in spotting outliers or extreme values.

In case the distribution is symmetrical, but markedly departs from normality in peakedness, some re-scaling of data may be necessary to justify

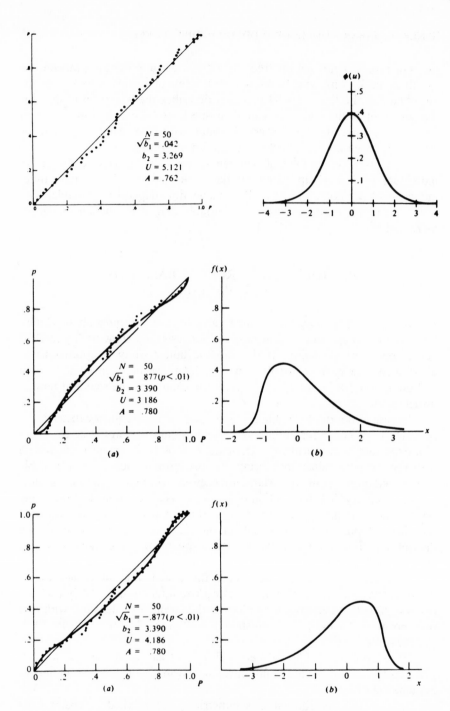

FIGURE 8. Plots of cumulative densities.

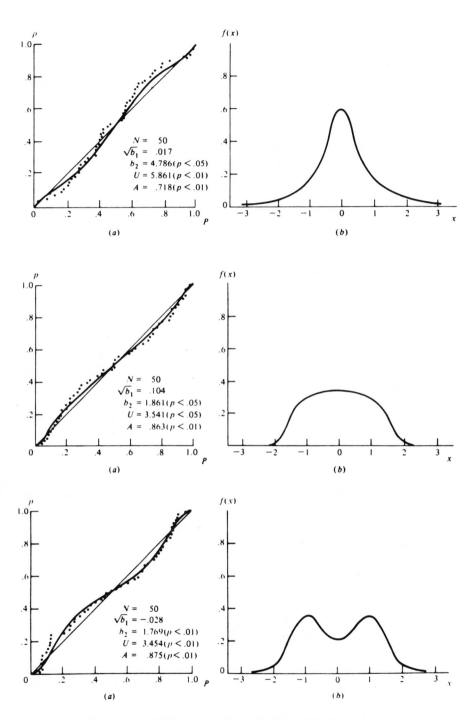

FIGURE 9. Plots of cumulative densities.

its approximation to normality. Otherwise, any individual difference must be derived indirectly from its own density distribution, not by referring to the standard normal distribution.

INDIVIDUAL DIFFERENCES BASED ON A
TIME-DEPENDENT VARIABLE

Given a time-dependent variable $X = f(t)$, we may attempt to fit a linear model, such as

$$X = a_0 + a_1 t$$
$$X = a_0 + a_1 t + a_2 t^2$$
$$X = a_0 + a_1 t + a_2 t^2 + a_3 t^3$$

or the like, depending on the degree of curvilinearity. In general, time t is a nonrandom fixed variable, and X is measured at certain fixed values of t. This is often called a polynomial model because the dependent variable X is expressed in a linear combination of various polynomial degrees of the independent variable t.

In many longitudinal studies of individual differences, patterns of growth in ability have shown definite dependence on age. Many human abilities grow steadily, plateau, and then decline gradually (Vandenberg, 1973). As has been observed in the field of economics, the growth in certain biological or mental attributes eventually exhibits some sort of diminishing returns.

When repeated measurements on the same group of individuals are impractical, replicated measurements on different groups at different times may be used, with caution. The best model thus fitted may indicate the trend or pattern of the group means. Its value in the study of the individual is limited if the within-group variation is quite large, compared with measurement errors.

INDIVIDUAL DIFFERENCES BASED ON TWO OR MORE
INDEPENDENT VARIABLES

Given a set of data on a dependent variable, say, Y and p independent variables Vs, we may build 2^p additive linear models, simply by inclusion or exclusion of each of the p variables. The number of feasible models will increase enormously if we decide to include any of the higher degree or cross-product terms. There are programs available that are capable of handling up to 100 original, transformed, and generated variables. The problem is not how to solve for the unknown parameters in the linear combination of variables that best fit the data. There are numerous accounts of how one can build and improve the models (Walberg, 1971; Ahlgren & Walberg, 1975; Walberg & Rasher, 1976; Daniel & Wood, 1980). There are suggestions of some of the steps we should take before and after fitting the model. If a theory-oriented model is hypothesized, our fitting of the model to the data is merely confirmatory. Otherwise, we may choose to explore with all possible models, if the number is reasonably small. If not, some steps may be taken before any regression analysis is performed.

1. Examine the correlation matrix. The variables that have high intercorrelation with the dependent variable, but low intracorrelation with the other independent variables are the most likely candidates to be included in the model. The rest can wait.

2. Examine the scatterplots. By examining the plot of the dependent variable versus the independent variables that are highly correlated, we may decide if any polynomial term should or should not be included.

3. Examine the three-dimensional plots. By examining the surface of the plots of the dependent variable with a pair of included independent variables, we can decide if the cross-product term should also be included. By observing the curvature—convex or concave—of the surface or the contour, some non-algebraic terms can be considered for inclusion.

Here are some steps to follow in the attempt to improve the fitted model:

1. Examine the standardized weights. The relative size of the weights on the standardized variates indicates the relative contribution to the maximized relationship with the dependent variable. Those independent variables with relatively small beta-weights may be dropped with little loss of information and a gain in parsimony for a reduced model.

2. Examine the plots of the observed versus the estimated values for the dependent variable. Such examination serves to double check the practical significance of the multiple correlation. Regardless of the level of the statistical significance of the correlation, the best linear model obtained would have very little value in application if the linear relationship were not convincingly visible from the plot. There may be room for additional variables.

3. Examine the plots of the residuals with the dependent variables and perhaps also with the other variables. If the residuals have any recognizable pattern, further improvement can be sought. If the size of the residuals are much greater than the measurement errors of the dependent variable, the dependent variable is not yet fully represented by the collected data. Some

essential variable has been neglected. If the size of the residuals, regardless of their pattern, are within the measurement errors of the dependent variable, no further improvement is needed. Any other fitting for further reducing of residuals might render the model more vulnerable on revalidation.

Two examples are given here to illustrate the simple steps we have taken to fit data with appropriate linear models. It is our intention to show the extensive use of graphs. In the eyes of beholders, a picture may tell more than a thousand words.

AN EXAMPLE OF LONGITUDINAL DATA

Given a set of Bock's (1975) data on the vocabulary growth of 64 pupils measured repeatedly on four occasions at 8th through 11th grade levels (see Table 2), the group means of 1.14, 2.54, 2.99, and 3.47 are, of course, significantly different. To study the trend of growth over time, a set of orthogonal polynomial coefficients were estimated. The model thus obtained

TABLE 2. Vocabulary Growth

Subject	Grade 8	9	10	11	Mean
1	1.75	2.60	3.76	3.68	2.95
2	.90	2.47	2.44	3.43	2.31
3	.80	.93	.40	2.27	1.10
4	2.42	4.15	4.56	4.21	3.83
5	−1.31	−1.31	−.66	−2.22	−1.38
6	−1.56	1.67	.18	2.33	.66
7	1.09	1.50	.52	2.33	1.36
8	−1.92	1.03	.50	3.04	.66
9	−1.61	.29	.73	3.24	.66
10	2.47	3.64	2.87	5.38	3.59
11	−.95	.41	.21	1.82	.37
12	1.66	2.74	2.40	2.17	2.24
13	2.07	4.92	4.46	4.71	4.04
14	3.30	6.10	7.19	7.46	6.02
15	2.75	2.53	4.28	5.93	3.87
16	2.25	3.38	5.79	4.40	3.96
17	2.08	1.74	4.12	3.62	2.89
18	.14	.01	1.48	2.78	1.10
19	.13	3.19	.60	3.14	1.77
20	2.19	2.65	3.27	2.73	2.71
21	−.64	−1.31	−.37	4.09	.44
22	2.02	3.45	5.32	6.01	4.20
23	2.05	1.80	3.91	2.49	2.56

Table 2 (*Continued*)

| Subject | Grade | | | | Mean |
	8	9	10	11	
24	1.48	.47	3.63	3.88	2.37
25	1.97	2.54	3.26	5.62	3.35
26	1.35	4.63	3.54	5.24	3.69
27	−.56	−.36	1.14	1.34	.39
28	.26	.08	1.17	2.15	.92
29	1.22	1.41	4.66	2.62	2.47
30	−1.43	.80	−.03	1.04	.09
31	−1.17	1.66	2.11	1.42	1.00
32	1.68	1.71	4.07	3.30	2.69
33	−.47	.93	1.30	.76	.63
34	2.18	6.42	4.64	4.82	4.51
35	4.21	7.08	6.00	5.65	5.73
36	8.26	9.55	10.24	10.58	9.66
37	1.24	4.90	2.42	2.54	2.78
38	5.94	6.56	9.36	7.72	7.40
39	.87	3.36	2.58	1.73	2.14
40	−.09	2.29	3.08	3.35	2.15
41	3.24	4.78	3.52	4.84	4.10
42	1.03	2.10	3.88	2.81	2.45
43	3.58	4.67	3.83	5.19	4.32
44	1.41	1.75	3.70	3.77	2.66
45	−.65	−.11	2.40	3.53	1.29
46	1.52	3.04	2.74	2.63	2.48
47	.57	2.71	1.90	2.41	1.90
48	2.18	2.96	4.78	3.34	3.32
49	1.10	2.65	1.72	2.96	2.11
50	.15	2.69	2.69	3.50	2.26
51	−1.27	1.26	.71	2.68	.85
52	2.81	5.19	6.33	5.93	5.06
53	2.62	3.54	4.86	5.80	4.21
54	.11	2.25	1.56	3.92	1.96
55	.61	1.14	1.35	.53	.91
56	−2.19	−.42	1.54	1.16	.02
57	1.55	2.42	1.11	2.18	1.82
58	−.04	.50	2.60	2.61	1.42
59	3.10	2.00	3.92	3.91	3.24
60	−.29	2.62	1.60	1.86	1.45
61	2.28	3.39	4.91	3.89	3.62
62	2.57	5.78	5.12	4.98	4.61
63	−2.19	.71	1.56	2.31	.60
64	−.04	2.44	1.79	2.64	1.71
Mean	1.14	2.54	2.99	3.47	2.53

Note. From *Multivariate Statistical Methods in Behavioral Research* p. 454 by R. D. Bock, 1975, New York: McGraw-Hill. Copyright 1975 by McGraw-Hill. Reprinted with permission.

TABLE 3. Univariate Statistics for Longitudinal Vocabulary Growth

Sample size	N = 64				N = 61			
Grade level	8	9	10	11	8	9	10	11
Mean	1.14	2.54	2.99	3.47	.98	2.42	2.82	3.38
SD	1.89	2.08	2.70	1.93	1.55	1.79	1.77	1.48
Skewness	.80	.79	.93	.69	-.28	.46	.24	.45
Kurtosis	2.31	1.13	1.52	2.81	-.65	.04	-.65	-.16
Minimum	-2.19	-1.31	-.66	-2.22	-2.19	-1.31	-.37	.53
Maximum	8.26	9.55	10.24	10.58	4.21	7.08	7.19	7.46
Range	10.45	10.86	10.90	12.80	6.40	8.39	7.56	6.93

Individuals removed for further analysis:

	8	9	10	11
No. 5	-1.31	-1.31	-.66	-2.22
No. 36	8.26	9.55	10.24	10.58
No. 38	5.94	6.56	9.36	7.72

is as follows:

$$X = 5.0696 + 1.6652t - .4599t^2 + .2230t^3$$

To the extent or range of available data, it can be concluded that the growth rate of vocabulary acquisition slows down as the subjects age.

To take a fresh look at Bock's data, proceed as follows:

1. Compute the summary statistics (see Table 3). All four groups of data on vocabulary growth show substantial departure from normality in symmetry and peakedness.

2. Check the distribution with stem-and-leaf diagrams. Extreme values are spotted from the graph for $N = 64$. By deleting the three outliers selectively, the summary statistics are recomputed and graphs rechecked (Figures 10 and 11). All distribute approximately as normal distributions. The group means for four occasions now become .98, 2.42, 2.82 and 3.38 for $N = 61$, all slightly reduced.

3. Plot X versus t (Figure 12). Here X shows a nonlinear upward trend that is supported by joining the group means on the bottom graph.

```
VARIABLE: GRADE11                                      VARIABLE: GRADE11

N              64      SUM         222.18     N              61      SUM         206.1
MEAN       3.47156     STD MEAN  0.240686     MEAN       3.37869     STD MEAN  0.189963
STD DEV    1.92549     VARIANCE   3.70751     STD DEV    1.48366     VARIANCE   2.20124
SKEWNESS   0.686415    KURTOSIS   2.81279     SKEWNESS   0.445388    KURTOSIS  -0.155737

STEM LEAF             #    BOXPLOT            STEM LEAF             #    BOXPLOT
  10 6               1        0                 10
  10                                            10
   9                                             9
   9                                             9
   8                                             8
   8                                             8
   7 57              2        I                  7 5               1        0
   7                          I                  7
   6                          I                  6
   6 0               1        I                  6 0               1        I
   5 66899           5        I                  5 66899           5        I
   5 0224            4        I                  5 0224            4        I
   4 788             3     +-----+               4 788             3     +-----+
   4 124             3     I     I               4 124             3     +-----+
   3 556789999       9     I     I               3 556789999       9     I     I
   3 00123334        8     *--+--*               3 00123334        8     *--+--*
   2 5566667788     10     I     I               2 5566667788     10     I     I
   2 12233334        8     +-----+               2 12233334        8     +-----+
   1 789             3     I                     1 789             3     I
   1 0234            4     I                     1 0234            4     I
   0 58              2     I                     0 58              2     I
   0                                             0
  -0                                            -0
  -0                                            -0
  -1                                            -1
  -1                                            -1
  -2 2               1        0                 -2
     +----+----+----+----+                         +----+----+----+----+
```

FIGURE 10. Stem-and-leaf display & box-whisker plot for $N = 64$ and $N = 61$ (11th grade).

VARIABLE: GRADE 8

```
N              61          SUM            59.89
MEAN       0.981803        STD MEAN    0.198035
STD DEV      1.5467        VARIANCE     2.39229
SKEWNESS  -0.281153        KURTOSIS    -0.64663

STEM LEAF                    #    BOXPLOT
  4 2                        1      I
  3 6                        1      I
  3 123                      3      I
  2 56678                    5      I
  2 00011222234            11     +------+
  1 555777                  6      I    I
  1 0112234                 7      *------*
  0 66899                   5      I  +  I
  0 11113                   5      I     I
 -0 3100                    4     +------+
 -0 96665                   5      I
 -1 432                     3      I
 -1 966                     3      I
 -2 22                      2      I
    +----+----+----+----+
```

VARIABLE: GRADE 9

```
N              61          SUM           147.87
MEAN        2.4241         STD MEAN    0.22958
STD DEV     1.79308        VARIANCE     3.21513
SKEWNESS   0.458419        KURTOSIS   0.0406394

STEM LEAF                    #    BOXPLOT
  7 1                        1      0
  6
  6 14                       2      I
  5 8                        1      I
  5 2                        1      I
  4 67899                    5      I
  4 1                        1      I
  3 56                       2      I
  3 0024444                  7     +------+
  2 5556666777             10      I    I
  2 012344                   6      *--+--*
  1 5777778                  7      I    I
  1 0134                     4     +------+
  0 557899                   6      I
  0 134                      3      I
 -0 4410                     4      I
 -0
 -1 3                        1      I
    +----+----+----+----+
```

VARIABLE: GRADE 10

```
N              61          SUM           172.31
MEAN        2.82475        STD MEAN    0.226758
STD DEV     1.77103        VARIANCE     3.13656
SKEWNESS   0.239264        KURTOSIS   -0.648544

STEM LEAF                    #    BOXPLOT
  7 2                        1      I
  6
  6 03                       2      I
  5 8                        1      I
  5 13                       2      I
  4 5667899                  7      I
  4 113                      3     +------+
  3 556788999                9      I    I
  3 133                      3      I    I
  2 66779                    5      *--+--*
  2 14444                    5      I    I
  1 55666789                 8      I    I
  1 11233                    5     +------+
  0 55677                    5      I
  0 224                      3      I
 -0 40                       2      I
    +----+----+----+----+
```

FIGURE 11. Displays for $N = 61$.

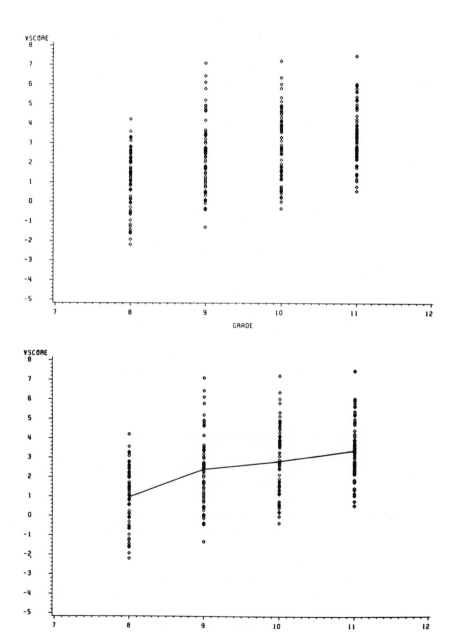

FIGURE 12. X versus t for vocabulary growth.

4. Perform an ANOVA to test the null hypothesis of no differences among four group means. With a value of $F_{3,240} = 23.41$, H_0 is rejected outright.

5. Explore with a series of linear models having various polynomials in t. We have conveniently coded the grades t with values of 8, 9, 10, and 11. The results are

  (a) For $X = -4.809 + .759t$, with $R = .455$, the model is significant with $F = 63.2$ at $p \ll 01$.

  (b) For $X = -24.575 + 4.979t - .222t^2$, with $R = .470$, the improvement by including t^2 is slight, but significant with $F = 4.4$ at $p < .05$.

  (c) For $X = -17.851 + 2.854t - .008t^3$, with $R = .470$, the gain by including t^3 is practically the same as by including t^2 in (b).

  (d) For $X = -191.446 + 58.491t - 5.898t^2 + .199t^3$, with $R = .478$, with insignificant improvement, we have a case of overfitting the data by having included both the square and the cubic terms of t.

6. Conclusion. Statistically, any of these polynomial models is significant at level $p \ll .01$. Model (a), which indicates a definite upward trend with respect to t may be selected as the best for our data, at least in the sense of parsimony. The nonlinear trend, although statistically significant, is not conclusive as far as the individuals are concerned. However, when we focus our interest on the individuals as a group at different grade levels, it is clear that vocabulary growth shows diminishing returns with time.

AN EXAMPLE OF CROSS-SECTIONAL DATA

To illustrate the steps of building linear models for a dependent variable as a function of several independent variables, we began with Anderson's (1970) analysis (see Walberg, 1971). Based on the given regression equation for Physics Achievement Z as a function of Student Ability X and Class Difficulty Y, we start with the estimated general linear model $Z = .43X + .28Y - .25XY + .14X^2 + .00Y^2$ for 63 females in high school physics classes.

1. Regenerate a set of data for $N = 60$. Start with two sets of normal deviates, one for X and one for Y, and compute a set for the dependent variable Z by adding about 5% of random errors, namely; $Z = .43X + .28Y + .14X^2 + .00Y^2 + .05N(0, 1)$. The set of data on X, Y, and Z is given in Table 4. We then proceed with this set of data, showing how to revalidate the given model with a new set of relevent data on the same variables.

TABLE 4. Cross-Sectional Data for $N = 60$

Observation	X	Y	Z	Observation	X	Y	Z
1	−1.38	−.28	−.11	31	.55	−1.02	−.13
2	.89	−1.02	.77	32	.46	−.17	.51
3	−.94	−1.65	−1.78	33	−.16	−1.89	−.41
4	.99	.48	1.39	34	−1.63	1.84	1.33
5	−.21	.07	−.59	35	.57	.63	.57
6	−.89	.14	−.03	36	−1.03	.13	−.96
7	.41	1.25	.76	37	.42	1.03	.57
8	.21	−.23	−.72	38	−3.65	.85	1.01
9	.34	.12	.67	39	.95	−.34	−.18
10	.18	1.04	−.43	40	−1.49	.58	−.87
11	.89	.80	−.61	41	−.42	.77	.22
12	2.73	−1.50	2.71	42	2.30	−1.27	2.42
13	1.23	−1.73	.64	43	.60	−.53	−.28
14	−.51	−1.43	−1.50	44	−.53	−.15	−.20
15	.41	1.39	0.26	45	.19	−.26	−.07
16	−1.06	.55	.45	46	−.38	.36	−.58
17	.34	−1.09	−.52	47	−.60	−1.55	−1.69
18	1.44	.62	1.79	48	−1.76	.56	.58
19	1.84	−1.58	1.74	49	.16	−.68	.01
20	−.78	−.18	−1.20	50	−.30	.63	.36
21	1.57	1.42	1.32	51	.25	.98	.69
22	.41	1.08	−.18	52	.22	−2.38	−.31
23	−1.92	.26	.31	53	−.64	.90	.20
24	−1.02	.20	−.06	54	1.93	−.55	2.44
25	−.20	−.81	−.25	55	.03	.45	1.09
26	−1.21	−1.15	−.53	56	.80	−1.09	.46
27	1.02	−.68	.53	57	−.31	−.13	.23
28	−.41	.57	.19	58	−.30	.68	.42
29	−1.08	−.38	−.62	59	1.63	1.26	.83
30	.99	1.80	1.34	60	−.64	.32	.60

2. Compute the summary statistics including the correlation matrix. With the dependent variable Z, we have $r_{ZX} = .510$ and $r_{ZY} = .205$. The linear correlation between Z at Y is, of course, very low. But Y should be included in the model, since the intracorrelation between the two independent variables X and Y is also very low, $r_{XY} = −.185$. It implies that there is little overlapping in contributions between X and Y.

3. Examine the scatter plots (Figure 13). There is one extreme value in X. Its elimination might raise the positive correlation between Z and X. However, we have decided to leave it there, since the same point is by no means an extreme in Y.

4. Examine the plot of Z versus X and Y (Figure 14). By observing the contours for given values of Y, we notice that Z is convexing upward

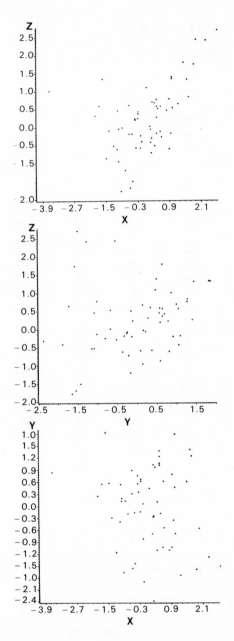

FIGURE 13. Scatterplots among variables: (a) Z versus X ($r_{zx} = .510$); (b) Z versus Y ($r_{zy} = .205$); (c) Y versus X ($r_{xy} = -.185$).

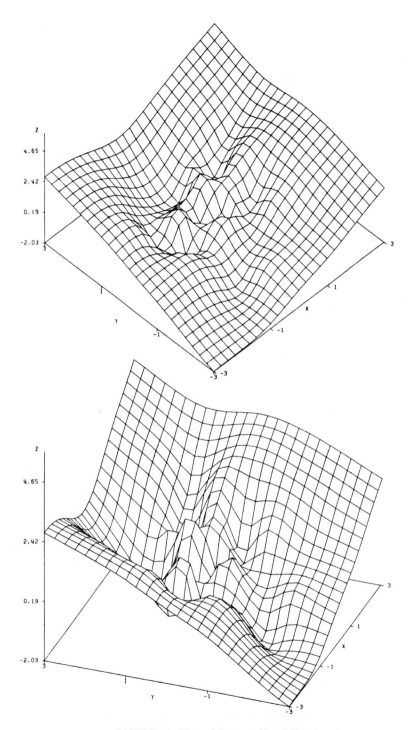

FIGURE 14. Plots of Z versus X and Y.

speedily, suggesting that X and X^2 should be included. By observing the contours for given values of X, we notice a definite upward trend with a slight tendency to concave downward, which suggests that Y might be included, but Y^2 may or may not be needed for our particular range of data. Meanwhile, the surface appears slightly twisted so that the cross-product of XY may be worth a trial, since we know that $r_{XY} = -.185$ is low compared with r_{ZX}, but noticeable as compared with r_{ZY}. We could have started to fit our data with a linear model such as $Z = a_0 + a_1X + a_2X^2 + a_3Y + a_4XY$. Nevertheless, we shall proceed in a stepwise fashion, just to show how well the various plots have enhanced our understanding of the relationship among the variables under study.

5. Explore with a selection of linear models. By the least-square method, we have obtained the optimized regression equations, each for one of the following general linear models:

(a) For $Z = .226 + .427X$, with $R = .510$.

(b) For $Z = -.079 + .0483X + .244X^2$, with $R = .748$, Z shows a definite upward trend at increasing rate of change of X.

(c) For $Z = .118 + .240Y + .129Y^2$, with $R = .254$, it is not statistically significant.

(d) For $Z = .234 + .475X + .292Y$, with $R = .594$, it is certainly not going to be just on a plane in space.

(e) For $Z = -.066 + .535X + .300Y + .247X^2 - .009Y^2$, with $R = .812$, the model is surely much improved.

(f) For $Z = -.024 + .519X + .381Y + .162X^2 - .005Y^2 - .255XY$, with $R = .849$, it is further improved. But by examining the regression equation in standardized beta-weights, $Z_z = .620Z_x + .403Z_y + .368Z_{xx} + .007Z_{yy} - .322Z_{xy}$ we may reduce the full model of five variates by eliminating the Y^2 term having such a low beta-weight as .007, with very little loss in its contribution to the model.

(g) For $Z = -.019 + .520X + .379Y + .163X^2 - .255XY$, with $R = .849$, we have at last obtained the "best" general linear model that fits our given set of data. By plotting the estimated values of Z versus each given set of X and Y, graphically, we have discovered that the new plots (Figure 15) are similar to the plots of the original model for Z as a function of X and Y (Figure 6).

6. Examine the plots of estimated Z obtained from the "best" model, with the observed Z. We may visualize the strong linear relationship between the estimated and observed values of Z, in reference to the maximized correlation of $R = .85$ or its square .72. It implies that about 30% of the variability in Z remains unaccounted for by the linear model, however good it may be (Figure 16).

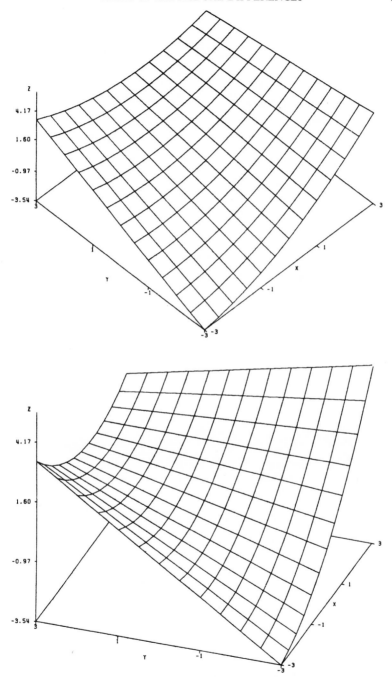

FIGURE 15. Plots of estimated Z versus X and Y.

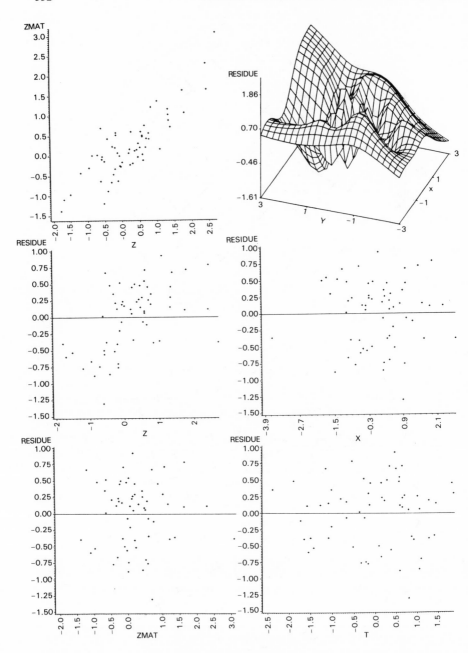

FIGURE 16. Plots of residuals.

7. Further plots of the residual versus Z show that residuals seem to increase for larger Zs. However, there is no observable pattern from the plots. It implies that there is probably nothing to gain by any further inclusion of variable based on our data on X and Y. In conclusion, as long as the residuals are within the measurement errors of Z, any further fitting with additional combinations of X and Y is unnecessary. Any improvement in prediction or estimation of the dependent variable Z will come from inclusion of other factors or variables not discussed here.

FINAL REMARKS ON GENERAL LINEAR MODELS

In the two simple working examples given in this chapter, we hope to convey what the techniques of building general linear models may contribute in the study of individual differences. Comparisons among group means by analysis of variance and covariance are doubtlessly important for their own sake. Studies of the linear relationship between a dependent variable with the linear combination of a set of independent variables may begin to provide us with the blocks for theory building that may someday enable us to put the pieces together.

Meanwhile, we maintain that a model that fits one set of data at a certain narrow range or region might not be readily applicable to another set of data at some other remote range or region. This may at least partially explain the many conflicting reports on the so-called aptitude–treatment–interaction studies. Furthermore, there is no reason to believe that any given pair of variables must always be linearly related. We should be willing to let the empirical data speak for themselves. We must be ready to explore further, with new models or new combinations of variables under study. And we are challenged to continue to improve the models until there is nothing to gain under the constraints we have on our measuring instruments.

As a final remark, there are numerous versions of programs for curve-fitting. With discretion, each can yield dividends. They save time and human resources. When properly used, the fitting of models permits us to explore the unknown, extending our horizon to areas that were once off-limits to us because of our inability to probe extensively or intensively.

ACKNOWLEDGMENTS

The authors are grateful to Professor R. Darrell Bock for his kind permission to reproduce the graphs, shown in Figure 8 and Figure 9, and to use data, as shown in Table 2, for illustrative analysis. Appreciation to the

UIC Computer Center for making computer time for extensive applications of SPSS and SAS packages is also acknowledged here.

REFERENCES

Ahlgren, A., & Walberg, H. J. Generalized regression analysis. In D. J. Amick & H. J. Walberg (Eds.), *Introductory multivariate analysis*, Berkeley, Calif.: McCutchan, 1975.

Anderson, G. J. Effects of classroom social climate on individual learning. *American Educational Research Journal*, 1970, 7, 135–152.

Bock, R. D. *Multivariate statistical methods in behavioral research*. New York: McGraw-Hill, 1975.

Daniel, C., & Wood, F. S. *Fitting equations to data* (2nd ed.). New York: Wiley, 1980.

Graybill, F. A. *An Introduction to linear statistical models*. New York: McGraw-Hill, 1961.

Johnston, J. *Econometric Methods* (2nd ed). New York: McGraw-Hill, 1972.

Tukey, J. W. *Exploratory data analysis*. Reading, Mass: Addison-Wesley, 1977.

Vandenberg, S. G. Comparative studies of multiple factor ability measures. In J. R. Royce (Ed.), *Multivariate analysis and psychological theory*. New York: Academic Press, 1973, pp. 149–202.

Walberg, H. J. Generalized regression models in educational research. *American Educational Research Journal*, 1971, 8, 71–91.

Walberg, H. J. A psychological theory of educational productivity. In F. H. Farley & N. J. Gordon (Eds.), *Psychology and education*. Berkeley, Calif.: McCutchan, 1981.

Walberg, H. J., & Rasher, S. P. Improving regression models. *Journal of Educational Statistics*, 1976, 1, 253–277.

9

Research Methods from Applied Behavior Analysis

THOMAS R. KRATOCHWILL, F. CHARLES MACE, AND STACY E. MOTT

Applied behavior analysis represents one of the major areas of research and practice in contemporary behavior modification or behavior therapy.[1] This area developed from work on the experimental analysis of behavior (cf. Day, 1976; Ferster & Skinner, 1957; Sidman, 1960; Skinner, 1945, 1953, 1957, 1969, 1974) and emphasizes the analysis of the effects of independent events (or variables) on the occurrence of specific behaviors (or responses). Research and practice in the field focus on behaviors that are clinically or socially relevant (e.g., academic skills and social behaviors) and adheres to certain methodological criteria (e.g., experimental analysis, observer agreement on response measures, social validation of therapeutic effects).

Relative to the other areas of contemporary behavior modification, behavior analysis methodology employs a more limited use of the term *behavior*. Typically, behavior refers to "the observable activity of the organism as it moves about, stands still, seizes objects, pushes and pulls,

---

[1] Several different approaches to behavior modification have evolved, and work in the field is not limited to applied behavior analysis as it is usually conceived. Contemporary behavior modification is characterized by neobehavioristic mediational S–R models, cognitive behavior modification, and social learning theory. Along with behavior analysis, each of these particular approaches to contemporary behavior therapy represents a unique focus on independent and dependent variables. The interested reader is referred to Kazdin and Wilson (1978) for a more detailed description of the differences in these various approaches.

THOMAS R. KRATOCHWILL ● Department of Educational Psychology, University of Wisconsin, Madison, Wisconsin 53706.   F. CHARLES MACE ● School of Psychology Program, Lehigh University, Bethlehem, Pennsylvania 18015.   STACY E. MOTT ● Department of Educational Psychology, University of Arizona, Tucson, Arizona 78712.

makes sounds, gestures, and so on" (Skinner, 1974, pp. 260–261). Although the focus of a behavior analysis is primarily on discrete classes of behavior, the individual is conceptualized as a total functioning organism. However, practical considerations usually militate against attempts to observe, measure, and relate all of the organism's responses taking place at one time (Bijou, 1976).

Intervention techniques associated with work in applied behavior analysis typically have been derived from operant laboratory research. The resulting principles of behavior (i.e., positive and negative reinforcement, punishment and extinction) have led to a variety of behavior-altering procedures such as time-out, response cost, shaping, fading, stimulus control, and others (Bijou, 1976; Kazdin, 1978; Sulzer–Azaroff & Mayer, 1977). As usually conceived, behavior analysis refers to the study of organism–environment interactions in terms of empirical concepts and provides a basis for understanding, predicting, and controlling behavior (Bijou, 1976).

In this chapter, we provide an overview of the methodology of applied behavior analysis. Included in the chapter is a discussion of the role of behavior analysis in the study of "individual differences" and associated characteristics of applied behavior analysis research, behavioral assessment, experimental design, criteria for data evaluation, and issues in generalizability of research data. Within the context of each area, conceptual and methodological issues are discussed and advantages and limitations of various approaches are examined.

BEHAVIOR ANALYSIS AND INDIVIDUAL DIFFERENCES

Behavior analysts are very interested in individual differences, but the field of behavior analysis approaches the issue of individual differences in a manner that is at variance with traditional approaches. A contrast between behavioral and traditional approaches on both conceptual measurement and methodological dimensions will help elucidate these differences.[2]

CONCEPTUAL/MEASUREMENT ISSUES

Historically, much of experimental psychology has been dominated by group approaches to the study of individual differences. The individual differences movement has used probability theory to estimate "true" scores

---

[2] What follows is a brief summary of the development of group or vagonotic methods. Interested readers are encouraged to refer to, Johnston and Pennypacker (1980) for a more detailed and complete story.

from measures of variability to define traits or characteristics. Thus, when Cronbach (1957) called for a marriage between correlational and experimental schools of research to produce research on aptitude–treatment interactions (ATI), he provided an impetus for the study of individual differences within this framework. In the typical ATI study in this area, an aptitude—that is, any characteristic of the person that affects a subject's response to treatment—is defined and measured (Cronbach, 1975). Some treatment is then implemented. The outcome is regressed onto a score recorded prior to treatment and if the regression line in the treatments differ in slope, ATI is said to have occurred. Cronbach (1975) reported on the progress in this area and a number of authors have reviewed the methodological and conceptual issues in this literature (e.g., Cronbach & Snow, 1977; Good & Stipek, 1983).

Research in the area of individual differences presents a system for conceptualizing and measuring human characteristics on the basis of variation in a set of measurements. Johnston and Pennypacker (1980) refer to this approach to defining and measuring phenomena as *vagonotic*.[3] Thus, from a vagonotic perspective, the measurement of an individual derives its meaning from the degree to which the score deviates from others' scores in a distribution.

Behavior analysis, in contrast, rather than defining a phenomenon on the basis of its variability, has embraced measurement techniques typically more indigenous to the natural sciences (Cone, 1981). The counting and timing of events according to absolute and standard units is referred to as *idemnotic* measurement (Johnston & Pennypacker, 1980).[4] This approach is reflected in the selection of dependent variables that are observable, quantifiable, and subject to concurrent, independent verification. Examples include rate per hour of discrete behaviors, the latency between the presentation of a stimulus and the subject's response, the distance between two stimuli, and the weight of an obese patient. In each case of idemnotic measurement, the meaning of an individual's score resides in its relation to its measurement scale rather than to its position relative to others in a distribution of scores. In this regard, variability is treated as a reflection of either variability in the organism, variability in the environment, or both.

[3] *Vagonotic* is derived from the Latin *vagare* (to wander) compounded with the Latin *notare* (to designate with brand or mark) and, hence, conveys the characteristics of instability in the meaning of the entity thus described (from Johnston & Pennypacker, p. 64).

[4] *Idemnotic* is derived from the Latin *idem* (the same) compounded with the Latin *notare* (to designate with brand or mark) and, thus, communicates the stability of meaning of a unit of measurement that is standard and absolute (from Johnston & Pennypacker, 1980, p. 71). A history of idemnotic measurement is not provided here; however, interested readers may consult Johnston and Pennypacker (1980).

As Johnston and Pennypacker (1980) note:

> In any experiment, this strategy takes two concurrent forms: reducing or eliminating variability in behavior by isolating and controlling those extraneous factors in the environment responsible for it and enlarging the remaining variability in behavior by deliberately arranging for occurrence of variation in some independent variable. The goal is to account for observed variability in behavior by its relation to known and controlled variation in the environment. The scientific enterprise thus becomes the search for the determinants of observed variability. Successful results of this search take the form of convincing demonstrations of controlling relations between manipulated environmental variables and resulting change or variation in behavior. Again we see that variability functions as the basic grist of the scientific mill—the raw material from which relational statements are made and verified (p. 209).

It can readily be observed that this very different approach to studying variability has important implications for how "individual differences" are conceptualized. Indeed, as mentioned above, the analysis of how individuals function as a result of treatments is implicit in behavior analysis research, but essentially, this whole area of investigation has not been integrated into what has conventionally been called individual differences.

The importance of work in this area has been emphasized by at least some individuals writing in the individual differences area. For example, Glaser (1967), in discussing individual differences in the study of learning, takes into account the analysis of functional relations between behavior and various controlling conditions. He also emphasizes the assessment of initial properties of the learner that interact with various types of learning. In doing this, the technology of assessment of initial stable baseline rates with repeated measurement over time became a recommended option for workers in the learning area. Despite this early recommendation, researchers have generally approached the study of individual differences very differently.

Since behavior analysis has as its major goal the understanding of the individual and his or her interaction with the environment, the study of group behavior is not considered as useful an approach in building a science of behavior. However, at this point we should emphasize that this relatively "pure" approach to experimental analysis is represented to varying degrees in professional work in the field. Indeed, although there are many examples of this approach (e.g., Bijou, 1976), there are many applications in the behavior analysis field, as specifically represented in the *Journal of Applied Behavior Analysis*, that do not embrace this basic form of methodology. Indeed, an implicit assumption of behavior analysis is that research will be conducted with a single organism or that a careful individual analysis of each organism in the experiment will take place. However, a perusal of applied research in the field suggests many deviation from this. Thus, despite an emphasis on analysis of the individual, many studies published in the applied behavior analysis field do not maintain the integrity of the individual analysis called for in methodological treatises on this topic.

METHODOLOGICAL CHARACTERISTICS OF APPLIED BEHAVIOR ANALYSIS

The differences between traditional and behavioral methods of studying individual differences are also based on the methodological focus of the two approaches. Basically, methodology of applied behavior analysis employs a time-series framework for analysis of the single case or small number of subjects (Kratochwill, 1978). (Throughout this chapter we will use the term *time-series design* to refer to that class of designs that involves repeated measurements of a dependent variable and introduction of one or more independent variables across a single subject or multiple subjects.) There are several unique characteristics of time-series design as used in behavior analysis that distinguish this methodology from other research methods used to study individual differences.

Repeated Measurement. A fundamental aspect of time-series methodology in behavior analysis research is the assessment of subject behavior over time. Measurement is scheduled more often and typically for a longer period of time than it is in group research approaches (as in repeated measures designs). Typically, data are collected prior to an intervention (baseline) and during one or more treatment intervention phases. Single or multiple measures may be gathered on a client (see our later discussion). For example, a child might be assessed for his or her spelling skills. The dependent variable monitored across time would be actual spelling performance defined in terms of units that are standard and absolute. Such measures would be made across time and the intervention would be evaluated by determining whether or not there was improvement on this dependent measure(s).

Monitoring Instrasubject Variability. When a subject's behavior is repeatedly measured across time, fluctuation in performance (i.e., variability) will become apparent. The level and trend of the dependent variables chosen for study are examined directly to make inferences about the course of behavior over time. Generally, stable measures of performance at baseline are considered necessary in order to attribute change to the independent variable. However, as noted by some authors (e.g., Parsonson & Baer, 1978), either stable measures or those that move in the opposite direction of anticipated changes from the treatment are necessary pre-conditions for an effective analysis of the dependent variables. Of course, the variability or trend itself might be a target for intervention. A researcher might be interested in reducing the variance in performance by some environmental manipulation as well as reversing the trend of a behavior deemed inappropriate (e.g., aggression, self-stimulation, increasing accuracy rate on academic tasks).

Specification of Controlling Conditions. A variety of conditions are specified in behavior analysis research. These usually include the independent variable, setting, or client characteristics (e.g., biological and reinforcement histories) and various assessment procedures. The task of the researcher is to manipulate one variable while holding others constant to determine effects on subject performance. Another usual task of the behavior analytic researcher is to combine variables to produce maximally effective treatments. However, this is sometimes done at a later research stage, after the effect of one particular variable has been established. In keeping with the behavior analysis tradition, specification of conditions in the experimental framework is considered essential for the control of variability and, ultimately, the reproduction of findings to establish the generalizability of results (Johnston & Pennypacker, 1980; Sidman, 1960).

Replication. Like other research in the social sciences, a major goal of behavior analysis research is to establish control of behavior. Conventional threats to internal validity are usually addressed by reproducing effects either within an individual or group or across clients, response measures, or settings. In each case, reproduction of effects is essential to determine if changes in the data either coincide with the treatment or are random. For example, in the most basic form of investigation, repeated measures of baseline performance are obtained (i.e., A_1 phase), followed by a treatment phase (i.e., B), and then by a treatment or intervention withdrawal (i.e., A_2). This basic $A_1/B/A_2$ design allows some inference about the effect of the treatment. Nevertheless, inferring that the treatment was responsible for the change in the behavior becomes more convincing as more systematic replication is built into the study. Thus, a researcher may extend this basic A/B/A design through several replications to increase inference for the effect of the intervention (this is discussed later in this chapter).

Design Flexibility. Time-series designs in applied behavior analysis allow a greater degree of flexibility in research than many traditional large $-N$ between group designs. For example, a researcher who determines that the application of some intervention was not effective can, in concert with the repeated measurement format of the design, alter the treatment so as to obtain the desired subject performance. After determining that one behavior or response measure is under the control of a certain independent variable, the researcher then continues with the experimental analysis until experimental control is established. A differential response to treatment can indicate the need to alter aspects of the intervention to make it more powerful and enhance or increase the chance of control of the experimental arrangements.

A major concern of researchers who are interested in studying individual differences is the generality of treatment effects observed in the experiment. In more traditional approaches, a researcher examines interactions between various aptitudes or traits and treatments. For example, it might be determined that children who are deficient in a certain aptitude, such as visual sequential memory, do better with a treatment consisting of slow pacing of instructional materials. The interaction between the aptitude and type of instructions suggests that one cannot generalize across all subjects, but rather that the researcher must indicate that there are individual differences in learning as a function of the measured aptitude or ability. Replication of research in this area may further refine or even restrict the types of conclusions that can be drawn. A further understanding of the relationship comes from testing the hypothesis from larger samples of the population.

In contrast to this approach, the behavior analysis researcher is primarily concerned with what happens at the level of the individual organism when he or she is exposed to the conditions of the experiment. In the above example, the particular interest could be in determining what prerequisite skills are necessary for a child to learn the material under certain specified conditions. A search for variability in behavior comes from a thorough understanding of the variables controlling the subject's behavior under the conditions of the experiment—that is, the level at which individual laws of behavior are established.

Establishing the generality of the effects is a primary concern for researchers from both camps. At first glance, the researcher focusing on the generality of group data (whether main effect or interaction) would appear to have the edge in establishing generality across subjects. Yet, behavior analytic researchers would argue that intersubject variability in group data will make it more difficult to understand the effect on the individual subject and ultimately will *obscure the search for controlling effects in the environment*. Thus, for traditional and behavioral researchers, the study of individual differences constitute two entirely different methods of investigation.

Behavior analytic researchers are interested in the generality of findings to a population. Once functional relations between environmental manipulations and the individual subject response are determined, replication (of variables, methods, processes) across subjects (and other response classes, settings, and species) can proceed. When it can be demonstrated that a treatment yields the same kind of orderliness in a population in different individuals in a population, subject generality has begun (Johnston & Pennypacker, 1980). Yet, individual differences in response to treatment will occur with unique environmental histories.

In behavior analyses, the search for generality occurs through the long process of replication (discussed in more detail later). One example of such efforts was presented by Johnston and Pennypacker (1980) who traced the history of the time-out (TO) paradigm (TO represents a class of procedures in which a period of time following a response is arranged to eliminate the reinforcement that is usually present, the effects of which are to reduce or decrease the response). Based on the early work of Skinner and Ferster, TO was extended into therapeutic interventions with children. Ferster's procedure consisted of the contingent application of TO for a specific response. A group of investigators focused on the use of ignoring as a TO from social reinforcement. The TO ignoring procedure has been used in studies dealing with delusional speech (Richard, Digman, & Horner, 1960); incorrect spelling and bad work habits (Zimmerman & Zimmerman, 1962); inappropriate crying, crawling, and isolate play (Harris, Johnston, Kelley, & Wolf, 1964); physical and verbal aggression (Brown & Elliott, 1965); inappropriate scratching (Allen & Harris, 1966); temper tantrums (Risley & Wolf, 1967); and incorrect responses to questions about magazine pictures (Barton, 1970). This line of research supports earlier theoretical research by Ferster (1958) that demonstrated the functional properties of the TO punishment procedure. Moreover, it blends into replication efforts in this area that have focused on other dimensions of TO (e.g., physical removal of the reinforcer, isolation as time out). Whether or not the same knowledge base would be available if group research methods had been used is an empirical issue and subject to considerable debate.

ASSESSMENT WITHIN APPLIED BEHAVIOR ANALYSIS

With its roots in the experimental analysis of behavior, applied behavior analysis has necessarily developed an approach to assessment that differs from traditional approaches (as noted above). In general, the traditional—that is, "trait" (psychometric) or "state" (dynamic)—approach to assessment has usually operated under the assumption that personality or behavior reflects enduring states or traits. This approach generally assumes that behavior is consistent across time and settings. Hence, the setting in which the individual functions is usually not a necessary focus of assessment. Thus, in traditional assessment, there is a reliance on the use of indirect, global measures that provide a description of personality functioning and etiology and allow for diagnosis or classification. Therefore, traditional approaches to assessment are characterized by a high degree of inference from assessment data and an emphasis on inter-individual or nomothetic comparisons (Hartmann, Roper, & Bradford, 1979). Behavioral assessment emphasizes a sampling of a person's behavior in a specific situation and assumes that this sample is a function of environmental conditions prevailing at the time of assessment. Thus, the behavioral approach to assessment uses more direct measures and attempts to assess target responses in the natural environment.

Behavioral assessment also has a broader purpose than most traditional assessment approaches. Although traditional assessment focuses primarily on diagnosis and classification, behavioral assessment is concerned with not only the identification of the problem, but also with the selection and *evaluation* of a treatment strategy. Thus, the primary functions of a behavioral assessment include (1) a description of the problem, (2) selection of a treatment strategy, and (3) evaluation of the treatment outcome (Ciminero, 1977).

The description of the problem within a behavioral assessment includes the specification of the behaviors to be modified as well as the variables controlling those behaviors. From this description of the problem, a treatment is selected that takes into account the information obtained about the behavior of concern and attempts to manipulate the variables that control it. Evaluation, the third purpose of a behavioral assessment, is a continuation of the assessment of the targer behavior of concern. Data collected before an intervention are compared to assessment data collected following the intervention. Thus, another characteristic of behavioral assessment is its reliance upon continuous assessment rather than on the infrequent type of assessment used in most traditional approaches (e.g., pretest-posttest IQ assessment to evaluate progress in special education).

Behavioral assessment can be thought of as a process that pulls the threads of problem identification, treatment selection, and evaluation into a coherent whole. Behavioral assessment thus is distinguished from traditional assessment not only by its focus on behavior as a function of the conditions under which it occurs, but also as an activity that permeates the entire process of an applied behavior analysis.

GENERAL METHODS OF BEHAVIORAL ASSESSMENT

The assessment of behavior can be accomplished in a variety of ways, but the three general approaches to assessment are (1) psychophysiological recordings, (2) self-report, and (3) direct observation of behavior. These three approaches correspond to the three modes of responding that can be assessed within a behavioral framework: (1) physiological, (2) verbal, and (3) motor responses. Thus, assessment within applied behavior analysis can include a variety of response modes or use a variety of methods. To the extent that these responses and methods are incorporated into a behavioral assessment, the total functioning of the individual will have been identified.

Traditionally, however, applied behavior analysis has relied primarily on *direct behavioral observations* as the assessment strategy. Indeed, a recent review of experimental articles published in the four major behavioral journals (*Behavior Research and Therapy, Behavior Therapy, Journal of Applied Behavior Analysis,* and *Journal of Behavior Therapy and Experimental Psychiatry*) revealed that 72% of all assessments used direct observation procedures (Bornstein, Bridgewater, Hickey, & Sweeney, 1980). Our primary focus will thus be on the use of direct observation in behavioral assessment; however, before this is discussed, a brief overview of the use of psychophysiological and self-report methods in behavioral assessment is in order.

Psychophysiological Assessment. Kallman and Feuerstein (1977) define psychophysiological measurement as "the quantification of biological events as they relate to psychological variables" (p. 39). The basis for using psychophysiological methods of assessment is the assumption that physiological responses are the same type of dependent variables as is overt behavior. As such, there is a difference between psychophysiological assessment and physiological psychology, in which the manipulation of the physical system is assumed to be an independent variable that influences overt behavior (Kallman & Feuerstein, 1977).

There are two reasons why physiological procedures would be used within a behavioral assessment. First, physiological recordings might measure a response that cannot be obtained in other ways. For example, if lowering a patient's blood pressure is the goal of an intervention, then physiological recordings must be used to record the effects of treatment on blood pressure. Second, physiological measures, through their relationship to some environmental variable, might be useful in the prediction and modification of behavior. An example of this use of physiological measures can be seen in a study by Lubav and Bahler (1976) that utilized biofeedback procedures to reduce epileptic seizures in several subjects. By measuring cortical activity via EEG recordings, these researchers were able to examine the type of activity (sensorimotor rhythm) and to provide feedback that would increase the activity that would interfere with seizures.

In general, psychophysiological measures can be either *direct* or *indirect.* Indirect measures, such as urine analysis to measure drug usage or blood alcohol levels to measure alcohol consumption, are used less often because they are not the behaviors that are the focus of an intervention. Direct measures, such as heart rate and blood pressure, are used more frequently because they provide an objective assessment of both initial behavior and the effects of treatment.

Although psychophysiological measures have a place in a behavioral assessment, their use is still in its infancy. Not only does the reliability, validity, and utility of this approach remain to be demonstrated, but the cost of the strategy prohibits widespread use. Nevertheless, many investigators consider psychophysiological measurement to be a vital and innovative addition to the array of behavioral assessment methods (Mash & Terdal, 1981).

Self-Report Measures. Although self-report measures are typically associated with a more traditional approach to assessment, they have nevertheless found a place within a behavioral approach as well. Although they are primarily used to assess the verbal response system, they can also be used to assess overt motor and physiological responses (Ciminero, 1977). However, the use of self-report measures within behavioral assessment is based on the assumption that they reflect some other observable behavioral phenomena (Tasto, 1977).

A variety of methods are subsumed under the general heading of self-reports. The most widely used, however, is the behavioral interview. Although many have criticized the use of interviews as a means of assessment, these criticisms have been based upon the type of data solicited—for example, reports of the client's early feelings about parents solicited within a psychoanalytic framework—rather than the method *per se* (Meyer, Liddell, & Lyons, 1977). Thus, interviews used within behavioral assessment differ from traditional interviews not in their execution, but rather in their content. A behavioral interview is conducted to elicit information regarding both the behavior of concern as well as the environmental factors controlling it. An example of an interview of this type is the format used by Bergan (1977) and his associates. Three phases of assessment are outlined in this behavioral consultation problem-solving format. These include problem identification, problem analysis, and the plan-evaluation interviews. Although the consultation approach to the behavioral interview is by no means a prototype for all such interviews, it nevertheless illustrates the way in which this method of data collection can be employed in a behavioral assessment framework.

Other infrequently used self-report measures within a behavior analysis framework include written surveys and inventories, such as fear survey schedules, reinforcement inventories, assertiveness scales, and marital inventories (Ciminero, 1977). Surveys and inventories enjoy a number of advantages over behavioral interviews, including a greater degree of standardization and objectivity as well as a lower cost and greater ease of administration. They are also, however, subject to many of the same problems as other assessment devices, such as inadequate reliability, validity, norms, standardization, and statistical analysis of data. When they are employed, their use is typically restricted to identifying potential targets for further behavioral assessment through direct observations.

A third type of self-report measure is self-monitoring. Self-monitoring, which refers to the client's continuous assessment of his or her own behavior in natural situations, is particularly suited to the assessment of private behaviors (e.g., sexual activity), which are beyond the ethical or technological limits of other methods. It also has the advantage of being available as an assessment method throughout the treatment program and, hence, is frequently used as an outcome measure as well. There are, however, a number of problems associated with self-monitoring, the most glaring of which are the possible unreliability of the data collected via this method and its potential reactive effects (Nelson, 1977a,b).

DIRECT OBSERVATIONAL SYSTEM

Three general types of observational systems can be used to observe behavior directly: narrative recording, event recording, and interval recording. These systems can be adapted to assess any of the response properties that are detailed in Table 1. These response properties are not, however, mutually exclusive—any or all of them may be relevant to the behavior of concern. Thus, in a behavioral assessment, any variety or combination of observation strategies may be used, depending on both the problem identified and the conditions controlling it.

Narrative Recording. Narrative recording is most frequently used at the onset of assessment if the investigator is unfamiliar with the behavior of client(s) being assessed. It involves recording, in a written or spoken (taped) form, the sequence of behaviors (both verbal and motor) being observed— hence narrative recording is usually a cumbersome and time-consuming method of assessment. Indeed, Holm (1978) estimated that approximately 15 hours were required to transcribe, code, and summarize a vocal narrative for each hour of actual observation. Nevertheless, narrative recordings are flexible measures of a variety of response topographies and often can yield such response properties as frequency, duration, and quality.

Although an attempt is made to record all behaviors occurring during the period of observation, narrative recordings are subject to a number of potential sources of unreliability. For example, the time required to describe one event may preclude the description of another when behaviors are occurring at a high rate. Thus, two observers may record different

TABLE 1. Response Properties

	Definitions	When appropriate
Frequency	Refers to the number of times that a response occurs within a specified period of time	When behaviors are discrete; when latency or duration are insufficient to describe the behavior
Duration	May refer to any of the following:	
	1. The interval between the onset and the cessation of the response (response duration)	When behaviors are continuous rather than discrete (response duration); when the time spent in an activity is of concern (response duration); when the time required for responding is of more concern than the response itself (response latency or interresponse interval)
	2. The interval between stimulus onset and responding (latency of a response)	
	3. The interval between successive responses (interresponse interval)	
Quality	May refer to any of the following:	
	1. Intensity or magnitude	When frequency, duration, or latency are insufficient to describe the response
	2. Accuracy of the response	
	3. Judgment of the acceptability of the response	
By-products of behavior	The physical (material) products of a behavior	When the outcome of the behavior rather than the behavior itself is of concern; when direct observation of the behavior is not possible

behaviors. In addition, observers may use different verbal descriptions, and subsequently disagree as to the coding of the protocols.

One method that can be used to avoid potential problems of unreliability is to provide observers with behavior codes or lists of descriptors to be used in the recordings (Cone & Foster, 1982). This strategy, however, would so stardardize narrative recordings that their flexibility would be reduced. If standardization of the recording procedure is desired, either event or interval recording would be a more appropriate method. Thus, narrative recording should be used when a detailed description of behavior is more important than the collection of data in a standardized form.

Narrative recordings also have the distinct advantage of simultaneously providing data, not only on the behavior of concern, but also on the antecedent and consequent events relevant to it. These measures are also a means by which participant observers can record data on low-frequency, but highly salient behaviors (Cone & Foster, 1982). Thus, narrative recordings, although potentially unreliable, have a number of advantages that make them a useful form of direct observation in applied behavior analysis.

Event Recording. Event recording involves the assessment of selected response properties for one or more kinds of operationally defined behaviors within an observation period. Event recording differs from narrative recording in that responses are selected before observations occur. It can be a highly objective and facile form of observation if the response definitions are adequate (see Table 2 for a description of an adequate response definition) and hence can be used by both independent and participant observers.

There are a number of limitations, however, in the use of event recording. First of all, if the response definitions are inadequate, then the reliability of data collected by two different observers will be low. Second, the technique is not recommended for behaviors for which onset and cessation are ill-defined, which, leads to low agreement among observers. Third, when behaviors are of a low frequency, there is a tendency for

TABLE 2. Criteria for an Adequate Response Definition

Objectivity: The degree to which the target behavior defined is observable, thus excluding target behavior definitions that apply to unobservable, underlying states or traits

Clarity: The degree to which the definition is readable and unambiguous and can be reliably paraphrased or repeated by experienced observers

Completeness: The degree to which the boundaries of the response are defined, i.e., what is to be included and what is to be excluded as an instance of a response. This criterion assures that few judgments as to whether or not an instance of a response has occurred must be made by observers

---

Note: From "Behavioral Definitions in Applied Behavior Analysis: Explicit or Implicit?" by R. P. Hawkins and R. W. Dobes in B. C. Etzel, M. LeBlanc, and D. M. Baer (Eds.), *New Developments in Behavioral Research: Method and Application* (1977). Hillsdale, N. J.: Laurence Erlbaum Associate. Copyright 1977 by R. P. Hawkins and R. W. Dobes. Adapted by permission.

observers to "nod off" and hence miss instances of the behavior (Cone & Foster, 1982). Event recording is also not very sensitive to changes in the duration of behavior and is therefore not well-suited to behaviors of variable duration. Finally, the summary data obtained from this form of observation may be misleading, as two observers may come up with identical totals for the behavior, but may have actually recorded different instances of it. This is less problematic for interval recording systems, which are frequently used in place of event recording.

Interval Recording. Of the three forms of direct observation, interval recording may be both the most useful and most reliable. Although it is similar to event recording, it differs in that the observation periods are divided into intervals, and categories of behavior are recorded as they occur within each interval. As with event recording, interval recordings also require the use of operational definitions to minimize ambiguities in the scoring of a response.

A variety of interval recording procedures can be used, depending upon the response properties of interest. *Whole interval* sampling involves the recording of behavior if and only if it occurs throughout the entire interval, thus giving an indication of the duration of the behavior of concern. *Partial interval* sampling, is used when the investigator is primarily interested in the frequency of behavior and, thus, involves scoring the behavior if it occurred within any part of the interval. The third type of interval recording procedure, *momentary sampling,* involves recording the behavior if it occurs at a certain point within the interval (usually at the beginning or the end). The choice of method would depend primarily upon whether the investigator wishes to estimate the frequency or the duration of the response of interest.

Interval recording, especially when short-duration intervals are used, has the advantage of identifying sequences of responding as well as disagreement between observers because observer data can be compared in terms of the intervals that were scored rather than in terms of an overall frequency measure. It also has the advantage of the recording of several behaviors simultaneously, thus yielding a larger amount of data than event recording. And, attending to transitions between the intervals, as well as to subject's behavior, decreases the likelihood that the observers' attention will wander and that instances of the response will not be recorded (Cone & Foster, 1982).

In summary, the three types of direct observation procedures differ not only in their methods, but also in the degree to which they produce reliable information (the issue of reliability will be discussed later). Thus, the selection of an observation strategy depends on a number of factors that will be discussed below.

General Considerations in Selecting an Observational System. A number of practical and conceptual issues must be considered in the selection of a particular observational system. In practical terms, the available resources (e.g., observers, recording equipment) may limit the type of system that can be used. For example, an event recording system may be the easiest method for participant observers to use because of its ease of implementation. The availability of coding systems that have already been developed by other investigators may also be a practical consideration for the use of a particular method. If the investigator is limited in the amount of time that can be spent on the development of an observation system, or if a system that meets research needs already has been developed, then he or she will choose an observation system from one that is available.

Another practical consideration is the frequency with which a behavior occurs. For example, as mentioned previously, the tendency for observers to "nod off" when behavior occurs at a low frequency might preclude the use of an event recording system in favor of an interval recording system.

Conceptual issues surrounding the selection of an observational system include the purpose for which data are being collected, the breadth of the data desired by the investigators, and the response property of interest (Cone & Foster, 1982). As mentioned earlier, if data are being collected to obtain initial information about the client's behavior in a particular situation, a narrative recording system may be the most useful for specifying various response topographies and antecedent and consequent events. Or if a range of target behaviors has already been identified and the investigator is interested in obtaining data on all of them, then an interval recording system that allows for the collection of data on several behaviors simultaneously might be selected. Third, although all three of the observational systems can yield data on various types of response properties, the selection of a particular observational system will depend upon the behavior and the research question being asked.

Target Behavior Selection. One of the most salient conceptual and methodological issues in behavioral assessment today is the selection of the behavior that is to be the target of an intervention. Traditionally, the approach to target behavior selection in applied behavior analysis has been to focus assessment and treatment of behaviors that are of applied or social importance (Baer, Wolf, & Risley, 1968). The criteria for such importance are usually that the behaviors

1. may be important to the client or to persons in contact with the client (e.g., parents, teachers, hospital staff);
2. are or eventually may be dangerous to the client or to others (e.g., aggressive behavior, drug addiction);

3. may interfere with the client's functioning in everyday life (e.g., phobias, obsessive-compulsive rituals); and
4. indicate a clear departure from normal functioning (e.g., bizarre performance, such as self-stimulatory rocking, age-inappropriateness performance, such as enuresis or thumb sucking among older children) (Kazdin, 1982, pp. 18–19).

Behaviors generally fall into one of these categories because they differ from "normal" in terms of their frequency, duration, or severity or because they are inappropriate in a particular environment. However, the judgment of the deviancy of a particular behavior is most frequently made by parents, teachers, or society at large and, hence, is inherently subjective. As a result, although there are many behaviors that would usually be agreed on as requiring treatment, there are equally as many behaviors that cannot be so clearly identified. In other words, when is a child's behavior "hyperactive" and when is it just "active?" Thus, the process of target behavior selection has become much more complex and must involve other criteria in addition to the requirement of the applied or social importance of a behavior (Mash & Terdal, 1981).

Behaviors targeted for change need not "deviate" from normal. Often behaviors are chosen because they are desirable, but the client could profit from an increase in these behaviors. For example, the client may participate in a project designed to increase creative behaviors, social skills, or even athletic proficiency. Thus, positive behaviors have often been the focus of behavior modification programs with children and adults.

The area of children's social functioning can be used as one example of the many issues surrounding the selection of target behaviors. In this area of research and practice, a distinction can be made between the global category of social competence, which refers to the global assessment of children's functioning, and social skills, which are those specific social behaviors that contribute to a child's social functioning (Hops, 1983). When one assesses a child's social functioning, reports concerning the child's level of social competence are usually obtained from the child's parents, teachers, or peers. At this level of assessment, a global impression of the child's ability to function in social situations is obtained. However, all the persons evaluating the child may not necessarily agree. For example, Gresham (1981b) conducted a series of factor analyses that indicated independent dimensions of social responses are obtained from peer ratings, peer nomination, and direct observations. Thus, even before specific social skills are identified as the focus of treatment, subjective evaluations at a global level have been inconsistent.

If, from a global evaluation, it appears that the child is not socially competent, the next step in assessment is to specify those social skills that should be the target of an intervention. The most frequently used selection technique has been to choose skills that, at least in terms of their face validity, have some relationship to social competence. However, researchers in the area of children's social skills have become increasingly aware of the disadvantages of randomly selecting social skills for assessment and intervention—such disadvantages as the lack of generalization and maintenance of the skills once they are taught as well as a lack of improvement in social competence as a result of skills training (Gresham, 1981a).

As a result, researchers and clinicians have begun to turn to alternative methods of selecting social skills for assessment and intervention. One such method is a reliance upon normative data indicating that certain skills are characteristic of normal social functioning. For example, in a recent study by Hendrickson, Strain, Tremblay, and Shores (1982), the choice of target behaviors—that is, play organizers, shares, and assists—was made upon the basis of data obtained in a previous study (Tremblay, Strain, Hendrickson, & Shores, 1981), indicating that these behaviors were the most likely to result in positive responding by a peer in a normal preschool setting. Another alternative method of selecting a target behavior is to use empirical evidence that certain skills covary with or are prerequisite to others. For example, Barton and Ascione (1979) conducted a study in which they found that training preschool children to share verbally resulted in an increase in physical sharing without specific training of that behavior, but that teaching physical sharing did not generalize to verbal sharing. Thus, if increasing both verbal and physical sharing was the goal of a social skills intervention, a cost-effective approach would be to select verbal sharing as the target behavior based upon these empirical data.

In summary, the area of children's social functioning provides a good background for illustrating the issues of target behavior selection in behavioral assessment. Although the criterion of applied and social importance is, and will continue to be, the major means of selecting a target behavior, it must necessarily be supplemented in some instances. Although subjective judgments of deviancy are useful as a means of identifying global areas in need of remediation, the selection of specific skills for assessment would ideally have an empirical basis. Reliance upon empirical evidence indicating that certain skills are characteristic of a normative group or that certain skills covary with or are prerequisite to others are two means of making target behavior selection more objective and empirically sound.

Conditions of Assessment. As mentioned earlier, one way in which behavioral and traditional assessment differ is that, in a behavioral approach, conditions of assessment are viewed as necessarily affecting assessment results. There are, however, a number of dimensions along which the conditions of assessment vary, including the setting in which the behavior is observed, the manner in which the behaviors of concern are elicited, the client's knowledge of whether or not behavior is being assessed, and the use of human observers versus automated devices to assess behavior (Kazdin, 1982).

Naturalistic versus Contrived Observations. Related to the issue of assessment in the natural environment is the manner in which the behavior of concern is elicited. Naturalistic observation, which can occur in either natural or analog settings, involves observing behavior as it naturally occurs. Thus, it is the method that is most likely to provide a valid index of performance. Naturalistic observation, however, also has a number of disadvantages that may prohibit its use. For example, a behavior might be of low frequency, be difficult to assess because of a lack of available resources, or require specific precipitating conditions that may or may not occur, thus making naturalistic observation impractical (Kazdin, 1982). Therefore, contrived observations that involve altering the assessment situation so that the behavior of concern will occur are an alternative when naturalistic observations become problematic. There are, of course, costs to the standardization of assessment conditions that contrived observations provide. For example, contrived situations might provide examples of behavior that have little resemblance to those that occur in the natural environment. If treatment gains were then based upon these contrived observations, it would appear that the treatment was successful, even though it might not have resulted in any meaningful changes in the client's life.

Obtrusive versus Unobtrusive Assessment. Observations can differ in the degree to which the client is aware that he or she is being assessed. Obtrusive observations—that is, those in which the client is aware of the assessment—are the most frequently used, both for the ethical considerations of informed consent as well as for the practical consideration of making observational data easier to obtain. However, the primary disadvantage of obtrusive observations is that they may be reactive (i.e., they may result in a change in subject performance merely as a result of their occurrence). Thus, occasionally, observations may be conducted unobtrusively or without the subject's awareness. Such unobtrusive measures pose serious ethical problems, however, when they are scheduled without the client's having consented to participate in either a treatment program or a research study (Kazdin, 1979).

Human Observers versus Automated Recordings. As the technology for directly observing behavior becomes more sophisticated, so too does the issue of human versus automated recording become more salient. Although automated recording devices have been used most frequently as measures of physiological responding (e.g., blood pressure, brain wave activity, skin temperature), there are automated recording devices that can be used to measure overt behavior as well. Such apparatus can detect when a response has occurred, the duration of the response, and other features of response performance (Kazdin, 1982), thus distinguishing them from such devices as tape recorders and stop watches that must still rely upon human observers to record the response. Automated recording devices have the advantages of reducing or eliminating human measurement error. As with any method of assessment, there are disadvantages to their use as well, including expense, the possibility of mechanical breakdowns, and their relative inflexibility in comparison to human observers.

Accuracy of Direct Observations. The accuracy of data obtained from direct observations is of primary importance to assessment, treatment selection, and evaluation. However, whenever human observers are used, there is the possibility that they will not record data accurately. Thus, the issue of the accuracy of direct observations is a salient one that must be taken into account when using this method of assessment.

Determining Observer Accuracy. Direct observation is designed to assess (1) the occurrence of behavior, (2) its repeated occurrence, (3) its occurrence in more than one setting, (4) its occurrence in comparison with other behavior, and (5) its occurrence as measured by alternative methods (Cone & Foster, 1982, p. 323). Hence, the accuracy of a direct observation procedure will be the extent to which it reports on these factors and, thus, correctly reflects the behavior of interest. Therefore, accuracy must be distinguished from the issue of observer agreement, which is a measure of how well the data from separate observers correspond, rather than whether or not the observer's data reflect the subject's actual performance. This distinction is illustrated by a study by Romanczyk, Kent, Diament, and O'Leary (1973), in which pairs of observers maintained a high level of agreement and yet obtained data that differed from that obtained by other pairs of observers. Thus, the assumption that observer agreement reflects observational accuracy may result in a serious error (Johnston & Penny-packer, 1980).

Assessment of the accuracy of direct observations, then, must occur independently of an assessment of observer agreement. Any method, however, must meet at least two requirements for assessing accuracy: (1) The observational system must be correctly implemented, and (2) there must be a correspondence between the data obtained and some pre-established criterion. A number of criteria can be used to assess observer accuracy, including data obtained from an automated recording device, a human performance that has been permanently recorded and for which a criterion protocol has been produced, or a performance that has been structured to match predetermined characteristics (Foster & Cone, 1980). For example, in the biological sciences, the accuracy of new instruments is determined by comparison to a standard or reference instrument the accuracy of which has been demonstrated. Analogously, behavioral observation may be compared to objective data obtained from an automated recording device (e.g., observation of motor activity may be compared to data from a wrist actometer worn during the period of observation). Or, alternatively, a videotaped protocol, for which consensual agreement among a number of independent observers has been obtained, can serve as a criterion against which the observations of a novice can be judged.

Sources of Inaccuracy and Possible Solution. A number of factors can affect the accuracy of direct observations, including (1) characteristics of the observation system itself, (2) observer characteristics, and (3) setting variables (Wasik & Loven, 1980).

Characteristics of the observation system, such as the complexity of the code and data collection procedure used, can affect data accuracy. For example, if a code is particularly detailed, or if response definitions are inadequate, this may result in either an inability of observers to record all instances of the behaviors in the code or a random application of the response definition to observed behaviors. The procedure itself may also affect accuracy. As mentioned earlier, an interval recording system might result in better observer attention than an event recording system. Solutions to the effects of the characteristics of the observation system then would include, for example, simplifying the behavioral code to make it more manageable by observers as well as clarifying the response definitions. In addition, careful attention must be paid to the selection of an observation system so that it is adequate for the type of data desired. For instance, if behavior occurs infrequently, an interval system may be more appropriate than event recording.

Observer characteristics, such as knowledge of experimental hypotheses, a tendency to develop idiosyncratic versions of the original behavior category, the amount of training and prior experience, and fatigue and boredom, can affect the accuracy of observational data as well (Wasik & Loven, 1980). Knowledge of the experimental hypotheses has repeatedly been shown to influence the results in the direction of these hypotheses (Kent & Foster, 1977). Observer drift, in turn, has also been shown to result in a tendency of paired raters to develop idiosyncratic versions of the behavior category that decrease the agreement between the data collected by different pairs of observers. The prior training and experience of the observers, as well as the type of training received, can also affect the accuracy of behavioral observations, with insufficient training and experience resulting in less accurate data. Fatigue and boredom are also factors that can affect data accuracy when the setting in which observation occurs is uneventful and routine or when the observer tries to code behaviors too often or for too long a period. These effects of observer characteristics can, however, be minimized in a number of ways. First of all, observers can be kept blind to the experimental hypotheses in order to minimize directional measurement error. Observers should also be rotated so that the phenomenon of observer drift does not occur. The training of observers should be examined to ensure that it is sufficient and that it provides the observers with numerous opportunities for practice. Finally, the time periods for observations should be short and infrequent enough so that fatigue and boredom are less likely to occur.

Characteristics of the setting in which data are collected can also affect accuracy. For example, such ecological variables, as the noise and activity levels of students in the classroom can interfere with the observer's ability to code behavior accurately. Perhaps, however, the setting variable that is most likely to affect the accuracy of data is the presence of the observer in the setting. In other words, the person being observed may react in such a way to these observations that the target behavior is altered in some way. For example, in a recent review of the literature on reactivity in behavioral observation, Haynes and Horn (1983) identified at least 10 reactive effects associated with behavioral observations. They include

1. Increases in behavior rates
2. Decreases in behavior rates
3. Differential effects on behavior rates for different behaviors of the same subject
4. Differential effects on behavior rates for different subjects
5. Increased variability in behavior rates
6. Systematic changes in behavior rates over time (slope)
7. Changes in behavior rates consistent with intrinsic or extrinsic demand conditions in the assessment situation
8. Orientation toward observers
9. Deficits in task performance
10. Changes in behavior rates by mediators in the subject's environment

Reactive effects can take many forms, and, hence, can seriously affect the accuracy of data obtained from direct observations. As a result, taking steps to minimize reactivity is highly recommended. For example, the use of participant observers (i.e., individuals who are normally a part of the subject's environment) would reduce the possibility that novelty or disruption of the environment would result in reactive effects. Another alternative is to obtain observations unobtrusively (e.g., video cameras or tape recorders could be utilized in place of an observer in the setting, or instructions could be given to observers to minimize their interactions with subjects as well as to "act neutral"). Other strategies include allowing for sufficient time for the dissipation of reactive effects and variability in the data or using a number of observers or various observation procedures so that any potential reactive effects will cancel out (Haynes & Horn, 1983).

Assessment of the Independent Variable. As discussed earlier, applied behavior analysis attempts to demonstrate or to identify a functional relation between an environmental event (an independent variable) and a behavior (a dependent variable). Implicit in this investigation is the assumption that the manipulation of the independent variable, when all other potentially influential effects (e.g., history, maturation, extraneous variables) have been controlled, will be responsible for changes in the dependent variable. The primary method of controlling for the effects of extraneous factors has been the technology of single-subject designs that ensure that the manipulation of the independent variable is responsible for observed changes in behavior. Missing from this method of control, however, is a means of ensuring that the independent variable that was manipulated was actually the variable described. In other words, the integrity of the independent variable cannot be established on the basis of the demonstration of a functional relation in a single-subject design. Such integrity can only be demonstrated through assessment of the independent variable or treatment method. Thus, assessment within applied behavor analysis must not only focus on the dependent variable or behavior of interest, but on the independent variable as well.

A number of problems may arise when investigators do not assess the independent variable within applied behavior analysis research. A major problem that occurs is that treatment ineffectiveness may be due to the failure of the experimenters to implement the treatment adequately. Inadequate treatment implementation may be the result of a procedure that was too weak (e.g., of an insufficient duration) or of a treatment that was not implemented as described. Unless the implementation of the treatment is assessed, however, the extent to which it was adequate will not be known. If the treatment was carelessly planned and implemented, no amount of care in research design and statistical analysis can compensate for it (Yeaton & Sechrest, 1981). Whereas it may be true that some treatments are relatively immune to the problems of weakness and inadequate implementation (i.e., as long as some attempt is made to implement the treatment it will be effective), until this immunity is demonstrated empirically, treatment should be monitored.

Recognition of the need to examine the integrity of treatment, however, is a recent development. Indeed, Peterson, Homer, and Wonderlich (1982), in a recent review of the literature, determined that the majority of articles published in the *Journal of Applied Behavior Analysis* did not assess the independent variable. Thus, in the majority of studies, the integrity of the treatment implementation is not known.

In order to ensure treatment integrity, Yeaton and Sechrest (1981) have suggested that investigators should first determine the level of integrity required and then institute a procedure to ensure this integrity. In other words, investigators must clearly define their treatment variable and then assess it throughout the course of treatment to determine if it is being implemented as described. To the extent that this is done within the applied behavior analysis literature, confidence in empirical data on treatment effectiveness will be increased.

BEHAVIOR ANALYSIS RESEARCH DESIGNS

Types of Behavior Analysis Designs

Some very basic core elements serve as a structure from which all behavior analysis designs are derived (Hays, 1981; Johnston & Penny-packer, 1980). Behavior analysis designs may be classified according to three general types: within, between, and combined series. Each of these designs, as well as their various advantages and limitations, will be described, and an example from the applied research literature will be presented.

Within-Series Designs: Simple and Complex Phase Changes. Within-series designs allow the examination of changes in level and trend of subject performance across various phases of the study. In the simple phase change design, the researcher compares measures at the point of phase change (i.e., intervention) for the differences in level or trend. The simplest form of the within-series design is an A/B strategy. Usually this format allows only weak inference for the effect of the intervention and can be regarded as pre-experimental (Kazdin, 1982). Confidence in a relationship between the intervention and dependent measures is increased when there are a series of *replications* of treatment over phases of the study. Thus, if the intervention effects can be demonstrated a second or third time by reinstating the B phase (e.g., in an A/B/A/B design), the researcher is more confident that alternative explanations (i.e., various threats to validity) are less plausible. The number of different strategies of reproducing treatment effects within subjects or groups can be used to compare different treatments, such as B and C (e.g., B/C/B, B/C/B/C designs).

More complex phase changes can also be scheduled in within-series designs. Essentially these strategies operate by the same logic as the simple phase change designs. The complex phase change designs are sometimes called interaction type designs because they examine the effects of multiple treatment components. Interactions refer to the effect of combining treatment components and requires that the investigator manipulate two or more variables separately or in combination (see Hersen & Barlow, 1976). In their basic form, these designs allow a comparison of the effects of adding or subtracting various treatment components. Thus, if a researcher is interested in comparing a social to a tangible reinforcement contingency, two different phase options are available. These include the B/B + C or B + C/B options in which B may be a social reinforcement and C may be a tangible reinforcement. As was true with the simple phase change strategy, the researcher has greater confidence in the effect of treatment when replication of the series occurs (e.g., B/B + C/B/B + C or B + C/B/ B + C/B). Generally, the complex phase change designs are useful when the investigator is interested in examining the treatment interactions and the development of treatment packages. Sometimes treatment effects will be additive, but sometimes certain therapeutic components will contribute more to the overall effect than other components. In such cases, the researcher is concerned with the optimal combination of components to produce the best treatment package.

An example of a simple phase change design occurred in an investigation by Broden, Copeland, Beasley, and Hall (1977) who conducted two experiments in a junior high school special education classroom with eight students. In experiment one, the investigators used an A/B/A/B design. During the first baseline phase, the rates of four types of teacher questions asked during eight class discussions were evaluated. The length of student answers, determined by counting the number of words, was recorded. During this phase, no attempt was made to alter teacher presentation or question types. Following this phase, the teacher was requested to increase the number of new questions and questions requiring multiple word answers during each class session. Thus, she was asked to increase the number of questions beginning with "why," because single word answers could not appropriately follow that question type. No specific instructions were issued to the students. Figure 1 is a record of the number of words used to respond to teacher questions. It can be observed that the number of words per response increased during the intervention phase. During the second baseline, the teacher was then asked to reduce the number of new and multuple word questions to approximately baseline levels. It can be observed in Figure 1 that in concert with this phase change, the numbers of words per response decreased. Subsequent implementation of the new and multiple word question phase (i.e., B_2) increased the number of word responses.

In the second experiment, the number of words used by students and the percentage of answers given in complete sentences, increased from less

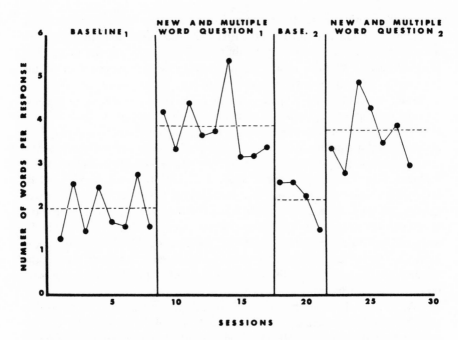

FIGURE 1. A record of the number of words used to respond to the teacher's questions. Baseline₁—before experimental procedures, new and multiple word questions₁—the teacher increased the number of new and multiple word answered questions; baseline₂—the number of new questions was reduced, new and multiple word questions were increased; baseline₃—the number of new and multiple word questions were increased. From "Altering Student Responses through Changes in Teacher Verbal Behavior" by M. Broden, C. Copeland, A. Beasley, and R. B. Hall, 1977, *Journal of Applied Behavior Analysis*, 10, p. 482. Copyright 1977 by M. Broden, C. Copland, A. Beasley, and R. B. Hall. Reproduced by permission.

than 5% to approximately 90% when the teacher instructed the students to answer using complete sentences and asked another pupil to answer using a sentence if the first one did not do so. Both experiments indicated that a return to baseline brought a return to low levels of verbal responding. Additional analysis demonstrated clearly that other, extraneous variables were not responsible for the observed increases in verbal responding.

It has been observed that the within-series withdrawal type designs can be used in situations in which the treatment is readily withdrawn. However, the withdrawal of treatment may not result in the anticipated changes in the dependent measures in the investigation. When this occurs, the logic of the design and experimental control are considerably compromised. Another limitation is that some measures may not deteriorate following removal of the intervention, especially when a skill has been learned. As a consequence, the design is usually inappropriate to evaluate certain types of academic or motor skill learning programs. Finally, certain ethical concerns may take priority over the experimental withdrawal needed to demonstrate treatment effects in this design. Where certain behaviors are aversive to the subject or others, it may be inappropriate to withdraw treatment to demonstrate the effects of the program.

Another complex phase change strategy has been called the changing criterion design. In this procedure, experimental control is established by bringing the level of the dependent measure under the control of arbitrarily set criteria (Hall & Fox, 1977; Hartmann & Hall, 1976). In the typical changing criterion design, a series of baseline observations is followed by an intervention and maintained throughout the treatment phase. However, at various points during the treatment phase, stepwise changes in the level of the dependent measure are set as criteria. In the usual form of this design, the criteria are linked with treatment contingencies. If the dependent measure reliably tracks the stepwise changes in the criteria, the internal validity of this design is strengthened in that various rival hypotheses related to change can be discounted.

A major feature that is necessary in drawing inferences from the changing criterion design is the demonstration of parallel changes in the dependent measure and criteria established during the treatment phase. Thus, in order to demonstrate parallel changes, the investigator must have each criterion phase of sufficient length to allow the dependent measure to stabilize before proceeding to the next phase. In fact, the size of the stepwise criteria must be large enough to distinguish the actual treatment effects from the variability in the phase series. It is also possible to further strengthen inference for an intervention effect by randomly varying the length, depth, and direction of the criterion shifts (Hayes, 1981). Essentially, this strategy exaggerates the control of the criteria and various contingencies associated with them on the dependent measure.

An example of this design is reported by Foxx and Rubinoff (1979) who conducted a study in which a treatment program to reduce excessive daily coffee drinking was implemented. In the study, three habitual coffee drinkers received an individualized changing criterion program that gradually reduced their daily caffeine intake to moderate and safer levels. The coffee consumers were required to self-monitor and plot their daily intake of caffeine. They also received various monetary rewards for not exceeding the treatment phase criteria and forfeited part of their pretreatment deposit if this occurred. Results of the program for Subject 1 are presented in Figure 2.

The figure shows that the subject's daily caffeine intake (reported in milligrams) was systematically reduced over treatment phases. The criterion

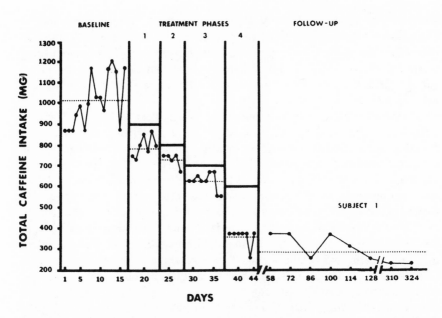

FIGURE 2. Subjects' daily caffeine intake (mg) during baseline, treatment, and follow-up. The criterion level for each treatment phase was 102 mg of caffeine less than the previous treatment phase. Solid horizontal lines indicate the criterion level for each phase. Broken horizontal lines indicate the mean for each condition. From "Behavioral Treatment of Caffeinism: Reducing Excessive Coffee Drinking" by R. Foxx and A. Rubinoff, 1979, *Journal of Applied Behavior Analysis, 12*, p. 339. Copyright 1979 by R. Foxx and A. Runinoff. Reproduced by permission.

level for each treatment phase was 102 mg of caffeine less than the previous phase. The solid horizontal lines in the figure indicate the criterion level for each phase; the broken horizontal lines indicate the mean for each condition. Generally, the results were similar for the other two subjects. In fact, the results of the studies indicated that the subjects' overall coffee drinking decreased from almost nine cups per day (or 1,100 mg of caffeine) during baseline to less than three cups per day (or less than 343 mg) at the end of the treatment. Essentially, this is a reduction of 69%. Also, the investigators noted that the treatment effect was maintained during a 10-month follow-up, which resulted in an average of 67% reduction from baseline.

Between-Series (Alternating and Simultaneous Treatment Designs). Two basic design types make up the between-series strategies. These include the alternating treatments design (ATD) and the simultaneous treatments design (STD). These are alternatives for the comparison of different interventions within the same subject. In a between-series strategy, two or more data series are compared across time. The comparisons made between the series take into account various features of the data (i.e., trend and variability) as the clients receive the various independent treatments.

The ATD exposes the subject to separate treatment components for equal periods of time (Barlow & Hayes, 1979). Generally, the treatments are alternated within a very short period of time, as for example from one session to another or from one part of the day to another. The sequence of times of the treatment exposure are determined either randomly or through counterbalancing. This tactic ensures that the subject receives equal exposure to the interventions, while providing a control for the effects of time and various setting differences. The ATD allows investigators to compare treatments in a relatively short period of time while avoiding some of the usual disadvantages of the aforementioned within-series withdrawal designs (i.e., need for a stable baseline, treatment withdrawal, and various other threats to internal validity). Nevertheless, the ATD does have some limitations. The most apparent one is that multiple treatment interference and logistical considerations must be taken into account when any two or more treatments are implemented. Generally, however, the ADT is a useful strategy for implementing treatments when investigators are interested in comparing two or more treatments relatively quickly.

In contrast to the ATD, the STD exposes the subject to interventions simultaneously (Kazdin & Hartmann, 1978). Nevertheless, the simultaneous availability of the treatment does not ensure that the subject will be exposed equally to the treatments under study (Kratochwill & Levin, 1980). Thus, rather than comparing the relative effectiveness of different treatments, as is the case in the ATD, the STD evaluates a subject's preference among different treatments. The STD could serve as a useful strategy for establishing a hierarchical ordering of treatments on the basis of their acceptability (Hayes, 1981).

An example of the ATD is reported by Ollendick, Matson, Esveldt–Dawson, and Shapiro (1980) who investigated the effectiveness of spelling remediation procedures in two investigations. In the first investigation, a procedure called positive practice over-correction plus positive reinforcement was compared to a positive practice alone and a no remediation control condition. In the second investigation, positive practice plus positive reinforcement was compared to a traditional corrective procedure, plus positive reinforcement in a traditional procedure when used alone. In the second investigation, the researchers compared the positive practice plus positive reinforcement procedures to a more traditional teaching tactic. Specifically, positive practice plus positive reinforcement was compared to a traditional corrective procedure with a traditional corrective procedure plus

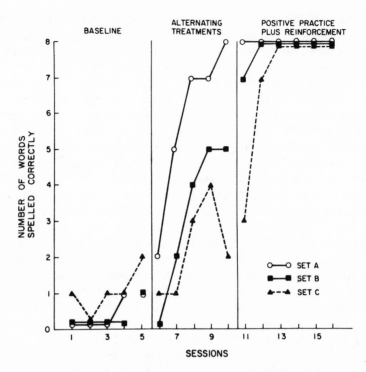

FIGURE 3. The number of words spelled correctly by Child 3 during the three experimental phases for the three sets of words. During the alternating treatment phase, words from Set A were assigned to the positive practice plus positive reinforcement condition; words from Set B were assigned to the traditional plus positive reinforcement condition; and words from Set C were assigned to the traditional alone condition. During the last phase, positive practice plus positive reinforcement was used with all three sets of words. From "Increasing Spelling Achievement: An Analysis of Treatment Procedures Utilizing and Alternating Treatments Design" by T. H. Ollendick, J. L. Matson, K. Esveldt-Dawson, and E. S. Shapiro, 1980, *Journal of Applied Behavior Analysis, 13*, p. 651. Copyright 1980 by T. H. Ollendick, J. L. Matson, K. Esvelt-Dawson, and E. S. Shapiro. Reproduced by permission.

positive reinforcement. Figure 3 shows the number of words spelled correctly by child 3 during the three experimental phases for the three sets of words employed in the investigation.

During the alternating treatment phase, words from set A were assigned to the positive practice plus positive reinforcement conditions; words from set B were assigned to the traditional plus positive reinforcement condition; and words from set C were assigned to the traditional alone condition. Results of the investigation show that the positive practice plus positive reinforcement was superior to the other conditions during the alternating treatments phase (see phase 2). The traditional plus positive reinforcement condition was more effective than traditional procedures alone, although it was less effective than the positive practice plus positive reinforcement condition. Also, when positive practice plus positive reinforcement was implemented for all time periods during the last phase, the child's spelling performance increased dramatically and was maintained at 100% accuracy.

Combined-Series (Multiple Baseline) Designs. The final design strategy can be called combined series because it permits comparisons both within and between series. One of the more common combined-series designs is called the multiple baseline design (MBD). In the typical MBD, a single within-series phase element (i.e., A/B) is replicated across two or more subjects, settings, or experimenters, thereby allowing a comparison between and within the A/B series. Control for the usual validity threats is achieved by staggering the treatment at different points across time. When changes are noted at the first A/B shift, and the remaining baseline series remain stable and unaffected, various threats to internal validity are less likely. For example, historical effects would typically be ruled out with successive replications across time. Thus, confidence in the intervention effect increases as replication series are conducted.

The MBD strategy has a number of advantages over other designs used in applied behavior analysis research. First of all, there is no *a priori* number of data series required for the design, and although some researchers recommend at least three series to establish internal validity, the researcher is not limited to this (of course, two series represent the minimum to achieve design integrity). Yet, the more series in which effects are demonstrated, the stronger the evidence for an intervention effect. The second positive feature of these designs relates to the nature of evaluating data sets across time in a single subject. An investigator can implement treatment in one phase and study generalized treatment effects across series. Yet, if this occurs, the investigator must employ different design tactics to rule out threats to validity, since the integrity of the design has now been compromised. For example, the researcher could shift to one of the withdrawal designs to demonstrate intervention effectiveness, thereby continuing to analyze generalizations separately (discussed later). In addition to these advantages, the MBD is often acceptable to individuals in applied settings who find that it fits naturally into monitoring behaviors, since it does not require withdrawal of treatment. Individuals working in applied settings are likely to object to treatment withdrawal in some of the within-phase series.

In a recent investigation, Poche, McCubbrey, and Munn (1982) examined the effects of an intensive training program on the tooth-brushing skills of three preschool children using an MBD across subjects. The authors used dependent measures involving plaque level indicators. A tooth-brushing program was broken down into 16 steps. It involved the actual manipulation of the brush in the mouth. Correct brushing included four criteria: (1) appropriate angle of bristles, (2) appropriate motion of brush, (3) appropriate tooth surface, and (4) minimum duration of brushing. The actual package program included instruction, a three-phase modeling procedure, physical guidance, and reinforcement. Figure 4 shows the number of tooth-brushing steps correctly performed by the three children during the baseline training and follow-up phases. As can be observed from the figure, the second subject, Holly, demonstrated virtually no skills, whereas Troy and Nancy had some of the skills before the intervention program started. Overall, the results show that the children completed an average of 8.6% of the steps before training as compared to an average of 95.8% of the steps found in the training program. Also, plaque levels decreased from an average of 58% during baseline to 24.6% following the training. The study has great significance in terms of teaching children a health-related skill.

SPECIAL DESIGN ISSUES

Evaluation of Psychoactive Medication. Researchers working in the applied behavior analysis field have frequently studied the influence of psychoactive medication on various response measures. Indeed, the areas of evaluation of drugs appear to be uniquely suited to the single case because of the many ideographic responses that are often found in children who are given medication. A number of designs are or can be used to evaluate psychoactive medications to determine their effectiveness.

When psychoactive medication is being evaluated in research settings, a number of issues have been identified that must be taken into account (Hersen & Barlow, 1976). These include such factors as placebo effects and blind assessments. First of all, a major factor to be addressed in the use of psychoactive medication is the residual effects of the medication once it is formally discontinued. Thus, medication may not always act the same way social interventions act when they are discontinued. The effects may continue to influence various behavior patterns as a result of biochemical changes that may carry over into subsequent experimental phases. The point is that the researcher must continue on to the next phase only when certain acceptable drug levels have been reached or when it can be determined that the drug present will not have a contaminating effect. This concern in applied research is especially evident when the researcher is trying to compare a psychoactive medication to a behavioral intervention. In

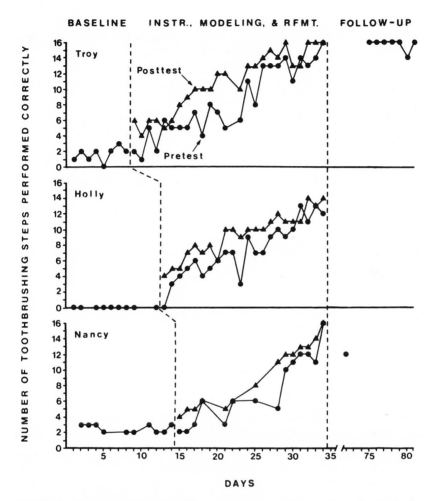

FIGURE 4. The number of toothbrushing steps correctly performed by the three children in the baseline, training, and follow-up conditions. From "The Development of Correct Toothbrushing Techniques in Pre-School Children" by C. Pouche, H. McCubbrey, and T. Munn, 1982, *Journal of Applied Behavior Analysis*, *15*, p. 318. Copyright 1982 by C. Pouche, H. McCubbrey, and T. Munn. Reproduced by permission.

such cases, the researcher is primarily interested in determining the effects of the psychosocial intervention independent of the biochemical effect of the drug.

A second major concern in psychoactive drug research relates to the expectancy or placebo effects that accompany drug administration. When research is conducted evaluating the effects of drugs it is usually desirable to include a placebo condition as a separate phase (i.e., A$_1$). When this type of evaluation occurs, the researcher can tease apart the effects of the drug as the result of factors in the environment serving to produce an effect when it is really not attributable to the drug. In such a design strategy, a researcher would implement an A/A$_1$ sequence to determine whether or not a placebo effect was evident. Following this sequence, the researcher would add an active therapeutic medication possibly followed by a behavioral intervention. Again, within-series involve manipulating one variable at a time when going from phase to phase.

A third issue to be addressed in drug research relates to the evaluation of blind assessments. There are two types of blind experimental arrangements. In the first type, labeled *single blind*, either the service provider or the subjects do not know whether or not they are receiving an active drug or a placebo. In the second type, *double blind*, neither know. Of course, a double-blind procedure is most desirable in applied research, but it is very difficult to effect.

For example, clients and/or staff working in applied settings might know when a drug is being administered, especially if it has dramatic effects on client behavior. Also, some medications have certain side effects that may alert the staff or the subjects to the fact that they are taking an active drug.

A variety of single case time–series designs can be used to evaluate psychoactive medications in applied research. A complete listing of all these designs is impossible here; however, the interested reader should consult Hersen and Barlow (1976) and Kratochwill and Mace (1984) for some examples of different designs that can be used to evaluate psychoactive drugs. Each of the designs raises a number of different issues regarding how medication might be evaluated and, thus, the researcher must select a design that answers the primary research questions.

An example of an investigation that evaluated the effects of psychoactive medication on a "hyperactive" preschool child was reported by Shafto and Sulzbacher (1977). These authors evaluated two treatment procedures: (1) food and praise contingent on appropriate play and (2) the effect of varying doses of methylphenidate (Ritalin) on the child's activity level. In addition, the authors monitored various social, verbal, and academic behaviors to determine the side effects of the treatment. Figure 5 shows the influence of various dosages of Ritalin and the teacher intervention on the frequency of activity changes during the free play period over a period of several months. The authors found that fewer free play activity changes occurred during contingent reinforcement phases while the medication had variable effects. These included increases in attention to task but at higher doses, decreasing intelligibility of speech and responsiveness to demands.

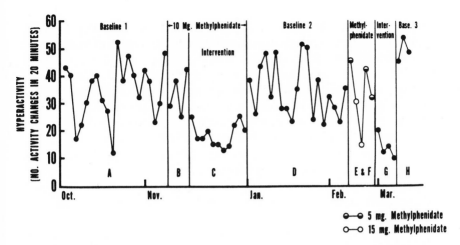

FIGURE 5. Influence of various dosages of methylphenidate and teacher intervention on daily frequencies of activity changes during free-play period. From "Comparing Treatment Tactics with Hyperactive Pre-School Child: Stimulant Medication and Programmed Teacher Intervention" by F. Shafto and S. Sulzbacher, 1977, *Journal of Applied Behavior Analysis, 10,* p. 17. Copyright 1977 by F. Shafto and S. Sulzbacher. Reproduced by permission.

In this investigation, the authors used an A/B/B + C/A/B/C/A design that does not allow strong inference regarding the effectiveness of either of the treatments used. Thus, the authors manipulated more than one variable (B/B + C) at a time in going from one phase to another. However, the authors did employ a double-blind procedure in that they established that neither the subject's mother nor any of the teachers knew the actual dosage on a particular day. Of course, no evaluation of a placebo condition was scheduled in this investigation.

STRATEGIES FOR ASSESSING GENERALIZATION

Once a causal relation is established between the independent and dependent variable, the applied researcher is usually concerned with the nature of generalization and the extent to which treatment effects generalize. Many authors have emphasized the importance of assessing (Baer *et al.,* 1968; O'Leary & Drabman, 1971) and programming generalization (Kazdin, 1976; Stokes & Baer, 1977).

Two primary types of generalization are of concern to behavior analysis researchers: the generalization of treatment effects across situations (*stimulus generalization*) and the generalization of treatment effects to other response measures (*response generalization*). When changes in the dependent variable occur in situations other than the treatment condition, stimulus generalization is said to have occurred. This may be the result of the subject's failure to discriminate changes in stimulus conditions (e.g., a different therapist providing the same intervention) or to the development of conditioned reinforcers that are capable of maintaining behavior after the original reinforcer is withdrawn. Response generalization, on the other hand, refers to changes in nontreated measures that can be attributed to the intervention. For example, a child's disruptive behavior may be reduced in the classroom and accompanied by an increase in certain academic response measures that were not the actual focus of the intervention.

Although the investigator may be interested in both stimulus and response generalization, the design used places some restrictions on the type of generalization that may be assessed (Kendall, 1981). The problem is that data patterns required to establish treatment effects may militate against those needed to confirm generalization. For example, consider an A/B/A/B design in which strong treatment effects occur during the first B phase. If treatment is subsequently withdrawn (second A phase) and the data remain unaffected, the researcher does not know if experimental control is lacking or if stimulus generalization has occurred. This often makes assessing stimulus generalization problematic with within-series simple and complex phase change designs. By contrast, however, evaluating response generalization with these types of designs is nonproblematic because data collected on other client measures may suggest that effects have generalized without jeopardizing the experimental validity. As indicated in Table 3, researchers may also find assessment of certain types of generalization problematic and others nonproblematic in certain time-series designs.

TABLE 3. Problematic and Nonproblematic Generalizations in Single-Subject Strategies

Single-subject strategies	Generalization	
	Problematic	Nonproblematic
Reversal	Treatment control or stimulus generalization	Testing for response generalization
Multiple baseline across situations	Treatment control or stimulus generalization	Testing for response generalization
Multiple baseline across behaviors	Treatment control or response generalization	Testing for stimulus generalization
Multi-element	Treatment control or stimulus generalization	Testing for response generalization

Note. From "Assessing Generalization and the Single Subject Strategies" by P. C. Kendall, 1971, *Behavior Modification, 5*, p. 311. Copyright 1971 by Sage Publications. Reprinted by permission.

Evaluation of response generalization is not limited to within-series designs. Response generalization with the ATD and STD may also be assessed by concurrent measures of nontarget behaviors. However, because experimental control depends on changes in treatment conditions, examining stimulus generalization may be troublesome. With the combined series designs, the MBD across situations or settings demonstrates control via behavior change that parallels the staggered introduction of treatment under different stimulus situations. This strategy makes assessment of stimulus generalization difficult, but response generalization is possible when concurrent measures are employed. In the case of the MBD across behaviors, the situation is reversed. Assessing generalization across different stimulus conditions is nonproblematic. However, since internal validity is linked to comparisons across behaviors, evaluating response generalization is typically not possible.

Several time-series designs have been developed to evaluate generalization of treatment effects. These include (1) *MBD plus generalization phases design* (Kendall, 1981), (2) *sequential withdrawal design* (e.g., Rusch, Connis, & Sowers, 1979), (3) *partial withdrawal design* (e.g., Vogelsberg & Rusch, 1979), and (4) *partial sequential withdrawal design* (Rusch & Kazdin, 1981).

One design layout (depicted in Figure 6) involves obtaining concurrent measurements on multiple behaviors (three, in this case) and staggering the intervention in conventional MBD fashion (Kendall, 1981). After the treatment effects are demonstrated for each behavior, a series of generalization tests or phases are instituted. During these phases, stimulus conditions may be systematically varied in order to evaluate the generalization of treatment effects to the new stimulus situations. For example, holding the

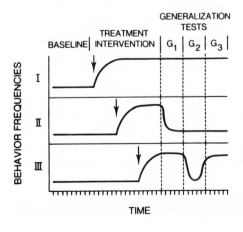

FIGURE 6. Hypothetical data for a multiple baseline design across behaviors with three generalization tests. From "Assessing Generalization and the Single-Subject Strategies" by P. C. Kendall, 1981, *Behavior Modification, 5,* p. 316. Copyright 1981 by P. C. Kendall. Reproduced by permission.

intervention constant, G_1 may represent treatment provided by a different experimenter, G_2 may be treatment provided in a different setting (e.g., different rooms), and G_3 may involve intervention using different materials (e.g., different reading books). The hypothetical data patterns appearing in Figure 6 represent possible outcomes. For behavior I, generalization is apparent across all three situations; for behavior II, generalization appears nonexistent; and for behavior III, effects were maintained in all but the G_2 phase. Data patterns in the latter two series may lead the investigator to develop additional intervention strategies targeted at situations in which effects did not generalize.

Each of the withdrawal designs for assessing generalization are used with multi-component package interventions. A package refers to an intervention program consisting of several distinct components. As separate components are individually withdrawn, data patterns are examined for the maintenance of treatment effects. That is, did therapeutic gains generalize to $N - 1, N - 2 \ldots N - N$ conditions? In the *sequential withdrawal design,* single components of a treatment package are withdrawn one at a time until all components have been discontinued. The effects of each $N - 1$ condition are evaluated in separate and consecutive experimental phases. This strategy has been used in conjunction with within-series withdrawal type designs (e.g., O'Brien, Bugle, & Azrin, 1972), as well as combined-series multiple baseline designs (e.g., Sowers, Rusch, Connis, & Cummings, 1980).

A variant of this procedure, referred to as the *partial-withdrawal design,* involves withdrawing any of N treatment components from one series in MBD (e.g., Vogelsberg & Rusch, 1979). If performance is maintained in the treatment withdrawal series, additional components may be withdrawn from the series or similar components withdrawn from other series. Whenever performance deteriorates, intervention efforts would focus on programming the generalization to the specific $N - 1$ condition (Rusch & Kazdin, 1981). This strategy provides information on how other series (i.e., behaviors, settings, or subjects) may respond to the withdrawal of specific components. It also often avoids the loss of all treatment gains that may occur with complete withdrawal of intervention.

The *partial-sequential withdrawal design* represents a combination of the sequential and partial withdrawal designs (Rusch & Kazdin, 1981). In this procedure, all or part of a multi-component treatment is withdrawn from one of the series in MBD. If the removal of the intervention results in decreased performance, a sequential withdrawal of specific components is instituted in the remaining series. Hypothetical applications of the partial-sequential withdrawal design appear in Figure 7.

In the first example (Figure 7a), the introduction of praise and prompts

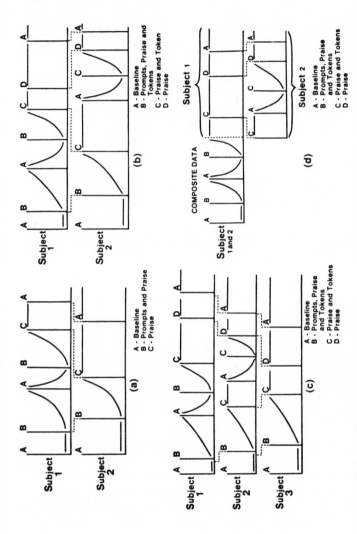

FIGURE 7. A systematic withdrawal of a two-component treatment across two subjects is represented in the upper left graph (a). Withdrawal of a three-component treatment across two subjects is indicated in the upper right graph (b). A systematic withdrawal of a three-component treatment across three subjects is shown in the lower left portion of graph (c). Finally, withdrawal of a three-component treatment across two subjects within ABAB reversal is depicted in the lower right portion of graph (d). From "Toward a Methodology of Withdrawal Designs for the Assessment of Response Maintenance" by F. R. Rusch, and A. E. Kazdin, 1981, *Journal of Applied Behavior Analysis*, 14, p. 137. Copyright 1981 by F. R. Rusch and A. E. Kazdin. Reproduced by permission.

(B) was staggered across two subjects. For Subject 1, the complete withdrawal of intervention produced a rapid loss of intervention gains. In order to avoid a similar loss in Subject 2, prompts only were withdrawn (C phase) followed by the withdrawal of prompts and praise (A phase) when effects were maintained. The application of this procedure to evaluate three-component interventions with two and three subjects are presented in Figures 7b and 7c, respectively. In both examples, when the complete withdrawal of intervention (prompts, praise, and tokens) resulted in performance losses for Subject 1, the package was reinstated, followed by sequential withdrawal of tokens (D phase) and praise (A phase). In Figure 7c, Subject 3 benefits from the knowledge gain in subjects and does not suffer from intervention losses. Finally, Figure 7d illustrates the use of this strategy with a within-series design using two subjects. Following an A/B/A/B sequence for both subjects, components were withdrawn one at a time for Subject 1. Like the other cases, when Subject 2 experienced performance losses with the removal of two components, both components were reinstated and sequentially withdrawn.

APPLICATION OF BETWEEN-GROUP DESIGNS IN APPLIED BEHAVIOR ANALYSIS RESEARCH

Rational for Group Designs. Traditionally, research in applied behavior analysis has emphasized single case time-series designs in which the effects of an intervention are evaluated on dependent measures for an individual subject. In contrast, most of the research in the social sciences has relied on between-group and within-subject group investigations. An overview of traditional group designs and their contributions to psychology is beyond the scope of this chapter. The interested reader is referred to studies that present these research options, as well as the advantages and limitations of this form of research (Kazdin, 1980b; Cook & Campbell, 1979).

Several advantages of between-group designs have been identified (see Kazdin, 1980b, 1982 for more detailed descriptions). To begin with, between groups designs can be useful to researchers when there is a concern with comparing two or more treatments. As noted in previous sections, there are difficulties in comparing two treatments for a single subject. For example, one treatment might limit what can be analyzed in a second treatment. Specifically, their juxtaposition across different phases for a single subject might vary. A treatment that employs a punishment contingency followed by a reinforcement contingency may even confuse the subject and result in deteriorated performance. Even the ATD has a problem of multiple treatment inteference, which is not adequately dealt with in the usual applications of this strategy. Thus, when treatments are compared in between-group designs, the researcher can evaluate separate treatments without an influence occurring on the other(s).

Another major positive feature of between-group designs is that the researcher can determine the magnitude of change between groups that have not been treated. If the investigator is interested in determining the magnitude of change in the treatment groups, relative to subjects who did not receive the intervention, a no-treatment control group can provide this type of information. Usually, such a group serves as a baseline for the evaluation of the performance of the treatment group. Technically, this strategy can be used in a time-series design when groups of subjects are randomly formed and when one of these groups serves as a no-treatment control. A major problem in time-series designs, and specifically an A/B/A/B type design, is that the researcher cannot make stable baseline estimates once an intervention has preceded it. In fact, it is reasonable to assume that the second baseline phase will always differ from the first baseline. Thus, between-group designs provide the researcher with an evaluation of a no-treatment group that has never received the intervention.

Another positive feature of between-group designs is that these types of methodologies can be used when a group of subjects is the primary focus of the intervention (e.g., large populations in cities, school districts, hospitals). It is possible that because of the limitations of repeated measures procedures, researchers simply cannot measure every one or all subjects over various phases of an investigation. Thus, between-group research designs might be appropriate to implement in the investigation when the investigator is interested in measurement on one or a few occasions in comparing large groups.

It should be emphasized that, in many cases, time-series research designs can be implemented with a group. It is possible to implement repeated measures across large populations when these data can be obtained. In fact, many applications in the *Journal of Applied Behavior Analysis* employ time-series methodology in the context of a group. Such applications have been used in A/B/A/B, within-series designs, as well as in between- or combined-series strategies.

Finally, between-group research is useful in generalizing intervention effects across subjects and settings. Once researchers have demonstrated strong independent variables in single-case research, it may be useful to investigate whether or not certain types of treatments hold up over diverse clients and settings. This type of research allows the investigator to promote generalization (this issue is discussed in the section on external validity). Examples of applications of between-group research will help the reader perceive their contribution to applied behavior analysis.

There are applications of group research, in applied behavior analysis, when it would have been useful for the authors to provide data on individual subject performance to elucidate more carefully aspects of why the treatment was successful and unsuccessful. In fact, in the *Journal of Applied Behavior Analysis*, group studies have been applied when analysis of a single-case study has not been well elucidated. An example of a study in this area is one reported by Bernal, Blinnert, and Schultz (1980) who evaluated the effectiveness of parent training in reducing conduct problems in children. A behavioral treatment group was compared to a client-centered parent counseling condition. The secondary issue addressed in the study was the relative effect of these two treatments in a comparison to a waiting-list control group. The waiting-list control group was an untreated condition during an eight-week period of treatment provided to the other groups. In the investigation, the familities of 36 five- to twelve-year-old, conduct problem children were assigned to the two treatment groups. However, the wait-list control assignment depended on the therapist's availability and so random assignment was technically not used. Graduate students trained in behavior modification procedures and supervised by senior staff conducted 10 treatment sessions for each family. The dependent measures consisted of parent reports and paper-and-pencil tests of child deviance as well as parent satisfaction. These measures showed a superior outcome for the behavioral over the client-centered and wait-control groups, but no differences between the latter two groups. The authors also found that at follow-up, there was no maintenance of this superiority of the behavioral treatment on these measures. On the other hand, what we believe to be the more important variable, home observation, showed no advantage of the behavioral over the client-centered treatment. Also, the two groups did not improve significantly more than the waiting-list control.

The authors indicated that the results of their investigation raised serious questions about the application of behavior modification procedures for conduct problem children. However, there are a number of limitations of this study that a careful analysis of a single subject's data might have clarified. First, if the researchers had presented individual data on the children and their responsiveness to treatment, leads would be provided on how to modify treatment in the future to effect change. Second, as noted above, one of the unique advantages of single-case time-series designs is repeated measurement over time. If repeated measures on each individual subject had been made, it would have been possible to see where performance deterioration occurred. This could lead to the more effective development of a treatment program to effect change in these children. Nevertheless, the investigation does show that group research is certainly considered in applied behavior analysis. However, whether or not between-group research is employed depends on knowledge in the area, concern among reviewers in the field, and the topic and its significance for applied work in the field.

Combined-Group and Time-Series Designs. Sometimes, between-group methodology is combined with the characteristics of single-case time-series methodology. In such cases, the researcher can reap the benefits of both methodologies to answer certain types of research questions. An example of this appeared in a study by Herman, DeMontes, Dominguez, Montes, and Hopkins (1977); these researchers evaluated the effectiveness of an incentive procedure to increase punctuality of six workers who were chronically late to work in a manufacturing company. The six workers in the experiment received a monetary bonus for every day they arrived on time. The authors used a within-series treatment design combined with a control condition. Results of the investigation suggested that the bonus was effective in reducing the instances of tardiness.

The intervention in this case demonstrated effectiveness, but the control condition provides some additional information that would otherwise have not been available. Specifically, the control group allowed assessment of the magnitude of the effects of the intervention. That is, the baseline and treatment conditions in the treatment group do not necessarily demonstrate what the level of tardiness would have been if treatment had never been introduced. Thus, the control group provides an estimate of the level of tardiness that actually demonstrated an increase over time. Herman *et al.* (1973) also added another dimension to the study that is a useful strategy when research is conducted with groups in applied behavior analysis. The authors presented, in separate figures, the fewest tardy incidents of a subject in a treatment group over the experiment. Also, the authors provided data for the individual who had the most incidents of tardiness during the experiment. These data provide an additional check on the effectiveness of the actual treatment program during the investigation and constitute a strategy that should be encouraged in applied research.

REPLICATION

In the context of research, behavioral measures also derive their meaning from the replication of experimental conditions. *Replication* refers to the reproduction of variables responsible for a particular behavioral effect. This may occur across different points in time, subjects, or environments. The purpose of replication is to examine collateral changes in the dependent variable associated with the replication of the independent variable. The resulting data patterns provide information regarding the reliability and generality of the phenomenon observed (Sidman, 1960).

Results are considered reliable when they are repeated with each manipulation of the independent variable. A researcher who can consistently reproduce a given pattern of data upon each introduction and withdrawal of treatment, for example, may conclude that the observed effect is both reliable and stable. Consumers of this information may then be confident that the procedures used will yield comparable results under identical or highly similar conditions. The generality of experimental findings, on the other hand, is assessed via replication efforts of a different sort. Rather than the identical replication of experimental conditions, selected aspects of the experiment are allowed to vary, while the remainder are held constant. An example in the behavior analysis literature is the finding that the stimulus characteristics of tokens used in token economies could vary widely and retain the qualities of a generalized reinforcer (Kazdin, 1982; Kazdin & Bootzin, 1972). Sidman (1960) referred to these two types of replication as direct and systematic, with direct replication dealing with concerns for the reliability of a phenomenon and systematic replication with its generality.

DIRECT REPLICATION

For the outcome of a given investigation to be believable, it must stand the test of replication. In behavior analysis research, this requirement is satisfied by reproducing a behavioral effect for a single individual. The term for demonstrating reliable effects for a single organism is intrasubject or *direct replication* (Sidman, 1960). When other subjects are treated, it is not for purposes of validating whether uncontrolled events peculiar to the original experiment may have produced the behavior change. As Sidman (1960) points out, failure to replicate effects with other subjects should generate further research rather than a recantation of the original finding.

Intrasubject replication is achieved by comparing an individual's performance under two or more conditions with setting variables held constant to minimize their influence during replication. As noted in the previous section, in a typical behavior analysis experiment, repeated measures of a target behavior are collected under baseline conditions and contrasted to performance measures during a particular treatment or intervention. Differential rates of behavior that correspond to baseline and treatment conditions suggest that the intervention produced an observable effect. The reliability of the effect, however, is determined by reproducing or approximating the original data pattern on another occasion. Numerous experimental designs discussed above have been developed for this purpose. Although the focus here is not to again review various design options, a design example will help illustrate the concept of direct replication.

Carr, Newsom, and Binkoff (1980) examined the functional relation between demand conditions and aggression in two mentally retarded children. Separate experimental sessions were held with each subject and involved placing the child under demand and no-demand conditions across alternating phases. Demands consisted of requiring the subject to sit quietly in a chair (Bob) or sit in a chair and complete a buttoning task (Sam). During no-demand conditions, the children were not required to engage in structured activities. Subjects experienced the two conditions in a sequence of $B_1/A_1/B_2/A_2$ (Bob) or $B_1/A_1/B_2/A_2/B_3$ (Sam) phases, where B = demands and A = no demands. For Bob, exposure to demands resulted in high rates of aggressive behavior, followed by a dramatic drop to zero rates when demands were withdrawn (A_1). Subsequent reintroduction of demands (B_2) yielded rates of aggression similar to those obtained in the initial B phase and were again eliminated by allowing Bob to leave the chair (A_2). A similar pattern of responding was evident in the second subject (Sam).

In this example, the relation between demand and no-demand situations on aggression was illustrated in the initial B_1A_1 sequence. The reliability of the phenomenon, however, was established when replication of the two conditions in the B_2/A_2 sequence reproduced data configurations quite similar to those obtained originally. Still greater confidence in the reliability of the effect was evident in the second replication of the demand condition (B_3) with Sam.

In contemporary discussions, the reliability of treatment effects is referred to as internal validity (cf. Campbell & Stanley, 1963; Cook & Campbell, 1979; Kazdin, 1980a,b; Kratochwill, 1978). Drawing valid conclusions regarding the reliability of a phenomenon requires that alternative explanations are untenable. Alternatives that rival the causal role of the independent variable are called threats to internal validity. Several authors have catalogued the various internal validity threats and discussed strategies to control or modify their influence (see Cook & Campbell, 1979; Kazdin, 1980b). The major threats to internal validity are listed and defined in Table 4. Many of these threats may be successfully dealt with via experimental design. Returning to the Carr et al. (1980) example, the impact of history, maturation, testing, instrumentation, and statistical regression is rendered implausible by the data patterns. For instance, it is unlikely that an event other than the change in demand conditions was responsible for the different rates of aggression across phases. Although it is possible that an extraneous aggression-suppressing event coincided with the withdrawal of demands, a second coincidence of this sort is improbable. Equally unlikely is the explanation that maturation processes produced the pronounced shifts in aggressive behavior. Seldom are maturational effects so abrupt, and moreover, reversals in development are rarely seen. Similarly, testing and instrumentation effects should accrue over the course of the experiment to produce a trend in the data, a characteristic not present in the

TABLE 4. Threats to Internal Validity

History	The occurrence of events extraneous to the experimental treatment that may affect the dependent measure
Maturation	Physical and/or psychological changes occurring within subjects that may affect the dependent measure over time. Becomes a threat to internal validity when such changes are not the focus of research
Testing	Changes in the dependent variable as the result of the process of measuring subject performance. May result from subjects having taken a pretest because of the reactivity of the measurement process
Instrumentation	Changes in the dependent measure as the result of the use of inconsistent measurement procedures over the course of evaluation. Instrumentation may occur when data collectors alter their method of recording performance as a result of experience, observer bias or drift, or the malfunction of mechanical recording devices. May also result from tests having unequal intervals leading to "ceiling" and "floor" effects
Statistical regression	If subjects are assigned to groups or treatment conditions on the basis of unreliable pretest or baseline measures, high scores will tend to decrease their performance over subsequent measurement occasions while the performance of low scores will increase. Regression always occurs toward the population mean of a group; thus, scores in the mid-range will likely be unaffected
Selection	When groups are formed by arbitrary rather than random methods, their differential performance may be due to prexisting differences between groups rather than actual treatment effects
Mortality	The withdrawal of some subjects observed at the pretest or baseline period before the final assessment may result in unequal groups. Observed effects may be attributed to differences in subject characteristics or subject response to treatment rather than the effects of the independent variable
Interactions with selection	The interaction of history, maturation, and/or instrumentation threats with selection resulting in spurious treatment effects. History-maturation may occur when subjects or groups experience different historical factors that influence performance. Maturation-selection results when subjects or groups mature at different rates to increase the disparity between groups over time. Selection-instrumentation occurs when performance is scored differently for different groups because of observer factors or tests with unequal intervals
Diffusion or imitation of treatments	When subjects in the experimental and control groups are free to communicate with each other, it is possible that subjects may exchange information about the procedures or conditions of their particular group. The validity of the experiment is, therefore, threatened because the groups are no longer independent
Compensatory equalization of treatments	When experimental treatments provide subjects with desirable services, administrators may find it unacceptable to "deprive" the no-treatment control group of these benefits and insist that comparable or compensatory services be provided. The intended contrast is thus nullified and causal statements about the independent variable are rendered invalid
Compensatory rivalry by respondents receiving less desirable treatments	When subjects are aware of their group status (i.e., experimental or control), those not receiving treatment may compete with their experimental counterparts. Observed effects may be the result of this rivalry, rather than the independent variable
Resentful demoralization of respondents receiving less desirable treatments	Control subjects aware that they are receiving less desirable treatment may respond by lowering their standard of performance. Between-group differences following treatment could not be attributed to the effects of intervention

Note. From "Experimental Research in Clinical Psychology" by T. R. Kratochwill and F. C. Mace, in A. E. Kazdin and A. S. Bellack (Eds.), *The Clinical Psychology Handbook* (1985, p. 135). New York: Pergamon Press. Copyright 1985 by Pergamon Press. Reproduced by permission.

study. And finally, intrasubject replication of the effects of demand conditions via the B/A/B/A design undermines the validity of a statistical regression hypothesis. If regression were going to occur, it would be expected on any of the repeated measurement occasions prior to a change in phases. Furthermore, reversals in regression patterns are unexpected because of the unlikely occurrence of central scores straying from the mean.

SYSTEMATIC REPLICATION

Once the reliability of a behavioral effect is established via direct replication, concern shifts to determining the extent to which the phenomenon is evident under conditions other than those of the original experiment. The generality of a functional relationship is assessed through *systematic replication* (Sidman, 1960). Systematic replication involves repeating an experiment while varying a limited number of its aspects. Should data patterns persist under varied conditions, conclusions can be extended to these areas.[5] Failure to reproduce the original findings, however, suggests that these varying aspects of the study are critical to the functional relations. Although this may appear to be cause for despair, additional research is often generated to determine the reasons for discordant results and efforts to amend the treatment to produce the desired outcome are made (Herson & Barlow, 1976; Sidman, 1960).

Much of the systematic replication in applied behavior analysis research is a progression of independent research efforts occurring over a period of several years. As noted in the beginning of this chapter, Johnston and Pennypacker (1980) summarized the development of the literature on time-out from reinforcement, a procedure commonly used to decrease behavior. The history of time-out was traced from its laboratory origins (e.g., Skinner, 1950) to its present status as a flexible treatment procedure having applications to a broad range of human problems. The maturity of the time-out literature is the result of scores of experiments that replicated past research while varying selected aspects of this problem. In the following section, several dimensions of research open to systematic replication are discussed.

DIMENSIONS OF SYSTEMATIC REPLICATION

Consumers of behavioral research want to know the circumstances under which a particular intervention or assessment procedure will be

[5] Campbell and Stanley (1963) refer to the generality of research findings as external validity. Factors that limit generality (and undermine systematic replication) are called threats to external validity. See Cook and Campbell (1979) and Kazdin (1980b) for more detailed accounts.

effective. Concerns for generality center around five major dimensions: subjects, behaviors, settings, procedures, and processes. In any given study, information regarding some or all of these dimensions is obtained, for it is the rare applied experiment that can isolate a solitary variable for systematic replication. Only through repeated experimentation are the limits of generality defined (Johnston & Pennypacker, 1980).

Across Subjects. Procedures that have little or no generality beyond a single case are generally of limited value to the applied community (Michael, 1974). Hence, there has been a movement in applied behavior analysis to develop robust assessment and intervention methods. A robust intervention, for example, would be one that is relatively impervious to individual differences in reinforcement history or biological makeup. In the time-out literature, the universality of the procedure has been clearly demonstrated by reproducing its functional effect in psychotic children (Tate & Baroff, 1966), retarded children (Barton, 1970; Peterson & Peterson, 1968), normal children (LeBlanc, Bushy, & Thompson, 1974), culturally deprived children (Wasik, Senn, Welch, & Cooper, 1969), and mentally retarded adults (Hamilton, Stephens, & Allen, 1967).

Across Behaviors. The majority of behavioral procedures in wide use today have demonstrated their application across a variety of behaviors. Each successful replication of an experiment across different subjects or behaviors within a subject extends the generality of the procedure across behaviors. The administration of a particular treatment to different subjects that share a response class (e.g., self-stimulation) yields information on how different response topographies may be affected. For example, Harris and Wolchik (1979) found that time-out reduced self-stimulation in two subjects whose topography consisted of repetitive contact (rubbing, stroking, or tapping) with an object or a body part. Subjects whose self-stimulation took other forms (e.g., turning objects, crumbling food, or extended and waving arms) were unaffected by a time-out procedure. For the latter two cases, overcorrection proved to be the treatment of choice.

Across Settings. Technically, changes in setting occur any time there are differences in materials, location, or persons present from one experimental session to another. In applied work, a certain degree of setting variability is inevitable. To the extent that treatment effects hold up under varying setting conditions, the generality of the intervention is strengthened. Several investigators, however, have isolated setting variables and examined their effects on behavior. In another study from the time-out literature, Wahler (1979) assessed the impact of time-out and differential attention at school and in the home. Following a period of baseline assessment in both settings, the treatment package was introduced in the home only with a corresponding increase in cooperative behavior. Subsequent intervention in the school produced similar improvement in the subject and, in doing so, extended the generality of combined time-out and differential reinforcement to an educational setting.

Across Procedures. No sooner are behavioral interventions developed than variations on the theme appear in the literature. With each successive variation and empirical examination, more knowledge concerning the generality of the treatment when the procedures are altered is obtained. In this regard, replication may yield information concerning the type, amount, or length of treatment required to bring about change. Since Skinner (1950) identified the suppressing effects of contingent darkness on key pecking, time-out has assumed a variety of forms. Among the variations shown to impact on behavior are removal of the subject from a reinforcing situation (e.g., Ayllon, 1963), withdrawal of social reinforcement (e.g., Risley & Wolf, 1967), and a contingent stimulus indicating the unavailability of reinforcement (e.g., Foxx & Shapiro, 1978). Other parameters of time-out receiving scrutiny are the duration of the procedure and the schedule of its application (Clark, Rowbury, Baer, & Baer, 1973).

Across Processes. A behavioral process refers to the functional relation between two or more variables (Johnston & Pennypacker, 1980; Sidman, 1960). The process occurring in time-out is the subject's particular target response followed by the contingent introduction or withdrawal or a stimulus that results in an interval of sparse reinforcement. In the overwhelming majority of studies, the effect of this process has been to decelerate the target behavior. Yet, time-out is not always successful in reducing response rates. Careful analysis of the process has revealed that time-out has predictable effects on behavior only when the density of reinforcement present in the "time-in" environment is taken into consideration. For example, Solnick, Rincover, and Peterson (1977) found that time-out had a negative reinforcement effect on tantrums, self-injurious behavior, and spitting when occurring is an impoverished (low reinforcement) environment. Enriching the reinforcement in the target setting resulted in the expected punishment paradigm. Thus, in this instance, systematic replication served to delimit the behavioral process of time-out and identify conditions that alter its nature.

METHODS OF SYSTEMATIC REPLICATION

As mentioned earlier, the goal of systematic replication is to assess the durability of a functioned relation when the dimensions of the original experiment are varied. Despite calls for evaluating the generality of behavior procedures, few researchers have channeled their efforts in this direction (an estimated 1%, according to Agras & Berkowitz, 1980). Available to the behavioral community are several experimental designs developed especially for this purpose (Kazdin, 1982). The design options discussed below include probe designs, between-series MBDs, within-series generalization phases, and within-series withdrawal designs.

Probe Designs. Probes are periodic measures taken under different conditions or of different behaviors of secondary interest to the investigator. Their primary function is to assess the generalization and/or maintenance of a behavioral effect in the absence of treatment. Because probes constitute intermittent rather than continuous data collection, they represent a relatively economical approach to assessment. Moreover, probes provide a means of evaluating the spillover effects of treatment to no-treatment situations. When individual differences are noted, further research may elucidate the factors that cause one subject to show a generalized response to treatment, whereas specific effects are found in another.

Tucker and Berry (1980) utilized probe measures in the evaluation of a training sequence to teach multihandicapped children to put their hearing aids on. The training procedure consisted of the following graded sequence of assistance provided by the trainer as needed: (1) no help, (2) verbal instruction, (3) demonstration and verbal instruction, and (4) physical guidance and instruction. Daily training sessions were conducted in an experimental room, and correct responses were reinforced with praise. The effectiveness of the training procedure was demonstrated using an MBD across subjects. During the training sessions, data patterns for Randy and Steve, and, to a lesser extent, Billy, resembled acquisition curves common in skill training studies. However, as Tucker and Berry point out, the validity of the teaching sequence resides in its generalization to the natural environment. For this reason, generalization probes were taken during baseline and training in residential areas and a classroom. In all subjects, generalization of training effects to natural settings occurred and at levels comparable to those achieved during the training sessions.

The characteristics of the MBD make it a natural tool for systematic replication. With each demonstration of the experimental effect with different subjects, settings, or behaviors, the generality of the phenomenon is strengthened. A study by Russo, Cataldo, and Cushing (1981) illustrates how the between-series multiple baseline method can be used to establish functional relations as well as their generality. Three retarded children were treated for noncompliance and severe behavior problems. Multiple baselines were obtained for compliance, crying, self-injurious behavior, and aggression during experimental sessions conducted by two different therapists. A compliance training procedure consisting of edible reinforcement and guided compliance resulted in marked increases in compliant behaviors when administered by either therapist. Moreover, the untreated baselines showed an inverse covariance with compliance, indicating that compliance training can result in collateral reductions in severe behavior problems. The authors' replication of this finding across two additional children with varying problem behaviors, as well as an additional therapist, produced convincing evidence for its generality.

Within-Series Generalization Phases. Another design option of within-series generalization phases was discussed in an earlier section. The technique involves conducting one or more generalization tests within a data series, usually after a treatment effect has been demonstrated. An example of this strategy is seen in a case study by Mace, Kratochwill, and Fiello (1983), in which severe aggression in a mentally retarded adult was eliminated via a positive treatment approach. Before intervention, the client had a long history of high rates of aggressive behavior occurring during occasions when he was separated from a state van (a stimulus acquiring reinforcing properties through association with outings into the community). Administration of a treatment package consisting of compliance training in the presence of the van and involvement in an activity incompatible with aggression was implemented. In subsequent phases of the study, the generalized effects of the treatment were assessed across four on-line residential staff, as well as in settings previously associated with serious aggressive acts.

WITHDRAWAL DESIGNS

A problem encountered by many behavior analysts is the loss of treatment gains following the withdrawal of the therapeutic variables. Kazdin (1982) notes that, although a reversal of performance patterns to baseline or near baseline levels is a natural consequence of treatment withdrawal, such losses may be prevented when treatment components are withdrawn systematically. The methodological response to this dilemma has been the development of strategies known as *withdrawal designs* as previously discussed.

The first of these methods to emerge was the *sequential-withdrawal design* (O'Brien et al., 1972; Rusch et al., 1979). The principle of this design is the successive withdrawal of components of a multicomponent treatment package after therapeutic results have been achieved. Fading the removal of treatment avoids an abrupt contrast between treatment and no-treatment conditions and enhances the prospects of maintaining the desired behavior. Moreover, dismantling interventions in this manner provides information regarding which components, if any, are necessary to maintain satisfactory performance.

The second strategy to evolve was the *partial-withdrawal design* (Russo

& Koegel, 1977). Similar in nature to the sequential-withdrawal design, the partial-withdrawal design removes the entire treatment from successive baselines in an MBD. In so doing, the investigator is given a preview of what to expect when intervention is withdrawn from the remaining baselines.

Sowers *et al.*, (1980) utilized the above strategies in the evaluation of a treatment package to teach retarded adults time-management skills. An MBD across subjects confirmed the benefits of the multicomponent intervention comprised of (1) pre-instruction in the use of a pictorial timecard, (2) instructional feedback (differential praise or corrective instructions) for on-time performance, and (3) the pictorial timecard that indicated lunch and break times. Using a *combined sequential-* and *partial-withdrawal design,* Sowers *et al.* (1980) sequentially withdrew pre-instruction (phase 3) and instructional feedback (phase 4) with a corresponding maintenance of on-time behavior in the first subject. When a similar strategy was employed with subject 2, however, he reverted to being late for his break during the latter part of phase 3. Punctual behavior was retrieved when the pre-instruction component was reintroduced to the training package (second phase 2). A second attempt at sequential withdrawal of pre-instruction and instructional feedback proved successful at maintaining a high percentage of on-time behavior using only the timecard as a prompt.

SUMMARY AND CONCLUSIONS

In this chapter, we have provided an overview of research methods in applied behavior analysis. In behavior analysis research the individual as a total functioning organism and his or her relation to the environment is studied. However, the behavior analytic approach is quite different than the more conventional approach to the study of individual differences. Behavior analysis research embraces several characteristics, including repeated measurement of the dependent variables, the monitoring of intrasubject variability, specification of controlling conditions in the environment, replication of experimental effects, and design flexibility in the analysis of independent variables. One major difference between traditional and behavior analytic study of individual differences pertains to the measurement system used. Traditional approaches rely on a vagonotic perspective in which the study of the individual derives its meaning from the degree to which a score deviates from other scores in a distribution. Behavior analysis relies on the counting and timing of events according to absolute and standard units—an idemnotic measurement. Several methods of assessment used in behavior analysis research were reviewed, including psychophysiological and self-report assessment methods, as well as direct observational methods. Special emphasis was placed on direct observational assessment and the methodological and conceptual issues surrounding this form of measurement.

Behavior analysis research designs can be developed from three basic types, including within series (e.g., A/B/A/B), between series (ATD and STD), and combined series (MBD). Each of these design types were reviewed, along with examples from the applied research literature. Special single-case time-series, as well as group designs, were presented along with the methodological considerations.

Replication is the heart of developing a knowledge base in the social sciences. In applied behavior analysis, direct and systematic replication is emphasized. Direct replication establishes the reliability of experimental effects, and systematic replication helps to establish the generality of findings across subjects, behaviors, settings, procedures, and processes. Various designs are used in the systematic replication process to help establish the generality of findings.

Behavior analysis research has made numerous contributions to both basic and applied research. We hope that researchers interested in the study of individual differences will consider both the contributions and the methodology of behavior analysis in future empirical work in this area.

ACKNOWLEDGMENTS

The authors express their sincere appreciation to Brian Iwata for his helpful comments on the manuscript and to Karen Kraemer for word processing the manuscript.

REFERENCES

Agras, W. S., & Berkowitz, R. Clinical research in behavior therapy: Halfway there? *Behavior Therapy*, 1980, *11*, 472–487.

Allen, K. E., & Harris, F. R. Eliminating a child's scratching by training the mother in reinforcement procedures. *Behavior Research and Therapy*, 1966, *4*, 79–84.

Allyon, T. Intensive treatment of psychotic behavior by stimulus satiation and food reinforcement. *Behavior Research and Therapy*, 1963, *1*, 53–61.

Baer, D. M., Wolf, M. M., & Risley, T. R. Some current dimensions of applied behavior analysis. *Journal of Applied Behavior Analysis*, 1968, *1*, 91–97.

Barlow, D. H., & Hayes, S. C. Alternating treatments design: One strategy for comparing the effects of two treatments in a single subject. *Journal of Applied Behavior Analysis*, 1979, *12*, 199–210.

Barton, E. S. Inappropriate speech in a severely retarded child: A case study in language conditioning and generalization. *Journal of Applied Behavior Analysis*, 1970, *3*, 299–307.

Barton, E. J., & Ascione, F. R. Sharing in preschool shildren: Facilitation, stimulus generalization, response generalization, and maintenance. *Journal of Applied Behavior Analysis*, 1979, *12*, 417–430.

Bergan, J. R. *Behavioral consultation*. Columbus, Ohio: Charles & Merrill, 1977.

Bijou, S. *Child development: The basic stage of early childhood*. Englewood Cliffs, N.J.: Prentice-Hall, 1976.

Bornstein, P. H., Bridgewater, C. A., Hickey, J. S., & Sweeney, T. M. Characteristics and trends in behavioral assessment: An archival analysis. *Behavioral Assessment*, 1980, *2*, 125–133.

Broden, M., Copland, C., Beasley, A., & Hall, R. B. Altering student responses through changes in teacher verbal behavior. *Journal & Applied Behavior Analysis*, 1977, *10*, 479–487.

Brown, P., & Elliott, R. Control of agression in a nursery school class. *Journal of Experimental Child Psychology*, 1965, *2*, 103–107.

Campbell, D. T., & Stanley, J. D. *Experimental and quasi-experimental designs for research*. Chicago: Rand-McNally, 1963.

Carr, E. G., Newson, C. D., & Binkoff, J. A. Escape as a factor in the aggressive behavior of two retarded children. *Journal of Applied Behavior Analysis*, 1980, *13*, 101–117.

Ciminero, A. R. Behavioral assessment: An overview. In A. R. Ciminero, K. S. Calhoun, & H. E. Adams (Eds.), *Handbook of behavioral assessment*. New York: Wiley, 1977.

Clark, H. B., Rowbury, T., Baer, A. M., & Beer, D. M. Time-out as a punishing stimulus in continuous and intermittent schedules. *Journal of Applied Behavior Analysis*, 1973, *6*, 443–456.

Cone, J. D. Psychometric considerations. In M. Hersen & A. S. Bellack (Eds.), *Behavioral Assessment: A practical handbook* (2nd ed.). New York: Pergamon Press, 1981.

Cone, J. D., & Foster, S. L. Direct observation in clinical psychology. In P. C. Kendall, & J. N. Butcher (Eds.), *Handbook of research methods in clinical psychology*. New York: Wiley, 1982.

Cook, T. D., & Campbell, D. T. (Eds.) *Quasi-experimentation: Design and analysis issues for field settings*. Chicago: Rand-McNally, 1979.

Cronbach, L. J. The two disciplines of scientific psychology. *American Psychologist*, 1957, *12*, 671–684.

Cronbach, L. J. Beyond the two disciplines of scientific psychology. *American Psychologist*, 1975, *30*, 116–127.

Cronbach, L. J., & Snow, R. E. *Aptitudes and instructional methods: A handbook for research on interactions*. New York: Irvington, 1979.

Day, W. F. Contemporary behaviourism and the concept of intention. In M. R. Jones (Ed.), *Nebraska symposium on motivation* (Vol. 23). Lincoln, Neb.: University of Nebraska Press, 1976.

Ferster, C., & Skinner, B. F. *Schedules of reinforcement*. New York: Appleton-Century-Crofts, 1957.

Foster, S. L., & Cone, J. D. Current issues in direct observation. *Behavioral Assessment*, 1980, *2*, 313–338.

Foxx, R. M., & Shapiro, S. T. The time-out ribbon: A nonexclusionary time-out procedure. *Journal of Applied Behavior Analysis*, 1978, *11*, 125–136.

Foxx, R. M., & Rubinoff, A. Behavioral treatment of caffeinism: Reducing excessive coffee drinking. *Journal of Applied Behavior Analysis*, 1979, *12*, 335–344.

Glaser, R. Some implications of previous work on learning and individual differences. In R.

M. Gagne (Ed.), *Learning and individual differences*. Columbus, Ohio: Charles E. Merrill, 1967.

Good, T. L., & Stipek, D. J. Individual differences in the classroom: A psychological perspective. In G. D. Fenstermacher & J. I. Goodlad (Eds.), *Individual differences in the curriculum: Eighty-second yearbook of the National Society for the Study of Education*. Chicago: University of Chicago Press, 1983.

Gresham, F. M. Social skills training with handicapped children: A review. *Review of Educational Research*, 1981a, *5*, 139–176.

Gresham, F. M. Validity of social skills measures for assessing social competence in low-status children: A multivariate investigation. *Developmental Psychology*, 1981b, *17*, 390–398.

Hall, R. V., & Fox, R. G. Changing-criterion designs: An alternative applied behavior analysis procedure. In B. C. Etzel, G. M. LeBlanc, & D. M. Baer (Eds.), *New developments in behavioral research: Theory, method, and application. In honor of Sidney W. Bijou*. Hillsdale, N.J.: Lawrence Erlbaum Associates, 1977.

Hamilton, J., Stephens, L., & Allen, P. Controlling aggressive and destructive behavior in severely retarded institutionalized residents. *American Journal of Mental Deficiency*, 1967, *7*, 852–856.

Harris, F. R., Johnston, M. K., Kelley, C. S., & Wolf, M. M. Effects of positive reinforcement on regressed crawling of a nursery school child. *Journal of Educational Psychology*, 1964, *55*, 35–41.

Harris, S. L., & Wolchik, S. Suppression of self-stimulation: Three alternative strategies. *Journal of Applied Behavior Analysis*, 1979, *12*, 185–198.

Hartmann, D. P., & Hall, R. A discussion of the changing criterion design. *Journal of Applied Behavior Analysis*, 1976, *9*, 527–532.

Hartmann, D. P., Roper, B. L., & Bradford, D. C. Some relationships between behavioral and traditional assessment. *Journal of Behavioral Assessment*, 1979, *1*, 3–21.

Hawkins, R. P., & Dobes, R. W. Behavioral definitions in applied behavior analysis: Explicit or implicit? In B. C. Etzel, J. M. LeBlanc, & D. M. Baer (Eds.), *New developments in behavioral research: Theory, method, and application*. Hillsdale, N. J.: Lawrence Erlbaum Associates, 1977.

Hayes, S. C. Single-case experimental designs and empirical clinical practice. *Journal of Consulting and Clinical Psychology*, 1981, *49*, 193–211.

Haynes, S. N., & Horn, W. F. Reactivity in behavioral observation: A review. *Behavioral Assessment*, 1983, *4*, 369–385.

Hendrickson, J. M., Strain, P. S., Tremblay, A., & Shores, R. E. Interactions of behaviorally handicapped children: Functional effects of peer social initiations. *Behavior Modification*, 1982, *6*, 323–353.

Herman, J. A., deMontes, A. I., Dominguez, B., Montes, F., & Hopkins, B. L. Effects of bonuses for punctuality on the tardiness of industrial workers. *Journal of Applied Behavior Analysis*, 1973, *6*, 563–570.

Hersen, M., & Barlow, D. H. *Single-case experimental designs: Strategies for studying behavior change*. New York: Pergamon Press, 1976.

Holm, R. A. Techniques of recording observational data. In G. P. Sachett (Ed.), *Observing behavior, Vol. 2: Data collection and analysis methods*. Baltimore, Md.: University Park Press, 1978.

Hops, H. Children's social competencies and skills: Current research practices and future directions. *Behavior Therapy*, 1983, *14*, 3–18.

Johnston, J., & Pennypacker, H. S. *Strategies and tactics of human behavioral research*. Hillsdale, N.J.: Lawrence Erlbaum Associates, 1980.

Kallman, W. M., & Feuerstein, M. Psychophysiological procedures. In A. R. Ciminero, K. S.

Calhoun, & H. E. Adams (Eds.), *Handbook of behavioral assessment*. New York: Wiley, 1977.

Kazdin, A. E. Statistical analysis for single-case experimental designs. In M. Hersen & D. H. Barlow (Eds.), *Single-case experimental designs: Strategies for studying behavior change*. New York: Pergamon Press, 1976.

Kazdin, A. E. Methodology of applied behavioral analysis. In C. A. Catania & T. B. Brigham (Eds.), *Handbook of applied behavior analyses: Social and instructional processes*. New York: Irvington, 1978.

Kazdin, A. E. Situational specificity: The two-edged sword of behavioral assessment. *Behavioral Assessment*, 1979, *1*, 57–75.

Kazdin, A. E. Acceptability of time-out from reinforcement procedures for disruptive child behavior. *Behavior Therapy*, 1980a, *11*, 329–344.

Kazdin, A. E. *Research design in clinical psychology*. New York: Harper & Row, 1980b.

Kazdin, A. E. *Single-case research designs: Methods for clinical and applied settings*. New York: Oxford University Press, 1982.

Kazdin, A. E., & Bootzin, R. R. The token economy: An evaluative review. *Journal of Applied Behavior Analysis*, 1972, *5*, 343–372.

Kazdin, A. E., & Hartmann, D. P. The simultaneous-treatment design. *Behavior Therapy*, 1978, *9*, 912–922.

Kazdin, A. E. & Willson, G. L. *Evaluation of behavior therapy: Issues, evidence, and research strategies*. Cambridge, Mass: Ballinger, 1978.

Kendall, P. C. Assessing generalization and the single-subject strategies. *Behavior Modification*, 1981, *5*, 305–319.

Kent, R. N. & Foster, S. L. Direct observational procedures: methodological issues in naturalistic settings. In A. R. Ciminero, K. S. Calhoun, & H. E. Adams (Eds.), *Handbook of behavioral assessment*. New York: Wiley, 1977.

Kratochwill, T. R. (Ed.) *Single-subject research: Strategies for evaluating change*. New York: Academic Press, 1978.

Kratochwill, T. R., & Levin, J. R. On the applicability of various data analysis procedures in behavior therapy research. *Behavioral Assessment*, 1980, *2*, 353–360.

Kratochwill, T. R., & Mace, F. C. Time-series research in psychotherapy. In M. Hersen, L. Michelson, & A. S. Bellack (Eds.), *Issues in psychotherapy research*. New York: Plenum Press, 1984.

LeBlanc, J. M., Bushy, K. H., & Thompson, C. L. The function of time-out for changing the aggressive behaviors of a preschool child: A multiple baseline analysis. In R. Ulrich, T. Stacknik, & J. Mabry (Eds.), *Control of human behavior* (Vol. 3). Glenview, Ill.: Scott Foresman, 1974.

Lubav, J. R., & Bahler, W. W. Behavioral management of epileptic seizures following EEG biofeedback training of the sensorimotor rhythm. *Biofeedback and Self-Regulation*, 1976, *1*, 77–104.

Lineham, M. M. Content validity: Its relevance to behavioral assessment. *Behavioral Assessment*, 1980, *2*, 147–159.

Mace, F. C., Kratochwill, T. R., & Fiello, R. A. A positive approach to the treatment of severe aggression: A case study. *Behavior Therapy*, 1983, *14*, 689–696.

Mash, E., & Terdal, L. *Behavioral assessment of childhood disorders*. New York: Guilford, 1979.

Meyer, V., Liddell, A., & Lyons, M. Behavioral interviews. In A. R. Ciminero, K. S. Calhoun, & H. E. Adams (Eds.), *Handbook of behavioral assessment*. New York: Wiley, 1977.

Michael, J. Statistical inference for individual organism research: Mixed blessing or curse? *Journal of Applied Behavior Analysis*, 1974, *7*, 647–653.

Nelson, R. O. Assessment and therapeutic functions of self-monitoring. In M. Hessen, R. M. Eisler, & P. M. Miller (Eds.), *Progress in behavior modification* (Vol. 5). New York: Academic Press, 1977a.

Nelson, R. O. Methodological issues in assessment via self-monitoring. In J. D. Cone & R. P. Hawkins (Eds.), *Behavioral assessment: New directions in classical psychology.* New York: Brunner/Mazler, 1977b.

O'Brien, F., Bugle, C., & Azrin, N. H. Training and maintaining a retarded child's proper eating. *Journal of Applied Behavior Analysis,* 1972, *5,* 67–72.

O'Leary, D. K., & Drabman, R. Token reinforcement programs in the classroom: A review. *Psychological Bulletin,* 1971, *75,* 379–398.

Ollendick, T. H., Matson, J. L., Esveldt-Dawson, K., & Shapiro, E. S. Increasing spelling achievement: An analysis of treatment procedures utilizing an alternating treatments design. *Journal of Applied Behavior Analysis,* 1980, *13,* 645–654.

Parsonson, B. S. & Baer, D. M. The analysis and presentation of graphic data. In T. R. Kratochwill (Ed.), *Single subject research: Strategies for evaluating change.* New York: Academic Press, 1978.

Peterson, L., Homer, A. L., & Wonderlich, S. A. The integrity of independent variables in behavior analysis. *Journal of Applied Behavior Analysis,* 1982, *15,* 477–492.

Peterson, R. F., & Peterson, L. R. The use of positive reinforcement in the control of self-destructive behavior in a retarded boy. *Journal of Experimental Child Psychology,* 1968, *6,* 351–360.

Poucher, C., McCubbrey, H., & Munn, T. The development of correct toothbrushing techniques in pre-school children. *Journal of Applied Behavioral Analysis,* 1982, *15,* 315–320.

Richard, H. C., Digman, P. J., & Horner, R. F. Verbal manipulation in a pyschotherapeutic relationship. *Journal of Clinical Psychology,* 1960, *16,* 364–367.

Risley, T. R., & Wolf, M. Establishing functional speech in echolalic children. *Behavior Research and Therapy,* 1967, *5,* 73–88.

Romanczyk, R. G., Kent, R., Diament, C., & O'Leary, K. D. Measuring the reliability of observational data: A reactive process. *Journal of Applied Behavior Analysis,* 1973, *6,* 175–186.

Rusch, F. R., Connis, R. T., & Sowers, J. The modification and maintenance of time spent attending to task using social reinforcement, token reinforcement, and response cost in an applied restaurant setting. *Journal of Special Education Technology,* 1979, *2,* 18–26.

Rusch, F. R., & Kazdin, A. E. Toward a methodology of withdrawal designs for the assessment of response maintenance. *Journal of Applied Behavior Analysis,* 1981, *14,* 131–140.

Russo, D. C., & Koegel, R. L. A method for integrating an autistic child into a normal public school classroom. *Journal of Applied Behavior Analysis,* 1977, *10,* 579–590.

Russo, D. C., Cataldo, M. F., & Cushing, P. J. Compliance training and behavioral covariation in the treatment of multiple behavior problems. *Journal of Applied Behavior Analysis,* 1981, *14,* 209–222.

Shafto, F., & Sulzbacher, S. Comparing treatment tactics with a hyperactive pre-school child: Stimulant medication and programmed teacher intervention. *Journal of Applied Behavior Analysis,* 1977, *10,* 13–20.

Sidman, M. *Tactics of scientific research.* New York: Basic Books, 1960.

Skinner, B. F. The operational analysis of psychological terms. *Psychological Review,* 1945, *52,* 270–277.

Skinner, B. F. Are theories of learning necessary? *Psychological Review,* 1950, *57,* 193–216.

Skinner, B. F. *Science and human behavior.* New York: Macmillan, 1953.

Skinner, B. F. *Verbal behavior.* New York: Appleton-Century-Crofts, 1957.

Skinner, B. F. *Contingencies of reinforcement: A theoretical analysis.* New York: Appleton-Century-Crofts, 1969.

Skinner, B. F. *About behaviorism.* New York: Knopf, 1974.

Solnick, J. V., Rincover, A., & Peterson, C. R. Some determinants of the reinforcing and punishing effects of time-out. *Journal of Applied Behavior Analysis,* 1971, *10,* 415–424.

Sowers, J., Rusch, F. R., Connis, R. T., & Cummings, L. E. Teaching mentally retarded adults to time-manage in a vocational setting. *Journal of Applied Behavior Analysis,* 1980, *13,* 119–128.

Stokes, T. F., & Baer, D. M. An implicit technology of generalization. *Journal of Applied Behavior Analysis,* 1977, *10,* 349–368. ⁓

Sulzer-Azaroff, B., & Mayer, G. R. *Applying behavior analysis procedures with children and youth.* New York: Holt, Rinehart and Winston.

Tasto, D. L. Self-report schedules and inventories. In A. R. Ciminero, K. S. Calhoun, & H. E. Adams (Eds.), *Handbook of behavioral assessment.* New York: Wiley, 1977.

Tate, B. G., & Baroff, G. S. Aversive control of self-injurious behavior in a psychotic boy. *Behavior Research and Therapy,* 1966, *4,* 281–287.

Tremblay, A., Strain, P. S., Hendrickson, J. M., & Shores, R. E. Social interactions of normal preschool children. *Behavior Modification,* 1981, *5,* 237–253.

Tucker, D. J., & Berry, G. W. Teaching severely multihandicapped students to put on their own hearing aids. *Journal of Applied Behavior Analysis,* 1980, *13,* 65–76.

Vogelsberg, J., & Rusch, F. R. Training three severely handicapped young adults to walk, look, and cross uncontrolled intersections, *AAESPH Review,* 1979, *4,* 269–273.

Wahler, R. G. Setting generality: Some specific and general effects of child behavior therapy. *Journal of Applied Behavior Analysis,* 1969, *2,* 239–246.

Wasik, B. H., & Loven, M. D. Classroom observational data: Sources of inaccuracy and proposed solutions. *Behavioral Assessment,* 1980, *2,* 211–227.

Wasik, B. H., Senn, K., Welch, R. H., & Cooper, B. R. Behavior modification with culturally deprived school children: Two case studies. *Journal of Applied Behavior Analysis,* 1969, *2,* 181–194.

Yeaton, W. H., & Sechrest, L. Critical dimension in the choice and maintenance of successful treatments: Strength, integrity and effectiveness. *Journal of Consulting and Clinical Psychology,* 1981, *49,* 156–167.

Zimmerman, E. H., & Zimmerman, J. The alteration of behavior in a special classroom situation. *Journal of the Experimental Analysis of Behavior,* 1962, *5,* 59–60.

10

Criterion-Referenced Assessment of Individual Differences

RONALD K. HAMBLETON

The field of criterion-referenced testing has developed quickly since the first papers on the topic by Glaser (1963) and Popham and Husek (1969). Glaser, and later, Popham and Husek, were interested in assessment methods that could provide information on which to base a number of individual and programmatic decisions arising in connection with specific instructional objectives or competencies. Norm-referenced tests were judged to be inappropriate because they provide information that facilitates comparisons among examinees on broad traits or constructs. These tests were not intended to measure specific objectives. And even if items in a norm-referenced test could be matched to objectives, typically there would be too few test items per objective to permit valid criterion-referenced test score interpretations.

Hambleton, Swaminathan, Algina, and Coulson (1978) reported that they had located over 700 papers on the topic of criterion-referenced testing between 1970 and 1978. Stimulating the advancement of criterion-referenced testing methods and practices was the desire by many decision-makers in education, industry, and the armed services to assess individuals relative to a set of objectives or competencies or a set of tasks or responsibilities defining a job, rather than relative to a specified group of examinees (i.e., a norm group). In criterion-referenced testing, individual differences are viewed in terms of mastery status (i.e., masters and non-masters). For example, the U.S. Army established the Skills Qualification Testing (SQT) Program (to assess the job competence of soldiers). Individual differences in job performance are not of any interest in the SQT Program. Instead, interest is centered on the identification of soldiers who

RONALD K. HAMBLETON ● Laboratory of Psychometric and Evaluative Research, University of Massachusetts, Amherst, Massachusetts 01003.

can (and cannot) meet the minimum standards of performance set for a particular job. The SQT Program is clearly a criterion-referenced testing program the goal of which cannot be met with norm-referenced tests.

The principal purpose of this chapter is (1) to describe the main technical advances in criterion-referenced test development and validation and (2) to compare these advances to the better known methods used with norm-referenced tests. In several of the earlier chapters, test scores (obtained from norm-referenced tests) were used to compare individuals. In this chapter, comparisons of individuals are of secondary importance, and when they are made, the comparisons are between individuals classified as "masters" and "nonmasters." Of central importance, instead, is the comparison of examinee performance to standards of performance set for well-defined domains of content.

At the outset, it may be helpful to highlight the main difference between this chapter and Chapter 11, by Bergan, Stone, and Feld. We will not assume a theoretical structure underlying the objectives or competencies we build tests to measure. The Bergan *et al.* approach is more psychologically satisfying in that a theoretical structure among the objectives of interest is either assumed or developed and that theory plays a central role in test validation.

The advances described in the present chapter are not tied to or generated from any theories of cognition. Because the advances do not depend on cognitive theories, the advances can be widely applied. Of course, when a suitable theory exists, it can guide the specification of objectives, test development, and validation investigations. The remainder of this chapter will be organized into seven sections: Definitions and Uses of Criterion-Referenced Tests, Norm-Referenced Testing versus Criterion-Referenced Testing, Content Specifications, Test Development, Standard Setting, Psychometric Characteristics of Criterion-Referenced Test Scores, and Summary.

DEFINITIONS AND USES OF CRITERION-REFERENCED TESTS

A criterion-referenced test (CRT) is constructed to permit test score users to assess examinee performance relative to one or more well-defined objectives (these objectives are also called competencies, tasks, outcomes, responsibilities) (Popham, 1978). The test score for an examinee on each objective measured by a CRT can be used (1) to describe examinee performance and/or (2) to assign the examinee to a mastery state.

At least 57 definitions of a criterion-referenced test have been offered in the literature (Gray, 1978). Popham's definition, though, is the most widely used. Several points about his definition deserve comment. First, terms such as objectives, competencies, and skills are used interchangeably in the field. Second, the objectives measured by a criterion-referenced test must be *well defined*. Well-defined objectives produce more valid items and usually improve the quality of test score interpretations because of the clarity of the content or behavior domains to which test scores are referenced. The definition does not restrict the breadth and complexity of a domain of content or behaviors relating to an objective. The intended purpose of a test will influence the appropriate breadth and complexity of domains. Criterion-referenced tests used in diagnosing performance deficiencies are typically organized around narrowly defined objectives, whereas year-end assessments will normally be carried out with more broadly defined objectives. For example, in the Maryland high school assessment, 12 broad objectives are used to cover the reading and mathematics skills required for high school graduation. Third, when more than one objective is measured in a test, examinee performance on each objective is usually reported. Fourth, Popham's definition does *not* refer to a cut-off score or standard. It is common to set a minimum standard of performance for each objective and interpret examinee performance by that standard. But the use of test scores for describing examinee performance is common, and standards are *not* needed for this type of score use. That a standard (or standards) may not be needed with a criterion-referenced test will surprise persons who have assumed (mistakenly) that the word *criterion* in "criterion-referenced test" refers to a "standard" or "cut-off score." In fact, the word *criterion* was used by Glaser (1963) and Popham and Husek (1969) to refer to a *domain of content or behavior* to which test scores are referenced.

Three additional points about criterion-referenced tests should be mentioned: (1) The number of objectives will, in general, vary from one test to the next; (2) the number of test items measuring each objective and the value of the minimum standard will, in general, vary from one objective to the next; and (3) a common method for making mastery/nonmastery decisions involves the comparison of examinee percent (or proportion-correct) scores on objectives to the corresponding minimum standards. With respect to point 3, when an examinee's percent score is equal to or greater than the standard, the examinee is assumed to be a "master" (M); otherwise the examinee is assumed to be a "nonmaster" (NM). There are, however, more complex decision-making models (Hambleton & Novick, 1973; van der Linden, 1980).

It is common to see terms like criterion-referenced tests, domain-referenced tests, and objectives-referenced tests in the psychometric literature. Popham's definition for a criterion-referenced test is similar to one Millman (1974) and others proposed for a domain-referenced test. There are no differences between the two if Popham's definition for a criterion-referenced test is adopted.

Objectives-referenced tests consist of items that are matched to objectives. The principal difference between criterion-referenced tests and objectives-referenced tests is that in a criterion-referenced test, items are organized into clusters with each cluster serving (usually) as a representative set of items from a clearly defined content domain measuring an objective. In an objectives-referenced test, *no* clear domain of content is specified for an objective, and the items are *not* considered to represent any content domain. Therefore, interpretations of examinee performance on objectives-referenced tests must be limited to the particular items on the test.

Criterion-referenced tests (domain-referenced tests, mastery tests, competency tests, basic skills tests, or certification exams, to give the alternative names) are in use in a large number of settings to address informational needs. For example, criterion-referenced tests are used in many elementary and secondary schools. Classroom teachers use test results to place a student in the correct school program, to monitor student progress, and to identify student deficiencies. Special education teachers are finding criterion-referenced tests especially helpful in diagnosing student learning deficiences and monitoring student progress. Criterion-referenced test results are also being used to evaluate various school programs. Although less common, criterion-referenced tests are finding some use in higher educational programs as well (e.g., those programs based upon the mastery learning concept). Also, criterion-referenced tests are in common use in military and industrial training programs.

A recent application of criterion-referenced tests involves microcomputers. Collections of test items (called "banks") are placed in computer memory and later can be selected by instructors for their criterion-referenced tests to assess student mastery. Either the computer can be used to provide the instructor with a hard copy of the test for reproduction or the microcomputer may be used to administer the test to each student at a computer terminal.

In recent years, it has become common for state departments of education and (sometimes) school districts to define sets of skills (or competencies) students must possess in order to be promoted from one grade to the next or, in some states, to receive high school diplomas. The nature of these criterion-referenced testing programs varies dramatically from one place to another. For example, in some states, students are held responsible for mastering a specified set of skills at each grade level; in other states, skills that must be acquired are specified at selected grade levels; and in still other states, only a set of skills that must be mastered for high school graduation is specified.

One of the most important applications of criterion-referenced tests is in the area of professional certification and licensure. It is now common, for example, for professional organizations to establish entry-level examinations that must be passed by candidates before they are allowed to practice in their chosen professions. In fact, many of these professional organizations have also established recertification exams. A typical examination will measure the competencies that define the professional role, and candidate test performance is interpreted relative to established minimum standards. Hundreds of professional organizations, including nearly all groups in the medical and allied health fields, have initiated certification and recertification exams.

NORM-REFERENCED TESTING VERSUS CRITERION-REFERENCED TESTING

Proponents of norm-referenced and criterion-referenced tests waged a battle in the 1970s. Proponents of norm-referenced tests argued, in part, that their tests could be used to infer examinee mastery/nonmastery states relative to implied or explicit objectives measured by their tests. Advocates of criterion-referenced testing typically argued that norm-referenced tests often did not measure the objectives of interest, or if they did, too few test items were used. Criterion-referenced test advocates, notably teachers and evaluators, argued strongly for the merits of criterion-referenced information over normative information. A third group argued that there was only one kind of achievement test from which both criterion-referenced and norm-referenced score interpretations could be made when needed.

Several changes took place in testing between 1970 and 1984: (1) The uses of criterion-referenced tests did increase substantially, and (2) there was a reduction in the number of administered norm-referenced tests. But, no one won the battle because it became clear that it is meaningful to distinguish between two kinds of achievement tests and that both kinds of tests play important roles in providing information for test users. Norm-referenced achievement tests are needed to provide reliable and valid normative scores for comparing examinees. Criterion-referenced achievement tests are needed to facilitate the interpretation of examinee performance relative to well-defined objectives and to compare examinees in terms of their mastery status.

Although the differences between these two tests for assessing individual differences are substantial, the two kinds of tests share many features. In fact, it would be a rare individual who could distinguish between them from just looking at the test booklets: The same item formats are used; the test directions are similar; and both kinds of tests can be standardized.

There are, however, a number of important differences. The first difference is *test purpose*. A norm-referenced test is constructed specifically to facilitate comparisons among examinees in the content area measured by the test. It is common to use age-, percentile-, and standard-score norms to accomplish the test's purpose. Since test items are (or can be) referenced to objectives, criterion-referenced score interpretations (or, more correctly, objectives-referenced score interpretations) are possible, but typically they are limited in value because of the (usually) small number of test items measuring the objectives of the test. Criterion-referenced tests, on the other hand, are constructed to assess examinee performance relative to a set of objectives. Scores may be used (1) to describe examinee performance and/or (2) to make mastery/nonmastery decisions. Scores can be used to compare examinees, but comparisons may have relatively low reliability if the score distributions are homogeneous.

The second difference is in the area of *content specificity*. Both norm-referenced and criterion-referenced test developers should prepare test blueprints or tables of specifications. It is even possible that norm-referenced test developers will prepare behavioral objectives. But criterion-referenced test developers must (typically) prepare considerably more detailed content specifications than those provided by behavioral objectives to ensure that their test scores can be interpreted as intended. This will be considered further in the next section. Thus, with respect to content specifications, the main difference between norm-referenced and criterion-referenced tests is in the degree to which test content must be specified.

The third difference is in the area of *test development*. Norm-referenced item statistics (difficulty and discrimination indices) play an important role in item selection. In general, items of moderate difficulty (*p*-values in the range .30 to .70) and high discriminating power (point-biserial correlations over .30) are most likely to be selected for a test because they contribute substantially to test score variance. Test reliability and validity will, generally, be higher when test score variance is increased. In contrast, criterion-referenced test items are only deleted from the pools of test items measuring objectives when there is evidence that these items violate the content specifications or standard principles of item writing or if the available item statistics reveal serious, noncorrectible flaws. Item statistics can be used to construct parallel forms of a criterion-referenced test or to produce a test to discriminate optimally between masters and nonmasters in the region of a minimum standard of performance on the test score scale (Hambleton & deGruijter, 1983).

The fourth and final major area of difference is *test score generalizability*. There is seldom any interest in generalizing from norm-referenced achievement test scores. The basis for score interpretations is the performance of some reference group. In contrast, score generalizability is usually of interest with criterion-referenced tests. There is seldom any interest in the performance of examinees on *specific* sets of test items. When clearly specified objectives are available, and it can be assumed that test items are representative of the content domains from which they are drawn, examinee test performance can be generalized to performance in the larger domains of content defining the objectives. This type of interpretation is (usually) of interest to criterion-referenced test users.

CONTENT SPECIFICATIONS

Behavioral objectives played a significant role in instruction and testing throughout the 1960s and 1970s. But, although behavioral objectives are relatively easy to write and have contributed substantially to the specification of curricula and jobs, they leave too much room for judgment in test development and test score interpretations. Popham (1974) described tests built from behavioral objectives as "cloud-referenced tests." Several suggestions have been made for addressing the deficiency in behavioral objectives and thereby making it possible to construct more valid criterion-referenced tests. Possibly the most versatile and practical of the suggestions, domain or item specifications, was made by Popham (1978). Domain specifications serve four purposes: (1) They provide item writers with content and technical guidelines for preparing test items; (2) they provide content and measurement specialists with a clear description of the content and/or behaviors that are relative to each objective, so that they can assess whether items are valid measures of the intended objectives; (3) they aid in interpreting examinee test performance; and (4) they clearly specify the breadth and scope of objectives. Some educational measurement specialists have even gone so far as to suggest that the emphasis on content specifications has been the most important contribution of criterion-referenced testing to measurement practice (see Berk, 1980).

Using as a basis the work of Popham (1978), Hambleton (1982) suggested that a domain specification might be divided into four parts:

Description—a short, concise statement of the content and/or behaviors covered by the competency

Sample Directions and Test Item—an example of the test directions and a model test item to measure the objective

Content Limits—a detailed description of both the content and/or behaviors measured by the objective, as well as the structure and content of the item pool (This section should be so clear that items may be divided by reviewers into those items that meet the specifications and those items that do not.) Sometimes clarity is enhanced by also specifying areas that are not included in the content domain description.

Response Limits—a description of the kind of incorrect answer choices that must be prepared when multiple choice items are used, or a list of scoring criteria when a performance is to be demonstrated. The structure and content of the incorrect answers or scoring criteria, in the case of performance items, should be stated in as much detail as possible.

Examples of domain specifications are shown in Figures 1 and 2. The first highlights the use of the format with a high school mathematics objective. The second demonstrates the use of the format with a reading skill that requires a particular performance to be demonstrated by examinees. Once properly prepared domain specifications are available, the steps in the test development process can be carried out.

Objective
The student will correctly identify the antiderivatives; the meaning, notation, and use of the indefinite integral; and will solve differential equations using indefinite integrals.

Sample Item
A certain curve passes through the point $(0, 4)$, and has slope (dy/dx) given by

$$\frac{dy}{dx} = \frac{1 + x + 3x^2}{y}$$

for each pair of x and y. The equation of the curve is:
(A) $y^2 = 16 + 2x + x^2 + 2x^3$
*(B) $y = 9 + 6x$
(C) $y = 2x + x^2 + 2/3x^3$
(D) $y = 2x + x^2 + 2x^3$

Contents Limits
1. Each item will consist of a problem statement at the seventh-grade reading level, an item stem, and four response choices.
2. The problems will consist of one of the following:
    a. Given a function $f(x)$, determining its antiderivative, stated in the form: "The antiderivative of the function . . . is," The words *indefinite integral* may be substituted for *antiderivative*.

FIGURE 1. A sample domain specification for an objective in a calculus course.

b. Determining the indefinite integral of a function stated in the form: "The indefinite integral

$$\int f(x)\, dx$$

is...," where $f(x)$ is a specified function.

c. Solving a differential equation with or without initial conditions, stated as, "The solution to the differential equation

$$\frac{dy}{dx} = \frac{f(x)}{g(y)}$$

is...." The functions $f(x)$ and $g(y)$ are specified. When an initial condition is specified, the phrase, "subject to the initial conditions $y = ...$ when $x = ...$," is added.

d. Solving a differential equation stated in the form of a word problem. This will be restricted to finding the equation of a curve given the general form of the slope and, given the velocity of a moving particle, finding an expression for the displacement s.

3. The functions to be integrated will be polynomials or simple rational functions of the form $u^{-n}(n \neq 1)$. Each term of the function to be integrated will be reducible to the form

$$\int u^n\, du\ (n \neq -1)$$

without the use of integration by parts, or partial fractions. Simple substitutions will be expected.

Response Limits

1. Each item will have one correct response and three incorrect responses.
2. The correct response will be randomly placed among the response choices.
3. The incorrect responses will be constructed using the common errors made by students such as ignoring the arbitrary constant, confusing formula for differentiation of x^n with that for integration of x^n, and inappropriate substitution of initial values in the solution.
4. The incorrect responses will not be less-reduced forms of the correct solution.

FIGURE 1 (*continued*)

The domain of content or behaviors defining the objectives that are to be included in a criterion-referenced test must be clearly specified. The mechanism through which the objectives are identified will vary from one application to the next. With high school graduation exams, on the one hand, the process might involve district educational leaders meeting to review school curricula and identifying a relatively small set of important

Objective
The student will present an oral report while following notes on a given seventh-grade literature subject

Administration
Individually Administered Performance Test

Materials
R/LA Standard 07-03 Teacher Directions

Directions
See R/LA Standard 07–03 Teacher Directions

Content Limits
1. The oral language skill includes preparing and following notes to present an oral report on a subject related to seventh-grade literature.
2. The directions will include a specified selection and a subject related to seventh-grade literature to be addressed in the talk.
3. The literary subject may be figurative language, historical accuracy, plot development, characterization, theme, author's purpose, or setting.

Response Limits
1. Student behavior includes preparing and using notes to present an oral report on a given topic related to seventh-grade literature.
2. The oral report will include an opening statement, details in logical order and a concluding statement.
3. The student will use appropriate pitch, stress, tone, and juncture in his or her voice.
4. The student will assume a natural posture, and face the audience.
5. The student will use grammar appropriate to Grade 7.

Scoring
1. Each student will present one oral report.
2. Teacher judgment will determine mastery according to the scoring criteria on the R/LA Standard 07–03 Teacher Directions.
3. For mastery, the student will perform at least 6 of the 8 criteria acceptably.

Specification Supplement
Students should be provided with books that have the required readings in them. If the books are *not* available, students should be provided with copies of the essential material.

FIGURE 2. A sample domain specification for a performance objective in a grade 7 language arts curriculum.

R/LA Standard 07-03 Teacher Directions

Administration

Individually administered performance test

1. Select a literary topic and a passage for each student according to the text the student is using
2. Read the directions to the students
3. Allow at least two class periods for the students to reread the passage and prepare notes
4. Time required: Approximately 5–10 minutes per oral report

Scoring criteria

Teacher judgment will determine mastery according to the following criteria: The student

1. developed content of report according to the assigned literary topic
2. presented an opening statement
3. presented the body of the talk in logical order
4. presented a concluding statement
5. produced notes which correspond to the speech presented
6. used appropriate stage presence (had natural posture, faced audience, made eye contact)
7. spoke distinctly and used vocal stress, tone, pitch, and juncture
8. used appropriate grammar for Grade 7.

For mastery, the student will perform at least 6 out of 8 of the above criteria acceptably.

Directions

The teacher says:

Next week you are to give an oral report on a passage from your literature text book. This afternoon, you are to prepare notes for your talk. First, you are to reread (title of work) and then make notes about (subject of report) for your talk.

Stimuli

Below are replacements for the blank spaces above.

1. "The Tell Tale Heart" that begins on p. 33 in *Introduction to Literature* (p. 46 in *Action*) and then make notes about the setting and plot development of the story
2. "Paul Revere's Ride" that begins on p. 197 in *Introduction to Literature* (p. 336 in *Focus* or p. 239 in *Action*) and then make notes about the use of figurative language in the poem
3. "The Fables of Aesop" that begins on p. 297 in *Introduction to Literature* (p. 54 in *Focus* or p. 350 in *Action*) and then make notes about the theme and author's purpose in writing the fables
4. "Dunkirk" that begins on p. 454 in *Introduction to Literature* (p. 246 in *Action*) and then make notes about the historical accuracy of the poem
5. "The Highwayman" that begins on p. 340 in *Focus* (p. 26 in *Action*) and then make notes about the use of figurative language in the poem

FIGURE 2 (*continued*)

broad objectives (e.g., study skills, mathematics concepts). On the other hand, within an objective-based instructional program, it is common for developers to divide a curriculum into broad areas known as "strands" and difficulty levels (which usually correspond roughly to grade levels). Next, for each strand–difficulty level combination, the sets of relevant objectives, often stated in behavioral form, are specified, reviewed, revised, and finalized. Finally, with certification or licensure exams, it is common to conduct a "role delineation study" or "job-study," first with individuals working in the area to identify the responsibilities, sub-responsibilities, and activities that define the role or job. Next, the knowledge and skills that are needed to carry out the role or job are identified, and later, validated. The validated or approved list of knowledge and skills serves as the objectives that need to be measured in the test.

TEST DEVELOPMENT

The main steps in building criterion-referenced tests will be reviewed first. Then, several of the steps (see Figure 3) that are handled differently from the steps in norm-referenced test development will be highlighted assessment of content validity (4) and item analysis (6c). Several other steps will be addressed in subsequent sections.

---

1. Preliminary considerations
   (a) Specify test purposes.
   (b) Specify groups to be measured and (any) special testing require-
       ments (due to examinee age, race, sex, socioeconomic status,
       handicaps, etc.).
   (c) Determine the time and money available to produce the test.
   (d) Identify qualified staff.
   (e) Specify an initial estimate of test length.

2. Review of objectives
   (a) Review the descriptions of the objectives to determine their
       acceptability.
   (b) Make necessary revisions to the objectives to improve their clarity.

3. Item writing
   (a) Draft a sufficient number of items for pilot-testing.
   (b) Carry out item editing.

FIGURE 3. Steps for constructing criterion-referenced tests.

4. Assessment of content validity
   (a) Identify a sufficient pool of judges and measurement specialists.
   (b) Review the test items to determine their match to the objectives, their representativeness, and their freedom from bias and stereo-typing.
   (c) Review the test items to determine their technical adequacy.

5. Revisions to test items
   (a) Based upon data from 4b and 4c, revise test items (when possible) or delete them.
   (b) Write additional test items (if needed) and repeat step 4.

6. Field test administration
   (a) Organize the test items into forms for pilot testing.
   (b) Administer the test forms to appropriately chosen groups of examinees.
   (c) Conduct item analyses, and item bias studies.

7. Revisions to test items
   (a) Revise test items when necessary or delete them using the results from 6c.

8. Test assembly
   (a) Determine the test length, and the number of forms needed and the number of items per objective.
   (b) Select test items from the available pool of valid test items.
   (c) Prepare test directions, practice questions, test booklet layout, scoring keys, answer sheets, etc.

9. Selection of a standard
   (a) Initiate a process to determine the standard to separate "masters" and "nonmasters."

10. Pilot test administration
    (a) Design the test administration to collect score reliability and validity information.
    (b) Administer the test form(s) to appropriately chosen groups of examinees.
    (c) Evaluate the test administration procedures, test items, and score reliability and validity.
    (d) Make final revisions based on data from 10c.

11. Preparation of manuals
    (a) Prepare a test administrator's manual.
    (b) Prepare a technical manual.

12. Additional technical data collection
    (a) Conduct reliability and validity investigations.

FIGURE 3 (*continued*)

Twelve steps for preparing criterion-referenced tests are offered in Figure 3. These steps were adapted from steps offered by Hambleton (1982). Some very brief remarks on the 12 steps follow:

Step 1—This step ensures that a test development project is well organized and that important factors that might affect test quality are identified early.

Step 2—Domain specifications are invaluable to item writers when they are well done. Considerable time and money can be saved later in revising test items if item writers are clear about their tasks.

Step 3—Some training of item writers in the proper use of domain specifications, and in the principles of item writing, is often desirable.

Step 4—This step is essential. Items are evaluated by reviewers to assess their match to the objectives, their technical quality, and their freedom from bias and stereo-typing.

Step 5—Any necessary revisions to test items should be made at this step and when additional test items are needed, they should be written, and step 4 repeated.

Step 6—The test items are organized into booklets and administered to appropriate numbers of examinees; the number reflects the importance of the test under construction. Appropriate revisions to test items can be made at this stage. Item statistics are used to identify items that may be in need of revision.

Step 7—Whenever possible, malfunctioning test items should be revised and added to the pools of acceptable test items. When substantial revisions are made step 4 should be repeated.

Step 8—Final test booklets are compiled at this step. When parallel forms are required, and especially if the tests are short, item statistics should be used to ensure that matched forms are produced.

Step 9—A standard-setting procedure is selected and implemented. The selection process must be documented.

Step 10—Test directions are evaluated, scoring keys are checked, and the reliability and validity of scores and decisions are assessed.

Step 11—For important tests, a test administration manual and a technical manual should be prepared.

Step 12—No matter how carefully a test is constructed or evaluated, reliability and validity studies must be concurrently carried out.

Of course, the thoroughness with which the steps are carried out depends on the intended uses of the test scores. An instructor preparing a criterion-referenced test may complete only a few steps. A state department of education preparing minimum competency tests should complete all the steps, with considerable attention to details.

ASSESSMENT OF ITEM AND CONTENT VALIDITY

Item validity is determined by considering three item features: (1) item–objective congruence (the extent to which an item actually measures some aspect of the content included in the domain specification), (2) technical quality, and (3) bias. Review forms for addressing the three features have been prepared by Hambleton (1980, 1984) and Roid and Haladyna (1982).

Item–Objective Congruence

Generally speaking, the quality of criterion-referenced test items can be determined by the extent to which they reflect, in terms of their content, the domains from which they were derived. Unless it can be said with a high degree of confidence that the items in a criterion-referenced test measure the intended objectives, any use of the test score information will be questionable.

The assessment of item–objective congruence involves obtaining the opinions of content specialists. Content specialists have the experience to determine the appropriate breadths of content areas of interest by reading a set of domain specifications or similar approaches for defining objectives or competencies. Although the parameters of the domains are often well delineated, usually some experience is required with curricula to use them correctly. Also, content specialists need to be able to determine the content match between items and the objectives they are intended to measure. To do this task effectively, in addition to having some experience with the relevant content, knowledge of the examinees is often very useful.

One procedure described by Hambleton (1984) for assessing item–objective congruence requires that content specialists rate item–objective match on a 5-point scale that ranges from poor (1) to excellent (5). The ratings data may be analyzed without employing any elaborate statistical procedures. Therefore, the rating form with the 5-point rating scale can easily be used in applied settings. The information needed is the mean and/or median rating assigned to the items by a group of content specialists. It is also possible to determine the "closeness" of each specialist's ratings to the median responses from all the specialists. When one differs substantially from the others and there is evidence of carelessness or incompetence on his or her part, the validity of the statistics will be enhanced if the "deviant" responses are removed from the analysis (Rovinelli & Hambleton, 1977).

Hambleton (1984) described a second procedure that can be used to obtain accurate opinions from content specialists. It involves a *matching task*. Content specialists are presented with two lists, one with test items and the other with objectives or domain specifications. The task is to indicate which objective he or she thinks each test item measures (if any). A contingency table can then be constructed by calculating the number of content specialists matching each item to each objective in the sets of items and the objectives being studied. The chi-square test for independence is commonly used to analyze data that are presented in a contingency table. A visual analysis of the contingency table will also reveal the amount of agreement among the specialists and the type and location of the disagreements. The "accuracy" of the ratings of each content specialist can be checked if a specified number of "bad" items (i.e., items not measuring any of the objectives) is introduced into the matching task. A content specialist's competence can be measured by the number of such items he or she detects.

Technical Quality and Bias of Test Items

The technical quality and bias of test items can be established at the same time as test items are reviewed for item–objective congruence. The nature of these reviews is identical to those of norm-referenced test development.

Content Validity

The content validity of a test is determined by ascertaining the representativeness of the test items of a specified domain of content. Whereas content validity is an essential characteristic of any achievement test (norm-referenced or criterion-referenced) because criterion-referenced test scores are referenced to the content domains, establishing content validity is extremely important. In order to determine content validity, (1) a clear statement of the content domain and (2) the presentation of the details about the sampling plan used in item selection are required. When test scores are reported at the objective level, the content validity of each sample of items measuring an objective must be determined.

Descriptions of content domains can range from identifying only broad areas of relevant content to identifying tightly defined domains in which every appropriate test item in the domain could be delineated. The former is unacceptable for criterion-referenced tests, and the latter is impractical in most instances. Popham's notion of a domain specification, which is both more reasonable and practical than other methods for specifying domains of content, falls somewhere in between. If relevant content is described clearly, then it will be clear what domain a set of items is intended to represent. Categories or multidimensional classification schemes can often be developed to delineate further the content in a domain specification;

then, content specialists can offer opinions on the representativeness of the selected test items. When representativeness has not been achieved, new test items can often be added to a test and, perhaps, others removed.

With respect to certification and licensure exams, content validity is often assessed by evaluating the test items in terms of their representativeness relative to a set of responsibilities, sub-responsibilities, and activities that define a professional role based on a role delineation study. The set of test items can be reviewed to determine how well they sample the responsibilities, sub-responsibilities, and activities identified in the role.

Another procedure for assessing content validity is Cronbach's duplication experiment, although this is rarely carried out because of the cost. This experiment requires two teams of equally competent item writers and reviewers to work independently in developing a criterion-referenced test. When the domain specifications are clear, and if item sampling is representative, the two tests should be equivalent. Equivalence of forms can be checked by giving both forms to the same group of examinees and comparing the two sets of test scores.

ITEM-ANALYSIS TECHNIQUES

It is in this area that there are substantial differences between constructing norm-referenced tests and criterion-referenced tests. When constructing norm-referenced tests, in addition to the usual concerns for content validity and technically sound test items, test items that contribute most to test score variability are preferred. As a result, item statistics play a critical role in item selection. However, when constructing criterion-referenced tests, test score variability is not a consideration; instead, it is viewed as an outcome of testing and something to be studied, and so item statistics play a small part in item selection, although they can be very helpful in detecting flawed test items. Identifying useful item statistics and determining how these statistics should be used are problems that have been addressed by several researchers (Berk, 1980a; Roid & Haladyna, 1982).

After the items have been tested using a group or several groups of examinees (pretesting or regular testing), many item statistics can be computed and interpreted. We prefer to use any of the item statistics that are chosen (1) to provide clues or "red-flags" for detecting items in need of revision or deletion and (2) to provide useful information for constructing single tests and parallel test forms.

Statistics that summarize and describe item effectiveness can be classified under two categories: (1) traditional and (2) criterion-referenced. Statistics in each category will be discussed in the next few pages.

Traditional Item Statistics

Traditional item indices are statistics developed from classical test theory that have been employed extensively with test items designed to discriminate among examinees. Since the test items are designed to assess some learner behavior and not to maximize the differences among examinees, traditional item indices are less meaningful for the purpose of examining test items. Therefore, this group of item indices should be carefully employed and augmented with other types of statistics. Three item indices will be discussed in this group: (1) the frequency of selection of distractors, (2) the item discrimination index, and (3) the item difficulty index. These are summarized in Figure 4. Guidelines for interpreting the statistics are summarized in Figure 5.

The statistics are the same ones used with norm-referenced tests, but their interpretation for and use with criterion-referenced test items are substantially different. Numerous researchers have offered *new* criterion-referenced test item statistics, they have been reviewed by Berk (1980a), but

---

Item Difficulty Level
p statistics, percentage of examinees answering an item correctly (include *all* examinees who were administered the item)

Adjusted p statistics, percentage of examinees (of those who reached the item) answering an item correctly. (This statistic has some merit, especially for items near the ends of tests, when the tests are speeded. Students who do not reach the test items are excluded from the analyses of these items. The modified p statistics are always higher than the p statistics—i.e., the items appear easier. Do the modified p statistics better indicate item difficulty levels in the population of students for whom the test is intended? It depends. When the test items are very difficult, the modified p statistics are less appropriate than the p statistics. When test items near the end of a test may range in difficulty, modified p statistics may be better. Anyway the truth lies somewhere in between the two statistical values and so having both is helpful. In summary, the modified p statistics are only of use when a test is speeded *and* with items appearing near the ends of tests).

Item Discrimination Level
Point biserial or biserial correlations (the biserials will always be somewhat higher). Biserials are a little harder to interpret; and they are harder to calculate—this is only a problem if you are preparing your own computer program. But, the important points do *not* concern which of the two is chosen. The two important points concern (1) choice of criterion and (2) interpretation of the statistics.

FIGURE 4. Summary of classical item statistics and techniques.

Choice of Criterion
Two criteria are possible: (1) total test scores and (2) objective scores. Some researchers would recommend that one additional step be taken: remove the item itself from the objective score so that the correlation is between the item scores and objective scores corrected for the bias that results when the item is included in the objective score. Perhaps this correction is not worth the trouble, even though the bias is substantial, because these item statistics are only "red flags" and the correction seldom if ever changes an assessment of item quality. And, for the second use (2) of the item statistics (building parallel-forms) the more dependable item discrimination indices obtained from the item-total test score correlations are available. Corrections to the total test scores are seldom considered when the tests are long since the bias is very small.

Interpretation of the Statistics
Of most interest is the identification of items with negative or low positive discrimination indices. Items with these values should be carefully reviewed for flaws. But, when item and/or test score variance is low, it follows that item discrimination indices will also be low and so "test score range restriction" is a more likely explanation than flawed test items. Norm-referenced test developers would automatically discard items with low discrimination indices. In building CRTs, the item statistics do not provide conclusive information about the ultimate merits of test items.

Effectiveness of Distractors
Percentage of high (top 25%) and low (bottom 25%) performers choosing each answer choice to items.
Issues. The above type of analysis can become very complicated if you worry about the percentage of students in the two groups (some like 27%, others 33%, etc.) and whether "high" and "low" groups of students should be identified from the total test score or objective score or corrected objective score, or external criterion (e.g., masters and nonmasters), etc. When you remember that the usefulness of the information is somewhat limited, probably it is best to choose the simplest approach: sort the examinees into high-and low-performing groups based upon total test score or objective score. The percentage of students in each group is not very important (as long as the actual number in each group is not too small) so use whatever your computer program provides.

FIGURE 4 (*continued*)

none of these statistics were found to contribute much to the identification of flawed test items. Every statistic recommended in this section can be obtained from a standard item analysis package—typically designed for use in constructing norm-referenced tests.

Evaluating the Effectiveness of Distractors. The frequency of selection of

Item Difficulty Levels

Of principal interest is the grouping of *p*-statistics for items measuring an objective. Study the outliers for flaws. Some test developers have assumed that *all* items measuring an objective must have a common *p*-value if they are to be valid. But, domains of content describing objectives can be broad and so such a restrictive assumption would be highly unreasonable. Therefore, expect some variation in difficulty levels but it should not be too great either (perhaps a range up to .40 may be acceptable). The average *p*-statistic for each objective should be studied to see if it is in the region on the percentage score scale corresponding to expectations of student performance. Reasons should be offered when the results are not as expected. Of concern is whether or not the results are "out of line" because of the invalidity of the test items.

Item Discrimination Levels

Look for the negative correlations. High or moderately negative correlations reveal items in need of major revisions (occasionally the problem is miskeyed items or multiple or no correct answers). Also, scrutinize items with low positive or low negative correlations. Check the standard deviations of item scores for these items, and when low ($\leq$.30), do not attach as much importance to the low correlations as compared to when the standard deviations exceed .30. Often the distractor analysis will help in revealing the reasons for low values since it will show the choice preferences of high- and low-performing examinees. Occasionally low negative correlations are obtained with items that are very easy.

Distractor Analysis

Identify distractors that none or few examinees selected; possibly these can be rewritten, especially if these distractors as written seem implausible. Study any distractors (incorrect answers) which attract more high- than low-performing examinees. Sometimes these distractors are "correct" also. Obviously, these choices can be rewritten. Also, any distractor that attracts a large percentage of students should be carefully studied. Possibly there is some irrelevant clue that many students used in selecting the choice. One caution: distractor analyses are not too useful with very easy test items.

FIGURE 5.   Interpreting classical item statistics.

the various answer choices can be tabulated from the field-test data. In general, attention should be focused on (1) distractors chosen by the upper ability group as the correct answer (it may be that the item was miskeyed) and (2) distractors not chosen by examinees (or by only a small percentage of them). These items should be red-flagged for further scrutiny. This does not automatically mean that the item needs to be revised. Each distractor may be functioning adequately, but the examinees used to collect the response data may have been skillfully instructed on the content material that was tested and, therefore, were better prepared to select the correct answer. Therefore, not much importance should be attached to distractor analyses with very easy items.

Item Discrimination Index. The discriminating power of a test item refers to how well the item distinguishes between examinees of high and low ability. There are several different kinds of item discrimination indices. The item total-test score point-biserial correlation is one popular indicator of an item's discriminating power. Any item with a negative discrimination should definitely be red-flagged for item revision. If an item has a very low positive discrimination index, it should be carefully reviewed for flaws, but not necessarily discarded as it would be in a norm-referenced test development project.

Item Difficulty Levels. Some authors have suggested that items measuring the same objective should have homogeneous difficulty levels (Popham, 1978). After the items are grouped by objective, their p values are compared to identify outliers. The deviant items are then flagged for careful review. The problem with comparing p values is that one cannot expect items measuring the same objective to have a single common p value. Some domains of content describing an objective are rather broad. Hence, variation in difficulty levels is expected, and determining the appropriate range of p values can be difficult.

Finally, for each objective, the average item difficulty across all items can be computed. Expectations about how difficult or easy the items should be, based on the ability level of the examinees, are stated. Discrepancies between the predicted and actual average p level may suggest that item improvements are needed.

Criterion-Referenced Statistics

The purpose of a criterion-referenced test is to describe what examinees can do, rather than how examinees should be ranked. Therefore, classical item statistics that were intended for use in the construction of norm-referenced tests must be interpreted differently with criterion-referenced tests. Also, several alternate indices have been proposed. Berk (1980a) gives a detailed account of the new indices found in the literature for use with criterion-referenced tests. Two of the most useful of the statistics will be discussed next.

The *pretest–posttest difference* index derived by Cox and Vargas (1966) that uses the same examinees before and after instruction is calculated as follows:

$$D = P_{\text{post}} - P_{\text{pre}}$$

where P_{post} is the proportion of examinees answering the item correctly on the posttest, and P_{pre} is the proportion of examinees answering the item correctly on the pretest. What is implied in the formula is that items given to uninstructed examinees should appear difficult (i.e., have low p values) and the same items given to instructed examinees should appear easy (Haladyna & Roid, 1981). The post-item difficulty should be relatively higher than the pre-item difficulty. Hence, the difference in the two difficulties can be used to detect aberrant test items. When the statistic is negative or zero, in addition to the obvious interpretation that the item is defective, several alternate hypotheses must be considered: (1) instruction is ineffective and/or (2) the test does not measure the objective of interest (Haladyna & Roid, 1981). Occasionally, problems are encountered when "uninstructed" and "instructed" groups are not highly correlated with "masters" and "nonmasters." For example, when an "uninstructed" group masters the objective measured by an item, the D index will necessarily be low because of the high performance level of the uninstructed group.

Popham (1978) suggested another approach for identifying items not affected similarly by instruction. The procedure begins by placing responses to each item into one of four possible categories of pretest–posttest results: (1) 00, examinee answers item incorrectly on both pretest and posttest; (2) 01, examinee answers item incorrectly on pretest and correctly on posttest; (3) 10, examinee answers item correctly on pretest and incorrectly on posttest; and (4) 11, examinee answers item correctly on both pretest and posttest. Then this process is completed across all examinees for every item.

Next, for all four cells, the median value is computed across all items measuring the same objective. Then these median frequencies are compared to each item's actual frequency via a simple chi-square test of significance. Large chi-square values indicate that an item's sensitivity to instruction was dramatically different from the group of items, and item improvement may be necessary (Popham, 1978).

STANDARD-SETTING

The most difficult problem in criterion-referenced testing concerns setting the cut-off score or, as it is sometimes called, the standard, on the test score scale to separate masters from nonmasters. The problem has no parallel in norm-referenced testing. It is now recognized by most criterion-referenced test users that there is no magic test score point waiting to be discovered as the standard by psychometricians. Rather, setting standards is ultimately a judgmental process that is best done by well-chosen individuals who (1) are familiar with the test content and knowledgeable about the standard-setting method they will be expected to use, (2) have access to item performance and test score distribution data in the standard-setting process, and (3) understand the social and political context in which the tests are being used (Hambleton & Powell, 1983).

PSYCHOMETRIC CHARACTERISTICS OF CRITERION-REFERENCED TEST SCORES

RELIABILITY ISSUES AND METHODS

It was noted earlier that criterion-referenced test scores are used, principally, in two ways: (1) to obtain descriptions and/or (2) to make mastery/nonmastery decisions. In the first way the precision with which domain scores are estimated is of interest. In the second way, the test–retest decision consistency or parallel-form decision consistency is of interest. It is clear that the usual approaches to assessing test score reliability (test–retest reliability, parallel-form reliability, and corrected split-half reliability) that are routinely applied to norm-referenced tests do not address directly either use and, therefore, are of limited value in the context of criterion-referenced measurement (Hambleton & Novick, 1973). It has been argued that classical reliability indices are not useful with criterion-referenced tests because the scores often are fairly homogeneous, and so classical reliability indices will be low. But this is not the real problem. If low reliability indices were the problem, the problem could be resolved by interpreting the indices more cautiously in light of homogeneous test score distributions or designing reliability studies to ensure more heterogeneous score distributions. Actually, norm-referenced test reliability indices are not useful with criterion-referenced test scores because they fail to provide the needed information on score and decision consistency.

The reliability topic has probably received more attention from psychometricians than any other in the criterion-referenced testing field. The interested reader is referred to Hambleton *et al.* (1978), and Berk (1980b) for recent reviews. A few of the more practical contributions to the topic will be considered next.

Reliability of Domain Score Estimates

The standard error of measurement associated with domain score estimates can easily be calculated. It is useful in setting up confidence bands for examinee domain scores. Fortunately, it is not influenced to any considerable extent by the homogeneity of examinee domain scores (Lord & Novick, 1968).

Another approach for determining the accuracy of domain score estimates was reported by Millman (1974). He suggested that the standard error of estimation derived from the binomial test model, given by the expression $[\hat{\pi}(1 - \hat{\pi})/n]^{\frac{1}{2}}$, can be used to set up confidence bands around domain score estimates. In the expression, n is the number of items measuring an objective and $\hat{\pi}$ is the proportion-correct score for an examinee.

Reliability of Mastery Classifications

Hambleton and Novick (1973) suggested that the reliability of mastery classification decisions should be defined in terms of the consistency of decisions from two administrations of the same test or parallel forms of a test. Suppose examinees are to be classified into mastery states (for example, mastery versus nonmastery, or achievement levels, denoted A, B, C, D, and F), Hambleton and Novick suggested the formula below to measure the proportion of examinees who are consistently classified on the two administrations:

$$p_0 = \sum_{j=1}^{m} p_{jj}$$

where p_{jj} is the proportion of examinees classified in the jth mastery state on the two administrations and m is the number of mastery states. In practice, m usually is equal to two. The index p_0 is the observed proportion of decisions that agree. Among the factors affecting the value of p_0 are test length, quality of test items, choice of cut-off score, group heterogeneity, and the closeness of the group mean performance to the choice of cut-off score. The p_0 statistic has considerable appeal and is easy to calculate.

The concept of decision consistency is a useful one with criterion-referenced tests, but the approach described above requires the administration of a single test twice or the administration of parallel forms of a test. In either case, test time is doubled. This approach is often difficult to implement in practice because of limited testing time. With norm-referenced tests, one way to avoid extra testing time in assessing reliability involves the use of the split-half method to determine the reliability of scores from a test that is one-half as long as the one of interest. Next, the Spearman-Brown formula is used, along with the split-half reliability estimate, to predict the reliability of scores with the test of interest. Unfortunately, the approach used with norm-referenced test scores cannot be used to assess consistency of decisions emanating from a single administration of a criterion-referenced test. A rather different approach for estimating decision consistency from a single administration was developed by Subkoviak (1976). Although the mathematical development of the formula is not comparable, Subkoviak's formula is the analog of the corrected split-half reliability index, which is used with norm-referenced tests to estimate parallel-form reliability from the administration of a single test.

VALIDITY ISSUES AND METHODS

Although many contributions to the criterion-referenced testing literature have been made since the late 1960s (for reviews, see Berk, 1980a; Hambleton *et al.* 1978; Millman, 1974; Popham, 1978), the important topic of criterion-referenced test score validity has been paid little attention by researchers. Very often, measurement specialists assume the validity of criterion-referenced test scores rather than make a special effort to establish the validity of the scores in any formal way. The argument seems to be that if the appropriate test development steps are carried out, a valid criterion-referenced test will necessarily result. But the validity of the resulting scores will depend on their intended use, in addition to the care with which the test was constructed. A review of 12 commercially prepared criterion-referenced tests was conducted by Hambleton and Eignor (1978). Not one of these test manuals included a discussion of what these authors felt was a satisfactory test score validity investigation. Evidence that the items matched the objectives was the only evidence the publishers reported concerning test score validity. No evidence of the accuracy of the domain scores or of the mastery and nonmastery classifications was presented.

Fortunately, the situation seems to be changing. Articles have now been published describing the nature of the validity questions and how they should be approached (Fitzpatrick, 1983; Kane, 1982; Hambleton, 1984; Linn, 1979, 1980; Madaus, 1983). Also, several exemplary validity studies have appeared in the literature (Kirsch & Guthrie, 1980; Ward, Frederiksen, & Carlson, 1980).

Many criterion-referenced test developers have argued that to "validate" their tests and test scores, it is sufficient to assess "content validity." Usually, opinions are obtained from persons with content expertise concerning the match between test content and the objectives a test is designed to measure. Since these experts focus on test content, the expression *content validity* is used to describe the nature of the activities carried out by the content specialists; but it should be clear that content validity refers to certain characteristics of the test content. Methods for approaching content validity assessment were described earlier in this chapter. The content validity of a test does not vary from one sample of examinees to the next, nor does the content validity of a test vary over time. However, any use of a test (whether *norm-referenced* or *criterion-referenced*) ultimately depends on the scores obtained from its administration, and the validity of the scores depends upon many factors (most especially, the intended use of the scores), in addition to test content. It is possible that examinee item responses and the resulting test scores do not adequately reflect or address the skills of interest, even though the test itself is judged to be content valid.

Fortunately, a wide assortment of methods (see Table 1 for a sampling) can be used to gather validity evidence relevant to the intended uses of a set of test scores:

1. *Intra-objective methods* include item analyses, the evaluation of test content (determination of item and content validity), and score reliability.
2. *Inter-objective methods* include what are often called "convergent" and "divergent" validity studies—studies to determine whether test scores correlate with variables they might reasonably be expected to relate to, and studies to determine if test scores do not correlate with variables they should not correlate with, respectively.
3. *Criterion-related methods* include prediction studies and studies of the relationships between test scores and mastery classifications and independent measures of performance, such as those that might be obtained from teachers, instructors, or supervisors.
4. *Experimental methods* include the determination of the sensitivity of test scores and mastery classifications to the effects of instruction on test content.
5. *Multitrait/multimethod studies* address what it is that a test actually measures.

The accumulation of validation evidence is a never-ending process. The amount of time and energy that should be spent on the validation of test scores and mastery classifications should directly relate to the importance of the testing program. Criterion-referenced tests that are being used to monitor student progress in a curriculum on a day-to-day basis will obviously demand less attention and fewer resources than will tests to be used to determine whether or not students graduate from high school or tests to be used to certify or license such professionals as family physicians, insurance salespersons, and clinical care nurses.

The brief section that follows describes several validity investigations that are unique to criterion-referenced tests.

Construct Validity Investigations

Construct validation studies have not been common in criterion-referenced measurement. This may be because criterion-referenced test

TABLE 1. Approaches for Assessing Validity

Approach	Description
Intra-objective	Measure of internal consistency at the objective level (e.g., KR-20)
	Item analyses
	Content specialists' ratings of item–objective congruence, bias, technical quality, and representativeness (content validity)
	Confirmatory factor analysis (Do the items fit a hypothesized structure?)
	Distractor analysis (for example, Do many of the high performers choose an incorrect answer choice?)
Inter-objective	Confirmatory factor analysis
	Scalogram analysis
	Convergent validity studies (includes studies of relationships between test scores and other tests that measure the same objectives or measure traits that should correlate with the objectives)
	Divergent validity studies (includes studies of relationships between tests that purport to measure different skills or traits)
Criterion-related (continuous or dichotomous criterion variable)	Correlation between domain score estimates obtained from the "actual" and the "lengthened" test (called "domain validity")
	Correlation of test scores with instructor ratings, on the job measures (or simulated on the job measures), self-ratings, or peer-ratings
	Comparison of examinee performance on the test before and after instruction
	Comparison of the score distributions or percent of masters for (1) "masters" and "nonmasters" (as identified by means other than the test itself), or, for example, (2) "uninstructed" and "instructed" groups of examinees
	Correlation between test scores and the number of years of preparation
	Correlation between test scores and examinee performance in real or simulated situations representing the same or similar content
	Bias studies to determine if unexpected differences arise due to race, ethnic background, sex, etc.
Experimental	Studies to investigate sources of possible invalidity such as degree of speededness (e.g., administer test with and without time limits to compare performance), clarity of directions, answer sheets, race and sex of test examiner
	Study of pre- and posttest performance with treatment and control groups
	Study of the influence of response sets and personality on test performance
Multitrait–multimethod	Simultaneous investigation of construct validity of several objectives utilizing two or more methods for assessing each objective

Note. From "Validating The Test Scores" by R. K. Hambleton in R. Berk (Ed.), *A guide to criterion-referenced test construction.* Baltimore, Md.: Johns Hopkins University Press, 1984. Reproduced by permission.

score distributions are often homogeneous (for example, it often happens that before instruction most individuals do poorly on a test and after instruction most individuals do well). Correlational methods do not work well with homogeneous score distributions because of the problems that arise from score range restrictions. But, as Messick (1975) has noted,

> Construct validation is by no means limited to correlation coefficients, even though it may seem that way from the prevalence of correlation matrices, internal consistency indices, and factor analysis (p. 858).

Construct validation studies begin with a definite statement of the proposed use of the test scores. A clearly stated use will indicate the kind of evidence that is worth collecting. Some of the investigations that could be undertaken to estimate the construct validity of a set of criterion-referenced test scores are described next.

Guttman Scalogram Analysis. It frequently happens that objectives can be arranged linearly or hierarchically on the basis of a logical analysis. Guttman scaling is a relevant procedure for the construct validation of criterion-referenced test scores in situations in which the objectives can be organized into either a linear or a hierarchical sequence. To use Guttman's scalogram analysis as a technique in a test score validation methodology, one would first need to specify the hierarchical structure of a set of objectives. To the extent that examinee mastery/nonmastery status on the objectives in the hierarchy is predictable from a knowledge of the hierarchy, one would have evidence to support the construct validity of the objective scores. On the other hand, in situations in which examinee mastery/non-mastery status is not predictable, one of three situations has occurred: The hierarchy is incorrectly specified, or the objective scores are not valid measures of the intended objectives, or both.

Factor Analysis. Factor analysis is commonly employed for the dimensional analysis of items in a norm-referenced test or of scores derived from different norm-referenced tests, but it has rarely, if ever, been used in construct validation studies of criterion-referenced test scores. One reason for this is that the usual input for factor-analytical studies are correlations, and correlations are often low between items on a criterion-referenced test or between criterion-referenced test scores and other variables, since score variability is often not very great. Also, inter-item correlations are often low because of the unreliability of item scores. However, the problem that results from limited score variability can, to some extent, be minimized by choosing a heterogeneous sample of examinees, for example, a group including both masters and nonmasters.

The research problem becomes a problem of determining whether or not the factor pattern matrix has a prescribed form. The prescribed form is set by the researchers and is based upon a logical analysis of the objectives and other research evidence concerning the structure of the objectives measured in the test. Evidence that the estimated structure among the variables matches the prescribed form will support both the research hypotheses and the validity of the scores as measures of the desired variables.

Experimental Studies. There are many sources of error that reduce the validity of an intended use of a set of criterion-referenced test scores, for example, clarity of test directions, test speedness, or level of motivation. Experimental studies of potential sources of error to determine their effect on test scores are an important way of assessing the construct validity of a set of test scores. Logical analyses and observations of testing methods and procedures can also be used to detect sources of invalidity in a set of test scores.

Multitrait—multimethod Approach. The category of construct validation would also include multitrait–multimethod validation of objective scores (Campbell & Fiske, 1959). Multitrait–multimethod validation includes any techniques addressing the question of the degree examinee responses to items reflect the "trait" (objective) of interest and the degree they reflect methodological effects.

Criterion-Related Validity

Even if scores derived from criterion-referenced tests are descriptive of the objectives they are supposed to reflect, the usefulness of the scores as predictors of, say, "job success" or "success in the next unit of instruction" cannot be assured. Criterion-related validity studies of criterion-referenced test scores do not differ in procedure from studies conducted with norm-referenced tests. Correlational, group separation, and decision accuracy methods are commonly used (Cronbach, 1971). Also, the selection of reasonable and practical criterion measures that do *not* themselves require extensive validation efforts remains as serious a problem in conducting validation studies with criterion-referenced tests as it is for norm-referenced tests. There are, however, two important differences. First, test scores are usually dichotomized (examinees above a cut-off score are described as masters, below as nonmasters). Second, and related to the first, instead of reporting correlational measures as is commonly done in criterion-related validity investigations with norm-referenced tests, readily interpretable validity indices reflecting the agreement between decisions based on the test and an external dichotomous criterion measure are reported.

Criterion-referenced test scores are commonly used to make decisions.

In instructional settings, an examinee is assumed to be a "master" when his or her test performance exceeds a minimum level of performance. Decision validity, which is simply a particular kind of criterion-related validity, involves (1) setting a standard of test performance and (2) comparing the test performance of two or more criterion groups relative to the specified standard.

One advantage of decision validity studies is that the results can be reported in a readily interpretable way (percentage of correct decisions). Alternatively, the correlation between two dichotomous variables (group membership and the mastery decision) can be reported and used as an index of decision validity. Other statistics are reported by Berk (1976), Hambleton (1984), and Popham (1978). Finally, the validity of a set of decisions will depend on several important factors: (1) the quality of the test under investigation, (2) the appropriateness and size of the criterion groups, (3) the characteristics of the examinee sample, and (4) the minimum level of performance required for mastery. All four factors will affect decision validity. Clearly, since a number of factors substantially influence the level of decision validity, it must be recognized that what is being described through a summary statistic of interest is *not* the test, but rather the *use* of the test in a particular way with a specified group of examinees. The same point applies equally well when norm-referenced reliability and validity indices are interpreted.

SUMMARY

In this chapter, we have highlighted several technical advances associated with criterion-referenced testing. Criterion-referenced testing primarily focuses on the problem of assigning individuals to mastery states that are described relative to well-defined domains of content. Although interest is centered on individual performance relative to the standards, individual differences in mastery status can serve as the dependent variable in a variety of research and evaluation studies.

At present, research is still under way on (1) methods for setting standards, (2) formats for reporting scores to maximize test score usefulness, and (3) approaches for describing objectives. New studies that offer a potential for the improvement of criterion-referenced testing practices include those on microcomputers for storing, administering, and scoring tests and studies with item response models for developing continuous growth or developmental scales to which objectives, test items, and examinees can be referenced.

REFERENCES

Berk, R. A. Determination of optimal cutting scores in criterion-referenced measurement. *Journal of Experimental Education*, 1976, *45*, 4–9.

Berk, R. A. (Ed.). *Criterion-referenced measurement: The state of the art*. Baltimore, Md.: Johns Hopkins University Press, 1980a.

Berk, R. A. A consumer's guide to criterion-referenced test reliability. *Journal of Educational Measurement*, 1980b, *17*, 323–349.

Campbell, D. T., & Fiske, D. W. Convergent and discriminant validation by the multitrait–multimethod matrix. *Psychological Bulletin*, 1959, *56*, 81–105.

Cox, R. C., & Vargas, J. S. *A comparison of item selection techniques for norm-referenced and criterion-referenced tests*. Paper presented at the annual meeting of the National Council on Measurement in Education, Chicago, 1966.

Cronbach, L. J. Test validation. In R. L. Thorndike (Ed.), *Educational measurement*. Washington, D.C.: American Council on Education, 1971.

Fitzpatrick, A. R. The meaning of content validity. *Applied Psychological Measurement*, 1983, *7*, 3–13.

Glaser, R. Instructional technology and the measurement of learning outcomes. *American Psychologist*, 1963, *18*, 519–521.

Gray, W. M. A comparison of Piagetian theory and criterion-referenced measurement. *Review of Educational Research*, 1978, *48*, 223–249.

Haladyna, T., & Roid, G. The role of instructional sensitivity in the empirical review of criterion-referenced test items. *Journal of Educational Measurement*, 1981, *18*, 39–53.

Hambleton, R. K. Test score validity and standard-setting methods. In R. A. Berk (Ed.), *Criterion-referenced measurement: The state of the art*. Baltimore, Md.: Johns Hopkins University Press, 1980.

Hambleton, R. K. Advances in criterion-referenced testing technology. In C. R. Reynolds & T. B. Gutkin (Eds.), *The handbook of school psychology*. New York: Wiley, 1982.

Hambleton, R. K. Validating the test scores. In R. Berk (Ed.), *A guide to criterion-referenced test construction*. Baltimore, Md.: Johns Hopkins University Press, 1984.

Hambleton, R. K., & deGruijter, D. N. M. Application of item response models to criterion-referenced test item selection. *Journal of Educational Measurement*, 1983, *20*, 355–367.

Hambleton, R. K., & Eignor, D. R. Guidelines for evaluating criterion-referenced tests and test manuals. *Journal of Educational Measurement*, 1978, *15*, 321–327.

Hambleton, R. K., & Novick, M. R. Toward an integration of theory and method for criterion-referenced tests. *Journal of Educational Measurement*, 1973, *10*, 159–170.

Hambleton, R. K., & Powell, S. A framework for viewing the process of standard setting. *Evaluation and the Health Professions*, 1983, *6*, 3–24.

Hambleton, R. K., Swaminathan, H., Algina, J., & Coulson, D. B. Criterion-referenced testing and measurement: A review of technical issues and developments. *Review of Educational Research*, 1978, *48*, 1–47.

Kane, M. T. The validity of licensure examinations. *American Psychologist*, 1982, *37*, 911–918.

Kirsch, I., & Guthrie, J. T. Construct validity of functional reading tests. *Journal of Educational Measurement*, 1980, *17*, 81–93.

Linn, R. L. Issues of validity in measurement for competency-based programs. In M. A. Bunda & J. R. Sanders (Eds.), *Practices and problems in competency-based measurement*. Washington, D.C.: National Council on Measurement in Education, 1979.

Linn, R. L. Issues of validity for criterion-referenced measures. *Applied Psychological Measurement*, 1980, *4*, 547–561.

Lord, F. M., & Novick, M. R. *Statistical theories of mental test scores*. Reading, Mass.: Addison-Wesley, 1968.

Madaus, G. (Ed.). *The courts, validity, and minimum competency testing*. Boston, Mass.: Kluwer-Nijhoff Publishing Co., 1983.

Messick, S. A. The standard problem: Meaning and values in measurement and evaluation. *American Psychologist*, 1975, *30*, 955–966.

Millman, J. Criterion-referenced measurement. In W. J. Popham (Ed.), *Evaluation in education: Current applications*. Berkeley, Calif.: McCutchan, 1974.

Popham, W. J. An approaching peril: Cloud referenced tests. *Phi Delta Kappan*, 1974, *56*, 614–615.

Popham, W. J. *Criterion-referenced measurement*. Englewood Cliffs, N.J.: Prentice-Hall, 1978.

Popham, W. J., & Husek, T. R. Implications of criterion-referenced measurement. *Journal of Educational Measurement*, 1969, *6*, 1–9.

Roid, G., & Haladyna, T. *A technology for item writing*. New York: Academic Press, 1982.

Rovinelli, R. J., & Hambleton, R. K. On the use of content specialists in the assessment of criterion-referenced test item validity. *Dutch Journal of Educational Research*, 1977, *2*, 49–60.

Subkoviak, M. J. Estimating reliability for the single administration of a mastery test. *Journal of Educational Measurement*, 1976, *13*, 265–276.

van der Linden, W. J. Decision models for use with criterion-referenced tests. *Applied Psychological Measurement*, 1980, *4*, 469–492.

Ward, W. C., Frederiksen, N., & Carlson, S. B. Construct validity of free-response and machine-scorable forms of a test. *Journal of Educational Measurement*, 1980, *17*, 11–29.

11

Path-Referenced Assessment of Individual Differences

JOHN R. BERGAN, CLEMENT A. STONE, AND JASON K. FELD

Assessment plays a critical role in meeting instructional needs related to individual differences in student competence. Assessment devices have long been central in determining the educational placement of students with special learning needs. Assessment techniques have also been used to diagnose individual learning problems and to place students in curriculum sequences (Glaser & Nitko, 1971).

Three major views regarding individual differences in competence are reflected in the questions educators ask assessment programs. The first, based on norm-referenced assessment, defines competence in terms of placement in a norm group. In this view, individual differences are conceptualized in terms of individual variations in norm group position. The second view, which relies on criterion-referenced assessment technology, defines competence in terms of the mastery of specific objectives and conceptualizes individual differences in terms of variations in mastery level. For example, students will generally differ in the proportion of skills mastered within a given content domain. Such differences are quantified through the use of domain mastery scores (Hambleton, Swaminathan, Algina, & Coulson, 1978). The third view conceives of competence in terms of educational progress during the course of instruction. It assumes that learning and development involve sequential changes in capability that reflect successively higher levels of functioning. Individual differences in competence are defined in terms of variations in position along paths of development. In this chapter, we discuss a new assessment technology,

JOHN R. BERGAN, CLEMENT A. STONE, and JASON K. FELD • Department of Educational Psychology, University of Arizona, Tucson, Arizona 85721.

path-referenced assessment (Bergan, 1981a), which was designed to measure individual differences by conceptualizing educational progress in terms of sequential changes in competence.

ORIGINS OF PATH-REFERENCED ASSESSMENT

Path-referenced assessment depends on the long-standing view that both learning and development involve sequential changes in capability that reflect successively higher levels of competence (see, for example, Gagné, 1962; Piaget, 1952). Three factors associated with this view contributed to the development of path-referenced assessment technology. The first had to do with the recognition of the sequential nature of learning in early conceptions of criterion-referenced assessment (Glaser, 1963); the second, recent advances in cognitive psychology that reevaluate the nature of cognitive structures and changes in those structures (e.g., Greeno, 1978; Siegler, 1983); and the third, the emergence of new mathematical models in a psychometric technology for path-referenced assessment.

THE INFLUENCE OF CRITERION-REFERENCED ASSESSMENT

Concern for the sequential nature of learning and development was linked directly to assessment technology, with the introduction of criterion-referenced assessment in the early 1960s (Glaser, 1963; Nitko, 1980). From its inception, the criterion-referenced approach assumed hierarchically ordered sequences of learning tasks. Moreover, many attempts were made to validate such sequences empirically. Unfortunately, these attempts were thwarted by the lack of appropriate statistical tools to test hierarchical hypotheses (Bergan, 1980; White, 1973). As the criterion-referenced approach was increasingly accepted, interest in sequencing waned. However, the sequential nature of learning is still recognized within the criterion-referenced framework (Nitko, 1980). Path-referenced assessment shares the early criterion-referenced assessment concern for sequential learning. It differs from the criterion-referenced approach in how learning and developmental sequences are conceptualized. The path-referenced approach also includes a concern for the assessment of progress not associated with criterion-referenced technology. This concern also involves a series of measurement issues (Rogosa, Brandt, & Zimowski, 1982) not dealt with in the criterion-referenced tradition. For example, path-referenced assessment requires a technology for quantifying change and for establishing norms for educational progress, whereas criterion-referenced assessment does not.

THE IMPACT OF COGNITIVE PSYCHOLOGY

New developments in cognitive psychology have had a marked effect on the technology of path-referenced assessment. In the early views of hierarchical sequencing, it was assumed that complex intellectual skills emerged from simpler component competencies (Gagné, 1962, 1970, 1977). Contemporary cognitive theory however, indicates that other forms of hierarchical sequencing also occur (e.g., Flavell, 1972). For instance, learning may involve the replacement of a simple rule by a more complex rule (Bergan, Towstopiat, Cancelli, & Karp, 1982). Thus, varying types of hierarchical sequencing suggest a need for item development techniques that go beyond the task analytical procedures (Gagné, 1970; Resnick, Wang, & Kaplan, 1973) used to identify component skills in criterion-referenced assessment. Path-referenced assessment technology constructs hierarchical sequences by identifying task demands (Newell & Simon, 1972) that reflect the types of change in knowledge structures.

Contemporary cognitive psychology has pointed out that different individuals may represent the same task in different ways. For instance, Lawler (1981) presented an addition problem (75 + 26) in two different ways to a young child. The first presentation was in the traditional vertical format found in elementary school worksheets. The second requested the child to add 75 cents and 26 cents. The child was unable to perform the carrying operation necessary to solve the first problem. However, she responded without difficulty to the second version indicating that three quarters, one more quarter, and a penny was "a dollar one." As this example shows, variations in task representation may affect the procedures used in task performance and, thereby, task difficulty. The example also illustrates the fact that task representation may be affected by the way in which a task is presented or modeled (Van Lehn & Brown, 1979). The concepts of task representation and task model have influenced the item generation technology of path-referenced tests. In particular, path-referenced technology makes provisions for different task models in item development. Model selection is influenced by assumptions regarding model effects on task representations.

Contemporary cognitive theorists have indicated the importance of distinguishing between hierarchical sequences involving the same general concept and sequences involving different concepts (Siegler, 1983). Single-concept sequences reveal the sequential development of increasingly refined rules that represent a deepening understanding of the concept under investigation. By contrast, different-concept sequences reveal developmental interrelationships among concepts. The within-concepts and between-concepts distinction has played a major role in determining the technology of path-referenced test construction. More specifically, item generation technology in path-referenced assessment includes provisions for the construction of task strands that are sets of tasks representing varying levels of competence for the same general concept (Bergan, 1981b). Hierarchical sequences are constructed both within and between strands.

A number of investigators (e.g., Bergan, 1980, 1983; Brainerd, 1979; Gelman & Gallistel, 1978; Wilkinson, 1982) have pointed out that, in many instances, development does not progress in stair-step fashion from one skill to another. Rather, individuals go through transition states in which performance is inconsistent. Inconsistent performance may reflect circumstances in which the individual selects different rules that may or may not be associated with accurate task performance (Brainerd, 1979). Inconsistency may also reflect conditions under which the individual has the necessary component capabilities for accurate performance, but cannot integrate them effectively (Wilkinson, 1982). Path-referenced assessment includes provisions for the double assessment of individual skills during item development, in order to identify instances of inconsistent performance associated with rule sampling and/or component integration problems.

THE CONTRIBUTION OF ADVANCES IN STATISTICS

Advances in statistical methodology greatly influence the development of path-referenced assessment procedures. New statistical techniques of relevance to path-referenced assessment are mostly latent variable models (Bergan, 1983; Bentler & Weeks, 1980; Jöreskog & Sorbom, 1979; Wright & Stone, 1979). These procedures can be used to

1. Test hypotheses regarding task sequencing
2. Assess progress along paths of development on a continuous scale
3. Measure educational progress resulting from instruction
4. Identify skills representing significant milestones in development
5. Reflect progress occurring across grade levels on a common scale assessing long-range development
6. Construct an adaptive measurement system that can accommodate a change in curriculum. Modifications in curriculum generally imply changes in skills targeted for assessment. Latent variable techniques can be used to place old and new versions of a test on a common scale so that student performance can be compared across time even when the curriculum is undergoing change.

PATH-REFERENCED ASSESSMENT TECHNOLOGY

Path-referenced assessment technology has four components. The first is a general model identifying the structure of knowledge in any given content domain. Path-referenced tests are theory driven. The general model makes it possible to link theoretical perspectives guiding item generation to the item construction process. The second component is a set of procedures for analyzing specific content domains in a way that reflects developmental sequencing for different categories of competence. The third component includes procedures that control the process of item construction. Items constructed for path-referenced tests must reflect hypotheses about the structure of knowledge in a content area specified through application of the general model. The development of items congruent with model hypotheses requires a new kind of item construction technology. The item generation component of the path-referenced approach provides that technology. The fourth component consists of the procedures used to establish the psychometric properties of path-referenced tests. These procedures include techniques used in item analysis, techniques used to establish the reliability and validity of path-referenced assessment devices, and techniques for norming path-referenced assessment instruments.

A General Domain Structure Model for Path-Referenced Assessment

The development of a path-referenced assessment test begins with a theoretical model of the structure of knowledge in the particular content area targeted for assessment. The general domain structure model, discussed in this section, makes it possible to design a theoretical model to guide the test development process for a particular content area.

The general domain structure model partitions any given broad domain of competence into an organized set of subdomains, hence its name. This competence partitioning involves the division of broad categories into successively narrower subcategories. For instance, the domain of mathematical knowledge can be divided into such subdomains as arithmetic and geometry. These can, in turn, be subdivided into smaller classes. For example, arithmetic includes the familar categories of counting, addition, and subtraction. The hierarchical nesting of categories in the model makes it possible to link general classes to highly specific categories of competence. Links from the general to the specific relate global constructs to operationally definable competencies that can be interpreted both by test developers and by the consumer of assessment information.

A developmental approach is fundamental to path-referenced assessment. As indicated, path-referencing describes competence in terms of positions along paths of development. The concept of developmental paths calls for theoretical perspectives on developmental change. In keeping with a developmental perspective, the model reflects a hierarchical ordering that represents developmental progressions. Developmental hierarchies are

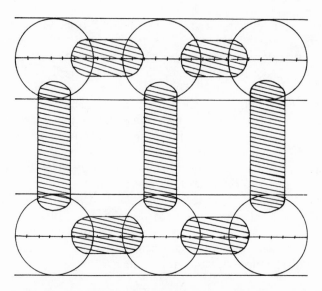

FIGURE 1. A general model showing basic characteristics of the structure of knowledge in the cognitive domain. The parallel lines on either side of the circles indicate dimensions in the cognitive domain. The circles indicate subdomains within dimensions. The tubular figures represent permability in the boundaries between subdomains and dimensions; the hatch-marked lines indicate continuous development within dimensions.

linked in the model to hierarchically nested categories of competence. This linkage organizes the well-defined subdomains of developmental progress into a set. Figure 1 illustrates the general structure of such a set.

Path Structure

The categorization of competencies in terms of a nested hierarchy involving varying levels of inclusiveness produces an interrelated set of subdomains. At some level in the categorizing process, it will be reasonable to assume that the subdomains under consideration reflect linear sequences of competencies. Such subdomains are called *paths*. Paths are conceived as categories of competence reflecting variations in task difficulty that can be represented on a linear scale. Paths are bounded by competency type, but not by variations in level of competence. For example, although a certain level of language development is necessary for reading, the allocation of reading and language to separate paths does not imply hierarchical ordering. Rather, language and reading are treated simply as different categories of intellectual competence.

In the domain structure model, paths are subdivided into components. The components, in turn, are broken down into subcomponents. The process of subdivision continues profitably until a set of tasks involving a common goal attained through the execution of an organized set of processes has been achieved. For example, numerical processes may be regarded as a subcomponent in the math path. Numerical processes may be subdivided into such categories as addition. Addition tasks have a common goal, the summing of numbers. Moreover, the attainment of that goal involves the execution of an organized set of processes constrained by the goal.

The term *task strand* is used in the model to refer to a class of tasks that have a common goal, and involve an organized set of processes directed toward attainment of that goal. A task strand represents the smallest subdivision of competence categories in a path structure. A task strand should reflect a single competence class. The use of task strands in the model makes possible the construction of development hierarchies both within the same general class and between classes of competence. Hierarchies within the same strand make it possible to assess a student's deepening understanding of a concept. Hierarchies between strands afford the opportunity to establish relationships across different classes of competence.

The specification of paths, component and subcomponent paths, and strands constitutes the path structure for the domain studied. The path structure provides boundaries for a nested hierarchy of subdomains reflecting different categories of competence. These categories imply developmental sequencing, but they lack specificity regarding the basis for such sequencing. The necessary specificity is provided by establishing a developmental structure for the domain.

Developmental Structure

The developmental structure in a domain indicates the ordering of tasks for each path in the domain. Assumptions about ordering for a given path are specified both within and between tasks strands associated with that path. Within-strand hypotheses make assumptions about an individual's deepening understanding of a concept associated with a path, whereas between-strand hypotheses designate developmental relations among different concepts in a path.

Developmental structure is conceptualized in terms of both continuous and discontinuous progress. Continuity and discontinuity perspectives on development may be thought of as different, but not necessarily incompatible views (Ausubel & Sullivan, 1970). Both positions are useful from a measurement point of view and, accordingly, both are reflected in the domain structure model. The concept of continuous development is congruent with the quantification of progress on a continuous scale. The idea of discontinuous growth suggests hierarchical subdomain boundaries within paths marking the achievement of developmental milestones.

In the domain structure model, hypotheses on developmental ordering are based in part on the consideration of the ways tasks are represented by the individuals performing them. The tasks within a path may be represented in different ways. For example, in the case of addition, the numbers to be added may be represented by concrete objects, such as blocks or by the physical manipulation of blocks. On the other hand, the numbers may be represented by written symbols and written performance using those symbols.

A task representation, first, designates the way in which the objects to be manipulated in the task are depicted. The term *object* is assumed to encompass internally stored symbolic phenomena and processes, as well as stimuli in the external environment (Newell & Simon, 1972). For example, in the case of the addition example given above, the objects (numbers) to be added were represented either by concrete objects, such as blocks, or by written symbols, internal representations of numbers. A task representation also designates the processes an individual uses in task performance. Processes may include both overt and covert behaviors. Moreover, the designation of process should take account not only the actual behaviours carried out in task performance, but also the set of possible behaviors (Newell & Simon, 1972).

Individuals who perform tasks as well as those who construct tasks, may represent them in different ways. Task construction is an important variable in test development because variations in construction are associated with variations in task representation accompanying task performance. A task construction invariably specifies the stimulus features of the task representing the objects upon which task actions are performed and generally implies a procedure used to perform the task. For example, a test may include a counting task in which the objects to be counted are represented by blocks. In addition, the task may also require that the procedure used to count involves touching the blocks one at a time while saying the appropriate numbers. Van Lehn and Brown (1979) use the term *model* to refer to the stimulus characteristics and procedures comprising a task construction. As indicated earlier, the way a task is modeled influences the way the task will be represented (e.g., Lawler, 1981). For example, a child confronted with the task of adding blocks may be more likely to represent the addition task through a counting strategy involving block manipulation than would the child presented with a verbal addition task.

Although models may influence task representations, they certainly do not determine them precisely. Individuals may represent tasks in ways that differ from those intended by task constructors. Nevertheless, task models can be used to form working hypotheses for task representations, and assumptions about the developmental sequencing of tasks may be based on such hypotheses. For instance, assume that the addition of concrete objects, such as blocks, is easier than verbal addition. The basis for this assumption is that individuals presented with verbal addition tasks will tend to represent the numbers involved as covert symbols. Of course, some individuals may represent the task concretely by such means as counting on their fingers. Nevertheless, the tendency to represent tasks symbolically suggests that verbal addition will be more difficult than concrete addition. The domain structure model uses task models to make assumptions about task representations associated with task sequencing.

Task representations related to a given model may vary as a function of cultural experience. For instance, some Mexican-American children represent subtraction tasks that would require borrowing for Anglo children, in ways that do not involve borrowing (Bergan & Henderson, 1979). The inclusion of the concepts of model and representation in the domain structure model increases the sensitivity of the model to culturally diverse representations associated with developmental progress.

Hypotheses about developmental sequencing are based primarily on specification of *task demands* associated with hypothesized sources of task difficulty. Task demands are task characteristics that influence the cognitive processes of task performance (Newell & Simon, 1972). Task demands may affect process in a number of ways. For example, demands may alter task complexity by such means as influencing the number of steps necessary to successfully perform the task. Task demands may also impose requirements with respect to component processes involved in task performance. Demands may also affect the types of rules required for task performance (Bergan *et al.*, 1982). In the domain structure model, developmental hierarchies are constructed by varying task demands. For example, a developmental path involving basic math skills would involve a task strand for counting. Demands creating differences in task difficulty within this strand would include variations in the range of numbers to be counted, variations in starting point (i.e., counting from one or counting on from a number greater than one), variations in the direction of counting (i.e., fowards or backwards), and increment variations (i.e., counting by ones or by multiples). These demands impose varying requirements on the individual with respect to the rules used to govern counting behavior (Bergan, Stone, & Feld, in press). For instance, when counting from one, a child may use a rule specifying that counting always begins with one. On the other hand, counting on from a number greater than one requires a more general rule specifying that counting may begin with a number within a range of values (Bergan et al., 1984). This example illustrates the situation in which development progresses with the replacement of a simple, but restricted rule, by a more general rule covering a broader range of counting tasks.

Domain Structure Analysis

The general model described above is used to construct specific path-referenced tests through domain structure analysis. Domain structure analysis specifies path structure and developmental structure for a particular domain of competencies. For instance, the specification of path structure and developmental structure for childrens' competency in mathematics would constitute a domain structure analysis. Domain structure analysis has a similar function to that of task analysis in criterion-referenced assessment. However, whereas task analysis focuses on specifying component skills linked to a given superordinate skill (Gagné, 1977; Resnick et al., 1973), domain structure analysis specifies hypothesized relationships among classes of competencies and provides information on developmental ordering that is not limited to sequencing related to component skills.

Path Structure Analysis

Domain structure analysis begins with the analysis of path structure— the subdivision of a path into components and subcomponents to yield a set of interrelated classes of competence of the type described for the general domain structure model. In category subdivision, it is assumed that component forms of competence have common properties that justify their inclusion in a superordinate competence category and unique properties that justify their status as separate subcategories within the superordinate category. Assumptions about commonality and uniqueness are based on similarities and differences with respect to the characteristics of tasks used in assessing competence and the corresponding processes involved in task performance.

In path structure analysis, the most general categories of competence for which measures are to be developed in the domain under examination are specified first. For example, we have recently developed a set of path-referenced measures in the cognitive domain for use in the Head Start Program (Bergan, 1981c). Math, reading, language, nature and science, and perception were specified as general categories of competence for which cognitive measures were to be constructed. The general categories of competence comprise the paths in a path structure. Each path is broken down into two or more components. In the case of Head Start math, these included numerical processes that involve, for example, simple addition, subtraction, and counting tasks and measurement processes that involve length and size comparisons, as well as a knowledge of time and money concepts. Each subordinate category is, in turn, broken down. The analytic process is continued until task strands have been produced, each representing a competency class involving tasks sharing a common goal.

As the subdividing of path categories into increasingly finer classes continues, competencies implied by the classes become increasingly explicit. Eventually, a point is reached at which it is possible to identify sets of task strands, each having a common goal and each capable of being characterized operationally. For example, in the case of Head Start math, the subdivision of numerical processes yields such familiar arithmetic classifications as counting, addition, and subtraction. Each of these classifications can be designated as a task strand within the math path.

The subdivision may be summarized through the use of tree diagrams, such as the one presented in Figure 2. The path name is at the top of the tree. The successive subordinate categories represent increasingly less inclusive subcomponents of the path.

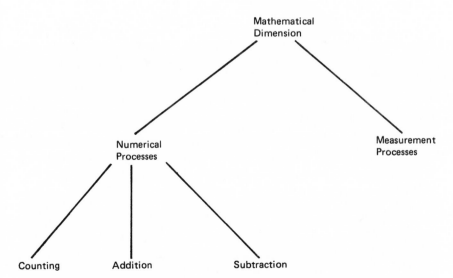

FIGURE 2. The categorical subdivision of the numerical processes subcomponent within the Head Start math measure.

The Analysis of Development Structure

Following the determination of path structure, developmental structure analysis is initiated. The task strand is the fundamental building block for establishing developmental structure. The first step in developmental structure analysis is to specify the task models to be included in each task strand in the structure. For example, the counting strand in the math path includes two models: counting with concrete objects and counting without concrete objects.

After the models have been specified, task demands are determined for each model. Demands for counting models include such variables as the range of numbers to be counted, the direction of counting (forward versus backward), and the starting number (one or a number greater than one). Task demands are chosen on the basis of two criteria. The first has to do with assumptions about their effects on cognitive functioning. For instance, the starting point in a counting task is specified as a demand because it is assumed to be associated with changes in cognitive structure (Fuson, 1982). When counting from one, children conceptualize the last number counted in terms of its cardinal value. The last number gives the number of things counted. Counting on from a number greater than one requires that the first number and the last number counted be conceptualized in terms of the cardinal property of the number (Fuson, 1982). It this were not the case, it would be impossible to relate the last number to the number of things counted. More specifically, the last number would always be greater than the number of times a counting word was assigned to an object in the counting process.

The second criterion involves their importance of developing competencies in other strands in the path. For example, starting point is not included as a task demand in the counting strand merely because it affects difficulty. The basis for its selection includes the fact that cognitive structures involved in counting on play an important role in the performance of other tasks in the math path. In particular, counting on is central to the acquisition of addition skills (Fuson, 1982). For instance, when young children are learning to add simple combinations such as 5 + 2, they tend to use a counting on strategy; a child might solve the 5 + 2 problem by saying *five* and then counting on *six, seven*.

After demands have been designated within strands, demand variations across strands within a path subcomponent are considered. In many cases, meaningful hypotheses can be formulated across strands. For instance, in the numerical processes subcomponent, certain counting tasks can be assumed to be subordinate to certain addition tasks. Similarly, addition tasks can be presumed to be subordinate to subtraction, multiplication, and division tasks. Although many cross-strand hypotheses may be meaningful, sometimes such hypotheses are not warranted and should not be advanced.

Two kinds of developmental hypotheses are associated with developmental structure analysis. The first involves variations in task difficulty, the second, the prerequisite ordering of tasks. The formation of these hypotheses heavily relies on information from the scientific knowledge base and information from current educational practice. For example, cognitive theory may provide a rationale for hypothesis formation. The age at which a particular set of skills is known to be acquired may also be considered, and, similarly, information on when certain types of skills tend to be taught in educational curriculums. Generation of developmental hypotheses completes the analysis of developmental structure. The next step is to produce items articulated to the structure.

ITEM CONSTRUCTION TECHNOLOGY

Domain structure analysis for a given path produces a structure representing an organized theoretical perspective regarding that path. In order to produce theory driven path-referenced measures, it is necessary to ensure that the items developed are congruent with the structure for the path. A new item construction technology is required to accomplish this.

Hambleton and Eignor (1979) developed an item construction technology for use in a criterion-referenced assessment that strongly influenced the technology presented in this section. Hambleton and Eignor adapted Popham's (1978, 1980) item-writing techniques to the problem of relating test items to instructional objectives unambiguously. The result is a domain specification strategy in which the specification of the class of items in a given domain is made concrete by the inclusion of item examples. Examples coupled with class specification provide item writers with clear guidelines for item construction.

The technology for path-referenced item construction is designed to relate specific items to the structures produced in domain structure analysis by linking item construction to task strands and task models. Hambleton's technology provides the basis for the construction of specific items within well-defined classes of tasks.

Strand Specification

The first step in the item construction process is to specify the task strands included in the path. Task strands are specified through the use of a form such as the one presented in Figure 3. Task strand specification requires, first of all, identification of the position of the strand in the domain

Dimension: Logical arithmetic processes
Component dimension: Numerical processes
Task strand: Addition

How objects are modeled
The stimulus materials used to represent the numbers may consist of the verbal presentation of two numbers to be added

Task demand variables
Variable: Range of sum
Description: The sum of the two numbers to be added
Subclass order by difficulty: (1–5) (6–10)

Estimated time/item: 15 seconds

FIGURE 3. Task strand form.

structure, by designating the path, component, and subcomponents to which the strand belongs. After its position has been determined, the strand is formally defined. Definition involves, first, specifying the common goal of the tasks within the strand. Goal specification requires a description of the desired outcome for the tasks in the strand and a designation, in general terms, of the processes required to achieve that outcome. For instance, in the case of addition tasks, the goal is to obtain a total by summing a set of numbers. Second, definition involves the designation of the objects to which the processes required for goal attainment are applied. For instance, in the case of addition, the objects to which processes are applied are numbers.

Model Specification

After strands have been defined, the task models to be included in them are listed. Each model chosen for strand inclusion is then justified. Models are specified by using a form such as the one shown in Figure 4. The first step in model specification is to summarize the position of the model in the domain structure, which includes labeling the path, components, subcomponents, and task strand with which the model is associated. The next step is to define the model. Model definition is based on a description of the manner in which task objects are represented in the model. For instance, in the case of addition, object representation may be concrete or verbal, by description in word problems, or by written specifications in paper-and-pencil problems. After object representation has been detailed, task-demand variables associated with the model are

---

Dimension: Logical arithmetic processes
Component dimension: Numerical processes
Task strand name: Addition

Task strand description
  Goal: Computation of the sum of numbers
  Object category: Numbers

Task models:
  Word Problems
  Verbal Problems
  Paper and Pencil Vertical Problems
  Addition with Objects

Justification for task models:
  These models are included because of their relationship to
  1. Educational experiences that children undergo in school
  2. More advanced numerical tasks (e.g., subtraction, multiplication)
  3. Instructional methods used in Head Start and elementary school settings
  4. Cultural diversity in how children represent addition problems

Estimated number of task strand items: 28

FIGURE 4. Task model specification form.

specified. Demand variables are established through assumptions about the processes believed to be used in performing tasks reflecting the model. Variables are listed and described briefly, and difficulty variations associated with them are indicated.

Task Specification

The next step in the item construction process is task specification. The tasks used in path-referenced tests are defined in terms of homogeneous item domains—domains that contains equivalent items (Macready & Merwin, 1973). Equivalence may be defined in different ways. In the present discussion, item equivalence implies that there are masters of the domain who tend to respond to all items correctly, nonmasters who tend to respond to none of the items correctly, and in some cases, individuals in transition between nonmastery and mastery who respond both correctly and incorrectly to the items in the domain. The steps taken in achieving task specification are based on the Hambleton and Eignor (1979) item domain specification procedures. Specification is implemented, using a form such as the one shown in Figure 5. The first step is to indicate the position of the task in the domain structure. Position is indicated by first labeling the path component and the subcomponent to which the task belongs. Then, the strand and model are indicated. After position has been specified, the task is

---

Dimension: Logical arithmetic processes
Component dimension: Numerical processes
Task strand: Addition
Task model: Verbal addition

Task
   The child is required to add 2 one-digit numbers to a sum less than or equal to 5

Description
   Stimulus materials: None (verbal presentation)
   Cultural considerations: not applicable

Directions
   Examiner says: "Now I want you to add some numbers. I'll ask you to add two numbers and you tell me the answer. How much is 2 and 3?"
      Cultural considerations: Directions for the task are administered in the language with which the child is most familiar (e.g., Spanish)
      Criterion response: The child says "5." To perform this task the child needs to
   1. Know the number chain through 5
   2. Be able to represent and combine 2 one-digit numbers with a sum less than or equal to 5

Alternative child representations
   Child may begin counting with the number 1 and add by couting all the numbers (i.e., *counting all*). Child may begin with one of the numbers given and add by counting from that point on (i.e., *counting on*). Child may use fingers, objects, etc., to help solve the problem (i.e., *concrete aids*). Child may use rote memory to solve problem (i.e., *number facts*)
      Cultural considerations: Alternative child representations provide a way for evaluating alternative paths and strategies toward competence in addition

Scoring criterion response:
   Correct response: Child says "5"

Scoring alternative representations:
   Child may be given credit for counting all, counting on, using concrete aids, or use of number facts even though his or her response is incorrect

Hypothesized appropriate age range: 3–5 years

FIGURE 5. Task sample form.

defined. Definition includes an operational description of the performance required. Task specification indicates the stimulus materials used, the directions provided, and the type of response required. It includes hypotheses about alternative ways children may represent the task and criteria for item scoring. Finally, task specification includes an example of an appropriate item.

The process of task specification provides the foundation for item writing. When items are written in accordance with task specifications, it is reasonable to assume that the items will fall within the class defined by the task. Similarly, the task will be linked to the appropriate model, and the model will be linked to the appropriate strand. Consequently, the items constructed for the test will, in all likelihood, adequately represent the structure from which they were developed.

PSYCHOMETRICS FOR PATH-REFERENCED TESTS

The development of path-referenced assessment instruments requires that fundamental questions involving item characteristics, reliability, and validity be addressed. Classical psychometric procedures are used to establish the psychometric properties of path-referenced instruments. However, recently developed latent variable techniques also play a major role in establishing the psychometric characteristics of path-referenced instruments.

Item Analysis

The first step in establishing the psychometric properties of a path-referenced test is to determine the characteristics of items proposed for use in the test. Both conventional procedures and latent trait techniques may be used profitably to conduct item analyses for path-referenced instruments. Item analyses may include the examination of item difficulties, discrimination indices, biserial or point-biserial correlations between each item and the total test, an analysis of item fit using latent trait techniques, and studies of item bias (e.g., Lord, 1980). Latent trait techniques used to determine item difficulty and fit deserve special comment. Latent trait techniques have the advantage of yielding estimates of difficulty that are independent of examinee ability. These estimates can be used to construct a linear scale of competence, making it possible to quantify path position and progress precisely. The analysis of fit for a given item deals with the question of whether or not responses to the item are consistent with the general pattern of responses observed for the test. Latent trait procedures assume that items in a given scale constitute a single latent variable or trait, which is congruent with the concept of developmental paths. Latent trait procedures provide a way to test the fit of individual items to a data set in a model which assumes all items reflect a single latent trait (Lord, 1980; Wright & Masters, 1982; Wright & Stone, 1979).

Performance Consistency

The utility of any measurement procedure depends on information about the consistency with which the variable being assessed is measured. The literature on criterion-referenced assessment and norm-referenced assessment yields two broad views regarding consistency related to measurement. The norm-referenced view focuses on consistency in individual variations in performance (Brennan, 1980). The criterion-referenced approach focuses on consistency related to domain mastery classification (Brennan, 1980; Hambleton & Novick, 1973; Subkoviak, 1980). Classical indices of reliability are used to assess consistency for norm-referenced tests. Decision consistency approaches (Subkoviak, 1980) and measures of dependability (Brennan, 1980) assessing consistency related to mastery classification have been suggested for use in criterion-referenced assessment. Both norm-referenced and criterion-referenced approaches to determining consistency are useful in path-referenced assessment. However, the fundamental path-referenced concern related to consistency involves the assignment of individuals and/or groups to path positions. It is of particular interest to know the extent to which an individual or the mean level of performance in a group would be assigned to the same position on a scale reflecting path position, if repeated measurements were made. It is also of interest to know the extent to which passing or failing particular items linked to path position implies passing or failing other items in the same class.

Latent trait techniques developed in connection with item response theory (Lord, 1980) play a major role determining performance consistency in path-referenced assessment (Hambleton, 1980a). Latent trait procedures can be used to establish confidence intervals for different ability levels reflecting variations in path position. These confidence intervals indicate a consistency in assignment to path position. A confidence interval associated with a particular ability level indicates the percent of testing occasions an individual's ability score would fall within the confidence band if repeated measurements were made. Consistency involving the probability of passing items in the same class is shown by item characteristic curves (Lord, 1980). The item characteristic curve for each item included in a test shows the relationship between variations in ability and the probability of a passing response for the examined item. Each item for which an item characteristic curve is established may be assumed to represent a subdomain of homogeneous items. For a particular path position and a particular item, a correct response probability indicates the proportion of items sampled from the subdomain that would be passed by an individual.

In some instances, it is useful to determine the dependability of decisions assigning individuals to mastery classifications associated with one or more cutoff scores in a path position scale. For example, progress along paths of development typically involves attainment of a series of developmental milestones. It may be useful to assess the dependability of decisions classifying individuals with respect to the attainment of these milestones. Criterion-referenced procedures can establish consistency in assignment to mastery states. Brennan's (1980) measures of dependability, based on generalizability theory (Cronbach, Glaser, Nanda & Rajaratnam, 1972), represent one useful approach to the problem of mastery state assignment. Brennan's measures focus on error variation defined in terms of the deviation of observed performance from one or more pre-established cut-off scores. One advantage to the Brennan technique is that it relates dependability in mastery classification to classical definitions of reliability and to notions about reliability in generalizability theory. For instance, Brennan (1980) has shown that coefficient alpha, which for dichotomous items is equivalent to the KR-20 reliability coefficient, is an upper bound to his dependability coefficient. A disadvantage of the Brennan approach is that his dependability measures do not have a direct, unambiguous meaning.

A number of decision consistency approaches have been suggested for use in mastery classification. These have been reviewed by Subkoviak (1980). Bergan (1983) has proposed a set of latent class models to be used in making mastery classification decisions. These procedures have a number of advantages. First, they yield a coefficient of agreement with a directly interpretable meaning. In particular, these models give the probability of agreement with respect to mastery classification. Second, these models allow the identification of sources of agreement and disagreement in classification. For example, agreement may be based almost exclusively on assignment to the mastery state, but not assignment to the nonmastery state. A disadvantage to the Bergan techniques is that they require multiple measurements. However, the problem of multiple measurements can be dealt with by splitting a test into parts, as in classical split-half reliability studies of internal consistency.

Classical reliability estimates may be of interest in path-referenced assessment for two reasons. First, as indicated above, classical measures of internal consistency (i.e., the KR-20 coefficient) provide an upper boundary for measures of dependability. Second, path-referenced assessment may include norm-referenced applications. For example, it may be of interest to compute percentile ranks for students at various age or grade levels and to link those ranks to path positions. This procedure would add more meaning to norm-referenced information. A knowledge of path position associated with percentile rank would make it possible to identify the kinds of skills that an individual attaining a specified rank would be likely to be able to perform.

Validity

Validity studies in path-referenced assessment include content, criterion-related, and construct validation. The literature on criterion-referenced assessment provides a starting point for the assessment of content validity in path-referenced assessment (see, for example, Hambleton, 1980; Hambleton & Eignor, 1979). This literature suggests that content validity be established through ratings assessing the extent to which items reflect the objectives they are intended to measure, through ratings of technical quality addressing such factors as item clarity, and through assessment of the extent to which the items reflect the domain to which they are assumed to belong (Hambleton, 1980). It may also be useful to assess the cultural content validity of path-referenced tests. A number of questions must be addressed in establishing cultural content validity. One is the extent to which item content is appropriate in light of the experiential background of the diverse groups with which the items are intended to be used. Special care must be taken to ensure that item difficulty is based on cognitive complexity rather than on content differences associated with cultural variations. A second question involves the extent to which item scoring allows for culturally diverse expressions of competence. A third is the extent to which items allow for linguistic diversity. A final consideration involves the extent to which the conditions of item administration take cultural diversity into account. For instance, some forms of questioning that are quite acceptable in one culture may be considered rude in another (Henderson & Bergan, 1976).

Criterion-related validity studies may include the full range of validity questions addressed in classical measurement theory. For instance, it may be of interest to know the extent to which path-referenced test scores correlate with teacher grades or with performances on norm-referenced tests.

Path-referenced measures differ from other forms of assessment in the requirements they impose with respect to construct validity. The domain structure analyses carried out in path-referenced assessment constitute a set of hypotheses to be tested. The empirical examination of these hypotheses comprises the construct validation of path-referenced instruments. Two fundamental questions must be addressed in construct validation. The first involves the validation of path structure. Path structure validation begins with an examination of relations among items assumed to reflect a single latent variable. There is no entirely satisfactory procedure for testing the hypothesis that a set of items can be conceptualized in terms of a single latent trait. A number of procedures have been suggested (e.g., Lord, 1980; Hambleton & Rovinelli, 1983). Factor-analytical procedures are among the most promising, often used techniques for assessing the uni-dimensionality of a set of items. The fundamental problem with the factor-analytical approach is that these procedures generally are designed to analyze continuous variables. Test items are categorical, often dichotomous. The use of tetrachoric correlations has been suggested for handling the problem of dealing with categorical variables under certain conditions (Lord, 1980). Christoffersson (1975) and Muthen (1978) have also developed a procedure that can be used with categorical item data, providing that one is willing to assume that each of the items reflects a continuum of competency. The Christoffersson and Muthen procedure has not been widely used, and its applicability in solving the problem of assessing unidimensionality is not known.

The second step in path structure analysis is to validate hypothesized relations among paths, components, and subcomponents in a structure. Confirmatory factor analysis procedures can be used here (Bentler, 1980; Jöreskog & Sorbom, 1979). These procedures have the advantage of making it possible to test specific hypotheses about the relationships among factors underlying intercorrelations among the measures being factor analyzed.

The second major construct validation question to be addressed in path-referenced assessment involves the validation of developmental struc-ture. This is initiated by examining the congruence between hypothesized ordering of items by difficulty with the ordering by difficulty revealed through the latent trait procedures. Latent trait procedures provide estimates of item difficulty that are independent of examinee ability. These estimates can be used to order items by difficulty. The Spearman rank order correlation can then be used to determine the relationship between the hypothesized and the observed ordering.

Validation of developmental structure is designed to include hypothe-ses about qualitative changes in competency, which can be tested using latent-class models (Bergan, 1980, 1983; Dayton & Macready, 1976). Latent-class models provide two criteria for determining qualitative changes in developmental level (Bergan, 1983). One is the prerequisiteness criterion (Gagné, 1962, 1977), that given suitable allowances for inconsistent responding on the part of examinees, no examinee should display mastery of a superordinate task in the absence of mastery of a prerequisitely related subordinate task. The second criterion is that when two task are ordered in a prerequisite fashion, there should be a class of individuals who display consistent mastery of the subordinate task in the absence of skill mastery with respect to the superordinate task. The second criterion is required because the prerequisiteness criterion does not distinguish between tasks that are equivalent and tasks that are ordered (Bergan, 1983). For example, if two tasks are identical, it would be expected that no one would pass one and fail the other.

Validation of hypotheses regarding qualitative developmental change affords a basis for defining hierarchically ordered subdomains for a developmental path. Items within a subdomain may vary in difficulty. However, items in different, hierarchically related subdomains not only vary in difficulty, they also should meet the criteria established for prerequisite ordering. This does not imply that hierarchical subdomains are always completely separate; some overlap may occur. For example, items at the highest level in a subordinate subdomain may not be prerequisitively ordered with respect to items at the lowest levels in the related superordinate domain.

Assessing Bias in Path-Referenced Instruments

Path-referenced assessment instruments may be subject to all types of bias that occur with other assessment techniques (see Berk 1982; Kratochwill, Alper, & Cancelli, 1980; Reynolds, 1982, for comprehensive discussions of test bias issues). However, certain types of bias are of special concern in path-referenced assessment instruments. These have to do, in the main with issues related to the construct validity of path-referenced tests. One potential source of bias in path-referenced assessment involves construct validity related to path structure. The fundamental assumption related to path structure is that the items comprising a development path reflect a single underlying trait or ability. Bias exists in a path-referenced assessment instrument to the extent that the assumption of unidimensionality does not hold across groups. Assumptions about path structure will also generally include hypotheses about relationships among paths and/or among components within paths. Bias is present to the extent that these assumptions do not hold across groups. Failure to validate assumptions about path structure across groups reflects bias because such failure may result in unfair test use. For example, consider the situation in which a path-referenced test is being used to individualize instruction for students from different ethnic groups. Suppose that the test treats certain

Hispanic groups. Under these circumstances, individualization plans based on test results could lead to instruction that would not effectively meet the needs of minority group students.

Construct validity issues related to developmental structure constitute an additional class of problems associated with test bias in path-referenced assessment devices. The fundamental assumption underlying the concept of developmental structure is that skill acquisition is developmentally sequenced. Unanticipated sequence variations associated with group composition significes test bias in path-referenced assessment. For instance, if black students acquired a series of mathematical skills in a different order than white students, and if the test used to assess mathematical competence assumed an order congruent with the observed developmental progression for whites, the test would be biased against black students. It is important to note that culturally related sequence variations can occur. As indicated earlier, developmental sequences may be affected by the manner in which the tasks in the sequence are represented in the cognitive structure of the individual. Cultural variations in task representation can occur. Such variations could lead to culturally related differences in the order of skill acquisition.

Construct validation hypotheses related to developmental structure may include assumptions about qualitative developmental progressions involving prerequisite ordering between tasks. Group-related variations in prerequisite ordering constitute a potential source of bias associated with path-referenced instruments. For instance, if two skills are prequisitively ordered for one group and not for another, multiple developmental progressions are indicated for the nonprerequisite group.

A final source of bias related to construct validity associated with developmental structure involves item bias. The concept of developmental structure assumes variations in item difficulty. The latent trait procedures used to establish item difficulties for path-referenced tests assume that those difficulties are independent of the ability levels of the examineees (Lord, 1980). Given this assumption, it is reasonable to expect that the probability of passing an item should be the same for individuals of the same ability from different ethnic groups (Lord, 1980; Shepard, 1982). To the extent that this is not the case, the item may be regarded as being biased. A variety of procedures have been developed for assessing item bias. These have been detailed in the literature (e.g., Berk, 1982; Lord, 1980; Osterlind, 1983; Hambleton, Martois, & Williams, 1983). Empirical analyses of item bias may lead to the discovery of items that do not function in the same way for different social or ethnic groups and also may stimulate the formation of hypotheses regarding the sources of group-related item differences. Such hypotheses can result in useful item revisions.

Norms for Path-Referenced Tests

It may be useful to establish norms for path-referenced instruments using established norm-referenced technology (e.g., Cochran, 1977; Thorndike, 1982). As indicated, it may then be useful to combine norm-referenced information with information about path position. Linkage levels may be linked to information about path position. Linkage of this kind provides a way to indicate the kinds of skills that students representing different relative standings in a norm group can perform. For example, it may be determined that a 4-year-old child scoring at the 84th percentile in his or her age group on a path-referenced mathematics tests is likely to possess certain basic number recognition skills, certain counting skills, and certain basic addition skills. Information of this type leads to a set of concrete referents linking group standing to skill level.

In addition to traditional status norms, it may be beneficial to establish progress norms for path-referenced tests. Progress norms indicate the relative standing of individuals in a suitable reference group with respect to gains in achievement occurring over a given time span. For example, progress norms might reveal that a Head Start program increased language development, placing the average student at the 84th percentile with respect to gains in language skill occurring over the instructional year. The development of progress norms requires valid information on growth trajectories that reflect changes in achievement occurring as a function of time. Recent advances in statistical technology have facilitated estimates of growth trajectories (Rogosa *et al.*, 1982). For example, Strenio, Weisberg, and Bryk (1983) have developed an empirical Bayes estimation procedure that can be used to construct growth curves in a way that takes advantage of information on individual background characteristics to improve growth parameter estimates.

APPLICATIONS OF PATH-REFERENCED ASSESSMENT

The final section of this chapter details the type of information afforded by path-referenced assessment, as well as how this information may be used by the instructional manager. An example employing latent trait and latent class analyses is given. These two procedures illustrate the critical features to path-referenced assessment, namely, the continuous scale as well as the developmental structure underlying path-referenced assessment instruments.

A PSYCHOMETRIC EXAMPLE

The psychometric example presented below describes latent trait and latent class analyses for one of six cognitive achievement measures being developed for use in the Head Start program. The measures have already gone through a developmental and a piloting phase. A relatively large field testing of the measures is currently in progress, the result of which will be final measures packages to be used in the management of the Head Start Program. The data to be described are from an item tryout of a mathematics measure conducted in Tucson, Arizona on children ranging in age from 5 to $6\frac{1}{2}$. However, to illustrate simply the analysis activities associated with developing path-referenced assessment instruments, only a few tasks from the math measure are used in the discussion. These tasks are briefly described in Table 1.

The tasks in Table 1 illustrate variations in skill difficulty based on

TABLE 1. Table of Task Descriptions for Selected Tasks

Name	Task example	
Counting 5	Child asked to count out loud from 1 to 10	
Counting 6	Child asked to count out loud from 1 to 20	
Counting 7	Child asked to start with 3 and count to 10	
Addition 8	Child is asked "How much is 5 plus 3?"	
Addition 9	Child is asked to do the problem	3 +1
Addition 10	Child is asked to do the problem	4 +3
Addition 12	Child is asked "Let's say you have three marbles and your friend has five. How many do you both have altogether?" Child is given blocks to help solve the problem	
Subtraction 5	Child is asked "How much is 7 take away 4?"	
Subtraction 6	Child is asked to do the problem	5 −2
Subtraction 7	Child is asked to do the problem	8 −5
Subtraction 10	Child is asked, "Let's say you have three marbles and your friend gives you some more. Now you have eight marbles. How many marbles did your friend give you?" Child is given blocks to help solve the task	

variations in task demands and task models. The counting 5 and counting 6 tasks provide an example in which task demand alterations affect performance. For these tasks, the demand variation is in the amount of knowledge of the number chain that is required. The counting 5 and counting 7 tasks illustrate the phenomenon of rule replacement discussed earlier. The task demand for this pair requires the replacement of a simple rule, expressing the idea that counting should start with the number one, by a more general rule that involves the idea that counting may start with any positive number. Thus, it might be hypothesized that the counting 5 task would be subordinate to both the counting 6 and counting 7 tasks. It is difficult to compare the variations associated with the counting 6 and counting 7 tasks, since two different demands are varied simultaneously.

The issue of varying task models is illustrated for the addition 8, addition 10, and addition 12, as well as for the subtraction 5, subtraction 7, and subtraction 10 tasks. In these task comparisons, the task models include a verbal presentation, a written presentation, and a word problem presentation. Because the written paper-and-pencil task involves identifying the necessary computation operation, as well as recognizing written numerals, it may be hypothesized that verbal and written tasks may be ordered by difficulty. However, since no change in the processes used to solve the tasks is evident, these tasks were not assumed to be prerequisitely related. In addition, it has been suggested that word problem tasks expressing active verbs in a story context should be easier than verbal problems not linked to a story (Carpenter, Moser, & Romberg, 1982). However, the data did not support this contention.

The task pairs, to this point, involve comparisons within task strands. However, difficulty differences may also occur between strands. Cross strand difficulty variations are illustrated in the counting and addition tasks. Strand comparisons produce variations in the processes involved in task performance, and it is these changes that are responsible for the variations in difficulty. The goal of counting tasks is to recite the number chain, whereas the goal of addition tasks is to compute a sum. Each of these goals has a set of integrated processes that are goal directed; hence, the set of processes associated with the counting tasks differ from those associated with the addition tasks. However, there are some processes that are common to both the counting and addition tasks. In fact, counting strategies have been shown to be used by individuals in solving addition problems (Fuson, 1982). Consequently, it would be expected that the counting tasks would be subordinate to the addition tasks.

Table 2 illustrates item analysis techniques for the tasks described above. The item analysis procedures include the application of latent trait techniques, which are fundamental to path-referenced task development.

TABLE 2. Item Statistics for Selected Tasks

Item name	Proportion correct	Item difficulty	Standard error	Discrimination index	Point-biserial r
Counting 5	.74	−2.25	.20	1.52	.57
Counting 6	.52	−.97	.18	1.63	.69
Counting 7	.56	−1.19	.18	1.78	.72
Addition 8	.24	.66	.21	1.31	.62
Addition 9	.20	.93	.22	1.57	.69
Addition 10	.20	.98	.22	1.45	.64
Addition 12	.20	.98	.22	1.40	.63
Subtraction 5	.11	1.81	.27	.85	.27
Subtraction 6	.09	2.13	.30	1.06	.37
Subtraction 7	.03	3.33	.47	1.26	.33
Subtraction 10	.07	2.32	.32	.95	.28

The Rasch model, which expresses the probability of a correct response in terms of a one item parameter (difficulty), was used in the analysis of the item tryout data. More complex latent trait models that take into account discrimination and/or guessing are being examined in the final field test phase of the measures development effort. The more complex latent trait models required larger samples than were available during the item tryout (Lord, 1980). The statistics for the selected tasks in Table 2 include the proportion correct, the latent trait model item difficulty estimate, its standard error, the discrimination index for an item, and the point-biserial correlation for each task.

The proportion correct index in Table 2 is a classical item difficulty estimate that provides a highly direct, familiar interpretation of test score data. It corresponds to the ratio of the number of individuals correctly answering an item to the total number of individuals attempting an item. From Table 2, it can be observed that few children passed the subtraction tasks, whereas a high percentage of children passed the counting 5 task.

One problem associated with the proportion correct index is that it depends on the sample and its ability level distribution. The latent trait model item difficulty estimate is useful because it overcomes this weakness. The latent trait approach constructs estimates that are assumed, for different samples taking the same test, to yield the same item difficulties except for a translation constant. The mean and variance of the difficulty estimates can be set to any desired value. The present difficulty estimates are centered at zero, a point reflecting average difficulty, and vary generally from −4.00, indicating very easy items, to 4.00, indicating very difficult items. For the tasks in Table 2, a wide range of estimates can be observed. As might be expected, the counting tasks were the easiest and the subtraction tasks the most difficult.

Upon examining the standard errors, we found a relatively high degree of precision associated with the assessment of the difficulty for the counting and addition skills. However, a lack of precision is observed for the subtraction tasks. This, however, is a function of estimating the parameter in the face of very little performance variability. For the subtraction tasks, very few children correctly solved any one problem. Although it appears that items that are too easy or too difficulty may contribute little to determining path position, a large sample would have yielded more variable performances and, thus, improved the estimates.

The discrimination index describes the slope of the relationship between an individual's ability and the probability of getting an item correct. From Table 2, it appears that some of the indices approximate a value of 1.00, which is expected under the one parameter latent trait model. When the index is greater than one, slight changes in ability produce proportionally greater changes than expected in the probability of getting an item correct. In other words, discrimination indices greater than one indicate that an item discriminates between low and high ability groups better than anticipated. The converse is true for discrimination indices less than one. The variability in the discrimination indices suggests that a two-parameter latent trait model, including both a difficulty and a discrimination parameter, may prove a better fit to the data than a one-parameter model.

The final statistic in Table 2 is the point-biserial correlation for each item. The point-biserial indicates how well any one item contributes to the total test. For the counting and addition tasks, the point-biserial correlations are relatively high. However, the point-biserial correlation for the subtraction tasks illustrate one disadvantage to its use. For items that have extreme difficulty level estimates, the point-biserials tend to be smaller than for items of moderate difficulty. The easy counting task and all the subtraction tasks show that point-biserial correlations are affected by task difficulty. Various latent trait techniques have been proposed to assess the relation of an item to the total test that overcome this shortcoming (Hambleton, 1983; Wright & Stone, 1979).

To discover developmental relationships associated with tasks, latent class models were used to assess equivalence and ordered relations among the various tasks. As it will be recalled, latent class models can be used to arrive at expected frequencies under the assumption that a model is true. These expected frequencies can then be compared with observed frequencies to test a model against the data. An equivalence relation (H_1) purports only individuals who tend to pass all items or tend to fail all items. A case in which there are individuals who tend to pass one task and fail the other is not considered. A homogeneous relation (H_2) among tasks might exist if there is a class of individuals who tend to pass task A and tend to fail task B. At the same time, there is a class of individuals who tend to pass task B and tend to fail task A. As can be seen, a homogeneous relation purports tasks that are of similar difficulty, and for which there is no clear trend as to which task might be learned first. Such a situation is certainly not as restrictive as the assumptions underlying equivalence relations.

Latent class models can also be used to assess two types of ordered relations among tasks: simple ordered relations (H_3) and prerequisitely ordered relations (H_4). Ordered relations involve tasks that vary in difficulty. For example, consider two tasks, A and B, with B the more difficult task. In addition to the mastery and non-mastery classes of an equivalence model, an ordered relation model purports the existence of a class of individuals who tend to pass A, but fail B. In addition, there is a class who tend to pass B, but fail A; however, the size of this class differs significantly from the size of the former class. In prerequisite relations, however, there is only one class, assuming the existence of a number of individuals who tend to pass A but fail B. Such a situation describes a relation in which task A is subordinate to task B. This state of affairs has often been interpreted as meaning that skill A must be learned before skill B can be learned. However, Bergan and Stone, (1981) have shown that it is possible to target instruction ahead of the learner's current ability. For some individuals who do not possess two prerequisitely related skills (A and B), teaching only task B can result in the learning of both skills. A complete description of the latent class models is given in Bergan, Stone, and Feld (in press).

Table 3 describes the latent class analyses for several comparisons among the selected tasks. These results can be used in conjunction with information from Table 2 to illustrate the continuous scale and developmental structure underlying tasks. Table 4 portrays this information for the selected tasks. The numbers along the left edge of the table represent the item difficulty parameters estimated under the Rasch model. The double lines indicate boundaries reflecting subordinate/superordinate relations or developmental milestones among tasks. For example, counting 5 is prerequisitely related to counting 6 and counting 7.

The scaling of items and learning sequences that Table 4 depicts can be used in a number of ways. For example, empirically validated learning sequences can be compared with existing curriculum. It seems reasonable to expect some congruence between a school's curriculum and how children develop competencies. Furthermore, developmental milestones can be identified within the analysis of learning sequences. These milestones

TABLE 3. Latent Class Analyses

Comparison	Preferred model	L^2	df	p	Conclusion
Counting 5—Counting 6	H4	8.18	7	<.50	Prerequisitely ordered
Counting 6—Counting 7	H2	5.84	6	<.50	Homogeneous
Addition 8—Addition 9	H2	6.96	6	<.50	Homogeneous
Addition 8—Addition 12	H2	3.54	6	<.50	Homogeneous
Addition 10—Addition 11	H2	5.60	6	<.50	Homogeneous
Subtraction 7—Subtraction 10	H4	8.74	7	<.50	Prerequisitely ordered
Counting 7—Addition 8	H4	10.03	7	<.50	Prerequisitely ordered
Counting 7—Addition 10	H4	9.48	7	<.50	Prerequisitely ordered
Addition 9—Subtraction 6	H4	6.75	7	<.50	Prerequisitely ordered
Addition 8—Subtraction 6	H4	12.15	7	<.50	Prerequisitely ordered
Addition 10—Subraction 7	H4	6.07	7	<.50	Prerequisitely ordered
Addition 12—Subtraction 10	H4	7.56	7	<.50	Prerequisitely ordered

TABLE 4. Latent Trait Scale and Developmental Structure for the Selected Tasks

3.5	
3.4	
3.3	Subtraction 7
3.2	
3.1	
3.0	
2.9	
2.8	
2.7	
2.6	
2.5	
2.4	
2.3	Subtraction 10
2.2	
2.1	Subtraction 6
2.0	
1.9	

TABLE 4. (*continued*)

1.8	Subtraction 5
1.7	
1.6	
1.5	════════════
1.4	
1.3	
1.2	
1.1	
1.0	Addition 10/12
.9	Addition 9
.8	
.7	
.6	Addition 8
.5	
.4	
.3	
.2	
.1	
.0	
−.1	
−.2	
−.3	════════════
−.4	
−.5	
−.6	
−.7	
−.8	
−.9	
−1.0	Counting 6
−1.1	
−1.2	Counting 7
−1.3	
−1.4	
−1.5	════════════
−1.6	
−1.7	
−1.8	
−1.9	
−2.0	
−2.1	
−2.2	Counting 5
−2.3	
−2.4	

TABLE 5. Table Relating Ability to
Skills

		b	$\theta_{pi}^* = .75^a$
Counting	5	−2.25	−1.15
	6	−.97	.13
	7	−1.19	−.09
Addition	8	.66	1.76
	9	.93	2.03
	10	.98	2.08
	12	.98	2.08
Subtraction	5	1.81	2.91
	6	2.13	3.23
	7	3.33	4.43
	10	2.32	3.42

[a] $\theta_{pi}^* = .75$ refers to what ability level is required for an individual to get 75% of the items representing the particular skill correct.

indicate that if an individual does not possess subordinate competencies, superordinate competencies are also not possessed. In conjunction with this, if an individual possesses superordinate competencies, then subordinate competencies are possessed as well.

The linking of an individual's ability level or path position to competencies possessed by the individual is a critical feature to path-referenced assessment. This is accomplished by relating the probability of passing an item, given its difficulty level, to an ability level. Table 5 illustrates this application for the items used throughout the example. For example, if a child's logit ability was discovered to be 2.08, then the odds are 3 to 1 that the child can correctly solve all the counting *and* addition tasks. Naturally, the odds would be greater with respect to the counting tasks only.

PATH-REFERENCED APPROACH TO THE MANAGEMENT OF INDIVIDUAL
DIFFERENCES

The management of individual differences may be thought of as a problem-solving process in which educators make decisions to guide instruction based on information about student's capabilities. In this sense, teaching may be considered to be an instructional management function in which the teacher is constantly engaged in decision-making processes at the classroom level (Berliner, 1983). The principal function of assessment in the decision-making process has been that of gathering information on student performance for the purposes of instructional management. Assessment provides the foundation for a broad range of management decisions at the classroom level of education programs. In particular, the application of path-referenced assessment to the management of individual differences provides information that can be used in a variety of management activities. These activities include decisions associated with the diagnosis of learner needs, decisions about individualizing classroom instruction, decisions related to educational placement in special programs, and the evaluation of individual progress.

Diagnosing Learner Needs

Path-referenced technology provides a perspective that links educational decisions to diagnostic information about the organization and patterning of change in student knowledge. In the path-referenced approach, diagnostic information gathered on current student status is tied both to possible future achievement and to past accomplishment, in order to facilitate the assessment of change. This dynamic view relates educational decision-making to the fundamental goal of enhancing student progress. Path-referenced assessment focuses on changes in capability over various time periods. As pointed out earlier, change is viewed as reflecting both continuous progress along paths of development and qualitative leaps representing the successive achievement of increasingly advanced levels of competence. The measurement of each of these types of change provides valuable diagnostic information to the instructional manager about individual differences. The first type of diagnostic information concerns what the student has accomplished at various points in the instructional process. For example, path-referenced test items, like criterion-referenced test items, are designed to be linked directly to the mastery of instructional objectives. The results of a path-referenced assessment communicate to the instructional manager those objectives that have been mastered by the student and those objectives that have not been mastered. Linking assessment to the mastery of objectives relates measurement directly to individual instruction. What is assessed is based on what is supposed to be taught the student. Moreover, what has been accomplished by the student is communicated in an unambiguous way to the instructional manager, thus facilitating instructional planning decisions for the student.

The second type of diagnostic information provided in path-referenced assessment is the path position of the student. The determination of current status in terms of path position implies the mastery of specific subordinate competencies in the past and charts the direction of learning that may occur in the future. The instructional decision-maker who knows what has been learned in the past and the direction learning may take in the future can use that information to determine individual learning needs. Both qualitative and quantitative information about path position are obtained with the path-referenced approach. Qualitative information on path position provides information about the achievement of milestones in the learning process. This information allows the manager to identify major categories of competency that have been mastered by the student or that may be targeted for future instruction. Quantitative information on path position makes it possible to quantify the amount of change that has taken place as the result of instruction. Information of this kind provides an unambiguous quantitative index that can be used to assess the effects of instructional programs on individual students.

The third type of diagnostic information provided in path-referenced assessment has to do with the distinction between deepening understanding of a concept and the hierarchical sequencing of different concepts. Siegler (1982) has pointed out that in determining changes in knowledge structures it may be useful to distinguish between hierarchically ordered sets of tasks applicable to the same general concept and ordered sequences reflecting different concepts. A focus on tasks related to the same concept reveals the sequential development of increasingly refined rules that allows the student to deepen his or her understanding of the concept being assessed (Siegler, 1982). For example, Bergan et al. (1984) designed a series of tasks to assess student knowledge of counting. The series included counting forward from one, counting on from a number greater than one, counting backwards, and counting by multiples. These tasks were shown to be hierarchically ordered and to reflect the acquisition of a series of increasingly general rules broadening the range of counting tasks that could be performed. The most restrictive rule required that counting always begin with the number one and proceed forward in increments of one. The most advanced rule allowed counting to start from a number greater than one, to proceed either forwards or backwards, and to include increments greater than one. The sequential acquisition of counting skills is not only important in its own right, but it is also useful in linking the development of counting to the mastery of other mathematical operations. For example, a number of studies (Fuson, 1982) have shown that counting on from a number greater than one aids in the development of addition skills. Consequently, taking account of the distinction between within-concept and between-concept sequences during the diagnostic process gives the teacher a clearer picture of the instructional needs of individual students.

Individualizing Classroom Instruction

Path-referenced assessment technology can be employed to guide the individualization of instruction. Information on the mastery of curriculum objectives linked to qualitative and quantitative information on individual differences in path position provides an empirical basis for individualizing classroom instruction. The instructional manager is not only given a detailed account of what the student knows, but also is apprised of the implications of that knowledge for both past and future learning. Information of this kind affords the basis for placing the student at the appropriate position in an instructional sequence, for designing instruction related to the rules that the student is using to perform academic tasks (Siegler, 1982), and for monitoring progress through the learning sequence.

As part of a measures development contract with the Administration for Children, Youth, and Families (ACYF) in the Department of Health and Human Services, the University of Arizona has constructed path-referenced measures of cognitive competencies for program management in Head Start. These measures reference an individual's performance to specific positions along empirically validated paths of development. In addition, Developmental Pathways Planning and Assessment Guides that relate directly to these measures have been constructed. The guides provide a way to link content reflecting specific instructional objectives to content representing broad educational goals. Three kinds of information are recorded in a Pathway to Development Guide: what is planned for instruction, what has been taught, and what has been learned. These categories of information provide the basis for instructional planning that is responsive to the learning needs of individual students. Planning information is provided for the individual student in the classroom and for each skill that is planned for instruction. Implementation of the Guide requires that the individual instructional plan indicate not only that a given skill has been selected for instruction, but also when instruction in that skill is likely to be provided to the student. Specification of teaching activity includes instruction that has been offered earlier in the school year and instruction that is currently being provided. Information on the individual student's mastery of instructional content is intended to reflect the student's mastery of skills in the classroom setting. Information on content mastery affords a basis for linking individualized planning decisions to the student's current level of skill. In addition, mastery information serves to check the validity of information obtained from formal testing programs that are used to help guide the planning of individualized instruction. The teacher using path-referenced strategies, including the implementation of the Pathways to Development Guides, is encouraged to take individual differences into account throughout the school year.

Placement in Special Programs

Students are generally placed in special programs through norm-referenced assessment. However, path-referenced assessment may also provide useful information for placement decisions. The general goal of special placement is to provide a program that is appropriate to the learning needs of the individual student. Path-referenced assessment affords relevant information for this purpose.

Path-referenced assessment information on the hierarchical ordering of academic skills affords information on the position of each student in learning sequences that have been targeted for instruction. In addition, data obtained through the Pathways to Development Guides provide the teacher with ongoing information about the skill levels of individual students. If instruction is well in advance of the level at which the student is functioning, or if it is well below the student's current level, plans may be made to make appropriate adjustments in instructional content or to place the student in a special program such that the level of skills targeted for instruction are congruent with the student's capabilities.

The path-referenced approach to placement decisions involves matching information on path position and progress to information on the learning opportunities available in specific instructional programs. A decision to place a student in a special program would imply that instruction congruent with the student's path position could be better provided in the special program than in other available programs. Moreover, information on a student's path position can be linked to instructional content specified in Developmental Pathways Guides. Such linkage makes it possible to determine the match between what is being taught in a particular placement and what the student knows. For example, suppose that a student were functioning in mathematics at a path position well below the other students in the class and that instruction available in a special education placement was congruent with the student's current level of functioning. Information of this kind would be extremely useful in making a placement decision.

Evaluation of Individual Progress

Evaluation at the classroom level affords the possibility of focusing on the accomplishments of the individual student. Nevertheless, it is important to remember that teachers may not always use information about the individual student in instruction. For example, when teachers group students for instruction, they tend to aim the level of instruction at the level of the group rather than at the level of the individual student. Path-referenced assessment is designed to focus attention on the individual student. This focus is achieved by providing the teacher with data on the individual student's path positions within various learning sequences periodically. Evaluation of an individual student provides the teacher with information on whether or not the goals of instruction have been achieved for that student. This information is obtained by establishing the congruence between competencies specified in objectives and current level of performance.

The evaluation of individual progress is generally concerned with determining changes in competence that can be attributed to instruction. Path-referenced assessment is designed to produce information about change that cannot be obtained in other ways. For example, indices of change provided in path-referenced assessment avoid the well-known problems asssociated with grade equivalent scores and other norm-referenced indices used to reflect change. See Angoff (1971), Horst (1976), and Linn (1981) for discussions of the difficulties associated with norm-referenced measures of change. The scales of continuous progress generated through path-referenced assessment are not linked to the relative position of a student in a norm group, as is the case with norm-referenced measures. Consequently, progress measured in terms of path-referenced scales can be interpreted unequivocally for all students, regardless of their relative standing in a norm group. Similarly, both quantitative and qualitative indices of path position provide an unambiguous link to the mastery of specific skills. Thus, if two students have the same path position score, it can be assumed that for that particular path they possess the same skills. More generally, knowledge of any particular path position score can be taken to indicate the kinds of skills possessed by the student.

Another type of information on individual progress afforded through path-referenced assessment is that on expected change. Path-referenced assessment can be used to generate progress norms (Bryk, 1983) indicating the amount of change expected for a given learner or a group of learners over a specific time span. Information from progress norms allows the instructional manager to determine the extent to which change is occurring for the individual within expected limits. Such information can be useful in establishing priorities and allocating resources for instruction. Moreover, information on expected gains can be used to determine the type of program that should be provided for the student, in the future.

FUTURE DIRECTIONS FOR PATH-REFERENCED ASSESSMENT

Path-referenced technology provides a new approach to the assessment of individual differences. Thus, it is of interest to speculate on the factors that might influence its evolution. Developers of school curriculum and assessment instruments have long recognized the need for sequencing sets of learning tasks into hierarchies. In the past, attempts at sequencing have been informal and accomplished largely through the implementation of task analysis procedures (Bergan, 1981a). Attempts made to validate these sequences empirically were thwarted because adequate technology to carry out such validation was not available. The technology afforded by the emergence of new mathematical models applicable to the assessment of individual educational progress has made the empirical validation of learning sequences possible. Moreover, advances in cognitive psychology, coupled with the need in schools to raise the quality of assessment procedures, has generated a requirement for change in the test construction process. Recognized need coupled with available technology suggests that conditions may be favorable for the development of path-referenced instruments. Although both need and technology are present, the construction of path-referenced instruments may be limited by special requirements associated with test development.

In the past, the conventional procedure for constructing assessment instruments has been for a group of curriculum content experts to define a content domain and then write assessment items under the direction of psychometricians. The character of the final test was determined largely by psychometric analyses conducted without content experts. Content validity was established before item analysis (Nunnally, 1978) and psychometric analyses were then used to determine the items included in the final instrument. Path-referenced assessment technology requires a new approach to the test construction process. The development of path-referenced instruments will be affected by the feasibility of and incentives for pursuing a new technology for test construction. The path-referenced approach to the assessment of individual differences differs from conventional approaches in that it is intended to determine developmental progress attributed to instruction. The requirement of determining developmental progress calls for theory-driven measures reflecting a developmental perspective. The construction of theory-driven measures calls for the combined efforts of people with special experience in cognitive developmental theory and curriculum areas and experts in the application of newly developed latent variable techniques used in measures validation. As implies here, the widespread development and utilization of path-referenced instruments requires a special technology for item construction. Items must be selected in such a way that coordinates item development with theoretical considerations, including the consideration of both path structure and developmental structure. Implementation of the path-referenced approach allows content specialists to generate hypotheses, from the theoretical perspectives they have developed, in ways that can be linked to formal instructions to data analysis specialists implementing statistical procedures used in measures validation. This approach makes it possible for content experts to control hypothesis testing related to these theoretical perspectives and also allows them to guide the refinement of measures through item revision. Given that path-referenced technology is utilized to some degree in assessment, it could influence future conceptions of individual differences. From a norm-referenced perspective, individual differences are based on assignment to group position. Group assignment provides information on where one stands, but not on how one got there or what one can do to change one's status. Path-referenced assessment would foster a perspective that would allow individuals to determine their current status against a standard reflecting the possibility of change or growth. In a society that is increasing its intellectual demands on its citizenry, the capability to conceptualize competence in a manner that fosters a view emphasizing change should be advantageous.

Finally, a path-referenced view suggests a number of research questions related directly to individual differences. One important set of research questions involving individual differences has to do with tailored testing. Tailored testing individualizes test administration to produce rapid and accurate estimates of individual ability. A path-referenced approach suggests the need for tailored testing research on accurate and rapid estimation of path position. As discussed earlier, the identification of path position is important for the purpose of individualizing instruction. Path position shows where an individual is in the development of specific competencies. Therefore, this construct can be used to describe the skill level of an individual. At the same time, it indicates the preferred level of instruction for a particular individual. There is also a need for research focusing on the identification of developmental paths and variations in path positions. Possible variations in the developmental paths of different individuals are of particular interest. For example, cultural background may be an important issue when the path individuals take in developing skills within an area we described. Variations in developmental paths may have implications for the design and/or sequencing of instruction. Just as people may take different routes from A to B, so many people learn skills in different sequences as they develop cognitive skills.

REFERENCES

Angoff, W. H. Scales, norms and equivalent scores. In R. L. Thorndike (Ed.), *Educational measurement* (2nd ed.). Washington, D.C.: American Council on Education, 1971, pp. 508–600.

Ausubel, D. P., & Sullivan, E. V. *Theory and problems of child development*. New York: Grune & Stratton, 1970.

Bentler, P. M. Multivariate analysis with latent variables. In M. R. Rozenweig & L. W. Porter (Eds.), *Annual Review of Psychology*, Vol. 31, Palo Alto, Calif.: Annual Review, 1980.

Bentler, P. M., & Weeks, D. B. Multivariate analysis with latent variables. In P. R. Krishnaiah & L. Kanal (Eds.), *Handbook of statistics*, Vol. 2. Amsterdam: North Holland, 1980.

Bergan, J. R. The structural analysis of behavior: An alternative to the learning hierarchy model. *Review of Educational Research*, 1980, *50*, 225–246.

Bergan, J. R. Path-referenced assessment in school psychology. In T. R. Kratochwill (Ed.), *Advances in school psychology* (Vol. 1). Hillsdale, N.J.: Lawrence Erlbaum Associates, 1981a.

Bergan, J. R. *Measuring cognitive growth in Head Start Programs* (Contract No. HHS-105-81-C-008). Paper presented at the annual symposium of the Society for Research and Child Development, Boston, Massachusetts, 1981b.

Bergan, J. R. *A domain structure model for measuring cognitive development* (Technical Report, Contract No. HHS-105-81-C-008). Tucson: University of Arizona, Center for Educational Evaluation and Measurement, 1981c.

Bergan, J. R. Latent-class models in educational research. In E. W. Gordon (Ed.), *Review of Research in education* (Vol. 10). Washington, D.C.: American Educational Research Association, 1983, pp. 305–360.

Bergan, J. R., & Henderson, R. W. *Child development*. Columbus, Oh.: Charles E. Merrill, 1979.

Bergan, J. R., & Stone, C. A. *Psychometric and instructional validation of domain structures*. Unpublished manuscript, Tucson: University of Arizona, 1981.

Bergan, J. R., Stone, C. A., & Feld, J. K. Rule replacement in the development of basic number skills. *Journal of Eucational Psychology*, 1984, *76*, 289–299.

Bergan, J. R., Towstopiat, O. M., Cancelli, A. A., & Karp, C. L. Replacement and component rules in hierarchically ordered mathematics rule learning tasks. *Journal of Educational Psychology*, 1982, *74*, 39–50.

Berk, R. A. *Handbook of methods for detecting test bias*. Baltimore, Md.: Johns Hopkins University Press, 1982.

Berliner, D. C. Developing conceptions of classroom environments: Some light on the T in the classroom studies of ATI. *Educational Psychologist*, 1983, *18*, 1–13.

Brainerd, C. J. *Piaget's theory of intelligence*. Englewood Cliffs, N.J.: Prentice-Hall, 1979.

Brennan, R. L. Applications of generalizability theory. In R. A. Berk (Ed.), *Criterion-referenced measurement: The state of the art*. Baltimore, Md.: Johns Hopkins University Press, 1980.

Carpenter, T. P., Moser, J. M., & Romberg, T. A. *Addition and subtraction: A cognitive perspective*. Hillsdale, N.J.: Lawerence Erlbaum Associates, 1982.

Christoffersson, A. Factor analysis of dichotomized variables. *Psychometrika*, 1975, *40*, 5–32.

Cochran, W. G. *Sampling techniques* (3rd. ed.). New York: Wiley, 1977.

Cronbach, L. J., Glaser, G. C., Nanda, H., & Rajaratnam, N. *The dependability of behavioral measurements: Theory of generalizability for scores and profiles*. New York: Wiley, 1972.

Dayton, C. M., & Macready, G. B. A probabilistic model for validation of behavior hierarchies. *Psychometrika*, 1976, *41*, 189–204.

Flavell, J. R. An analysis of cognitive developmental sequences. *Genetic Psychology Monographs*, 1972, *86*, 279–350.

Fuson, K. C. An analysis of the counting-on solution procedure in addition. In T. P.

Carpenter, J. M. Moser, & T. A. Romberg (Eds.), *Addition and subtraction: A cognitive perspective*. Hillsdale, N.J.: Lawrence Erlbaum Associates, 1982.

Gagné, R. M. The acquisition of knowledge. *Psychological Review*, 1962, *69*, 355–365.

Gagné, R. M. *The conditions of learning* (2nd ed.). New York: Holt, Rinehart & Winston, 1970.

Gagné, R. M. *The conditions of learning* (3rd ed.). New York: Holt, Rinehart & Winston, 1977.

Gelman, R., & Gallistel, C. R. *The child's understanding of number*. Cambridge, Ma.: Harvard University Press, 1978.

Glaser, R. Instructional technology and the measurement of learning outcomes: Some questions. *American Psychologist*, 1963, *18*, 519–521.

Glaser, R., & Nitko, A. J. Measurement in learning and instruction. In R. L. Thorndike (Ed.), *Educational measurement* (2nd ed.). Washington, D.C.: American Council on Education, 1971.

Greeno, J. G. A study of problem solving. In R. Glaser (Ed.), *Advances in instructional psychology*, (Vol. 1). Hillsdale, N.J.: Lawrence Erlbaum Associates, 1978.

Hambleton, R. K. Test score validity for standard setting methods. In R. A. Berk (Ed.), *Criterion-referenced measurement: The state of the art*. Baltimore, Md.: Johns Hopkins University Press, 1980.

Hambleton, R. K. (Ed.) *Applications of item response theory*. Vancouver, British Columbia: Educational Research Institute of British Columbia, 1983.

Hambleton, R. K., & Eignor, D. R. *A practitioners guide to criterion referenced test development, validation, and test score usage*. Prepared for the National Institute of Education and Department of Health, Education, and Welfare, 1979.

Hambleton, R. K., Martois, J. S., & Williams, C. *Detection of biased items with item response models*. Paper presented at the meeting of the American Educational Research Association, Montreal, 1983.

Hambleton, R. K., & Novick, M. R. Toward an integration of theory and method for criterion-referenced tests. *Journal of Educational Measurement*, 1973, *10*, 159–170.

Hambleton, R. K., & Rovinelli, R. J. *Assessing the dimensionality of a set of test items*. Paper presented at the annual meeting of American Educational Resources Association, Montreal, 1983.

Hambleton, R. K., Swaminathan, H., Algina, J., & Coulson, D. G. Criterion-referenced testing and measurement: A review of technical issues and developments. *Review of Educational Research*, 1978, *48*, 1–48.

Henderson, R. W., & Bergan, J. R. *The cultural context of childhood*. Columbus, Oh.: Charles E. Merrill, 1976.

Horst, D. P. *What's bad about grade-equifalent scores*. ESEA Title 1 evaluation and reporting system (Technical Report No. 1). Mountain View, Cal.: RMC Research Corporation, 1976.

Jöreskog, J. K., & Sorbom, D. *Advances in factor analysis and structural equation models*. Cambridge, Mass.: ABT, 1979.

Kratochwill, T. K., Alper, D., & Cancelli, A. A. Nondiscriminatory assessment: Perspectives in psychology and special education. In L. Mann & D. Sabatino (Eds.), *Fourth review of special education*. New York: Gardner Press, 1980.

Lawler, R. W. The progressive instruction of mind. *Cognitive Science*, 1981, *5*, 1–30.

Linn, R. S. Measuring pretest–posttest performance changes. In R. A. Berk (Ed.), *Educational evaluation methodology: The state of the art*. Baltimore, Md.: Johns Hopkins University Press, 1981.

Lord, F. M. *Applications of item response theory to practical testing problems*. Hillsdale, N.J.: Lawrence Erlbaum Associates, 1980.

Macready, G. B., & Merwin, J. S. Homogeneity within item forms in domain-referenced testing. *Educational and Psychological Measurement*, 1973, *33*, 351–360.

Muthen, B. Contributions to factor analysis of dichotomous variables. *Psychometrika*, 1978, *43*, 551–600.

Newell, A., & Simon, H. A. *Human problem solving.* Englewood Cliffs, N.J.: Prentice-Hall, 1972.

Nitko, A. J. Distinguishing the many varieties of criterion-referenced tests. *Review of Educational Research*, 1980, *50*, 461–485.

Nunnally, J. C. *Psychometric theory.* New York: McGraw-Hill, 1978.

Osterlind, S. J. *Test item bias.* Beverly Hills, Cal.: Sage Publications, 1983.

Piaget, J. *The child's conception of number.* New York: Humanities Press, 1952.

Popham, W. J. *Criterion-referenced assessment.* Englewood Cliffs, N.J.: Prentice-Hall, 1978.

Popham, W. P. Content domain specification/item generation. In R. A. Berk (Ed.), *Criterion-referenced measurement: The state of the art.* Baltimore, Md.: Johns Hopkins University Press, 1980.

Resnick, L. B., Wang, M. C., & Kaplan, J. Task analysis in curriculum designs: A hierarchically sequenced introductory mathematics curriculum. *Journal of Applied Behavioral Analysis*, 1973, *6*, 679–710.

Reynolds, C. R. Methods for detecting construct and predictive bias. In R. A. Berk (Ed.), *Handbook of methods for detecting test bias.* Baltimore, Md.: Johns Hopkins University Press, 1982.

Rogosa, D., Brandt, D., & Zimowski, M. A growth curve approach to the measurement of change. *Psychological Bulletin*, 1982, *92*.

Shepard, L. A. Definitions of bias. In R. A. Berk (Ed.), *Hanbook of methods for detecting bias.* Baltimore, Md.: Johns Hopkins University Press, 1982.

Siegler, R. S. The rule-assessment approach and education. *Contemporary Educational Psychology*, 1982, *7*, 272–288.

Siegler, R. S. Five generalizations about cognitive development. *American Psychologist*, 1983, *38*, 263–277.

Strenio, J. F., Weisberg, H. I., & Bryk, A. S. Empirical Bayes estimation of individual growth curve parameters and their relationship to covariates. *Biometrics*, 1983, *39*, 71–86.

Subkoviak, M. J. Decision-consistency approaches. In R. A. Berk (Ed.), *Criterion-referenced measurement.* Baltimore, Md.: Johns Hopkins University Press, 1980.

Thorndkike, R. L. *Applied psychometrics.* Boston, Mass.: Houghton Mifflin, 1982.

Van Lehn, K., & Brown, J. S. Planning nets: A representation for formalizing analogies and semantic models of procedural skills. In R. E. Snow, P. A. Fredrico, & W. E. Montague (Eds.), *Aptitude learning and instruction: Cognitive process analyses.* Hillsdale, N.J.: Lawrence Erlbaum Associates, 1979.

White, R. T. Learning hierarchies. *Review of Educational Research*, 1973, *43*, 361–375.

Wilkinson, A. C. Partial knowledge and self-correction: Developmental studies of a quantitative concept. *Developmental Psychology*, 1982, *18*, 876–893.

Wright, B. D., & Masters, G. N. *Rating scale analysis.* Chicago: Mesa Press, 1982.

Wright, B. D., & Stone, M. H. *Best test design: Rasch measurement.* Chicago: Mesa Press, 1979.

Index

467